S0-BDP-129

Second Edition

Handbook for Public Relations Writing

Thomas Bivins

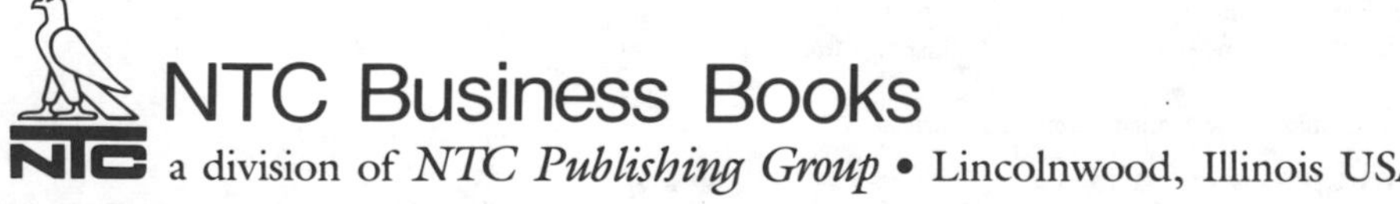
NTC Business Books
a division of *NTC Publishing Group* • Lincolnwood, Illinois USA

Library of Congress Cataloging-in-Publication Data

Bivins, Thomas
Handbook for public relations writing / Thomas Bivins — 2nd ed.
p. cm.
Includes index.
ISBN 0-8442-3263-7. — ISBN 0-8442-3264-5 (pbk.)
1. Public relations—United States. 2. Public relations—United States—Authorship. I. Title.
HM263.B48 1991
659.2—dc20 90-23548

1992 Printing

Published by NTC Business Books, a division of NTC Publishing Group
4255 West Touhy Avenue
Lincolnwood (Chicago), Illinois 60646-1975, U.S.A.

Manufactured in the United States of America.

2 3 4 5 6 7 8 9 VP 9 8 7 6 5 4 3 2

Contents

User's Preface

This is a handbook for those who, by intention or by accident, find themselves in the position of having to write for public relations. It is designed to be of aid to both the beginner and the advanced public relations writer. In it, you will find most of the forms of PR writing including news releases, backgrounders, broadcast scripts, magazine and newsletter articles, brochures, and print advertising copy.

This latest edition has been extensively revised to include, among other topics, expanded coverage of newsletters and brochures and techniques for their production as well as their writing. Since most practitioners, at one time or another, have had to put these "simple" pieces together from scratch, it is essential that you know both how to write for them and how to design them. In addition, the section on house publications has developed into a chapter-length discussion focusing entirely on magazines, including layout tips. A chapter on annual reports, not covered at all in the first edition, has been added. You will also find a completely revised chapter on speeches and presentations geared specifically to public relations practitioners, and a new chapter on printing and typesetting. A chapter on using computers in the PR writing process, including tips on word processing *and* desktop publishing, has been added in recognition of the tremendous impact this technology is having on the entire communications industry.

Most importantly, an entirely new chapter on writing precedes all the others. It covers the basic elements of writing for public relations including how to write both informative and persuasive messages. And, as in the previous edition, you will find a complete section on grammar and one on style geared toward the PR practitioner working within a business environment. Included in them are examples of work common to such an environment including correspondence, memoranda writing, sections from orientation materials, and most of the everyday types of writing that any public relations practitioner is called on to produce.

This new edition is the result of much input from readers. Many of you have indicated areas that you would lilke to see covered. I have done my best to respond to those recommendations in the belief that a true handbook should meet the needs of its users. This revision could not have been accomplished without the help of my editor at NTC, Anne Knudsen, whose expert copy editing frequently led me to a closer examination of my topics, a rethinking of my direction, and a general reorganization. I believe that this edition of the handbook truly meets the needs of today's public relations writer.

Many of the recommendations contained in this handbook are based on years of experience as a writer, both in public relations and in general business practice. It is my belief that any PR writer worthy of the name should become familiar with all forms of writing—from business letters to press releases. After all, good writing is good writing, no matter what the form. The truly good writer is able to work in any medium, like the good artist.

A handbook should be something that you can put on your shelf or desk, or in your briefcase and refer to when you have questions concerning public relations writing. This book is an attempt to put most of the reference material that you, as a public relations writer, would need to successfully complete the work which is so vital a part of your chosen profession—writing.

CHAPTER 1

Writing for Public Relations

Fine writing is next to fine doing...

John Keats

All public relations practitioners write at some time. Public relations is, after all, communication, and the basic form of communication is still the written word.

Regardless of the prevalence of television and radio, the written word is still powerful. Even the events we witness on television and hear on the radio were written down originally in the form of scripts. News anchors on television are not recounting the day's events from memory; they are reading from a teleprompter.

It is no wonder today's employer values an employee who can communicate through the written word. Employers want people who can write and communicate ideas—who can pull complex or fragmented ideas together into coherent messages. This requires not only technical skill, but also intelligence. It also requires a love of writing. Be forewarned: The subjects of public relations writing can seem to many to be crashingly dull; however, for writers who love their craft, the duller the subject, the greater the challenge. Even the most mundane subject can shine with the right amount of polish.

So, the place of writers in public relations is assured. From the president or vice president of public relations to the lowliest office worker, writing will be a daily part of life. From enormously complex projects involving dozens of people and whole teams of writers to the one-person office cranking out daily press releases and weekly newsletters, writing will continue to be the number one concern of public relations. Through it, your publics will come to know you and, for better or worse, develop a permanent image of who you are. It is in your best interest and that of the people you work for to ensure that this image is the one you want to portray.

What is needed before you begin to write, however, is knowledge. Being able to spell and string words together effectively does not make a good writer. A good writer must be able to think. A good writer must be aware of the world around us and understand how his or her writing is going to affect that world.

It is absolutely essential that you think before you write, otherwise your writing will be only empty words, disconnected from reality, or, worse, unintentionally misleading or false.

What Is Public Relations Writing?

All public relations writing attempts to establish positive relations between an organization and its various publics—usually through image-building techniques. Most writing in the realm of public relations falls into two rather broad categories:

- Uncontrolled information,
- Controlled information.

Uncontrolled Information

Information which, once it leaves your hands, is at the mercy of the media, is *uncontrolled.* In other words, the outlet in which you want it placed has total editorial control over the content, style, placement, and timing. Such items as press releases are totally uncontrolled. Others, such as magazine articles, may receive limited editing but are still controlled as to placement and timing.

Controlled Information

Information over which you have total control as to editorial content, style, placement and timing, is *controlled.* Examples of controlled information are institutional and advocacy advertising, house publications, brochures, and broadcast material (if it is paid placement). Public service announcements (PSAs) are controlled as far as message content is concerned, but uncontrolled as to placement and timing.

Naturally, the categories overlap. The trick is to utilize each in a cohesive mix with a single, unified message in mind.

The Tools of the Public Relations Writer

As with any trade, public relations writing makes use of certain tools through which messages are communicated. The most common are listed here.

- **News releases**—both print and broadcast. This is the most widely used of all public relations formats. News releases are used most often to disseminate information for publicity purposes and are sent to every possible medium, from newspapers to radio stations.
- **Backgrounders**—basic information pieces providing background as an aid to reporters, editors, executives, employees, and spokespersons. This is the information used by other writers and reporters to "flesh out" their stories.
- **Public service announcements (PSAs)**—the broadcast outlet most available to public relations. Although its paramcters are limited, additional leeway can be gained by paying for placement, which places it in the category of advertising.
- **Advertising**—the controlled use of media ensuring that your message reaches your public in exactly the form you intended and at the time you want. Advertising can be print or broadcast.
- **Articles and editorials**—usually for newsletters, house publications, trade publications, or consumer publications. In the case of non-house publications, PR articles are submitted in the same way as any other journalistic material. Editorials can be either paid for, as are Mobil's editorials and *Fables*, or submitted uncontrolled and vie for placement with other comments from other parties.
- **Collateral publications**—such as brochures, pamphlets, flyers and other direct marketing pieces. These are usually autonomous publications which should be able to stand on their own merits but which can be used as supporting information for other components in a package. They might, for instance, be part of a press packet.
- **Annual Reports**—one of the most-produced organizational publications. Annual reports not only provide information on the organization's financial situation, they also act as a vehicle for enhancing corporate image among its various internal publics.
- **Speeches and presentations**—the interpersonal method of imparting a position or an image. Good speeches can inform or persuade and good presentations can win support where other, written, methods may fail.

Although these are not the only means for message dissemination at the disposal of the public relations writer, they are the most used. Knowing which to use requires a combination of experience, research, and intuition. The following chapters do not purport to teach you these qualities. What they do attempt to do is to provide you with a framework, or template, from which you will be able to perform basic tasks as a public relations writer. The rest is a matter of experience, and no book can give you that.

Writing for Public Relations

All forms of writing for public relations have one thing in common—they should be written well. Beyond that, they are different in many ways. These differences are related primarily to intent, style, format and medium. Corporate magazines and newsletters, for example, employ standard magazine writing style (which is to say, a standard magazine style of journalism). Newsletter writing, on the other hand, is leaner, shorter, and frequently uses a straight news reporting style. Folders (commonly referred to as brochures) are, by nature, short and to the point. Copy for posters and flyers is shorter still, while pamphlets and booklets vary in style and length according to purpose.

There are basically only two reasons for a public relations piece to be produced: information or persuasion. The approach to writing these pieces depends to a great extent on the purpose to which the piece is to be put. But, before you even put pen to paper (or text to screen), you have to begin the whole process from an organizational perspective. This means planning.

Almost all writing goes through, or should go through, several stages before it reaches completion. Before you start writing, a plan by which your message will ultimately reach its intended audience and accomplish its intended purpose has to be developed. One of the most useful techniques for planning written communication is *management by objectives* (MBO). MBO allows you to set objectives in advance for your written communication and provides you with the criteria you need to measure the message's effectiveness all along the way. By adapting an MBO approach to writing, you can derive at least three processes—planning, writing, evaluation—you must go through to achieve success in your written communications.

The **planning process** includes:

- Developing a problem/issue statement,
- Researching the topic,
- Analyzing the target audience,
- Setting objectives and criteria for evaluation,
- Choosing the appropriate medium or media.

The **writing process** includes:

- Setting message strategy,
- Setting a style and organizing the message,
- Writing the message.

The **evaluation process** includes:

- Testing the message in advance of distribution,
- Evaluating the message during and following the program.

The Planning Process

Developing a Problem/Issue Statement

The first step in any MBO-based plan is to define the issue or problem. Working without a precise definition of the issue is analogous to writing a college term paper without a thesis statement—you have no clear direction to show where you are going and, thus, no way to determine whether you have gotten anywhere when you're finished.

The terms *issue* and *problem* are relatively interchangeable depending on how you view the situation. *Issue* is a more generic term and covers both problems and opportunities; however, many in public relations persist in viewing most responses in terms of problems. For our purposes, we will use the term *issue* as being more inclusive.

The first step in defining the issue is to develop an **issue statement**. An issue statement is a precise definition of the situation including answers to the following.

- What is the problem or opportunity you are going to address?
- Who are the affected parties? At this point, it is only necessary to list the concerned parties. A precise definition of publics is the next step in the planning process.
- Is this issue of immediate concern (one needing to be addressed right now), impending concern (one that will have to be addressed very soon), or potential concern (one that you are tracking as needing to be addressed in the near future)?
- What are your strengths and weaknesses as regards this issue?

In answering these questions, you should take care to be as precise as you can. Succinctness is important to clarity, and clarity is of primary importance in the planning process. It is often wise to answer these questions in outline form, then, working from the outline, develop an issue statement. Consider the following example. It is necessarily simplistic for demonstration purposes. Most issue analysis at this stage is far more complex; however, the approach is the same and the need for precision and succinctness is nonetheless important.

1. Issue: Your company has recently developed a new line of educational software targeted to school-aged children from first grade through high school. Development was time-consuming and expensive, and was based on previous research showing a marked trend in education toward computers in the classroom. Marketing and advertising of the new software will be taken care of by your company's marketing department and its outside advertising agency.From a public relations perspective, however, you see an opportunity to capitalize on the growth in educational computers by raising the awareness of key publics as to the importance of this trend and by tying your company's name to that growth.

Preparing a Direction Sheet

Obviously, the first step any public relations practitioner takes before begining to write is research. Every practitioner needs to understand thoroughly the audience, message, and medium for each communication. Intuition will not suffice. It is important, therefore, to lay the groundwork for any written piece by beginning with a *direction sheet*. No public relations writer should begin an assignment without one. It is really a series of questions to which you should have answers when you begin an assignment.

A basic direction sheet might include the following information:

• Subject of the piece. Is it going to be a new product publicity piece, an announcement of employee promotions, or news about a special event such as a fund raiser or a grand opening?

• Format. What form will the information take? Is it to be a press release, a magazine article, a television PSA, or a brochure?

• Objective. What do we hope to accomplish by producing this piece? Do we want to educate the general public concerning our hiring policies? Do we want to make engineers aware that we have developed a new product for their use? Do we want to promote the Olympics by associating ourselves with the event?

• Intended audience. Exactly who is our target public? Is it housekeepers, businesspeople, children, staff members? Who we decide to communicate with will determine the form of the message and probably the medium.

2. Affected publics: Your publics have already been determined in part by the markets who will be using your new line of software. They are: Educators, administrators, parents, and students.
3. Since this is an opportunity and not a problem, timing is essential. Most opportunities require that you act quickly in order to capitalize on them. Your software is already developed and a marketing program developed. You need to move in advance of, or, at the very least, simultaneously with, the marketing effort.
4. Your strengths include the availability of existing marketing research that has already determined your target publics, advance knowledge of how the new software will enhance the educational process so that you can focus on those elements, and a wide-open opportunity to set the scene for your product through some public relations advance work.

• Angle. An all-important consideration. This is usually just a general idea at the beginning. The angle is one of the toughest components to establish. It has to be new and interesting. In a print ad, it could be a bold headline. In a television PSA, it might be a scenic shot juxtaposed with abrasive audio. In a radio PSA, it might be a humorous context. Whatever the angle, it will serve as the hook and establish the context of the message.

• Key ideas. These are the salient points you wish to make through your communication. Establishing key ideas is important because these will serve as a sort of outline for writing. It is imperative to cover all or most of the key ideas if your message is to be successful.

• Length. This depends to a great extent on format. The decision on length should be as specific as possible in order to eliminate misunderstandings between the party requesting the piece and the writer. Press releases, for instance, can be anywhere from one to five pages. Article length is usually determined by the publication for which it is intended. Brochure length varies according to layout.

• Deadline. This is the all-important element and usually the most inflexible. Unfortunately, in public relations writing as in most writing, the finished product is needed yesterday.

When you receive an assignment, try to get as much information as you can filled out on your direction sheet. Once you have left your "client," it becomes increasingly difficult to get back in touch. It is always a good idea to gather as much information as possible in one sitting. This means, be prepared ahead of time with a complete list of questions.

Weaknesses might include competition, potential perception of vested interest in any philanthropic effort you might suggest, and the necessity to move almost immediately because of the availability of the product.

An issue statement based on this information might look like the following.

> The recent development of our new line of educational software and the coincidence of current trends in educational computing present an opportunity for our company to align itself as a leader in modern education. To do so, we will need to raise the level of attention of key publics concerning the importance of computers in the classroom in such a way that we become closely associated with the trend . We are in a unique position to alert educators, administrators and parents to the multiple uses of classroom computers and the availability of educational software as an answer to many current classroom problems. A well-placed publicity effort outside of and separate from our marketing plan could help pave the way for eventual increased sales of our software. This publicity effort should not seem to be connected to our product; however, we should not appear to hide our interests in increased sales either. A joint effort with an educational nonprofit organization might be the best approach to take.

This issue statement covers all of the questions posed earlier. The only qualitative difference between the original answers provided to the questions and this statement is the narrative format of the statement. Stating the issue in this form helps others to conceptualize what you already understand, and sets the groundwork for further analysis of the issue.

Researching the Topic

Obviously, as is the case in all forms of writing, you must know your topic. Research techniques can run the gamut from formal research, such as surveys and questionnaires, to simply checking the library.

Most public relations writers have access to organizational research material, and so much of the research can be accomplished in house. You can check with various departments for information on your topic and obtain previously published material from in-house and other sources. After you have been at this type of work for a while, you will undoubtedly have a well-stocked "swipe file" in which you have collected everything you (or anyone else) has ever written about your subject area. In essence, you become a standard journalist gathering background information for a story. You should never start writing until you have sufficient background on your subject.

Interviews

For many articles, human interest is important. This is where interviews come in. First-hand information is always best when you can get it. Interview those intimately involved with your topic and use their information when you write. Interviewing is a special skill and it takes a lot of practice. Who you interview will have a great deal to do with how informative or interesting your interview will be. Although you can't always control who you interview, you can prepare so that you can make the most out your meeting.

Analyzing the Target Audience

Imagine holding a complex conversation with someone you don't know at all. If you are trying to persuade that person of your point of view, you will have a better chance if you know his or her predispositions in advance. The same holds true for written communication. In order to write for an audience, you have to know that audience intimately.

What you need to know about your target audience depends to a great extent on what your objectives are. As discussed previously, public relations writing is typically used for either information or persuasion. A lot depends on which of these two uses your particular piece will be put to. Persuasive publications, for example, usually rely on the "look" as the element that first hooks the prospective reader. "Slick" brochures or print ads are obviously designed with this in mind. On the other hand, think of all those publications you've seen at government agencies or received through the mail as a result of having requested information. They frequently are less glitzy, more straightforward, and simpler in style. They don't have to be designed to attract your attention or persuade you to pick them up. They are designed to inform you, and they assume that you have already chosen to read them.

Developing a reader profile

Knowing for whom you're writing is probably the most important factor in setting message strategy. The success of your writing will be determined, to a great extent, on how well you've "aimed" your message. The best way to write is to write for an imagined reader, an individual to

Tips for a successful interview.

- Do your homework. Collect background information on the people you're going to interview, as well as the topics. Don't be embarrassed by your own ignorance of the topics; however, the better you know the topics, the more time you can save by asking for confirmation or denial of specifics, rather than asking for in-depth explanations.

- Prepare your interviewees in advance of the interviews. Contact them well in advance, set a convenient time for the interview (convenient for them, not you), and make sure they know exactly what you are going to cover and why. That way, they can also prepare for the interview by gathering pertinent information—or, at the very least—their thoughts. Ask if you can talk with them, not interview them. A talk puts people at ease—an interview can make them tense and formal.

- Write down a list of questions that you want answered, working from the general to the specific. But, remember, be prepared to let the interview range according to the interviewees' responses. Often, an answer will open new areas of inquiry or suggest an angle you hadn't thought of before. Be ready to explore these new avenues as they come up.

  Ken Metzler, journalist, educator and author of *Creative Interviewing* claims that the best interviewers should not only expect surprises, but should ask for surprises in their willingness to explore rather than follow a strict set of questions.

- If you are going to use a tape recorder, check to make sure that your interviewee is comfortable with being taped, and that you have fresh batteries or that an electrical outlet is available. And, even though you are taping, always take notes. This physical activity usually puts the interviewee at ease by showing that you are listening, and it serves as a good backup if your recorder stops functioning or your tape runs out.

  Your recorder should not occupy the space between you and your subject. Move it a little to the side, but make sure the microphone isn't obstructed. The space between you and your subject should be free of any object that may be a source of distraction. (You

whom you are speaking directly. In order to understand this individual, you need to know him or her personally. To do this, you will have to develop a profile of this "typical" reader.

There are a number of methods for collecting information on your target audiences, ranging from fairly expensive formal research through secondary research gathered from such sources as the library or your own organization, to simply asking the person who gave you the assignment

should also keep your note pad in your lap, if possible, or simply hold it.)

• Break the ice. Open your interview with small talk. Try a comfortable topic, such as the weather, or, if you know something about your interviewee, a familiar topic that is nonthreatening. For example, if you know your interviewee is an avid golfer, ask if he or she has had a chance to play much lately. Almost any topic will do—in fact, most of the time, something will suggest itself naturally.

• As your interview progresses, don't be afraid to range freely, but return occasionally to your pre-set questions. Although the information you gather exploring other avenues may add greatly to your collection of relevant facts, remember to cover all the ground necessary for your article.

• If you are ever unsure of a quote or think you might have misunderstood it, ask your subject to repeat it. Even if you are taping the interview, accuracy on paper and in your own mind is worth the slight pause.

• Finally, be prepared to have to remember some key conversation after your interview is officially over. Most of us are aware of the phenomenon that Ken Metzler calls the "afterglow effect," when dinner guests, for example, stand at the door with their coats on ready to go and talk for another 30 minutes. The same thing usually happens in an interview. You've turned your recorder off and put your pad away, and on your way out the door, you have another ten minutes of conversation. In this relaxed atmosphere, important comments are often made. Remember them. As soon as you leave, take out your pad and write the comments down or turn on your recorder and repeat the information into it. However, always make sure that your interviewee is aware that you are going to use this information as well. Don't violate any assumed "off the record" confidences.

Remember, get as much as you can the first time out. Most interviews range from 30 minutes to two hours. A follow-up interview, providing you can get one, will never be as fruitful or relaxed as the first one.

who the audience is. Many writers are put off by the notion of having to gather hard-core information about their readers. Unfortunately, many a message has totally missed its audience because it was not built around this information.

If you can't afford the luxury of a formal survey, try gathering demographic information from other departments within your own organization. For example, if your organization has a marketing department and your publication is external, you might be able to extract some solid audience demographics from existing marketing research. And, don't discount the value of a visit to the library.

Government documents such as the *American Statistics Index* (*ASI*) can be invaluable sources. *ASI* is a compendium of statistical material including the US census and hundreds of periodicals that can be obtained directly from the sponsoring agencies or, often, from the library itself. *ASI* also publishes an alphabetical index arranged by subject, name, category and title.

Other sources of market information include the Simmons Market Research Bureau's annual *Study of Media and Markets*. This publication includes information on audiences for over a hundred magazines, with readership delineated by demographic, psychographic, and behavioral characteristics. When using secondary research such as this, be aware that you will find much information that is not directly applicable to your target audience. You not only have to know where to look, but you also have to know how to decipher what you read and apply it to your needs.

There is one other important factor to consider at this point: How your target audience feels about your subject. In most persuasive endeavors, there are three types of audiences: those already on your side, those opposed to your point of view, and those who are undecided. Most persuasive appeals are, or should be, aimed at the last group.

As most experienced persuaders know, convincing the hard-core opposition is not a reasonable objective. Persuading those already on you side is like preaching to the converted—unless you want to stir them to some action, it is a waste of time. Thus, most persuasion is aimed at the undecided. Remember, however, that even the undecided have opinions. Those opinions may not be fully crystallized, and this leaves this group particularly open to persuasion.

Anticipating readers' expectations

Once you know who your audiences are and how they feel about your subject, there is one final question that must be answered if you expect to be successful: Why are they going to be reading your publication? If you don't know why your audience is reading your publication in the first place, you certainly can't know what they expect to get from it. Ask yourself some questions.

1. What does your audience know about your topic already? Never assume they know anything about your subject; however, don't talk down to them. How do you reach a compromise? Find out what they

do know. Remember, people like to learn something from communication. It is best, however, to limit the amount of new information so as not to overwhelm your readers.

2. What is your audience's attitude toward you? Remember the three basic audiences for any persuasive piece? You'll need to determine whether your audience is on your side, against you, or unconvinced. This is a primary concern. To the extent possible, it is also a good idea to try to determine what your audience's image of you or your organization is. Determining audience attitude is often an expensive proposition because it usually requires formal research. However, if the best you can do is make an educated guess based on a small focus group or even on intuition—that's better than nothing at all. It is much easier to convince others when you know that you already have credibility with them.
3. Is your publication to be used in a larger context? In other words, is your publication part of a press kit, for instance, or a direct-mail package, or one of many handouts at a trade show? This knowledge will determine your readers' level of attention and their receptiveness. Always consider the surroundings in which your piece will be used if you want it to have the maximum impact.

Setting Objectives and Criteria for Evaluation

Objectives relate to the purpose of your message and should be realistic and measurable. For public relations writing, there are three types of objectives: informational, attitudinal and behavioral.

Informational objectives are used most often to present balanced information on a topic of interest to your target audience. For instance, if you are simply attempting to let your employees know that your organization has developed a new health care package, your objective might read something like this:

> To inform all employees of the newest options available in their health care benefits package by the end of the October open enrollment period.

Notice that the objective begins with an infinitive phrase. Objectives should always be written this way. Notice, too, that the number of employees is addressed ("all"), and a specific time period for the completion of the objective is also included. In a complete communications plan, this objective would be followed by the proposed tactic for its realization and a method by which its success could be measured. For example:

> To inform all employees of the newest options available in their health care benefits package by the end of the October open enrollment period by placing informational folders in each employee's paycheck over the next two months. Personnel will keep a record of all employees requesting information on the new health care plan during the open enrollment period.

If your objective is attitudinal or behavioral rather than informational, your message is probably going to be persuasive. There are three ways you can attempt to influence attitude and behavior.

- You can create an attitude or behavior where none exists. This is the easiest of these three because, if none exists, there is usually no predisposition on the part of your target audience.
- You can reinforce an attitude or behavior. This is also relatively easy to do because your target audience already believes or behaves in the way you desire.
- You can attempt to change or alter an attitude. This last is the most difficult to accomplish and, realistically, shouldn't be attempted unless you are willing to expend a lot of time and energy on an, at best, dubious outcome.

An example of an attitudinal objective might be:

> To create a favorable attitude among employees concerning the changeover from a monthly pay disbursement to a twice-monthly pay disbursement.

Methods for measuring this type of objective range from informal employee feedback to formal surveys of attitudes some time after the changeover has gone into effect.

An example of a behavioral objective might be:

> To increase the number of employees in attendance at the annual company picnic by 25 percent by mailing out weekly reminders to the homes of employees four weeks prior to the picnic.

Obviously, measuring the effectiveness of this objective is easier; however, if you don't see an increase in attendance, you will have to do some serious research into the reasons why. And, be aware that these reasons might not involve your message or its presentation at all. You might have simply picked the Sunday of the big state fair to hold your picnic. The lesson here is, don't ever conclude that your message is automatically the problem without exploring all variables affecting its desired results.

Choosing the Appropriate Medium or Media

Any *assumptions* you make concerning the most appropriate medium for your message could be disastrous. As in all stages of the planning process, selecting the right medium or media is a decision that should be based on sound knowledge of a number of factors. Public relations educators Doug Newsom, Alan Scot and Judy VanSlyke Turk in their book, *This Is PR: The Realities of Public Relations*, have suggested a series of important considerations to be used in choosing the right medium for your message:

- **What audience are you trying to reach and what do you know about its media usage patterns and the credibility ratings for each medium?** Many target audiences simply do not watch television or listen to the radio. Others don't read newspapers regularly or subscribe to magazines. You need to know, first off, whether your intended audience will even see your message if it is presented in a medium they don't regularly use. Research tells us, for example, that businesspeople read the newspaper more than do some other groups, and rely on it for basic news and information. Other groups may rely on television almost exclusively for their news and information. For each of these groups, the credibility of the medium in question is vital. For example, businesspeople cite newspapers as a more credible source for news and information than television; however, for many people, television is far more credible.
- **When do you need to reach this audience in order for your message to be effective?** If time is of the essence, you'd best not leave your message for the next issue of the corporate magazine.
- **How much do you need to spend to reach your intended audience and how much can you actually afford?** It may be that the only way to achieve the result you're looking for is to go to some extra expense such as a folder with more glitz or a full-color newsletter. Although every job has budget constraints, it's best to know from the start exactly what it will take to accomplish your objectives.

After these tough questions have been answered, you will still need to ask four others:

- **Which medium (of those you've listed in response to your first three questions) reaches the broadest segment of your target audience at the lowest cost?** The answer to this question will give you a "bottom-line" choice of sorts because cost is the controlling factor in answering it. It might be that you can reach all of an employee audience with an expensive corporate magazine, but two-thirds of it with a less expensive newsletter.

- **Which medium has the highest credibility and what does it cost?** Here, the correct answer will give you the additional factor of credibility which is key if your audience is discriminating at all. There are always those for whom the least credible of sources is still credible (otherwise, gossip tabloids would go out of business). But, for the honest communicator, credibility is important to the success of any future messages.

- **Which medium will deliver your message within the time constraints necessary for it to be effective?** Again, a critical letter distributed company-wide may be a lot more timely than a well-written article in next month's corporate magazine.

- **Should a single medium be used or a combination of complementary media (media mix)?** Remember, each element in an overall communications program may require a specialized medium in order for that portion of the message to be most effective.

Obviously, the more you know about your audience, the better you will be at selecting just the right medium for your message. However, you must also understand that certain media criteria often dictate message and message format. For instance, brochures "demand" brevity, as do flyers and posters; corporate magazines allow for fuller development of messages; newsletters offer more space than folders but less than magazines; pamphlets offer space for message expansion and place fewer demands on style; and annual reports require strict adherence to SEC (Security and Exchange Commission) guidelines. You must also consider cost, lead time for writing, editing, layout, typesetting, pasteup, printing, and distribution.

In short, selecting the most appropriate medium for your message is a complex endeavor. Be forewarned, therefore. No assumptions should be made about the acceptability of any particular medium. Until you have considered, at the least, the questions posed earlier, you will probably only be guessing on your choice of an ideal medium.

The Writing Process

Setting Message Strategy

Message strategy has to do with your approach to developing a message, or messages, that will reach and have the desired effect on your targeted audiences. Following the MBO method of organization, your message strategies should logically follow your objectives and contribute either directly or indirectly to them. You will need to develop individual message strategies for each of your target publics, based on what you have learned about them through your research. Remember, the strategy or strategies you employ will be determined, to a great extent, by your audience's makeup, predispositions and perceived needs.

Sandra E. Moriarty, in her book *Creative Advertising*, has described five basic message strategies (which she calls *stratagems*) that can be used as summary statements describing the general orientation of an overall creative strategy.

- **Information**. An information strategy is usually a straightforward statement of fact, best used on audiences interested enough to seek out the information you can provide. This strategy is frequently employed for such messages as new product announcements, consumer awareness campaigns, and public information programs. It is also used for supplemental messages (such as position statements) to persuasive campaigns.
- **Argument**. Argument strategy assumes that there are at least two sides to the issue you are addressing. Messages are usually persuasive in nature and require an audience that is already interested in the issue and able to process information fairly well. Argument strategy makes frequent appeals to reasoning and logic and is best structured to reach either those who are already convinced or those who are neutral and open to reasoning.
- **Image**. Image strategy is used to develop or maintain a strong, memorable identity for a person, idea, product, or organization. It attempts to "bundle" perceptions into a single concept or symbol representing the subject of the message. The best image strategies result in a perception that the image itself *is* the subject, not just a symbolic representation of the subject. This technique is frequently used to publicize political candidates and to promote parity products

that depend on a connotative association in order to differentiate them from competitors.

- **Emotional strategies**. Emotional strategies are generally intended to persuade. They are best used for messages aimed at those who are either neutral or already on your side, and will rarely convince the hard-core opposition. Emotional strategies depend on the use of emotionally laden words, images, or style elements, such as the structure of a speech or the use of certain "hot buttons" in a message. Most of us think of emotional strategies as useful only in the context of emotionally charged issues; however, everything from political candidates to soft drinks can be sold through emotional appeal, or through association of the "product" with emotions, such as patriotism or romance. Even humor can be seen as an emotional strategy because typically it makes us *feel* good about the message.
- **Entertainment**. Entertainment strategy is commonly used in advertising because it is particularly effective when communicating in highly competitive and cluttered environments. Remember, however, that, like humor, entertainment can be an excellent strategy for "selling" your ideas, philosophies, or whatever, regardless of the medium or format. The entertainment value of a message helps it gain and maintain attention.

Persuasive pieces are usually heavy on the positive attributes of your service, product or point of view. They need to be written in terms the audience can relate to and frequently benefit from a use of words with emotional impact. Information pieces can get away with far fewer emotionally packed words and are frequently longer. After all, their aim is to inform; the assumption is that the audience is already convinced of, or at least interested in, the subject.

An informative piece should be balanced and complete. Its purpose is to let readers in on something they may not know or may have an incomplete picture of. The intent may be to publicize a new product or service, to set the record straight on a vital issue affecting your organization, or simply to let your readers know what's happening in your organization. Whatever the intent, the informational publication has to stick to just that—information. If your point of view is so strong as to evoke opposition, you probably should be writing a piece to persuade.

Setting a Style and Organizing the Message

To a large extent, style refers to format. Style is usually, but not always, predetermined by what medium you will use. If, for example, you are writing for a newsletter or house magazine, your choices will usually be limited to either straight news or feature. If you are writing a press release, your style will always be straight news. If you are writing for broadcast, the style will be that of a script.

Style also refers to grammatical and semantic usage. These topics are extensively covered in **Chapters 13** and **14**. Rather than refer to these two chapters only when you have a question, it is a good idea to review at least the style chapter at this point.

The same advice applies to organizing your message. Rather than repeat here much of what is explained later in **Chapter 14** on style, why not read it now, before proceeding?

Writing the Informative Message

Writing informative messages is one of the most straightforward tasks in pubic relations writing. Informative messages should be balanced and non-biased in presentation. Naturally, you can put your own "spin" on anything you write, but in the information piece, you should keep to the facts. Most audiences will see through a persuasive piece thinly disguised as information. This is one of the major objections journalists voice concerning press releases. They often say that much of what they receive is really advertising (persuasion) in disguise.

When writing an informative piece, ask yourself some questions.

- Why would my target audience want to know about this topic?
- What would they want to know about it?
- Is the topic tied to a particular strategy? If so, what strategy? If it is part of an overall persuasive campaign, why am I using an informative approach?
- How much material should I leave for "further information?"
- Am I expecting any results from this approach? Make your objectives clear enough to be measurable so that you can later evaluate the results of information dissemination effectively.

The most valid objective of information is to raise the level of knowledge or understanding of your target audience. The reason behind PR writing may be ultimately to persuade, but in informative pieces, bias should be kept to a minimum.

Writing the Persuasive Message

Writing a message that persuades is not easy. First, you have to have a crystal-clear understanding of what it is you want your readers to do in response to your persuasive effort. This means that you have to be able not only to convey your message in the clearest possible terms, but also be responsive to opposing points of view.

It is important to note here that the persuasive message is normally audience centered. Persuasive strategy is based on who your audience is and how they feel about your topic. The piece should inform, and while informing, persuade. The approach you use probably will be based on audience analysis—how receptive your audience is to either an emotional or a rational appeal. Historically, audiences react best to a combination of both. There are times, however, when a purely emotional or purely rational appeal will be most effective.

Remember, a hostile audience usually won't be convinced; a sympathetic audience doesn't need to be convinced; and, an undecided audience is as likely to be convinced by your opposition as by you. Different strategies will be employed for each of these audiences. For instance, if you are writing for a friendly audience, an emotional appeal may work very well. For an undecided audience, a rational appeal supported by solid evidence may work best. If your audience is neutral or disinterested, you'll have to stress attention-getting devices. If they are uninformed, you'll have to inform them. And if they are simply undecided, you'll have to convince them.

For persuasive messages it is important to understand the psychological state of your audience and build your message around this. This audience-centered approach includes three basic techniques: the motivated sequence, the imagined Q & A, and messages aimed at attitude change. We will discuss each of these briefly.

The motivated sequence

The motivated sequence is common tactic used by persuaders and involves the following five steps.

1. **Attention**. You must first get the attention of your audience. This means that you have to open with a bang.
2. **Need**. Next, you have to establish why the topic is of importance to the audience. Set up the problem statement—a brief description of the issue you are dealing with.
3. **Satisfaction**. Present the solution. It has to be a legitimate solution to the problem.
4. **Support**. You have to support fully your solution and point out the pitfalls of any alternatives. Otherwise, your audience may not be

able to comprehend completely the advantages of your solution over others.

5. **Action**. Finally, call for action. Ask your audience to respond to your message, and make it as easy as possible to take action.

The imagined Q & A

In the imagined Q & A, the message is structured into a series of questions that the audience might have, followed by your answers to each. Ask yourself the questions your audience might be asking you.

- **Why even talk about this subject**? Tell them the importance of your topic to them. Tie your topic to their concerns.
- **For example**? Don't just leave them with your point of view. Give them examples. Support your proposal.
- **So what**? Let them know what all of this means to them, and tell them what you want them to do.

Messages aimed at attitude change

Many novice writers assume that all they are obligated to do in a persuasive piece is present their side. This is a dangerous assumption, especially if the opposing side has sound arguments of its own. Any persuasion piece should cover all sides. If your arguments really are sound, they will stand up to comparison.

You may assume that your audience is at least familiar with opposing viewpoints. In most cases, it is advisable to address counter arguments only after you have presented your own side. When writing any piece that aims to change audience attitudes, try using the following guidelines.

1. State the opposing view fairly. Make your audience believe that you are fair-minded enough to understand that there is another side and that you're intelligent enough to understand it.
2. State your position on the opposing view. Now that you've shown that you understand the other side, state why you don't think it's right—or, better yet, not totally right. This indicates that you find at least some merit in what others have to say—even the opposition.
3. Support your position. Give the details of your side of the argument. Use logic, not emotion. Show that you are above such tricks; however, don't avoid emotion altogether. Try to strike a balance while leaning toward logic and emotional control.

4. Compare the two positions and show why yours is the most viable. If you've done your work well up until this point, then your audience will already see the clear differences between the two sides. Strengthen their understanding by reiterating the differences and finishing with a strong statement in support of your arguments.

The Evaluation Process

Now is the time to test your message. You'll need to test it on several levels in order for your assessment to be accurate.

First, do your messages reflect your original objectives as set during the planning process? You should ask yourself why each message has been developed. If the answer relates to accomplishing one of your objectives, then the message has succeeded at that level.

The adequacy of your selected target audience, choice of medium, and message strategy can be tested at the same time. The best approach is to test your message and medium on members of your target audience.

Focus Group Testing

Focus group testing has become a fairly common practice for those in advertising, marketing and public relations. The technique requires that you assemble a small group (usually not more than ten or so) from your target audience, present them with the message, and ask for their reactions. Your approach can be fairly formal (a written questionnaire to be filled out following the presentation), or informal (open-ended questions asked in an open discussion among the participants). The key is to design your questions in advance and to cover all the areas you need to analyze. Be sure to explore whether your message's language is appropriate to your audience. Is it difficult to follow or have too much jargon or too many technical terms? Does your audience understand the message? Does the message speak to them, or do they feel it is meant for someone else? Is the medium appropriate? Would your readers take time to read the message if it came to them in the mail? As an insert in their paychecks? In the corporate magazine? Answers to these questions should give you a fair idea of how your larger audience will react to your message.

The best way to set up a focus group is to hire a moderator who is experienced in asking these questions and interpreting the responses properly. Don't assume that because you are the writer, and the closest to the project, that you can interpret audience feedback clearly. In most cases, you are not the one best suited to act as the focus group's moderator.

Readability Formulas

Readability formulas analyze everything from the level of education needed to understand a message to the number of personal pronouns used (a measure of the level of friendliness of the tone of your message). Two of the most common readability formulas are described here.

The Gunning Fog Index

1. Select a sample of 100 words from the middle of your message.
2. Count the number of sentences and divide that number into 100 to find an average sentence length (ASL).
3. Count the number of words consisting of three syllables or more in the 100 words. Do not include proper nouns, compound words like *typesetting*, or words that end in *ed* or *es*.
4. Add the totals from steps 2 and 3 and multiply by 0.4.

The resulting score approximates the number of years of schooling required to read the piece. College graduates usually can read at about a score of 16 while most best sellers are written at 7-8. Obviously, if your piece is intended for vertical distribution, such as a company magazine, you will need to reach an "average" audience. Newspapers, for instance, write at about the sixth-grade level.

The Flesch Formula

1. Select a sample of 100 words from the middle of your piece.
2. Count the number of sentences; divide that *into* 100 to find the average sentence length (ASL).
3. Count the number of syllables in sample and divide this figure *by* 100 for the average word length (AWL).
4. Plug the resulting figures from steps 2 and 3 into the following formula:

   Readability = 206.835 – (84.6 x AWL) – (1.015 x ASL)
5. Interpret the scores based on the following scale:

70–80 = very easy (romance novels)
60–65 = standard (newspapers, *Readers Digest*)
50–55 = "intellectual" magazines (*Harpers, The Atlantic*)
30 and below = scholarly journals, technical papers

This formula is based on ease of reading determined, to a large extent, by the length of words. This assumes that polysyllabic words slow down and often confuse the reader. Other formulas guage the degree of familiarity by noting personal pronouns, for instance.

This sort of evaluation is known as *preparation evaluation*. Obviously, it can only tell you if the message and the way it's packaged and presented are acceptable to your target audience. What it won't tell you is whether or not your audience will respond to your message. You'll have to wait for that.

Survey Techniques

There are a number of methods for judging the effectiveness of your communication once it is distributed, ranging from expensive to relatively inexpensive, and from complex to simple. Let's take the simplest first: readership surveys.

Readership surveys are simple questionnaires, usually included with your publication (as in a corporate magazine or newsletter), that seek to find out whether anyone out there is paying attention. A few, plainly put questions—about what interests your readers the most, the least, what they would change if they could, what they would include or leave out—will tell you a lot. Most commercial publications run the occasional readership survey just to make sure they're operating on the same wavelength as their readers.

On the more expensive level are formal, statistical surveys measuring everything from whether your readers are actually receiving your message to whether or not they're changing their attitudes or behaviors because of it. These surveys are best left to highly qualified specialists who will ask the right questions and properly interpret the answers. The results can be invaluable, particularly with persuasive messages. Remember, behavioral change can often be easily measured in increased sales of your new widget, attendance at the company picnic (remember to factor in the free beer as a contributing variable), more votes for your candidate, or a decrease in the number of complaint letters you receive on an issue. Attitude change, on the other hand, is more difficult to measure but, nonetheless, equally important.

Modern survey techniques, contrary to what critics say, can accurately define attitudes and measure shifts in them. Because of the complexity of the operation, however (and the need to perform both a pre- and a post-survey in order to have something to compare), you will have to pay the price. Good research isn't cheap.

The Legal Aspects of PR Writing

All those who deal in public communication are bound by certain laws. For the most part, these laws protect others. We are all familiar with the First Amendment rights allowed the press in this country. To a certain degree, some of those rights transfer to public relations. For example, corporations now enjoy a limited First Amendment protection under what is known as *commercial speech*. Commercial speech, as defined by the Supreme Court, allows a corporation to state publicly its position on controversial issues. The Court's interpretation of this concept also allows for political activity through lobbying and political action committees.

But, as with most rights, there are concomitant obligations—chief among them is the obligation not to harm others through your communication. The most important "don't"s for public relations writers concern slander or libel (defamation), invasion of privacy, and infringement of copyrights or trademarks.

Defamation

Defamation is the area of infringement with which writers are most familiar. Although it is variously defined (each case seems to bring a new definition), defamation can be said to be any communication that holds a person up to contempt, hatred, ridicule, or scorn. One problem in defending against accusations of defamation is that there are different rules for different people. It is generally easier for private individuals to prove defamation than it is for those in the public eye. Celebrities and politicians, for example, open themselves to a certain amount of publicity, and, therefore, criticism. While a private individual suing for libel must only prove negligence, a public figure must prove malice. In order for defamation to be actionable, five elements must be present.

- There must be communication of a statement that harms a person's reputation in some way—even if it only lowers that person's esteem in another's eyes.
- The communication must have been published or communicated to a third party. The difference here is that between *slander* and *libel*. Slander is oral defamation, and might arise, for example, in a public speech. *Libel* is written defamation, though it also includes broadcast communication.
- The person defamed must have been identified in the communication, either by name or by direct inference. This is the toughest to prove if the person's name hasn't been used directly.

- The person defamed must be able to prove that the communication caused damage to his or her reputation.
- Negligence must also be shown. In other words, the source of the communication must be proved to have been negligent during research or writing. Negligence can be the fault of poor information gathering. Public figures must prove malice—that is, the communication was made with knowing falsehood or reckless disregard for the truth.

There are defenses against defamation. The most obvious is that the communication is the truth, regardless of whether the information harmed someone's reputation or not.

The second defense is *privilege*. Privilege applies to statements made during public, official or judicial proceedings. For example, if something normally libelous is reported accurately on the basis of a public meeting, the reporter cannot be held responsible. Privilege is a tricky concept, however, and care must be taken that privileged information be let only to those who have right to it. Public meetings are public information. Concerned individuals only have a right to privileged information released at private meetings.

The third most common defense is *fair comment*. This concept applies primarily to the right to criticize, as in theater or book critiques, and must be restricted to the public interest aspects of that which is under discussion. However, it also can be construed to apply to such communications as comparative advertising.

Privacy

Most of us are familiar with the term *invasion of privacy*. For public relations writers, infringing on privacy is a serious concern. It can happen very easily. For example, your position as editor of the house magazine doesn't automatically give you the right to use any employee picture you might have on file, or divulge personal information about an employee without their prior written permission.

Invasion of privacy falls roughly into the following categories.

- Appropriation is the commercial use of a person's name or picture without permission. For instance, you can't say that one of your employees supports the company's position on nuclear energy if that employee hasn't given you permission to do so—even if they do support that position and have said so to you.

Private facts about individuals are also protected. Information about a person's lifestyle, family situation, personal health, etc., is considered to be strictly private and may not be disclosed without permission.

- Intrusion involves literally spying on another. Obtaining information by bugging, filming or recording in any way another's private affairs is cause for a lawsuit.

Copyright

Most of us understand that we can't quote freely from a book without giving credit, photocopy entire publications to avoid buying copies, or reprint a cartoon strip in our corporate magazine without permission. Most forms of published communication are protected by copyright laws.

The reasons for copyright protection are fairly clear. Those who create original work, such as novels, songs, articles and advertisements, lose the very means to their livelihood each time that novel, song, or advertisement is used without payment.

All writers need to be aware that copyrighted information is not their's to use free of charge, without permission. Always check for copyright ownership on anything you plan to use, in any way. You may want to rewrite information, or paraphrase it, and think that as long as you don't use the original wording you are exempt from copyright violation. Not so. There are prescribed guidelines for use of copyrighted information without permission. You may use a portion of copyrighted information if:

- It is not taken out of context,
- Credit is given to the source,
- Your usage doesn't affect the market for the material,
- You are using the information for scholastic or research purposes,
- The material used doesn't exceed a certain percentage of the total work.

Just remember, never use another's work without permission.

Trademarks

Trademarks are typically given for the protection of product names or, in certain instances, images, phrases or slogans. For example, several years ago, Anheiser Busch sued a florist for calling a flower shop "This Bud's For You." The reason, of course, is that the slogan was commonly recognized as referring to Budweiser beer. The Disney studios have jealously guarded their trademarked cartoon characters for over fifty years and their trademark appears on thousands of items. Charles Schultz' Peanuts characters are also used for hundreds of purposes, all with permission. Even advertisments that mention other product names are careful to footnote trademark information.

One of the main reasons for trademark protection is to prevent someone not associated with the trademarked product, image or slogan from using it for monetary gain without a portion of that gain (or at least recognition) going to the originator. Another important concern is that the trademarked product, image or slogan be used correctly and under the direction of the originator. Certain trademarked names, such as *Xerox*, *Kleenex* and *BandAid*, have for years been in danger of passing into common usage as synonyms for the generic product lines of which they are part. The companies that manufacture these brand names are zealous in their efforts to ensure that others don't refer, for example, to photocopying as "xeroxing," or to facial tissue as "kleenex." In fact, one of the legal tests for determining whether a brand name has become a synonym for a generic product line is whether it is now included in dictionaries as a synonym for that product.

As harmless as it may seem, using the term "xeroxing" in a written piece to refer to photocopying, or the simple use of a cartoon character on a poster announcing a holiday party may be a trademark violation. The easiest thing to do is to check with the originator before using any trademarked element. Often, the only requirement will be either to use the true generic word (in the case of a brand name), or mention that the image, slogan or name is a trademarked element and give the source's name.

***Copyright**—Used to protect copy of any length. Can be either "noticed"—or marked—without actual federal registration (which limits protection under the law) or with registration (which expands the degree of legal protection).*

***Registered Trademark**—Used to protect any word, name, symbol, or device used by a manufacturer or merchant to identify and distinguish his goods from those of others. This mark indicates that the user has actually registered the item with the federal government, allowing maximum legal protection.*

TM

***Trademark**—Similarly used, but as a "common law" notice. In other words, material marked this way is not necessarily registered with the government and thus has limited and not full protection.*

Exhibit 1.1—Symbols for Protected Material

Learning to Adapt

One of the trademarks of a good writer is the ability to adapt to the needs of the audience, the message, and the medium. Public relations writing, unlike many other forms of writing, requires this flexibility. In the following chapters, you will find a variety of writing styles utilized in different formats. The key to writing for public relations is to learn these formats and adapt your style to each as needed. The road to becoming a good public relations writer is filled with side tracks. It is quite easy to let yourself become specialized. The trick to becoming the best kind of writer is not to let that happen. The greater the variety of writing styles you can learn to use well, the better your chances of becoming an excellent writer will be.

CHAPTER 2

Media Relations & Placement

And do as adversaries do in law,
Strive mightily, but eat and drink as friends.

William Shakespeare

Public relations practitioners are professionals. So are journalists. Professionals, in the ideal sense, work together for the public welfare. Why, then do public relations people see members of the media as adversaries, going out of their way to dig up the dirt? And why do reporters—whether print or broadcast—often see public relations people as "flaks," paid to run interference for their clients?

Actually, there is a little truth in both points of view and there are a number of legitimate complaints on both sides. Public relations people often are charged with covering up or stonewalling, while reporters often do seek only the negative in any issue. Obviously, this is far from a perfect relationship between professionals.

Part of the problem stems from a lack of real understanding in both camps of how the other operates. There is little you can do to make journalists find out more about PR, but you can do much to improve your own knowledge of how the media operate, what media people want from you , and what they are capable and not capable of providing.

The Stumbling Blocks

Know What News Is

The most common stumbling block to a good working relationship between public relations and media professionals is a mutually agreeable definition of the concept of *news*. Research has shown that most journalists judge news value based on at least some of the following characteristics:

- **Consequence**. Does the information have any importance to the prospective reading, listening, or viewing public? Is it something that the audience would pay to know? Remember, news value is frequently judged by what the audience is willing to pay for.
- **Interest**. Is the information unusual or entertaining? Does it have any human interest? People like to transcend the everyday world. Excitement, even vicarious excitement, often makes good news.
- **Timeliness.** Is the material current? It it isn't, is it a whole new angle on on old story? Remember, the word *news* means "new." This is one rule frequently broken by public relations practitioners. Nothing is more boring than yesterday's news.
- **Proximity**. For most public relations people seeking to connect with the media, a local angle is often the only way to do it. If it hits close to home, it stands a better chance of being reported.
- **Prominence**. Events and people of prominence frequently make the news. The problem, of course, is that your company president may not be as prominent to the media as he or she is to you.

If your story contains at least some of the above elements, it stands a chance of being viewed as news by the media.

Know Their Jobs

Remember the adage, "Know thine enemy"? It definitely applies to knowing the media.The media are a powerful force, and they can do a lot for you—or a lot against you. The determining factor may well be how much you know about and appreciate their jobs.

To that end, you should learn all you can about the media outlets and the individuals with whom you will be dealing on a regular basis. Having some journalism experience goes a long way toward understanding the frustrations of the job. Journalists have a tough life. I know—so do *you*. But, they are much less tolerant of people who don't understand them than you probably are. Many public relations practitioners have had prior journalistic experience or education.

Talk to journalists. Ask them for their guidelines on gathering news. Get to know how they write and what they choose to write about. Know their deadlines and keep them as if they were your own. In a way, they are. At the same time, try to let media people know what you do. Show them your style. Ask them for hints on how to make it more acceptable to their needs. Everybody likes to be asked their professional opinion.

A word needs to be said here about courting the press. Most journalists who deal in hard news don't react well to being courted. That is, they aren't likely to change anything they think or write because you invited them out to lunch. Although we've all heard stories about unethical journalists, I prefer to assume that every reporter has professional scruples. You should too. They may well go out to lunch with you, especially if you have a story that may interest them, but, they are very likely to pick up their own checks. The sole exception might be the trade press. Trade journalists are used to receiving samples of products that they are writing about. The editor of a plastics industry trade journal might have a desk full of everything from pieces of new plastic to lengths of rubber hose, or actual products made from new compounds. They usually look at these, not as gifts, but rather as evidence of the application or existence of new products. In fact, one of the stages product publicity goes through involves having the trade media "test" new products. The results usually end up in what is known as "roundups"—articles written by the trade media on a number of similar products, contrasting their pros and cons. Everything from small parts to whole pieces of expensive equipment are loaned out to the various trade publications for these purposes. These products are normally sent on a 90-day loan and returned after the testing is completed. For most media, though, the golden rule of media relations is, "Let them know you by your work, not by your checkbook."

Working with Media People

Finally, there are a few basic rules of thumb that will help you in dealing with the media.

- Always be honest. It takes a lot of hard work to build credibility, and nothing builds credibility like honesty. It only takes one mistake to ruin months of credibility building. If you are honest with the media, they will be fair to you. But, remember, fair to them means balanced and objective. They will tell all sides of a story, even the negative. You should be willing to do the same.
- Give media people what they want, not what you want. Ideally, they can be the same thing. The key, of course, is to make your information newsworthy, following the criteria listed earlier.
- Along the same lines, don't bombard journalists with a daily barrage of press releases. Nothing that happens that often is newsworthy. The reporters and editors who receive your releases know this and are very likely to stop reading your information.

- Don't plead your case or follow up on stories. The nature of publicity is to let the media handle it once you have released it. If you want more control than that, take out an ad.

Media Placement

Knowing the media will go a long way toward enhancing your chances of placing valuable information with them. But, you can't rely on personal contact for everything. Placing PR materials with the media requires up-to-date information on all of the possible outlets for your materials. Naturally, the number and type of media outlets will depend on your business. If you are in the automotive industry, trade journals will be a vital link between you and your publics. If you work for an organization that is strictly local, then your media contacts will be limited to the local media. Local interest news will be important, too, within the communities in which your plants or offices are located. If you work for a regional or even a national operation, then your contacts will expand accordingly. Whatever media you deal with, it is important to keep updated lists and directories that meet your particular needs with the least amount of waste information.

Directories and Media Lists

A good directory is an indispensable tool for the media relations specialist. Directories come in all sizes and address almost every industry. Publishers of directories offer formats ranging from global *checkers* that include a variety of sources in every medium, to specialized directories dealing with a single medium.

There are a number of excellent directories for media placement. Here are some of the major ones.

- *Bacon PR and Media Information Systems.* A series including *Bacon's Publicity Checker* (two volumes covering editorial contacts in the US and Canada, magazines organized by industry, daily and weekly newspapers, and all multiple publisher groups); *Bacon's Media Alerts* (a directory of editorial profiles covering editorial features and special issues, often planned months in advance, for both magazines and newspapers); *Bacon's Radio/TV Directory* (a listing of every TV and radio station in the US, listed geographically); and *Bacon's International Publicity Checker* (editorial contact information on magazines and newspapers in 15 Western European countries).

- A series published by Larrison Communications that includes *Medical and Science News Media*; *Travel, Leisure and Entertainment News Media*; and *Business and Financial News Media*.
- *Editor & Publisher*. Several media guides, including the well-used *Editor & Publisher International Yearbook* (a collection of newspapers divided into dailies and weeklies and covering everything from local and national publications to house organs and college papers).

Since the prices of these directories can range into the hundreds of dollars, you will need to be fairly selective.

When choosing a directory, there are some key points to keep in mind.

1. The directory should be current. If it is not updated at least once a year, its uses are limited.
2. The directory should cover the geographic area in which you operate and in which you want your organization's message to go out. You may not need a national directory if your operation is strictly local or statewide. Many states publish directories of all kinds of information, like almanacs, that include media addresses.
3. If your primary target is trade publications, then you need to choose a directory that lists them. Standard Rate and Data Service, for instance, publishes a constant stream of listings, including business and industry directories.
4. If you are a heavy user of broadcast media, your directory should include broadcast listings.
5. The directory should list names of editors, news directors, etc., and their addresses. Make sure these are current. Nothing is more embarrassing to you and more infuriating to them than to receive a press release addressed to the previous editor.
6. Make sure the circulation is listed for print publications and listening/viewing audience for broadcast outlets. You don't want to waste an excellent story on a tiny circulation trade when you might have reached a much larger audience.

Directories are essential, but they are not the only tools you will need to keep up to date with media relations. Media lists are vital to your job. They are a more personal tool than directories since they contain details about local contacts and all the information you need to conduct business in your community. Media lists may include regional and even nationwide contacts depending on the scope of your operation. A media list, once compiled, has to updated by hand at least once a month. This is usually a minor job and can be handled very efficiently by clerical staff once the list is compiled. It only takes a 30-second phone call to each of the media outlets on your list to verify names and addresses. In the long run, the routine of updating will pay off.

In compiling a media list, you will need to include most of the following items.

1. Name of the publication, radio/TV station, particular show (for talk shows), etc.
2. Names of editors, reporters, news directors, etc.
3. Addresses, including mailing and street addresses if they are different. You may need to hand deliver a press release on occasion, and this can be difficult if all you have is a PO box number.
4. Telephone and FAX numbers for the media outlets as well as for each of the people you have on your list. Many media outlets can now accept computer-generated press releases through normal telephone lines or satellite-transmitted video or audio actualities. Include details in your media list.
5. Any important editorial information such as style guidelines, deadlines, times of editions (morning/evening), dates of publication for magazines, times of broadcasts, use of actualities, photo requirements, use of facsimile or electronic transmission (and applicable phone numbers).

If you use a computer for record keeping, it is a great way to compile and maintain a media list. Computer software designed specifically for media lists (such as *PR Works* for the Macintosh) is also now available.

Placement Agencies

Placement agencies are outfits that will take your information, such as a press release, and send it out to a great many media outlets using their regularly updated media lists and computerized mailing services. Many of these firms guarantee hundreds of mailings per release and, in fact, mail out hundreds of releases for you—at a tidy cost.

Placement agencies will provide you with a great many more mailings than you might have gotten from your personal mailing list, but much of what is mailed out is not correctly targeted and ends up as waste coverage. As any business editor will tell you, the majority of press releases received are not relevant to the publication, and many originated from placement agencies in other states. You are often better off targeting those media with which you are most familiar and who you know are at least interested in your information.

The sole exception might be the newer, computerized firms such as PR Newswire. Organizations such as this send out your release electronically, over a newswire—just like the Associated Press. Media outlets can subscribe (free of charge) to the service and will receive your release—along with hundreds of others—sorted by subject and other descriptors. They can scan by subject, look at the lead only, or pull up the whole release. This method severely reduces the amount of paper they have to plow through and guarantees at least subjects of interest to them. Your advantage is that you can target locally, regionally or nationally. Of course, the price of placing the release increases with its coverage.

Fit Your Information to Your Outlet

It is essential to know as much as possible about the media outlet to which you are sending your information. Never submit information blindly to publications or stations you've never read, watched or listened to. Picking a trade publication out of *Standard Rate and Data* just because it has a large circulation doesn't ensure that it is the type of publication in which you want to see your story.

The key, of course, is to read the publication, watch the TV station, or listen to the radio station first. By doing so, you also will learn about the outlet's style and will be able to tailor your release accordingly.

If you are writing for a trade journal, don't automatically assume that the one you have chosen is similar in style to others in the industry. Remember that publications are often differentiated by their styles when they deal with similar subject matter.

Understanding Radio and Television

Before placing information on the radio, you will need to understand the concept of format. Whereas placement of your message on televition requires a familiarity with the various program offerings of the stations you are dealing with, placement on radio is usually determined by the format of the station—usually designed around the type of music it plays or information it provides. For example, some stations play only Top-40 hits. These stations usually cater to a teenage audience. If a teen audience is your target public, then you might want to consider sending your information to a Top-40 station. Other stations might provide a news-only format, or a jazz format, or a classical music format.

Determining what radio station you place your message on depends on what your target audience listens to, and that is determined through audience research. If, for instance, your target audience regularly listens to jazz, then you would be best served to place your message on a station using a jazz format. Examine the formats and styles of all publications or broadcast shows you would like to accept your information. Prepare your material in a style as close to theirs as you can. For example, if you are pre-recording PSAs (public service announcements) for use on various stations, you might want to put a different music track on each spot depending on the format of the station with which it will be placed. Nothing is quite so jarring to listeners of a classical music station than to have their entertainment interrupted with a message surrounded by a rock music background. While a rock music station might carry a spot with a classical music background, the opposite is probably not true.

Any radio sales manager will be able (and quite willing) to provide you with detailed analyses of the station's listening audience. All you have to do is to match your target audience profile with its listener profile.

Television is much easier to figure out. It is a medium that reaches the broadest segment of the population. Rather than depending on formatting to attract a single audience, television depends on different programs and times of day to attract different audiences.

To determine which television station to use, you will first need to know how far its signal reaches (commonly referred to as *reach*). Just like radio, a TV sales manager will be able to give you detailed statistics on viewing audiences by time of day and program.

You will need to consider the following questions before you write for either radio or television.

1. If radio, what format does the station use? If television, what programs are appropriate to your message?
2. Will the station take taped actualities (for interviews or reactions)? If so, what kind of tape? Reel-to-reel? Cassette? If it is video for television, will the station want one-inch tape, or three-quarter- or half-inch cassette? Can they use slides? How about slide-tape?
3. What length spot will the station use? 10-, 20-, 30-, or 60-second spots?
4. Who will write the copy? Will you write and submit it or will you simply give the station the information? Will the station use scripts you have written for its announcers to read?

5. Will the station provide production services or will you have to have your message prerecorded?
6. How much lead time does the station need? For production? For placement?

All of these considerations, and probably a few more, will have to be taken into account before you can work successfully with the broadcast media. Note that all this information should be included in your media list.

Broadcast Cover Letter

Before you send any information to a radio or television in station in the form of a "spot" (a written script or pre-recorded message designed specifically for broadcast), make sure it is accompanied by a cover letter explaining the content, and a mail-back card of some kind through which the station can let you know when and if your spot was aired. **Exhibit 2.1** is a generic example of such information.

Exhibit 2.1—Cover letter and mail-back card

The American Tuberculosis Foundation
1212 Folger Street
New York, New York 00912

Dear Program Director:

Smoking and lung disease are illnesses that affect all of us in some way. The recent concern over second-hand smoke has resulted in considerable debate. In an effort to help "clear the air," the American Tuberculosis Foundation hopes you will run the enclosed radio/TV spots for the education of your listening/viewing audience.

Since our campaign started in January, over 300 radio/TV stations around the country have responded by airing the "Your Good Health" spots. We hope that you will join them in serving your listening/viewing audience.

For your convenience, we have provided you with a mail-back card. By filling out this important evaluation, you will help us to better serve our common interests in the future.

Thank you,

MAIL-BACK CARD: "YOUR GOOD HEALTH"

I have aired or intend to air the following spots: (circle appropriate length).

10 sec. 20 sec. 30 sec. 60 sec.

Radio Television

The spots aired the following times and dates:

Day	Times

CHAPTER 3

Press Releases & Backgrounders

Though it be honest, it is never good to bring bad news...

William Shakespeare

The press release has been called the workhorse of public relations. Every day, thousands of press releases are sent out all over the country to newspapers, magazines, and radio and television stations. Some newspaper editors receive as many as a thousand a month. Of these, only a minuscule number are ever used, and most of these are severely edited. Why, then, do public relations professionals, and the people who employ them, continue to use press releases? Because they are still effective. They are still used by newspapers and trade journals to pass along information about events and occurrences that reporters might not otherwise have the time or the inclination to cover.

The key to effective press releases is not so much in the writing, although we will concentrate on that, but in the placement. As we saw in the previous chapter, knowing when something is newsworthy and when it is not, and knowing your contacts in the media and their schedules and guidelines, are the most important elements of press release writing.

As a writer of press releases, you will become a reporter. It is essential that you understand journalistic style in order to present your releases in the proper format. Remember that reporters and editors are used to seeing one style of writing on a daily basis. That style fits their papers and they are unlikely to print anything that doesn't conform. Remember, too, that although the reporter is responsible only to his or her editor, you are responsible to both the editor and the people you work for. This means that you must accommodate the style of the newspaper and the needs of your employer. It is not an easy fence to walk, but as a public relations practitioner, you have to try to keep your balance.

What is a Press Release?

A press release is information that you wish released to the press, usually the print media. Although all press releases have format in common, there are different emphases.

- Basic **publicity releases** cover any information occurring within an organization that might have some news value to local, regional or even national media.
- **Product releases** deal with specific products or product lines. These are usually targeted to trade publications within individual industries. They can deal with the product itself, consumer use of the product, or a particular business or marketing angle.
- **Financial releases** are used primarily in shareholder relations; however, they are also of interest to financial media and many local, regional, and national general media have financial highlights sections.

Writing a Press Release

The style of the press release is that of the straight news story: it begins with a lead, expands on the lead and proceeds to present information in decreasing order of importance . This "inverted pyramid" style allows an editor to perform his or her job—that is, edit—from the bottom up.

The Lead

The lead is all important. You are competing for the editor's attention with scores of other press releases. A quick glance at the lead should tell the editor whether he can use your release or not. Note, however, that a publicist's lead is likely to differ from one written by a newspaper reporter. The following examples, written for a local newspaper, will serve to explain the difference.

> *Publicist's Lead:*
> Francis Langly, former Director of Research and Development at Rogers Experimental Plastics Company, will be awarded the prestigious Goodyear Medal on June 6 in Indianapolis at a banquet held in his honor. Awarded by the American Chemical Society, the Goodyear Medal is the premier award for work in the field of specialty elastomers.

> *Reporter's Lead:*
> Francis Langly, 24 Cedar Crest Drive, will receive the Goodyear Medal at the annual meeting of the American Chemical Society. The conference is being held in Indianapolis on June 6.

Although neither of these examples is particularly—public relations releases rarely are—there are still reasons for the differences in content and style. Consider these questions.

1. Why is the address left out in the publicist's lead?
2. Why is Langly's title included in the publicist's lead?
3. What is the difference between the phrases "will receive" and "will be awarded"?
4. What is the significance for the publicist in pointing out that the Goodyear medal is the premier award in the field?

Answers to these questions illustrate the differences between hard news and publicity and between the publicist's and the journalist's objectives.

As every journalist knows, the lead is the hook that entices the reader into your story. For the public relations practitioner, too, the lead is a hook to entice the editor into running your release. Don't ever get the notion that any press release you send out will automatically be printed or that it will even be printed the way you wrote it. The fact is, that even if you have written the most appealing press release ever seen at the *Daily Planet*, editors feel an obligation to edit. You will be lucky to have the information in your release placed. This should not deter you from writing a good lead, however, and a good release. First, you have to sell the editor before your release will ever be seen by anyone else.

Editors often take less than 30 seconds to peruse a press release. A lot depends on how you present yourself in the headline (title) and the lead. Most editors use several measures to determine whether your release will be used. Who you are, as regards your past record of providing only legitimate news, is the first important consideration. Once past that, your headline or title should tell them whether your release is important to them or not (more on this later). Finally, your lead should summarize the relevancy of your story.

The *summary lead* is by far the most common type. A good summary lead will answer the key questions—who, what, when, where, why and how. The delayed lead is used to add drama to a news story; however, this type of lead is usually reserved for feature stories and is not appropriate for straight news.

Before you write the lead, you must first decide on a theme. Try to determine what is unique about the event covered by your release. Although press releases should generally be considered as straight news stories, and must be informative, they don't have to be boring. To illustrate, look at the lead from a release distributed by the Electronic Producers Association.

> "The present condition of the software market is such that companies involved in software development should be able to capitalize on current economic trends. This means that new product development should allow the earliest investors a significant niche in the market." This statement was made by Mr. James L. Sutton, President of Associated Products Corporation, during a speech at the Fall convention of the Electronic Products Producers Association held in Syracuse, New York.

Now consider this revised version of the same lead.

> A leading electronics industry executive declared today (October 21) that the computer software market is wide open to new investors.
>
> "The present condition of the software market is such that companies involved in software development should be able to capitalize on current trends," said James L. Sutton, President of Associated Products Corporation. "This means that new product development should allow the earliest investors a significant niche in the market."
>
> Sutton's prediction of a dynamic market was made in a speech given at the Fall convention of the Electronic Products Producers Association in Syracuse, New York.

Notice how the second lead has broken up the quote and used the proper journalistic form for attribution. The opening paragraph has been rewritten to include most of the pertinent information:

Who? A leading electronics industry executive.

What? Declared a wide-open computer software market.

When? Today (October 21). Notice the inclusion of the actual date in parentheses. This is to let the editor know that the "today" you are speaking of is October 21. If the paper receives the release on October 20 but doesn't publish the information until October 22, they will need to correct the copy to read "yesterday."

Where? Left until the final paragraph. (It isn't always necessary to squeeze all of the information into the first graph.)

Why? Included in the explanatory paragraph following the lead. Of all the information, why is the most likely to be left out of the lead because it usually takes the most explanation and invites the interested reader to look further.

How? In a speech. Also left for the final graph.

The thing to remember is that you are responsible for the ordering of points in your lead and in your press release. The more interesting you can make the information by order of presentation, the better it will read. Notice also how much shorter the sentences *seem* in the revised version. In fact, there is only one more sentence than in the original, but because the quote is broken up and the attribution placed in the middle, the sentences seem much shorter. Although it is wise to present most of the key information early in the release, only the most important elements need appear in the lead. The rest can follow in logical order.

Using Quotations

Quotations add interest to your press release. It is always good to obtain usable quotations and then to place them at appropriate spots throughout the release. Note that it is never a good idea to begin a press release with a quote. Since press releases are considered straight news stories, a quote fails to come to the point soon enough. As was seen above, quotes need not be written as complete sentences, followed by the attribution; they can be broken up by the attribution. You don't need to follow every quotation by an attribution, especially if it is understood that the same person quoted earlier is still being quoted. A good rule of thumb is to repeat an attribution if more than one paragraph has elapsed since it was last given. Of course, if you change the source of the quotation, you will need to designate the change by a new attribution. Don't be afraid to work with the form of attribution, and don't use the same form each time. Consider the following:

> Johnson, a long-time trucker, doesn't like the strike. "This layoff has really affected my family," *he said*. The strike has been in effect for three months. "We're down to eating beans out of a can," *he said*. Johnson has three small children and a $150 a month house payment. "I don't know what I'm going to do about my bills," *he said*.

The form of attribution (...*he said*) is correct but its repetition is monotonous. There are a number of ways of attributing a quotation that can add variety to releases. For example, you can simply paraphrase points of the quote, combine quotes, or simply use one attribution *between* two quotes. Look at this revised version.

> Johnson, a long-time trucker, doesn't like the three-month-long strike. "This layoff has really affected my family," he says. "We're down to eating beans out of a can."
>
> Johnson, who has three small children and a $150 a month house payment says he doesn't know what he's going to do about his bills.

Notice that the tense of the attribution has also been changed to the present. Press releases need to sound as timely as possible which includes using the present tense in attributions if possible. If you are dealing with a story that is obviously past, then attribution must reflect this.

Most newswriting classes and most journalists adhere to the rule of using only the last name in an attribution. Press releases, on the other hand, must follow the conventions set up by the originating organization. In most cases, even if you do insist on attributing a quotation to "Mr. Jones" or "President Smith," the news editor will delete the honorific. You will have done your job by using the conventions of your employer. In the long run, that is all you are expected to do.

Accuracy

The accuracy of quotations is obviously important, but while public relations writers can have some leeway, reporters must be absolutely accurate. An illustration will help explain. Suppose you work for Rogers Experimental Plastics Company. You are writing a release on a new product line and are quoting the company president. You have interviewed the president and he knows you are writing the release. He is also aware of what he said. However, since he will probably be reviewing the release before it is sent out, he will correct anything he doesn't like. As a writer and an employee, you have the creative ability and leeway to "invent" a quotation as long as he approves it. No employer will fault you for putting well written words in his mouth. Suppose the president had said:

> I don't think anything like this new plastic has ever been seen—at least not around this area of the world. It may be the greatest thing since sliced bread and who knows how much money we'll make from it.

You may actually write in your release:

> Paul Johnson, President of REPC, is excited about the new product. "We've come up with a totally new concept in plas-

> tic," he says. "I expect that the market for 'Plagets' in the West will be tremendous."

All you've done is tidy up the quotation and make it more interesting. Remember that you may "doctor" only quotations that will be checked for accuracy and approved by the party to whom they are attributed. It is a good rule to make sure that anyone you interview receives a copy of the finished release before it is distributed. There is nothing like a libel suit for sobering up a writer. Of course, one legitimate way of presenting unclear or clumsy quotations is to paraphrase or use indirect attribution. This is fine for news stories written by reporters, but press releases can benefit a great deal from well-written quotations.

Press Release Format

Although public relations practitioners often incorporate the conventions of their organization into their press releases, there is a standard press release format.

1. Press releases are typically written on plain, white bond paper with no decorative border.
2. Margins are one to one-and-a-half inches on all sides.
3. The address of the sender is placed in the upper left-hand corner of the first page. This identifying block should include the complete address, name of the contact person (usually the person who wrote the release), and a telephone number. It is especially important to include a night telephone number as well as a daytime number. Remember, newspapers don't shut down at night and if an editor wants to use your release but needs further or clarifying information and can't reach you, the release may get dumped.
4. The release date appears on the right margin, slightly lower than the bottom of the address block. This portion provides the editor with exact information concerning the appropriate timing for the release. More about release dates later.
5. The body of the release begins about one-third of the way down the page allowing some white space for comments or notes from the editor. If there is to be a title, and titles are entirely optional, it should come between the address block and the body of the release, flush left. Typically, the title does not extend beyond the address block

by more than a few characters, which usually means that it will be stacked (broken into two lines on top of each other). The title should be in all caps, single spaced, with the last line underlined.

6. The body of the press release is double spaced. Never single-space a press release. Paragraphs are usually indented with normal spacing between graphs. Some companies prefer no indention and triple-spacing between graphs but the standard is indented.
7. If the release runs more than a page, the word "more" is placed in brackets or within dashes at the bottom of the page.
8. Following pages are identified by a slug-line followed by several dashes and the page number at the top of the page, usually either flush left or right.
9. The end of the release is designated in one of several ways. Use the word "end" or the number "30" either in quotation marks or within dashes, or the symbol # # # # #.

Timing and Dating Releases

When do you want your release to be published or broadcast? If you have just written a release about an important meeting which will be held tomorrow (January 23) but you don't want the information which will be presented at that meeting to reach the public prior to the meeting, you will have to say so on your release. Although it is wise not to send out releases too far in advance of an event, it is also wise to be as timely as possible—which means getting your release to the paper beforehand.

There are a number of ways of designating release dates and times and all of them belong below the address block, flush right.

1. **Release with no specific time frame.** By far the most common type of release and usually designated by *For Immediate Release*. Other phrases include *For Release on Receipt* or *For Release at Will*. It is unnecessary to add a date to this type of release statement.
2. **Release with specific date.** An example would be *For Release January 23 or Thereafter*, or if you need to be even more specific, *For Release January 23, 10:00 p.m. or Thereafter*. Other options are *Hold for Release, Friday, January 23, 10 a.m.*, or *For Release after 10:00 a.m., Friday, January 23*. This type of release statement could be used, for instance, if you want all the media to carry it at one time; or if the event is actually occurring at a future date but you want to release the information early.

Company or Client Name
and Address Here
Contact: (Your Name)
Day Phone:
Night Phone:

Release Date and Time

THE TITLE GOES HERE, ALL UPPER
CASE AND UNDERLINED LIKE THIS

The Point of Origin Dateline Goes Here -- The body of the release should begin one-third of the way down the page so as to leave enough room for the editor or copy person to write remarks.The release proper should be all double spaced for ease of readability and editing.

Be sure to use normal indents and consistent spacing between paragraphs. It is not necessary to triple space between graphs.All information should be presented in descending order of importance, ending with the least important items in case last-minute editing results in the bottom of your release being lopped off.

Remember to leave at least one-inch margins all around, but resist the urge to leave huge right-hand margins in order to stretch your information. It usually looks like you're writing in a column.

When you arrive at the bottom of the first page, leave at least a one-inch margin and indicate either the end of your release (-30-) or that more information follows (-more-). If more information follows, try not to break paragraphs or sentences in the middle. Never break a word and complete it on the next page

-30-

Exhibit 3.1—Press release format

Datelines

Datelines are used to indicate the point of origin of your press release if, for some reason, that is important. Datelines are important to foreign correspondents to enable readers to appreciate that a story originated at the location where it happened. For public relations practitioners, a dateline may serve the same purpose. It alerts the editor to the fact that your release concerns an event either reported from or happening at a certain geographical location. Datelines should be placed immediately preceding the opening of your release proper, on the same line.

> Springfield, OH—Rogers Experimental Plastics Company (REPC) has announced the development of a versatile new plastic widget which has the potential for use in a number of industries from automotives to electronics.

Note that if the city is well known, there is no need to include the name of the state (New York, Los Angeles, etc.). In the case of a city whose name may be popular in a number of states, you would want to designate the state, (as in the example above to differentiate Springfield, OH, from Springfield, OR, or Springfield, KY, or any number of Springfields). However, if the release is intended for a statewide press only, you can get by with just the name of the city. If there is any possibility that confusion might arise from use of the city name only, include the state (Moscow, Idaho or Moscow, USSR?).

Exclusives and Specials

If your release is an exclusive (intended for only one paper) make sure the editor knows it. Remember that an exclusive can only be sent to one publication. A special, on the other hand, is a release written in a certain style, intended for a specific publication, but being released elsewhere as well. Both designations should be noted immediately below the release information as follows:

> For Immediate Release Exclusive to the Daily Planet
> For Release February 24 or Thereafter Special to the Daily Planet

Local Interest

Local media outlets like local stories. For most public relations writers, press releases can almost always be oriented to a local audience. The real problem is finding just the right local angle—the one that will entice the newspaper into running the story. Some basic rules of thumb will help you in your placement:

1. If you are releasing a story with national as well as local interest , try to construct your release so that any local information is

Deer Point Development, Inc.
Box 1387
Deer Point, Michigan 72493
Contact: Warren Bailey
Day Phone: (714) 858-6635
Night Phone: (714) 645-1765

For Immediate Release
Special to the Deer Point Sentinel

NEW PLANT TO OPEN IN DEER POINT

A new plant designed to manufacture high tech components for automobiles is scheduled to be opened in late July according to Eleanor Maston, president of Deer Point Development, Inc. (DPD).The two-building facility will encompass over 55,000 square feet and be housed on a five-acre plot near the Doe River.Maston's company was instrumental in the planning, acquisition of land, and contracting of firms for the construction of the new plant. The plant will be owned and operated by Auto-Tech, Inc. of Albatross, Maine—a long-time member of the automotive peripherals industry.

Maston predicts that over 800 new jobs will be created by the plant's construction. "Auto-Tech has assured us that they intend to hire the majority of their plant workers from the local community," she says. "They plan to bring in only a bare-bones management crew from the outside to begin with, and train local people from the ground up."

According to Maston, DPD first learned of the scheme last December when Auto-Tech president Wilson Klatchki contacted her.The New England-based company was seeking to expand into the high-tech industry and needed a plant close to the major automobile manufacturers in Detroit. Deer Point seemed like the perfect solution.

-more-

Exhibit 3.2—Exclusives and specials

interspersed throughout the release. This way, it will be difficult to cut out the national information, which might not be of interest to a local editor, without harming the local angle.

2. Avoid commercial plugs. Editors recognize advertising instantly and will simply round-file (trash) your release. Keep your local angle newsworthy.

3. If you are sending only to local media and you reference a local city in your release, omit the name of the state.
4. Above all, don't strain to find a local angle where there is none. Nothing is worse than a transparent local interest angle.

Suppose that you are assigned to write a release that has national importance and you want to target it for a local paper, the *Seattle Times*. You know from your interview with William J. Hoffman, chief systems engineer of Associated Products Corporation of Syracuse, N.Y. that he went to high school and college in Seattle. Based only on this little bit of knowledge, the piece can be localized. In addition, you could try to place a version of the release in the *Lincoln High Review* and another version in the University of Washington *Husky* (the alumni paper). Your leads might look like this:

> For the *Seattle Times*
> William J. Hoffman, Seattle native and Chief Systems Engineer for Associated Products Corporation (APC) of Syracuse, N.Y., has been credited with developing a revolutionary educational software line.
>
> For the *Lincoln High Review*
> William J. Hoffman, a Lincoln High School graduate and former president of the LHS Electronic's Club, has been credited with developing a revolutionary educational software line.
>
> For the *University of Washington Husky*
> William J. Hoffman, a University of Washington graduate with honors in Engineering, has been credited with developing a revolutionary educational software line.

You might think that the Lincoln High School angle is too much of a strain. If you do, don't use it. Every angle, however, is worth, at least, some consideration. You'll be surprised how your placements can multiply if you ask the right questions in your interviews and construct the right angles from the answers.

Remember, though, that the focus of your release isn't always the local angle. That is only the hook. Don't slight your real story in favor of the local angle, no matter how interesting it is. In the samples above, for instance, Hoffman is the angle, but the software is the story. The trick is to lead with the angle, move to the story, and keep the two so intertwined that any editor will have difficulty separating them.

Product Press Releases

Product publicity often has little or nothing to do with advertising. In its strictest sense, advertising refers only to the purchasing of time or space in which to run a message. Product publicity is not paid for. It is a far more subtle art. You must be able to construct informative passages concerning a given product without actually "pitching" the product. This is not an easy task. The minute an editor detects a sales pitch, the release gets pitched.

Most product publicity goes through several stages: product introduction (usually via press releases to trade media), articles in which the product is reviewed after testing (written by the trade publications themselves), and "user articles" (submitted by the public relations writer focusing on actual users of the new product). This section covers only product introduction releases.

Product releases serve a multitude of purposes, from pure information about a single product, to publicity for other companies and other products. It is quite common to mention contributing manufacturers in a product release. For example, if you develop a basic plastic that is then used by a leading headphone manufacturer in their product design, it is usually acceptable to mention their use of your product. There is always the chance that the headphone manufacturer will reciprocate. In fact, many such joint arrangements are formalized when products are publicized. Consider the release in **Exhibit 3.3** about a new water cooler.

Can you tell who the publicity is for? From the address block you learn that the company which manufactures the fountain is sending out the release; however, a second company is also mentioned. The manufacturer of the ice maker is given some free publicity. In many cases, this is a good thing to do. Obviously, you don't want to give your competition a helping hand, but it never hurts to help your friends. Often, it's difficult to tell what the real publicity point is in a product release. If the above release had been written and distributed by an agency or by FREON, Inc., then the "bottom line" publicity would actually be for the ice maker, through publicity for the fountain. This is not an uncommon approach in product publicity and is not normally considered unethical.

Organization of Product Press Releases

Product press releases are arranged slightly differently from other releases. Although they certainly follow the normal inverted pyramid style of decreasing order of importance, they are quite obvious in their inductive approach to the product definition. In other words, product releases normally proceed from a general statement concerning the product (often an announcement that the product is on the market) to specific information about the product's attributes, characteristics and applications. The end of the release is usually reserved for company background—full name, relationship to parent or subsidiary companies, and branch locations or the location at which the specific product is made. The release in **Exhibit 3.4** reflects this pattern of organization.

Tall Drink of Water, Inc.
435 Lasado Circle
Watertown, NY
Contact: Myrna Hofman
Phone: (121) 393-1222

For Immediate Release

NEW FOUNTAIN DISPENSES
COLD, HOT, AND ICE WATER

Watertown, NY—A new water fountain which dispenses cold water, hot water, and ice has been marketed by Tall Drink of Water,Inc. (TDW) of Watertown, NY. The new fountain, which already is appearing in offices across the country, operates on an entirely new system for compartmentalizing water supplies.

According to TDW president and co-founder, Willis Reed, the new fountain represents four years of hard work. "We spent a lot of time on this new fountain," he says. "It's a whole new concept in water fountains. We did some initial research on office water consumers and found that they wanted not only cold water, but also hot and iced water as well."

The new fountain uses a system of valves which pass the water from the building plumbing system through the fountain in a series of stages. The incoming water is captured first in a central reservoir. From this central pool, the liquid is siphoned off to the cold water tank. This tank feeds the main drinking spout for normal water needs. Ice is produced in a refrigerated tank located next to the cold water reservoir and dispensed through a separate opening in the side of the fountain. On the opposite side of the fountain is the hot water dispenser which feeds off a heater tank located above the main reservoir.

-more-

Exhibit 3.3—Product Press Release

Fountain—2

"It's the addition of the ice maker which makes our fountain unique," says Reed. "We use a Handy-Ice III manufactured by FREON,Inc. in Asbury Park, NJ," he says. "The Ice III produces ice at a rate that far exceeds anything else on the market today. A number of other manufacturers already make dual purpose fountains,but ours covers the entire range of drinking needs."

Reed indicates that the new fountain will probably be marketed in areas with noticeable seasonal shifts. "We expect that areas that have pronounced seasonal temperature fluctuations will have the greatest need for our fountain," he says. "But almost any office where people have different tastes in beverages is a potential market." Reed explains that in any given office environment, 75 percent of the staff will be satisfied with just plain water; however, the other 25 percent will use a fountain for making hot drinks such as tea and soup in the winter and iced drinks in the hot months. He also expects that the very availability of such a fountain will increase its usage.

Those interested in installing TDW's new fountain may do so on a 90-day free basis by contacting the Marketing Department at the following address:

Tall Drink of Water, Inc.
435 Lasado Circle
Watertown, NY 10056

# # # # #

Rogers Experimental Plastics Company
1234 Elastomer Drive

Springfield, Ohio
Contact: Patricia Williams
Days: (419)784-9982
Nights: (419)453-6542

For Immediate Release

VERSATILE NEW PLASTIC WIDGET
HAS INDUSTRY-WIDE APPLICATIONS

Rogers Experimental Plastics Company (REPC) has announced the development of a versatile new plastic widget with the potential for use in a number of industries from automotives to electronics. The new widget, dubbed "Plaget," is a vacuum-molded elastomer product displaying characteristics of both plastic and rubber.

"We've worked for almost five years on this widget,"says Raoul Simpson, materials engineer for Rogers. "We think 'Plaget' will revolutionize the way designers think about widgets from now on." Simpson led the team that developed "Plaget" and has already begun experiments designed to test its broad range of applications. "We already know it can be used in the automotive industry replacing the heavy two-piece metal widgets now being used," he says. "We suspect that it will be useful in a number of related and unrelated industries including electronics as a more cost-effective replacement for fiberoptics."

The key element to the success of "Plaget" is its ability to withstand temperature extremes and its resistance to oil and abrasive chemicals. And because of its characteristic conductive nature, it has the potential for a number of applications in the electronics industry.

-more-

Exhibit 3.4—Product Press Release

Writing News Releases for Broadcast

Radio is meant to be heard and television is made to be seen and heard. That means you have to write for the ear or for the ear and eye. Simplification is the key to broadcast writing. Because it is harder to absorb the spoken word than the written word, concepts need to be pared down to the bare bones. Sentences must be shorter, speech more colloquial, and complex

"Plaget"—2

Paul Johnson, president of REPC, is excited about the new product. "We've come up with a totally new concept in plastic widgets," he says. "I expect that the market for 'Plagets' in the West will be tremendous."

Rogers Experimental Plastics has been developing plastics products for uses in industry since its founding in 1979. It is located in Springfield with a subsidiary in Cleveland.

# # # # #

issues distilled to their essence. One of the major advantages of using broadcast media is its repeatability. Listeners may hear or see a message many times in the course of a single day or a single week. Even so, you must learn to write as though your audience will only hear or see your message one time.

Consider the differences between these two releases—one meant for print, the other for radio.

Print:
INDIANAPOLIS, June 6—Francis Langly, former Director of Research and Development for Rogers Experimental Plastics Company (REPC), today received the American Chemical Society's (ACS) Goodyear Medal—ACS's most prestigious award—for his work in the field of speciality elastomers.

Radio:
At an awards luncheon in Indianapolis today, a Wilmington native received the highest honor of the American Chemical Society. The prestigious Goodyear Medal—awarded for work in the field of specialty elastomers—went to Francis Langly, former Director of Research and Development for Rogers Experimental Plastics Company.

Although both releases are of approximately the same length, there are some noticeable differences which raise some interesting questions:

1. Why doesn't the broadcast release start with a dateline?
2. Why not use the abbreviations ACS and REPC in the broadcast release?
3. What is the reason for beginning the broadcast release with the location rather than the name as in the print release?

Datelines are not needed in broadcast releases because they won't be read. Although they might still indicate the point of origin, once they are committed speech, the point of origin usually becomes clear through the narrative.

Abbreviations are too confusing when heard on the air. It is always advisable to use the entire name, unless the abbreviation has become commonplace usage.

Finally, beginning with location in broadcast helps set the scene. This is peculiar to broadcasting and is a carryover from drama in which a scene is set prior to any dialogue.

Use the medium to your advantage. If you are using radio, set the scene first, then populate it with real people and easy-to-understand facts. Remember, a news release for radio or television is just that—news. It is intended for the same purpose as a press release—to be used as news. The closer to acceptable news style it is, the better your chances of getting it broadcast. Prepare your releases for broadcast media using the same format you would use for a print release. **Exhibit 3.5** illustrates this.

After reading the broadcast release in **Exhibit 3.5**, ask yourself some questions.

Society for Needy Children
4240 Welxton Ave.
Newhope, MN 78940
Contact: Lucille Bevard
Day Phone: 438-8743
Night Phone: 544-9745

For Immediate Release

A little girl stood for the first time today to receive a new teddy bear and a check for $75,000 from the Society for Needy Children. Eight-year-old Mary Patterson accepted the check on behalf of the children at the St. Mary Martha's Children's Hospital. The money represents the culmination of a year-long fund-raising drive by the Society.

The money is earmarked for a new ward to be devoted exclusively to the treatment of crippling diseases in children. One of the first beneficiaries will undoubtedly be little Mary who has been disabled by congenital arthritis since birth. Along with her new teddy bear, Mary and the other children at the hospital will be using a new physical therapy center which was donated by a matching grant from the Friends of St. Mary Martha's.

Hospital Administrator, Lois Shelcroft says that the check and the new therapy center are just the first step, and that the Society for Needy Children has promised to continue its fundraising efforts on the hospital's behalf in the coming year. Society spokesperson, Jane Alexander, says that the next fund-raising drive, scheduled to begin in September, will provide funding for a new lab.

# # # # #

Exhibit 3.5—Broadcast Release

- Why is paraphrase used instead of direct quotation in this release?
- Does the lead establish a sense of place prior to coming to the point?
- Can you locate all the elements of a lead within the release?
- Are they where they should be in order of importance?
- If you were a news announcer, what additional information would you want to have before you ran this story?

Remember, no matter what the type of press release, it is still information you will lose control over once it is sent out to the media. They are your primary audience. You must learn to write for them first. To the extent that you do this, your releases will have a greater chance of reaching any other audience.

Backgrounders

Backgrounders are in-depth information pieces. As the name implies, they provide background information for anyone wishing it—reporters, ad copywriters, speech writers, and editors. Backgrounders are almost always prepared by the public relations staff. A good backgrounder is comprehensive yet concise. It should never be used to espouse company policy or philosophy. That is reserved for controlled media, such as ads, and editorials.

Backgrounders frequently accompany press releases in press kits. They usually supply enough information so that the media can fill in any gaps left by the release. Often, they are just insurance against getting called in the middle of the night by a reporter who is editing your press release and in the need of some "background." Other times, they are important "sales pieces," setting up an historical need for a new product (see, for example, **Exhibit 3.6**). In order to make a backgrounder comprehensive, the public relations writer must research as many sources as possible, including old articles, brochures, reports, press releases and materials published outside the organization. Backgrounders can also benefit from personal interviews. As with press releases, backgrounders are more readable if they contain firsthand information.

Organization

Backgrounders should begin with a statement of the issue being addressed. Since it is not a news story or press release, it need not be presented as a lead nor need it follow the inverted pyramid style. Most backgrounders, however, do follow a basic pattern.

1. Open with a concise statement of the issue or subject on which the accompanying press release is based. Try to make it as interesting as possible. This opening statement should lead logically into the next section.

2. Follow the opening with an historical overview of the issue. You should trace its evolution—how it came to be—and the major events leading up to it. It is permissible here to use outside information. For instance, if you were writing a backgrounder on a new surgical technique, you would want to trace briefly the history of the technique's development and tie this in with information on techniques that had been used in the past. It is advisable to name your sources in the body of the text when appropriate. Readers of backgrounders want to know where you got your information.
3. Work your way to the present. This is the meat of your backgrounder. You want to explain the issue you opened with and its significance. Be factual. Remember, a backgrounder is an information piece, not an advertisement, or the place to sell your company's philosophy.
4. Present the implications of the issue being discussed and point the direction for future applications. Even though a backgrounder is a public relations piece, it needs to be carefully couched in fact-based information.
5. Use subheads where appropriate. Subheads negate the need for elaborate transitions and allow you to order your information logically. Subheads need to be carefully chosen and should contribute to understanding.
6. Most backgrounders are four or five pages in length. Let your information dictate your length; however, don't become long winded or pad your document. Editors will recognize fluff immediately. The object of a backgrounder is to provide information and answer anticipated questions, nothing more.

The backgrounder in **Exhibit 3.6** was used as an accompanying piece to a press release touting the advantages of a fire-resistant latex foam for use in upholstered furniture and mattresses.

- How does it follow the recommendations for writing a backgrounder?
- How does it differ?
- Does it trace the history of the issue adequately?
- Does it bring the reader up to the present and cover the current status of the issue?

Contents, Not Structure, Pose the Most Fire Hazards

Losses to unwanted fires are costing billions of dollars and claiming thousands of lives each year in the United States. The National Fire Protection Association handbook states: "Fire resistive construction is an important life-safety measure. However, severe fires may occur in the contents of fire resistive buildings, and highly combustible decorations and interior finish materials may more than offset the value of noncombustible structurals." In fact, of all the contents common to residential, commercial and institutional occupancies, the most often underestimated is the hazard from burning upholstered chairs and mattresses.

Although the many desirable features of a fire resistive building cannot be overlooked, there is no such thing as a "fireproof" building. Regardless of the construction type, there are always combustibles within the building. Generally, contents fires present a greater life safety hazard to building occupants than the eventual ignition of the structure. In fact, the cause and early stages of fires are related to the building contents and interior finish materials and not the structure.

No matter what the construction type, the contents fire must be controlled in order to achieve life safety. A parallel may be drawn between a contents fire in a fire resistive building and a fire in a furnace. The contents are the fuel and the building is the furnace.

Statistics Show Furniture Fires on the Rise

The Consumer Products Safety Commission recently stated that in 1981 there were about 62,000 bedding fires which caused 930 fatalities. Another 35,000 fires in upholstered furniture took 1,400 lives prompting the Commission to declare that these materials are the "biggest killer of all the products under the jurisdiction of the agency."

The National Bureau of Standards had earlier reported that mattresses, bedding and upholstered furniture were involved in 45 percent of the fatal fires they reviewed where the materials first ignited could be identified. They concluded that "any inroads that can be made into the furniture problem promises greater fire-death reduction than any other type of strategy."

Exhibit 3-6—Backgrounder

Building Design not the Answer

As for building design, recent well-publicized fires have resulted in new provisions to building fire codes; however, over 90 percent of the buildings that will be in use in the year 2000 have already been built. Reliance on these new fire codes for personal safety may, in fact, be unwarranted.

Although building design and fire protection devices are important, they do not guarantee the safety of the occupants. Many fires develop too rapidly for fire systems, such as sprinklers, to control. Fires can spread past a sprinkler head to another area before the sprinkler head operates. Another fire might smolder for hours, producing deadly smoke and gases but not enough heat to cause operation for the sprinkler system. In addition, property loss is most closely related to fire-resistant building materials which would have to be incorporated into future structures. Building contents most strongly affect human safety.

Fire Reduction Not Yet a Reality

A decade ago, the National Commission on Fire Prevention and Control reported that fire was a major national problem, ranking between crime and product safety in annual cost. They were appalled to find "that the richest nation in the world leads all the major industrialized countries in per capita deaths and property loss from fire." The efforts of this commission focused attention on fires and resulted in the establishment of a goal to reduce the nation's fire losses by 50 percent in the next decade—that was in 1972.

Recent fire loss data from the National Fire Prevention Association suggests that we have performed poorly in our efforts to reduce the nation's fire losses. Multiple death fires, killing three or more people, have increased 70 percent in the past decade. In fact, fatalities in this group rose 37 percent between 1972 and 1980, and fires in this category are increasing at an average rate of 7.5 percent a year.

The estimated property loss from just building fires in the United States during 1980 was about $6 billion, an increase of almost 7 percent from 1980. Further analysis of the estimated 1981 fire loss data shows that:

— Educational facilities lost $184 million, an increase of 82.2 percent over 1980 figures.

— Institutional facilities lost $38 million, up 52 percent.

— Areas of public assembly lost $356 million, up 9.2 percent.

— And residential occupancies, such as hotels, motels and apartments, lost $3.3 billion, up 7.1 percent from 1980.

Judging from this data, it is apparent that the goal of reducing fire losses by 50 percent has not been met. In fact, fire losses appear to be steadily increasing in most cases. Why? In answering this question, some important points must be taken into consideration:

— Contents may more than offset the value of noncombustible building materials, and

— the flammability properties of the contents are critical to life safety.

Although most new buildings are constructed in accordance with a national building code such as the National Fire Protection Agency (NFPA) 101 Life Safety Code or a similar code, no national code regulates upholstered seating or mattresses. And despite the existence of a Federal mattress flammability standard, its effectiveness has been questioned by both the Consumer Products Safety Commission and the National Bureau of Standards. As a result, a concrete fortress could be built according to code and filled with furniture which burns like gasoline. Larger buildings can contain tons of such furniture.

The Burden of Safety is on the Buyer

In the absence of codes specifically meant for furniture, the burden of safety falls on the person selecting furniture for a residence, commercial structure or installation. Greater care must be taken to select the most fire-resistant furniture available for a particular need. In judging these needs, the hazards to which the furniture might be exposed should be considered, such as the likelihood of cigarette burns, openflames, proximity of fuel or other combustibles, and population density. For example, in areas with a high level of vandalism, materials with a good open flame resistance might be needed, while furniture prone to accidental ignition may only need to be cigarette resistant.

The ultimate test of any furniture is, of course, how it will perform in an actual fire. It is obvious that fire-resistant structures are not enough to ensure life safety. If the nation's fire losses are to be reduced, then the potential hazards of furnishings must be considered.

# # # # #

Could you tell from reading this backgrounder that it was meant to "sell a product"? Probably not, unless you knew in advance that it was part of a product-related press kit. The object of a backgrounder is to provide background, not to "sell" anything. In the case of this particular backgrounder, information is provided concerning fire safety and the need for purchasers of upholstered furniture to be aware of the dangers of fire. The next step is to present the readers with a suggested action. This can, and often does, come in the accompanying product press release. Thus, the trick to writing backgrounders is to make them relate to your subject without actually "pushing" your product, philosophy, or service.

Case Study: Associated Products Corporation

The following information pertains to a mythical company. Additional information will be presented in subsequent chapters. Use this and the additional information to complete all assignments.

Background

You work in the Public Relations Department of the Marketing Division of Associated Products Corporation (APC), located in Syracuse, New York. APC is a large company with several divisions, each manufacturing a different product. The Marketing Division handles all the marketing for all of the products company wide. As part of the Marketing Division, the Public Relations Department is charged with handling the company's image with its various publics including consumers.

The Electronics Division of APC has just developed a new line of educational software for both IBM and Apple computers. The software, called InfoQuick or IQ, is a series of programs designed as teaching aids for a variety of curricula from first grade through high school.

The development of the IQ series was an ambitious undertaking costing millions of dollars. Not only were educators in a number of fields consulted, but the best programmers available were hired to develop the software. At this point, the first programs have been developed for grades 1–12 in history and science, and in math for grades 9–12.

Advertising is being handled by an outside agency. The new software line will be marketed under a blanket educational "road show" demonstrating its uses in schools, shopping malls, and trade shows in addition to the agency advertising. This will all be handled in-house by the Marketing Division and the Public Relations Department.

The Product

Since the advent of the personal computer scarcely ten years ago, a major market has developed in software. Companies ranging from the manufacturers of the personal computers on which the software is to be run to independent companies whose sole product is software have entered this very lucrative market. Each year in the US, over $10 million in software is purchased by owners of business and personal computers. Of that $10 million, some $2 million is spent on educational software. The major buyers are individuals who purchase the software for their children. Schools account for roughly four percent of purchases.

The range of software available includes game-oriented programs designed to stimulate the otherwise reticent learner. Recent studies conducted at California University have shown that problem learners have benefited the most from this type of program. The recent video game fad has added impetus to the market by providing a vehicle for learning. Many programs have already been developed utilizing the video game approach to learning. It has been found that students become more involved and acquire knowledge faster when the learning process is interactive.

The major thrust at this time appears to be the development of cohesive and comprehensive software packages which can be used by a varied age group at different levels of education. As part of a major study carried out last year by California Research Institute (CRI), teachers in grades 1–12 were questioned as to the educational needs of their students. Forty-five percent stressed the need for more student-teacher interaction, given large class sizes and brief class periods. Among the 1200 respondents in the CRI study, 35 percent knew something about computers, 10 percent owned their own personal computers, and 55 percent rated themselves as having little or no knowledge of computers. However, even among those who expressed no knowledge of computers, there was a strong willingness to accept computer technology as a suggested solution to the student-teacher interaction problem.

Name of software package: InfoQuick or IQ

Areas developed to date:

History programs, grades 1–12
Science programs, grades 1–12
Math programs, grades 9–12

Sample software programs

History

1. Famous Historical Personalities Series

Meet Mr. Franklin
Meet Mr. Lincoln

These programs explore historical figures as if they were living people. The students must interact with them in simulated computer conversations. By learning about the characters, the students will learn something about the period in which they lived and the policies they helped develop and influence.

2. Famous Documents Series
Writing the Constitution
Mapping the Way West

These programs require the student to actually write or create a map while exploring the reasons behind specific historical events. A student, for instance, might be asked to write what he or she might include in the constitution if it were to be written today. The Way West program teaches basic mapping skills while learning the historical significance of the westward expansion. Students will get to read and work with the treaties that created our country piece by piece.

Science

1. *Big Bones*—All about dinosaurs, with special computer graphics of dinosaurs and their skeletal structure.
2. *Small World*—All about the inside of the atom, with special computer graphics of atomic structure.
3. *Guts*—All about human biology, including skeletal structure, digestive system, circulatory system and muscles.

For High School:

Advanced programs in all Math, Science, and Social Studies areas such as *Algebra IQ, Chemistry IQ, Geometry IQ, etc.*

Software development is continuing and a complete series is expected in all grade levels within two years.

Market Testing

During the concept and development of InfoQuick (IQ), the proposed product was tested "in the field" through a series of programs in target schools. The educators who were hired initially to work in the concept stages of development, were also utilized in the pre-marketing test stages. Three schools were chosen for the test: one each on the East Coast, in the Midwest, and on the West Coast. The schools were selected as reflective of the national average for student enrollment, socio-economic stratum, and cultural balance.

Although it was impossible to select a perfectly "average" school or group of schools, the aim was to test the marketability of IQ on the type of student and school which would be most likely to use the finished product. A high school, junior high, and elementary school were chosen and one complete curriculum package was tested in each school as follows:

Location	**Grade**	**Program**
East Coast	fourth	*Big Bones*
Midwest	seventh	*Meet Mr. Lincoln*
West Coast	eleventh	*Algebra Plus*

The results were analyzed and the programs were moderately revised to adjust to recommendations from teachers and students. The remainder of the programs were designed along the guidelines resulting from these test situations.

The Project

The company realizes that to sell educational software, there must be a demand. To help generate increased demand, and to enhance its status as a corporate good citizen, APC has contacted the National Education Association (NEA) and arranged to work with them on a project that will introduce children to computers. The proposed APC/NEA project will emphasize learning problems, computer skills, and the importance of new technology to education. The project slogan is "Johnny *can* learn to read." The emphasis will be on both the learning of computer skills and learning from computers. APC has donated $1 million to NEA as seed money to get the project underway. Although the public relations aspects of promoting the company through the NEA project and marketing aspects of launching the new IQ line are somewhat separate, there is some overlap.

In addition to the advertising, APC will be working closely with NEA in developing and releasing information and organizing special events to educate the public about computers (and by extension, IQ). NEA proposes to develop a speaker's bureau composed of computer trained educators who will be available nationwide as tutors for other educators and for students. The idea is to set up workshops for educators first, followed by basic demonstrations for students. Part of the APC seed money will go toward supplying computers for the training sessions. Another portion will go into an NEA fund which will help defray the cost of a school or school district's purchase of a computer system.

Some facts:

- More than 2000 school districts in the U.S. have access to or own their own computer system.
- Statistics show that high school graduates with computer skills are likely to obtain higher-paying jobs than those without.

- The National Institute for Scholastic Testing has released a study showing that students between the ages of 7 and 14 have the ability to acquire computer skills readily and absorb information more quickly when it is embedded in a fun-oriented, interactive format such as a computer program.

The NEA

The National Education Association (NEA) is an organization of professional educators in the United States, with more than one million members. The NEA was founded in 1857 as the National Teachers Association and was chartered by Congress in 1906. It is composed of four departments, 16 national affiliates, and 11 associated organizations, each representing an area of specialized interest. Its general aim is to promote the welfare of all professional educators, including both teachers and administrators; however, it has also been a leader in educational innovation and reform.

The Speaker's Bureau

Utilizing the $1 million APC grant, the NEA has assembled a number of speaker-instructors to augment their new program of educating teachers and students in the use of computers as a learning tool. The services of the group, called "Byte of the Apple," are available nationwide by writing care of the National Education Association, Box 1776, Washington, D.C. 00716.

A speaker-instructor will come to the school, present a training session to the teachers and students who will be using the computers, and provide the school or school district with the means for applying for a computer teaching facility of their own from NEA/APC. The training sessions can be adapted to individual needs. The workshop normally includes one four-hour session for teachers only. The next day (or that afternoon if a one-day workshop is desired) another four-hour session will be held involving selected students, allowing teacher-student interaction. Included in the training sessions will be an explanation of how computers work, how they fit into the various curricula, how to teach with a computer, and selected software recommendations for future reference. Initial handouts will include a pamphlet presenting an overview of what the speaker-instructor will be talking about.

Should the school adopt the new computer learning program and order a computer learning center of its own, it will also receive complete print support in the form of workbooks, instruction manuals, and posters concerning computers and software.

The Company

Associated Products Corporation was founded in 1956 as Apex Frozen Foods. In 1960, the company purchased Traxton Electronics and changed its name to Associated Products Company. Since that time, APC has acquired four more concerns: Johnson Paper Company in 1962, LLD Packaging in 1965, Trading Post Textiles in 1965, and Philcronics Electronics in 1970. The current president, James Sutton, took over from the company founder, Alex Cordel, in 1975. Cordel is now Chairman of the Board for APC. Under Sutton, APC has developed several new products including IQ software, a new line of facial tissues, and a new stereo headphone which folds up to fit in the palm of your hand. It has also developed innovative packaging designs for perishable items such as milk, other dairy products, and fresh fruit juices.

Currently, APC is in the midst of negotiating a deal to purchase Value Rent-a-Car. Since its founding in 1956, APC has grown to a position as one of the top 500 corporations in the country. Its total profit last year was $456 million, up 24 percent from the previous year. Its stock has been consistently strong. At the present time, Alex Cordel holds 43 percent of the company stock with the rest divided among about 4500 investors.

The People

William J. Hoffman

William J. Hoffman, chief systems engineer, heads the research team that developed the new IQ software. Hoffman has been chief systems engineer at APC for 10 years and is a native of Seattle, Washington where he attended Lincoln High School and the University of Washington. While at Lincoln High, he was the president of the electronics club and the chess club. At the University of Washington, he majored in engineering and graduated with honors in 1966. Hoffman has worked for APC since 1967 and was promoted to chief systems engineer in 1974. Here is a sampling of his statements made in a recent interview concerning the development of the new software.

> "We've been working on IQ for about five years now. Me and the others on the team think we've got something big here."
>
> "This package is designed to cover an entire educational career, from first grade through high school. It took a lot of sweat to come up with program ideas and information enough to cover that amount of time, skill levels, and grade levels."

"I got to work with pretty smart people outside the computer field for a change, and I think we all learned a lot in the process."

"I think I always knew that this is what I would do. Even in high school, before computers were everyday things, I was interested in the concept of computers and programming."

"This kind of creative engineering is what I like to do the most. I could easily do this for the rest of my life."

James L. Sutton, President of APC

James Sutton has been president of APC since 1975 when he was promoted from senior vice president of marketing. Sutton is a native of Deerborn, Ohio, and graduated from Ohio State University in 1969 with a business degree. He was instrumental in coming up with the idea for a new software line and has developed successfully other product lines for the various divisions of APC since he assumed the presidency. Here is a transcript of a recent interview.

Interviewer: Mr. Sutton, I understand that this new educational software, InfoQuick, that APC has developed is an entirely new concept. How so?

Sutton: Well, it's new in that it is so expansive. That is, it covers so many subjects over so many grade levels. We designed it to be used with children all the way from the first grade through high school. Educational software isn't exactly new, but IQ is like a textbook company providing all the textbooks needed for a child through his entire educational career. We cover everything from spelling to higher math, including calculus and algebra. Our programs also have the advantage of being interrelated because they're produced by a single company.

Interviewer: Do you see that interrelatedness as being a problem? I mean, doesn't that amount of interrelatedness lead to a sort of tunnel vision—like being taught the same courses by the same teacher all your life. Wouldn't you tend to see only one side of everything?

Sutton: Not really. What we've done is to hire the top programmers and educators in the area of software curriculum development to work on our project. Each discipline—history, math, science, etc.—is covered by a number of experts in the field, not a single person. What I'm talking about when I speak of interrelatedness is our ability to reference across a number of courses by computer. In other words, the student using one program of the IQ series will be guided to related topics in other subject areas much the same way you are guided by cross-references in the library card catalog.

Interviewer: You've obviously spent a lot of time and money on this project. Why do you think it will be successful— especially in the light of the recent drop-off of interest in video games?

Sutton: Part of the reason is that we are "selling" (if that's the right word) our curriculum to schools and educators. We have to first convince them that the IQ system of learning is easy and fun. Which brings me to another point. One of the reasons for developing IQ in the first place is to take some of the load off the teacher.

We have statistics showing that an average teacher in a, say fourth-grade class of 30 students, spends approximately only 10 minutes a day with each student individually. Students who need more than that 10 minutes either have to take up time outside of class or try to get the needed in-depth information from their textbooks—or their parents.

IQ helps provide that needed personal attention because of its interactive format. Look at it this way: what is the reason for questions at the end of a chapter in a standard textbook? They're supposed to stimulate the student to "interact" in a sense, with the book. But the book doesn't really respond in the truest sense of the word. It merely houses the answers to the questions while the student carries out any action that is taken.

On the other hand, when a student works with a computer loaded with an IQ program, he is interacting with it. The computer not only asks questions, it provides the student with hints, advice, and guidance. IQ programs explore various facets of each subject by quickly leading the student through an assignment, for instance. It can actually teach, ask questions, and guide the student in his search for the answers.

Interviewer: Could you give me a concrete example of what you mean?

Sutton: Sure. We have a program already developed called *Meet Mr. Franklin* in which the student will actually carry on a computer initiated conversation with Benjamin Franklin.

Interviewer: You mean, they actually hear Ben Franklin talk?

Sutton: No. What happens is that the computer introduces Franklin to the student as if it were the person himself. The program is designed for younger students, fourth to sixth grade, and makes heavy use of computer graphics. Graphics have become very sophisticated today. The Franklin program opens with a picture of Ben Franklin who introduces himself on the screen. From that point on, the student is actually involved in a conversation with him.

Franklin tells him about his life and the times in which he lived, punctuated with graphic displays of objects, maps, and documents of the period. At certain points throughout the lesson, the student is prompted to ask questions of Franklin. Depending on the question selected, from a list on the computer screen, Franklin will then respond.

Again, what's most exciting about the entire package is its interrelatedness. On the Franklin program, for instance, the student will be referred to other programs in the history series for that age group. You can go from the Franklin program to one on Washington, or Jefferson, or Adams and begin to get different perspectives on the same historical era.

Interviewer: To change the subject slightly—I understand that APC is now involved with the National Education Association in a joint project concerning computers.

Sutton: Yes, and again, we're very excited by the prospects of working with such a large and important group. As I've said many times before, we're strong an education here at APC—and that's not just PR talk. I wouldn't be where I am today without my education and I want to do everything I can to see to it that other children get the chance to get the best education possible.

We've given the NEA a rather large grant to get them started on a program of teaching seminars all over the country. They'll set up a speaker's bureau of educators in the area of computer learning who will travel to requesting schools and explain the benefits of computer education.

They'll hold workshops for teachers and students and provide the computers needed to get started on their own programs. Part of our donation will help pay for these computers.

Interviewer: Is this tied in with your software marketing effort?

Sutton: Not directly, no. But, of course, they're related. I'd look like a fool if I told you that they're not. But the money APC's donated to the NEA is a no-strings-attached grant. We're not requiring that they use our software or even mention it in any way. The money is a gift. We're not even asking for sponsorship identification.

Interviewer: Why this sudden push by APC in education, especially computer education?

Sutton: Because we live in a different age than we did when I grew up. Kids today need to know how to cope with the "information age." They need to know how to work with computers. I don't want this generation to be replaced by these machines—I want them to learn to master them.

I believe our joint project with the NEA will give them that chance. I also believe our new software will teach them the same basics I learned as a kid while showing them the wave of the future. We're committed to this course. We've pumped a lot of time and money into it, and we all want to see it work.

Assignments: Press Releases and Backgrounders

Assignment 3-1: Press Release

Write a press release on APC's involvement with NEA and its proposed program to educate children through computers. This is to be a jointly-approved release and cannot mention APC's new software line. The proposed publics are educators, parents, and students. The release will be distributed by the NEA placement service to newspapers, educational publications and school districts around the US. Your address is: Associated Products Corporation 1800 Avenue of the Americas Syracuse, NY 10025 Contact: (your name); Day telephone: (315) 758-9836; Night telephone: (315) 653-5467

Before you begin, develop several different leads— One emphasizing APC; one emphasizing the NEA; and one emphasizing the APC grant.

Read the background materials thoroughly then list items you would include in your release in the order in which they would appear in your release. Do this for each of the leads you have prepared. Remember to use an inverted pyramid style in which the least important information will appear at the end of your release. Arrange your information in the form of an outline.

Using your outline as a guide to organization, write the release.

Assignment 3-2: Press Release

Write a second release on the development of the product itself. The company needs to get some mileage out of the personal angle. Although development and description of the software is the focus of the second release, the angle should be the people who were in charge of development. Prepare one release for the *Seattle Times* and another for the *Deerborn Sentinel.*

Remember, the story is the software; the angle is the person you are using for human interest. Naturally, the leads for the two releases will have to be localized. Consider such approaches as using a dateline, leading with the name, leading with the software, or leading with a piece of local information (from the biographies). Develop one lead for each of these possibilities.

Develop an outline for each lead as you did in **Assignment 3-1**.

Assignment 3-3: Backgrounder

Prepare a backgrounder of no more than three pages explaining the current marketing strategy of APC. Try to couch the "sales pitch" in the light of software development in general. In addition, try to utilize previous information about the company and the people involved to help "flesh out" your backgrounder. Remember, this is a background piece and will probably be used to fill in gaps in editors' knowledge about the company and the market in general. Remember also, that backgrounders need to follow a logical pattern in development. It is not sufficient simply to string information together.

The strength of a backgrounder is in its organization. Before you begin your backgrounder, develop an outline, including a thesis statement in the form of an interesting lead.

CHAPTER 4

Brochures & Press Kits

I've got a million of 'em

Jimmy Durante

What most people refer to as brochures are technically called folders, but since the term "brochure" has fallen into common usage, we'll stick with it here. Brochures are usually formed of a single sheet of paper folded one or more times. The folded brochure may be stored conveniently in a pocket, making it literally pocket sized. However, it doesn't have to be. Part of the fun of designing a brochure is choosing its size and number of folds. Although writing for a brochure implies that you already know what size and shape the finished product will be, you can also write first and then determine the size and shape that fits your copy. As with any in-house publication, you can work it either way, fitting copy to design or design to copy. You should take the approach that works best for you, though you may need to cut costs by trimming your copy, or accommodate mandatory information by expanding it. Longer copy is best suited to other formats such as booklets or pamphlets. In any event, brochure copy is usually abbreviated.

Exactly how abbreviated, no one seems to know, for the length of a brochure varies enormously. Information is the key. Most brochures are used to arouse interest, answer questions, and provide sources for further information. Even when used as part of a persuasive campaign, brochures are seldom persuasive in and of themselves; they are support pieces or part of a larger media mix. Brochures can serve as stand-alone display rack literature, as a component of a press kit, or as part of a direct-mail packet. They can vary in length and size and are usually limited only by budget, talent and imagination.

Before you begin to write, you need to determine exactly what your message is. Are you trying to inform or persuade? Is a brochure the best medium for your message? Who is your intended audience? Your format and your style must match your audience's expectations and tastes.

Before You Write

Know Your Intended Audience

You can refer to **Chapter 1** for detailed information on target audiences. But you can begin by assuming that your audience will be seeking or processing an abbreviated amount of information. Most readers understand that brochures aren't intended to provide long, involved explanations.

There are several audience-centered considerations you should make before you begin writing.

- Is your audience specialized or general? If it is specialized and familiar with your subject, you can use the trade language or jargon familiar to them, no matter how technical it might be. For example, in a brochure on a new chemical product (a copolyester, let's say) you can deal with durometer hardness, temperature-related attributes, resistance to pollutants and weather, and stress characteristics. None of these concepts should be new or surprising to a specialized audience of chemical engineers or designers who use polymers. On the other hand, if your audience is a lay audience, you will have to deal in generalities.

  Here are two examples of a piece on an imaginary copolyester—one for a technical audience (engineers) and one for a less specialized audience (retailers of a manufactured product made from the raw product).

  Technical:
  The results of laboratory testing indicate AXON II® polyester elastomer is resistant to a wide variety of fuels including leaded and unleaded gasoline, Gasohol, kerosene and diesel fuel. With a hardness range of 92A to 72D durometer, tests show the most fuel-resistant type of copolyester to be the 72D durometer with the other family types also showing an impressive amount of fuel resistance.

  General:
  AXON II® polyester elastomer offers design potential plus for applications in a variety of industries. On the toughest jobs, AXON II® is proving to be the design material of the future. Its

unique properties and flexibility in processing make it applicable in areas previously dependent on a range of other, more expensive, products.

- Are you persuading or informing? If you are persuading your audience, you can use the standard persuasive techniques covered in **Chapter 1** including emotional language, appeal to logic, and association of your idea with another familiar concept. As with print advertising, the tone of the brochure (whether persuasive or informative) is set in the introductory headline. For example, here are two cover titles or headlines from two brochures on graduate programs in journalism. The first is persuasive and the second informative.

  Persuasive:
  Is one graduate program in journalism better than all the others?
  Yes.
  The University of Northern Oregon.

  Informative:
  Graduate studies in journalism
  at the University of Northern Oregon.

  Regardless of your intent, the brochure copy should always be clear on what you expect of your audience. If you are trying to persuade, state what you want the reader to do—buy your product, invest in your stock, vote for your candidate, support your bond issue. Persuasion only works if people know what it is you want them to be persuaded about.

- How will your audience be using your brochure? Is it intended to stimulate information on a topic for which detailed information can be obtained in another form? Are you going to urge readers to send for more information? Is it meant to be saved as a constant reminder of your topic? Many health-oriented brochures, for example, provide information meant to be saved or even posted for reference, such as calorie charts, vitamin dosages and nutrition information. If your brochure is designed to be read and discarded, don't waste a lot of money on printing. On the other hand, if you want it to be saved, not only should you make the information valuable enough to be saved, but also the look and feel of the brochure should say "don't throw me away." The same is true of any publication. Newspapers, by their inexpensive paper and rub-off ink, say "read me and then throw me away,." while a magazine like *National Geographic* says "throw *me* away and you'd be trashing a nice piece of work."

Determine a Format

Format refers to the way you arrange your brochure—its organizational characteristics. As with everything else about brochures, format can go two ways: you can fit format to your writing or you can fit your writing to a predetermined format. For instance, if you are told to develop a Q & A (question and answer) brochure, you'll have to fit both writing and design to this special format. On the other hand, if you are writing a persuasive piece, you might decide to go with a problem-solution format, spending two panels of a six-panel brochure on setting up the problem and three on describing the solution.

Some organizational formats work well in brochures, some don't. Spatial organization (up to down, right to left, east to west), which can work well in book form or in magazine articles, doesn't seem to fit in a brochure. Neither does chronological organization. The reason for this may be the physical nature of the brochure itself. Magazine and book pages are turned, one after the other; and each page contains quite a lot of information. A brochure demands a more concentrated effort, one that is less natural than leafing through pages. Because each panel is limited in space, development has to take place in "chunks." Organizational formats that require continuous, linked development or constant referral to previous information aren't suited to brochures.

Pick a format that is suited to brochure presentation, or design your brochure to suit your format. Creative brochure design is part of the fun of working with this type of publication.

Position Your Brochure

Is your brochure to be used as part of a larger communication package (a press kit, for instance), or is it meant to be a stand-alone piece? If it is part of a larger package, then the information contained in the brochure can be keyed to information elsewhere in the package. If it is a stand-alone piece, it will need to be fairly complete—and probably longer. Knowing how your brochure fits into a larger communications program helps you to position it properly. *Positioning* refers to placing your piece in context as either part of some larger whole or as a standout from other pieces.

The only other consideration to make here concerns writing style. The brochure needs to mimic the style of the package of which it is a component. Obviously, this doesn't mean that it should read like a magazine because it is packaged with a magazine, but it should resemble the companion pieces as closely as possible. If the other pieces are formal, the brochure should be formal; if they are informal, the brochure should be also. The key is consistency.

Decide on Length

Succinctness is an art. Almost all writers are able to write long, but very few can write short without editing down from something originally longer. Your information will probably be edited a number of times to make it as spare and succinct as possible, because short copy is the ideal for brochures.

Your copy must be short because of space limitations, in order to leave enough white space for aesthetic value, for type size considerations (for example, a brochure for senior citizens must utilize a fairly large typeface), or for cost considerations. Whatever the reason, you must learn to write short and edit mercilessly.

The copy in **Exhibit 4.1** was originally written for a brochure explaining the entire program of the Public Relations Student Society of America in detail. Clearly, a brochure written this way would be aimed at those who are already aware of the program and its basic offerings and now want more detail. As you read through it, notice that parts are in italics. This is text that could be edited out to produce two, slightly different versions of the same information.

While both versions could be viewed as informational, the edited version is slightly more persuasive. Its intent is to pique the reader's interest so he or she will send for more information. The long version assumes that the reader has already achieved the "aware" level common to the adoption process (see **Chapter 1**) and is now in the interest stage, while the edited version makes that awareness its chief objective. The copy shown here is used as an example of editing. In a real situation, you would have to create two distinctly different brochures in which information, if repeated at all, is done so in a completely different way.

Obviously, the longer copy is much longer and would need a larger format to accommodate everything and still appeal aesthetically. It was designed to fit a three-fold, 8.5" x 22" format. The shorter version will fit into a more open format, possibly a one- or two-fold that contains some white space (see **Exhibit 4.2**).

The key to editing the longer copy is to realize exactly how much a prospective graduate student would need to know about your program. If you include too much in a piece designed to merely attract attention, you may lose your readers. On the other hand, if you don't provide enough basic information, you may never pique their interest. Although the edited elements may in fact influence the final decision-making process, they may not be important in the awareness stage of the adoption process. Once you have decided on the purpose of your brochure, writing and editing become a much easier job.

A professional association

The Public Relations Student Society of America (PRSSA) is the student-run wing of the Public Relations Society of America (PRSA), the largest professional public relations organization in the nation. There are more than 4,300 students in 150 chapters at colleges and universities all across the United States.

The primary goal of PRSSA is to provide students with learning experiences that support coursework taken in public relations and related areas. Although PRSSA is a student-run organization, PRSA still plays an important and active role in its activities.

Each PRSSA chapter is counseled by a professional advisor and a faculty advisor (both members of PRSA) and is sponsored by a professional chapter. Here at the University of Oregon, PRSSA receives the full support of our parent chapter in Portland as well as a national network of professional and student services.

The student connection

Members of the University of Oregon PRSSA attend a number of events each year including the national conference (where members from all 150 PRSSA chapters meet to exchange ideas and attend seminars and workshops), the annual PRSSA Assembly, local and regional workshops and seminars sponsored by PRSA and PRSSA, and the yearly District Conference here in the Northwest.

We belong to the Northwest District along with PRSSA chapters from Central Washington University, Washington State University and the University of Idaho. Each year, we gather for a three-day conference where we exchange ideas and attend workshops and seminars given by public relations professionals.

The professional connection

PRSSA members also make invaluable contacts with public relations professionals all over the Northwest through field trips, professional workshops on subjects such as resume writing and portfolio presentation, PRIDE internships (which carry national recognition) and the Professional Partners

Exhibit 4.1—Brochure Copy

Program, in which students are matched with public relations professionals in the Portland, Salem and Eugene areas.

PRIDE stands for Public Relations Internships to Develop Expertise. PRIDE internships are specially designed for members of PRSSA only, and offer PRSSA students an opportunity to develop their knowledge of public relations through close relationships with practicing professionals.

The PRIDE internship requires a contractural agreement between the student and his or her internship supervisor and the student's faculty advisor.

At the end of a successful PRIDE internship, the student's contract is sent to PRSSA national headquarters in New York, which then sends the student a certificate of completion. Although more complex than a standard internship, PRIDE internships offer a more formalized insurance that the student will be working on coordinated projects specifically related to public relations.

The Professional Partners Program matches *PRSSA students with PRSA* members in an informal, information-sharing partnership.

Students interested in the program fill out a form indicating their area of interest (i.e., special events, corporate PR, agency PR, etc.). The student is then matched with a partner practicing in that area.

Throughout the school year, the student and his or her professional partner meet informally to discuss the field of public relations, the professional's work, the student's particular interests and public relations in general. The usual method is through lunch meetings in the city in which the professional works, occasional visits by the professional to Eugene, and PRSA monthly luncheons in Portland. In addition, professional partners frequently share a workday in which the student gets to observe his or her partner in action on the job.

Joining PRSSA

Joining PRSSA is easy. All you have to be is interested. You'll receive a membership certificate, a reduce-price subscription to the most widely read professional publication in public relations, *Public Relations Journal*, and a chance to become a member of PRSA at a reduced fee when you graduate .

So, if you think PRSSA has something for you—or even if you just want to know more about us—let us know. Just talk to any member, come by a meeting, or see Dr. Bivins in room 206 Allen Hall.

It could be the most professional move you'll ever make.

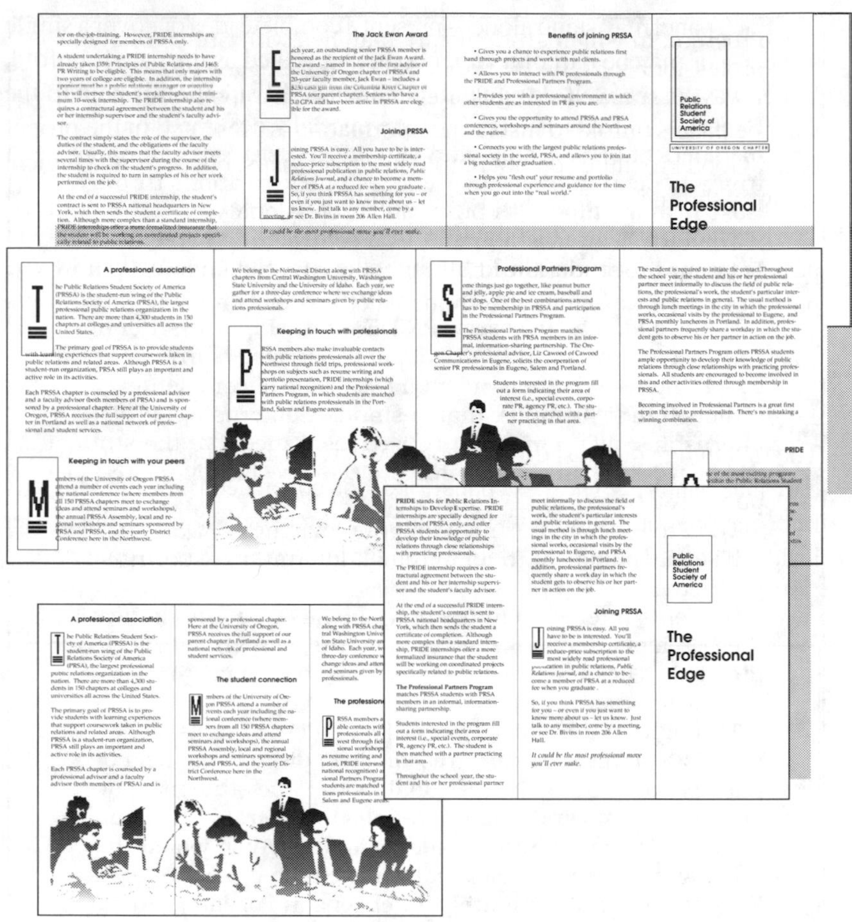

Exhibit 4.2—Editing Brochure Copy

Whether you write for a specific size or you fit the size to the amount of information you have (especially if your boss simply can't live without that detailed explanation of how beneficial your new widget is to Western technology), your copy will have to fit that unique characteristic of the brochure—the number of folds.

Brochures are designated by how many folds they employ. A two-fold, a sheet with two creases, has six panels—three on one side and three on the other. A three-fold has eight panels, and so on. Each fold adds two or more new panels. Although some very interesting folds have been developed, the usual configuration consists of panels of equal size (see **Exhibit 4.3**).

Each panel may stand alone—present a complete idea or cover a single subject—or may be part of a larger context revealed as the panels unfold. Either way, in the well-designed brochure careful attention is paid to the way the panels unfold to insure the information is presented in the proper order. Good brochures do not unfold like road maps, but present a logical pathway through their panels (see **Exhibit 4.4**).

Research indicates that the first thing a reader looks at in a direct mail package is the brochure. The last thing is the cover letter. Exactly how you present the brochure may determine whether it gets read or gets thrown away.

The Order of Presentation

The first thing you must do is establish where the front panel is and where the final panel is. The first panel or front cover need not contain any information, but it should serve as an "eye catcher" that draws the reader inside. It should employ a "hook"—an intriguing question or statement, a

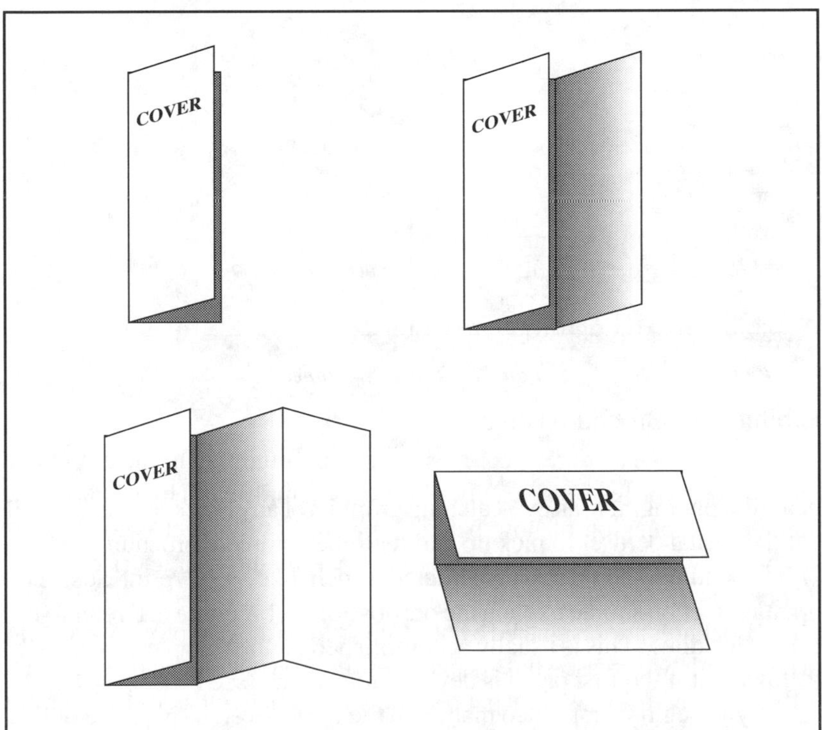

Exhibit 4.3—Typical Brochure Folds

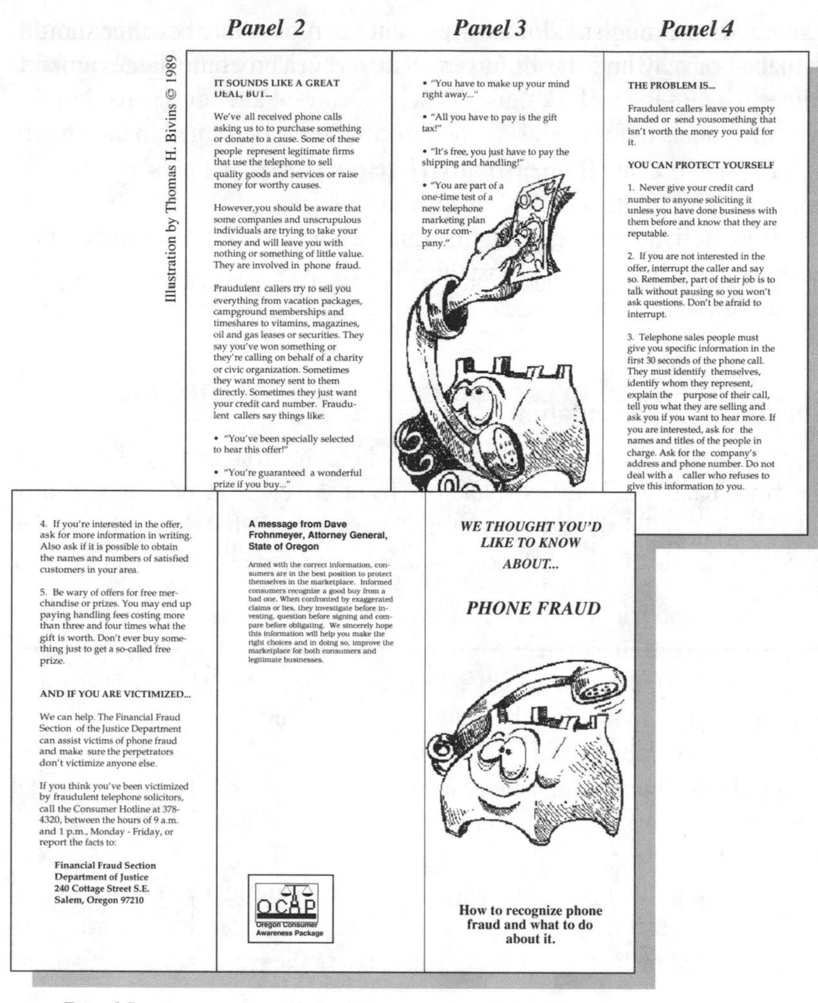

Panel 2

Illustration by Thomas H. Bivins © 1989

IT SOUNDS LIKE A GREAT DEAL, BUT...

We've all received phone calls asking us to to purchase something or donate to a cause. Some of these people represent legitimate firms that use the telephone to sell quality goods and services or raise money for worthy causes.

However,you should be aware that some companies and unscrupulous individuals are trying to take your money and will leave you with nothing or something of little value. They are involved in phone fraud.

Fraudulent callers try to sell you everything from vacation packages, campground memberships and timeshares to vitamins, magazines, oil and gas leases or securities. They say you've won something or they're calling on behalf of a charity or civic organization. Sometimes they want money sent to them directly. Sometimes they just want your credit card number. Fraudulent callers say things like:

- "You've been specially selected to hear this offer!"
- "You're guaranteed a wonderful prize if you buy..."

Panel 3

- "You have to make up your mind right away..."
- "All you have to pay is the gift tax!"
- "It's free, you just have to pay the shipping and handling!"
- "You are part of a one-time test of a new telephone marketing plan by our company."

Panel 4

THE PROBLEM IS...

Fraudulent callers leave you empty handed or send yousomething that isn't worth the money you paid for it.

YOU CAN PROTECT YOURSELF

1. Never give your credit card number to anyone soliciting it unless you have done business with them before and know that they are reputable.

2. If you are not interested in the offer, interrupt the caller and say so. Remember, part of their job is to talk without pausing so you won't ask questions. Don't be afraid to interrupt.

3. Telephone sales people must give you specific information in the first 30 seconds of the phone call. They must identify themselves, identify whom they represent, explain the purpose of their call, tell you what they are selling and ask you if you want to hear more. If you are interested, ask for the names and titles of the people in charge. Ask for the company's address and phone number. Do not deal with a caller who refuses to give this information to you.

Panel 5

4. If you're interested in the offer, ask for more information in writing. Also ask if it is possible to obtain the names and numbers of satisfied customers in your area.

5. Be wary of offers for free merchandise or prizes. You may end up paying handling fees costing more than three and four times what the gift is worth. Don't ever buy something just to get a so-called free prize.

AND IF YOU ARE VICTIMIZED...

We can help. The Financial Fraud Section of the Justice Department can assist victims of phone fraud and make sure the perpetrators don't victimize anyone else.

If you think you've been victimized by fraudulent telephone solicitors, call the Consumer Hotline at 378-4320, between the hours of 9 a.m. and 1 p.m., Monday - Friday, or report the facts to:

Financial Fraud Section
Department of Justice
240 Cottage Street S.E.
Salem, Oregon 97210

Panel 6

A message from Dave Frohnmeyer, Attorney General, State of Oregon

Armed with the correct information, consumers are in the best position to protect themselves in the marketplace. Informed consumers recognize a good buy from a bad one. When confronted by exaggerated claims or lies, they investigate before investing, question before signing and compare before obligating. We sincerely hope this information will help you make the right choices and in doing so, improve the marketplace for both consumers and legitimate businesses.

OCAP
Oregon Consumer Awareness Package

Panel 1

WE THOUGHT YOU'D LIKE TO KNOW ABOUT...

PHONE FRAUD

How to recognize phone fraud and what to do about it.

Exhibit 4.4—Brochure Logic

beautiful photograph, an eye-catching graphic, or any other device that will get the casual peruser to pick up and read the complete brochure.

Brochures should be constructed much like good print ads. The opening section should explain the purpose of the brochure and refer to the title or headline. This is usually accomplished on the first panel or shortly following it if the first panel is devoted to a visual (see **Exhibit 4.4**).

If you begin your printed matter on the front cover, its headline or title becomes very important. Most informational brochures use a title simply to tell what's inside. After all, most people looking for information don't want to wade through a lot of creative esoteria. A brochure headline should be to the point. "Blind" headlines are of no use in a brochure. For example:

Reaching for the stars?

Is this headline for a product (maybe telescopes)? A service (astrology)?

In the Air Force, you can reach for the stars!

Now, both the intent and the sponsor are clear. For the information-seeking reader, a blind headline *might* work; however, if you really want to be sure—and if you want to pick up the browser as well—avoid them.

The second panel, at least in a two-fold brochure, is the first panel of the inside spread. Its job is to build interest. It is usually copy heavy, and may contain a subhead or crosshead. In fact, panels may be laid out around crossheads. But make sure the reader knows which panel follows which. Never let your copy run from panel to panel by breaking a sentence or a paragraph, or (worst of all) a word in half. Try to treat each panel as a single entity with its own information. This isn't always possible, but it's nice to strive for.

The rest of the inside spread (panels three and four) carries the main load. It may be constructed to present a unified whole with words and graphics bleeding from one panel to the next, or the panels may retain their individuality.

The back panels (panels five and six) serve various purposes. Panel five may be used as a teaser or short blurb introducing the inside spread, or it may be incorporated into the design of panel two (especially useful since this panel is often folded in and seen as you open the front cover). It may also simply continue the information begun on panels two, three and four. Panel six may be left blank for mailing or contain address information. It doesn't usually contain much else.

Most of us are used to seeing two-folds folded so that the far right panel (inside panel four and outside panel five) is folded in first with the far left panel (outside panel one and inside panel two) folded over it. But this has always presented problems. For instance, what do you put on panel five? It is the first panel you see when you open the cover, yet it is technically on the back of the brochure. You can use it as a teaser, or simply as the informational panel that follows the inside spread. Or, you can experiment with the fold (See **Exhibits 4.5** and **4.6**). So much depends on the presentation of your information, and because they are folded, brochures are among the hardest collateral pieces to present properly. If readers are even slightly confused, you've lost them.

Exhibits 4.5 and **4.6**—Traditional and Non-traditional Folds

The standard two-fold folder places the cover on the far right panel of the outside spread. Panel five (inside panel four) folds in first (see below).

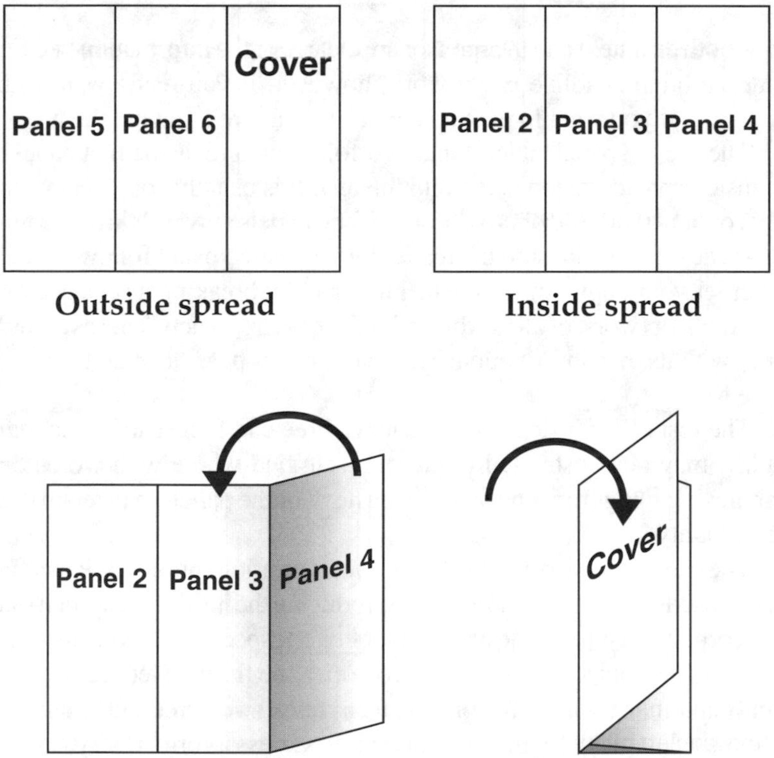

Panel 5 | Panel 6 | Cover

Outside spread

Panel 2 | Panel 3 | Panel 4

Inside spread

Panel 2 | Panel 3 | Panel 4

Cover

This traditional fold requires two "unfolds" to access the inside spread—the cover and panel five; however, panel five may or may not be intended as part of the inside spread. More often, it follows panels two–four, yet it appears as the first panel seen when the folder is opened.

Crossheads

Crossheads should be used liberally in a brochure. They help break up copy and give your brochure a less formidable appearance. Studies have shown that copy formed into short paragraphs, broken by informative crossheads, gives the reader a feeling that he or she can read any section independently without being obligated to read the entire piece. While in some instances

The standard two-fold folder is redesigned here placing the cover in the center of the outside panel. This allows panel two to fold inside (see below).

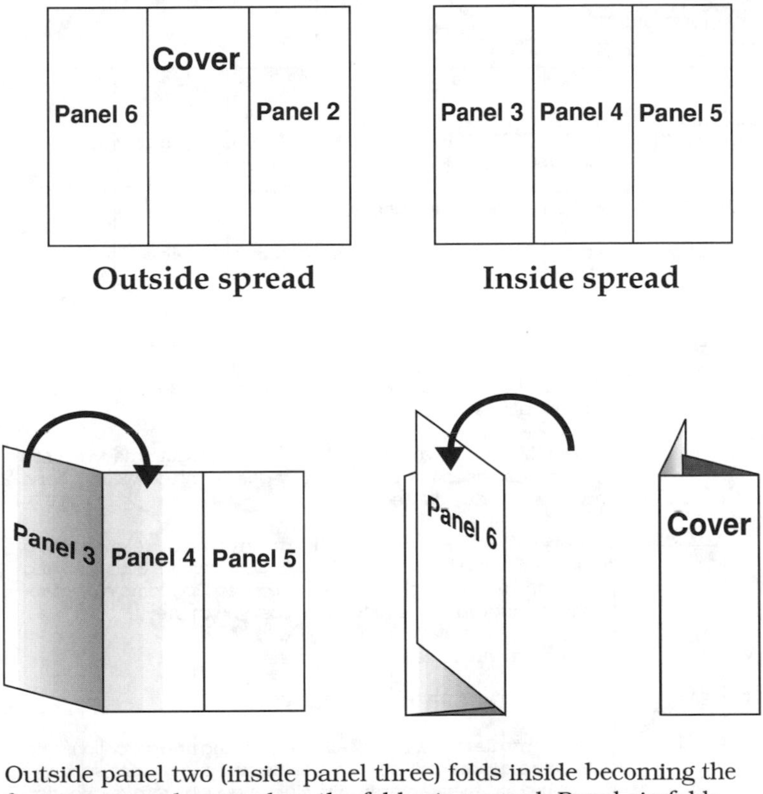

Outside spread

Inside spread

Outside panel two (inside panel three) folds inside becoming the first copy panel seen when the folder is opened. Panel six folds over it to become the back (or mailer). This presents the center outside panel as the cover and sets up two "unfolds" to get to the inside spread; however, there is no doubt that panel two (even though it is folded inside) is the first panel to be read. This fold alleviates the "panel five" problem of the traditional fold.

this may be self-defeating, reading one pertinent paragraph is often better than reading none; and, if you run your copy together in one long, unbroken string, you're going to limit readership to a hardy few. Aesthetically, your brochure will simply look better with the increased white space crossheads can add. And, white space encourages readership as well.

Copy Format

As you create your brochure, you may have to present the copy to others for approval. It helps to place it into a format that conveys the look of the

"Phone Fraud"
3-fold folder
Attorney General

PANEL 1

HEADLINE: WE THOUGHT YOU'D LIKE TO KNOW ABOUT (graphic splits head line here) PHONE FRAUD

VISUAL: Stylized graphic of telephone

SUBHEAD: A consumer guide to your rights and obligations when dealing with telephone sales

PANEL 2

SUBHEAD: WHAT IS PHONE FRAUD?

COPY: We've all been asked to purchase something or donate to a cause over the phone.

Most of the people who contact us represent legitimate firms that use the telephone to sell quality goods and services or raise money for worthy causes.

However, there are companies that are involved in telemarketing fraud. According to the Federal Trade Commission, telemarketing fraud is the use of telephone communications to promote goods or services fraudulently. And this can cost you money!

VISUAL: Cartoon drawing of telephone receiver

SUBHEAD: WHAT ARE THEY TRYING TO SELL YOU?

COPY: Fraudulent sales callers try to sell us everything from vacations and time-share condominiums to vitamins and magazines subscriptions. They say they represent film clubs, vacation resorts, charities, magazine and book clearing houses, and even churches. Sometimes they want money sent to them directly, or sometimes they just want your credit card number. (This is especially dangerous because they can charge any amount they want with your number.)

-more-

Exhibit 4.7—Brochure Copy Format

finished product. Obviously, the best way to show anyone how a finished piece will look is to mock it up; however, copy often must be approved prior to any mockup, so indicating headlines, visuals and copy blocks in the order in which they appear is an important visual aspect of the brochure copy format. Indicating headlines and visuals will enhance continuity between the writer and the designer if they are different people (See **Exhibit 4.7**).

This is as far as most writers go; however, if you work for a small firm or nonprofit agency, you may be solely responsible for producing collateral pieces from writing to layout.

Phone Fraud--Page 2

SUBHEAD: WHAT DO THEY SAY TO YOU?

COPY: Although fraudulent sales callers may have vastly different products or services to sell, there are frequently similarities in their "pitches." These pitches often sound very professional. Sometimes, you are even transferred from person to person to make it sound more like a business setting. Do the following lines sound familiar?

--"You've been specially selected to hear this offer!" (How was the selection process made?)

--"You'll get a wonderful prize if you buy..." (How much is this prize worth?)

--"You have to make up your mind right away..." (They make it seem like this is a now or never opportunity.)

--"It's free, you just have to pay the shipping and handling!" (If they get only $7.00 shipping and handling per person and con 100 people into paying up front, they make $700!)

--"But first, I'll have to have your credit card number to verify..." (To verify what and why?)

PANEL 3

SUBHEAD: WHAT HAPPENS THEN?

COPY: If it is a fraudulent sales call, you sometimes actually receive the merchandise--but it is often over priced, of poor quality, or the wonderful prize you won is usually a cheap imitation.

Or, if you've been asked to invest in something, it may turn out to be non-existent.

Or, you find out the worthy cause you donated to only got a tiny part of your actual donation while the caller got the bulk of it.

Or, unauthorized charges start appearing on your credit card bills.

-more-

Remember, you can write first and then develop a length and size to fit your editorial needs, or you can limit your copy to a pre-set design and size. Either way, you have to be aware of copyfitting requirements (see **Chapter 9** for details on copyfitting). Once you know how much you must write, stick to your guns. If you find that you have written more than will fit your original design concept, you can increase the number of folds and, thus, the number of available panels, or edit your copy.

If your supervisor isn't clamoring for every ounce of information you can provide in 93.5 square inches of space, stick with editing your copy. The best brochures are almost always the short ones.

Phone Fraud--Page 3

PANEL 4
SUBHEAD: HOW CAN YOU PROTECT YOURSELF?

COPY: 1. First of all, always find out who is calling and who they represent. Ask how they got your name. Ask who is in charge of the company or organization represented. Get specific names and titles. Ask for the address and telephone number of the firm calling you. Be extremely cautious if the caller won't provide that information.

2. Be cautious if the caller says an investment, purchase or charitable donation must be made immediately. Ask instead that information be sent to you.

3. Be wary of offers for free merchandise or prizes. You may end up paying handling fees greater than the value of the gifts. And, don't ever buy something just to get a free prize.

4. If you're interested in the offer, ask for more information through the mail. Also ask if it's possible to obtain the names and numbers of satisfied customers in your area.

5. If you're not interested in the offer, interrupt the caller and say so. Remember, part of their job is to talk without pause so you can't ask them questions. Don't be afraid to interrupt.

PANEL 5
SUBHEAD: WHAT DO YOU DO IF YOU'RE VICTIMIZED...
Report the facts to :

Financial Fraud Section
Department of Justice
240 Cottage Street S.E.
Salem, Oregon 97210

KICKER: REMEMBER, YOU HAVE RIGHTS. DON'T BE VICTIMIZED BY TELEPHONE FRAUD!

PANEL 6
HEADLINE: HOW TO RECOGNIZE PHONE FRAUD AND WHAT TO DO ABOUT IT, FROM THE STATE OF OREGON ATTORNEY GENERAL'S OFFICE

-30-

Three approaches that are *not* options for squeezing in extra information are decreasing the proposed point size of your typeset copy, eliminating planned white space or graphics, and reducing the size of your margins. Any one of these will severely reduce the aesthetic value of your brochure and deter or prevent the reading of it.

Remember, simplicity, conciseness and succinctness are the keys to success. Come to the point quickly, elaborate only to the degree absolutely necessary, and get out—leaving your reader with a feeling that he or she has read something that means something.

The Press Kit

One of the most common methods of distributing brochures and other collateral information pieces is via the press kit. Press kits are produced and used for a wide variety of public relations purposes. They are handed out at product promotion presentations and press conferences; they are used as promotional packages by regional or local distributors or agencies; and they are part of the never-ending stream of information provided by organizations in an effort to get their messages out. When a press kit, or press packet, is used properly, it can effectively aid message dissemination by adding the right amount of unduplicated information to the media mix.

The press kit (also called the *media kit* or *information kit*) is usually composed of a number of information pieces enclosed within a folder. The cover usually indicates who is providing the kit and its purpose. A press kit should include the following items at the bare minimum:

- A cover letter explaining what the kit is about;
- A table of contents;
- A press release;
- A backgrounder or, at very least, a fact sheet.
- One or two other information pieces such as:
  —Already-printed brochures
  —Company magazines or newsletters
  —An annual report
  —A feature story or sidebar, if appropriate to the subject matter
  —A biography (or biographies) and accompanying photos

Anything fewer than these items is a waste of folder space. If you have only a few items to disseminate and wish to avoid the cost of producing folders, use plain, manuscript-sized envelopes. They are cheaper than folders; you might already have them in stock with your address printed on them; and they are ready for mailing.

The contents of a press kit can vary greatly depending on the intent of the kit. For example, the contents of a *media kit* distributed by the American Lung Association to its regional offices contained the following items:

- Cover letter
- Table of contents
- Clipsheet (photos and logos for newspaper placement)
- Magazine ad folder with sample return order card
- Magazine drop-in ad instructions
- Suggested cover letter for magazine ad folder
- Newspaper clipsheet instructions
- Captioned photo
- Direction sheets titled "How to get the best use of TV PSAs" and "How to get local ID on TV spots"
- Radio scripts (tapes sent with kit)
- Radio usage report and cover letter
- Report of use card
- Radio station phone call (scripted inquiry used to contact radio station program directors)
- Radio PSA distribution report card
- Television scripts (tapes sent with kit)
- Storyboard for TV spot
- Cover letter for TV stations
- TV PSA delivery report card
- Report of use card for TV PSAs
- Supply service memo and order form for more of any of these items

In contrast, a *press kit* for a corporate product introduction briefing included these items:

- Press release on the new product
- Color photo and cutline (caption)
- Press release on the product content (the material used to manufacture the product)
- Black and white photo and cutline of other products made from the manufactured material
- Press release describing another application of the material
- Black and white and color photos of that application
- Backgrounder on the material
- In-house magazine article tear sheet on the material
- Color brochure on the material and its uses
- Press release on new materials being developed
- Hard copy of the product presentation speeches

Press kits can serve many purposes and should include enough information to meet the needs of their audiences. The key to assembling a useful kit is to keep in mind the needs of those receiving the information.

If you are providing a press kit to the media for a press conference, it should include some of the following items:

- A cover letter explaining the kit and a table of contents listing each item in the kit, with each item listed as appearing on the right or left side of the folder.
- A basic facts sheet outlining the participants a the press conference, the relevant dates, and any facts or figures which might be unclear.
- A backgrounder explaining the relevance of the current topic in an historical context.
- Press releases of about one and one-half pages for both print and broadcast media. Give both releases to each reporter.
- Any feature stories or sidebar-type information that might be of interest to reporters. Be sure it is relevant.
- Any photos or other visual materials which might add to the stories. Include cutlines.
- If any individuals play an important part in the event the press conference covers, include biographies on them as well as photos.
- Include any, already produced information pieces which might be of interest to the media, such as brochures, in-house publications, etc.

Once you have assembled a press kit, make sure that all of the media get a copy, even those reporters who do not attend the event your press kit is designed to cover. Press kits are most effective when used with a good, up-to-date media list. By labeling your press kits before the event to be covered with the name of the various media outlets, you will know immediately after the event who showed up and who needs to have their kits mailed.

Case Study: Associated Products Corporation

Using the background provided in **Chapter 3**, complete the following assignments.

Assignment 4-1: Brochures

You have been assigned to produce two brochures—one for APC introducing the new IQ software package, and one for NEA/APC introducing the "Byte of the Apple" speaker's bureau. The first brochure will be product oriented while the second will be service oriented. You may continue the motif you have established in your previous package components for the second brochure or develop a new one. The first brochure must not appear to be related to the NEA brochure. The first brochure should be a two-fold; the second, a one-fold. The two-fold brochure should be designed to fit on an 8 1/2" x 11" inch piece of paper. The one-fold should fit on 8 1/2" x 7 1/2" paper. Prepare a completely scripted brochure with headlines, visuals, and copy blocks. Attach a "dummy" brochure layout designating positions of headlines, visuals, and copy blocks.

Assignment 4-2: Brochures

Spec the type for your two brochures. Assume that you will be using 11-point type leaded 2-points. You must make sure your copy will fit the specified blocks on your layout. Prepare a layout and a worksheet on copyfitting for each brochure.

Assignment 4-3: Press kits

Assume that you are charged with assembling a press kit for InfoQuick, to be distributed at a product press conference announcing the new software. The press conference is to be held at the Downtown Hotel in the Sheridan Room at 10:00 a.m. on Tuesday, November 17. Attending will be APC President James Sutton and project head William Hoffman. Both will give short talks and take questions from the trade media present.

Make a list of items you would include in this kit, including any you may have already produced and any you would recommend be produced specifically for the kit. In addition, write a cover letter, to be included in the press kit, explaining the purpose of the press conference. Also, put together a table of contents for your press kit, listing the items in the kit in the order in which they are to be placed in the kit.

CHAPTER 5

Newsletters

I really think you should consider a newsletter.

Garry Trudeau

Every day in the United States thousands of newsletters are published and distributed to hundreds of thousands of readers. It is estimated that some 50,000 corporate newsletters alone are published each year in this country. Most newsletters are internal publications in the sense that they reach a highly unified public—employees, shareholders, members, volunteers, voting constituencies and others with a common interest. In fact, if you ask any self-respecting communications professional for the most effective means of reaching a primarily internal audience, the response will most likely be the newsletter.

Determining the Focus and the Need

Newsletters are as varied as the audiences who read them; however, they do break down into two categories, each based on *distribution.* Which category a newsletter falls into usually determines its focus. Newsletters that are distributed within a corporation are usually considered **vertical** publications because they are intended for everyone from the mailroom clerk to the CEO. Newsletters that are distributed to a more narrowly defined group with a common interest (such as newsletters on management techniques within a certain industry, or technical publications within an industry) are called **horizontal** publications.

Vertical Publications

There are three main types of vertical publications.

- **Association newsletters** help a scattered membership with a common interest keep in touch. Profit and nonprofit associations and almost every trade association in the United States publish newsletters for their members, often at both national and regional levels.
- **Community group newsletters** are often used by civic organizations to keep in touch with members, announce meetings, and stimulate attendance at events. The local YWCA or Boys Club newsletter might announce their schedules, while a community church group newsletter distributed throughout surrounding neighborhoods might be a tool for increasing membership.
- **Institutional newsletters**, perhaps the most common type of newsletter, are usually distributed among employees. Used by both profit and non-profit organizations, they are designed to give employees a feeling of belonging. They frequently include a balanced mix of employee-related information and news about the company.

Horizontal Publications

There are also three main types of horizontal publications.

- **Publicity newsletters** often create their own readers. They can be developed for fan clubs, resorts (some resort hotels mail their own newsletters out to previous guests), and politicians. Congressional representatives often use newsletters to keep their constituencies up to date on their activities.
- **Special interest newsletters** developed by special-interest groups tend to grow with their following. *Common Cause*, for instance, began as a newsletter and has grown into a magazine representing the largest lobbying interest group in the United States.
- **Self-interest or "digest" newsletters** are designed to make a profit. The individuals or groups who develop them typically offer advice or present solutions to problems held in common by their target readers. These often come in the form of a sort of "digest" of topics of interest to a certain profession. In the public relations profession, for instance, you'll find *PR Reporter, PR News, Communicate, O'Dwyer's Newsletter, Communication Briefings*, and many more.

Why a Newsletter?

Why indeed? Most newsletters address an internal public, with the exception of those that target single-interest groups—such as professionals and executives—outside a formal organizational structure. The goal of most newsletters, then, is communication with a largely internal public.

Downward and Upward Communication

In the ideal organizational structure, communication flows vertically (upward and downward) and horizontally. The newsletter is a good example of downward communication. It fulfills part of management's obligation to provide its employees formal channels of communication. Upward communication provides employees a means of communicating *their* opinions to management. Ideally, even downward communication channels such as newsletters permit upward communication through letters to the editor, articles written by employees, surveys, and so forth. Newsletters can also provide horizontal communication, but this type of newsletter is rarely produced *within* an organization; rather it originates from outside.

Newsletter or Something Else?

But, why a newsletter instead of a magazine, booklets, bulletin boards, or (heaven forbid) more meetings? There are several questions you can ask yourself when deciding whether a newsletter is the publication that best suits your purpose.

- What *is* the purpose of the publication? Is it to entertain? Inform? Solicit?
- What is the nature and scope of the information you wish to present? Longer information is probably better suited to a longer publication such as a magazine; shorter, to brochures or folders. If your information is strictly entertaining or human interest, it may also be better received within a magazine format.
- Who, exactly, are you trying to reach? All employees from the top down? A select few (the marketing department, the credit department, the vice president in charge of looking out windows)?
- How often do you need to publish it to realize the objectives you set in answering the previous questions? Newsletters are best suited to situations requiring a short editorial and design lead time.

Keep in mind also that newsletters are best for small publication runs and information that needs a quick turnover. They handle information that is considered necessary but disposable (much like a newspaper, which in a sense the newsletter mimics). However, this is *generally*, but not *universally* true. Many fine newsletters are designed to be kept. Health and financial newsletters, for instance, are often hole-punched so that the reader can save them in ring binders. For the most part, though, they are considered disposable.

Setting Objectives and Strategies

Newsletters, like any well-managed publication, will achieve best results if objectives are set and all actions follow logically from them.

Newsletter Content

To determine a newsletter's content, you must first know your audience. Is it totally internal, or a combination of internal and external? Your audience and its interests will dictate, to a large extent, the topic and direction of your articles.

Depending on the type of newsletter you are publishing, the focus will be broad or narrow. For example, when you write for an internal, employee public, you must carefully balance information with entertainment. You must please management by providing information it wants to see in print and you must please the employees by providing information they want to read. Otis Baskin & Craig Aronoff, in their book *Public Relations: The Profession and the Practice*, present a rule of thumb for an appropriate mix in an internal publication (not necessarily a newsletter) aimed primarily at an employee audience.

- 50 percent information about the organization—local, national and international
- 20 percent employee information—benefits, quality of working life, etc.
- 20 percent relevant noncompany information—competitors, community, etc.
- 10 percent small talk and personals

Given that most newsletters are fairly short, such a complete mix may be impractical; however, a close approximation will probably work. Remember, though, that this mix is only appropriate for vertical publications such as institutional newsletters.

By comparison, most horizontal publications tend to focus on items of interest to a more narrowly defined target public. For example, a newsletter for telecommunications executives may concentrate on news about that industry, omitting human interest items, small talk or industry gossip. In fact, almost every newsletter targeted to executives contains only short, no-nonsense articles. The reason, of course, is that busy executives simply don't have the time to read the type of article that interests the average employee.

How to Set Objectives

Objectives relate to your publication's editorial statement. Editorial statements shouldn't be pie-in-the-sky rhetoric; they should reflect the honest intent of your publication. If your intent is to present management's story to employees, then say so up front. An editorial statement can be an objective, or it can serve as a touchstone for other objectives.

For example, from the editorial statement in the previous paragraph you could reasonably derive an objective such as "To raise the level of awareness of management policies among all employees by *X* percent over the next year." Or, "To provide an open line of upward and downward communication for both management and employees." Whatever your objectives, make sure they are measurable. Then, you can point to your success in reaching them over the period of time you specified. You should also have some means by which to measure the success of your objectives. If your objective is simply "To present management's message to employees," how will you measure its success or failure? Don't you want to find out if just presenting the message was enough? How will you tell if anyone even read your message, or, if they did, whether they responded in any way?

Make your objectives realistic and measurable, and once you have set them, follow them. Use them as a yardstick by which to measure every story you run. If a story doesn't help realize one of your objectives, don't run it. If you just can't live without running it, maybe your objectives aren't complete enough.

Writing for Newsletters

Most newsletters are journalistic in style. They usually include both straight news and feature stories and range from informal to formal depending on the organization and its audience. Usually, the smaller the organization, the less formal the newsletter. Large corporations, on the other hand, often have a very formal newsletter with a very slick format combining employee-centered news with company news.

The responsibility for writing the newsletter is almost always handled in house, although some agencies do produce newsletters on contract for organizations. In-house personnel tend to be more in tune with company employees and activities. Sometimes the writing is done in house and the production, including design, layout, and printing, is done by an agency.

If you do produce your own newsletter, you are limited only by money and imagination. A standard newsletter is usually 8 1/2" x 11" or 11" x 17" folded in half. It averages in length from two to four pages and is frequently folded and mailed. Many are designed with an address area on the back for mailing (see **Exhibits 5.1** and **5.2**).

Length of articles varies. Some newsletters contain only one article, while others include several. An average, four-page newsletter uses about

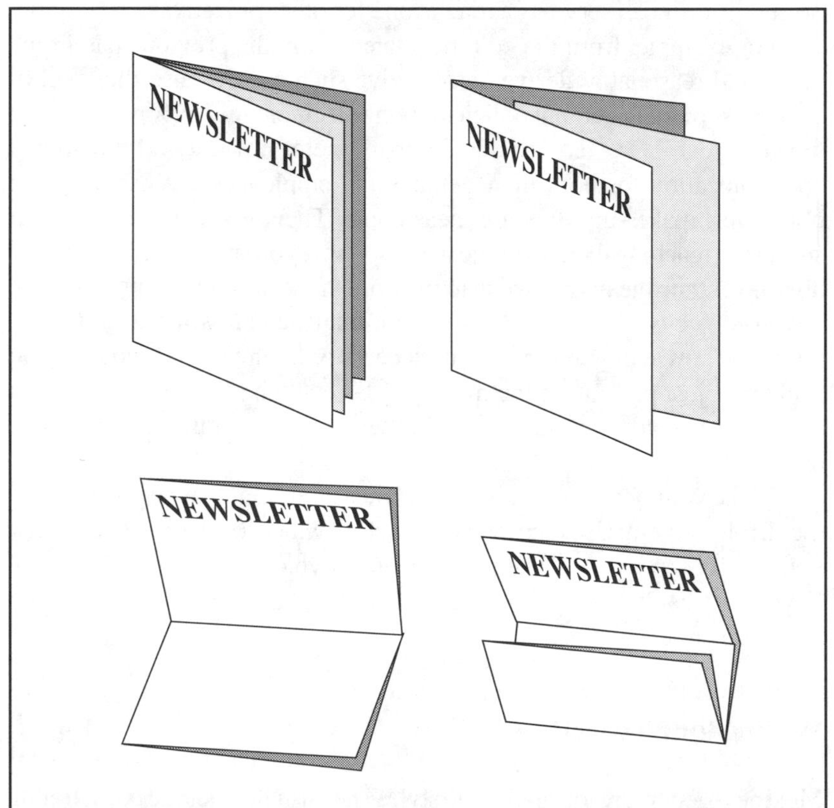

Exhibit 5.1—Newsletter Folds

Clockwise from upper left: standard 11 x 17, four-page folded and stapled; standard 11 x 17, single fold with one-page loose insert; standard 11 x 17 folded in thirds for mailing as-is or inserted into business envelope; standard 11 x 17 folded in half for mailing.

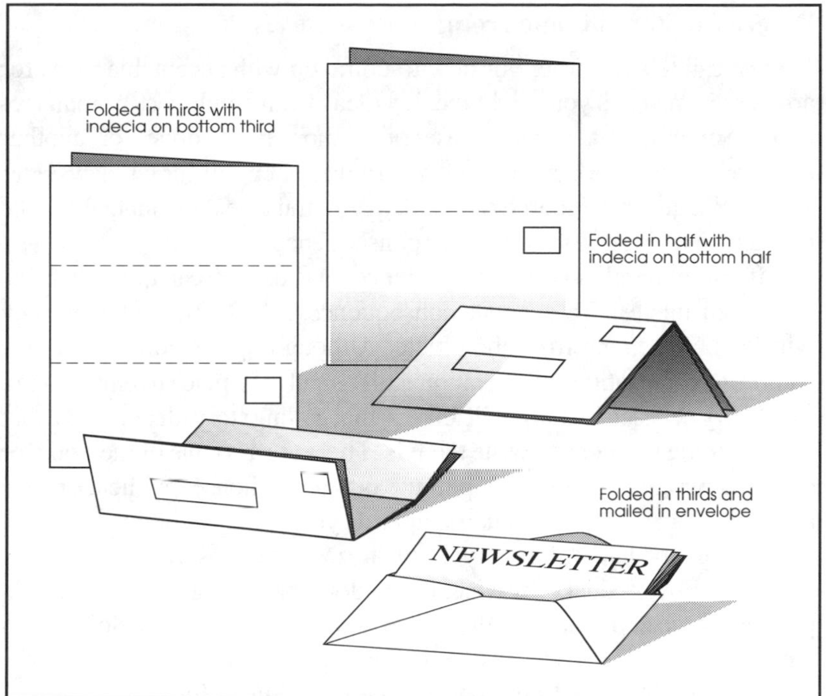

Exhibit 5.2—Newsletter Mailing Options
Clockwise from bottom: standard 11 x 17, four-page folded in thirds and mailed in business envelope; standard 11 x 17, single folded in thirds with Post Office indecia on bottom third (usually folded and stapled); standard 11 x 17 folded in half with indecia on bottom half (usually folded and stapled).

2,000 words of copy. Depending on the focus of the newsletter, articles can range in length from "digest" articles of less than 100 words to longer articles of 600 words for newsletters that cover only one or two topics per issue. The trend today is toward shorter articles, especially for the newsletter aimed at the businessperson or corporate executive. Even for the average employee, newsletter articles usually need to be brief. Most newsletters make use of simple graphics or photographs. While most are typeset (or, increasingly, desktop published), many are simply typed.

Because newsletters inform and entertain, articles should be written in an entertaining way. Usually, news about the company or strictly informational pieces utilize the standard news story style, except that there is no need to use the inverted pyramid because newsletter stories are seldom edited for space from the bottom up. Employee interest pieces tend to use the feature story style. Feature-type articles for newsletters should be complete, with a beginning and an ending.

Where Do Stories Come From?

No one can tell you where or how to come up with acceptable ideas for articles. Sometimes you might receive ideas from employees or management. Sometimes a news release or a short piece done for another publication will spark enough interest to warrant a full-blown newsletter article. Whatever the source of the idea, you must next evaluate the topic based on reader interest and reader consequence.

If you're familiar with your audience's tastes, you can quickly determine their interest. To evaluate consequence, ask yourself whether they will learn something from the article. Although light reading is fun for some, an organizational publication isn't usually the place to engage in it.

Every newsletter editor will tell you that getting story ideas isn't all that hard. Finding someone to write them is. There are a couple of methods for enlisting writers. If you are putting out an in-house publication, try assigning "beats" just like a newspaper. If you're lucky enough to have a staff, assign them to different types of stories—perhaps by department or division, or by product or service. If you don't have a staff, rely on certain people in each department or division to submit stories to you. Sometimes the simple promise of seeing their name in print is enough inducement.

You can also send employees a simple request form, spelling out exactly what you are looking for. The return information will be sketchy, but you can flesh it out with a few phone calls (see **Exhibit 5.3**). This is an especially good method of gathering employee-related tidbits that don't deserve an entire story but should still be mentioned. Another method for organizing your shorter stories is to group them according to topic. For example, group all stories relating to employee sports, or all stories about employee community involvement, or promotions, and so on.

Of course, if your publication is a narrowly focused horizontal publication, you may end up doing most of the research and writing yourself. Many such newsletters are truly one-person operations. Because desktop publishing allows a single person to act as reporter, editor, typesetter, and printer, this type of publication is enjoying a rebirth.

Whatever system you use to gather stories, as editor you will probably be doing most of the writing as well as the editing.

Researching Stories

If you write most of your own stories, you know that every topic must be researched thoroughly. The first step in a normal research process is to do

Employee Information Form
For Newsletter Articles

Employee Name: ______________________________

Department: ______________________________

Position: ______________________________

Do you have any information pertaining to promotions, awards, service recognition, etc.that might be of interest to fellow employees? If so, please give details below.

Do you have any story ideas for the employee newsletter?
Please list your suggestions below.

If you are directly involved in any of the above information, would you be willing to be interviewed?

Would you be willing to write any or all of an article relating to any of the ideas mentioned above?

Please return this form to the Corporate Communications Department, #302.

Exhibit 5.3—Employee Information Form

a "literature search" to determine whether your article has already been written. If it has, but you still want to explore the topic for your specific audience, then try another angle.

Next, gather background information. Try to get specifics. You can't write about something you don't know a lot about personally. It also pays to get first-hand information. Interview people who know something about your topic. Not only will you get up-to-date information, but you may end up with some usable quotes and some new leads. (See **Chapter 1** on interviewing tips.)

Don't forget the library. Many a fine article has been written based on a library visit. Library research is among the most valuable, and one of the cheapest, forms of research. In any event, most articles will be fairly complete and accurate if you do a little background research and conduct an interview or two. Since newsletter articles are usually short, this is about all the information you can use.

Writing the Lead

Now that you've got story ideas and done some research, where do you go next? Always start at the beginning. A good lead is just as important to a newsletter piece as to a news story. It's still the hook that entices the reader into reading the complete piece.

Although to a great extent newsletters depend on design to attract readers, the well-written article is what draws them back. Like any good story, the newsletter article should have a definite beginning, middle, and end. Of course, if the article is written like a straight news story (inverted pyramid) it will begin with a tight lead and taper off as it progresses. In both cases, the lead is the key.

Your lead must tell the reader what the story is about. It is not necessary to cram everything into the lead; however, you must include enough information so that the reader doesn't have to search for your topic. For straight news articles, the lead needs to come right to the point with the facts up front. For a feature, the delayed lead may be used. In this type of lead you create ambience, then place your story within the environment you have created. Other techniques include leading with a quote and placing it in context, or using metaphor, simile, analogy, anecdote and other interest-getting devices. Although most of us forgot these literary tools the minute we left freshman composition, we shouldn't assume that good writing can get along without them. Look over the following literary uses of metaphor, simile and analogy and then compare them with the newsletter article leads that follow them.

- A **metaphor** literally says that one thing *is* another:

  ...cauliflower is nothing but a cabbage with a college education. (Mark Twain)

  Tree you are,
  Moss you are,
  You are violets with wind above them. (Ezra Pound)

- A **simile** says that one thing is *like* another:

  Though I must go, endure not yet
  A breach, but an expansion,
  Like gold to airy thinness beat. (John Donne)

  In time of peril, like the needle to the lodestone, obedience, irrespective of rank, generally flies to him who is best fitted to command. (Herman Melville)

- **Analogies** make hard-to-understand ideas easier to grasp by placing them in reader context; or, in the following example, by making a point of view more understandable through humor:

  Soap and education are not as sudden as a massacre, but they are more deadly in the long run. (Mark Twain)

The following leads show even the most mundane subject is of interest to someone and deserves the most interesting treatment possible. Pay particular attention to the number of scene-setting or descriptive words used in these leads.

Leading with a quote:

"Steelhead trout are an elitist fish; they're scarce, big, beautiful and they're good fighters," says Bob Hooton, Fish and Wildlife biologist responsible for steelhead on Vancouver Island. (*Salmonid*, newsletter of the Canadian Dept. of Fisheries and Oceans)

Leading with an anecdote:

When teachers, lawyers and other well-seasoned professionals tell you to leave work at the office, take their advice. If you don't, you will end up sleeping with your work—and only with your work—every night. (*PReview*, newsletter of the University of Delaware PRSSA)

If past experience is an indication, the telephones at our Client Services Center in Laurel, Maryland, will rarely stop ringing on December 16. That day the Center begins accepting calls for appointments to review diaries from the Fall 1982 radio survey. (*Beyond the Ratings*, national newsletter of Arbitron)

April 1st marks the beginning of a new era in banking—and a new dawn of satellite communications. On that day a clerk in Citicorp's Long Island, N.Y. office will make history by picking up the phone and dialing a Citicorp office in California. (*Telecommunications Week*, national newsletter published by Business Research Publications, Inc.)

Leading with an analogy:

Your living room may be a high-crime area—if that's where you watch TV. A study to be published in October by The Media Institute finds that TV crime is far more violent than real life crime... (*Business and the Media*, national newsletter published by The Media Institute)

You've heard the adage "two heads are better than one." What about 40? The Division's plants, more than 40 of them, are "putting their heads together" in the form of a Division-wide information sharing project recently released. (*Action Connection*, employee newsletter of Weyerhaeuser Packaging Division)

Like almost everything else, the image of the chemist is changing. Once thought of by many as a world of burbling test tubes and vials of questionable looking liquids, chemistry is changing to meet the technical and environmental needs of the microchip age. (*Current News*, employee newsletter of Delmarva Power)

Setting the scene:

It's 5:30 on a Monday afternoon and you've just finished one of *those* days. Not only did the never-ending pile of work on your desk cease to go away, but you just received two additional "A" priority assignments. On top of that, the phones wouldn't stop ringing and the air conditioning wouldn't start working, even though the temperature hit 95. (*Spectra*, employee newsletter of the SAIF Corporation)

It's pretty quiet at Merwin Dam in southwest Washington. Two generators are running. The water level is down a little so folks along the reservoir can repair some docks while the weather stays nice.

For the 21 people working at the dam, it's business as usual. But, there is a subtle change. There's no longer a threat hanging over their heads that Pacific might not own or operate the dam. The court case that could have forced Pacific to give it up was finally resolved at the end of February. (*Pacific Power Bulletin*, employee newsletter of Pacific Power)

Cramming Mom, Dad, the kids and perhaps a pet together in a car, camper, cabin or hotel for a two-week vacation will either bring day-to-day tensions to a boil—or draw everyone wonderfully closer.

The key to a successful vacation is preparation. With adequate planning, you can return home a stronger family—not a carload of bitter enemies. (*Bottom Line/Personal*, a digest-type newsletter for subscribers published by Boardroom Reports, Inc.)

Leading with a metaphor/simile:

Recession fears faded like Presidential Candidates this spring. Markets were jolted by the February employment release which showed an increase in employment of over 500,000.... The mood has gone full circle as there is renewed focus on the strength of the economy with its 5.4 percent unemployment rate, and the whiff of higher inflation in the air. (*Northwest Business Barometer*, a quarterly economic review for customers from U.S. Bank)

News Style

Remember the inverted pyramid we used when writing press releases in **Chapter 3**? It's just as valid for news stories written for newsletters. The inverted pyramid makes sense for short, straight news stories. Consider the straight news story in **Exhibit 5.4** that appeared in a student newsletter.

Notice how the story opens with a straight news lead, much like a press release, and covers the basic who, what, when, where, and how of the story.

Counselors' Association 'hires' PRSSA

The American Mental Health Counselors Association (AMHCA), a representative association for community counselors, has hired PRSSA to develop and implement a series of communication projects.

The projects began last spring when a committee of five PRSSA members developed a PR plan for AMHCA. The comprehensive plan is targeted at present and potential members. The two main objectives of the plan are to strengthen AMHCA as a membership organization and to create awareness of AMHCA among its target audiences.

After receiving approval for the plan from AMHCA board members, PRSSA was asked to develop more specific projects. This fall, a committee of eight PRSSA members worked on two projects. The first was to develop a logo and slogan for AMHCA to be used on all informational materials. The logo, now finished, symbolically represents the safety and shelter of a hearth, utilizing a stylized Hebrew symbol for home and well being. The second project involved redesigning an existing AMHCA brochure. The committee developed a whole new layout and cover design.

The committee will also continue to develop projects winter and spring terms. The main project will be a series of brochures for AMHCA. The brochures will range from information on membership to information on mental health counseling. Other upcoming projects include writing a series of public service announcements to be broadcast nationally for Mental Health Week in March.

"Overall, the project has been a great experience for all of us involved," said committee chairperson, Wendy Wintrode.

Exhibit 5.4—Straight News Story

Although the most common straight news lead is the *summary lead*, other types are also used. In the *delayed lead*, the point of the story is delayed slightly while an interesting angle is developed or a character is set up through a quote, or a scene is set through description. For example:

> School children all over the country will soon be learning the three *R*'s on a *C* thanks to a $1 million grant from Associated Products Corporation (APC). APC has recently donated the money to set up a fund for the purchase of educational computers that, when combined with APC's newest software, will teach reading, 'riting, and 'rithmetic in a whole new way—on computers.

If this reads less like straight news than the preceding story's lead, then you've discovered why a delayed lead is rarely used in straight news. Delayed leads most often appear in feature-type stories because they are excellent ways to set a scene, introduce a character, or simply attract and hold attention.

Feature Style

Feature style is usually less objective and provides less hard information than straight news style. Features generally take a point of view or discuss issues, people and places. The style is more relaxed, more descriptive and often more creative than straight news style. Look at the opening paragraphs of the feature story in **Exhibit 5.5**. This story is on the same topic as the previous straight news example, but the approach is extremely different.

Clearing up the confusion over mental health

What's the difference between a therapist, psychologist, psycho-therapist, psychiatrist, and a counselor? If you don't know, you're among the millions of people who are confused about the multi-tiered mental health counseling field.

In an effort to clear up some of the confusion, the American Mental Health Counselors Association (AMHCA) has "hired" a university student group to produce a public information campaign for them.

The Public Relations Student Society of America (PRSSA) at the University of Oregon has been retained by the Association to develop a program of information that will better define the various roles contained under the umbrella term "mental health counselor." Jane Weiskoff, regional director of AMHCA says that the confusion seems to stem from a misconception over what constitutes a "counselor." "In the mental health profession, there is a perceived hierarchy," she says. "Psychiatrists are seen as being at the apex of the field with psychologists, therapists, and other counselors falling into place under them. We'd like to clarify and possibly alter that perception."

Part of the plan, which has already been produced and approved, is to establish and maintain contact with current AMHCA members through a series of brochures and an updated and redesigned association newsletter. These informational pieces will carry the message that mental health counselors come in a variety of forms with a variety of educational and training backgrounds, and that each of these levels is suited to certain types of counseling. The goal is to establish credibility for certain of the counseling functions not fully recognized at this time by the general public and the mental health profession....

[*for illustration purposes, part of the story has been deleted here.*]

... If committee chairperson Wendy Wintrode has her way, the term "mental health counseling" will soon have a completely different, and definitely more expanded, definition. "We want everyone to know that professionalism doesn't begin and end with a small clique at the top—it is the guiding force behind the entire field of mental health counseling."

Exhibit 5.5—Feature-style Article

The facts are still here, but the focus in on creative information presentation. The lead is a question (a typical delayed lead strategy). Answering that question becomes part of the story itself. Quotes are used liberally. They not only validate and lend credibility to the subject discussed, they add human interest.

Human interest is a key characteristic of much feature writing. It can be simple inclusion of the human "voice" in a story, or it can be an entire *profile,* featuring a single person. Although the term profile usually refers to a feature story done on a person or on one aspect or issue relating to a person, individual companies or products may be profiled as well.

The following is from a profile on a corporate legal department and its head. Notice how the scene is set in the lead before the subject is introduced.

> Sitting behind a cluttered desk, boxes scattered around the office—some still unopened—is the new head of Associated Products Corporation's Law Department, Ed Bennett. Ed is a neat man, both in appearance and in speech. As he speaks about the "new" Law Department, he grins occasionally as though to say, "Why take the time to interview someone as unimportant as a lawyer?" That grin is deceiving because, to Ed and the other attorneys who work for Associated Products Corporation, law is serious business.

To add human interest is merely to add the human element to a story. Information without this element is only information. With it, information becomes more interesting, more personal, more attuned to reader's experiences. As a further example, consider the following broadcast news lead.

> A little girl stood for the first time today to receive a new teddy bear and a check for $75,000 from the Society for Needy Children. Eight-year-old Mary Patterson accepted the check on behalf of the children at the St. Mary Martha's Children's Hospital. The money represents the culmination of a year-long fundraising drive by the Society.

And, if you're trying to reach people with your message—I mean really reach them—injecting human interest is often the best way to do it.

Writing the Story

Once the lead is conceived and written, the story must elaborate on it. If possible, make points one by one, explaining each as you go. Get the who, what, when, where, and how down in the most interesting way possible—but get to the point early.

The body of the article must support your main point, hopefully already made in the lead, and elaborate on it. Anticipate questions your reader might have, and answer them satisfactorily. Remember to utilize logical transitional devices when moving from one point to another. Subheads, while technically sound, don't alleviate the need for thoughtful transitions.

Back up your statements with facts and support your generalizations with specifics. Although newsletter articles seldom use footnotes, they are not completely inappropriate. Usually, however, citation can be taken care of in the body of the text. If, however, you are quoting someone, be sure to use attribution. Don't just give the person's name. A person's title or job may lend your quote authority if that person is considered knowledgeable or an expert on your subject.

In a feature, cover the news angle in a more people-oriented way. Use color, paint word pictures to help readers hear, smell, and feel the story. If your story has a possible human-interest angle, use it. It helps your readers relate to the message through other human beings. Above all, don't be afraid to experiment with different approaches to the same topic. Try a straight news approach, then a human-interest angle or maybe a dramatic dialogue. In every case, try to make your story specific to your audience. Remember, they are major players in your scripts, in reality or vicariously (see **Example 5.6**).

Formatting Your Content

Depending on the nature of your publication, contents can vary widely. Here are some of the most common editorial inclusions.

- **Articles**
- **Table of contents**: Usually run on the first page.
- **Masthead**: Gives publication information (editor, publisher, etc.) and usually run on the second or back page.
- **Announcements**: Usually as boxed information, but sometimes run as regular columns for job placement, promotions, etc.
- **Letters:** If the publication is designed for two-way communication, a letters column is a common addition.
- **Editorial**: Can be in the form of a "President's Column," a signed editorial from management or the publication's editor.
- **News Notes**: A quick (and brief) look at what's happening—often a boxed item or sometimes run in very narrow columns as *marginalia*.

- **Mailer**: This is the spot reserved for mailing labels, postage-paid information and return address; however, it is often used as a place to put masthead information.
- **Calendar**: Upcoming events of interest to readers.

Although there are variations on these elements, most newsletters include at least some of these items.

Fully Loaded

Playing Tag with the Competition

Can the lowly load tag become a competitive advantage? Several plants are learning the answer is yes, if it's a load tag produced on BOXIS. BOXIS, the Packaging Division's Box Information System, has been around a while, and most plants are currently using computer generated load tags. But Portland folks, among others are getting a feel for just how useful BOXIS load tags can be – for themselves and their customers.

"Most load tags are handwritten, often difficult to read," notes Don McLaurin, BOXIS manager in Tacoma. "BOXIS produces a computer generated tag that's easy to read, even in dark warehouses."

But the beauty of the BOXIS load tag is more than skin deep. It also carries bar code information, the foundation of automated operations that improve productivity and customer service.

For instance, while an order is still being produced, load tags help the finishing department run more smoothly. According to Portland's Chuck Goodrich, production supervisor, the load tag's bar coding has helped Portland increase strapper throughput 15 to 20%.

"As a unit comes down the line, a laser scanner reads the bar code information on the load tag. The information is used by a computer to set the strapping pattern, automatically strap the unit, and send it down the correct spur line," Chuck explains.

Automated strapping is an easy way to make sure the load is strapped to the customer's specs. It also can improve finishing department productivity, decrease bottlenecks at the strapper, and free employees to dress the load and correct problems before they happen.

"It has really made a big difference," adds Chuck. "Before, the line would get so backed up, we'd have to put three people on the strapper. Now, we're able to run it smoothly most of the time with just one person."

Another advantage of the bar code system is that it provides instant access to order status.

"By simply scanning the bar code on a completed unit, we can tell a customer exactly how many units of the order have been completed that moment," explains Don. But load tag customer service doesn't stop there. Packaging Division customers are learning how our load tags can help them with computerized inventory and other needs.

Tom Booth, production planner at Salinas, says the flexibility of the load tag and help from information systems expert Del Green allowed them to quickly and easily modify the load tag when a key agricultural customer, Bud of California, asked them to add a special numeric inventory code.

"Hey, this is a competitive business," Tom says, "and anytime you can provide an additional service – particularly when it doesn't cost much – that's a real advantage. The customer was very, very pleased."

Brendan Doherty, Charlotte sales rep, says a customized load tag was one factor solidifying Charlotte's position in a trial with Kimberly Clark. "We developed a special corner tag that included a calendar. They were impressed. We're still on a trial basis, but it looks very good. The load tag is an advantage that sets us apart just that much more.

That's not the end of the story; BOXIS users are still learning just what the system can do. But one thing's certain: once they see Weyerhaeuser load tags, customers are beginning to request similar load tags from all their packaging suppliers.

A major Rochester customer, Central New York Bottle, liked the tag so much they asked competitors to produce a similar one. "This customer buys $5 million of corrugated a year," says senior sales rep John McCormick. "We are currently a minority supplier. But this could easily gain us $200,000 in new business because our competitors are scratching their heads wondering how they will do it."

"They don't have the system.'

Exhibit 5.6—The Newsletter Story

How Much Is Enough?

How many articles to run depends on the focus and length of your publication, but fortunately, newsletters are extremely flexible. If you run a four-page newsletter but you always have more information than room, you can expand to six or eight pages. A one-page insert (loose, or run on a larger sheet with a brochure-type fold) will give you enough room for two or three more stories—more if your articles are short (see **Figure 5.7**).

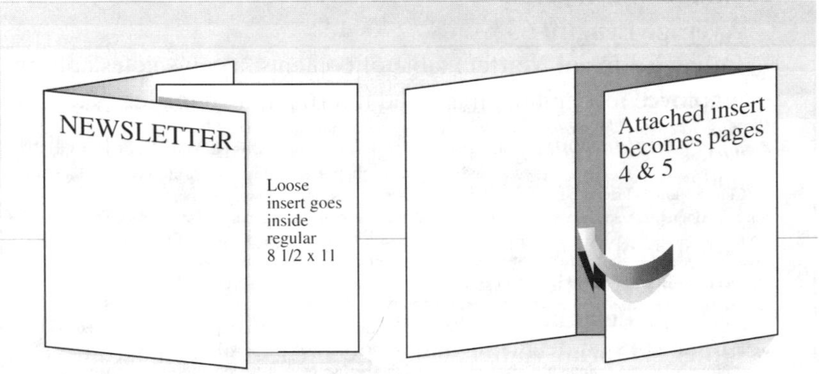

Exhibit 5.7—Newsletter Inserts

A one-page addition (printed both sides) can be inserted as a loose page into a standard four-page newsletter; however, many of these loose pages fall out or become lost during distribution or reading. If you opt for an attached page as part of a two-fold format, the last page should fold inward.

There is truly no set figure for how much is enough; however, here are some contents from a variety of newsletters.

- *Oregon Columbia IABC Ampersand:* A regional monthly association newsletter of the International Association of Business Communicators.
  Number of Pages: 4
  Number of Articles: 4
  Average Length: 500 words
  Other Editorial Matter: table of contents, announcements, masthead, help wanted.

- *Action Connection:* A monthly institutional newsletter for employees of the Weyerhaeuser Paper Company Packaging Division.
  Number of Pages: 8

Number of Articles: 7
Average Length: 447 words
Other Editorial Matter: recognition by plant site, employee recognition, masthead.

- *Resource:* A monthly institutional newsletter for employees of the Western Wood Products manufacturing Division of Georgia Pacific.
  Number of Pages: 4
  Number of Articles: 5
  Average Length: 65 words
  Other Editorial Matter: table of contents, a news notes column, employee recognition, masthead information on mailer.
- *The Sampler from Response Analysis:* A digest newsletter for clients and prospective clients featuring articles on research findings from Response Analysis Corporation of Princeton, New Jersey.
  Number of Pages: 4
  Number of Articles: 10
  Average Length: 252 words
  Other Editorial Matter: table of contents, editorial, masthead.
- *Northwest Business Barometer:* A quarterly economic review for customers from the Department of Economics, U.S. Bancorp.
  Number of Pages: 8
  Number of Articles: 6 (Divided geographically and topically)
  Average Length: 850 words
  Other Editorial Matter: News notes called "Random Thoughts." Masthead information is included as part of the nameplate or banner.
- *N.E.T.M.A. (Nobody Ever Tells Me Anything):* An employee/public news briefs newsletter from Eugene, Oregon, Development Department/Business Development Division.
  Number of Pages: 4
  Number of Articles: 14 (digested news type)
  Average Length: 90 words
  Other Editorial Matter: a list of publications of interest to the business community, business community recognition column, calendar of events, trivia column.

Making Your Articles Fit

Most newsletters lead off with the most topical or interesting story on the front page—much like a newspaper. Your choice of lead article will be based on management dictates or your assessment of reader interest.

Before you begin to lay out your newsletter, you should list all your potential articles, their lengths, and approximate placement by importance/interest in the newsletter. This way, if space gets tight, you can edit from the bottom up. A secondary choice is to carry over articles that aren't "time bound"—that is, articles that could just as well wait for the next issue. And, finally, you can edit each story until *all* of them fit in the space you have. This assumes that some information in each article is superfluous which, under ideal editorial circumstances, shouldn't happen. But, as any experienced editor can tell you, there is always something you can cut.

Standing columns—articles such as editorials or employee recognition that recur from issue to issue—should already have a reserved space in your layout. It is in your best interest to allot a certain amount of space to these recurring articles and stick to it. That way, your other articles will have the space they need and deserve.

If you run out of space and can afford it, consider adding two pages (a single page run on both sides) either as an insert or an extra fold. If you only have enough copy to add literally one page (a single sheet printed only on one side) don't do it. Nothing is as unattractive as a publication page printed only on one side.

Editorial Considerations for Display Copy

Display copy, from an editorial viewpoint, includes headlines, subheads, captions, and pull quotes. Each of these elements has to be written for best effect. Ideally, each should contribute to the article to which it refers by adding to, elaborating or amplifying on, or drawing attention to information already presented in the article.

Writing Headlines

Headlines are important to any publication, but especially so for newsletters. Headlines should grab the readers' attention and make them want to read the article. They should be informative and brief. Here are some guidelines that should help you in constructing good headlines.

- Keep them short. Space is always a problem in newsletters. Be aware of column widths and how much space that sentence-long headline you are proposing will take up. Every column inch you devote to your headline will have to be subtracted somewhere else. Headlines don't have to be complete sentences, nor do they have to be punctuated unless they are.

- Avoid vague words or phrases. Your headline should contribute to the article, not detract from it. Cute or vague headlines that play on words should be left for entertainment publications like *Variety* (famous for its convoluted headlines). Don't use standing heads for recurring articles such as "President's Message" or "Employee Recognition." It is better to mention something of the article's content in the headline, such as "Packaging Division wins company-wide contest."
- Use short words. Nothing is worse than a long word in a headline that has to be hyphenated or left on a line by itself. You can always come up with an alternative that is shorter.

Writing Subheads and Crossheads

Subheads are explanatory heads, usually set in a smaller type (or italics), that appear under the headline. For example:

ACME buyout impending
Statewide Telecom makes takeover bid

In most cases, a headline is sufficient; however, there are times when a rather lengthy subhead is necessary, especially if the headline is brief or cryptic.

'A drama of national failure'
A best-selling author talks about reporting on AIDS

Subheads should be used sparingly, if at all, and only for clarity's sake.

Crossheads are the smaller, transitional heads within an article. You shouldn't need them in a typical newsletter article. About the only time they might be useful is in a longer article—perhaps a newsletter devoted to a single subject. Crossheads should be very short and should simply indicate a change in subject or direction. Most writers use crossheads in place of elaborate transitional devices. Since space is always a consideration, using a crosshead instead of a longer transitional device will save you several column inches.

However, if you do use crossheads, make sure that more than one is warranted. Like subpoints in an outline, crossheads don't come solo. Either delete a single crosshead, or expand your points to include another one.

Writing Captions

Captions, or cutlines, are the informational blurbs that appear below or next to photographs or other illustrations. They are usually set in a smaller point size. Like headlines, they should contribute to the overall information of an article, not detract from it.

Keep captions brief. Make sure they relate directly to the photograph. (The best captions also add information that may not be included in the article itself.)

If your caption is necessarily long, make sure it is clear. If you are naming a number of people in a photo, for example, establish a recognizable order (*clockwise from the top, right to left, from the top, from the left*, etc.)

Captions, like headlines, should not be vague or cute. You simply don't have enough space to waste developing that groaner of a pun you've been dying to try out.

Writing Pull Quotes

Pull quotes are relatively new to newsletters. Traditionally a magazine device, they draw a reader's attention to a point within an article. They almost always appear close to the place in the article from which the quote is taken.

Pull quotes don't have to be actual quotes, but they should at least be an edited version of the article copy. Pull quotes usually suggest themselves. If you have a number of good quotes from an interviewee, you can always find a good one to use as a pull quote. Or, if you simply want to stress an important point in an article, use it as a pull quote.

Pull quotes can also create white space or fill up unused space left over from a short article. A good pull quote can be as long or as short as you want and still make sense. They can span several columns, be constrained to a single column, head the page, appear in the center of a copy-heavy page, or help balance some other graphic element on the page.

Remember, good pull quotes reflect the best your article has to offer. A mundane pull quote is wasted space.

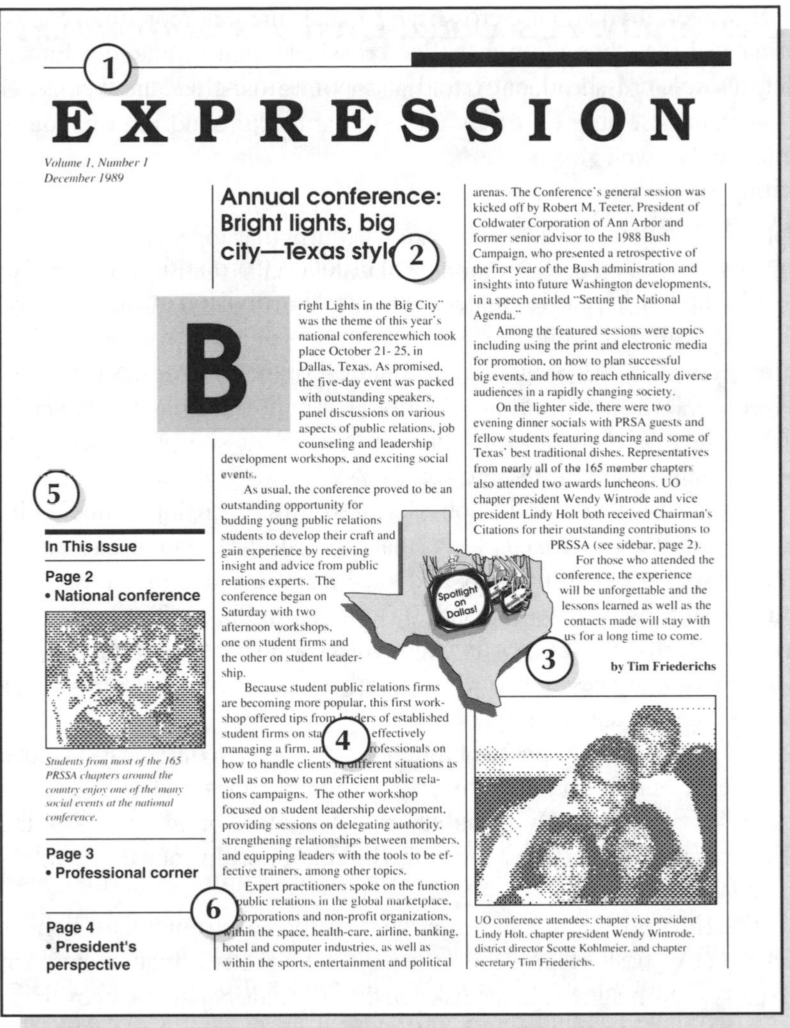

1

EXPRESSION

Volume 1, Number 1
December 1989

Annual conference: Bright lights, big city—Texas style

2

Bright Lights in the Big City" was the theme of this year's national conferencewhich took place October 21- 25, in Dallas, Texas. As promised, the five-day event was packed with outstanding speakers, panel discussions on various aspects of public relations, job counseling and leadership development workshops, and exciting social events.

As usual, the conference proved to be an outstanding opportunity for budding young public relations students to develop their craft and gain experience by receiving insight and advice from public relations experts. The conference began on Saturday with two afternoon workshops, one on student firms and the other on student leadership.

Because student public relations firms are becoming more popular, this first workshop offered tips from leaders of established student firms on sta[rting and] effectively managing a firm, an[d from p]rofessionals on how to handle clients in different situations as well as on how to run efficient public relations campaigns. The other workshop focused on student leadership development, providing sessions on delegating authority, strengthening relationships between members, and equipping leaders with the tools to be effective trainers, among other topics.

Expert practitioners spoke on the function [of p]ublic relations in the global marketplace, [c]orporations and non-profit organizations, within the space, health-care, airline, banking, hotel and computer industries, as well as within the sports, entertainment and political arenas. The Conference's general session was kicked off by Robert M. Teeter, President of Coldwater Corporation of Ann Arbor and former senior advisor to the 1988 Bush Campaign, who presented a retrospective of the first year of the Bush administration and insights into future Washington developments, in a speech entitled "Setting the National Agenda."

Among the featured sessions were topics including using the print and electronic media for promotion, on how to plan successful big events, and how to reach ethnically diverse audiences in a rapidly changing society.

On the lighter side, there were two evening dinner socials with PRSA guests and fellow students featuring dancing and some of Texas' best traditional dishes. Representatives from nearly all of the 165 member chapters also attended two awards luncheons. UO chapter president Wendy Wintrode and vice president Lindy Holt both received Chairman's Citations for their outstanding contributions to PRSSA (see sidebar, page 2).

For those who attended the conference, the experience will be unforgettable and the lessons learned as well as the contacts made will stay with us for a long time to come.

by Tim Friederichs

UO conference attendees: chapter vice president Lindy Holt, chapter president Wendy Wintrode, district director Scotte Kohlmeier, and chapter secretary Tim Friederichs.

5

In This Issue

Exhibit 5.8—A Newsletter Front Page

Some of the more important editorial elements of a typical newsletter front page are: 1) The banner or name of your newsletter. Make sure it neither overpowers your front page nor is overpowered by other elements on the page. 2) The headline. Typically there should be only one major head on the front page. Make it large enough to draw attention, but not so large as to overpower your banner. 3) Photos and illustrations. Don't scrimp on size. Draw attention to your stories with large photos and illustrations. Just make sure they are of a quality worthy of the attention. 4) Body copy. Flush left if columns are wide (2 or 3 columns), justified if narrow (4 or more columns). 5) Table of contents. Don't assume it has to be boxed. Try an open format for a change. 6) Rules. Use them to delineate your columns, or to set items apart.

Case Study: Associated Products Corporation

The following is additional information to be used for the newsletter assignments. Be sure to review the original background information in **Chapter 3** as well.

APC Electronics Division

The Electronics Division of Associated Products Corporation is located in White Plains, N.Y., and is a major manufacturing division of the company. APC was originally called Traxton Electronics and electronics is still its primary concern. Although the headquarters of the company is located in Syracuse, N.Y., the Electronics Division was moved to White Plains in 1979 to take advantage of a relatively new plant site purchased from another manufacturing firm the year before.

The new Electronics Division is located on a ten-acre lot outside White Plains but still within the city limits that provides the city with substantial tax revenue from both property and local income taxes. In addition, the division employs 800 workers, 350 from White Plains. The remainder have transferred from other divisions (or headquarters as in the case of executives) or are new hires, who specialize in electronics, from various parts of the state and country.

The division is composed of four buildings and two large parking lots. The largest building is given over to assembly lines and is where the electronics are physically manufactured. The other buildings house the offices, research labs, meeting rooms, a large auditorium, and the facility's cafeteria.

The InfoQuick software (a product of the Electronics Division) is created in two basic stages. First, the physical diskette is manufactured in two parts—the magnetic inner disk and the synthetic paper outer covering. The magnetic disks are then bulk coded with the software information from a master program, much like a record is stamped on an assembly line. Of course, the transfer is made electronically instead of physically. The disks are then covered with the outer sleeve and sealed, all by machine. The only workers involved in the process are those who run the primary machines; however, a number of assembly line people are involved in the final packaging in which the software is inserted into boxes and wrapped in cellophane for shipping.

Robert McArthur, Electronics Division Manager

Senior vice president and division manager, Robert McArthur, has been with APC for over ten years. Before coming to APC, McArthur was assistant vice president for manufacturing at Philcronics (another electronics firm which was purchased by APC in 1974). He has a close working relationship with APC president, James L. Sutton, and sits on the executive board of the company. Although he had no hand in either the idea or the development of InfoQuick, McArthur is playing a major role in the manufacturing process. As division manager, he is responsible for the mass production of the software, including raw materials purchase, quality control, and meeting production deadlines. Some quotes:

> "I agree with Jim [Sutton] when he says that this idea is revolutionary. I've raised two kids myself [McArthur's wife died in 1970] and I know firsthand how difficult it is to keep them interested in learning."
>
> "The Electronics Division is *the* division at APC (don't tell Harve Johnsen over in the Paper Products Division I said that) and we pump a lot of money into R&D [research and development] to support that claim. Without R&D, we wouldn't have IQ on the market today. It takes a lot of thinking and sweating to come up with that kind of product."
>
> "If it didn't have a market, we wouldn't make it. Let's face it—if we can't make any money, then we go out of business. I mean, I appreciate what IQ is going to do for kids all over the country, but it's also going to make us a bundle."
>
> "The people who work here in the White Plains plant are a great bunch of folks—all 800 or so of them. Every single worker knows his job and does it. We don't get a lot of flack from the line people. They know that in today's economy, their lucky to have jobs. I don't mean to sound high and mighty, but that's the bottom line. It doesn't mean that we try to get away with anything, we don't. They get top money and honest treatment."
>
> "We're thinking of instituting a profit-sharing plan sometime this year. The employees already know about it and they're real pleased. It gives them incentive to work hard, put in a full day, and come up with cost-saving ideas. They know that they'll profit too."

Ellen Burke, Assembly Line, Electronics Division

Ellen Burke is an assembly line worker for the Electronics Division. She's been with APC for four years, is married and has one child, three years old. Some quotes:

> "Some people don't like assembly line work, but I don't mind it. I try to understand what it is I'm doing. I don't just go through the motions eight hours a day."
>
> "This InfoQuick stuff is a great idea. I understand that President Sutton came up with it. Good for him. My daughter will be going to school in a few years, and I sure want her to get to use it."
>
> "The profit-sharing plan we've been hearing about is a great idea. I could use a little profit. Not that I don't get paid good money. I do. But, when I get part of the profits, then the company kind of belongs to me too—and everybody else around here."

Lorna Allen, Programmer III, Electronics Division

Lorna Allen is a computer programmer hired by APC five years ago when work on the IQ line began. She had just received her masters in computer science from Cornell and was job hunting. Along with eight other programmers, Allen was responsible for coming up with the technical requirements necessary to put the educational ideas into computer language. Some quotes:

> "I was extremely lucky to have been hired by APC right out of graduate school. Now, I'll be able to stay on here in the Electronics Division as long as IQ is carried as a product line—which we all hope will be a long time."
>
> "When we first began, we only had the barest of ideas how we'd proceed. What evolved was an excellent working relationship between the programmers and the educators we hired as consultants."
>
> "We've really done something to be proud of here—not only as computer programmers, but as inventors. I mean, I feel kind of like Ben Franklin or Thomas Edison—a pioneer in my field."

Assignment 5-1: Newsletters

As part of your job as public relations writer for APC, you must contribute articles for the employee newsletter, *APC Action*. You have been assigned the task of writing an article of 500 words (it will be this month's feature article) on the new IQ software line and APC's involvement with NEA. Since there is a lot of information, you will have to concentrate on keeping to the point (500 words is only about two typed pages).

This is an employee newsletter. You should try to make the article newsy but interesting. Look for an angle that you think might attract the employee—something they may all have in common. Since this is a feature story, use feature article construction.

Assignment 5-2: Newsletters

Most school districts subscribe to a national newsline featuring news of interest to educators. Individual districts often put out their own newsletters based on newsline information, sometimes using stories from the newsline *in toto*. You should write a brief news story (about 250 words) on the NEA speaker's bureau for the newsline. Use standard news story format (inverted pyramid).

Assignment 5-3: Newsletters

You've been given the assignment of writing a newsletter feature for the corporate monthly newsletter about the Electronics Division at White Plains plant and its involvement with the IQ line. This can be an all-purpose article because it's as much about the plant and the division as it is about the software. The article is to be about 600 words.

CHAPTER 6

Magazines & Trade Publications

The magazine in the end will be the most influential of all departments of letters.

Edgar Allen Poe

When we speak of magazines most of us think of our favorite consumer publication (*Time, Newsweek, National Geographic,* the *Atlantic*, etc.); however, for our purposes, we are speaking primarily, but not exclusively, of the **house publication**. Recent research has shown that house publications are the *least* looked to form of organizational communication. Guess what's first? Face-to-face communication. That's not surprising, but it doesn't mean that the house magazine is dead. What it does mean is that it should *contribute* to open communication rather than be relied upon as the sole source. In addition, it plays another role. Unlike most print media an organization might have access to, the house publication is a totally controlled medium—that is, the organization producing it has sole editorial control. The company can go on record through its house organ, state its position on a controversial issue, or simply tell its story its way. In other words, the house organ is still a good public relations tool.

The typical house organ is meant for an internal public—usually employees, shareholders, and retirees. Sometimes, though, it is offered to the external public. A publication like *Exxon USA* stresses a broader emphasis with articles often dealing with the industry as a whole and subjects of interest to those outside the company. Because the house organ is, at bottom, still a public relations piece, its thrust remains company oriented. Even a seemingly unrelated story will, in some way, eventually relate to the organization.

The house publication is usually in either magazine or newspaper format (or sometimes a hybrid called a "magapaper"). Both communicate with their various publics efficiently. Unless the company is large enough to produce a slick, in-house publication, the house organ will be sent out to an agency for design and printing. Sometimes the agency will even provide writers to work up the stories; however, the best articles still come from writers inside the company who know and work with the people they write about.

Content and Format

Like their smaller cousin, the newsletter, house magazines usually present the following editorial mix:

- 50 percent information about the organization—local, national and international
- 20 percent employee information—benefits, quality of working life, raises, etc.
- 20 percent relevant noncompany information—competitors, community, etc.
- 10 percent small talk and personals

How you organize these elements is important. You should lead your reader through your magazine in a logical order, and one that is pleasing and most interesting to him or her.

There is no single organizational format for house magazines. What is important is that you find a place for all relevant information, a place inclusive enough to house similar information from issue to issue.

Before you even start (or if you're overhauling an existing publication) you need to set some objectives. To make sure your reasons for publishing a house magazine are realistic, ask yourself some questions.

- Are my goals and objectives consistent with the goals and objectives of the organization itself? What am I really trying to get out of this? The temptation is very real, especially for creative people, to produce a magazine for simple ego gratification. Don't succumb to it. Have good, solid reasons for publishing.
- Can I attain these objectives through another, more effective, method? Can I achieve good downward communication through an existing newsletter or more frequent meetings?

- Can I attain these objectives in a more *cost-effective* way? House magazines are expensive to produce. As usual, your budget restrictions will have the final say.

Once you have answered these questions, and you have satisfied yourself that your prospective audience will benefit from your publication, you can decide on its proper organizational format.

Most house magazines contain very much the same type of editorial information as newsletters. The following items are listed in the approximate order in which they might appear (allowing for overlap in the case of articles).

- **Table of contents**: Usually run on the front page.
- **Masthead**: Gives publication information (editor, publisher, etc.) and usually run on the table of contents or second page.
- **Editorial**: Can be in the form of a "President's Column," a signed editorial from management or the publication's editor.
- **Letters:** If the publication is designed for two-way communication, a letters column is a common addition.
- **News Notes**: A quick (and brief) look at what's happening around the organization. You can get a lot of these in two or three pages. This is a good place for employee information as well.
- **Articles:** News and feature articles make up the bulk of the magazine and should have a consistent order of their own. For instance, the cover story should always appear in the same approximate location each issue.
- **Announcements**: Usually boxed, but sometimes run as regular columns for job placement, promotions, etc. This is another good place for employee interest pieces.
- **Calendar**: Upcoming events of interest to readers.

Remember, there is no hard and fast rule for formatting your magazine; but stick to whatever method you choose. Your readers look for consistency. If the format changes every two issues, you'll quickly lose them.

Writing Articles

House publication articles range from straight news to complete fiction, and include everything in between. Most, though, are either straight news or feature. Since straight news has been covered adequately in earlier chapters, we will concentrate on feature writing here.

A feature can be construed as almost anything that isn't straight news. In fact, *feature* has several meanings. As used in the term "feature story," it simply means the main story or cover story in the publication. In its broader sense it means an article that features something as its central point or theme. This something may not necessarily be the message of the story or its publicity angle. It is most often the story itself. For example, you've been asked to do a story on a new product—say, a plastic lining that can be used as a bed for soil or sod to keep it from eroding or slipping. Instead of doing a straight news story on the product itself, you opt to do a feature story on a user of the new product. Maybe you find a golf course that's using the new underliner to rebuild its greens and the focus of the story becomes the golf course. The publicity angle or the message about the new product becomes almost secondary. Featuring the golf course adds an extra dimension to your product story and sets it in context. In fact, the most useful element of a feature story approach is that it presents a context. Not every straight news story can do that.

A vast array of writing styles can justifiably be called "magazine writing." Articles or ideas for articles that don't seem to fit one particular magazine format, or even one section of a magazine, may well fit into another. For example, let's say you interview an employee on a job-related topic such as benefits. In the course of your conversation you discover that he builds model ships for a hobby and, in fact, has won several competitions. You actually gather enough information for a how-to article on building model ships as well as enough for a feature on the employee. Neither of these ideas may fit into the story you originally set out to do; however, they may fit into another section on employees or one on hobbies. The lesson, of course, is never discard information just because it doesn't fit into your present assignment. Even if the tone or style of the article or information doesn't seem to fit one category, it may well fit another.

Although several standard types of feature articles are appropriate for magazines, the most common is the *profile*.

The Profile

The profile is most typically a feature story written specifically about a person, a product or service, or an organization or some part of it. It literally profiles the subject, listing facts, highlighting points of interest, and—most importantly—tying them to the organization. Regardless of the subject of your article, you are writing for a specific organization and the article must have some bearing on it—direct or indirect.

The personality profile

Personality profiles are popular because people still like to read about other people, whether these people are just like them (so they can easily relate) or very different (so they can aspire or admire). Of course, a personality profile should do more than just satisfy human curiosity, it should inform the reader of something important about the organization itself by putting it in the context of a biographical sketch. For example, this lead was written for a brief profile on an award-winning engineer:

> When Francis Langly receives the Goodyear Medal this spring, it will represent the symbolic crowning of a lifetime of dedication to the field of chemistry. Awarded by the Rubber Division of the American Chemical Society, the Goodyear Medal is the premier award for work in the field of specialty elastomers—an area that Langly helped pioneer. When Langly makes his medalist's address to the gathering in Indianapolis in May, his comments will be a reflection of almost 50 years of innovation and development which began in 1938 when he joined Rogers Experimental Plastics Company as a research chemist.

What does this say about the organization? It implies, for one thing, that the company is obviously a good one to have such a well-respected person work for it for so long. A profile like this calls attention to the merits of the organization by calling attention to someone who has something to do with it—or, in some cases, to someone who benefits from its services or products. Consider the following lead:

> Guy Exton is a superb artist. His oils have hung in galleries all over the country. But, for nearly five years, he couldn't paint anything. In order to paint, you typically need fingers and a hand, and Guy lost his right hand in an auto accident in 1983. But now, thanks to a revolutionary new elastomer product developed by Rogers Experimental Plastics Company, Guy is painting again. He can grip even the smallest of his paint brushes and control the tiniest nuance through the use of a special prosthetic device designed by Medical Help, Inc. of Franklin, New York. The device, which uses REP's "Elastoflex" membrane as a flexible covering, provides minute control of digits through an electro-mechanical power pack embedded in the wrist.

One of the most common types of personality profiles is the Q & A (question and answer format). This style typically begins with a brief biographical sketch of the person being interviewed, hints at the reason for the interview, and sets the scene by describing the surroundings in which the interview took place. For the remainder of the piece, speakers are tagged Q or A. Sometimes, the interviewer is designated with the magazine's name (for example, *The Corporate Connection* might be shortened to *CC*). Likewise, the interviewee might be designated by his or her last name.

The descriptive narrative tells the story of the individual being profiled from a second-person point of view. Naturally, quotes from the subject may be included, but sometimes a successful profile is simply a biographical sketch, and won't necessarily need them. The profile in **Exhibit 6.1** is a mixture. Although there are some brief quotes, most of the profile is simple biography.

A Lifetime of Service

When Francis Langly receives the Goodyear Medal this spring, it will represent the symbolic crowning of a lifetime of dedication to the field of chemistry. Awarded by the Rubber Division of the American Chemical Society, the Goodyear medal is the premier award for work in the field of specialty elastomers—an area that Langly helped pioneer. When Langly makes his medalist's address to the gathering in Indianapolis in May, his comments will be a reflection of almost 50 years of innovation and development which began in 1938 when he joined Rogers Experimental Plastics Company as a research chemist.

Born in Brooklyn, New York, in 1915, Langly received his BA in chemistry and his PhD in organic chemistry from Cornell in 1939. His first position at REPC was in the Chemical Department at the Experimental Station near Ravenswood, Vermont. At the outset of World War II, he was working on the synthetic rubber program addressing the problem of an adhesive for nylon tire cord for B-29 bomber tires. These studies eventually culminated in the development of the vinyl pyridine adhesives so widely used today.

Langly's background in organic chemistry led to his transfer to the Organic Chemicals Department at the Johnson Laboratory in Stillwater, Oklahoma, where he discovered the first light-fast yellow dyes for cotton; and during the next 10 years, he led the task force that developed dyes for the new synthetic fibers that were fast becoming a mainstay of American fashion.

From his work in dyes, Langly moved on to work in fluorine chemical research. The small research team he headed is credited with the discovery of a family of new elastomers. The team at that time had, what Langly calls, "a very special business in fluorine chemicals," but no solid applications yet for these quickly developing products. Langly and his group knew that they had something distinctly different and new in the field of elastomers. To an inventor, of course, the invention comes first. It didn't seem to trouble him that there was little or no market at that time for these new products. "There was no surprise in development," Langly says. "We understood the properties of the products we were developing and were sure that markets would eventually open up."

continued on next page

Exhibit 6.1—Personality Profile

Chief among these early fluorelastomers was "Axon," a polymer that could resist extremely high temperatures, toxic chemicals, and a broad range of fluids. Other products, however, were gathering attention in industry and defense and the company was eager to market these already-accepted materials. In fact, the "Axon" project was sidetracked in the early 1950s when it was thought that the Langly research team could be better utilized in work on an already existing product. In a way, this turned out to be a profitable diversion. Although the proposed research turned out to be a dead end, a small pressure reactor system that had been designed to build EP rubbers was converted to make fluoropolymer and used as a pilot plant to produce "Axon."

According to Langly, "you rarely have a chance to fill a vacuum with something entirely new." And "Axon" was entirely new. The Air Force had been searching for some time for a product that could withstand very low and very high temperatures and was impervious to oil for use as engine seals on jet aircraft. "Axon" fit the bill perfectly. The Air Force quickly adopted it for use in jets, and the product went commercial for the first time in 1959.

When interest in space led the United States into the space race in the late 1950s, "Axon" gained another and larger market for use in rocket engine seals. Because of its ability to seal against "hard" vacuum, "Axon" was one of the first rubbers that could be used in space.

As the markets for "Axon" continued to expand—to automotives, industry, and oil exploration uses— Langly progressed through a series of promotions. When the Elastomer Chemicals Department was formed in the mid-1960s, he was transferred to corporate headquarters in Freeport as Assistant Director of Research and Development.

Until his retirement in 1979, Langly continued to develop his interest in the field of elastomers. To date, he has 35 patents issued in his name and some 15 publications. In the 25 years since the birth of "Axon," Langly has seen the product grow to its present status as the premium fluoroelastomer in the world with a new plant recently opened in Belgium providing the product for a hungry European market.

But, Langly numbers the discovery and development of "Axon" as only one in a long line of accomplishments attained during his half-century of work in the field of chemistry. Since his retirement, he has remained active in the field, working in art conservation, developing new techniques for the preservation of rare oil paintings. In a year and a half of work with the City Museum in New York, he set up a sciences department for the conservation of paintings. He is currently scientific advisor for the Partham Museum in Baltimore. He continues to consult, working closely with industry. He serves as expert testimony at court trials involving chemicals. And, he has given a speech before the United Nations on rubber.

Yet, Langly remains low key about his accomplishments and his current interests. "I'm just trying to keep the fires going," he says. Despite this modesty, it is apparent to others that when Francis Langly receives the Goodyear Medal this year it will represent, not a capstone, but simply another milestone in a lifetime of service.

The product or service profile

Profiling a product or service means describing it in a way that is unusual in order to draw attention to the product and the organization. This is often done in subtle ways. For example, the personality profile on the artist Guy Exton is really a way of mentioning a product. Clearly this doesn't detract from the human-interest angle, but it does accomplish a second purpose (probably the primary purpose) which is publicity. The same techniques you use in other article types can be used in profiling products.

The organizational profile

In the organizational profile, an entire organization or some part of it is profiled. The organizational profile and the personality profile are accomplished much the same way, except that you need to interview a number of key people in the unit you are profiling in order to obtain a complete picture of that unit. The following profile looks at an entire company providing a unique service, and a department within a large corporation (**Exhibit 6.2**).

The Legal Department at APC

Sitting behind a cluttered desk, boxes scattered around the office—some still unopened—is the new head of Associated Products Corporation's Law Department, Ed Bennett. Ed is a neat man, both in appearance and in speech. As he speaks about the "new" Law Department, he grins occasionally as though to say, "Why take the time to interview someone as unimportant as a lawyer?" That grin is deceiving because, to Ed and the other attorneys who work for Associated Products Corporation (APC), law is serious business.

Questions of law are rarely debated around APC. According to Ed, when something is not legal, it simply is not legal. No vote is taken by anyone; no decision needs to be arrived at. For this reason, "house counsel" (those attorneys who work for and in companies rather than for individuals) are often thought to be against all suggestions—paid to say no to projects or suggestions. This isn't so, says Ed. "It just so happens that a number of things that people wish to do must meet certain requirements. In most cases," he says, "it's not a question of 'you can't do it' but rather a matter of 'you have to do it this way.'"

According to Ed, this often puts the bearer of this news in an awkward position—much like the messenger who brings the Chinese Emperor bad tidings and has his head cut off for his efforts. It is a lot better in Ed's mind to make the adjustments to a particular project now than to wait until they can no longer be made and find out that the entire project is unworkable.

In APC's Law Department, each attorney handles a specific area dealing with particular projects. Like many of the other

continued on next page

Exhibit 6.2—Organizational/Departmental Profile

departments in APC, Law is experiencing a period of transition. Consequently, specific areas of assignment are only tentative. Still, the four-man legal staff now employed by APC is specialized to the extent that each member has an area of expertise in which he or she works a majority of the time.

Dennis Silva, newly arrived at APC from work with the State, is involved primarily with local and state government matters. Gary Williams is involved primarily in contractual matters, often between APC and other large companies. Keith McGowan has been handling research and certain other issues frequently dealing with the Federal Government.

Ed, just recently elected Vice President and General Attorney, describes his role as that of a player-coach. Aside from his specific responsibilities, he must also present the legal overview of the company's actions, and accept the consequences of his advice. "Along with responsibility comes accountability," he says.

Ed, who has been with APC for nearly two years, was assistant center judge advocate at Walter Reed Army Medical Center prior to coming to APC. He received his Juris Doctor from the University of Pennsylvania Law School and graduated from the College of William and Mary. Before coming to work for APC, Ed was a judge advocate officer at the Headquarters, U.S. Army Fort Dix, New Jersey from 1972 to 1975.

Together with the three other attorneys, Ed helps comprise a relatively small department. Despite its size, it may well be one of the most important functions within the company. "The myriad of legal and regulatory requirements, particularly in a business like this, creates a jungle," Ed says. "It is impossible to get to the other shore of this particular river by rowing in a straight line. There are cross currents and tides with the wind blowing from a hundred different directions."

The metaphor may be mixed, but the point is clear. According to Ed, the various State and Federal regulations governing our operations are, by no means, consistent. Neither, frequently, are the goals of the company as expressed by the input of each of the departments. Consequently, it is also the responsibility of the Law Department to make uniform, or parallel, the various desires of the company.

"The end is always the same though," says Ed. "It is not to turn out neat legal briefs which, though often well researched and executed, are not useful if a manager can neither understand nor conform to them. It is to strike a balance between our own professional conscience and the utilitarian nature of the work."

"Of course," says Ed, "we'd like to spend six months on each item, carefully researching it, but by then we have lost the element of timeliness which is often equally important."

The people who make up the Law Department are, in the highest sense, professional. In fact, they have a professional responsibility quite separate from the company. Every attorney is a member of a bar association, and thus has imposed upon him the Code of Professional Responsibility unique to his profession. "We are not exempted," says Ed, "simply because we are 'house counsel,' from the dictates of that Code." Thus, their advice has to be correct, or as correct as it can be under prevailing circumstances. All of APC's attorneys are members of

continued on next page

at least one bar and some are members of up to four.

The role of the APC attorney is similar to that of the "outside" attorney in that they are here to represent the company in legal matters. But APC's Law Department does more than that. It not only represents the company when it gets into difficulty, but expends a great deal of time and effort in keeping the company out of difficulty. To that end, the house counsel of APC must maintain sufficient contact with the company, its people, and its activities in order that it may render timely advice and thus prevent difficulties.

In a way, the modern attorney is still much like his medieval predecessor, who, hired to represent his client on the field of combat, used every honorable devise in his power to win. Perhaps the armor and shield have been replaced by the vested suit and briefcase, but the same keen edge that decided many a trial-by- combat is still very much apparent. Never draw down on an attorney. They are still excellent swordsmen.

Writing the Story

Magazine articles, unlike straight news stories, must have a definite beginning, middle, and end. Developing these elements takes patience, practice and organization.

The Lead

Always start at the beginning. A good lead is just as important to a magazine piece as it is to a news story. You must hook your reader into reading further and you must keep his or her interest through to the end.

In your lead, you must tell the reader what the article is about. You don't have to cram everything into the lead; however, you should include enough information so that the reader doesn't have to search for the topic. Consider the following leads.

A lead for a horse-racing trade:

For some time now, the sound of heavy machinery has been echoing through the rolling green countryside and heavily forested groves of Eastern Maryland. But that sound will soon be replaced by the sound of galloping horses as they take to

> the newly banked turns and straightaway at what is being billed as "the most innovative thoroughbred training and sports medicine facility in North America."

One for the hospital industry:

> The scene is a standard hospital room designed with fire safety in mind: a very low fuel load, floors of asbestos tile, walls of gypsum board on steel studs and a ceiling of fiberglass panels. The hospital is built in accordance with the National Fire Protection Agency Life Safety Code and has received the Joint Commission on Accreditation of Hospitals maximum 2-year approval.
>
> Late in the evening, a patient ignites the contents of his trash can which, in turn, ignite the bed clothes and, eventually, the mattress. The ensuing fire is a disaster, and despite the correct operation of all fire systems, multiple fatalities occur and the entire hospital wing is a total loss. Why? There are no fire standards on the upholstered furniture in this hospital and the mattresses meet a federal code designed to retard fires from smoldering cigarettes, not open flames.

A lead for a new product aimed at highway engineers:

> You're traveling along at high speed—the familiar "clackety-clack" of the rails beneath your feet. But wait a minute. You're not on a train, you're in an automobile, and that familiar sound beneath your feet is the result of deteriorating pavement joints that have been repaired with the usual "hot pour" method.

And an article for golf course superintendents:

> Valleyview Country Club had a problem—the twelfth hole was sinking again. For almost 40 years, the facilities people at Valleyview had been rebuilding the green. In fact, it had been rebuilt three times over that period of time, but each time with the same results—in a matter of a few years, the green would begin to sag again. This time, it was almost bowl-shaped and was acting as a funnel for rainwater that was draining from its outer edges into its concave center.

Although you may not have guessed it, each of these leads comes from articles announcing new products or new applications for established products. Remember, even the most mundane subject can benefit from a creative treatment. Your readers will only read your story if they like your lead.

The Body of the Article

The body of your article should contain all the information your reader needs to understand what you are trying to say. Obviously, it's in your best interest to present your ideas clearly. Working from an outline is the best way to ensure that you have covered all your key points in a logical order. (Several methods for organizing an outline are presented in **Chapter 14**.)

The body of the article must support your main point (hopefully already made in the lead) and elaborate on it. You should anticipate questions your reader might have, and answer them satisfactorily. Remember to utilize logical transitional devices when moving from one point to another. Subheads, while technically sound, don't alleviate the need for thoughtful transitions. Back up your statements with facts and support all generalizations with specifics. Although magazine articles seldom use footnotes, they are not completely inappropriate. Usually, however, citation can be taken care of in the body of the text.

Articles for house publications tend to be shorter than consumer magazine articles or even trade journals. The average length of most house publications (magazine format) is around twelve pages. Article length runs about 1,000 words or less for features (about four typed pages). Considering that magazine column width is about 14 picas for a three-column spread, and that articles are usually accompanied by photographs or artwork and headlines, subheads and blurbs—a 750-word article may cover several pages.

In **Exhibit 6.3** notice the organizational concept and transitional devices that move the article from point to point, and the contributions of the lead and ending.

The Ending

The most powerful and most remembered parts of your article will be the beginning and the end. Good endings are as difficult to write as good beginnings. However, there are only a few ways to wrap up an article and bring your readers to closure (a sense that they are satisfactorily finished): summarize your main points (summary ending), refer back to the beginning in some way (referral ending), or call for action (response ending), although this last is rarely used in magazine article writing. Consider the following leads with their respective endings.

Posing a question in the lead/summary ending

Lead:

Name the oldest civilization in North America. If your anthropological information is such that you pinpointed the Aleut peoples of Alaska, you are both well-informed and correct.

Ending:

"Intellect and knowledge, technical skills, helpfulness, and concern for the truth are still the hallmarks of Aleut culture,"

APC's Answer Man

The lead paragraph incorporates many of the basic elements of a news-type lead including who, what, where and how. It also delays the discovery of the topic until the second sentence by setting the scene first.

You might have noticed, if you've been in the new headquarters building at Associated Products Corporation long, a rather harried figure dashing madly up and down the halls. That man with the worried expression is Dave Martin. Dave, in a sense, is the ombudsman for APC's new building. He's the man who fields all the complaints, large and small, that have to do with everything from desk positioning to major malfunctions.

The second paragraph is the "bridge" from the lead to the body of the story. It begins with a factual statement and ends with another teaser.

Dave's official title reads: Manager, Headquarters Facilities and Services. This constitutes a promotion for Dave who was Manager, Technical Services. It also constitutes quite a lot of "heartburn."

Paragraphs 3 through 6 follow a sort of chronological order based on the construction of the new building, and provide background information

The job was almost a matter of evolution for Dave, who became associated with the project through working with Bob Allen, Project Manager for the new building. Dave continually found himself involved with planning of space allocation, since this was a natural carry over from his former job. He cites the speed at which the building was completed as one of the major factors for his almost sudden immersion in the project.

An undertaking of this magnitude usually takes years to complete. The space layout itself, which usually takes six to eight months, only took six to eight weeks. Dave and the planners worked night and day setting up seating arrangements for each department. These arrangements had gone through each department weeks before but had to be thoroughly scrutinized by the architects and planners before implementation.

Dave realizes, of course, that not everyone is going to be completely happy with his or her particular arrangement, but no major changes can be made until after the first of the year. There are several reasons for this. "The move itself will take up to 60 days to complete," says Dave, "during which time furniture will constantly be arriving." According to Dave, each piece has been designated for a particular spot in the new building, and last minute changes would only serve to confuse further what will doubtless be a confusing move as it is.

Telephones have already been assigned to particular individuals and can't be moved, and the special ambient lighting fixtures built into the desks provide light for a specific grouping of furniture. Moving a desk would mean disrupting the lighting scheme for a particular area which would affect more than just one person. All of these factors lead Dave to stress acceptance of the new floor plan, at least for the time being. According to Dave, psychological adjustment to new surroundings normally takes about 30 days. A great deal of complaints handled prior to that time are likely to be adjustment oriented. Those are the complaints he would like to avoid initially.

Paragraphs 7 and 8 come back to the subject (focusing on the human angle) and expand on his position and point of view.

Dave's new position will have him on the fourth floor as part of the Industrial Relations Department, where he will be in charge of the expanded reproduction facilities as well as Office Services, which handles supplies, PBX operation, mail service, and messenger service.

Dave is going to be monitoring almost every aspect of the new building. He will handle the janitorial contract, the plant contract (yes, Virginia, there will be greenery inside too) and snow removal. As Dave says, "If the building has a problem during the day, I'll hear about it first." Dave's only concern right now is that he will receive too many complaint calls like "I don't want to sit next to Joe," or, "I can't see the window from here." With all of the major problems involved in a move of this magnitude (by the way, he's also in charge of getting everybody into the building) Dave doesn't need to hear the "personal" problems each employee is bound to have.

The closing paragraph refers to the opening paragraph as a technique for gaining closure.

So, if you see this man with the harried expression in his eyes rushing around the halls of APC's new headquarters building, have a heart. Remember that Dave, like a modern-day Atlas, bears the weight of six floors on his shoulders. Just say "hi," give him a smile, and learn to live with your new desk for a while.

Exhibit 6.3—Organizing the Article

observes the Connecticut anthropologist, Laughlin. Such virtues are valuable assets, ever more useful as the 21st century approaches, and the bedrock on which the best that is Aleut may find permanence and continuity.—Richard C. Davids for *Exxon USA*

Setting the scene in the lead/referral ending

Lead:

For one emotion-filled moment on July 28, when the Olympic torch is lit atop the Los Angeles Memorial Coliseum, this sprawling California city will be transformed into an arena of challenges and champions. But that magic event, shared with two billion television viewers around the world, will mark more than the beginning of the XXIII Summer Olympic Games.

Ending:

For GTE employees worldwide, perhaps some of that special thrill can be shared by just watching the Games on television, and knowing that whenever gymnastics, fencing, water polo, volleyball, yachting or tennis are televised, those images and sounds will have passed through the hands of 425 fellow employees—GTE's Team at the Olympics.—Bill Ferree for *GTE Together*

An anecdotal lead/summary and referral ending

Lead:

In 1737, Benjamin Franklin wrote in the Pennsylvania Gazette of an auroral display so red and vivid that some people thought it was a fire and ran to help put it out.

Ending:

Although the effects of auroral activity on the lower levels of the earth's atmosphere are more apparent, the effects on the upper atmosphere are not, and we are only now beginning to understand them. With more understanding, we may eventually view the aurora with a more scientific eye, but until that day comes, it still remains the greatest light show on earth.—Tom Bivins for *National Bank of Alaska Interbranch*

Writing Headlines

Writing headlines for magazines is much like writing headlines for newsletters, but there are some exceptions. First, some definitional differences. A **headline**, strictly speaking, is for news stories, while a **title** is for features. For example, a news story on a new product might read like this:

New software will 'revolutionize education' says APC president

Now, contrast that headline with the following title:

Talking to the past— Learning about the future

The headline tells something about the story, so that even the casual reader can glean some information from reading it alone. The title, on the other hand, entices the reader or piques his or her interest. Therefore, a basic rule of thumb for writing headlines and titles is: use headlines for news articles and titles for feature articles. And, as with all writing, try to be clear. If your headline or title confuses the readers, they won't read on.

Editing Your Article

Magazine articles probably get, and deserve, the most editing of the various types of writing discussed in this book. Length has something to do with it, but more than that, it's the freewheeling attitude of some article writers (especially novices) that contributes the most to this need. Since many writers of basic company publications end up dealing with pretty dry topics, an assignment to do an article for the house magazine might be seen as an invitation to creativity. This usually leads, in turn, to a looser style, wordiness, and lack of organization. Whatever the reason, even the best-written article can benefit from intelligent editing.

A quick word here about the term "intelligent editing." This implies that you are being edited by (or are yourself, if you're doing the editing) someone who knows about writing—both grammar and style. Unfortunately, as many of us who have worked on in-house publications for years know, editors are often chosen because of their position within the organizational hierarchy (or the obligatory approval chain) and not for their literary talents. One of the best (if perhaps a little cynical) rules of thumb for dealing with "inexpert" editing is to ignore about 80 percent of it. You quickly get to recognize what is useful to you and what is not. Basically, editing that deals with content balance and accuracy is usable. Most strictly "editorial" comment is not. A vice president's penchant for ellipses or a manager's predilection for using *which* instead of *that* are strictly stylistic preferences (and often ungrammatical). In many cases, even if you do ignore these obligatory edits, these same "editors" won't remember what they said when the final piece comes out. A rule of thumb for most experienced writers is to try to avoid being edited by non-editors. If you can't, at least see how much you can safely ignore.

As for editing yourself, there are several methods for cutting a story that is too long, even if you don't think you can possibly do without a single word.

- Look at your beginning and end to see if they can be shortened. Often we write more than we need by way of introduction or closing when the real meat is in the body of the article.
- If you used a lot of quotes, cut the ones that are even remotely "fluff." Keep only those that contribute directly to the understanding of your story.
- Are there any general descriptions that, given later details, may be redundant? Cut them.
- Are there any details that are unnecessary given earlier general descriptions? Cut them. (Be careful not to cut both the general description *and* the details.)
- Are there any people who can be left out? For instance, will one expert and his or her comments be enough or do you really need that second opinion?
- Finally, look for wordiness—instances in which you used more words than you needed. This type of editing hurts the most since you probably struggled over that wording for an hour and went through your thesaurus 20 times.

Your goal is to get the article into the size you need without losing its best parts or compromising your writing style. **Exhibit 6.4** shows how some of these guidelines can be applied.

Exhibit 6.4—Editing an Article

Take a close look at this article and notice to what degree the edited sections add to the article. If they add indespensible information, they shouldn't be edited out.

DGA Wins UL Certificate

The sign on the door reads "Grade 'A' UL Central Station." To the people at Dallas General Alarm (DGA) and to the hundreds of businesses and homes they protect, this means the availability of some of the best alarm and intrusion detection systems in the country. In fact, almost every improvement made to DGA over the past few years has had as its goal the attainment of UL certification.

In 1924, Underwriters Laboratories, Inc. began offering a means of identifying burglar alarm systems that met acceptable minimum standards. The installing company can apply for investigation of their services and if found qualified, may be issued UL certification.

To the customer, this certification can mean a large reduction (sometimes up to 70 percent) in insurance premiums, depending on the exact grade and extent of the UL approved service used.

These four paragraphs, although adding additional information, can be cut without loss to the overall information impact of the story since they deal with details that we can actually get along without. Naturally, given enough space, we would opt to leave the story intact.

However, Dallas General Alarm doesn't sell only UL service. "We sell and lease our systems on the merit of the system and the particular need of the customer," says Dave Michaels, director of quality control for DGA. "Of course, those who do have the UL Grade 'A' system installed can usually pay the extra cost entailed with the savings they make on insurance alone."

What makes this Grade "A" system so effective that insurance companies charging sometimes thousands of dollars a year in coverage are willing to cut 40, 60 or even 70 percent off their premiums?

"The UL people are really tight on their standards," says Michaels. "They conduct a number of 'surprise' inspections of DGA on a regular basis. If we fall down in any of their requirements, we get our certification cancelled."

DGA has its own tight security system consisting of television monitors on all doors and verbal contact with people entering their offices. The central control room is always manned and locked. A thick, glass window allows the operators on duty to personally check all people entering the premises. Other UL requirements are extra fire proofing for the building itself and a buried cable containing the thousands of telephone lines used to monitor the various alarm systems which run out of the building. The cable is unmarked, preventing the adventurous burglar from cutting it and thus disabling the hundreds of systems served by DGA.

The over-a-thousand customers who either lease or by alarm or detection systems from DGA range from some of the biggest businesses in Dallas, to private residences. In addition, all of the schools in the Dallas area are monitored from the DGA central station against break in and vandalism.

The monitoring devices, located at the DGA central control, vary from a simple paper tape printout to actual voice communication with the premises being protected. For instance, the card-key system used by Atlantic Richfield Company allows access to certain areas through the use of a magnetic card inserted into a slot in the door. Access is forbidden to those lacking the proper clearance and the number and time of the attempted access are printed out at the DGA central station.

Trade Journals

Trade journals are a valuable source of information for those who work within a specific industry. They provide news and stories dealing with the concerns and products of that industry. Trades accept product press releases readily and are an excellent target for placement. They usually have a section devoted specifically to new products and will normally place your release, edited of course, in this section.

By far, the most impressive system is the "Hyper Guard Sound System" which allows the central station operators actually to listen into a building or home once the system is activated. If the building is entered, the sound sensitive system is activated causing an alarm to go off at the DGA central station. By the use of microphones installed on the premises, the DGA operators can then determine the presence of an intruder. The owners, of course, sign in and out verbally when they open and close. Most of these customers also carry the special "holdup" feature of this system which allows them to trigger, unnoticed, an alarm in the event of a robbery.

"We tried out a lot of other sound-activated systems," says Michaels, "but the 'Hyper Guard' made by Associated Products Corporation is the best I've ever seen." Michaels says that the Hyper Guard system is probably 20 times more sensitive than most other brands DGA has tried. "And, in our business, sensitivity is a key component of a successful detection."

Whatever you do, don't edit out the purpose for writing the article in the first place. In this case, it's mention of a product.

Once an alarm is received from any of the hundreds of points serviced by DGA, it is only a matter of seconds before security guards, police, ambulance or fire department are notified and on their way. DGA maintains direct, no-dial lines to all of these agencies.

DGA currently contracts with Smith-Loomis which dispatches two or three security guards to each of DGA's calls. "Our average response time is under 4 1/2 minutes," says Dave Michaels. "Of course, we often have to wait on the owner to show up to let us in." Michaels says that if DGA keeps a key to the premises, another 10 percent often can be taken off on insurance premiums because it allows a faster response time and a higher apprehension rate. "Recently, we got two apprehensions in three alarms at a local pharmacy," he says. "We roll on every suspicious alarm. UL only allows one opening and one closing time per business unless prearranged," says Michaels. "This way, we know exactly when there should be nobody on the premises."

DGA offers a number of different systems. Some respond to motion, and some to sound. There are systems with silent alarms and systems on sight alarms fit to frighten the toughest intruder; and, DGA also handles smoke and heat detection systems. But, the key to a UL Grade "A" certified system, says Michaels, is the central control. "That's the added factor in a Grade 'A' system," he says. "We know immediately when something has occured, and we respond."

Frank Collins, president of Southwestern Gemstones, Inc., has had his Grade "A" system since September. "I was robbed last year of over $400,000 worth of merchandise," he says, "and I was uninsured. That won't happen again." Collins is impressed with his system.

From his office in the Calais Building, Collins can watch everyone who enters his showroom via television monitor. A telephone allows visitors to identify themselves from outside the front door before entry. The showroom itself is an impressive array of precious gems and gold and a great many antique art objects, frequently hand-made turquoise and silver pieces. "I got the complete works," Collins says, "audio sensors, motion sensors, TV monitor, everything," resulting in a good-sized cut in his necessarily high insurance premiums. For the many high-risk businesses served by Dallas General Alarm, the UL Grade "A" system seems to be the answer.

Here is a good example of an extra character who can be deleted without substantial loss to the story. Although this kind of testimony adds credibility to any story, in this case, the story is about DGA and their spokesperson actually provides the first-person credibility we need for our purpose – which is to get one of our products mentioned.

"We don't expect more than a couple of hundred customers for the UL system over the next few years," says Dave Michaels, "but that's all right. Our customers know their needs and they know that they can't get a better system for the price." Collins smiles. "For the three or four dollars a day this system costs, they couldn't even afford a guard dog."

For those desiring more attention, trades also accept articles written on products, concepts and services of interest to their specific audiences (i.e., the industries they serve). These are normally submitted in the manner of any freelance magazine article. First, you query the journal by letter explaining that you have an article idea, what it is, and why you think it might fit the journal's format and be of interest to its readership. If you receive a positive response, send the article, carefully following the journal's editorial style. Trade journals, like consumer magazines, often

tors can then determine the presence of an intruder. The owners, of course, sign in and out verbally when they open and close. Most of these customers also carry the special "holdup" feature of this system which allows them to trigger, unnoticed, an alarm in the event of a robbery.

"We tried out a lot of other sound-activated systems," says Michaels, "but the 'Hyper Guard' made by Associated Products Corporation is the best I've ever seen." Michaels says that the Hyper Guard system is probably 20 times more sensitive than most other brands DGA has tried. "And, in our business, sensitivity is a key component of a successful detection."

Once an alarm is received from any of the hundreds of points serviced by DGA, it is only a matter of seconds before security guards, police, ambulance or fire department are notified and on their way. DGA maintains direct, no-dial lines to all of these agencies.

DGA currently contracts with Smith-Loomis which dispatches two or three security guards to each of DGA's calls. "Our average response time is under 4 1/2 minutes," says Dave Michaels. "Of course, we often have to wait on the owner to show up to let us in." Michaels says that if DGA keeps a key to the premises, another 10 percent often can be taken off on insurance

premiums because it allows a faster response time and a higher apprehension rate. "Recently, we got two apprehensions in three alarms at a local pharmacy," he says. "We roll on every suspicious alarm. UL only allows one opening and one closing time per business unless prearranged," says Michaels. "This way, we know exactly when there should be nobody on the premises."

"For the th
dollars a
system c
couldn't e
a guar

DGA offers a num
tems. Some respond t
sound. There are syst
and systems on sight
the toughest intruder;
smoke and heat detec
key to a UL Grade
says Michaels, is the c
the added factor in a G
says. "We know imm
thing has occured, ar

Frank Collins, president of Southwestern Gemstones, Inc., has had his Grade "A" system since September. "I was robbed last year of over $400,000 worth of merchandise," he says, "and I was uninsured. That won't happen again." Collins is impressed with his system.

From his office in the Calais Building, Collins can watch everyone who enters his

23

Security is a full-time job for Dallas General Alarm

by Ellen Hart

Technology and common sense blend to provide a thoroughly modern security service

The sign on the door reads "Grade 'A' UL Central Station." To the people at Dallas General Alarm (DGA) and to the hundreds of businesses and homes they protect, this means the availability of some of the best alarm and intrusion detection systems in the country. In fact, almost every improvement made to DGA over the past few years has had as its goal the attainment of UL certification.

In 1924, Underwriters Laboratories, Inc. began offering a means of identifying burglar alarm systems that met acceptable minimum standards. The installing company can apply fo rinvestigation of their services and if found qualified, may be issued UL certification.

To the customer, this certification can mean a large reduction (sometimes up to 70 percent) in insurance premiums, depending on the exact grade and extent of the UL approved service used.

However, Dallas General Alarm doesn't sell only UL service. "We sell and lease our systems on the merit of the system and the particular need of the customer," says Dave Michaels, director of quality control for DGA. "Of course, those who do have the UL Grade 'A' system installed can usually pay the extra cost entailed with the savings they make on insurance alone."

What makes this Grade "A" system so effective that insurance companies charging sometimes thousands of dollars a year in coverage are willing to cut 40, 60 or even 70 percent off their premiums?

"The UL people are really tight on their standards," says Michaels. "They conduct a number of 'surprise' inspections of DGA on a regular basis. If we fall down in any of their requirements, we get our certification cancelled."

DGA has its own tight security system consisting of television monitors on all doors and verbal contact with people entering their offices. The central control room is always manned and locked. A thick, glass window allows the operators on duty to personally check all people entering the premises.

Other UL requirements are extra fire proofing for the building itself and a buried cable containing the thousands of telephone lines used to monitor the various alarm systems which run out of the building. The cable is unmarked, preventing the adventurous burglar from cutting it and thus disabling the hundreds of systems served by DGA.

The over-a-thousand customers who either lease or by alarm or detection systems from DGA range from some of the biggest businesses in Dallas, to private residences. In addition, all of the schools in the Dallas area are monitored from the DGA central station against break in and vandalism.

The monitoring devices, located at the DGA central control, vary from a simple paper tape printout to actual voice communication with the premises being protected. For instance, the card-key system used by Atlantic Richfield Company allows access to certain areas through the use of a magnetic card inserted into a slot in the door. Access is forbidden to those lacking the proper clearance and the number and time of the attempted access are printed out at the DGA central station.

By far, the most impressive system is the "Hyper Guard Sound System" which allows the central station operators actually to listen into a building or home once the system is activated. If the building is entered, the sound sensitive system is activated causing an alarm to go off at the DGA central station. By the use of microphones installed on the premises, the DGA opera-

Dave Michaels of Dallas General Alarm sits in front of the main counsole from which dozens of businesses are monitored daily. The slightest sound will set off an alarm at this console and, if a burglary is deemed to be in progress, police or security officers are dispatched within minutes of the alarm. The sound-activiated system is manufactured by the Electronics Division of APC.

22

Security is a full-time job for Dallas General Alarm

by Ellen Hart

Technology and common sense blend to provide a thoroughly modern security service

The sign on the door reads "Grade 'A' UL Central Station." To the people at Dallas General Alarm (DGA) and to the hundreds of businesses and homes they protect, this means the availability of some of the best alarm and intrusion detection systems in the country. In fact, almost every improvement made to DGA over the past few years has had as its goal the attainment of UL certification.

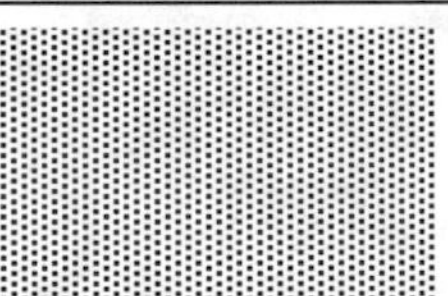

Dave Michaels of Dallas General Alarm sits in front of the main counsole from which dozens of businesses are monitored daily.

In 1924, Underwriters Laboratories, Inc. began offering a means of identifying burglar alarm systems that met acceptable minimum standards. The installing company can apply for investigation of their services and if found qualified, may be issued UL certification.

To the customer, this certification can mean a large reduction (sometimes up to 70 percent) in insurance premiums, depending on the exact grade and extent of the UL approved service used.

The over-a-thousand customers who either lease or by alarm or detection systems from DGA range from some of the biggest businesses in Dallas, to private residences. In addition, all of the schools in the Dallas area are monitored from the DGA central station against break in and vandalism.

The monitoring devices, located at the DGA central control, vary from a simple paper tape printout to actual voice communication with the premises being protected. For instance, the card-key system used by Atlantic Richfield Company allows access to certain areas through the use of a magnetic card inserted into a slot in the door. Access is forbidden to those lacking the proper clearance and the number and time of the attempted access are printed out at the DGA central station.

By far, the most impressive system is the "Hyper Guard Sound System" which allows the central station operators actually to listen into a building or home once the system is activated. If the building is entered, the sound sensitive system is activated causing an alarm to go off at the DGA central station. By the use of microphones installed on the premises, the DGA operators can then determine the presence of an intruder. The owners, of course, sign in and out verbally when they open and close. Most of these customers also carry the special "holdup" feature of this system which allows them to trigger, unnoticed, an alarm in the event of a robbery.

"For the three or four dollars a day this system costs, they couldn't even afford a guard dog."

"We tried out a lot of other sound-activated systems," says Michaels, "but the 'Hyper Guard' made by Associated Products Corporation is the best I've ever seen." Michaels says that the Hyper Guard system is probably 20 times more sensitive than most other brands DGA has tried. "And, in our business, sensitivity is a key component of a successful detection."

Once an alarm is received from any of the hundreds of points serviced by DGA, it is only a matter of seconds before security guards, police, ambulance or fire department are notified and on their way. DGA maintains direct, no-dial lines to all of these agencies.

DGA currently contracts with Smith-Loomis which dispatches two or three security guards to each of DGA's calls. "Our average response time is under 4 1/2 minutes," says Dave Michaels. "Of course, we often have to wait on the owner to show up to let us in." Michaels says that if DGA keeps a key to the premises, another 10 percent often can be taken off on insurance premiums because it allows a faster response time and a higher apprehension rate. "Recently, we got two apprehensions in three alarms at a local pharmacy," he says. "We roll on every suspicious alarm. UL only allows one opening and one closing time per business unless prearranged," says Michaels. "This way, we know exactly when there should be nobody on the premises."

DGA offers a number of different systems. Some respond to motion, and some to sound. There are systems with silent alarms and systems on sight alarms fit to frighten the toughest intruder; and, DGA also handles smoke and heat detection systems. But, the key to a UL Grade "A" certified system, says Michaels, is the central control. "That's the added factor in a Grade 'A' system," he says. "We know immediately when something has occured, and we respond."

"We don't expect more than a couple of hundred customers for the UL system over the next few years," says Dave Michaels, "but that's all right. Our customers know their needs and they know that they can't get a better system for the price." Collins smiles. "For the three or four dollars a day this system costs, they couldn't even afford a guard dog."

22

have a sheet of "author's guidelines" explaining their style, average length, manuscript requirements and so on. Follow these guidelines explicitly if you want to get published or get your client the publicity you were hired to provide.

The variety of trade journal articles is immense. They can range from feature-type articles using human interest, through straight news stories on products and services, to light fluff articles on travel and entertainment. In order to determine what style best fits your idea and their magazine, obtain a copy of the publication and read it thoroughly. Never submit an article to a magazine you haven't read.

Get a copy of one of the numerous "publicity checkers" which list all of the publications by industry. Almost every industry has a trade journal, sometimes a number of them. For instance, there are trades for golf course groundskeepers, race track owners, thoroughbred breeders, paper manufacturers, supermarket owners, table waiters, bartenders, railroad workers, airline workers, and almost every other trade imaginable. One or more of these will fit your needs.

Exhibit 6.5 (facing page)—Edited Pages

As you can see from these layhouts, the unedited version of the DGA story takes up approximately one and a half pages including pull quote, photo and caption. The edited version (opposite page) takes up only a single page including a reduced photo, edited caption, and the full-sized pull quote.

Case Study: Associated Products Corporation

Use the background provided in **Chapters 3** and **5** to complete these assignments.

Assignment 6-1

You have been charged with developing a magazine article for APC's house publication, *APC Plus*, a magazine that goes out to all of APC's subsidiaries and is read by about 1000 employees. Like the newsletter article you wrote in **Assignment 5-1**, it should be on the new IQ software line and APC's involvement with the NEA. You can use the same theme or angle, or come up with another one. You should use a feature style, but don't omit the newsworthy product-development information. Your article should be about 750 or 800 words in length. You should come up with a headline, but subheads, photo recommendations, and other fillers are optional.

The most difficult part of this type of writing is organizing the information. Organization is usually dictated by the lead. Look carefully at your information, decide on an angle, and write several trial leads to see if they indicate a direction for your story. Once you have decided on a lead, produce an outline of exactly where you want to go with your story and what you want to include. Try a topic sentence outline in which you write the complete topic sentence for each section.

Assignment 6-2

Take the information you have gathered on James L. Sutton and write it into a profile. Sutton obviously is the angle, but, again, IQ is the publicity "bottom line."

Your profile is to be submitted to *Computer World* magazine's "People in Computing" section. *Computer World* is a consumer trade publication with a circulation of 150,000.

Along with the profile, you will include a picture of Sutton working at a computer terminal with the new software; a picture of a classroom of students using computers; and a publicity of one of the new software packages.

Assume you have spoken on the telephone with the editor of *Computer World*, Fran LeFavre, and she showed some interest in the story idea.

Attach a letter mentioning your conversation along with the article. The address is:

Computer World
One, Presidents' Circle
Chicago, IL 60640

You have also received from *Computer World* a brief sheet of "Author's Guidelines." These guidelines are as follows:

1. Most of the articles submitted to *Computer World* are meant for a lay audience, one which, though familiar with computing concepts, is not technically oriented. Therefore, your information should be free of all but the most basic jargon.
2. Articles should be no more than 2,000 words for cover story material, and features. Articles for the "Business Briefs," "People in Computing," and "Inside Computing" sections should be no longer than 800 words.
3. All articles should be typed on plain white bond paper in plain type. Lines should be double-spaced and all formulae and symbols should be clearly designated.
4. References should be limited to those which can be easily mentioned within the text. Please do not footnote.
5. Attachments (photos, transparencies, charts, schematics, etc.) should be included as appendices following the article with clear designations within the article as to placement.

Make sure that your article follows these guidelines closely.

CHAPTER 7

Annual Reports

Never ask of money spent
Where the spender thinks it went.
Nobody was ever meant
To remember or invent
What he did with every cent.

Robert Frost

Annual reports are probably the least read of all house publications. Recent research indicates that about half the shareholders who receive them spend less than 10 minutes looking at them. And 15 percent of all stock analysts don't read them at all. So why is corporate America spending $5 billion a year producing annual reports?

Part of the reason is that the federal government requires it. The Securities Exchange Act of 1936 requires publicly traded companies to provide their investors with a yearly financial statement. This law also requires that an annual report be delivered to stockholders no later than 15 days before the annual meeting. Quarterly reports also have to be filed.

Beginning in 1980, the Securities and Exchange Commission (SEC) mandated that additional information be added, including financial data covering the past five years, and an expanded discussion and analysis of the company's financial condition. It's not surprising, then, that annual reports increase in size and complexity each year—so much so, in fact, that a few years ago General Motors asked the SEC to allow them and other companies to develop and file an abbreviated, "summary" annual report.

In 1987, the SEC ruled that companies could indeed publish such a report as long as they included all of the elements required by law as either appendices to the abbreviated report or in another formal document, such as the already required Form 10-K. Critics worry that this new flexibility allows companies to selectively cut bad news from its most visible communication vehicle. They argue that most stockholders will read *only* the annual report, believing it complete. Although some companies have experimented with the "summary" annual report, at this writing, most companies still produce the lengthy report already familiar to stockholders.

Annual Report Audiences

When you produce an annual report, you're writing for a primarily internal audience, one with a vested interest in the well-being of your organization. That's why many annual reports gloss over the bad news, even though research shows that most stockholders would feel a lot better about a company if it were open and honest with them.

However, stockholders aren't the only audience for annual reports. These organizational summaries are excellent information sources for media people, especially financial reporters. They also provide valuable background for financial analysts, potential stockholders, nonshareholding employees and customers, and opinion leaders such as legislators and community leaders.

Before you write an annual report, you must first decide which of these audiences you are writing for. Don't ever assume that you are talking only to shareholders; rank the other potential audiences in order of their importance to you and be sure to address them, too.

Annual Report Contents

No two annual reports are alike; however, the SEC does require certain elements be present including:

- Certified financial statements for the previous two years
- An explanation of any difference between these financial statements and statements filed in another form with the SEC
- A summary management analysis of operations for the past five years
- Identification of the company directors' principal occupations
- Stock market and dividend information for the past two years
- Notice of Form 10-K availability
- A brief description of both business and line-of-business in the "audited footnote." This all appears in the footnote itself.

- Any material differences from established accounting principles reflected in the financial statements
- Supplementary inflation accounting

The form this information takes is what makes annual reports different from each other. To accommodate the SEC guidelines, annual reports have developed certain standard mechanisms for housing the required information.

- A description of the company including its name, address (headquarters, subsidiaries and plant sites), its overall business, and a summary of its operations, usually in both narrative and numerical form.
- A letter to stockholders including an account of the past year's achievements, an overview of the industry environment and pertinent markets, and a discussion of future business and investment strategies.
- A financial review as set forth by SEC regulations listed above.
- An explanation and analysis of the financial review that outlines the factors influencing the financial picture over the past year.
- A narrative report covering anything from a discussion of subsidiaries to details on corporate philanthropy. Many companies use the annual report as a forum in which to discuss social issues or beat their own public relations drum, as it is one of the best publicity tools available.

Writing for Annual Reports

There are generally two ways to produce an annual report: you can write it in house, or you can farm it out to an agency. Frankly, agencies—including those that specialize in annual reports—produce the bulk of these publications. However, with the advent of desktop publishing, more organizations are considering in-house writing and production.

No matter who writes it, the bulk of an annual report is taken up with tables, charts and flashy photographs. In fact, critics charge, annual reports often try too hard (and too blatantly) to sweeten a bitter financial pill with a lot of pretty sugar coating. Many annual reports do stand guilty of this, but countless others perform a valuable informational service to shareholders and members. In fact, because they *are* good message vehicles, a great many nonprofit organizations are now producing annual reports even though they don't really have to. The modern annual report has become a major tool in any organization's public relations arsenal.

Writers produce only a small portion of the annual report, but it is the portion most read by shareholders—the president's letter and the narrative report.

The President's Letter

There are some really awful president's letters in annual reports. The reason most cited is the SEC guidelines telling them what they have to talk about. Fortunately, these guidelines don't tell writers *how* to talk about what they *have* to talk about. There is no reason these letters have to be crashingly dull, wordy and confusing. What impresses the everyday shareholder is honesty, a straightforward writing style, and no fluff.

Both of the following examples opt for the "numbers up front" approach on the mistaken belief that readers want it that way.

> [Company name] expanded its financial base in 19__ and substantially increased the number of property interests in its investment portfolio. A $47 million common stock offering, completed in June, plus a $40 million public offering of mortgage notes and common stock purchase warrants in December 19__ were among the financial resources which permitted [company name] to increase the number of its property interests to 191 by adding 99 real estate investments during the year.

•

> The year 19__ was a successful one for [company name]. Net income was up substantially, over 27 percent greater than 19__'s results, to a record $305.6 million, as the economy moved into a strong recovery. On a per share basis, our earnings were $9.50, an increase of 13 percent, reflecting both the issuance of additional common stock during this past year, as well as the preferred stock issued during 19__.

The next example at least begins with an interesting image of a "corporate renaissance."

> We are in the midst of a corporate renaissance and 19__ was a strong reflection of the growth, diversification, and enthusiasm that typifies [company name].
>
> We had a record performance in 19__ in many areas. For the first time, net income exceeded $1 billion, at $1.2 billion. Sales reached an all-time high of $13.4 billion—up more than $2 billion from the 19__ level. The list of records also included earnings per share at $6.47; and operating income, which at $2.3 billion was up 69 percent from the previous record.

And what about bad news? This letter buries it under a barrage of industry buzzwords such as "maximizing profitability."

> [Company name] continued its strategy of maximizing profitability in basic markets and businesses in 19__. All these areas of the Corporation had a truly excellent year. Unfortunately, the property and casualty reinsurance lines of the Insurance Group, which are not a part of our basic long-term strategy, incurred continuing heavy losses, significantly lowering our overall profitability. Reflecting this impact, [company name]'s consolidated net income of $106.3 million was about flat with 19__, although earnings per share increased marginally to $4.02 from $3.96 reflecting a slightly reduced number of common shares outstanding.

Finally, here's a letter that approaches a mixed year with an interesting, number-free narrative approach.

> External forces produce both opportunities and challenges—and 19__ had its share of both for [company name] and its businesses.
>
> During the year, some of the external forces facing our four business segments served to expand revenues and growth. Others had a dampening effect, calling for effective countermeasures.
>
> The mix of forces at work included... [bulleted list follows]
>
> We worked to take advantage of those external forces that offered opportunities, and to overcome the challenges posed by others.

If you can write the letter yourself, and simply route it for the president's approval, you'll get better results than you would if the president drafts it. When you do it yourself, keep in mind a few points. Because most of the rest of the report is numbers, it's best to keep numbers in the letter to a minimum. Keep your letter short, and keep its language friendly and simple. This way, you'll be able to cover the SEC bases without boring your readers.

The Narrative Report

The body of the annual report is your only chance to write anything without numbers—or, at least, with a minimum of numbers. Here is where you get to describe the company, its operations, its people (a favorite focus of many reports), and its future in detail. The only problem is one of space. Remember, you can't leave out anything required by the SEC. And you don't want to leave out anything that really makes your company look good.

One of the best ways to decide on content is to have the people in charge of the various divisions or subsidiaries submit brief lists of the year's highlights from their "down in the trenches" perspective. Make your needs known in plenty of time to get responses from your contacts. And leave the final compiling and writing to one person so that the entire report has a single style.

A quick word about that style. Depending on a company's image, the style of an annual report can vary greatly. Some are formal to the point of being stiff. Others are too informal and leave shareholders with a feeling that the company is being loosely run. The best and most appropriate style is somewhere in the middle.

As with the president's letter, you don't have to begin your narrative report with numbers. In fact, it benefits greatly from a little introduction. There is no reason why annual reports have to be boring reading. The following introductions to the narrative report sections of two different annual reports are fairly good examples of what can be done to lend a modicum of interest to an otherwise often dull subject.

> To come up with a winner in global competition, you have to provide the highest quality... the greatest number of choices... and the most innovative solutions to a customer's needs, regardless of location.
>
> In meeting that challenge, [company name] uses a system of "global networking" to choreograph its worldwide response by product, function, and geographic area. Networking teams enable [company name] to draw upon its resources around the world and to respond quickly no matter where customers may be headquartered.

•

> There are many ways to define shareholder value... and many ways that companies strive to create it. But at [company name[, the strategy has been three pronged:
>
> - Utilizing existing resources within the company to diversify into four separate businesses.
> - Acting on opportunities to build and strengthen these existing businesses.
> - Keeping abreast of trends that hold promise for the future.

Use numbers to *augment* your narrative—don't let numbers be the entire focus. Although annual reports are intended to spell out a company's financial environment, they communicate more often with average people than financial analysts. Financial analysts won't rely on an annual report as their sole information source. Many shareholders will, so it has to be written in a style they will understand.

Striking just the right tone, in both writing and design, is the most important ingredient in producing an annual report. In fact, so much depends on design that many annual reports emphasize the form the expense of its function.

Design for design's sake is still common. Be careful not to let your "look" overpower your written information. Ideally, form and function should work together to achieve a real sense of the company that readers care enough to own part of.

CHAPTER 8

Writing for Television, Radio & Audio-visual Media

The play's the thing...

Hamlet

Broadcasting is pervasive. Since the advent of radio, people have become more and more dependent on the broadcast media for their information and entertainment. Today, more than ever before, the public views the world through the window of the television. The average American family spends more than six hours a day watching television, and, according to recent research, they find it the most credible news source by a wide margin. Radio reaches more people each day than any other medium with more than 444 million radios in American homes and cars.

For the public relations practitioner, utilization of these two powerful and influential media is often restricted. While approximately 90 percent of the non-advertising content of print media is informational, 90 percent of the non-advertising content of broadcast media is entertainment. There is simply very little time available for news-related items. Radio usually airs news, but often in an abbreviated format. Each of the 30-minute network television news shows has only 22 minutes of actual news which would fill about one-quarter of the front page of a daily newspaper.

There are some obvious advantages to using the broadcast media, however. They reach millions of people each day. Moreover, television and radio involve their audiences more than print does, and can be highly memorable. People tend to react more personally to broadcast than they do to other media. Think of the influence television celebrities have on the youth of today. Consider the power of newscasters such as Peter Jennings or Dan Rather in influencing opinion.

Reaching Broadcast Audiences

Getting public relations material aired on network radio and television is difficult; however, local broadcast media offer some avenues for the experienced practitioner.

There are five basic methods for the public relations writer to reach broadcast audiences: News releases (see **Chapter 3**), video news releases (VNRs), radio and television tapes and actualities, interviews and talk shows, and public service announcements or corporate advertising.

Video News Releases

Video news releases are a fairly new phenomenon. Originally, they were simply pre-packaged publicity features meant to be aired on local, regional, or national television. Now they have become staples of many local news shows searching for time-filling informational pieces.

The entertainment industry was among the first to recognize the potential in producing their own videos for publicity purposes. For example, the publicity department for a new motion picture would produce a tape including collages of footage from the film in varying lengths, special "behind the scenes" looks at production, and interviews with key stars. Each of these segments would have both an "A" and "B" sound track. The "A" sound track would contain both music and voiceover. The "B" sound track would contain music only. The varying lengths would allow a station to air a segment suited to its particular time requirements. The choice of sound tracks would allow the station to drop in its own announcers' voices to give the piece a local feel.

It is in local television that VNRs are most successful. Filling an hour with local news is sometimes difficult for programmers, and program managers are constantly seeking out "fillers" to plug 30-, 60-, or 90-second holes in newscasts. In fact, a recent A.C. Nielson poll showed more than 75 percent of all TV stations regularly used VNRs.

Organizations and their PR agencies and departments have been quick to capitalize on this opportunity. The key is to produce fillers in various lengths that have certain news value yet are not time bound. This way, stories can be produced, packaged and mailed to stations around the country with no fear that the news will be old before it is received. Medialink, a New York-based company, developed the nation's first dedicated video newswire and has become a leading distributor of VNRs, with Medialink wires in over 600 television newsrooms around the country. This type of distribution network allows organizations to get even the post time-sensitive news on the air soon enough to be effective. For example, a company can stage an important news conference, tape interviews and visuals from the event, combine this with pre-produced or stock footage of the company, and send it out via satellite all over the country in a matter of hours.

There are some problems with this infant publicity vehicle, however. A major criticism in the news industry is that much of what is packaged as video "news" releases is really advertising in disguise. This may be true, in part—VNRs are an excellent means of plugging a product while wrapping it in a soft news format. The same thing, of course, has been done for years in product-oriented articles for trade publications; however, the difference is that VNRs are being sent to mainstream media outlets who trade in hard news, not product publicity. The old advertising adage, "buyer beware," should hold here. Alert journalists should always be aware of the publicity angle inherent in any sort of release—print, video, or otherwise. On the PR side, practitioners won't gain any media support by deliberately disguising product plugs as hard or soft news. The best approach is to tag clearly any VNR as to its sponsor and content and let the media do the gatekeeping.

Writing for video news releases

How you write for a VNR depends on the format of the release. Taped press conferences and the like should follow a straight news format, much like straight news print releases. Features should follow feature style. Most of the techniques discussed below also apply to writing for VNRs. Simply be aware of the format and target media, and conform to their accepted styles. Remember, as with all other media, the broadcast media will accept only that which fits their needs and format.

Radio and Television Tapes and Actualities

Radio and television rely heavily on taped actualities in covering the news. An actuality is simply a firsthand account, on tape, of a news event. Actualities lend credibility to any newscast. They may feature newspeople describing the event, interviews with those involved in the event, or they may simply provide ambience or background for a voiceover. Rarely will the public relations writer be in the position to provide a finished actuality to a radio or television news program. Most of the time, he or she will act as the intermediary or spokesperson for the organization. Or, the PR practitioner may arrange a taped interview with another company spokes-person, typically outside of the public relations department. In some cases, the medium may be interested enough to send out a reporter or news team to cover an event firsthand. In that case, the public relations practitioner usually acts as liaison arranging the schedule and making sure that everything is in order for the taping.

Interviews and Talk Shows

It may be that a radio or television station has a local talk show or similar vehicle for which information about your organization is suitable. The public relations practitioner, here again, usually acts as liaison, arranging the interview for a spokesperson, getting preparatory materials together, and making sure the spokesperson gets to the interview or talk show on time. As the media specialist, you may also be called on to coach the spokesperson or even write his or her responses.

Public Service Announcements and Corporate Advertising

There is a difference in the way the broadcast media treat PR materials prepared by profit-making organizations and those provided by non-profit organizations. Realizing that profit-making organizations don't usually need free air time, the Federal Communications Commission (FCC) requires them to purchase time, even for messages presented in the public interest. Free public service time, on the other hand, is available only to legitimate non profit organizations.

Corporate Advertising

Corporate or institutional advertising takes three basic forms depending on the purpose of the message.

1. **Public interest** usually provides information in the public interest such as health care, safety, and environmental interests. In order to have these placed for free, they have to meet stringent guidelines.
2. **Public image** tries to sell the organization as caring about its employees, the environment, the community and its customers. Unlike the public service ad, the public image ad will always focus on the company and how it relates to the subject.
3. **Advocacy advertising** presents a definite point of view. This may range from political to social, and positions, by inference, the company as an involved citizen of the community or the nation.

The object of corporate or institutional advertising is not usually to sell a product, but rather to promote an idea or image. All forms of corporate advertising are, in fact, image advertising since, in each, the organization is projecting an image of itself as concerned, caring and involved. Image advertising has become as important to most organizations as product advertising, and most major advertising agencies now handle as much image advertising as sales promotion.

Public Service Announcements

Like corporate public interest advertising, the public service announcement or PSA is aimed at providing an important message to its target audience. However, unlike corporate advertising, even that done in the public interest, the PSA is reserved strictly for non profit organizations—those that qualify as non profit under federal tax laws.

Remember, however, that public service announcements and image advertising, while different under the law, are identical in format and style. They are both an attempt to sell something, whether it's a product, an idea or an image. What follows is applicable to both.

Writing for Television

Broadcast messages, whether paid-for advertising or PSAs, are called *spots*. Producing a complete television spot is usually beyond the expertise of the public relations writer and is best left to professional film and video production houses. Many practitioners, however, prefer to write their own scripts, so a knowledge of the proper form is essential. A good script tells the director, talent, or anyone reading it exactly what the spot is about, its message, and the image it should convey. In a well-written script, virtually nothing is left to the imagination. A good, working knowledge of film and video techniques is necessary if you are to be able to visualize your finished product and transmit that vision to someone else. Before beginning a script, therefore, you need to become familiar with some basics of television production and the language of script writing.

Basic Concepts

Television spots are produced either on film or videotape. Since both formats involve similar aesthetics, a discussion of one will serve to cover both. Television spots, and all commercials and programs for that matter, are composed of a series of scenes or shots joined together by transitions. A scene usually indicates a single locale, so that a 30-second commercial might be composed of a single scene which is in turn composed of several camera shots. Or, a 30 minute program might be composed of many scenes composed of many camera shots. These scenes and shots are joined by transitional devices usually created by switching from one camera to another (a form of on-the-spot editing), or in the case of a single-camera production that is edited later, by switching from one kind of shot to another. The script tells the director, camera operators, and talent what sort of composition is required in each shot.

Camera shot directions are scripted in a form of shorthand. The most common designations are described below. For our purposes, we will assume that the shots are of a person.

CU or **closeup**—A shot which takes in the neck and head but doesn't extend below the neck.

ECU or **extreme closeup**—A much tighter version of the CU, usually involving a selected portion of the object, such as the eyes.

MS or **medium shot**—A shot that takes in the person from about the waist up.

Bust shot—A shot of a person from the bust up.

LS or **long shot**—A shot of the entire person with little or no room at the top or bottom of the screen.

ELS or **extreme long shot**—A shot with the person in the distance.

There are variations on these basic shots, such as **MCU** or **medium closeup**, **MLS** or **medium long shot**, **2-shot** or a shot of two people, **3-shot** a shot of three people, etc. When designating shots in scripts, you need to be in the ballpark—you don't have to have it down to the millimeter. Whatever you write in your script may ultimately be changed by the artistic collaboration between the director and the camera operators.

Camera shots are accomplished in one of two ways: by movement of the optical apparatus (or lens), or by movement of the camera itself. The most common designations for lens movement are *zoom in* and *zoom out*. Physical movements are as follows:

Dolly in/out—Move the camera in a straight line toward or away from the object.

Truck right/left—Move the camera right or left, parallel to the object.

Pan right/left—Move the camera head to the right or left.

Tilt up/down—Move the camera head up or down.

Each of these movements creates a different optical effect, and each will impart a different impression to the viewer. Dollies and trucks, for instance, impart a sense of viewer movement rather than movement of the object being filmed or taped. The camera becomes the viewer. This type of shot is frequently called **point of view** or **POV**. Pans and tilts appear as normal eye movement, much as if the viewer were moving his or her eyes from side to side or up and down. Remember that the camera is actually the eyes of the viewer limited by the size of the screen.

Transitions are the sole domain of the director and editor. In the case of a studio production, such as a live talk show, the director and techinical director work together—the director giving transitional directions, and the technical director following those directions by electronically switching between the cameras. Transitions in field productions and single-camera productions are taken care of in post-production editing through a coop erative effort between the director and the editor. The following are the most used transitions:

Cut—An instantaneous switch from one shot to another.

Dissolve—A gradual replacement of one image with another.

Wipe—A special effect in which one image is "wiped" from the screen and replaced by another. This was used extensively in silent movie days and in adventure films of the 1930s and 1940s.

Fade—A gradual change, usually to or from black designating either the beginning or end of a scene.

Other shorthand notations are specific to audio directions. The most common are:

SFX or **sound effects**.

SOF or **sound on film—**The sound source is the audio track from a film.

SOT or **sound on tape**—The sound source is the audio track from a videotape or audio tape.

SIL or **silent film**.

Music up—Signifying that the volume of the music bed is raised.

Music under—Signifying that the volume of the music bed is lowered, usually to allow for narration.

Music up and out—Usually designating the end of a production.

VO or **voice over/voice only**—Indicating that the speaker is not on camera.

OC or **on camera**—Indicating that the speaker or narrator can be seen. This is usually used when the speaker has been VO prior to being OC. In other words, it indicates that he or she is now on camera.

Writing for the Eye

When you write for television, you write for the eye as well as the ear, which means that you have to visualize what you want your audience to see and then put that vision on paper. Your image must be crystallized into words that will tell others how to re-create it on tape or film.

In order to end up with the best possible script, you must begin with an idea. Try to think in visuals. Take a basic concept and try to visualize the best method for presenting it to others. Should you use a studio or film outdoors? Will you use ambient sound or a music background? Will you have a number of transitions or a single scene throughout? Answering these questions and others will help you conceptualize the television spot.

Television Scripts

Script Treatment

Once you have a basic idea in your head of what you would like to say, the next step is to write a *script treatment*. A treatment is a narrative account of a television spot. It is not written in a script format but may include ideas for shots and transitions. The key is to keep it informal at this point.There will be plenty of time to clean it up in later drafts.

Exhibit 8.1 is a treatment for a promotional ad for a documentary to be shown on television.

Working Scripts and Shooting Scripts

The next step is to sharpen your images in a working script. The working script should include all of the information necessary for a complete understanding of your idea. In it, you should begin to flesh out camera shots, transitions, audio—including music and sound effects—and approximate times. The working script is still a draft, but in it you should begin to solidify your ideas. The shooting script is constructed from the working script. The director will use it to produce your spot for television. In it you must include all of the proposed camera shots, transitions, narrative, audio of all types, and acting directions.

"IDITAROD"
30 second promo
Treatment

Opening shot of dog team against setting sun across long stretch of tundra. Cut to flashes of finish line hysteria, dogs running, racers' faces frozen or exhausted, stretches of open ground, trees, checkpoints, etc., perhaps terminating at starting gun. Images continue under narration.

Voice over: WHAT MAKES SOME PEOPLE SPEND LITERALLY AN ENTIRE YEAR TRAINING BOTH THEMSELVES AND THEIR DOGS, OFTEN WITH HEARTBREAKING RESULTS? WHAT DRAWS A PERSON TO DOG SLED RACING? IS IT A MYSTIQUE UNIQUE ONLY TO ALASKA, OR IS IT SOMETHING COMMON TO ALL PEOPLE AT ALL TIMES?

Cut to closeup of winner of last year's Iditarod race… exhaustion… joy… satisfaction. Zoom in to freeze-frame of face.

Voice over: JOIN US FOR A TWELVE HUNDRED MILE RACE ACROSS ALASKA WHEN NATIONAL GEOGRAPHIC PRESENTS "IDITAROD": THE RACE ON THE EDGE OF THE WORLD.

NGS logo… super day and time.

#####

Exhibit 8.1—Television Script Treatment

Here are some guidelines that will help you as you move through both working and shooting scripts.

1. Open with an attention-getting device: an interesting piece of audio, an unusual camera shot, or a celebrity. The first few seconds are crucial. If your viewers are not hooked by then, you've lost them.
2. Open with an establishing shot if possible—something that says where you are and intimates where you are going. If you open in a classroom, for instance, chances are you are going to stay there. If you jump too much, you confuse viewers.

3. If you open with a long shot, you should then cut to a closer shot, and soon after, introduce the subject of the spot. This is especially applicable if you are featuring a product or a celebrity spokesperson.
4. Vary shot composition from MS to CU throughout and somewhere past the midpoint of the spot, return to a MS, then to a final CU and a super (superimposition) of logo or address. (A *super* involves placing one image over another.)

PRODUCTION: A.P.P.L.E. 9/17 Revised — Page 1 of 33

PRODUCER: University of Alaska
Media Services

VIDEO	AUDIO
Scene opens with aerial view of grassy area on which is displayed 5 boxes of different sizes and colors. Cut to ground level view as camera pans over boxes. They are labeled: non-renewable resources, hazards, ownwrship, and land use. Shot should end on non renewable resources box with a tight shot. Pull back to catch entrance of mime. This should be an edit so that the other boxes are no longer in the shot.	ALASKA'S LAND IS PRETTY COMPLEX AND UNDERSTANDING IT CAN BE COMPLICATED. THERE ARE A FEW BASIC THINGS, HOWEVER, THAT YOU SHOULD KNOW SO THAT WHEN THE TIME COMES FOR YOU TO MAKE DECISIONS ABOUT LAND, YOU CAN MAKE GOOD ONES.
	YOU SHOULD KNOW ABOUT RESOURCES, RENEWABLE AND NON-RENEWABLE. YOU SHOULD KNOW WHO OWNS THE LAND NOW AND WHO MIGHT OWN IT IN THE FUTURE AND HOW THEY USE IT. AND YOU NEED TO KNOW ABOUT THE LAND'S OWN NATURAL HAZARDS SO THAT YOU CAN USE IT WITH CAUTION IF YOU HAVE TO. YES, USING THE LAND CAN BE COMPLEX, BUT IT CAN ALSO BE VERY INTERESTING.

-more-

Exhibit 8.2—Television Working Script

5. Don't call for a new shot unless it adds something to the spot. Make your shots seem like part of an integrated whole. Be single-minded and try to tell only one important story per spot.

Although a director will feel free to adapt your script to his or her particular style and to the requirements of the production, you should leave as little as possible to the imagination.

Exhibit 8.2 is a page from a working script. Notice the difference between it and the shooting script version in **Exhibit 8.3**.

PRODUCTION: A.P.P.L.E. 9/17 Revised Page 1 of 33

PRODUCER: University of Alaska
Media Services

VIDEO	AUDIO
ELS moutain range, AERIAL	(ambient sounds of birds)
Camera PANS range, descends through wooded area, zeroing in on the edge of a grassy clearing.	(sound of wind)
DISSOLVE to LS grassy clearing	
Colorful objects can be made out scattered within the clearing.	
DISSOLVE to MLS grassy clearing	
At ground level, camera slowly PANS across objects and stops on box labeled "non-renewable resources."	
DISSOLVE to MS mime	
Camera PANS as mime enters scene and approaches box.	
DISSOLVE to CU mime and box FREEZE FRAME as mime starts to open box.	NARRATOR: ALASKA'S LAND IS PRETTY COMPLEX AND UNDERSTANDING IT CAN BE COMPLI-CATED. THERE ARE A FEW BASIC THINGS, HOWEVER, THAT YOU SHOULD KNOW SO THAT WHEN THE TIME COMES FOR YOU TO MAKE DECISIONS ABOUT LAND, YOU CAN MAKE GOOD ONES. YOU SHOULD KNOW ABOUT RESOURCES, RENEWABLE AND NON-RENEWABLE.
	-more-

Exhibit 8.3—Television Shooting Script

Accompanying Scripts

The accompanying script is the version sent with the taped spot to the stations who will run it. It is written on the assumption that the shooting script has been produced as it was originally described. The accompanying script is stripped of all but its most essential directions. It is intended to provide the reader a general idea of what the taped spot is about and is to be used only as a reference for broadcasters who accept the spot for use.

PRODUCTION: Iditarod   DATE: 9/17/78   Page 1 of 1

PRODUCER: Northstar Associates

VIDEO	AUDIO
Open on LS dog sled racing into setting sun. Series of quick CUTS of finish line excitement, checkpoints, racing, and scenery.	(National Geographic music up)
Narration begins as series of shots of winning team flash by.	NARRATOR: WHAT WOULD MAKE A MAN SPEND LITERALLY AN ENTIRE YEAR TRAINING BOTH HIMSELF AND HIS DOGS, OFTEN WITH HEARTBREAKING RESULTS?
Quick series of CUs and MSs of woman racer.	WHAT DRAWS A MAN OR WOMAN TO DOGSLED RACING? IS IT A MYSTIQUE UNIQUE ONLY TO ALASKA, OR IS IT
PAN of faces in crowd at finish line.	SOMETHING COMMON TO ALL PEOPLE AT ALL TIMES?
CUT to CU of winner's face showing joy and exhaustion.	
FREEZE FRAME of face MATTED on magazine cover.	JOIN US FOR A TWELVE-HUNDRED MILE RACE ACROSS ALASKA WHEN NATIONAL GEOGRAPHIC PRESENTS "IDITAROD: THE
SFX logo.	RACE ON THE EDGE OF THE WORLD."
SUPER station air date.	(music up and out)

Exhibit 8.4—Accompanying Script

It is customary to send out taped spots in packages that include a cover letter explaining what the package is, a form requesting the receiver to designate when and how often the spot is used, and an accompanying script for each spot. Sometimes a storyboard is also sent with an abbreviated frame-by-frame summary of the major points, both audio and video, of the spot. The accompanying script in **Exhibit 8.4** was sent with the finished promo seen as a treatment in **Exhibit 8.1**.

The American Tuberculosis Foundation
1212 54th St. NE
New York, NY 00123

"Your Good Health"
30 Second TV Spot — Page 1 of 1

VIDEO	AUDIO
Open on CU of Young woman's face against a neutral background. She is smoking.	NARRATOR: (VO) YOU KNOW THE DANGERS OF CIGARETTE SMOKING.
Woman looks unconcerned. She takes another puff as she talks	SMOKING CAUSES HEART DISEASE, EMPHYSEMA, AND CANCER. BUT DON'T STOP SMOKING JUST BECAUSE YOU MIGHT DIE FROM IT.
Pull back to MS to reveal child of about 4 yrs. looking up at her.	STOP SMOKING BECAUSE SOMEONE YOU LOVE MIGHT DIE FROM IT. WHEN YOU SMOKE AT HOME, YOUR CHILDREN BREATH THE SAME CANCER-CAUSING SMOKE YOU DO… AND THEY DON'T HAVE ANY CHOICE. THEY CAN'T DECIDE TO QUIT SMOKING. BUT YOU CAN. IF YOU WANT TO STOP SMOKING, WRITE US. WE'LL SEND YOU A
Child covers his mouth and coughs	FREE PROGRAM THAT WILL HELP YOU STOP IN 30 DAYS.
Slow zoom to CU woman, still holding cigarette. Looks concerned.	REMEMBER, SOMEONE YOU LOVE CARES ABOUT YOUR GOOD HEALTH.
	# # # # #
Fade to black, super address	

Exhibit 8.5—"Talking Heads" Script

Choosing a Style

The two styles most common to television spots are *talking heads* and *slice-of-life*. In a *talking heads* spot, the primary image appearing on the television screen is the human head—talking. This style is often chosen for reasons of cost—talking heads spots are relatively cheap to produce—but it can be very effective. **Exhibit 8.5** is an example.

Talking heads spots have criticized for being boring or unexciting, but this does not need to be the case.The key is to make what is said forceful and memorable while, at the same time, introducing enough camera movement and varied shot composition to make the video image visually ineresting. By incorporating the simplest of camera movements into your scripts, you can hold the attention of the audience long enough to impart your verbal message. With this in mind, read through **Exhibit 8.5** and notice how closely the subtle camera movements are tied to the verbal message.

As its name implies, the *slice-of-life* television spot sets up a dramatic situation complete with a beginning, middle, and end. In the slice-of-life spot, the focus is on the story, not the characters. The message is imparted through an interesting sequence of events incorporating but not relying on interesting characters. Slice-of-life spots, usually use a wide variety of camera movements and post-production techniques, such as dissolves and special effects. Although this type of spot is often shot with one camera, the effect is one of multiple cameras due to the post-production process. Slice-of-life spots may be more difficult to produce than talking heads spots, but they are just as easy to script. (See **Exhibit 8.6**.)

Timing Your Script

How do you know when you have written a script that will end up running only 60 seconds on the television screen? Timing a script isn't easy and requires a certain amount of "gut feeling." The best way to time a script is to read through what you have written as if it were already produced. Always exaggerate your delivery. You usually talk faster than you think you do. Pause for the music, sound effects, and talent reactions. You also need to simulate movements as if they were occurring on screen. If your script calls for the talent to walk up a classroom aisle, for instance, walk the equivalent distance while you read the narrative. This type of "live action" walkthrough will give you a ballpark idea of how long your script will be when finally shot.

Remember, the director will ultimately make the adjustments necessary to fit your script into the required time slot; but, it's always in your best

Institute for Higher Education
Box 1873
Washington, D.C. 19806

"Payoff"
60 Second TV Spot

Page 1 of 3

VIDEO	AUDIO
Open on MLS large crowd shot, city street,people walking. We see a young man in front of crowd as it stops at crosswalk.	(Music up: "You've Earned Your Chance") "THE CITY'S HOT, THE DAY'S BEEN LONG,
Continue MLS as light changes and crowd crosses.	BUT YOU'VE BEEN OUT THERE HANGING ON.
ARC LEFT and AROUND as young man crosses street and FOLLOW shot behind him as he reaches other side.	THE FACES START TO LOOK THE SAME, YOU WONDER IF THEY KNOW YOUR NAME.
CUT TO MLS as young man stops in front of building, checks address on slip of paper in his hand, and enters.	THERE'S ONE MORE SHOT BEFORE YOU'RE THROUGH.
CUT TO MS young man as he rushes to squeeze into elevator.	YOU KNOW YOU'RE TIME IS COMING DUE. IT'S YOUR TURN NOW, YOUR DUES ARE PAID.
CUT TO MCU young man looking uncomfortable in crowded elevator. He looks to right and left as others ignore him.	YOU'VE EARNED YOUR CHANCE, YOU'VE MADE THE GRADE."
CUT TO MS of elevator doors opening as young man exits, looks both ways and turns screen left.	(Lyrics end, music under)
CUT TO MS of young man pausing before door, checking number, and entering.	
CUT TO MLS young man entering front office. Secretary is seated at desk and glances up as he enters room.	
CUT TO CU secretary's face	SECRETARY: MAY I HELP YOU?
	-more-

Exhibit 8.6—Slice-of-life Script (continued on following pages)

interest (as far as your reputation as a writer is concerned) to be as close as possible.

Cutting Your Script

Cutting a script means understanding the message you want to impart thoroughly, and then making sure that it is still intact after editing. Remember, a 30-second spot is half the length of a 60-second spot. That

"Payoff"
60 Second TV Spot

VIDEO	AUDIO
CUT TO CU young man's face	MAN: YES. I'M HERE FOR AN APPOINTMENT WITH MR. ALDRICH.
CUT TO 2-SHOT secretary and young man	SECRETARY: YOU MUST BE MR. ROBINSON. MR. ALDRICH IS EXPECTING YOU. I'LL LET HIM KNOW YOU'RE HERE. WHY DON'T YOU HAVE A SEAT. I'M SURE HE'LL BE RIGHT WITH YOU.
Follow MS young man as he seats himself. He picks up a magazine and begins to read.	ANNOUNCER: YOU'VE PREPARED FOR THIS MOMENT FOR FOUR YEARS. NOW IT'S PAYOFF TIME. YOU'RE CONFIDENT AND POLISHED. YOU'VE GOT A COLLEGE
CUT TO MCU young man as he glances at office door.	EDUCATION AND THE TRAINING YOU NEED TO GO WHERE YOU WANT TO GO, AND DO WHAT YOU WANT TO DO IN LIFE. YOU HAD THE INSIGHT AND THE DRIVE TO BETTER
CUT TO CU young man's face exuding confidence	YOURSELF THROUGH HIGHER EDUCATION, AND NOW IS THE MOMENT YOU'VE WAITED FOR.
CUT TO MLS as office door opens and interviewer steps out to shake young man's hand.	-more-

may sound obvious, but 30 seconds lost out of a 60-second spot can result in the deletion of a lot of valuable set-up and development time. That 10 seconds you took to pan slowly around the classroom scene now has to go. What do you do instead? Here are some guidelines for cutting your script.

1. Always begin with the longer script. It is easier to cut down than to write more.
2. Look first at the opening and closing sections to see if you can eliminate long musical or visual transitions or fades.

"Payoff"
60 Second TV Spot   Page 3 of 3

VIDEO	AUDIO
CUT TO CU interviewer's face	INTERVIEWER: MR. ROBINSON? I'VE BEEN LOOKING FORWARD TO MEETING YOU.
CUT TO CU young man's face, smiling.	I'VE GOT TO TELL YOU--YOU'RE JUST THE KIND OF PERSON WE'RE LOOKING FOR. WE'VE GOT A LOT TO TALK ABOUT.
CUT TO MEDIUM 2-SHOT as two men chat	
LOSE focus and SUPER address	
FOCUS on MEDIUM 2-SHOT as two men enter office and close door behind them.	ANNOUNCER: MAKE YOUR DREAMS A REALITY. GO TO COLLEGE. EDUCATION PAYS OFF. FOR MORE INFORMATION, WRITE:
	INSTITUTE FOR HIGHER EDUCATION BOX 1873 WASHINGTON, D.C. 19806
	(Music and lyrics up)
	"YES, YOU'VE EARNED YOUR CHANCE, NOW GIVE IT ALL YOU'VE GOT."
	# # # # #

3. Next, check for long dissolves or other lengthy transitions within the body of the script to see if these can be replaced with shorter transitional techniques, such as cuts, or eliminated altogether.
4. See if you can eliminate minor characters. Cutting a character with only one or two lines will save you a lot of time.
5. See if you can eliminate any narrative assigned to your major spokesperson. Leave only the key message, slogan, any necessary contact information—and enough narrative transition to allow for coherent development.

Institute for Higher Education
Box 1873
Washington, D.C. 19806

"Payoff"
30 Second TV Spot Page 1 of 2

VIDEO	AUDIO
Open on LS young man entering front office. Secretary is seated at desk and glances up as he enters room.	
CUT TO CU secretary's face	<u>SECRETARY</u>: MAY I HELP YOU?
CUT TO CU young man's face	<u>MAN</u>: YES. I'M HERE FOR AN APPOINTMENT WITH MR. ALDRICH.
CUT TO 2-SHOT secretary and young man	<u>SECRETARY</u>: YOU MUST BE MR. ROBINSON.MR. ALDRICH IS EXPECTING YOU. I'LL LET HIM KNOW YOUR'RE HERE. WHY DON'T YOU HAVE A SEAT. I'M SURE HE'LL BE RIGHT WITH YOU.
Follow MS young man as he seats himself He picks up a magazine and begins to read.	<u>ANNOUNCER</u>: YOU'VE PREPARED FOR THIS MOMENT FOR FOUR YEARS. NOW IT'S PAYOFF TIME. YOU'RE CONFIDENT AND POLISHED. YOU'VE GOT A COLLEGE EDUCATION AND THE TRAINING YOU NEED TO GO WHERE YOU WANT TO GO, AND DO WHAT YOU WANT TO DO IN LIFE.
CUT TO MCU young man as he glances at office door.	
CUT TO CU young man's face exuding confidence	-more-

Exhibit 8.7—Edited Script

6. Finally, try out the cut-down version on someone who hasn't seen the longer version to make sure it flows and makes sense.

Read **Exhibit 8.7**, the 30-second version of the "slice-of-life" spot in **Exhibit 8.6**. Notice what was left out and what remains. Is the message still clear? Did the "story" lose anything in the cutting?

"Payoff"
30 Second TV Spot Page 2 of 2

VIDEO	AUDIO
CUT TO MLS as office door opens and interviewer steps out to shake young man's hand.	ANNOUNCER (CONT.): YOU HAD THE INSIGHT AND THE DRIVE TO BETTER YOURSELF THROUGH HIGHER EDUCATION, AND NOW IS THE MOMENT YOU'VE WAITED FOR.
CUT TO CU interviewer's face	INTERVIEWER: MR. ROBINSON? I'VE BEEN LOOKING FORWARD TO MEETING YOU. I'VE GOT TO TELL YOU—YOU'RE JUST THE KIND OF PERSON WE'RE LOOKING FOR. COME
CUT TO 2-SHOT as both enter office and shut door behind them.	IN. WE'VE GOT A LOT TO TALK ABOUT.
	ANNOUNCER: MAKE YOUR DREAMS A REALITY. GO TO COLLEGE. EDUCATION
SUPER Address on door	PAYS OFF. FOR MORE INFORMATION, WRITE:
	INSTITUTE FOR HIGHER EDUCATION BOX 1873 WASHINGTON, D.C. 19806
	-30-

Writing for Radio

The radio spot, like the television spot, must be absolutely clear in order to be understood—both by the listener and by the broadcaster who will be airing it. Remember, radio scripts are written for the ear. You must be clear and simple, reducing ideas to their essence. Radio may be the most flexible of media because it can rely on the imagination of the listener to fill in visuals. In radio, it is possible to create virtually any scenario which can be imagined by the audience. With the appropriate sound effects, you can have elephants perform on stage, or lions in your living room; you can position yourself in the middle of the Amazon jungle or on the highest mountain peak. Radio spots are also much cheaper to produce than television spots and can be changed on much shorter notice. Lengths of radio spots vary. Where television spots are typically either 60- or 30-seconds in length, radio spots are anywhere from 10-seconds to 60-seconds and any length in between. The standard lengths for radio spots are:

10 seconds or about 25 words
20 seconds or about 45 words
30 seconds or about 65 words
45 seconds or about 100 words
60 seconds or about 125 words

Live Radio Announcements

The simplest type of radio spot is the spot announcement involving no sound effects or music bed and meant to be read by station personnel. This type is usually sent in a package of two, three, or four spots and can be general in nature, geared to a specific program or tied to some specific time of the year or holiday.

Like television scripts, radio scripts must be uniformly formatted. Never send a spot on a 3" x 5" card. Although most stations will transfer the information from a spot announcement to a card for ease of handling, you should always send your spots on standard bond paper. Some other rules include:

1. Head up your spot with the name of the originating agency and its address and telephone number. Include a contact.
2. Title your spot and give the length at the beginning, not the end.
3. Because spot announcements are never more than one page in length, you may be able to get more than one per page. The standard is usually five or six 10-second spots per page; two 30-second spots

per page; and one 60-second spot per page. As with press releases, end all spots with # # # # #.

4. Type all radio spots upper case, double-spaced for ease of reading. Talent directions, if there are any, should be upper and lower case in parentheses.

Since spots are typically written as a series, it is necessary to develop a theme which will carry over from spot to spot. This is best accomplished

The American Tuberculosis Foundation
1212 Street of the Americas
New York, NY 00912

"YOUR GOOD HEALTH" :10 SEC. LIVE RADIO SPOTS

THE AMERICAN TUBERCULOSIS FOUNDATION AND THIS STATION CARE ABOUT YOUR GOOD HEALTH. DON'T SMOKE... SOME WHO LOVES YOU, WANTS YOU TO QUIT.

# # # # #

(station call letters) AND THE AMERICAN TUBERCULOSIS FOUNDATION CARE ABOUT YOUR GOOD HEALTH. IF YOU SMOKE, TRY TO STOP. IF YOU'RE THINKING OF STARTING, THINK TWICE.

# # # # #

SMOKING NOT ONLY HARMS YOUR LUNGS, IT HARMS THE LUNGS OF THOSE AROUND YOU. SOMEONE YOU LOVE WANTS YOU TO QUIT. THE AMERICAN TUBERCULOSIS FOUNDATION CARES ABOUT YOUR GOOD HEALTH.

# # # # #

IF YOU'RE THINKING OF STARTING TO SMOKE... THINK TWICE.SMOKING HARMS YOU AND THOSE YOU LOVE. THE AMERICAN TUBERCULOSIS FOUNDATION AND THIS STATION CARE ABOUT YOUR GOOD HEALTH.

# # # # #

GOOD HEALTH MEANS TAKING CARE OF YOURSELF. DON'T START SMOKING. AND IF YOU ALREADY SMOKE... TRY TO STOP. SOMEONE YOU LOVE CARES ABOUT YOUR GOOD HEALTH. A MESSAGE FROM (station call letters) AND THE AMERICAN TUBERCULOSIS FOUNDATION.

# # # # #

Exhibit 8.8—Live Radio Spots (continued on following pages)

by the use of key ideas and phrases, repeated in each spot. The concepts and ideas should be such that they can be developed more fully as the spots increase in length and time.

The spots in **Exhibit 8.8** employ some standard methods for creating a cohesive series. Whenever you produce a series of spots, they should reflect a continuity of theme and message. Ask yourself these questions about the spots:

1. What is the underlying theme or concept throughout the spots?

The American Tuberculosis Foundation
1212 Street of the Americas
New York, NY 00912

"YOUR GOOD HEALTH" :30 SEC. LIVE RADIO SPOTS

DO YOU SMOKE? IF YOU DO, DO YOU REMEMBER WHEN YOU STARTED? MAYBE YOU WERE A TEENAGER AND YOUR FRIENDS THOUGHT IT MADE THEM LOOK "ADULT." WHATEVER THE REASON, SMOKING ISN'T GROWN UP ANY MORE... IT'S JUST PLAIN STUPID. THE AMERICAN TUBERCULOSIS FOUNDATION AND THIS STATION WANT YOU TO KNOW THAT SOMEONE YOU LOVE CARES ABOUT YOUR GOOD HEALTH. WE WANT YOU TO HAVE THE CHANCE TO ACT LIKE A GROWN UP.IF YOU'D LIKE TO STOP SMOKING,WRITE US.
OUR ADDRESS IS:

THE AMERICAN TUBERCULOSIS FOUNDATION
BOX 1892
NEW YORK, NEW YORK 00911

#####

WHEN YOU SMOKE, YOU'RE NOT JUST HURTING YOURSELF, YOU'RE HURTING THOSE AROUND YOU... AND MAYBE EVEN SOMEONE YOU LOVE. THE AMERICAN TUBERCULOSIS FOUNDATION WANTS YOU TO KNOW THAT YOU CAN QUIT. WE'VE DEVELOPED A PROGRAM THAT WILL HELP YOU STOP SMOKING IN 30 DAYS, AND WE'LL SEND YOU THAT PROGRAM FREE. ALL YOU HAVE TO DO IS WRITE US AT:

THE AMERICAN TUBERCULOSIS FOUNDATION
BOX 1892
NEW YORK, NEW YORK 00911

WE CARE ABOUT YOUR GOOD HEALTH.

#####

2. How is this theme carried out from spot to spot?

3. What are the key ideas and phrases that are repeated in all the spots?

Notice that the longer spots elaborate on the theme in some way. The shorter spots, especially the 10-second spots, are the basic message—often only the phrase or idea which will be repeated in the longer spots. The longer spots, particularly the 60-second spot, can take time for development and enumeration of points barely mentioned in the shorter versions.

The American Tuberculosis Foundation
1212 Street of the Americas
New York, NY 00912

"YOUR GOOD HEALTH" :60 SEC. LIVE RADIO SPOT

SMOKING CAUSES HEART DISEASE, EMPHASEMA, AND CANCER.BUT DON'T STOP SMOKING JUST BECAUSE YOU MIGHT DIE FROM IT. STOP SMOKING BECAUSE SOMEONE YOU LOVE MIGHT DIE FROM IT. THAT'S RIGHT... SECOND-HAND SMOKE IS A PROVEN CONTRIBUTOR TO HEALTH PROBLEMS IN NON-SMOKERS. WHEN YOU SMOKE AT HOME, YOUR CHILDREN BREATH THE SAME CANCER-CAUSING SMOKE YOU DO... AND THEY DON'T HAVE ANY CHOICE. THEY CAN'T DECIDE TO QUIT SMOKING. BUT YOU CAN. IF YOU WANT TO STOP SMOKING, WRITE US. WE'LL SEND YOU A FREE PROGRAM THAT WILL HELP YOU STOP IN 30 DAYS. WRITE:

THE AMERICAN TUBERCULOSIS FOUNDATION
BOX 1892
NEW YORK, NEW YORK 00911

(repeat address)

REMEMBER, SOMEONE YOU LOVE CARES ABOUT YOUR GOOD HEALTH.

#####

"As-Recorded" Spots

Unlike the television spot, radio spots come not only in different lengths but in different formats. Television spots are rarely written to be read by a television announcer as a drop-in as are radio spots. The radio spot, on the other hand, can be pre-recorded, utilizing many of the same techniques as television—sound effects, music beds, multiple talent, sound fades and dissolves, and changes in scenes. Of course, these effects are more difficult to pull off when you are restricted to audio only, but the challenge is in the trying.

Northwest Library Association
1342 Placer Ave.
Seattle, WA 98901

"Werewolf" 30 Sec. PSA—As Recorded

(sfx: sounds of wind, howling and footsteps running)

WOMAN: DID YOU HEAR THAT? IT SOUNDED LIKE A WEREWOLF!
MAN: DON'T WORRY. WE'RE SAFE.

(sfx: loud sound of bushes rattling and sudden snarling)

WOMAN: (very frightened) IT IS A WEREWOLF! WHAT ARE WE GOING TO DO?
MAN: (reassuringly) I TOLD YOU NOT TO WORRY.I HAD PLENTY OF GARLIC ON MY PIZZA TONIGHT,REMEMBER?
WOMAN: (sarcastically) I CERTAINLY DO.
WEREWOLF: (in terror) GARLIC! (screams)

(sfx: sounds of rapidly retreating footsteps and howling fading into distance)

WOMAN: (relieved) HOW ON EARTH DID YOU KNOW THAT GARLIC WOULD FRIGHTEN A WEREWOLF AWAY?
MAN: I READ IT IN A BOOK AT THE PUBLIC LIBRARY.
WOMAN: (sarcastically again) AND DID THIS BOOK EXPLAIN THE EFFECTS OF GARLIC ON YOUR DATE?
MAN: WHOOPS...
ANNCR: YOU'D BE SURPRISED WHAT YOU CAN LEARN AT YOUR PUBLIC LIBRARY. GIVE READING A TRY... IT MAKES GOOD SENSE.
MAN: (voices fading as couple walks away) OH,COME ON CAROL, IT SAVED OUR LIVES DIDN'T IT... I'LL CHEW SOME GUM... I'LL BRUSH MY TEETH...

# # # # #

Exhibit 8.9—As-Recorded Radio Spot

As-recorded spots are produced by the originating agency and are ready to be played by the stations receiving them. They are usually sent in the format used by the particular stations or on reel-to-reel tape which will probably be transferred to the proper station format. As with television spots, an accompanying script is sent along with the standard cover letter and response card.

As-recorded radio spots differ in format from television scripts but contain much of the same information. However, if you are basing your radio spots on already produced or written television spots, you will need to transfer the video cues to audio cues. For instance, if you are using a celebrity spokesperson who is easily recognizable on your video spots, she will have to identify herself on radio. Scene setting, which can be easily enough accomplished on video, will have to be taken care of verbally or through sound effects for radio. Consider the example in **Exhibit 8.9**.

Other Audio-visual Media

Slide Presentations

Writing for other types of audio-visual productions is a natural extension of radio and television writing. Scripts employing slides as visual accompaniment are formatted similarly to television scripts, with visuals on the left and narration on the right. There are several types of presentations utilizing slides and sound. Among the most common are:

1. Live narration (usually in the form of a scripted speech) accompanied by slides. This is the form of many presentations ranging from educational to sales promotion. The slides can be changed by hand, or by remote control.
2. Taped audio with slide accompaniment. The simplest method is to change slides manually as you play a tape. More elaborate systems allow for audio tones to signal slide changes automatically. The advantage of taped audio is that virtually any sound technique that can be used in radio can be used for slide/tape presentations, including music, sound effects, multiple voices, etc. Some systems don't even require a screen but can be viewed on a built-in television-like screen.

   For organizations with limited budgets, the slide-tape combination is an excellent way to produce an inexpensive television spot. Some stations may even produce your presentation on videotape for you if submit your slides and audio script. Of course, you can also produce the audio tape yourself and send it with your slides to the stations.

3. Slides and audio dubbed to videotape. This allows the presentation to be viewed on a VCR (video cassette recorder) and simplifies the logistics of lugging around slides, projectors, screens, and audio tapes. If slides are committed to videotape, you might want to go the

Slide Script
"Building the Future" Page 1 of 5

1. Graphic—"BUILDING THE FUTURE ON THE PAST" over University coat-of-arms	1. BUILDING THE FUTURE ON THE PAST. THESE WORDS REFLECT BUTLER UNIVERSITY'S COMMITTMENT TO INNOVATIVE RESEARCH AND EDUCATIONAL PROGRAMS.
2. Aerial shot of campus	2. A COMMITMENT TO DEVELOP THE PROMISE OF IDEAS INTO THE FOUNDATION OF HUMAN PROGRESS.
3. Same, with "RESEARCH" and "TEACHING"supered	3. THIS COMMITMENT TAKES MANY AND VARIOUS FORMS REFLECTING THE INTELLECTUAL DIVERSITY OF THE CAMPUS COMMUNITY.
4. Psychology researcher with experimental subject	4. IMPORTANTLY, THE BOLD AND UNCOMPROMISING INQUIRY SO TYPICAL OF RESEARCH AT THE UNIVERSITY MORE OFTEN THAN NOT PROVIDES THE BASIS FOR THE BEST IN TEACHING AND PUBLIC SERVICE.
5. IEC researcher testing solar cell	5. IT HAS BEEN SAID THAT THE FUTURE IS PURCHASED BY THE PRESENT.

-more-

Exhibit 8.10—Slide/Tape Script

extra step and have the slides shot by studio cameras incorporating movement into the production. This is accomplished by panning, zooming, tilting and dissolving from camera to camera while taping the slides projected onto screens in the studio.

4. Multi-media presentations utilizing slides, movie projectors and videotape. This type of presentation is extremely complex and usually left for the production studio; however, scripting is frequently done in house.

Society for Needy Children
4240 Welxton Ave.
Newhope, MN 78940

Contact: Lucille Bevard
Day Phone: 438-8743
Night Phone: 544-9745

SNC FUNDRAISER NETS $75 THOUSAND   For Immediate Release

:90 Seconds	A little girl stood for the first time today to receive a new teddy bear and a check for $75,000 from the Society for
Tape Roll (SIL)	Needy Children. Eight-year-old Mary Patterson accepted the check on behalf of the children at the St. Mary Martha's Children's Hospital. The money represents the culmination of a year-long fund-raising drive by the Society.The money is earmarked for a new ward to be devoted exclusively to the treatment of crippling diseases in children. One of the first beneficiar-ies will undoubtedly be little Mary who has been disabled by congenital arthritis since birth. Along with her new teddy bear, Mary and the other children at the hospital will be using a new physical therapy center which was donated by a matching grant from the Friends of St. Mary Martha's. Hospital Administrator, Lois Shelcroft says that the check and the new therapy center are just the first step...
(SOT: Shelcroft :20)	(CUT TO SHELCROFT INSERT OUTRO: "... continue next year.")
	The next fundraising drive, scheduled to begin in September, will provide money for a new lab. # # # # #

Exhibit 8.11—Broadcast Release Script

Like the television script, the audio-visual script should be easy to follow. Visuals appear exactly opposite their audio counterparts, often with numbers corresponding to the slide placed within the script narration to indicate the exact point at which the slide will be changed.

The major difference between audio-visual scripts and television spots is length. Slide presentations are usually longer with fewer visual changes. To keep them lively, count on changing slides every five to ten seconds. Much depends on the type of presentation. For instance, if you are presenting the annual budget report, you might be severely limited as to the type and number of slides shown. Viewers need time to read and digest the information contained on the slides. As a rule, if the slide contains written information, gauge the amount of time it will take to read it by reading it aloud. If you are dealing strictly with visual images and not words, then the five to ten second time allotment should be just about right. A lot depends on the pace and subject of the narration. Slides used for television presentation, especially, should change frequently. If they do not, then some other sort of movement should be incorporated into the production to compensate.

Exhibit 8.10 is a slide/tape presentation that accompanies a fundraising appeal to corporate sponsors from a major university. See if you can discern where best to place the slides within the narration. What do you see as the theme or focus of this first page? Can you tell who the intended audience is from the tone and focus?

Broadcast Releases

Sometimes, you will be asked to provide a broadcast release with accompanying visuals. The format is very much like a television or slide script. **Exhibit 8.11** is based on a broadcast release from **Chapter 3** (**Exhibit 3.5**) The visuals have been written in.

Case Study: Associated Products Corporation

Use the background information provided in Chapter 3 to complete these assignments.

Assignment 8.1: Television

You have been assigned to develop a complete promotional package which will be used by APC and NEA to stimulate interest in computer learning skills. As part of the package, write a 60-second television spot (in the form of a shooting script) employing the talents of a celebrity of your choosing. The spot should focus on the place of computers in today's society and the importance of computing skills to children of all ages.

The spot will be generic in nature and will not mention the new APC/NEA program. You have total control at this point as to the angle and message. Try to be as creative as you can. Try also to use the unique talents of whatever celebrity you have chosen to their fullest. It will be necessary to develop some sort of slogan or catch phrase which will be used in all of your broadcast media spots. The slugline for TV and subsequent radio spots will be:

For more information on computer learning skills and your child write:

The National Education Association
Box 1776
Washington, D.C. 20012

Before you begin the actual scripting, develop a treatment for your proposed script. It should be no more than one page and include preliminary ideas of narrative, talent, camera movement, shot composition, and sound effects.

Assignment 8.2: Television

Take the 60-second spot you have written and cut it to 30-seconds. In doing so, remember to include the most pertinent information and maintain the flavor of the original 60-second spot as much as possible. Focus on the main ideas and basic concept that make your 60-second spot work.

Assignment 8.3: Radio

You must develop, as part of a complete broadcast media package, radio spots on APC/NEA, using the theme you developed for your TV spots. You must first create a series of spot announcements to be read by radio station personnel. You will need 10-, 30-, and 60-second spots highlighting the information presented in your TV spot but without the celebrity.

Assignment 8.4: Radio

In addition, you will need to develop two "as recorded? spots—one 30- and one 60-second using your celebrity talent's voice in some way. Remember to maintain consistency of theme by keying on the main points and using a thematic slogan if possible.

Assignment 8.5: Radio

As part of your everyday work for APC, you have been assigned to produce publicity for a joint venture with the American Red Cross to sponsor a cardio-pulmonary resuscitation (CPR) education and awareness campaign. This campaign is to emphasize the importance of Red Cross CPR training to the community and to the individual. Other campaigns have been held around the country over the past eight months, resulting in approximately 50,000 individuals being trained.

The first event is to be a kick-off "CPR Awareness Day" to be held in Bellevue State Park on Sunday, November 4. Present will be members of local paramedic units from the local area as well as Red Cross volunteers.

The "Day" begins at 1:00 p.m. with introductions and refreshments. An initial demonstration will be made to all attending, then individuals will break up into groups headed by the trainers. Each group will learn the basics of CPR. At the end of each hour-long training session, participants will receive certificates of completion in CPR training from the Red Cross.

At 5:00, the rock group "Plastic Umbrella" will perform.

Your assignment is to make up three promotional radio spots of 10, 30, and 60 seconds in length to be read live . Remember, these need to reflect a conversational style since they will be read aloud on the air. For the 60-second spot, you may want to create an interesting "hook."

CHAPTER 9

Print Advertising

...we by tracing magic lines are taught, how to embody and to color thought.

Anonymous

For writers, there can be no truer proving ground than the print ad. Aldous Huxley once remarked that trying, through words on paper, to sell something to someone who doesn't want to buy it is the hardest task a writer can set himself. The fact of the matter is, most print ads don't get read at all. Readers have a tendency to skip over ads that they find of no immediate interest. While television, and radio to an extent, play to "captive" audiences, not so a magazine or newspaper. Gone are the devices used by the electronic media to interest the reader. In print advertising, there is no catchy music score or flashy moving image; no slick camera angles or intriguing sound effects—only the printed word and the overall effect of layout and design. Don't feel, however, that print advertising is a waste of time. On the contrary, it offers the reader the luxury of perusing at leisure. Print can be most effective as a vehicle for information too complex or lengthy for television or radio.

Public relations practitioners do not usually spend a great deal of time writing for product or service advertising; however, corporate America spends billions of dollars a year in advertising aimed not at selling products but at creating or enhancing image. This means that more and more PR writers are responsible for producing ad copy. There is also a trend in public relations toward a more complete integration with other communication functions. Marketing, advertising, and public relations all share common goals when it comes to the organization in which they work. Flexibility is the key. Being able to produce copy for corporate advertising is just another aspect of being a complete public relations writer.

Writing Print Advertisements

Whether designed for broadcasting or for the printed page, corporate advertising falls into the same three forms mentioned in **Chapter 8**: Public service, public image, and advocacy advertising. While the focus of these forms is identical from broadcast to print, the format and execution is quite different. Print ads are composed of three primary elements: headline, visual, and copy.

Headlines

Like the press release, the print advertisement has to be sold on its appearance, but to a different audience—the public. To the writer, this means that the reader has to be hooked in some way into reading the ad. The best place to start is the beginning.

Aside from an eye-catching visual, nothing attracts a reader like a good headline. Recent research indicates that the headline is often the only thing read in a print ad. David Ogilvy, in his book *Ogilvy on Advertising,* says that "On the average, five times as many people read the headline as read the body copy."

Headlines come in all shapes and sizes and need be neither long nor short to be effective. What they do need to be is interesting. Consider the following headlines gathered from a number of consumer magazines.

YOUR DYING IS YOUR RESPONSIBILITY.

The Hemlock Society

THE WAY SOME OF US PERCEIVE AIDS,
YOU'D THINK YOU COULD GET IT
BY JUST TOUCHING THIS PICTURE.

Pediatric AIDS Foundation

FOR 50 YEARS,
TEXACO HAS BEEN HAVING A LOVE AFFAIR
WITH THE MOST PASSiONATE WOMEN.

•

FOR 50 YEARS,
TEXACO HAS BEEN ASSOCIATING
WITH THE MOST VILLAINOUS CHARACTERS.

FOR 50 YEARS,
TEXACO HAS BEEN SUPPORTING
THE MOST HEROIC MEN.

•

FOR 50 YEARS,
TEXACO HAS BEEN YOUR
TICKET TO THE MET.

(A series of small ads placed in the upper right-hand corner of succeding pages)
Texaco

Research conducted by Starch INRA Hooper, the advertising research firm, concludes that what the headline says is of more importance than its form or design. However, inclusion of certain elements was found to increase readership.

- A headline addressing the reader directly.
- A headline referring to a specific problem or desire.
- A headline offering a specific benefit.
- A headline offering something new.

Of course, not all readers will be interested by all headlines. Print ads, like other forms of communication, are intended for a target public. A print ad for the preservation of bald eagles by the Sierra Club may not get much readership among nonconservationists (or poachers). All good headlines, however, have certain attributes in common.

- They should be specific. Try to avoid vague phrases or references that mean little or nothing to your reader.
- They should be believable. If you make them appear unbelievable, you should do so only in an effort to entice the reader into reading further.
- They should be simple. A good headline sets forth one major idea. The time to elaborate is in the body of the ad, not the headline.

There are several ways to construct your headlines to help them attract readers.

- Introduce news value into your headline. News invites readership. Any time your ad can appear newsworthy, your readership will increase. The headline "Why reforming our liability system is essential if America is to succeed in overseas markets," appeared on a two-page ad by AIG. Headlines such as these appear as lead-ins to articles and appeal to readers who are interested in informative advertising.

- Target your message by using a selective headline which pinpoints the exact public you are trying to reach. An ad run by Metropolitan Life featured a small child on crutches and the headline, "If you forget to have your children vaccinated, you could be reminded of it the rest of your life." This headline obviously appeals to its target audience—parents. It might or might not appeal to unmarried people with no children.
- The testimonial approach features a firsthand quotation. "Rock the boat!" is the headline on one of a series of ads featuring first-hand employee testimonies about Texaco and its products. This ad features a chemist talking about innovation. A testimonial headline is particularly useful if spoken by a well-known celebrity. Many non-profit agencies now utilize the talents of various celebrities to sell ideas. Paul Newman speaks out against nuclear weapons, Charlton Heston speaks on behalf of the nuclear deterrent, and numbers of celebrities urge us to become foster parents or pen pals to underprivileged children.
- The curiosity headline invites the reader to read further in order to answer a posed question. "Do we really want to return to those good, old-fashioned days before plastics?" comes from an ad on recycling from Amoco.
- The command headline orders the reader to do something. "Make a life or death decision" refers to the right to die and is from a series of single-column magazine ads from the Hemlock Society. In most cases, this type of headline isn't actually commanding you to do something, it is simply suggesting that you think about it.

Of course, there are other types of headlines less used than these, but most fall into one of these categories. Remember, the headline is the hook. Write a good headline, and half your job is already done.

Visuals

You don't absolutely have to have a visual in a print ad, although most of us are used to seeing one. Many good advertisements have been carried off with words only. For instance, the Chase Manhatten Bank once ran an ad with a very large headline comprised of a single word "WOLF!" The rest of the ad, run without a visual, spoke of the necessity of "crying wolf" occasionally in order to draw attention to the vanishing capital situation in the U.S. today.

If you do decide that you need a visual, make it a good one. The choice of visual is not always the prerogative of the writer. In most cases, that part is taken care of by the art department or agency; however, every writer of print advertising has something in mind when creating an ad. It is virtually impossible to come up with snappy copy and have had no visual in mind. It is your job to communicate your ideas for visuals to the people who will be charged with producing the final ad. You don't have to be an artist—all you need to do is provide a rough sketch (a *thumbnail*) and a narrative description of the visual with the ad copy. The headline, visual and body copy should work together to make a single point.

Body Copy

Good body copy is hard to write. Don't let anybody tell you otherwise. You can bet the best examples of good ad copy are the ones that took the most time, effort, and revision. Good body copy is easy to spot. It uses a minimum of adjectives and relies heavily on nouns. It uses verbs to keep things moving along. Most of all, it follows a logical order of presentation.

Good body copy begins with a bridge from the headline (an expansion of the headline idea), continues with the presentation of major points, and ends with a recapitulation of the main point, a call for action (overt or implied), or both. Sometimes, a device known as a "kicker" is used to reiterate the message of the headline. A kicker is usually a slogan or a headline-type phrase coming at the end of the body copy. Consider this ad (written by a student) concerning nuclear waste disposal.

> **BURYING THE MYTH ABOUT NUCLEAR WASTE IS TOUGHER THAN BURYING NUCLEAR WASTE.**
>
> One of today's biggest misconceptions is that nuclear waste can't be disposed of safely. This just isn't true. With today's technology, we can safely bury nuclear wastes deep underground, imprisoning them in a series of safeguarding barriers, designed so that even if one should fail, the waste would still be contained. Nuclear waste disposal can be as safe as taking out the trash. It simply requires good sense. So please, bury the myth, and we'll bury the waste.

Notice, first of all, that the headline is interesting and plays on the term "burying" to designate both the disposal of nuclear waste and the disposal of a misconception. The lead sentence in the body copy elaborates on the headline by explaining exactly what "myth" is referred to. A presentation of the main points follows the lead sentence and explains how technology helps insure safety. The ad wraps up with a direct reference back to the headline and a call for action. All of the components necessary for a successful ad are present. (See **Exhibit 3.1**.)

Notice too that the copy is limited. "Brevity is the soul of virtue" to the ad copywriter. Unfortunately, not all public relations advertising can fit so neatly into so few words. It is the nature of public relations to be informative. This often requires detail of the kind that can only be presented in the print media and at length.

Longer public interest ads—often running to one or more pages—can provide detailed explanations and will be read, but only by those intensely interested in the topic. Others, not interested enough to read through an entire ad of this type, might still skim it for highlights or, at the very least, appreciate the fact that the sponsoring agency felt that the issue was important enough to spend money advertising it.

Aside from logical order of presentation, there are some basic guidelines which will help you to write good body copy.

1. Stick to the present tense when possible. This will make your message seem timely and active.
2. Remember that you are speaking to one person. Unlike television and radio ads which reach a mass audience simultaneously, print is read by one person at a time. Use a familiar voice. Use personal pronouns. Involve the reader. Say "we" or "our" instead of "the Company" or "the industry." Make the readers understand that you are one of them.
3. Use the active voice. Don't say "A proposal was made whereby nuclear waste can more effectively be disposed." Say instead, "We've proposed a new method for disposing of nuclear waste."
4. Use words that will be familiar to your readers. On the other hand, don't speak down to them. Assume that they know something about your subject but are looking to your ad to increase their knowledge. If you use a necessarily difficult word or phrase, explain it. Remember, readers like to think that the people explaining or giving advice are smarter than they are, but not a whole lot smarter.
5. Although the average sentence length for ease of readability is about 16 words, vary your sentence length for variety. Varying paragraph length, too, will lend your ad an appearance of readability.

Nuclear Waste
Quarter-page Newspaper

HEADLINE:	Burying the myth about nuclear waste is tougher than burying nuclear waste.
VISUAL:	Silhouette of grass with cutaway for copy -- implying copy is placed in hole in ground simulating nuclear waste.
COPY:	One of today's biggest misconceptions is that nuclear waste can't be disposed of safely. This just isn't true. With today's technology, we can safely bury nuclear wastes deep underground, imprisoning them is a series of safeguarding barriers, designed so that even if one should fail, the waste would still be contained. Nuclear waste disposal can be as safe as taking out the trash. It simply requires good sense. So please, bury the myth, and we'll bury the waste.
SLUG:	Committee for Energy Awareness

-30-

Exhibit 9.1—Print Ad Format

The ad copy here clearly shows how the ad is to be laid out as well as how it is to read. The laid out ad appears here at right.

Northrim Associates
Quarter Page, newspaper
"You Probably Know"

VISUAL: Cartoon line drawing of Grizzly Bear with fly fishing gear and waders standing in stream.

HEADLINE: You probably know that the Alaskan Grizzly eats hundreds of pounds of salmon a week.

COPY: But did you know that he is also a superb fisherman, catching dozens of salmon a day from mountain streams? If your sport is fishing and wildlife watching, come to Alaska this summer. Aside from some of the best fishing in the world, we've also got some of the most beautiful scenery, friendly people, and wild life.

If you've never been to the "Last Frontier," you'll find it the experience of a lifetime; and if you're coming for a return visit—welcome back! Consider Alaska this summer. Start by writing:

Department of Tourism,
State of Alaska,
Juneau, Alaska 99504.

We can help with all your travel arrangements, and even find you a campground—free of bears.

KICKER: Alaska: The first choice—the last frontier.

# # # # #

Exhibit 9.2—Print Ad Format

Many readers who do not have time to pour over long, unbroken passages will read shorter paragraphs. To this end, subheads are useful to point to especially informative passages.

6. Use contractions. People talk that way, so why not write that way—as if you were speaking to them. An exception would be the contracted form of *there is—there's*. The contraction reads awkwardly and is too often used ungrammatically instead of *there are*.
7. Always punctuate properly, even in headlines. Think about what punctuation does. It makes the reader pause and denotes a change or variance in emphasis. Stay away from the exclamation point and don't use ellipses or "leaders."
8. Avoid clichés and try not to use vague words or phrases. People like to feel that they understand you.
9. Never say anything controversial that you don't back up with facts or evidence. Unsupported statements will hurt your credibility.

Ad Copy Format

Print ads, like other forms of public relations writing, require the proper format for presentation. Most print ads, however, will not be sent directly to the media as mere copy but rather as a complete ad, ready to be published (camera-ready). Nevertheless, it is necessary to format your ad copy so that the agency or department handling the assembly of the final product understands what it is you are trying to do. Fortunately, the format for ad copy is similar to other formats such as brochures, posters, and direct mail pieces. It is easily adapted to any form of copywriting which requires a mixture of headlines, visuals, and text. The key is to make sure you designate clearly all of the elements at the right-hand margin so that a reader can see what element of the ad he or she is reading at the time (see **Exhibit 9.2**).

It is okay to describe the visual in some detail, although too much detail might be confusing. You simply need to impress on your readers exactly what you, the writer, had in mind for the finished product.

Ad Layout Formats

Some public relations writers, especially those in limited-budget, non-profit organizations, find themselves in sole charge of some forms of advertising and must design ads as well as write the copy for them. It is best to know how to proceed *before* you're assigned the task. Even if you don't lay out your own ads, it's a good idea to become familiar with the most common ad formats so that as you write, you can conceptualize exactly how your copy will fit into the finished product. The following represent the most common print ad formats in use.

Picture window is probably one of the most popular styles for print ads. The visual dominates this format and usually takes up the top or bottom two-thirds of the page. Normally, the headline is a single line followed by body copy in two or three columns.

KABUKI

Lorem ipsum dolor sit amet, consectetuer adipiscing elit, sed diam nonummy nibh euismod tincidunt ut laoreet dolore magna aliquam erat volutpat.

Lorem ipsum dolor sit amet, consectetuer adipiscing elit, sed diam nonummy nibh euismod tincidunt ut laoreet dolore magna aliquam erat volutpat.

Lorem ipsum dolor sit amet, consectetuer adipiscing elit, sed diam nonummy nibh euismod tincidunt ut laoreet dolore magna aliquam erat volutpat.

Ut wisi enim ad minim veniam, quis nostrud exerci tation ullamcorper suscipit lobortis nisl ut aliquip ex ea commodo consequat.

Duis autem vel eum iriure dolor in hendrerit in vulputate velit esse molestie consequat, vel illum dolore eu feugiat nulla facilisis at vero eros et accumsan et iusto odio dignissim qui blandit praesent luptatum zzril delenit augue duis dolore te feugait

nulla facilisi.Lorem ipsum dolor sit amet, consectetuer adipiscing elit, sed diam nonummy nibh euismod tincidunt ut laoreet dolore magna aliquam erat volutpat. Ut wisi

Lorem ipsum dolor sit amet, consectetuer adipiscing elit, sed diam nonummy nibh euismod tincidunt ut laoreet dolore magna aliquam erat volutpat.

Ut wisi enim ad minim veniam, quis nostrud exerci tation ullamcorper suscipit lobortis nisl ut aliquip ex ea commodo consequat.

Duis autem vel eum iriure dolor in hendrerit in vulputate velit esse molestie consequat, vel illum dolore eu feugiat nulla facilisis at vero eros et accumsan et iusto odio dignissim qui blandit praesent luptatum zzril delenit augue duis dolore te feugait nulla facilisi.

KABUKI

Copy heavy Places the emphasis on the copy rather than on the visual. For messages that are complex in nature and require detailed explanation, this is one of the best formats to use. In corporate advocacy advertising, copy heavy ads are very common.

Silhouette or **copy fit** usually has the copy "wrap around" an open (as opposed to framed or bordered) piece of art. Copy fit takes an expert in typesetting. This isn't something a beginner will normally feel comfortable with, but a good copy fit ad can exude an air of unity that may not be found in other layouts.

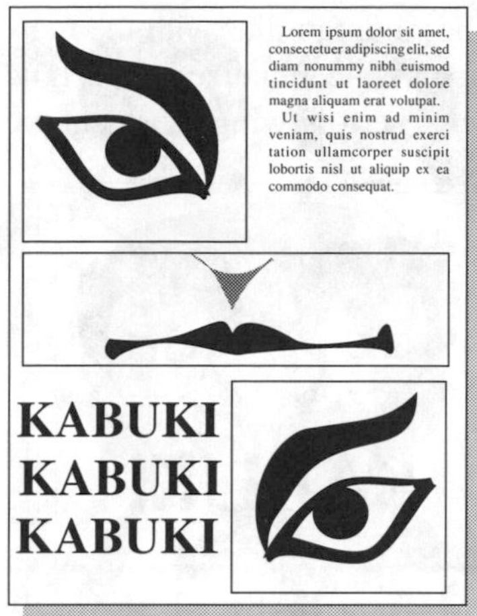

Mondrian is named after the Dutch artist who developed the style. This style is, again, not for the beginner. Mondrian divides the ad space into rectangles of various sizes into which headlines, copy and visuals are placed. Balance is the key here.

Frame or **donut** refers either to framing copy with a visual or framing a visual with copy.If the perimeter is open at either the top or bottom, the layout is sometimes called **horseshoe**.

Circus is definitely the domain of graphic designers. It takes an expert to balance this layout well. This format often utilizes both framed and silhouetted visuals along with *copy fit* body copy and numerous subheads.

Multi-panel or **cartoon** is exactly what it says. In this format, the panels are usually of equal size. Sometimes the panels tell a sequential story. Multi-panel does not always have to frame each picture in the sequence. Some multi-panel layouts use a series of open, or silhouetted visuals—often a repeated image which changes gradually as it progresses.

Type Specimen relies on the effect of a special or enlarged typeface in place of or as the primary visual element. Again, it takes an expert designer or typographer to handle a type specimen design.

Copyfitting

In print advertising, copyfitting is the method by which those who are responsible for the final production of a print ad manage to fit headlines, visuals and copy into a pre-set space. It is not an easy task.

For the public relations writer, copyfitting may at first appear to be either beyond his capabilities or a waste of his time. After all, isn't the art director or ad agency going to take care of the technical end? All you have to do is write, right? Wrong. Suppose you are a one-person public relations office for a non-profit agency. Every day you churn out pages of copy for press releases, fund-raisers, newsletters and, yes Virginia, print ads. You can't afford the luxury of an outside agency or even of having the printer lay out your ads for you. You have to do it yourself. Here are some guidelines.

Sizing Copy

There are two reasons for fitting copy accurately: to determine how much space a given amount of copy will take when set in type; and to determine how much copy to write to fill a predetermined space. Both methods are discussed here.

Before you begin, you must know:

- The typeface, type size, and amount of leading to be used.
- A character-per-pica (CPP) count for the type face.
- The total number of characters in the original copy.
- The column width of the typeset copy.

Type face is the name of the style of type you are using. Typefaces come in either *serif* or *sans serif* styles. Serifs are those little cross strokes at the end of lines on letters. Each typeface (there are probably thousands of them) has a name: Times Roman, Garamond, Helvetica, Bodoni, etc. They also usually come in bold, demi-bold, light, italics or any number of other designations of line width or slant. Although selecting a type style involves familiarity with a great number of faces, the beginner need only reference a few. Most people quickly develop favorites and rely on them for most of their printing jobs. The trick is not to become so attached to a single type face that you never experiment.

Type size is the important element in copyfitting. Type is measured in points (72 points = 1 inch). Points indicate the vertical size of a letter. The point size of a given alphabet is determined by the size of its capitals—usually anywhere from 6 to 72 points. Type size for publications, for instance, usually ranges from 8 to 12 points, while most ads are set in 12 to 14 point body copy. The point size is determined to a great extent by readability. Anything below 8 points is pretty difficult to read.

Leading refers to the amount of space between the lines of type. Sometimes type is set solid—without leading. Leading improves readability. A block of bold type set solid might be too dark in appearance while a block of light type or italics might be easier to read. Most of the time, type is leaded one or two points. Point size and leading are usually indicated together. Twelve-point type leaded two would be written 12/14 and would be spoken of as "twelve over two" or "twelve leaded two."

Character-per-pica count (CPP) tells us how many characters of a given typeface of a given point size that will fit into a pica. A pica is a typesetter's measurement used to indicate the space into which the copy will be fit (6 picas = 1 inch). Measured horizontally or vertically, one pica equals 12 points. Thus, one line of 12 point type would take up one pica vertically. If a block of type is set solid, 100 lines of 12 point type would take up 100 picas or about 16-2/3 inches. Character-per-pica count is the horizontal measurement and is usually determined by consulting a type book or a typesetter. Most type books include a CPP. The CPP for 10 point Helvetica, for instance, is 2.4 which means that you can get 2.4 characters of 10 point Helvetica into one pica measured horizontally. If your copy is 10 picas wide and is set in 10 point Helvetica, than the number of characters per line will be 24.

If you need to determine copy depth (vertical measurement of a block of copy) a simple formula is:

$$\frac{\text{Lines of type x (point size + leading)}}{12} = \text{Copy depth in picas}$$

Thus, if you used 10-point type with 1-point leading (10/1), 100 lines of type would be:

$$\frac{100 \text{ x } (10 + 1)}{12} = 91.7 = 92 \text{ picas}$$

To determine how many characters are in your original copy, you will need to know whether your typewriter is using 10 or 12 characters per inch. Many electric typewriters have adjustable pitches. If your typewriter uses a 10 pitch format, for instance, you will get 10 characters per inch (CPI)—12 pitch yields 12 CPI. To determine the total number of characters in your typed copy, first measure an average line width. If you are using a 10 pitch format and your line width is 6 inches, you are getting about 60 characters per line (CPL). Next, count the number of lines on a page including partial lines as whole lines. Finally, count the number of pages of copy you have. The formula is:

line width in inches x characters per inch x lines per page x number of pages

Sample Copyfitting Problems

If you know the copy width

Suppose you want to set 2,500 characters of original copy in 10-point Times Roman. You know that your copy width when set in type will be 20 picas. How many lines of copy will you have?

1. CPP x line width (in picas) = CPL (characters per line)

   2.4 x 20 = 48 CPL

2. $\frac{\text{Total characters in original copy}}{\text{CPL}}$ = Number of lines

   $\frac{2500}{48}$ = 52.08 = 52

Now, you have 52 lines of copy set in 10-point Times Roman and you decide to lead it 1-point. What will the depth be in picas?

1. (Point size + leading) x number of lines = Depth in points

   (10 + 1) x 52 = 572 points

2. $\frac{\text{Depth in points}}{12}$ = Depth in picas

   $\frac{572}{12}$ = 47.66 = 48 picas

If the copy had been 10-point leaded 2 or 10/2, what would the copy depth have equaled? (Remember, there are 12 points to a pica.)

If you know the copy depth

If you know that you have to fill a specific depth with copy, how do you determine how wide it will be, based on the known number of characters in your original unset copy? Suppose your depth is to be 50 picas and the total number of characters in your original copy is still 2,500. You are going to set your type in 10-point Helvetica leaded 2.

1. $\frac{\text{Total number of characters}}{\text{Number of lines}}$ = CPL

   $\frac{2500}{50}$ = 50 lines

2. $\frac{\text{Characters per line (CPL)}}{\text{Characters per pica (CPP)}}$ = Line width in picas

   $\frac{50}{2.4}$ = 20.83 = 21 picas wide

If you know how much space you have to fill

Suppose you have to write enough copy to fill a predetermined amount of space on the finished layout. Let's say you have to fill a space 35 picas wide by 105 picas deep. If your typewriter gives you 10 characters per inch, set it to a 60-space line or 60 characters per line. Now, to determine now many lines at 60 characters each you will have to type to fill the ad space, use this formula. (Assume that you will have your copy set in Garamond 12-point, unleaded. Thus, the depth in picas will equal the number of lines.)

1. CPP x line width = CPL (characters per line)

   2 x 35 = 70 CPL

2. CPL x depth of proposed copy = Total characters (Remember, this is assuming that you are setting 12-point type.)

   70 x 105 = 7,350 characters

3. Typed lines needed will equal total characters divided by typewriter characters per line, thus:

   $\frac{7350}{60}$ = 122.5 or 123 typewritten lines

If you had decided to use a typeface that is 12-point leaded 1 (12/1), you would have to compensate for the difference in point size including leading and the depth in picas. The CPP remains the same, so step one remains the same.

2. $\frac{\text{Number of lines in picas}}{\text{point size + leading}}$ x 12 = Lines of type

   $\frac{105 \times 12}{(12 + 1)}$ = 96.92 or 97 lines of type

3. Lines of type x CPL = Total characters

   97 x 70 = 6790 total characters

4. Typed lines needed will equal total characters divided by typewriter characters per line.

   $\frac{6790}{60}$ = 113.16 or 113 typewritten lines

Marking the Copy

Typesetters can't read minds, although sometimes they come very close. In order for your instructions to get across to the typesetter, you must mark your copy indicating type style, size, and any other information pertinent to how you want your finished typeset copy to look. Some necessary indications are:

- Name of type style (font or typeface—Garamond, Helvetica, Bodoni Bookface, etc.)
- Weight of the typeface (bold, medium, light, etc.)
- Point size and leading.
- Column width and depth.
- Special instructions such as flush right or flush left, etc.

On the first page of copy, indicate any instructions pertaining to all copy. For instance, if you want all copy to be flush left, this is the place to indicate it. For each block of copy requiring a separate notation, indicate that instruction in the left margin, directly next to the relevant copy.

Designate your type style, point size, leading, margin format and column by using a shorthand notation understood by most typesetters and printers.

First, draw a horizontal line with a vertical line crossing it left of center:

- In the upper right quarter, indicate type style and weight (medium, bold, italic, etc.)

- In the upper left quarter, specify point size.

- In the lower left quarter, indicate leading.

10 Helvetica
14 [18 picas]

- In the lower right quarter, indicate margin format and column width.

10	Helvetica
14	Centered

10	Helvetica
14	[18 picas

- Special column designations should be indicated if needed (center, stacked, etc.). Flush right/left is indicated by [or] , ragged right/left by or .

Times 12 point

Suppose you want to set 3000 characters of original copy in 12-point Souvenir Medium (CPP = 2.3). You know that your copy width when set in type will be 20 picas. How many lines of copy will you have? You decide to lead your copy 1-point—what will the depth be in picas?

Times 10 point

Suppose you want to set 3000 characters of original copy in 12-point Souvenir Medium (CPP = 2.3). You know that your copy width when set in type will be 20 picas. How many lines of copy will you have? You decide to lead your copy 1-point—what will the depth be in picas?

Palatino 12 point

Suppose you want to set 3000 characters of original copy in 12-point Souvenir Medium (CPP = 2.3). You know that your copy width when set in type will be 20 picas. How many lines of copy will you have? You decide to lead your copy 1-point—what will the depth be in picas?

Exhibit 3.3 —Typeset Copy

As you can see, a difference in one-point can save considerable space (Times 12 versus Times 10). Changing type faces, even if you keep it in the same point size, can also save space (Palatino 12 versus Times 12).

Case Study: Associated Products Corporation

Assignment 9.1: Copyfitting

Suppose you want to set 3,000 characters of original copy in 12-point Souvenir Medium (CPP = 2.3). You know that your copy width when set in type will be 20 picas. How many lines of copy will you have? You decide to lead your copy 1-point—what will the depth be in picas?

Assignment 9.2: Copyfitting

Suppose your depth is to be 40 picas and the total number of characters in your original copy is still 3,000. You are going to set your type in 10-point Times Roman leaded 2. What will your line width be in picas?

Assignment 9.3: Copyfitting

You have to fill a space 25 picas wide by 90 picas deep. Determine now many lines at 60 characters each you will have to type to fill the ad space. (Assume that you will have your copy set in Goudy 12 point, unleaded.)

Use the information provided in Chapter 3 for the following assignments.

Assignment 9.4: Print Ad

As part of an overall promotional package for APC/NEA, including television, radio and now print, you are to write copy for a full-page magazine ad to be run in four color. The theme should be the same as or linked to the theme you developed for the radio and television spots to add continuity to your promotion. You will need to come up with a headline, visual idea, and body copy. You may or may not choose to include a kicker or some other standard ending device. Include a thumbnail sketch in the upper right-hand corner of your copy indicating placement of headline, visual, and body copy.

Assignment 9.5: Print Ad

Restructure your full-page, four-color magazine ad for newspaper. The visual will be in black and white—the size of the finished ad is to be 5 x 9 inches. The typeface will be 12-point Goudy Oldstyle with 1-point leading. You first need to determine if your original copy will now fit in this reduced space. It is up to you to come up with a copy block shape and size. If you need to trim your copy to fit the space, do so. If you need to rethink the visual and come up with another one, do that too; but remember to try to keep your components consistent. The format for the copy is the same as for the last assignment. Attach your formulas for working out the copyfitting to the copy. Include all measurements. Be sure to include a thumbnail on the copy.

CHAPTER 10

Speeches & Presentations

There are two times in your life when you are totally alone: When you die, and just before you give a speech.

Anonymous

Speech writing is putting words into someone else's mouth; and that's not an easy task. It requires that you know the person for whom you are writing intimately. You need to know his or her style of speaking, body language, tone of voice, speech patterns, and, most importantly, personality. When you write a speech, you become the person you are writing for, and, to an extent, that person will become you at the moment he or she begins to speak your words.

Thus, speech writing is a truly collaborative effort. It requires the absolute cooperation of all parties involved. Think of famous speeches you have heard or read: Patrick Henry's "Give me liberty or give me death," Winston Churchill's "Blood, sweat and tears," John F. Kennedy's "Ask not what your country can do for you," and Martin Luther King's "I have a dream." Often, famous speeches such as these were written by the speakers themselves, but just as often, they were collaborative efforts by the speakers, professional speech writers, and others with valuable input into the process. As in other forms of public relations writing—*everybody has something to say about what you write.*

Types of Speeches

The public relations speech is as varied as are the purposes to which the speech will be put. In fact, speeches are usually classified by purpose.

- A speech to inform. This type of speech seeks to clarify, instruct, or demonstrate.
- A speech to persuade. This is designed to convince or influence and often carries a call to action.
- A speech to entertain. This type covers almost everything else including celebrations, eulogies, and dinner speeches.

The type of speech you use will be determined largely by the topic and the audience. The method of delivery and the degree to which the speech relies on audio-visual aids will also depend on these factors.

Modes of delivery

There are four basic modes of delivering a speech:

- extemporaneous delivery
- impromptu delivery
- scripted delivery
- memorized delivery

In the first two types, the public relations writer is responsible primarily for the research and compilation of information, usually in outline form. The speaker then studies the notes carefully and is theoretically prepared to speak knowledgeably and fluently on the topic. Speeches to be delivered from script or from memory can be written entirely by the public relations writer. For all modes of speaking, the primary responsibility of the public relations practitioner, after the speech is prepared, is to coach the speaker. This means, of course, that you must know how to give a good speech yourself. If you don't, and many public relations people don't, find someone who can and have them coach the speaker. This often means hiring outside professionals to do the job. It may be costly, but in the long run, it is well worth the effort.

Preparation and Writing

Preparation is the most important element in any type of presentation. Although some of us are able to speak "off the cuff," it is a dangerous habit to get into. Think of the politicians who have lost elections because of candid "off the record" remarks or unwise ad libs. It is extremely important that you prepare in advance everything that you will say and do during a presentation. Don't leave anything to chance.

The "nuts and bolts" of an effective presentation include:

- Specific purpose;
- Clear understanding of your audience;
- Well organized ideas;
- Adequate support;
- Effective delivery.

Specifying Your Purpose

Keep two important principles in mind. First, the speech should be results oriented.Think of the effect you want it to have on the audience. Decide whether you want your audience to be persuaded, informed, or feel entertained by your presentation.

Second, the purpose of your presentation should be the basis for all the other decisions you make. This means that the way you organize your ideas, the kind of audio-visual support materials you use, even the way you deliver the presentation, will hinge on why you are giving it in the first place.

Analyzing Your Audience

Your presentation is given for your listeners. Even if you think it is the best presentation you have ever given, if it doesn't affect them, it will have failed.

Analyze the occasion: the reason why this group is together at this time and what they expect to hear from you.

Analyze the people: what experience and knowledge about the subject do they bring to your presentation? What is their attitude toward the subject? Toward you?

Organizing Your Speech

Good organization lets your audience know that you know what you're talking about. There's nothing worse than a seemingly confused speaker. Not only do you lose credibility, but you also waste valuable time. Remember, no one will sit still for long—especially if you're not making sense. And, the only way to make sense is to be organized.

It is worth repeating that the best way to organize a speech is to think of its *purpose*. Use that purpose as the basis for deciding what goes in your speech, how you structure it, what data you present, even for deciding your style or wording.

Here is a typical speech format.

I. Introduction

A. Attention-getter—Tell people why they should listen.

B. Establish rapport—Create a bond with your audience. Show them what you have in common.

C. Preview—Tell people what they are going to hear.

II. Body/discussion

A. Main points, arranged logically (usually in order of importance).

B. Data supporting each main point.

III. Conclusion

A. Review—Summarize the key points the audience has heard.

B. Memorable statement—Create a desired "frame of mind" that will stay with the audience.

C. Call for action (if applicable).

Building a speech is like building anything else. You've got to have a solid foundation. It helps if what you build has a look of continuity, coherence and completion. No one likes a structure that looks haphazard or loosely constructed. For speechmakers, a solid structure implies a solid idea.

You can see from this outline that in speeches, it pays to be repetitious. Tell people what you are going to do, do it, then tell them what you have done.

Most writers find it easier to work on the **body** of the presentation first, before thinking upa snappy introduction and conclusion.

The body of a speech may be developed in a number of ways:

- Chronological—Organized by time. For example, cover first this year's events, then next year's.
- Spacial—Organized by direction. For instance, talk about your company's development as it moved from the East Coast, across the nation, to the West Coast.
- Topical—Organized by topic. Cover ideas that are related to each other together, then move on to the next set of ideas.
- Cause and effect—Organized by need/fulfillment. Describe "what we need" and then "how to get it."

- Problem/solution—Organized by question/answer. Describe the problem and then the solution, or vice versa.

Pay attention to how you word the main points you want to make. Work for parallelism, balance and good transitions between main points. (Notice how the five types of organization described above begin with parallel openings. Notice, too, that they are balanced both in length and sentence structure.)

With the body of the presentation in hand, attack the **introduction**. A good introduction is relevant to the audience and occasion, involves the audience personally, positively disposes them towards your presentation, and stimulates them.

A good introduction does not begin with "Today I want to talk to you about...," nor does it necessarily mean tell a joke. Good introductions can be questions, unusual facts, good examples, stories, illustrations, metaphors, analogies, or any one of a number of other devices.

Now to the **conclusion** of your presentation. Remember the advice: Tell them what you are going to do, do it, then tell them what you have done. The conclusion is the time to tell them what you have done. You should summarize, repeat or reiterate the main points of your presentation. Finish with a memorable statement that makes the purpose of the speech clear and positions the audience firmly on your side. (Note: You do not have to say "thank you.")

Supporting Your Ideas

Look at every presentation as though it were a plant. The roots are the good ideas you have. The stalk or stem is the organization of those ideas so that they flow well and fit nicely. Now for the fine detail: the pattern of the leaves, the shape and texture of the flower.

The detail or support you use to fill out your presentation must be sufficient to ensure that your listeners know precisely what you mean but should not be so overwhelming that you lose your audience in detail.

Your support must be relevant to your listeners. If it makes no sense to them you will fail to get their attention, gain their good will or persuade them to your view. Use any kind of support that is appropriate to your purpose and ideas. Facts and statistics are almost mandatory for many business presentations. Examples and illustrations, however, can often make those hard numbers "come alive." Quotations from a source your listeners respect can add proof that what you are saying is true. Analogies and metaphors can often be used to make concrete that which is abstract by bringing the abstraction down to human terms. Preachers use these two devices all the time. Remember, use enough support and detail to do the job but no more.

Delivery

Finally, you are standing in front of your listeners. Now it is your job to make your ideas come alive.

Here is the secret of effective delivery: thorough preparation and lots of practice.

You cannot deliver a presentation effectively if you don't know what you want to say. That means preparation. The only way you can become an expert is to practice. There is no shortcut!

Okay. You are thoroughly prepared and well practiced. Now you must stand and do two things. First, stick to what you have practiced. Don't get distracted. Don't "throw away" your prepared presentation for an impromptu effort. Second, keep your eyes on your audience. Look at them.

Summary Sheet

One of the best ways to organize is to develop a summary sheet. Include at least the following information:

- **The audience:** Ages, size, educational background, demographic characteristics?
- **The Purpose:** Inform, persuade, reinforce attitudes, entertain "After listening to my speech, audience members will..."
- **Organization of the Speech:** Chronological, spatial, topical, cause and effect, problem-solving?
- **Supporting materials:** Statistics, wuotations, case histories, analogies, hypothetical illustrations, anecdotes?
- **Purpose of introduction and conclusion:** Gain interest, create need for listening, summarize, call for action?
- **List of visual aids:** Which media, what content, integration into speech?

Exhibit 10.1—Summary Sheet

Watch their reactions to what you say. Don't get engrossed in your script. In fact, try not to use a script. Use an outline or brief notes.

Don't get engrossed in your audio-visual material. Watch the audience, not the screen. Even if your are using 35 mm slides in a black room, look out at your audience. You won't be able to see them well, but it is important they get the feeling you can.

Another piece of advice: look relaxed, even if you aren't. Smile, frown, move your arms, look around the room at everyone. Try to feel as though you are in the middle of a lively conversation with a group of friends. It will do wonders for your delivery.

Remember:

- **Specific purpose**: without it you're lost.
- **Analyze audience**: your listeners are the key to your success.
- **Organize ideas**: your presentation must make sense.
- **Good support**: give your ideas vigor and import.
- **Effective delivery**: make your ideas come alive.

Using Audio-visual Support

We live in an increasingly visual society today. Most of us watch TV or go to the movies. Our magazines and newspapers are increasingly visually oriented today. It's hard for an audience to maintain attention, even with the most persuasive of speakers, without something to look at. Used as integrated components of a speech, audio-visual materials can help keep the audience's attention and add valuable information.

Use audio-visual support for impact—to develop audience interest and hold its attention. Use it for effectiveness—to help your listeners remember more, longer. Don't use it simply because it is there. Use it only if it enhances your presentation.

Briefly, if you do use audio-visual support:

- Be sure it adds to your presentation.
- Do not let the support control the presentation. Your ideas must come first.
- Be sure to rehearse the presentation with the audio-visual materials. Learn how to use them.
- Do not talk to the visuals, talk to the audience.

- Talk louder—you are competing with the visuals for audience attention.
- Stand clear—remember, visuals must be seen to be useful.

The most common support materials used with speeches are:

- **Visual support**: Charts, graphs, diagrams, samples, handouts, photographs.
- **Audio support**: Recordings.
- **Audio-visual support**: Films, videotape, slide/tape programs.

Slide Shows

A good slide presentation can add zip and clarity to information that may be otherwise dull. It requires that you be well organized, know your audience and follow a few simple rules.

Rule 1: Define your objective. Be sure you know what you want to accomplish; what changes you want to take place in your listeners; what behavior you want to affect.

Rule 2: Analyze your audience. Are they ignorant or expert? Do you aim for the "lowest common denominator?" The middle? The top? The more you know about them, the easier it is to make that decision.

Rule 3: Work from an outline. Keep it simple and make it a concise summary of the major points and supporting materials needed to reach your objective with this audience.

Rule 4: Decide what mood or treatment you want. A light, humorous treatment may mean cartoons and a comic narration. Are you going to threaten? Cajole? Be very low-keyed? Mood makes a difference in how you use color and pacing.

Rule 5: Write a script, if you plan to use one.

Rule 6: Plan your slides.

- Convert material designed originally for publication to slide format.
- Use a series of slides or charts, disclosed progressively, to build up complex ideas.
- Keep all copy and symbols simple and legible. Projected letters should be at least two inches high and one-half inch wide.
- Make all copy slides short and to the point. Include no more than

15 or 20 words or 25 or 30 pieces of data per slide.

- Never use more than fifteen words on a slide.
- Limit each slide or chart to one main idea.
- Keep slides simple and bold. One idea per slide.
- Make your slides legible from a distance. The number of feet from presenter to rearmost viewer, multiplied by .04, is the minimum height of a letter projected on a screen. (30 x .04 = 1.20 feet)
- Use charts and graphs rather than tables. Tables almost always look complicated and confusing.
- Use variety in layout, color, charting and graphics for change of pace.
- Avoid mathematical formulas or equations on slides.
- Keep photographs uncluttered.
- Plan to keep moving. Leave slides up only long enough for the audience to read. Remember, they are there to supplement and support your words and ideas.
- Enlist the aid of a competent audio-visual specialist.

Rule 7: Edit your slide presentation.

- Are all major points covered?
- Does the content of each slide fit the narration?
- Are all slides legible?
- Are colors bold and effective?
- Does each slide depict one idea and one idea only?
- Is there good continuity from slide to slide?
- Does the program add up to form a visually coherent and pleasing presentation?

Rule 8: Rehearse, rehearse, rehearse.

Rule 9: Be sure to visit the room where you will be making the presentation to make sure the projector is there and in working order. Run through your program to make sure all is as you want it.

Rule 10: Slide programs are almost always given in darkened rooms.

The only other light will be the one on the lectern you use. That means you must make a special effort to force yourself to look out into a blackened room at people you may be unable to see. Don't lose eye contact with them because they can see you just fine.

Handling the Q & As

Anticipation is the key to successful question and answer periods. If you're the type of speaker who has to have everything written out in advance, then Q & A is not for you. You need to know whether you can handle thinking, analyzing, and speaking off the cuff before you "throw yourself to the lions." The best hedge against blowing a Q & A session is practice. It's advisable to have someone who is familiar with the topic you cover in your presentation work with you on possible questions in advance. That way, you have at least some idea of what to expect when you face the real thing. The following advice will help you when you do.

1. Repeat the question or paraphrase it in your own words.
2. Make sure you understand the question before answering it. Seek clarification if necessary.
3. Don't lie, fabricate or distort. If you don't know the answer, say so—but do so from a position of strength, not weakness.
4. Refer to any visual aids that will help you answer the question.
5. Be concise—don't give another speech.
6. Don't allow a questioner to take you on tangents. Stick to the main points of your speech..
7. Don't allow an individual questioner to monopolize the Q & A session.

Case Study: Associated Products Corporation

Background for Speech Assignment

The corporate level group of Associated Products Corporation is considering a three-day retreat. The purpose of the retreat is to:

- "Energize" corporate staff;
- Delve into interpersonal issues affecting productivity (e.g. trust, openness, sensitivity, political power plays);
- Create increased group cohesiveness;
- Provide an opportunity for staff members to learn more about one another; and
- discuss long range corporate strategy in a relaxed setting.

The Company and Staff

Use previous background on the company. In addition, look at the following specifics about the corporate staff.

The corporate staff is composed of 48 people: 30 men and 18 women. APC prides itself on being young and innovative. The median age of the corporate staff is 34. Thirty percent have college degrees.

Members of the corporate staff have strong feelings (pro and con) about having a three-day retreat. Many have expressed the view that the retreat could turn into a "warm and fuzzy" group encounter.

APC has never gone on a company retreat. James Sutton, the president, recently read in an airline magazine that corporate retreats might be a good idea for some companies. He has passed the copy of the magazine on to all members of the staff. The following are excerpts from the magazine.

- Of the companies who have gone on company retreats, 70 percent report unqualified success; they are already planning next year's retreat.
- Some company officials return from the retreat as casualties. They learn things about themselves that may be traumatic.
- The best retreats are those that have an agenda.
- None of the companies reported allowing spouses to attend the retreat. And some spouses expressed concern about their mates attending the three-day retreat.

- Most of the companies (30 percent) reported using an outside consultant to design and "lead" the retreat.
- The 70 percent who report unqualified success point to such indices as: increased profits, increased staff commitment, healthier and more productive working climate, and lack of game playing and political maneuvering.
- Retreats are usually outside the city where the home office is located (within a two-hour driving radius).
- All corporate officers surveyed agreed that, if held, the retreat must be compulsory, not voluntary.
- Retreats cannot "cure" a sick company. Sick companies tend to return from retreats sicker than they were before. "Healthy" companies, or those on the road towards health, tend to return from retreats healthier.
- Successful retreats are predicated upon individuals opening up and disclosing those issues which trouble them.
- The average cost of a retreat in 1980 was $80.00 per staff member per day.
- Many companies view a retreat as a fringe benefit for employees.
- Progressive, as opposed to conservative, companies believe in the value of retreats.
- Successful retreats require advance preparation within the corporate staff itself. Staff members approach the retreat with the "right" attitude.
- Over the last ten years, the number of companies which have held retreats has declined slightly.

Assignment 10.1: Speech

You head a task force that will review the pros and cons of holding a corporate retreat. Present the case that APC should go on the retreat, *or* present the case that APC should not go on the retreat.

You will present your speech to the corporate staff of which you are a member. The staff will vote after hearing all proposals.

Your presentation should be 10 minutes in length and you can use any visual aids that you deem necessary. It will be delivered in the small company auditorium; amphitheater arrangement. Complete the Summary Worksheet that follows. It may also be used as a guide in preparing future presentations.

Summary Worksheet

Preliminary questions

I. What are the expectations of this audience?

Towards me?

Towards my topic?

Towards this specific situation (i.e. any extenuating circumstances which should be considered)?

II. How do I expect my audience to be affected by my presentation?

The general purpose of my presentation will be to inform, persuade, reinforce certain ideas, entertain?

The specific thesis: After listening to my speech, the audience will...?

The body of the speech

III. What is the best structure to follow given I and II above?

Should my presentation be arranged chronologically? spatially? topically?

By cause and effect? By problem/solution?

The structure I have chosen is the best in this particular situation because...

IV. What are the three or four main points suggested by the specific structure?

A.

B.

C.

D.

V. How will I support the main points?

Will I use statistics, examples, analogies, case studies, direct quotations?

A will be supported by:

B will be supported by:

C will be supported by:

D will be supported by:

VI. How should I adapt my language and word choice to suit audience expectations?

To what extent should I use jargon and buzz words?

To what extent should I be conscious of defining certain words?

VII. Should I use any visual aids?

What should be visualized?

How will it be visualized?

Why is it being visualized?

VIII. How should I introduce the speech?

Why should my audience listen to this message?

How will my audience benefit by listening to me?

How can I make my audience want to listen?

You should listen to me because...

IX. How should I conclude the speech?

How do I relate the conclusion to the main points I have covered?

In conclusion...

Once you have completed the worksheet, write the speech. Begin with the body of the speech and leave the introduction and conclusion until last.

CHAPTER 11

Working with Printers

Knowledge is of two kinds. We know a subject ourselves, or we know where we can find information upon it.

Samual Johnson

The relationship between the writer-designer, typesetter, and printer is supposed to be a symbiotic one. This might lead you to believe that everyone in the trio gets along. Don't believe it for a minute. Typesetters and printers are professionals in their own rights, and, as such, are very likely to have their own, often very different ideas, of what you need.

The trick to working successfully with typesetters and printers is to know what your are talking about. There's no substitute for knowledge. The key is to try out several typesetters and printers and work with those who not only give you the best deal, but who also are willing to give you guidance. This is not an easy process, but it does pay off in a lower frustration factor in the long run. Knowing how to spec type and select the proper typeface will help you out with typesetters. They are generally willing to do exactly what you say, no matter what it looks like when finished. Their job is to set in type what you have given them as copy according to your written and verbal explanations. Well-marked copy will go a long way toward alleviating any misunderstandings between you and your typesetter. You have to know a bit more about the printing process, however, in order to get along with your printer. Every writer can tell you horror stories about printers who, after seemingly understanding exactly what *you* want, proceed to print exactly what *they* want. This is not to say that it is hard to get along with printers. It simply means that you have to know what you want and be able to explain it to someone who knows printing inside-out.

Printers can be an invaluable aid in selecting papers, inks, printing methods, bindings and so on. You can get what you want if you know how to ask for it.

Printing Processes

Many writers simply entrust the choice of printing methods to the printer. Most collateral pieces and many newsletters are simply offset printed, which is one of the fastest and cheapest methods to get good quality printing today. Other, quick-print methods will usually result is a loss of quality. If you want to impress your readers, use a quality offset technique. Other, more detailed printing jobs, such as embossing or special paper shapes, may require specialty printing. Be advised that specialty printing is costly. Make sure that you are willing to bear the extra cost before you decide on that gold-foil stamp on the cover of your new brochure. Although there are a number of printing processes available to you, probably the two you will have most contact with will be **offset lithography** and **quick printing**.

Offset Lithography

The most common printing process used today is offset lithography. The process is based on the principle that oil and water don't mix. In offset lithography, the nonprinting area of the printing plate accepts water but not ink, while the image, or printing, area accepts ink but not water. During the printing process, both water and ink are applied to the plate as it revolves. It is named *offset* printing because the plate isn't a reverse image as in most printing processes. Instead, the plate transfers its positive image to an offset cylinder made of rubber (which reverses the image), and from there to the paper (see **Exhibit 11.1**). Because the plate never comes in contact with the paper, it can be saved and used again and again, saving cost on projects that have to be reprinted periodically—unless, of course, you make changes.

Most PR documents will be printed this way. It is relatively inexpensive, compared to other processes, and it results in a high-quality image. Although small press runs of 1,000 or less can be made using offset lithography, it is especially cost-effective for larger runs, since presses are capable of cranking out hundreds of copies a minute.

Quick Copy/Print

The so-called *quick copy* or *quick print* process involves two methods of reproduction.

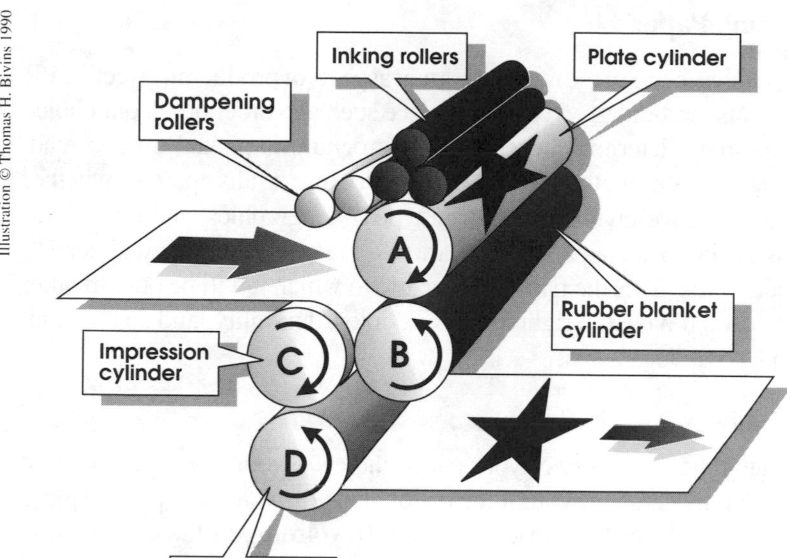

Exhibit 11.1—Offset Printing

Offset gets its name from the indirect, "offsetting" printing process, in which the printing plate's image is "offset" to a rubber blanket which puts the ink on the paper. Notice how the type and image go from positive to negative to positive again.

Quick print involves a small cylinder press using paper printing plates. The plates are created using a photo-electrostatic proccss that results in a raised image created with toner (much like the toner used in photocopy machines). This raised image takes the ink and is imprinted directly onto the paper.

Quick copy is really xerography, and has made tremendous inroads into the quick print area. The larger model photocopiers used in this process can crank out multiple copies, collate, and often staple them.

Neither of these processes is useful for two-color work, but both are cheap and fast. If you are going to use quick copy, reserve it for rush projects or those that won't suffer from single-color xerography. Be aware, also, that there can be major differences between photocopiers, and even between copies run on the same machine. A copier that ran your last job beautifully may not repeat the same quality the next time if the toner hasn't been changed recently. Don't be afraid to ask for a test print of your most difficult page to make sure the blacks are really black and there is no fade out on any part of the page.

Choosing Paper

Paper choice is one of the most important aspects of producing effective PR documents, particularly a collateral piece such as a brochure. Your choice of paper may determine whether your brochure is picked up and read, whether it lasts more than one or two days before it falls apart, or whether it even works well with your chosen type style, graphics, and ink color.

When choosing a paper, there are two major criteria you will need to consider. First, does the paper suit the use to which it will be put? In other words, does it have the right look, feel, color, durability, and so on. And, second, what does it cost?

Suitability

In judging the suitability of your paper choice to your job, you must first determine the nature of your information. Do you want your printed piece to last and be passed from reader to reader? If you do, you'll want to choose a durable stock that will take constant opening, closing and general handling without tearing. Some pieces are printed on relatively cheap and lightweight stock and are meant to be thrown away soon after reading (flyers, one-shot announcements, etc.). Others need to be more permanent. A brochure outlining company benefits to employees, for example, is one that probably will be kept and used over and over again. It will need to be on a heavier and more durable stock. A company magazine printed in four-color will need a durable paper since the publication will probably be passed on to other readers.

Aside from durability, three other factors need to be considered in judging the suitability of your paper: weight, texture, and color.

Weight

Papers come in various weights. Weight is determined by taking 500 sheets of a given type of paper and weighing it. Although a heavier weight usually indicates a thicker stock, it doesn't have to. One 25-pound bond paper may be thicker than another. Likewise, a newsletter printed on one 60-pound stock may be lighter and less durable than another stock. The best way to judge weight versus thickness is to handle the paper for each type of stock personally. Most printers have hundreds of samples of paper stock and can help you select the proper weight and thickness you want for your job.

Texture

Texture is also an important consideration when choosing a paper. Heavily textured paper may impart a feeling of quality or a feeling of roughness, depending on the paper stock and the method of manufacture. Basically, paper breaks down into two broad categories for texture: *matt finish* and *coated finish.* Matt finish ranges from a paper with a rather smooth but nonglossy surface to heavily textured paper. *Coated stock* refers to any paper that is "slick" or "glossy." Again, the range is considerable. Photographs often reproduce better on coated stock, which is what most magazines use. On the other hand, using a matt stock will soften the color and give a photograph an entirely different feeling. Some heavily textured stock may not take ink well but may be perfect for foil stamping or embossing. The best way to tell if your idea will work on a certain texture stock is to ask the printer, look at some choices, and come to an informed decision.

Color

Paper color has to complement all the other graphic elements of your collateral piece: typeface, ink color, photographs and artwork. It will also set the mood of your piece. Color preference is a very personal matter. Remember, however, that you are producing pieces to be read by certain target publics who may or may not like your color choice. Thus, to an extent, color choice is a matter of gauging your intended audience's reaction to it. Research has shown, for instance, that business people will not respond to questionnaires printed on hot-pink paper (not much of a surprise). They will respond to beige and various shades of white, but respond very little to pale blue and green. All colors carry connotations for most people. You need to stay away from outrageous combinations and any color you judge might not get the response you want from your information piece.

Cost

This may well be the determining factor in your paper choice. Don't despair, though, just because your budget may be limited. Paper comes in thousands of weights, colors and textures; and one of them will fit your cost restrictions. Also remember that a few extra dollars on a good grade paper may well pay off in the long run by impressing your readership.

Selecting Paper for Computer Laser Printing

Paper is probably the least thought about part of laser printing. Most of us simply opt for whatever is handy. The fact is, some papers are made specifically for laser printers, and some papers definitely should be avoided.

Ask yourself three questions when you pick laser printer paper.

- Will the laser copy be used as a finished piece or for reproduction?
- Does the paper say what you want it to say? In other words, what is its look and feel?
- Does the paper run well in your printer?

Keeping in mind the paper specifications presented earlier in this chapter, the following rules of thumb should help you select the proper paper for your needs and your printer.

- Brighter paper reproduces well on laser printers. (This doesn't mean *whiter* paper; there are varying degrees of brightness even among white papers.) Brighter papers are also good for reproduction masters. In fact, several manufacturers make papers specifically for laser printer output that will be used for reproduction. Also, since it's hard to predict the degree of darkness of your printer, the brighter the paper, the more contrast you're likely to have between the print and the paper. In general, avoid colored paper; however, some interesting effects can be obtained with lighter colors such as gray and beige.
- Stay away from heavily textured paper. The heavier the texture, the more broken your type will look, because it will be harder for the toner to adhere to the paper's surface. Texture also affects any large, dark areas such as screens and display type. Some texture, like that found in bond paper and linen stock, is fine. The trick here is to experiment.
- Avoid heavy papers like cover stock, generally 90 pounds or more, unless you like removing jammed paper from your printer. On the other hand, extremely light papers, such as onion skin, may stick to the rollers or jam as they feed into the printer. Don't experiment much here. Just settle for a text-weight paper (generally around 60 pounds) and consign the choice of cover paper to your commercial printer.
- Use a fairly opaque paper, especially if the laser-printed copy is to be your final version. If you use a paper with high opacity, be sure it isn't also heavily textured.
- Don't expect heavily textured papers to retain their texture. Unlike offset presses, laser printers flatten the paper as it moves through the printer. In most cases, any texture will be lost.
- By the same token, don't use embossed or engraved papers in your laser printer since they might jam the mechanism and will flatten out anyway.

- Make sure your paper is heat resistant. Since laser printers work in temperatures of around 400° F, certain letterhead inks may melt or stick and any metal or plastic will certainly ruin your printer. Above all, don't use acetate in your laser printer unless it has been specifically designed for your particular printer.

Choosing Ink

Choosing an ink can be a nightmare for the novice. Even the most experienced designers often have a short list of their favorite inks. Inks come in virtually limitless color combinations. And, each color will be affected by the paper it is printed on. Coated (slick) paper will result in brighter colors while matt finish paper will soften the color. The texture of the paper also affects ink color, as does using colored paper.

There are no easy ways to learn what inks to use. The best way for a beginner to choose an ink is to look at other work done using the same ink/paper combination. Also, obtain a copy of the Pantone Color Matching System. It's really just a color sample book, much like the ones you see when you pick out a house paint, but it is the most commonly used system among printers and designers. You'll be amazed at the variety of colors available to you. Don't be embarrassed, however, to stick to the basic colors to begin with. They are usually the safest to work with. Your printer will usually have a Pantone book you can use while there. Pantone's address is on the sample book. Just write them and ask about obtaining your own copy.

If you don't want any surprises, ask to see samples of work your printer has done using different papers and inks. Most printers take great pride in their work and will be more than happy to share it with you.

Color Printing

Color brings an added dimension to any publication, whether it's as simple as a second color to help accent, unify or dress out a publication, or as complete as full-color. To use color effectively, you should have a rudimentary understanding of how the different color processes operate.

Spot Color

Spot color is the placement of a second color (black—or whatever the primary inking color—being the *first*) in a publication. (Note that in printing, black is counted as a color.) Unless you're using a multicolor press, applying the second color means an additional press run. That translates to more ink, materials, handling and press time and money.

In two-color printing, two sets of printing plates are made, one for each color run. Often, a designer will use the second color for the art and graphic highlights—such as dropped-initial letters—and use the black (or other first color) for the type. This also means that you have to create two originals, one for the black plate and one for the second color. This is not an easy process for most people and is usually left to a designer or printer. Check with your printer first and see what their needs are regarding two-color printing.

Process Color

Process color or **four color** is used for reproducing full-color artwork or photography. This illusion of full color is accomplished by optically mixing the three primary colors—yellow, red (actually **magenta**) and blue (called **cyan**)—along with black. Four color plates are shot through a screen to reduce solid areas to printable, graduated dot patterns. Because each color is shot through a slightly different angle screen, the screened halftone of each blends through the overlaid dot patterns.

During printing, each color is applied separately, one plate at a time and one color atop the others. The quality of this four-color overprinting method largely depends upon the quality of the original work, the quality of the cameras, plates and printing press used, and upon the skills and professionalism of those who operate the equipment. Process color is best left to your printer to handle for you. As always, ask in advance.

Binding

With binding, as with everything else, if you want to know what to expect, ask your printer and seek out samples on your own. Basically, there are two types of binding: that used for relatively thin publications such as magazines and pamphlets, and that used for thicker publications such as books. We'll only discuss those most applicable to public relations output here.

Regardless of what you are binding, it will probably be organized into **signatures**. Signatures are groupings of pages printed on both sides, usually sixteen to a signature, but sometimes less, as long as they're in multiples of four (pages printed for binding are usually printed four to a two-sided sheet of paper).

After signatures have been collated, they may be bound. Among the most common bindings that public relations people are likely to use are *saddle stitching*, *perfect binding*, or *spiral binding*. More traditional forms of binding, such as *case binding* (for hardcover books) are reserved for publications you want to last longer than you.

***Saddle stitching** is a simple, inexpensive procedure that nests the signatures atop one another and drives two to three staples through the spine and cover of the publication. Magazines and annual reports are most often bound this way.*

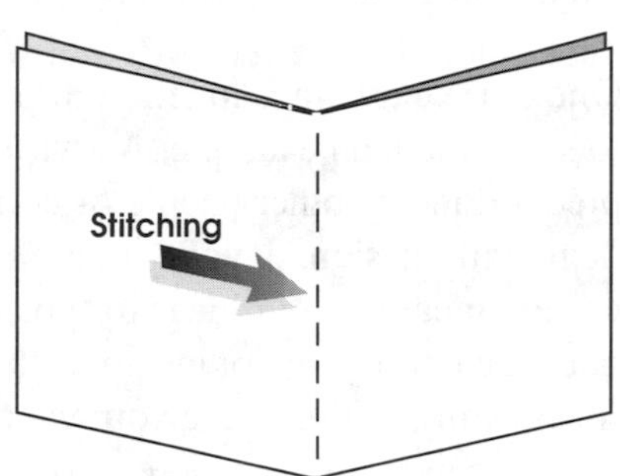

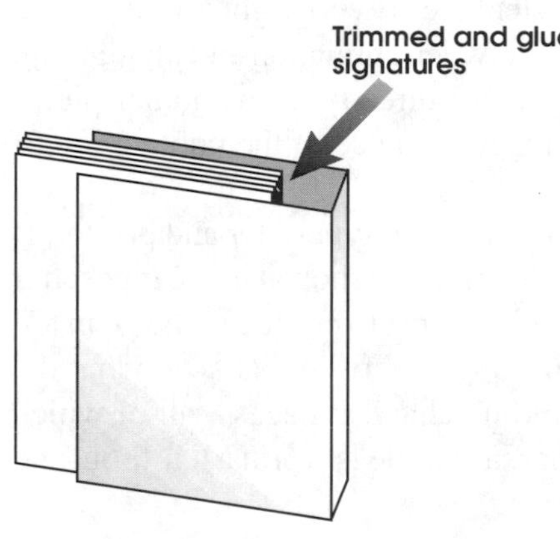

*Publications that are expected to receive a great deal of use and/or be around for a while are more likely to be perfect bound. In **perfect binding**, the backs of the collated signatures are trimmed or ground off and dense adhesive is applied. While it's still sticky, a bonding/lining is placed atop the adhesive and the cover is glued on. The adhesive maintains its flexible bonding strength for a long time. Most paperback books and some hardcover books are perfect bound. Hefty magazines and annual reports are sometimes bound this way as well.*

***Spiral binding** doesn't look all that good, but it does have the benefit of opening flat. Any reference publication would benefit from spiral binding. Holes are drilled or punched through the gutter of the publication after the signatures have been collated and trimmed, and either wire or plastic is inserted or "spun" through the holes.*

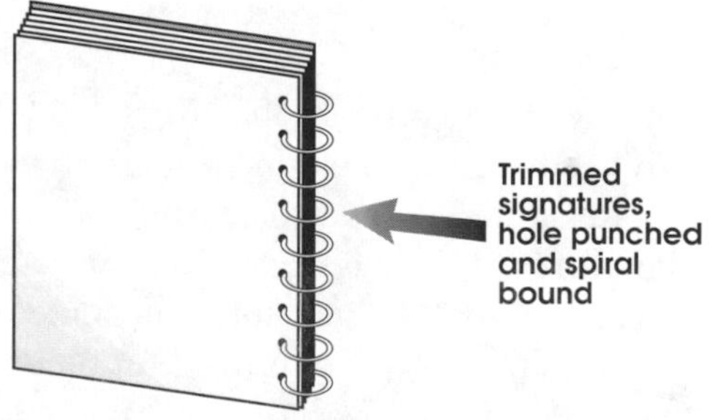

Most quick printers can do saddle stitching and spiral binding; however, only larger printers will be able to do perfect binding.

Swipe Files

One of the best ways to tell your printer or typesetter what you want is to show them an example. A **swipe file** is a collection of your favorite pieces done by other people or companies. They will help you a great deal with design, layout ideas and writing style, as well as with communicating your ideas to typesetters and printers. You may find a particular brochure, for instance, that is exactly the right size and design for the information piece you want to produce. You may decide to use similar paper, ink color, or even design. Most graphic artists, designers, and printers use ideas generated from a variety of sources. However, don't plagiarize your source. Don't steal the artwork right off the source brochure. Be careful to differentiate between emulation and plagiarism. If you do decide that you must "borrow" directly from another piece, obtain permission from its originator in advance of the publication of your piece.

Keep a swipe file of samples to show your typesetter and printer. If you find a piece that you would like to emulate, show it to the typesetter and printer to get an idea how much it will cost to produce. They can tell you what the type is, whether your copy will fit in that size, what the paper stock is, weight, color ink, and mechanical needs—all of which will affect the price. For the beginner, a sample is worth a ten-thousand word explanation.

CHAPTER 12

Public Relations Writing & the Computer

And now I see with eye serene
The very pulse of the machine.

Wordsworth

Every day in the United States, and around the world for that matter, hundreds of thousands of publications are created for and by organizations. These publications are aimed at a variety of audiences: employees, shareholders, members, volunteers, communities, and countless others, and come in dozens of shapes and sizes—newsletters, brochures, magazines, annual reports, pamphlets, booklets, posters, flyers, and direct mail pieces are just a few.

Anyone assuming the responsibilities of putting together a publication for an organization has quite a lot to learn. But, the availability of computer software and hardware designed specifically to augment that task has made the job, if not easy, at least manageable by a single person.

Probably the most revolutionary invention of the last century has been the computer. Scarcely fifty years ago, a computer able to do the simplest calculations took up an entire room. Today, even the most complex work can be done at your desk. When the microcomputer became commonplace only a very few years ago, it seems that life changed for millions of people. For the publishing industry, however, the most significant change followed invention of the hardware itself. The microcomputer changed the way we do nearly everything; page-layout software programs changed the way we think about and execute publications.

One of the earliest, some say the first, page-layout programs was *PageMaker*, invented by Paul Brainerd (now president of Aldus Corporation) and a handful of friends. Its original target audience was newspaper publishers. When that audience proved to be basically unreceptive, Brainerd turned to business. As it turned out, page-layout software revolutionized the way organizations thought about in-house publication. What once had to go through the traditional writing, editing, typesetting, pasteup, and printing processes could now be done in a fe, simple steps.

What is Desktop Publishing?

Although it took several long years for "desktop publishing" to catch on, it is now sweeping the country. The term **desktop publishing** is a bit of a misnomer because "publishing" involves much more than just the writing and laying out of a publication—which is all the software claims to do. True publishing entails *all* the printing and production stages, testing the product in its respective markets, creating a marketing and distribution plan, and the myriad other details that make publishing a complex and often risky business. What this software, and the increasingly sophisticated hardware, allow is the involvement of fewer intermediaries in the publication process.

As Paul Brainerd once quipped, "A desktop publishing program won't make you a designer." What the revolution in computer publishing has done is provide the writer, editor, and designer with another tool to better accomplish their respective jobs. *Without the knowledge and experience gained through a study of the basics of writing, editing and design, however, even the best computer hardware and software won't help you.*

The computer has made a tremendous difference. Word processing programs, once cumbersome and nearly impossible to work with, allow us to write, delete, move whole copy blocks, copy between files, index, outline and do other tasks that once took hours and days to accomplish on a typewriter. The computer has allowed writers and editors to facilitate their work through the on-line interchange of information (or exchange of disks). Editors can now edit on screen, and the writer can watch—if he or she or he has the nerve. And, the designer and artist can see their work come to life on the screen and have it instantly delivered into their hands as fast as a laser printer can print. Working together, writers, editors, designers, and artists have made the most of this revolutionary tool.

Desktop Publishing and Public Relations

The first great benefit of desktop publishing is actually a by-product of an earlier revolution—word processing. It is rare to find an office without a computer capable of word processing. The typewriter, while not obsolete, is used less and less. Word processing has allowed the public relations writer to write and edit copy, spell check the work, run grammar programs to check for style problems, and even apply readability formulas to the work.

How to Choose a Word Processing Program

Since word processing burst upon the scene, software programs have abounded. The earliest programs were cumbersome and quirky. Now they run the gamut from highly sophisticated to simple. With so many options, how do *we* choose a word processing program? Most of us just use the one that came with our computer. In fact, we tend to become almost religiously devoted to the first program we learned. The reason is that it is time consuming and often frustrating to have to learn a new program; and old habits, formed when we learned to use our first program, are hard to break. At the rate software is being updated, it's enough just to keep up with the changes in the program we are using.

Even if you learned on a particular program, there comes a time when it might not do everything you need. At $200 to $500 a whack, "trying out a program" could be a costly practice. Here are a few tips for deciding on just the right word processing program for you.

Pick a program that meets *all* of your needs, not just some of them. First, decide if ease of use is more important than certain special features. The more features incorporated into the program the more difficult it will be to learn and use. For example, do you need a program that indexes to write copy for a newsletter? Maybe you can find a program that will serve both purposes and still be easy to use.

If you are switching to a Macintosh-compatible word processing program from a PC-based program, or vice versa, be prepared for some changes in your software. Although many people can handle both systems with ease, most prefer one over the other. Not every program that works well on one is going to work as well on the other. If you are choosing a word processing software for your Macintosh based on how wonderful you thought the PC version was when you used it, think again. The *modus operandi* of the Macintosh computer is sufficiently different from that of the PC to render across-the-board program comparisons as useless as comparing apples and oranges (pun intended).

Pick a program that will not limit document size. Although you will probably be working with short documents, it pays to use a program that will allow long documents without tying up primary memory on your computer. For instance, some word processing programs use primary memory to store the file you are working on. Once you fill that primary memory, you're done—whether you like it or not. You are forced to save very small files to disk each time. Eventually, you're going to want to work on longer documents.

Pick a word processing program that is compatible with your page-layout program. This is a key feature of any word processing program for a desktop publisher, especially if you are going to be using your word processing program to produce the text for desktop publishing. Incompatibility can cause some real problems, and the fact that there are levels of incompatibility makes it even more difficult to match up your programs. For example, some word processing files can't be transferred at all to your page-layout program. Others will transfer, but only as "text" files. That means your original formatting is lost. Some display other quirks when transferred, such as losing everything bold or italicized. Read the documentation that came with you page-layout program. It will tell you not only which word processing programs work with it, but also which versions.

Compatibility problems also occur among other types of programs for many of the same reasons. One solution is to use software manufactured by the same company for everything. That's nice in theory, but most of us find that any given software company excels in one or two areas and not all of them. For instance, Aldus was the first into the market with a page-layout program, *PageMaker*. In fact, it became the industry standard for Apple computer systems. However, if you work on PCs, you might find other programs more responsive, such as *Ventura Publisher* from Xerox, or Quark *Xpress*. And although you might find some auxiliary programming from the same company for use with your page-layout program (Aldus also makes *FreeHand* for instance), it's not realistic to expect that you'll find them all. Some computer hardware comes with bundled software—packages containing "everything you'll need" for your new computer. Don't be fooled. There is no *one* company with a corner on the market for any given type of software.

Pick a program that is compatible with the programs of the other people who will be working with you. Nothing is more frustrating than knocking off a 3,000-word article only to discover your layout artist uses a page-layout program that won't accept your word processing program's format. Many word processing programs have built-in converters or translators allowing files written in one program format to be transferred to another format. However, formats don't usually convert *in toto* and leave many problems, such as no paragraph indents or missing type style commands in the newly converted version of the file.

Compatibility across hardware system types is also a problem, especially if you are working on a mixed system with some people using IBMs and others Macintoshes. If you are all linked through a local area network (LAN), sharing a system should cut down on transfer problems. Most networks support convert programs allowing you to use Macintosh-generated files on PCs and vice versa. In addition, there are hardware converters available that can transfer data among disparate system types or even disk sizes and formats, and the newest Macintosh comes with a built-in convert program allowing it to read directly from PC disk formats.

Read software reviews for straightforward information on the strengths and weaknesses of potential software purchases. A number of reputable magazines, including *PC World, BYTE, MacUser, Macworld, Publish* and many others, provide monthly reviews of both software and hardware. But don't just take the word of reviewers and friends. Obtain a test version and try it out. Many software companies will gladly send you a sample of their program to test out before you purchase. They are fairly complete as to the various functions they'll perform, but normally don't allow you to save your work. In other words, they give you just enough to whet your appetite.

Remember, selecting the right word processing program is one of the most important decisions you make as a desktop publisher. It pays to take your time. If you try to project your needs as far ahead as possible now, you will save yourself a lot of heartburn later on.

Design and Layout

One of the key changes desktop publishing has brought about is the speed with which any publication can be laid out. That's because in computer layout, all your tools are in your computer and your drafting or layout table and pasteup board are on your computer screen.

The techniques here are based primarily on Apple *Macintosh* hardware and Aldus *PageMaker* page composition program, but may be roughly transferrable to other systems and software. However, our point is not to detail the use of one system over another, but to demonstrate the versatility of the computer in layout.

There are a number of basic advantages to computer page layout that you need to be aware of before you plunge into designing and formatting publications on your computer.

Placing text and graphics

The primary advantage of computer page layout is the ability to place text and graphics right on the page from word processing or illustration programs. Although other page-layout programs require you to create a frame in which you then place text or graphics, *PageMaker* allows you to place these items directly on the page, anywhere you want them. Once there, they can be manipulated in a number of ways. You can also place text one column at a time or in *PageMaker's* textflow mode which allows it to flow uninterrupted from page to page until it is completely placed. Text can be confined to any size column or stretched across columns by a simple movement of the mouse. Once on the page, text can be made longer or wider by manipulating the *handles* that are part of each *PageMaker* element.

Graphics, such as those imported from Aldus *FreeHand*, are placed in roughly the same way. By moving the mouse pointer to the position on the page where you want the graphic to appear and holding down the mouse button while dragging diagonally, you may designate the size you want the graphic to be when it is placed. This will then constrain the placed element to that area (in the case of text) or size (in the case of a graphic).

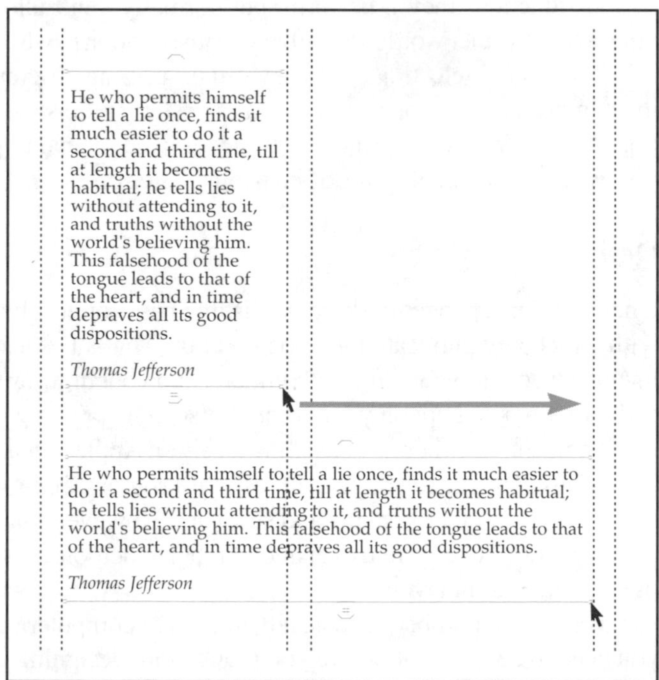

Exhibit 12.1—Stretching Text.

The beauty of computer layout is the ease with which you can manipulate the various elements on the page. Placing text in most layout programs is as easy as designating the space and importing the existing text copy. In PageMaker, *you don't even have to designate the space in advance.*

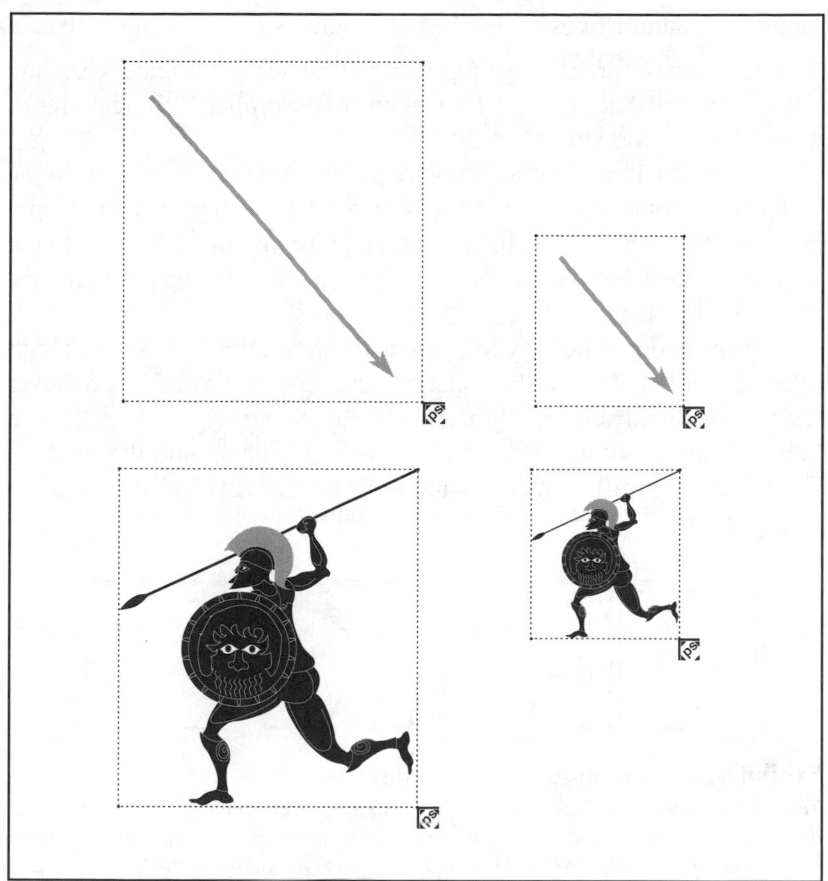

Exhibit 12.2—Placing Graphics.

Graphics placement in PageMaker *can be restricted to a specific place on the page or a specific size. Keep in mind, however, that stretching the graphics block without holding down the shift key will result in a distorted graphic.*

Once placed, the graphic may be sized, cropped or otherwise adjusted depending on the software used to produce it. Graphics placed from PICT or EPS formats can be sized proportionally in *PageMaker* by simply holding down the *shift* key while dragging a corner handle. Paint-type graphics can also be sized without loss or compression of shading patterns if you hold down both the *command* and *shift* keys as you drag. If you don't hold down the *shift* key or *command* and *shift* keys while executing these maneuvers, the images will distort. Many programs also now include a text-wrap function that allows you to literally wrap text around a placed graphic.

Using Lines and Boxes

Today, even word processing programs now allow you to create boxes and lines, but not all that long ago this was one of the primary selling points of a page-layout program.

Although it is possible to import or place boxes and other such simple patterns from other programs, it is easier to create them in the page-layout program. Boxes do have to be moved each time you make an adjustment to type or format, but it's a easier to move them in a computer program than on a pasted-up piece of paper.

Drop shadows are easy to create and can be effective if they are not overused. In *PageMaker*, drop shadows are produced by adding a darker shaded box slightly diagonally and to the rear of your original box. Be sure your top box is not transparent, and delete the line around the shadow. Experiment with different shades and don't assume that black is the best for a drop shadow.

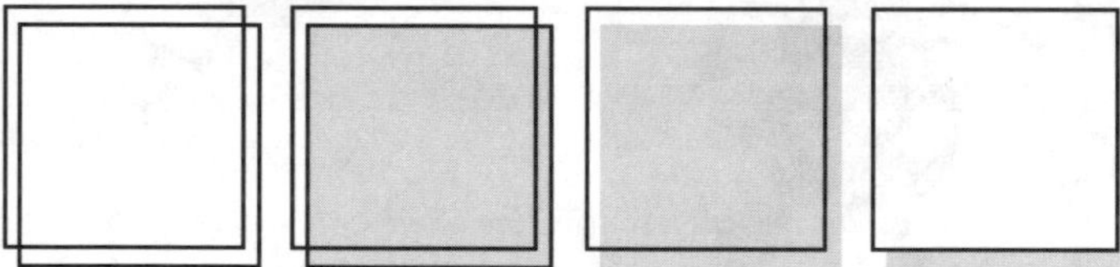

Exhibit 12.3—Creating a Drop Shadow

To create a drop shadow in a program such as PageMaker, *simply draw a box, duplicate it by copying and pasting; place one box slightly at a diagonal to the other and overlapping; shade the lower box; delete the line around it; fill the top box with white and make sure it's brought to the front.*

Tint blocks, boxes that are filled or shaded, should also be used with care. Very small type or type with thin serifs won't print well over a tint block, especially on a laser printer. Use a light shade (no more than 20 or 30 percent) and a type size of at least 12 point. If your final product will run on a Linotronic, be aware that fills or shades will appear darker than on a laser-printed copy. A 40 percent fill that looks fine on a LaserWriter will be too dark for a copy block on a Linotronic.

Like type size, line thickness is usually given in points. This is convenient since line width is much narrower than you would want to measure in inches. The standard seems to be 1 point; however, experiment with line thickness and use what seems most appropriate to your purpose. For example, some programs designate "hairline" as well as .05- and 1-point line thicknesses at the narrower end of the range. Hairlines are

Lorem ipsum dolor sit amet, consectetuer adipiscing elit, sed diam nonummy nibh euismod tincidunt ut laoreet dolore magna aliquam erat volutpat. Ut wisi enim ad minim

Lorem ipsum dolor sit amet, consectetuer adipiscing elit, sed diam nonummy nibh euismod tincidunt ut laoreet dolore magna aliquam erat volutpat. Ut wisi enim ad minim

Lorem ipsum dolor sit amet, consectetuer adipiscing elit, sed diam nonummy nibh euismod tincidunt ut laoreet dolore magna aliquam erat volutpat. Ut wisi enim ad minim

Lorem ipsum dolor sit amet, consectetuer adipiscing elit, sed diam nonummy nibh euismod tincidunt ut laoreet dolore magna aliquam erat volutpat.

Exhibit 12.4—Tint Blocks

Tint blocks are useful graphic devices for attracting attention; however, remember that shaded boxes will darken when run on a Linotronic. *As you can see below, the darker the box, the more difficult it is to read the copy. Clockwise from the top, the shades are 10%, 20%, 40% and 30%.*

excellent for the lines used in coupons or fill-in-the-blanks forms. You'd be surprised how thick a 1-point line looks in these forms. On the other hand, a 2-, 4-, or 6-point line is quite a bit thicker *looking* than a 1-point line. Use the thicker settings sparingly. (See **Exhibit 12.5**.)

Grids, Master Pages and Templates

Once you're familiar with your page-makeup program, you can experiment with actual publications. You can be producing simple publications in no time once you've mastered three devices: **grids**, **master pages**, and **templates**. The creative use of these devices can be used to add consistency to your publications page by page and issue by issue and can save you time and frustration.

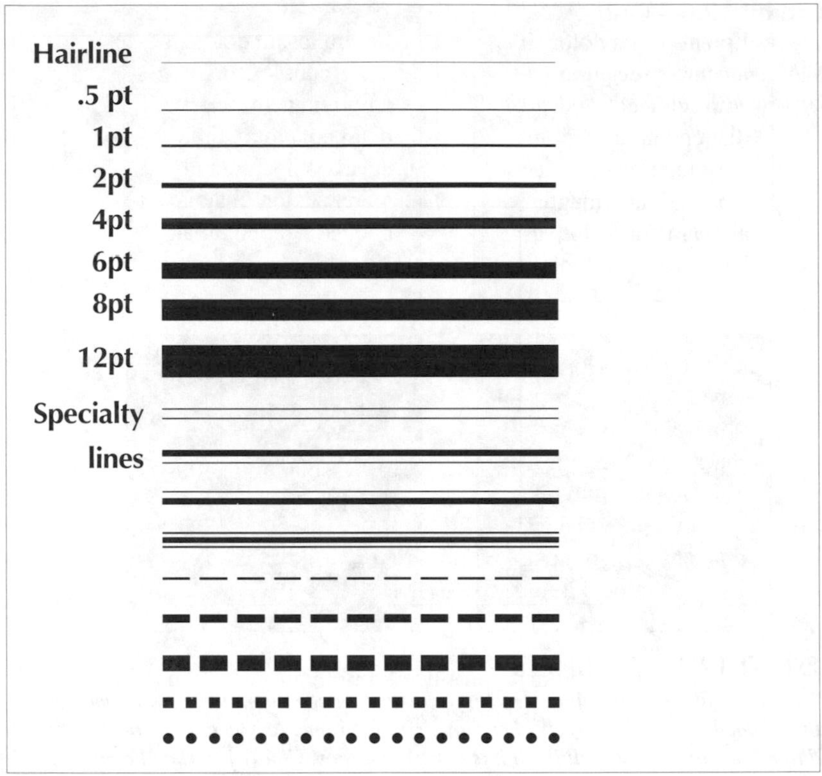

Exhibit 12.5—Lines

TIP: On most screens, lines below 1 point don't show any smaller than the 1-point line. Sometimes, blowing the page up to 200 or 400 percent shows the difference. The best way to judge the differences, however, is to print out a proof sheet and look for yourself.

Grids

Grids are guides around which you build your publication. Their importance to layout can't be over stressed. Grids are not, as some graphic artists will tell you, confining. They do not stifle creativity or limit your imagination. They aid you in balancing your publication from page to page, or from spread to spread.

A grid is composed of a series of non-printing horizontal and vertical lines. They can appear directly on the page you are working on or remain invisible until you call them up. They are variably adjustable and can be moved about to suit your needs. Programs such as *PageMaker* use columns as the basic grid unit, while other programs, such as Letraset's *ReadySetGo*, set up grids as a series of vertical and horizontal rectangles.

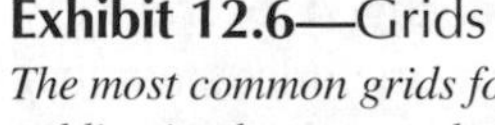

Exhibit 12.6—Grids

The most common grids for publication layout are the three-column magazine page (bottom) and the three-column brochure page (top right).

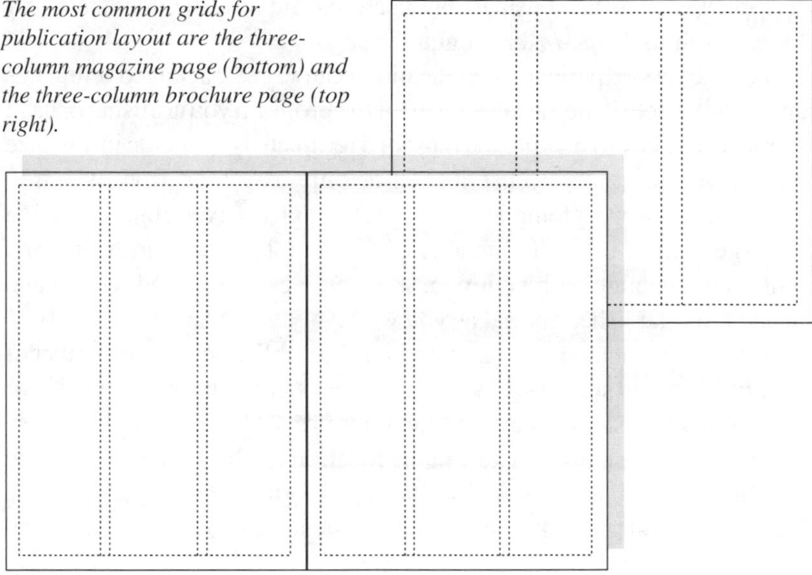

For longer or regularly produced publications, such as a weekly newsletter or monthly house magazine, grids are indispensable. Even for smaller publications such as brochures, grids keep your margins consistent and your layout balanced.

Master pages

Master pages are created (on *PageMaker*) at the beginning of the layout process and consist of any elements you want to repeat from page to page—not just grids, but also page headers, numbers, rules and other graphic elements. Every page is then overlaid by the master page elements unless otherwise overridden.

Master pages also hold the basic grid on which each page is built including columns, margins and other space dividers.

Templates

Templates are probably the most useful tool for the editor who publishes a large periodical publication on a recurring basis. Templates allow you to save all of the grid elements, master pages, and style elements that will be reused each time, saving time and frustration. Templates were originally developed as tutorials for page-layout programs and later as specialty offerings packaged as guidelines for certain types of publications, such as memos, newsletters, brochures, etc. Aldus packaged several early sets for newsletters and business publications and now includes a number of these with its *PageMaker* program.

For the less-experienced publication editor, pre-packaged templates can be a great help if they are designed for the program you are using or have access to. The key to making the most of a template is to decide in advance whether you are going to use it as-is or only as a base from which to experiment. Not every template is flexible enough for experimentation, but if you are aware of the limitations of the templates you are using and comfortable enough with your own skills, you can work both within and outside the established format as you wish.

A template includes the basic grid for the publication and a number of **place holders** and **spacers**. Place holders are usually samples of display or body type executed in the face, style and size pre-set for that template. They appear exactly or approximately in the location on the page in which you would use them if you made absolutely no format changes. Again, the flexibility of your prepackaged templates depends a lot on your abilities and willingness to experiment.

Once you have the experience, creating your own custom templates is simple enough. The more you know about your page-layout program, the easier it will be. Although your program will dictate the exact way in which you build your template, the following process—based on *PageMaker*—can be transposed to other software programs.

1. Establish page size, orientation and margins in your *page setup* function. For example, if you are developing a template for a tabloid-sized newsletter, indicate *tabloid*, margins, number of pages and beginning page number. Most templates are composed of two or three pages—a cover page and sample inside pages. If you have certain sections or departments with special heads or boxes, you can include these as well; however, try to keep your template to as few pages as possible and add special features when you begin to construct your actual issue. Normally you'll want to set up your front page separately from the inside pages with masthead and other recurring elements already in place.
2. Set the measurement system you wish to use. Most prepackaged templates and most professional layout artists use points and picas. You may use whatever system you are most comfortable with. However, since you will undoubtedly be working with printers and typesetters, you might as well get used to their measurement system.

3. On your *master pages,* establish column number and width as well as any recurring elements that you want to appear on succeeding pages. For example, if you establish a three-column format, it will repeat on every page thereafter unless suppressed on a page-by-page basis. In addition, most programs, including *PageMaker*, also allow you to indicate page number placement which then automatically numbers your pages. Other elements, such as boxes or rules, can be included here as well. You may either lock these elements, including margins and column guides, or leave them and adjust them on a page-by-page basis. Remember, what you put on your master pages will appear on every page after that, but it isn't carved in stone and can be suppressed, or changed at any time.
4. Create your *style sheet*. Establish all of the parameters for each of the type styles you will be using and that you want to remain consistent from issue to issue. For instance, you might set your body text style at 10-point Times, justified with auto leading; your headline style at 24-point Avant Garde bold, centered with 25-point leading; your pull quotes at 14-point Avant Garde bold italic, centered with auto leading; and your captions 10-point Times italic, flush left with auto leading. You may also set such parameters as tabs, indents (both for paragraphs and whole subsections), hyphenation and so on. The beauty of a style sheet has already been explained, but when combined with a template, it becomes an indispensable tool for the publication's editor or designer.
5. Create **place holders**. Place holders combine the advantages of a style sheet with a visual representation of where elements are usually placed in a given publication. For example, to create a headline place holder, simply type in the word "Headline" in the size and style that you wish your finished headline to be. To insert your finished headline, just place your text cursor, highlight the place holder word, and type in your headline. It will appear in the size and style of the place holder. Place holders can be used in place of or in conjunction with a style sheet. Some people prefer just to use a style sheet because of the flexibility it allows. Place holders tend to pre-establish a design in your mind and are better for those who *need* a design pre-established.
6. Certain graphic elements such as imported art or special boxes can sometimes placed on the *desk top* beyond the edges of the pages, cut and placed in the *clipboard* file (held only as long as your computer is switched on) or placed in a *scrapbook* for later use. Admittedly,

elements saved this way take up more disk space; but if you use them a lot, yet don't want to lock them into any particular place on your layout, try "putting them to the side."

7. Once you have constructed your template, be sure to save it as a template. If you save it as a regular publication, any subsequent changes you make to it while laying out an issue will remain. If saved as a template, it will open only an untitled copy each time. Changes made to that copy can then be saved as a separate issue of your publication.

Remember, templates aren't cut in stone—they're only etched on your computer's memory. But the templates exist to bring continuity and consistency to a publication. One of the pitfalls of computer layout is the ease with which changes can be made. *Resist the urge to change your publications just because it's easy*. Make changes infrequently. Make sure each change has a legitimate rationale, and then make sure you can live with the change once you've made it.

Preparing Your Layout for Printing

The final stage of layout is the *mechanical*, the finished layout that goes to the printer. Again, the computer has revolutionized this process. If you are diligent, exact, and working with a limited range of graphics, you can literally present your printer with a mechanical in one piece—*with no pasted-up parts*. Computer imagesetters, such as the Linotronic 300, print out your layouts onto paper exactly as you have designed them, ready to be shot into printer's negatives. You can even go directly to negative film from a Linotronic, saving the cost of shooting negatives from a positive mechanical—but only if you are completely satisfied with your layout.

Assuming you are working in black and white, there are several ways to construct your mechanical, or camera-ready layout.

1. You can have it run *entirely* off a Linotronic, either from your computer disks or through a network or telephone line hookup. This implies that all of the elements on your mechanical are computer generated—word-processed text and display type; borders, boxes and rules produced in your page-layout program; photos scanned, cropped and sized in either a photo manipulation program—such as *Image Studio*—or right in your layout program; illustrations created in a paint, draw, or illustration program and imported or placed in your layout program; and any color separations already performed by your software.

Masthead

36pt. headline placeholder

18pt. subhead placeholder

24pt. column headline placeholder

This is a 12pt. bold byline placeholder

This is a 12pt. body text placeholder composed of Times Roman set flush left

This is a 12pt. caption placeholder of Times Roman italic

APC **Action**

A revolution in the making

New software may turn the tide in education

APC moves up Page 2

A penny for your thoughts Page 3

More on software Page4

Exhibit 12.7—Working with a Template

The template above is representative of the basic template found accompanying programs such as PageMaker. *Using this template, the newsletter page (inset) was created. You will find that adjustments will usually have to be made to typeface and size.*

2. You can run the basic mechanical (text, display type, rules and boxes) on a Linotronic and have photos and art shot separately and stripped into the negative before the printing plate is made. If you don't have a scanner or access to electronic clip art, this is probably the closest you'll get to having the whole thing done in one step. Even at this level, the savings in typesetting and pasteup alone are worth it.

3. You can run your mechanical on a laser printer at either of the above two levels. This assumes you either don't have access to a Linotronic, or you don't feel that the extra quality is needed for your particular publication. Some very nice newsletters and brochures can be offset printed directly from laser-printed mechanicals. The difference to the trained eye (or anyone with a magnifying glass) is the type. It bleeds badly at larger point sizes and can even look fuzzy at smaller sizes. But if you're on a shoestring budget, this is a great compromise.

Exhibit 12.8—Basic Printing Loop

A single-person operation can get by with a computer and a printer—preferably a laser printer—for jobs that don't require the finished quality of imagesetting.

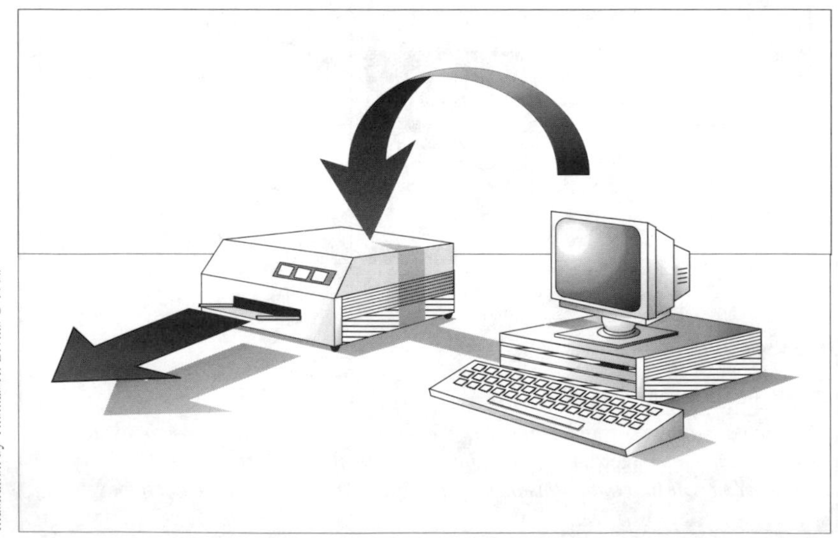

Setting Up a Desktop Publishing System

Getting started with desktop publishing means having to make a lot of complex choices. You not only have to pick the best software for the job, you also have to pick the best hardware to run your software. Hardware choices for desktop publishing especially are dictated by your needs and your pocketbook, although your personal preference is undoubtedly a factor. For example, if you have already been working on a PC (IBM or compatible), don't assume that you'll have to switch to Apple Macintosh just to get involved in desktop publishing. Software layout programs such as *Ventura Publisher* and Quark *Xpress* can turn your PC into a superb desktop publishing system. And, with the advances in special add-ons to non-*PostScript* laser printers, you can now rival the output of a standard *PostScript* printer with your PC system.

Exhibit 12.9—Advanced Printing Loop

An advanced desktop printing loop might include a computer and any peripheral devices, such as a scanner. The finished publication is sent to an output device such as a laser printer for drafts, or to an imagesetter such as a Linotronic for final output. The camera-ready output can be run either on paper (equivalent to a PMT) or on negative film ready for plate making.

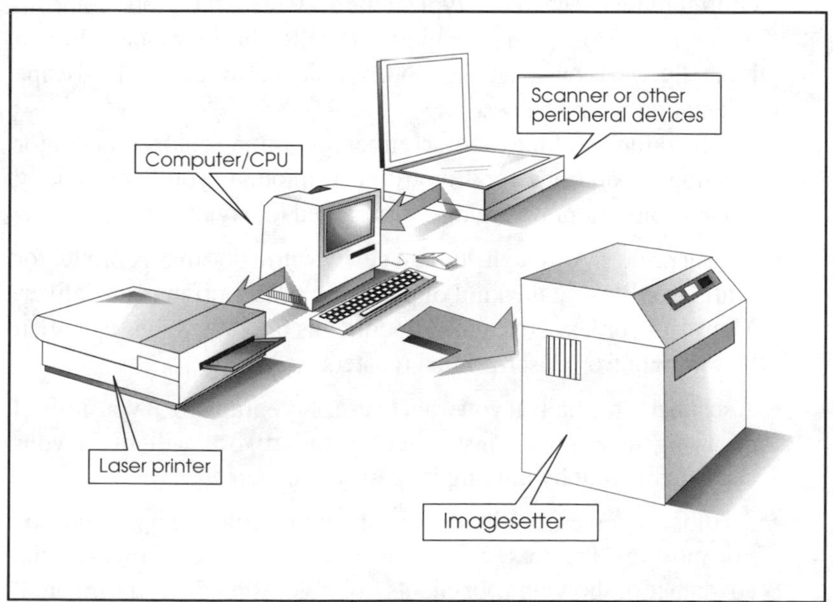

Hardware

Whether you're starting from scratch or adding to an existing system, at the very minimum, you'll need the following hardware:

- A computer with enough RAM to handle today's complex programs (at least 1 MGB, more if you can afford it).
- At least a 20 MGB hard drive. The fact is, most layout programs now require a hard drive to work, and you're going to need the storage space and room to work.
- At least one floppy disk drive for backup file storage.
- A monochrome monitor.
- A printer. For the beginner who will be sending, or taking, final output to a Linotronic, a dot-matrix will do for rough drafts.

If you aspire to a more advanced system, you'll probably be considering the following as either basics or add-ons:

- A high-resolution monitor. Although you can certainly get by with less, if you're going to be working with photographs at any time, you'll want a monitor that will show you a complete range of grays.

  And, if you're going to be working on ads or publications with large page sizes, double-page spreads, or just want to see an entire page at once and still be able to read the body type—look into buying a large-screen monitor. These vary in price (none are cheap) and configuration. The most typical large-screen monitors come in either landscape (wide) or portrait (tall) configurations. If you typically work on magazine and newsletter spreads, a landscape orientation would be best.

  If you are working in color (either for printing color comps or for creating separations for Linotronic printouts), you'll eventually want a color monitor. Again, be prepared to pay the price.
- A laser printer. Although you can get by with a dot-matrix printer for drafts, you'll want the kind of precision a laser printer can deliver. Many of your less prestigious documents or publications can often be run right from laser-printed masters.
- A scanner, especially if you want to use photographs or if you're tired of trying to calculate just where your artwork will fit in your computer layout by holding it against your screen.
- A color printer, especially if you want to run color comps or proofs. For most art directors, a color printer isn't needed; however, the advantage of showing your clients full-color comps can't be ignored.

Of course, there is always something you can add—a more expensive computer, expanded memory, a better laser printer, a graphics tablet, and so on. Just make sure that you will get your money's worth out of that fancy, new piece of hardware before you buy it.

Software

These days, you can purchase a word processing program that will do a bit of page layout (simple blocks, columns, lines, etc.), or a layout program that will do a bit of word processing. But what you really want is the best of each, since no one program can yet deliver in all areas.

As with hardware purchases, buy what you need to do the job, but be aware of your future needs. Software, unlike hardware, isn't easily extended by adding a peripheral device. If you buy into a word processing program that will only do short documents (because that's all you do right now), you'll have to buy a whole new program later if you decide you need greater capabilities. Plan ahead and purchase software that you can use both now and in the predictable future.

Again, there are basic needs and more elaborate needs. For the beginning desktop publisher, the following types of programs are recommended at a minimum:

- A good word processing program—one that will serve your current *and* future needs. The industry standards are relatively expensive — such programs as *WordPerfect* for the PC and Microsoft *Word* for the Mac have become leaders in word processing for good reason. These, and others like them, have limited layout capabilities and can sometimes even use imported graphics. The key to their success, however, is the fact that they can adjust to longer and more complex documents easily. For example, both *WordPerfect* and Microsoft *Word* can perform various indexing, sorting, and text calculation functions, as well as execute excellent spell checks.

    Remember, word processing programs are also a matter of taste, but don't assume that your favorite PC-based program will be as good in its Macintosh version. It's been our experience that there are good PC word processing programs and good Macintosh word processing programs, and *they are different programs entirely*. Read some reviews, try out sample programs, and, above all, project your needs as far ahead as you can.
- A page-layout program. As with the word processing program, what's good for the goose isn't necessarily good for the gander.

What works well on a Macintosh doesn't necessarily work well for a PC desktop publishing system. Industry standards such as *PageMaker* (for the Macintosh) and *Ventura Publisher* and Quark *Xpress* (for the PC) are your best bet. Don't skimp on quality. A low-end page-layout program will give you low-end results—if you survive the frustration factor.

Aside from these basic requirements, the serious publication director will want access to various add-on programs that will enhance the job and reduce the number of intermediaries involved in the publication process. Take a look at these software extras.

- A graphics program (or programs). This is an area in which your talent is the deciding factor. For those with little or no artistic or design talent, some basic (but fairly inflexible) programs are best. Object-oriented programs such as *MacDraw* and *Cricket Draw* provide clean, *PostScript*-printable lines, but are limited to basic and somewhat static forms. Of course, bit-mapped images can be created on a number of paint programs, including *MacPaint* and *FullPaint*, but they aren't for polished publications.

  Judging by the multiplicity of newspaper graphics being generated using *MacDraw*, you might think it is a superb artist's tool; however, programs such as Adobe *Illustrator* and Aldus *FreeHand* are actually the software of choice for experienced designers and artists. Be warned, these programs are not for the inexperienced designer. They are complex to learn and use, but the results can be astonishing.

- A color graphics program. If you work in color, this can be useful. However, the two most popular programs mentioned above, *Illustrator* and *FreeHand*, can also be used in color and can produce color separations. Although a color graphics program such as *PixelPaint* or *Modern Artist* can be fun to use, especially if you have a color monitor, they are truly luxuries if you already own an illustration program. And, since they produce bit-mapped images, they are of limited use in publications.

- A photo manipulation program such as *Image Studio* or *Digital Darkroom*. If you have a scanner and work with photos on a regular basis (either as finished art or simple placeholders for the screened art), you'll want one of these programs. They allow for the kind of fine tuning many scanners don't provide, including brightness and contrast adjustments, gray-scale manipulation, photo retouching, and myriad other tasks. These programs are not toys; they are serious graphics tools that, as they become more sophisticated, may actually replace the traditional methods of working with photographs.

- A font editing/creation program such as *Fontographer* or *Letra Studio* allows you to create your own type fonts. These are terrific fun for novice and experienced type designers alike, but they can be difficult to learn if you know absolutely nothing about type. They are especially good for developing logotypes and creating special letters for illustrations.

The Proof Is in the Pudding

There's a lot to be said for that old saw. Ultimately, your final, printed publication is going to determine how successful your desktop publishing system is—and a lot of that success depends not on your hardware and software, but on you.

You are the final ingredient in this system. Your energy, talent, interest, and organizational abilities will be the final determinant in the success or failure of your ads. Truthfully, you can get by on a lot less than you think you can if you possess the right attitude and the requisite abilities. Fancy hardware and expensive software only enhance and streamline a process you should already have down to a fine art.

The fact is that most excellent publications are still laid out the "old-fashioned" way. Nothing substitutes for being able to accomplish the task this way. (For instance, what happens when the power goes out or your only computer breaks down?) Don't get the wrong idea—computers have made and are continuing to make a tremendous difference in publishing. Just remember—that multi-thousand dollar system you sit down in front of every day is only a tool. Simply holding a brush in your hand doesn't make you an artist, the same as sitting in front of a typewriter doesn't make you a writer. Dedication, hard work, and talent will.

Take a hard look at your layouts and ask yourself a few questions:

- Are they already the best they can be without the addition of desktop publishing? If they are, you probably already know the basics and are ready for desktop publishing. If they're not, why not? Will the technology help the look or simply add to the clutter? Be honest. Don't expect desktop publishing to give you something you don't already possess.
- What, exactly, do you expect desktop publishing to add to your layouts or the process of developing them? Again, if you're looking

for an answer to your design problems, check out your own abilities first. On the other hand, if you're expecting the technology to streamline the process and save you some money—it probably will.

- Will the savings you accrue be offset by the cost of the system? It takes a lot of savings in typesetting to counterbalance a $25,000 investment.
- Are you willing to take the time needed to make you an expert on your system? If you aren't willing to become an expert, you're wasting your money. Anyone can learn the basics (or just enough to cause trouble). If you're serious about desktop publishing, you'd best dedicate yourself for the long haul. Be prepared to immerse yourself in the process, the programs, and the machinery. The more you know, the more streamlined the process becomes.

Above all, don't set yourself up for frustration. Realize the limitations of your system and of desktop publishing in general. Understand how it works and why it does what it does. You don't have to become a "computer nerd" to gain a fairly complete understanding of your hardware and software. The more you know, the less frustrated you'll be when something does go wrong. Most of the frustration of working with computers comes from not knowing what's happening in software or hardware problem situations. Keep those technical support hotline numbers close at hand and use them. Don't be afraid to ask questions, but read your manuals first so you'll know what to ask.

Finally, take it all with a grain of salt. Don't talk to your computer. You probably don't talk to your typewriter. They're both just tools of the trade. Misuse them, and your shortcomings will become apparent to everyone who looks at your ads. Use them wisely, and they'll show off for you.

CHAPTER 13

The Basics of Grammar

Let schoolmasters puzzle their brain,
with grammar, and nonsense, and learning;
good liquor, I stoutly maintain,
gives genius a better discerning.
Oliver Goldsmith

Writing is a technical skill as well as an art and, as such, it demands a thorough understanding of grammar. Unfortunately, most of us still have some rather uncomfortable memories of grammar lessons in either grade school or high school. Others believe that we can write intuitively, without any formal knowledge of grammar. This is a dangerous belief because it leads to a false sense of security and often a misunderstanding of the basic rules of grammar.

The simple fact is, those who know and understand grammar are better writers than those who don't. Obviously, no one wants to start at the beginning of a grammar text and wade all the way through it in order to gain a better understanding of how to use a comma. With that "roadblock mentality" in mind, the following brief discussion of grammar is offered as a shortcut.

Please don't assume that this is a definitive text. It is not. It is merely a reference for those using this book. In it, you will find a number of helpful hints and a few rules of thumb which will serve to set you on the right track. The key, of course is recognizing when you need help. As a public relations writer, you will never want for editors who point out your errors, even though some are no better at grammar than you are. It is in your best interest to learn the rules and use them. Writing without a knowledge of grammar is like falling into the water without a knowledge of swimming—in either case, your chances of surviving in the medium are slim.

Parts of Speech

The parts of speech are simply the categories in which words belong. Most words are classified in three ways:

- By their grammatical function (such as *subject*, *object*, etc.);
- By their grammatical form (such as the *s* form added to the end of plural nouns);
- By their meaning (such as the names of things as in the case of *nouns*, or statements of action as in the case of *verbs*).

No matter what category we place words in, some of them will end up as more than one *part of speech*. Take the word *place* for instance.

> *As a noun*
> This advanced version of PSO-1 will certainly take the *place* of older compounds in plastics' manufacturing.
>
> *As a verb*
> In a startling move, John Rivers, Mayor of Edmonton, has decided to *place* his hat in the ring for the governor's race.
>
> *As a modifier*
> *Place* settings of plastic spoons were totally inappropriate at the company picnic considering that roast beef was being served.

Parts of speech are categorized according to what they do. The following groups represent the basic parts of speech in English.

Nouns

Nouns are words that name a person, place or thing. Subjects of sentences are usually nouns, as are objects of verbs and prepositions.

> Associated Products *Corporation* (APC) of *Syracuse, N.Y.* today announced a joint *venture* to educate American school *children* in the *uses* of *computers*.

Keep in mind that although most nouns form the plural by simply adding *s*, some, such as *sheep*, and *woman*, are irregular.

Pronouns

Pronouns substitute for nouns, but in order to understand exactly what noun a given pronoun is substituting for, we have to look for its antecedent.

> Tom said that *he* was going out for a while, but *he* left no forwarding address or indication when *he* would return.

In this sentence, it is clear that the pronoun *he* refers to the antecedent, *Tom*. But in the following sentence, the pronoun *you* refers to anyone who might take the action.

> *You* would have to be a fool to come to work dressed for the weather outside when the air conditioner still insists it's winter.

Indefinite pronouns (*everybody, anybody, someone*) act like nouns and therefore take no antecedent . These, like the *you* in the sentence above, refer to whomever takes the action.

Verbs

Verbs are action words, as we were told so many times in grade school; but what they really do is make a statement about the subject of the sentence. For public relations writers, choosing the right verb tense is all important. For instance, stating that the president of APC "has announced" an important project has a different effect on readers than saying he "announced" an important project. Both use a past tense form, but the first is much more immediate. The nuances are subtle, but they are definitely there.

The following tenses are the most common for regular verbs.

- **Present tenses** express actions that are happening now or that are habitual. The *simple present tense* might most commonly be used in print ad copy.

  > Associated Products Corporation *Announces* a Breakthrough in Educational Software.

  The present progressive tense uses a **present participle** (the *-ing* form). This implies immediacy and is used in press releases. Note that you need to include a specific time the event is to take place, otherwise the sentence implies it is taking place *now*.

  > James L. Sutton, a native of Deerborn and president of Associated Products Corporation of Syracuse, New York, *is announcing* the development of a new educational software line at a two o'clock press conference this afternoon (May 25).

- **Present perfect tense** indicates an action carried out before the present and completed in the present. It can also be used for an action which was begun in the past and continues in the present.

  > James L. Sutton, a native of Deerborn and president of Associated Products Corporation of Syracuse, New York, *has announced* the development of a new educational software line.

This tense is the perfect choice for some press releases because it implies immediacy, yet ties the action to the past. It has the benefit of being non-specific and doesn't call for the inclusion of a date.

- **Past tenses** express actions that took place in the past.

> James L. Sutton, a native of Deerborn and president of Associated Products Corporation of Syracuse, New York, *announced* the development of a new educational software line at a two o'clock press conference today (May 25).

Again, note that the use of the past tense in this lead is followed by a specific time.

The **past perfect tense** expresses actions completed *before* other past actions occured. Compare the use of the past perfect and the simple past tense in this press release lead.

> James L. Sutton, a native of Deerborn and president of Associated Products Corporation of Syracuse, New York, *had announced* the development of a new educational software line just before he *announced* his resignation from the company.

- **Future tenses** express an action that will occur in the future.

> James L. Sutton, a native of Deerborn and president of Associated Products Corporation of Syracuse, New York, *will announce* the development of a new educational software line at a two o'clock press conference today (May 25).

A specific time is called for here too.

The **future perfect tense** indicates actions that will be completed before a specified future time.

> James L. Sutton, a native of Deerborn and president of Associated Products Corporation of Syracuse, New York, *will have announced* the development of a new educational software line before he resigns.

Obviously, some of these tenses are more common than others in public relations writing. The point, however, is that they each carry an implied meaning as well as an explicit meaning.

Adjectives and Adverbs

Adjectives and **adverbs** are the modifiers. Adjectives modify nouns or words acting as nouns, and adverbs modify other adverbs, adjectives, verbs, and most other words. We will look in detail at these parts of speech later on.

Prepositions and Conjunctions

Prepositions and **conjunctions** are used to connect parts of a sentence. A *preposition* usually relates a noun, pronoun or phrase to some other part of the sentence.

> The ancient cities *of* Sodom and Gomorrah have long since vanished *from* its shores. (*Cities* is related to *Sodom and Gomorrah*; *vanished* is related to *shores*.)

> Sitting *behind* a cluttered desk, boxes scattered *around* the office—some still unopened—is the new head of the Law Department. (*Sitting* is related to *desk*; *boxes* is related to *office*).

A **conjunction** is used to join words, phrases, or clauses together. In using conjunctions, never forget that these simple words carry meanings of their own as well as show relations between the sentence parts that they connect.

> The project is a joint effort of the National Education Association *and* Associated Products Corporation of Syracuse, New York. (*And* joins the *NEA* with *APC*.)

> The Lincoln High School graduate has been chief systems engineer since 1974, but he says the new project has given him a rare opportunity to work with designers outside the computer field. (*Since* links the first clause with a specific date; *but* joins two main clauses.)

Sentences and Clauses

Words are the basic unit of written English. Good writers manage to string these units together to form coherent clauses, which in turn form complete sentences. The type (and therefore the complexity) of sentence we write depends on the type and combination of clauses we choose to make up the sentence.

Independent Clauses

Independent clauses, sometimes called **main clauses**, always have a subject and a verb and make a statement independent of the rest of the sentence. A sentence always has one main clause, and sometimes it has more than one.

There are several frequently used words that serve to separate independent clauses. These are called **coordinating conjunctions**. The most common coordinating conjunctions are: *and, but, so, for, yet, or, nor*. A comma is usually used before a coordinating conjunction separating independent clauses.

> A recent study shows that students between the ages of 7 and 14 have the ability to acquire computer skills readily, *and* they will be more marketable when they graduate from high school.
>
> The program is designed to benefit a small segment of the public, *but* the public relations "fallout" will be apparent for years.

Conjunctive adverbs, like coordinating conjunctions, join complete clauses which are linked by a common idea. And, like coordinating conjunctions, they possess meanings of their own. Make sure that you are using the correct conjunctive adverb for your transition—one that indicates the relationship between the clauses. The most common conjunctive adverbs are:

accordingly	however
also	likewise
besides	moreover
consequently	nevertheless
else	otherwise
furthermore	then
hence	therefore

> The announcement came as a complete shock to those present; consequently, few questions were asked. (*Consequently* implies that the second clause is a result of the first.)
>
> There are many possible excuses for not getting to work on time; however, John chose to say he had been kidnapped by terrorists and was only released an hour ago. (*However* indicates that what happened in the second clause happened in spite of what happened in the first.)

Subordinate Clauses

Subordinate clauses, sometimes called dependent clauses, contain ideas that are less important than those in the independent clause. A subordinate clause relies on an independent clause for meaning, and is frequently introduced by a **subordinate conjunction** such as:

although	unless
as	until
because	when
how	where
though	whether

Subordinate clauses also act as parts of speech (adjectives, adverbs, nouns). The sentence must contain an independent clause or it will not be a complete sentence.

> When he arrived... (Subordinate clause, but not a sentence.)
>
> When he arrived, the meeting was already underway. (Subordinate clause followed by an independent clause, thus a sentence.)
>
> The meeting was already underway when he arrived. (Same here except that the subordinate clause is positioned last.)

Sentences are classified by the number of subordinate or main clauses they contain. The basic classifications are: **simple**, **compound**, **complex**, and **compound complex**.

A **simple sentence** has a single main clause.

> You can do something to help save the whales.

A **compound sentence** has two or more main clauses.

> You can do something to help save the whales, and you can earn money doing it.

A **complex sentence** has a main clause and one or more subordinate clauses.

> By doing something to help save the whales, you can also earn money.

A **compound-complex sentence** contains two or more main clauses and one or more subordinate clauses.

> By doing something to help save the whales, you can earn money and they can continue to live in peace.

Case

Case is confusing; no doubt about it. Case is used to indicate the function of nouns and pronouns in a sentence. For instance, in the sentence "He gave me a week's vacation," the *nominative* case form *he* indicates that the pronoun is being used as subject; the *objective* case form *me* shows that the pronoun is an object; the *possessive* form *week's* indicates that the noun is a possessive.

Personal pronouns (*I, you, he, she, it*) have different forms for the nominative, possessive, and objective cases. The following table will help clear up the differences.

Singular	**Nominative**	**Possessive**	**Objective**
First Person	I	my, mine	me
Second Person	you	your, yours	you
Third Person	he, she, it	his, her, hers, its	him, her, it
Plural	**Nominative**	**Possessive**	**Objective**
First Person	we	our, ours	us
Second Person	you	your, yours	you
Third Person	they	their, theirs	them

Probably the most troublesome use of case involves the **relative pronoun,** *who*. In both the singular and plural forms, *who* is the nominative case, *whose* is the possessive case, and *whom* is the objective case.

Nominative

Use the nominative case to indicate the subject of a verb. In formal English (which usually means anything you write short of a personal memo or note), try to adhere to the following rules.

1. Use the nominative case of the pronoun after the conjunctions *as* and *than* if the pronoun is the subject of an understood verb.

    Hoffman obviously felt that they were better off than he (was.). (*He* is the subject of the verb *was*, which is understood.

2. Use the nominative case for the subject of a clause even though the whole clause may be the object of a verb or preposition. This only applies to clauses. (Compare this rule to the use of the objective case discussed later.)

    Sutton has stated that he will give a bonus to whoever accomplishes the task first. (*Whoever* is the subject of the verb *accomplishes* in the clause of which it is a part.)

3. Use the nominative case of the personal pronoun after forms of the verb *be* (*is*, *are*, *were*, *have been*). This is a tough rule to follow, however, since even good speakers these days tend to use less formal forms. In this instance, it is usually permissible to be more informal, especially when a contraction is involved. Let the expectations of your audience be your guide.

   Formal:
   It was I. I thought it was he. It was not we.

   Informal:
   It's me. I thought it was him. It wasn't us.

4. Use the nominative case following the infinitive *to be* when the infinitive has no expressed subject. Again, the informal form is commonly used instead.

   Formal:
   I would not want to be he.

   Informal:
   I would not want to be him.

Possessive

Most nouns have a common form which is changed to show possessive by simply adding *'s*, as in *worker/worker's*. In the possessive case, *'s* should be used with nouns that are animate objects. For inanimate objects, use the *of* construction.

> Sutton's leadership has inspired a number of workers in their creative endeavors.
>
> The value of the dollar has increased dramatically over the past month.

Objective

The objective case is particularly troublesome for some writers. Following a few basic rules should iron out the difficulties.

1. Use the objective case for the object of a verb, verbal (gerunds and participles), or preposition.

   Whom did you see about the irregularity in your typewriter? (The verb *see* already has a subject, *you*, so *whom* is the object of the verb.)

   I saw *him*. (*Him* is the object of the verb *saw*.)

   Visiting *them* was the highlight of the convention. (*Them* is the object of the gerund *visiting*.)

Two of *us* were reprimanded for being late this morning. (*Us* is the object of the preposition *of*.)

Whom does he want to nominate for president? (*Whom* is the object of the infinitive *to nominate*.)

As a contrast, consider this sentence:

Who do you suppose convinced him to run? (*Who* is the subject of the verb *convinced* which already has an object, *him*.)

2. In formal English, *whom* is always used in the objective case; however, informal English permits the use of *who*. We have become so used to using who, it is now difficult to switch to *whom* in formal writing. Again, think of the expectations of your audience.

   Formal:
   Whom are you seeing this morning?

   Informal:
   Who are you seeing this morning?

3. One of the more confusing constructions is the use of the objective case after the conjunction *and*.

   They found Sheila and me locked in an embarrassing grip behind the filing cabinet. (Not *Sheila and I. Me* is the object of the verb *found*.)

   You must choose between him and me. (Not *he and I. Him* and *me* are objects of the preposition *between*.)

4. After the conjunctions *than* and *as*, use the objective case only if it is the object of an understood verb.

   This company needs him more than me.

   By using the objective case, the sentence is understood to mean "This company needs him more than it needs me." If we were to use the nominative case, the meaning of the sentence would be altered:

   "This company needs him more than I (need him)."

Adjectives and Adverbs

Adjectives and **adverbs** are words which qualify meanings. Without them, descriptive writing would be impossible. Consider the following sentence:

Sutton is a *neat* and *energetic* man who speaks *glowingly* of his *latest* project.

Remove the adjectives and adverbs and you are left with:

> Sutton is a man who speaks of his project.

The key to the proper use of adjectives and adverbs in PR writing is to avoid overusing them. The more adjectives and adverbs you use, the less credible your writing becomes.

> Sutton is an excruciatingly neat man who speaks in absolutely glowing terms of his latest project.

Adjectives are words that modify nouns or noun substitutes. Never use an adjective to modify a verb, another adjective, or an adverb.

> She was terrible upset when he spilled coffee on her new dress. (*Terrible* is an adjective and thus cannot modify *was upset.*)

> She was terribly upset when he spilled coffee on her new dress. (*Terribly* is an adverb.)

> She jumped very quickly to her feet when he spilled the coffee. (*Very* is an adverb modifying the adverb *quickly.*)

There are two basic types of adjectives: **descriptive** and **limiting**. **Descriptive adjectives** name some quality of an object, such as a *white* house; a *small* car; or a *worn* carpet.

Limiting adjectives restrict the meaning of a noun to a particular object or indicate quantity. There are five kinds of limiting adjectives:

> *Possessive: My* suit; *their* office

> *Demonstrative: This* suit; *that* office

> *Interrogative: Whose* suit? *Which* office?

> *Articles: A* suit; *an* office; *the* office

> *Numerical: One* suit; *second* office

Nouns as Adjectives

Sometimes a noun can be used as an adjective, but it is advisable to avoid this use, other than in such commonplace uses as *horse* race, *theater* tickets, *show* business.

And, make sure that you are using the proper form of a noun when you intend it as an adjective:

> *Wrong:*
> The Taiwan plant opened on schedule in October.

> *Right:*
> The Taiwanese plant opened on schedule in October.

Linking Verbs

One of the most confusing areas of adjective/adverb usage comes when we have to deal with *linking verbs*. Linking verbs connect the subject of the sentence with the subject complement (the word that modifies the subject).

The most common linking verbs are: *be, become, appear,* and *seem*. Others pertain to the senses, such as *look, smell, taste, sound,* and *feel*. Modifiers which follow linking verbs refer back to the subject and should be in the form of an adjective and not an adverb.

> Joan looks pretty today. (*Pretty* modifies *Joan.*) Joan looks great, but she smells bad. (*Great* and *bad* both refer to *Joan.*)

One of the most common errors is "I feel badly" in place of the correct form, "I feel bad."

> *Wrong:*
> I felt badly about the loss of your mother.
>
> *Right:*
> I felt bad about the loss of your mother.

The selection of an adjective or adverb as a modifier will alter the meaning of your sentence. Use an adverb after the verb if the modifier describes the manner of the action of the verb.

> The man looked suspiciously at her. (The adverb *suspiciously* modifies the verb *looked.*)
>
> The man looked suspicious. (The adjective *suspicious* modifies the subject *man.*)

In the first example, the verb *looked* expresses action and must be modified by an adverb. But in constructions like "He looks tired" or "He feels well," the verbs serve, not as words of action, but as links between the subject and the adjective.

The choice of an adjective or an adverb thus depends on whether or not the verb is being used as a linking verb. Ask yourself whether you want to modify the subject or the verb. And, be careful you don't alter the meaning of your sentence.

Degrees or Quantity

Adjectives and adverbs also show degrees or quantity by means of their **positive**, **comparative**, and **superlative** forms.

- The **positive** form expresses no comparison at all: *slow, quickly.*

- The **comparative** form permits a comparison between two (and only two) nouns by adding *-er* or the adverb *more* to the positive form of the word: *pretty, prettier; rapid, more rapid.*
- The **superlative** form involves a comparison between three or more nouns by adding *-est* or the adverb *most* to the positive form: *pretty, prettiest; rapid, most rapid.*

As a rule of thumb, most adjectives and a few one-syllable adverbs form the comparative and superlative forms with *-er* and *-est*. Two-syllable adjectives often offer a choice, as in *lovelier, loveliest* and *more lovely, most lovely*. Adjectives and adverbs of three or more syllables usually use *more* and *most* (*more assiduous*, not *assiduouser*).

Some adjectives and adverbs are absolute in their meaning and can have no comparison. These are words like *final, unique, empty, dead*, and *perfect*. However, you may imply that something is *not quite empty* or *not quite perfect* by using the adverb *nearly*. (This letter is *more nearly* perfect than the other.)

Agreement

Subject/Verb

What's wrong with the following leads?

> Associated Products Corporation (APC) in conjunction with the National Education Association (NEA) have announced a new project entitled "Johnny can learn to read."

> The National Education Association (NEA) in cooperation with the Associated Products Corporation (APC) are co-sponsoring a program that is designed to educate school children with computers.

The verbs *have announced* and *are cosponsoring* don't agree with the subject. The problem, of course, is that the writers have mistakenly assumed a *compound subject*, which normally requires a plural verb form. What we have here are two singular subjects. A singular subject requires a singular verb and a plural subject requires a plural verb.

The following types of constructions often cause trouble in subject-verb agreement.

1. When words or phrases come between the subject and the verb, the verb agrees with the subject of the sentence, not with the noun in the intervening expression.

Wrong:
The first two hours of the day was boring.

Right:
The first two hours of the day were boring.

2. When a sentence has a singular pronoun, the singular pronoun takes a singular verb.

    Wrong:
    Everyone involved in the transfer think that APC made the right move.

    Right:
    Everyone involved in the transfer thinks that APC made the right move.

3. A sentence that has two or more subjects joined by *and* always uses a plural verb.

    Wrong:
    Both the IRS and Associated Products considers the agreement fair.

    Right:
    Both the IRS and Associated Products consider the agreement fair.

    However, when the parts of the subject refer to the same thing, the verb form is singular.

    Right:
    His editor and friend recommends that he pursue a career other than writing. (Assumes that the editor and friend are the same person.)

    Right:
    His editor and friend recommend that he pursue a career other than writing. (Assumes that the editor and friend are two different people.)

    Right:
    My husband and lover was there to help me.

    Wrong:
    My husband and lover were there to help me. (Unless, of course, they are two different people.)

4. A sentence which has two or more subjects joined by *or* or *nor* has the verb agree with the subject nearest it.

    Wrong:
    Neither the board members nor the CEO were there.

    Right:
    Neither the board members nor the CEO was there.

5. In a sentence with a *collective* noun (*assembly, committee, jury, mob, herd*) a plural verb should be used to indicate that individual members of the group are acting separately.

    The *committee* has reached a consensus.

If you wish to indicate the individual actions of a collective group, use an additional noun.

    The committee *members* returned to their offices.

6. In a sentence with a *predicate* noun (one that usually follows the verb but says something about the subject) the verb agrees with its subject, not the predicate noun.

    Wrong:
    Status and pay is a prime force behind the "Yuppie" movement.

    Right:
    Status and pay are a prime force behind the "Yuppie" movement. (*Prime force* is the predicate noun.)

Antecedents

An **antecedent** is a word or group of words referred to by a following pronoun. The following general rules apply to the selection of proper pronouns for agreement.

1. Use a singular pronoun to refer to antecedents such as:

any	man
anybody	neither
anyone	one
each	person
either	somebody
every	someone
everybody	woman
everyone	

Everybody held *his* breath as the ball dropped signifying the new year had begun.

Each of the participants brought *his* own expertise to bear on the problem.

The problem with sentences like the one above is that the use of *he* as a pronoun might be construed by some to be sexist. The use of *he* or *his* to denote a group of unspecified gender composition is a delicate one. One way to avoid this rather awkward situation is to recast the sentence.

The *crowd* held *its* breath as the ball dropped signifying the new year had begun.

The *participants* brought *their* own expertise to bear on the problem.

2. With a collective noun as an antecedent, use a singular pronoun if you are considering the group as a unit. If you are considering the individual members of the group separately, add another noun to indicate individual actions.

   The *committee* has finished its work for the day.

   The committee *members* have decided to finish their work for the day.

3. If two or more antecedents are joined by *and*, use a plural pronoun to refer to them. If two or more singular antecedents are joined by *or* or *nor*, use a singular pronoun to refer to them. If one of two antecedents joined by *or* or *nor* is singular and one plural, make the pronoun agree with the nearer.

   Jack and Jim have finished their work.

   Neither Jack nor Jim has finished his work.

   Neither the department head nor the secretaries have finished their work.

Faulty Pronoun References

Faulty references of pronouns frequently present problems. The answer is to avoid sentences in which there are two possible antecedents for a single pronoun.

Unclear:
Jack told Carl that he was ungrateful. (Is *he* Jack or Carl?)

Clear:
Jack said to Carl, "You are ungrateful."

Clear:
Jack confessed to Carl that he was ungrateful.

Also avoid the indefinite use of *they*, *you*, and *it*.

Informal:
In smaller offices, they do not have great problems of communication.

Formal:
In smaller offices, the problems of communication are not great.

Informal:
In some states you are not permitted to walk against traffic.

Formal:
Some states do not permit pedestrians to walk against traffic.

Informal:
It says in the newspaper that Monday will be warmer.

Formal:
The newspaper says that Monday will be warmer.

Dangling Constructions

A **dangling construction** is one in which the second clause in a sentence does not logically modify anything in the first, although it seems to at first glance. The real problem is that most people understand the sentence despite the dangling construction.

Two of the most common types of modifiers are **participles** and **gerunds**. These parts of speech are called **verbals** and are words that are derived from verbs but are normally used as nouns or adjectives. Verbals often cause trouble because they *look like* verbs; however, they can act only as modifiers or as nouns. They can never, by themselves, transmit action.

A **participle** is the form of a verb which ends in *-ing* in the present form and in *-ed* or *-en* in the past form. A participle can act as an adjective.

Perspiring heavily, the man ran wild-eyed into the oncoming truck. (*Perspiring* is an adjective modifying *man*.)

When using participles as adjectives, make sure that they have a noun or a noun substitute to which they relate; otherwise, there is nothing to modify, and a dangling construction results.

Dangling participle:
While hunting in the woods, several deer were shot. (This means, literally, that several deer were hunting in the woods.)

Corrected version:
While hunting in the woods, we shot several deer.

Dangling participle:
The afternoon passed quietly, watching the words on the screen of the word processor scroll slowly by. (This means, literally, that the afternoon watched the word processor.)

Corrected version:
She passed the afternoon quietly, watching the words on the screen of her word processor scroll slowly by.

A **gerund** is the form of a verb which ends in *-ing*. The gerund is always used as a noun.

> Taking your medicine is better than avoiding the consequences of your acts. (*Taking* is a noun and the subject of the sentence.)

One of the most common problems with verbals is that we often think we are using a gerund (as a noun and therefore as the subject of a sentence) when we are really using a participle (which requires a subject).

Gerund as subject:
Reading a good novel is a thoroughly engrossing experience.

Dangling participle:
Reading a good novel, time passed quickly. (This means that time was reading the novel.)

Corrected version using a participle:
While reading a good novel, Tom didn't realize that time was passing so quickly. (*Reading* modifies *Tom.*)

Corrected version using a gerund:
Reading a good novel causes time to pass quickly. (The subject of the sentence is *reading a good novel.*)

Parallel Structure

Another common problem for writers is handling **parallel structure** correctly. In a sentence that has parallel structure, each of the phrases and clauses is structured in the same way. This helps keep the meaning of sentences clear.

Notice the correct use of parallel structure when the elements in a sentence are joined by a coordinating conjunction.

Wrong:
Bob likes working late and to take charge of everything.

Right:
Bob likes working late and taking charge of everything.

Or:
Bob likes to work late and to take charge of everything.

Wrong:
Ginny is bright, with a quick wit, and has a college degree.

Right:
Ginny is bright, has a quick wit and a college degree.

Or:
Ginny is bright, with a quick wit and a college degree.

In sentences that make comparisons, parallel structure is sometimes difficult to achieve. Make sure that you complete *all* comparisons. This often can be done simply by repeating a word or two.

Wrong:
He is as pernicious, if not more pernicious, than I am.

Right:
He is as pernicious as, if not more pernicious than, I am.

If you read the first sentence without the parenthetical comparison, you'll see that it doesn't make much sense.

He is as pernicious than I am.

Now read the corrected version the same way.

He is as pernicious as I am.

Another common mistake is to leave out one of the terms of the comparison. This can alter the meaning of a sentence.

Wrong:
I admire her more than Jane.

Right:
I admire her more than Jane does.

Or:
I admire her more than I admire Jane.

In some sentences, the meaning may be drastically altered by omitting a necessary word.

Mr. Grant helps around the office by filing and making his own coffee. (Does Mr. Grant file his coffee?)

Mr. Grant helps around the office by filing and *by* making his own coffee.

Difficulties also arise in sentences that use *and, who* or *and, which* clauses.

Wrong:
They bumped into Marge at the top of the stairs, an unlit passageway at best and which is dangerous at worst.

Right:
They bumped into Marge at the top of the stairs, which is an unlit passageway at best and which is dangerous at worst.

Note that the second *which* can be left out as long as the first is present. Another option might be:

> They bumped into Marge at the top of the stairs—an unlit passageway at best, and dangerous at worst.

The **correlatives** *either-or, neither-nor, not only-but also, both-and*, and *whether-or* require parallel constructions.

> *Wrong:*
> You are either late or I am early. (This makes the adjective *late* parallel with the clause *I am early*.)
>
> *Right:*
> Either you are late or I am early. (Now we have two parallel clauses.)
>
> *Wrong:*
> Philbert not only has been understanding to his secretary, but also to his wife. (A verb parallel with a preposition.)
>
> *Right:*
> Philbert has been understanding not only to his secretary, but also to his wife. (Two parallel phrases.)

Larger elements also need to be parallel. This is especially important in writing where lists or "bulleted" items are used. It is necessary that all items in a series be kept parallel. Note the following problems with parallel structure.

> In using the following program, we have set certain long-range objectives. These include:
> - Informing children of the voting process.
> - Increasing voter participation in the future.
> - Increasing voter understanding in the future in the home as well as in the classroom.
> - Promote patriotism by having people become involved in the U.S. government.
> - Promote teaching of the governmental processes in schools and in the home.

The problem is that the first three items begin with gerunds (remember those?) and the last two begin with verbs. Change the last two to gerund forms (*promoting*) and the structure is parallel.

> General Goals:
> - Gear programs to specified target audiences.
> - Program elements to be evaluated.
> - Design a program which is easy to use and understand and which is interesting.
> - Testing of all elements by target audiences.

The problem here is that two of the items begin with verbs, one begins with a gerund, and one begins with a noun. To correct this structure, the second item should read, "*Evaluate* program elements," and the fourth item shoud read, "*Test* all elements by target audience."

> Some notable economic/financial highlights of 1983 were:
> • Increased GNP of approximately 6.2% (fourth quarter to fourth quarter)
> • A drop in unemployment from 10% to 8.2% by year-end — Inflation (C.P.I.) of approximately 4.0% (December to December)
> • Corporate profits up approximately 15% on average and still rising
> • A strong U.S. dollar.

By converting each of the items to phrases beginning with nouns, we would achieve parallel structure. Thus:

- An increased GNP...
- A drop in unemployment...
- A rise in corporate profits...
- A strong U.S. dollar

Related to parallel structure is the problem of *mixed construction*. The most common error results from shifting from one verb tense to another or from one "person" or "voice" to another in pronoun references.

Mixed:
My secretary told me she *would* have the letter for me as soon as she *can* get to the word processor.

Fixed:
My secretary told me she *would* have the letter for me as soon as she *could* get to the word processor. (or *will-can.*)

Mixed:
People are always making mistakes. *You* could avoid most of them by thinking before *you* act.

Fixed:
We are always making mistakes. *We* could avoid most of them by thinking before *we* act.

Mixed:
A man (or male of the species) *is* a complex being, and *he is* quite territorial. *They are* constantly on the alert for competitors.

Fixed:
A man (or male of the species) is a complex being, and *he is* quite territorial. *He is* constantly on the alert for competitors.

Punctuation

Internal punctuation is possibly the most complex area of grammar because it is so open to interpretation.

Internal punctuation marks indicate the relationship of elements within a sentence. In English, five punctuation marks are used for this purpose: **commas**, **semicolons**, **colons**, **dashes**, and **parentheses.** Using these marks correctly requires adherence to certain rules. The only options are those which allow the writer nuances in meaning. For example, consider this unpunctuated sentence:

> Woman without her man is an animal.

Now, place two commas setting off *without her man* as a parenthetical element and you have:

> Woman, without her man, is an animal.

Place a period setting off *woman* as a statement, make *without her* an introductory phrase, and you have:

> Woman. Without her, man is an animal.

As you can see, punctuation is all important to meaning. How well we punctuate may mean the difference between being understood and being misunderstood.

Commas

The simplest reason for using a comma is to indicate a pause. Commas are most commonly used to separate main clauses joined by a coordinating conjunction.

> I was tied up all morning with work, and I had a meeting just before lunch.

> Marvin could not make it to the ten o'clock meeting, but he sent his secretary to take notes.

The only exception to this rule is when one or both of the clauses are very short.

> Just ask me and I'll go.

The bottom line is, if in doubt—use a comma. Ultimately, it is better to use punctuation than leave it out and cause possible confusion.

Don't mistake a compound *subject* for a compound *sentence*. A compound subject does not require a comma.

> Both the obnoxious tasting potato salad and the equally horrible hot dogs were provided by the company food service crew.

Commas are used to separate introductory clauses and phrases from a main clause.

> When he saw the approaching storm, he quickly ran to the cellar and locked himself in.
>
> In an office of so many functions, she remains functionless.

The comma may be omitted, however, after very short introductory clauses or phrases unless this omission may lead to misunderstanding, as in the following examples.

> After dark streets in the poorer section of town begin to empty.
>
> After dark, streets in the poorer section of town begin to empty.
>
> When you return gifts will be waiting for you under the tree.
>
> When you return, gifts will be waiting for you under the tree.

Commas are used to set off transitional expressions such as, *for example*, *on the other hand*, *in fact*, or *secondly*. Normally, these occur at the beginning of the sentence and are followed by a comma.

> In fact, Jones was so intoxicated that he couldn't even sign his name.
>
> For example, the number of schools receiving aid under the new computer loan program has doubled in the past six months.

Commas also separate items in a series (usually called a **coordinate series**).

> Eudora spoke haltingly, quietly, and quickly.
>
> The woods are quiet, dark, and deep.
>
> It is a dark, dank, foreboding place to work.

There is an option in this case. Many people always include the final comma after the *and* in a coordinate series. Others always leave it out. It's up to you, of course, but remember to leave it in if there is any chance of confusion.

> Perry used his windfall to purchase a number of new items including an automobile, a new television, some antique books and furniture. (Was the furniture antique too?—insert a comma.)

Remember to group items joined by *and* and separate these groupings by commas.

> Perry used his windfall to purchase a number of new items including an automobile and tires, a new television and VCR combination, and a remodeled sailboat.

Use a comma to separate **coordinate adjectives**. When using a series of coordinate adjectives, make sure you have grouped the adjectives for your exact meaning.

> He sat behind a long, polished, mahogany desk and smiled his best Cheshire Cat smile. (This means that he sat behind a mahogany desk which was both long and polished.)

> He sat behind a long, polished mahogany desk and smiled his best Cheshire Cat smile. (This means that he sat behind a long desk of polished mahogany as opposed to unpolished mahogany.)

Be sure that all coordinate adjectives refer to the noun they modify. If one or more of the adjectives refers to another adjective in the series, don't separate it from the adjective to which it refers with a comma.

> It was a dark red house. (Was the house dark, or was it a dark shade of red?)

Set off **nonrestrictive elements** with commas. Do not set off **restrictive elements** with commas. A nonrestrictive element is a word or group of words that is a supplement to, rather than an integral part of, the basic word or group of words it modifies. If the words or phrases can be omitted without changing the meaning of the sentence, they are nonrestrictive and must be set off by punctuation. If the words or phrases may not be omitted without impairing the sense of the sentence, they are restrictive and must not be set off.

> Bank employees, who are highly paid, can afford vacations to the Virgin Islands. (This applies to all bank employees and is therefore nonrestrictive.)

> Bank employees who are highly paid can afford vacations to the Virgin Islands. (This applies only to those bank employees who are highly paid and is therefore restrictive.)

It's appropriate here to mention two words—*that* and *which*— that often cause some confusion. The key to understanding exactly when each should be used is knowing whether they represent a restrictive or nonrestrictive element within the sentence. *That* is the defining or restrictive pronoun while *which* is the nondefining or nonrestrictive pronoun.

The copier *that* is broken is on the third floor. (Indicates which copier we are talking about.)

The copier, *which* is broken, is on the third floor. (Indicates some additional information about the copier in question.)

When speaking of people, always use *who*.

That crowd from the Marketing Department, *who* are on the third floor, just barricaded themselves in the lounge. (Refers to the clique, not necessarily the entire department.)

That crowd from the Marketing Department, *which* is on the third floor, just barricaded themselves in the lounge. (Refers to the whole department.)

That crowd from the Marketing Department *that* is on the third floor just barricaded themselves in the lounge. (Refers to a specific Marketing Department.)

Semicolons

Semicolons are normally used as substitutes for commas when a relationship exists between two clauses yet the ideas are strong enough to appear almost as separate sentences. Semicolons can be used in place of commas when separating main clauses joined by a coordinating conjunction, especially when the clauses already contain commas.

Joan, the best secretary in the office, won the secretary of the month award; but Anne, Becky, and Ruth were all given honorable mentions.

Semicolons should also be used to separate main clauses not joined by a coordinating conjunction, especially if the two clauses show a strong relationship of ideas.

Fred is a total flake; every day he proves it more.

Never join sentence elements of unequal grammatical rank. Always make sure both clauses are main clauses.

Wrong:
Fred is a total flake; although he is sincere.

Right:
Although Fred is a total flake, he is sincere.

Use a semicolon to separate main clauses joined by a conjunctive adverb.

John was late for work this morning; however, he brought doughnuts.

Dr. Howard has published several works over the past ten years; therefore, he is considered an authority.

Colons

Colons are overused in most writing. The colon is most appropriately used to separate two main clauses, the second of which amplifies the first.

On the door of the men's room was posted a sign: Off limits due to bi-functional overload.

Note that the first word of a complete sentence following a colon may be capitalized or not—one of the few options in the correct use of grammar. The most common use of the colon is as a means of introducing a list.

Sales of the "Gaftex" plastic elbow have increased as follows:
- 20% in January
- 30% in May
- 10% in July.

A number of new applications have been discovered including: automotive, industrial, aerospace, refined foods, and retail sales.

In the last example, you could do just as well by omitting the colon altogether.

Dashes and Parentheses

Dashes and **parentheses** are used in place of commas to either add or subtract emphasis. They are used to set off parenthetical expressions that abruptly interrupt the structure of the sentence. The choice of which marks to use is entirely up to you. Most writers, however, use dashes to set off statements that they wish to emphasize, and parentheses to set off less emphatic statements.

Emphatic:
The bottom line—as the boss often said—is the bottom line.

Less Emphatic:
The bottom line (as the boss often said) is the bottom line.

No Emphasis:
The bottom line, as the boss often said, is the bottom line.

Dashes can also be used to prevent confusion when commas might lead to a misreading.

Confusing:
Two women, Jane and Myrna, run the entire department from the confines of a small office on the third floor. (This could be misread [and there is always someone who will misread it] to mean four women— two unnamed and Jane and Myrna.)

Clear:
Two women—Jane and Myrna—run the entire department from the confines of a small office on the third floor.

When using parentheses, make sure to include any punctuation that normally would be used in the sentence without parentheses.

> Because she went to lunch early (nine o'clock), she was docked one hour's pay.

And if the matter within parentheses is a complete sentence, place a period within the parentheses.

> Whatever the reason, Fred chose not to attend. (He frequently pulls this maneuver.)

Don't confuse brackets with parentheses. Brackets are used to set off editorial corrections or explanations within quoted matter. They are sometimes necessary (but only rarely) to set off items in parentheses from items already set off by parentheses.

> The letter opened, "Dear Fiends [sic] and Romans."

> He [the manager of public relations] spoke at great length and with something less than aplomb.

> The bottom line (as the boss [Mervin Smirks] often said) is the bottom line.

Quotation Marks

Quotation marks are almost always properly used. What is misused are the punctuation marks either placed inside or outside the quotation marks. In the United States, internal punctuation, such as commas, is placed *inside* the quotation marks.

> "There is no use in working today," he said.

Periods are also placed inside quotation marks.

> According to Tom, "Work is the only true medicine for depression."

Colons and semicolons should be placed inside the quotation marks.

> According to Tom, "Work is the only true medicine for depression;" however, Tom is frequently wrong.

Always place a dash, question mark, or exclamation point inside the marks when it applies only to the quotation. Place it outside the quotation marks when it applies to the whole statement.

> He said, "Will I see you tomorrow?"
>
> Did he say, "I'll see you tomorrow"?

Remember not to place a period after the quotation marks if another final punctuation mark has been used inside the quotation marks. The same applies to internal punctuation if by placing a called-for punctuation mark you end up with more than three punctuations.

> The program, entitled "Johnny can learn to read!" will be available to most of the country this fall.

Normally, you would be required to put a second comma setting off the parenthetical element; but, in this case, that would leave you with three punctuation marks. The comma can be eliminated without disturbing the message.

Apostrophe

The **apostrophe** is used in several different ways, but you must remember to be consistent when you do use it. Use an apostrophe to indicate the omission of a letter.

> can't
> the summer of '42

Use an apostrophe to form the plurals of letters, numbers and words used as words.

> Cross your t's and dot your *i*'s.
> Count to 10,000 by 2's.
> Don't use so many and's when you write.

Don't use an apostrophe before the *s* indicating decades.

> 1960s
> 1980s
> the '90s

Use an apostrophe to indicate the possessive form of a word. Place it before the *s* in the singular form and after the s in the plural form.

> The boss's desk was absolutely spotless. (Only one boss.)
> The bosses' desks were absolutely spotless. (Many bosses.)

Hyphen

The **hyphen** is a useful punctuator, but is often confused with the dash when typed on a typewriter. (Most computers have both a dash and a hyphen.) On a typewriter, two hyphens equal one dash (-- = —).

Use a hyphen for compound words that are not yet accepted as single words. Many of the words we accept today as being single, unhyphenated words, started as two separate words, and then became compound words joined by a hyphen.

> base ball > base-ball > baseball

The only accurate way to determine whether a word is hyphenated or not is to check a recent edition of a dictionary.

Use a hyphen to join two or more words which act as a single adjective before a noun. Don't hyphenate two adjectives if they follow the verb.

> Arthur is a well-known philanthropist, which is amazing considering that he only makes $10 thousand a year.
>
> That Arthur is a philanthropist is well known.

Omit the hyphen when the first word is an adverb ending in *-ly*.

> He managed to glue the entire typewriter back together using quick-drying cement.
>
> He managed to glue the entire typewriter back together using quickly drying cement.

Use a hyphen to form compound numbers from 21 through 99 and to separate fractions.

> twenty-nine
> two-thirds

Use the hyphen with the prefixes *self, all, ex,* and the suffix *elect*.

> self-important
> all-conference
> ex-mayor
> president-elect

And use the hyphen to avoid ambiguous or awkward combinations of letters.

> *belllike* should be *bell-like*
> *recreate* means to enjoy leisure time; *re-create* means to create anew.

Mechanics

There are several areas we haven't touched on yet which serve to complete this discussion of grammar. They are: The use of **italics**, **capitalization**, and **numbers**.

Italics

Italics are a tricky business for the public relations writer. When writing news releases, for instance, the PR writer has to act as, and follow the guidelines of, a journalist. According to the *Associated Press Style Book and Libel Manual*, for instance, there are several rules for using italics (or underlining, which is the typist's substitute for italics).

For example, AP style does not allow for italics for the titles of books, records, and newspapers. It would have you place these in quotation marks. *The New York Times* thus becomes "The New York Times." And, for magazines, *Newsweek* would become, simply, "Newsweek."

Now, AP style is anything but consistent and is intended largely for journalists; and, as public relations writers, there are times when we have to write in acceptable journalistic style. However, most PR writers probably spend as much, or more, time writing copy for items which will be printed (house magazines, newsletters, brochures, etc.) as they do writing releases for the print media. As any typesetter will tell you, anything that is to be set in italics is so designated by the copywriter by underlining. In the long run, it will probably be to your benefit to become familiar with both AP style and accepted standard usage for italics. It will undoubtedly save you and your typesetter some problems later on.

The following rules, therefore, though they may stray from AP style, reflect standard English grammar usage—not AP style—for italics and use of quotation marks for publications.

- Use italic (underlining) to indicate the titles of entire publications.

  The New York Times
  Time magazine (Note that the entire name of the magazine is *Time*, not *Time Magazine*.)

  The Sun Also Rises (Note that the movie version of this book would be enclosed in quotation marks.)

- Use quotation marks to indicate a chapter from a book, an article in a newspaper or magazine, or a cut from a record album (the title would be in italics as it is a complete publication).

The article, "I Was a Teenage Corporate Executive" appeared in the June issue of *Forbes*.

Billy Joel has had several number one hits including "Keeping the Faith" from his album *Innocent Man*.

- Italicize letters, words, and numbers used as words.

  Your *r* s look very much like your *n*s.

  When you use the word *dedicated*, exactly what do you mean?

- Use italic to add stress or emphasis to certain words (but don't overuse it).

  I was speaking of *your* bad habits, not mine.

Capitalization

Capitalization is a tricky business unless you adhere to some basic rules of thumb. First of all, capitalize proper nouns and common nouns used as proper nouns.

1. Specific persons, races, and nationalities:

   William, Mary, American, Asiatic

2. Specific places:

   Dallas, Iran, Peoria

3. Specific organizations, historical events, and documents:

   Democratic National Committee
   Taft-Hartley Act
   Civil War
   NAACP

4. Titles when they precede a proper noun.

   Professor Wilson
   Dr. James Arlington
   President George Bush

   When titles follow the name, capitalize them only if they represent a title and not a job description.

   John Smith, President, Bank of the North

   John Smith, the president of the Bank of the North, was conspicuously absent from the meeting.

5. Common nouns when used as an essential part of a proper noun.

    University of Delaware (Not in "The university was overrun with bigots.")

    General Motors Corporation (Not in "The corporation stands to lose millions this year.")

6. An exception is usually made for State and Federal governments.

    The state encompasses some three-million square miles. (Speaking of the state as a land mass.)

    The State refused to reinstate voting rights to over 400 criminals. (Speaking of the government.)

    The Federal Government ran roughshod over the territory for over 40 years.

7. Capitalize geographic locations when they refer to the locations themselves and not to a compass direction.

    The Northeast is seriously overcrowded yet maintains a vast amount of virgin forest.

    If you travel northeast from here, you are bound to come to a fast food restaurant.

Numbers

Numbers are a sticky subject. Different style books and grammar approach numbers from a variety of ways. Probably the best method to use is laid out in *The Associated Press Style Guide*. What follows is a distillation.

1. Spell out all numbers from one through nine. The numbers 10 and above should be written as numerals. There are, of course, exceptions.
    - Spell out numbers at the beginning of sentences, regardless of the size of the number. (This doesn't apply to dates.)

        Forty people attended the meeting held in a closet-sized room.

        1986 is going to be a good year.

    - Spell out numbers to represent rounded figures or approximations.

        About two or three hundred were in attendance.

        He was obviously in his nineties.

    - Spell out fractions.

        one-fourth, two-thirds, seven-eighths

- Spell out numbers preceding a unit modifier containing a figure.

  five 9-inch toothpicks
  seven 1/2-inch pieces of plastic

2. Use figures to represent numbers in the following cases:

   - When numbers below 10 appear in the same sentence but refer to the same general subject as larger numbers.

     Melissa sent out for 3 sandwiches, 20 cups of coffee, and 4 small bags of pretzels, but she wanted them within five minutes. (The number five does not refer to the same general subject and so does not have to be written as a numeral.)

   - When numbers refer to parts of a book, they should be figures.

     Chapter 2, page 75, paragraph 4

   - When numbers precede units of time or measurement, they should be written as numerals.

     3 x 5 card
     9 o'clock or 9:00
     15-yard penalty

Spelling

Spelling is a problem. No doubt about it—many of us simply cannot spell. Part of the problem is our language. English, historically, is made up of many languages: Latin, French, Dutch, German and many others. Often there seems to be no logic to the way words are spelled in English.

For instance, the letter *a* can have many different phonetic sounds, as in *ran*, *air*, *day*, *papa*, or *lathe*. On the other hand, different combinations of letters are often sounded alike: *rec(ei)ve*, *repr(ie)ve*, *rep(ea)l*. There seems to be no logical reason for the difference in the sound of *c* in *citizen* and *cat* or the *g* in *regal* and *regency*. Some letters don't seem to belong in the word at all as in *i(s)land*, *recei(p)t*, and *de(b)t*. And then there are the words for which pronunciation would seem to be impossible if we didn't grow up knowing the difference: *through*, *bough*, *trough*, *though*.

Of course, knowing all this doesn't necessarily help the chronic poor speller. Knowing that *sight* comes from Anglo-Saxon, *site* from French, and *cite* from Latin doesn't help us unless we spell by context and recognize the differences in meanings of these words.

For the problem speller, there is, however, some hope. That hope lies in correct pronunciation, recognition of differences in meanings and spellings, and the memorization of some of the rules of spelling.

Correct Pronunciation

Correct pronunciation can act as an invaluable aid to spelling. Many words are commonly mispronounced leading to misspelling. The following list is by no means exhaustive, but it does contain some of the most often mispronounced words.

arctic	interest
athletics	irrelevant
boundary	mathematics
candidate	mischievous
cavalry	nuclear
comparable	prejudice
desperate	quantity
disastrous	temperature
grievous	veteran
incidentally	

Note that some of these words do have more than one pronunciation. If you have trouble spelling them, you should cultivate the pronunciation which helps you with spelling.

Many words in English sound alike but are spelled differently. These are called **homonyms** and the spelling must be derived from the meaning within the sentence.

ascent = a climb	assent = to agree
all ready = everyone is ready	already = by this time
all together = as a group	altogether = entirely
altar = a place of worship	alter = to change
capital = governing city, or wealth	capitol = a building
council = an assembly	counsel = to advise
bare = stripped or naked	bear = to carry or a stuffed Teddy
course = a path or way	coarse = rough textured
complement = that which completes	compliment = praise
principal = chief or most important	principle = a belief or rule
stationery = writing paper	stationary = not moving
weather = the elements	whether = if

Spelling Rules

Unfortunately, the only way for many of us to improve our spelling is to memorize the rules. This may sound impossible, but knowing some of the rules that pertain to your particular area of weakness can aid you immeasurably.

1. Write *i* before *e* except after *c*, or when sounded like *a* as in *eighty* or *sleigh*.

   belief neighbor
   ceiling receive
   deceive thief
   feign vein
   field

Naturally, there are some exceptions: *financier, species, fiery, weird*.

2. When using prefixes, add the prefix to the root of the word without doubling or dropping letters.

   *dis*appear
   *dis*satisfaction
   *un*necessary

3. Drop the final *e* before a suffix beginning with a vowel but not before a suffix beginning with a consonant.

   care + ful = careful
   come + ing = coming
   entire + ly = entirely
   fame + ous = famous
   ride + ing = riding
   sure + ly = surely

   In some words, keep the final *e* to keep a *c* or *g* soft before an *a* or *o*.

   change + able = changeable
   courage + ous = courageous
   notice + able = noticeable

   Again, there are some exceptions: Some words that take suffix *-ful* or *-ly* drop the final *e*.

   awe + ful = awful
   due + ly = duly
   true + ly = truly

   And some words taking the suffix *-ment* drop the final *e*.

   acknowledge + ment = acknowledgment
   judge + ment = judgment

4. The final *y* is usually changed to *i* except before a suffix beginning with *i* (usually *ing*).

   cry + ing = crying
   happy + ness = happiness
   hurry + ing = hurrying
   funny + er = funnier
   hurry + ied = hurried
   study + ing = studying

5. Double the final consonant before a suffix which begins with a vowel when a single vowel precedes the consonant, and the consonant ends an accented syllable or a one syllable word.

    format + ed = formatted (*a* is a single vowel preceding the consonant but the word is accented on the first syllable.)

    sad + er = sadder (*a* is a single vowel preceding the consonant and the word is one syllable.)

    stoop + ing = stooping (The word is one syllable but the consonant is preceded by two vowels.)

6. Sometimes, adding a suffix like *-ity*, *-ation*, or *-ic* can help you spell the base word by showing you the pronunciation.

    similar — similarity
    moral — morality
    symbol — symbolic
    grammar — grammatical

The bottom line is that good spelling can become a habit. Once you have learned to spell a certain word correctly, you shouldn't have any more trouble with it. There are some steps which might help you to spell troublesome words, however, and prevent you from using ingrained misspellings.

1. Look closely at a word which is giving you trouble and say it to yourself, taking care to pronounce it carefully and correctly.
2. Divide the word into syllables taking care to pronounce each one.
3. Always try to visualize the correct spelling before you write the word.
4. Write the word down without looking it up.
5. Now, look the word up to see if you spelled it correctly. If you did, cover the word and write it again. Write it one more time just to be sure you have it down. If you've written it correctly all three times, chances are you won't have any more trouble with it in the future. If you had some problems with any one of the three writings, go over the word again starting with step one.
6. Finally, make a list of words which give you trouble. Go over the list frequently using the above method until you have eliminated them one by one. If you are a chronic misspeller, this can seem an almost never-ending job, but one well worth the effort.

CHAPTER 14

The Basics of Style

Proper words in proper places,
make the true definition of style.
Jonathan Swift

Why study style? Why spend time on something that you should have learned in school a long time ago? The problem is, not many of us learned to write the way we do in school—instead, we learned on the job, picking up bad habits and having those habits further ingrained by people who couldn't put it down much better than we could. That's why it's important to pause for a few moments and check our writing style to see if we have acquired any bad habits that might be corrected, even at this late date.

That's the purpose of this section—to help you understand some of the accepted methods of "good" style and to apply those methods to your personal writing style. We don't want you to change an already good writing style. What we would like to accomplish is an increased awareness of how to change those things that you would like to change while leaving the good parts intact. I've tried to make this section as painless as possible by providing you with the most appropriate areas of style in the most abbreviated way. And with brevity in mind, let's go on to the lessons.

Working with Words

Formal vs. Informal

All of us think we know how to use a dictionary. It's part of every writer's library. The problem is that a lot of people don't *use* their dictionaries and assume rather than check the meanings and spellings of words. This leads, of course, to misinterpretation of written materials by readers.

One of the biggest problems in using dictionaries is deciding whether or not a word is appropriate in context. For instance, a word that might be entirely appropriate in informal English might not be appropriate in formal English. Dictionaries can be of some help. Most provide guidance in selecting the right word. For instance, a dictionary might label the word *swipe* as a colloquial or informal alternative to mean *steal* or *plagiarize*. You wouldn't want to use it in a formal, business letter. This brings us to our first rule: Avoid using informal words in formal writing.

> *Informal:*
> It seems that Mr. Jordan swiped the information on the new plastic widget from a brochure he found in his files.
>
> *Formal:*
> It seems that Mr. Jordan plagiarized the information on the new plastic widget from a brochure he found in his files.

It's usually safe to assume that if a word is unlabeled in your dictionary, it is considered to be in general usage and therefore formal.

For the public relations writer, contractions (which are usually considered informal usage) can be useful. Frequently, you can take on a familiar tone with your target audience by using contractions. For strictly formal documents, it is still a good rule to write out the complete word or phrase instead of its accepted contraction. Words like *can't*, *won't*, *isn't* should be written out as *cannot*, *will not*, and *is not.*

Jargon

All industries have their jargon. Banks call Certificates of Deposit "CDs," journalists call paragraphs "graphs," police call a record of arrests a "rap sheet," and highly technical industries develop an entire dictionary of shorthand notations. Reserve jargon for external information pieces only if they are to be read by experts in the field. For internal pieces, jargon is usually acceptable. For the lay reader, use jargon only if you are able to explain its usage in lay terms. It is wise to follow this procedure unless you are sure that your jargon has become accepted general usage.

When jargon becomes cumbersome, it overrides meaning. What we commonly refer to as "legalese" and "bureaucratese" are really overuse of jargon. The result is ambiguity.

> *Jargon:*
> Do not discharge your mechanical device releasing its base-metal projectile until such time as the opposing force has decreased the distance between your two positions to a point allowing visual recognition of the delineation between the

occular components of the aforesaid opponent and recognition of the opaque, globular housing thereof.

General:
Don't fire until you see the whites of their eyes.

Words like impact and input have now become jargon to many industries. They sound "trendy" to many people and give them a false sense of belonging to a select group of "experts."

Jargon:
I have asked Ms. Pomeroy to input the latest cost figures so that we may have the results by 4:00 this afternoon. (A noun misused as a verb.)

General:
I have asked Ms. Pomeroy to enter the latest cost figures so that we may have the results by 4:00 this afternoon. (A verb used correctly.)

Jargon:
The severe downturn in the economy has negatively impacted our industry. (A noun misused as a verb.)

General:
The severe downturn in the economy has negatively affected our industry. (A verb used correctly.)

Did you recognize any other examples of jargon in the above examples? What are they and how would you change them to a more general style?

In your efforts to write clearly and concisely, remember that the object of written communication is to communicate. In other words—don't "fuzzify."

Exactness

Exactness is an art. Most of us tend to "write up" when we assume a formal style. But when we "write up," we lose precision. What we should strive for is clarity, and clarity can be achieved most easily by using exact words. Most of our writing is read by people who know something about us and what we do, but we cannot always assume that to be the case.

Denotative and connotative meanings

One way to avoid confusion is always to use words whose denotative meanings most closely match those understood by our audience. The *denotative* meaning of a word is its "dictionary" meaning and, of course, the best way to determine that is to look the word up. The first example following uses the wrong word.

> *Wrong:*
> The employees were visibly effected by the president's speech on benefits. (*Effect* means result.)
>
> Right:
> The employees were visibly affected by the president's speech on benefits. (*Affect* means influenced.)
>
> *Wrong:*
> As a manager, Marvin was fine; but as a human being, he had some severe problems dealing with sex differences among his department members. (Sex usually refers to biological differences or the act itself.)
>
> *Right:*
> As a manager, Marvin was fine; but as a human being, he had some severe problems dealing with gender differences among his department members. (*Gender* has become the accepted term for the differences in roles related to the total experience of being either male or female.)

Naturally, your choice of words will depend on exactly what you mean. Perhaps Marvin, in the second example above, has some sexual hangups, but you don't want to indicate that if his problem is really with roles performed by his employees.

Connotative meanings are those your audience may associate with words in addition to or instead of their dictionary meaning. Connotation is the result of automatic associations your audience makes when interpreting some words. For example, you may intend the word *dog* to mean a four-footed, warm-blooded animal of the canine species. To audience members whose past associations with dogs has been positive, a picture of a particularly friendly dog may pop into mind. For some who may have had negative experiences—such as being bitten by a dog—the association may be entirely the opposite of what you intend. Although there is no way to guard against all such associations, there are certain words or phrases that you should avoid as being *too* vague in connotation to be useful to you as a communicator.

Think of the different connotative meanings for words such as *liberal*, *conservative*, *freedom*, *democracy*, *communism*, and *patriotism*. Words with multiple connotations may not be the best words to select if you are striving for exactness.

Some words or phrases may have little or no connotation, such as *place of birth*. The denotative meaning of this phrase is clear, but there is little connotative meaning. However, if we replace the phrase with the word, *hometown*, not only does the denotative meaning become clear, but the word also gains a definite connotative meaning—usually a positive one.

Specific words vs. general and abstract

Exactness requires that you be specific. Writing in generalities is even worse. When we read something which has been written in general, nonspecific terms, we can't help but feel that something is being left out—perhaps on purpose.

General words are indefinite and cover too many possible meanings, both denotatively and connotatively. Specific words are precise and limited in definition.

General	**Specific**
car	Honda, Accord LX
people	Delawareans
animal	cat
precipitation	rain

Abstract words deal with concepts or ideas which are intangible, such as *freedom* or *love*. Use these words, but make sure that they are not open to misinterpretation.

> "Enjoy the freedom of 7-Eleven!" (Does *freedom* mean that you pay lower prices, can shop 24-hours a day, have ample parking, preserve the American way each time you shop there, or what exactly?)

One of the parts of speech (remember those?) affected the most by inexactness is the adjective. A number of adjectives are extremely general in nature and impart little or no additional meaning to a noun, thus negating their function.

> *General:*
> Marisa, please take this report to word processing and tell them it's a rush job. (Show me something that isn't a rush job!)
>
> *Specific:*
> Marisa, please take this report to word processing, and tell them we need it by 3:00 this afternoon. (Now, word processing has a specific deadline.)

Keep it fresh

At one time, all expressions were original; however, that was probably a long, long time ago. Today, we're frequently stuck with trite or overworked expressions or clichés. The problem with these is that they may be entirely overlooked by your reader who has probably seen them a thousand times.

> *Trite:*
> Nine out of ten times Harcourt is wrong in his instant analysis of a problem.
>
> *Better:*
> Most of thc time Harcourt is wrong in his instant analysis of a problem.
>
> *Trite:*
> Harcourt is claiming his latest plan is a viable option in controlling employee absences.
>
> *Better:*
> Harcourt is claiming his latest plan is a solution to the problem of employee absences.

Public relations, like many other forms of writing, including journalism, has developed certain stock expressions which some might consider to be clichéd. Many of these are acceptable shortcuts that aid understanding.

> John Smith, *a native of* Chicago...

or

> Chicago *native* John Smith...

Generally, these semantic shortcuts impart the correct meaning without being vague or appearing trite. Other phrases have become clichéd through overuse, and have subsequently lost their meaning.

> The head of programming says this new product will keep APC *on the cutting edge.*
>
> James Sutton, president of Associated Products Corporation, *announced today* (May 25) the release of a new line of plastic widgets.

The key is to recognize trite, overused expressions and clichés and understand when they can be useful and when they can hurt your message. Remember, good writers avoid worn out words and opt instead for fresh usage.

Wordiness

Being too "wordy" is a habit that most of us fall into at one time or another. Perhaps, as was mentioned above, we once thought it meant we were writing in a formal style. Actually, the opposite is true. Formal English should be no more wordy than informal English. In fact, it should be even more precise because it is formal. As a writer, you will find that the best way to eliminate wordiness is through editing. You probably already have more editors than you need, but your best editor is still you. You can eliminate a lot of shuffling of papers up and down the channels of communication for approvals if you perform some surgery early on. When you edit, strike out the needless phrases and words that add no additional information to your work, and clarify with precise words.

> *First draft:*
> I would appreciate it if you could set up a meeting for sometime in the late afternoon, mid-week, for our next, important get-together.
>
> *Revised draft:*
> I would appreciate it if you could set up a time sometime late Wednesday afternoon for our next meeting.
>
> *Final draft:*
> Please set up a 3:00 meeting for next Wednesday.
>
> *First draft:*
> We would like to attempt to schedule our very next company picnic to be held in or around the city of Wilmington in order to facilitate transportation by employees to the site.
>
> *Revised draft:*
> We want to schedule our company picnic in Wilmington to make it easier for employees to get to.

Naturally, you don't want to be brief to the point of abruptness, but you can see what exactness can do in the editing process. The key is to make sure that all important information is covered in enough detail to be useful to the reader.

Unfortunately, we often over-clarify in an attempt to make our messages understood; however, much of what we write is simply redundant or not needed for clarification.

> The in-basket is completely full. (How can it be incompletely full?)
>
> Johnson has come up with a most unique design for dismantling the employee pension fund. (It's either unique or it's not.)
>
> The meeting date has been set for March 31, the last day of the month.

Emphasis

Organization of words within a sentence, sentences within a paragraph and paragraphs within a larger work is key to clear writing style. We typically organize based on the importance or weight assigned to these words, paragraphs or larger elements. By placing them in a prescribed order, we give the thoughts they represent emphasis.

Following are some of the standard methods for gaining emphasis.

- Place the most important words at the beginning or end of the sentence.

  Unemphatic:
  There was a terrific explosion in the Xerox room that shook the whole building. (*There* is an unemphatic word in an emphatic position.)

  Emphatic:
  A terrific explosion in the Xerox room shook the whole building.

- The end of a sentence is also a strong position for emphasis.

  Unemphatic:
  I know Tom was the one who stole the stapler.

  Emphatic:
  I know who stole the stapler—Tom.

- Increase emphasis by arranging ideas in the order of climax. Rank items in a series by order of importance, building from the least important to the most important.

  Jill was abrasive, lazy, undedicated, and basically ill-equipped to deal with her co-workers. (In this case, *ill-equipped* is used to sum up Jill's other attributes.)

  Watch out for an illogical ranking of ideas. If done unintentionally, this could cause some unwelcome hilarity.

  Because of his brief exploration of the casinos, Jerry became morose, despondent, melancholic, and lost twelve dollars.

- Gain emphasis by using the active rather than the passive voice. The active voice indicates that the "doer" of the action is the most important element in the sentence; the passive indicates the "receiver" is the most important.

  Unemphatic:
  Not much is being done to defray health benefit costs by the employer.

Emphatic:
The employer is not doing much to defray health benefit costs.

Unemphatic:
The study, accomplished by the Financial Department, showed a sharp decline in quarterly earnings.

Emphatic:
The Financial Department's study showed a sharp decline in quarterly earnings.

- Add emphasis by repeating key words or phrases. Such repetition not only adds emphasis, but often serves as a memory stimulant.

  I am afraid that false hopes were raised by these negotiations, false indications of changes which may not occur, and false expectations on the part of management as to its ability to fulfill false promises.

  Don't mistake repetition for emphasis with redundancy. The difference is in the added strength of the statement.

- Add emphasis by balancing sentence construction. Balanced structure occurs when grammatically equal elements are used to point to differences or similarities. The usual construction is one in which two clauses indicate parallel elements.

  Knowing the health hazards and still smoking is freedom of choice; not knowing and smoking is victimization.

  Working here is boring; not working here is unemployment.

- Increase emphasis by varying sentence length. Constant sentence length creates monotony, and monotony creates disinterested readers. Although this rightly belongs under the longer elements we will cover next, you should consider the value of varying sentence length within the space of two or three sentences viewed as a unit.

  I have discovered that the content employee is dedicated, remains on the job longer, suffers fewer illnesses, creates fewer problems, and rarely complains. In short, he is productive.

  I understand. You have a number of assignments due simultaneously, your secretary is out sick, your copier is broken, and you cannot get an outside line. I still need it now.

Working with Sentences

Sentence Length

A good rule of thumb for determining proper sentence length is to keep sentences at about 16 words long. Naturally, you're not going to count each word you write, but you get the idea. Short sentences are easier to read. This is also the case with word length. Nobody wants to stop and ponder a beautifully constructed word of eight syllables. On the other hand, too much of anything can lead to monotony. The key to good style, then, is to vary sentence length. Don't string together short, choppy sentences if they can be joined to form more interesting, compound sentences.

> *Monotonous:*
> Harvey walked into the office. He sat down. He began to type on his 1923 Underwood. It was the typewriter with the black, metal carriage. Harvey hated typing this early in the morning. He was never fully awake until at least 10 o'clock.

> *Varied:*
> Harvey walked into the office, sat down and began to type on his 1923 Underwood with the black, metal carriage. He hated typing this early in the morning, since he was never fully awake until at least 10 o'clock.

Notice that related ideas are linked as compound sentences. Linking unrelated ideas is an easy mistake, and sounds silly.

> Harvey walked into the office, sat down and began to type on his 1923 Underwood. It was the typewriter with the black, metal carriage, and he hated typing this early in the morning. (What does his typewriter having a black, metal carriage have to do with Harvey's dislike for early-morning typing?)

Another easy method of preventing monotony is to alter the beginnings of your sentences. In other words, don't always write in the subject-verb-object order. One of the best ways to vary this order is to use a subordinate clause first.

> Because of his dislike for early-morning typing, Harvey never showed up at work prior to 10 o'clock.

> Starting out early, Harvey walked two blocks at a brisk pace, then collapsed.

> Before you start on that report, come into my office for a little chat.

And don't forget—beginning a sentence with a conjunction is perfectly acceptable. Remember, though, that even conjunctions have meanings and usually infer that a thought is being carried over from a previous sentence.

> Not only was Harvey later than usual, he was downright tardy. And I wasn't the only one to notice. (Implies that the information is being added to the previous thought)
>
> Not only was Harvey later than usual, he was downright tardy. But I was probably the only one who noticed. (Implies a contrast with the previous thought.)

With a little reworking, even a series of clauses strung together because they are related can be fixed up. Remember, conjunctions can be useful but not if they are overused.

> *Clauses strung together:*
> Francine is always on time, and she frequently comes in before regular office hours, and she never leaves before quitting time.
>
> *Reworked into a complex sentence:*
> Francine is always on time, frequently coming in before regular office hours and never leaving before quitting time.
>
> *Clauses strung together:*
> He ran down the street, and then he stopped at the main entrance, and he took a deep breath, and then he went inside.
>
> *Reworked into a compound predicate:*
> He ran down the street, stopped at the main entrance, took a deep breath, and went inside.

Working with Paragraphs

As the sentence represents a single thought, so the paragraph represents a series of related sentences. There is no set number of sentences you should include in a paragraph; however, paragraph length is shorter today than in the past. Short paragraphs invite readership while long paragraphs "put off" the reader. The key, of course, is coherence, which means that ideas must be unified. You can give unity to your paragraphs in several ways.

Make each sentence contribute to the central thought. The first sentence should generally express the theme of the paragraph. Although the thematic statement may actually appear anywhere in the paragraph, the strongest positions are at the beginning or the end; and the end is usually reserved for a transitional lead into the following paragraph.

> Our annual operating budget is somewhat higher than expected due to the increase in state allocations to higher education this fiscal year. The result will probably be an increase in departmental allowances with the bulk of the increase showing up in the applied sciences. Although Arts and Sciences have been "holding up" well, we don't expect that they will be able to maintain this independence for long. As a result, their departmental budgets will also reflect this positive financial shift. Next year's outlook is a different story.

The lead sentence sets the theme for the entire paragraph, which is this year's budget. The final sentence indicates that the next paragraph will probably deal with next year's budget. What you want to avoid are unrelated sentences. If they are truly unrelated, then they deserve a paragraph of their own. If they are slightly related, then the relationship needs to be pointed out.

Arrange sentences in a logical order, and provide smooth transitions between them indicating their relationship. There are several ways to group sentences to show ranking.

- **Time order** and chronological order are sometimes synonymous, although chronological order often implies a direct mention of time or dates.

> The growth of communication in the northernmost regions of America was rapid and coincided roughly with the development of the land itself. In 1867, shortly following the Civil War, the first telegraph line was strung between Dawson Creek and Whitehorse. By the turn of the century, the lines had been extended through to Seattle, on the Southeastern coast, and Anchorage, along Prince William Sound. The First World War saw a flurry of development as military involvement increased in the region. And with this involvement, came a windfall of communication development which lasted until 1959.

Time order is appropriate when explaining the steps involved in an action.

> Changing a typewriter ribbon is a relatively easy task, even for an office executive on a Saturday afternoon. First, pull the ribbon-release lever, and remove the old ribbon. Throw it away. Remove the new ribbon from its box, insert it onto the spindles provided for it and snap it down. Next comes the hard part. Pull out enough ribbon to place around the ribbon guides against the platen and thread it through the "slots" in the guides. Return the ribbon-release lever to its original position. You are now ready to type.

- **Space order** implies movement from one location to another: right to left, up to down, east to west, high to low, and so on.

  It rained all day yesterday. The weatherman had shown in glaring detail how the jet stream would carry the warm, moist low front from the snow-filled Cascades of the Northwest, over the Rockies, onto the plains, and finally into my backyard on the Atlantic coast. Apparently, it hadn't lost anything in the transition.

- **Order of climax** means that arrangement follows from the least important element to the most important element in the paragraph, or in ascending order of importance. Most of the time, the climax is the concluding sentence.

  If the clerical staff is uncomfortable with the workload, their immediate supervisors are the first to know. Middle managers are often reluctant to act on "workload" problems, but if pressured, will pass on complaints to executive officers. If the problem isn't handled to the satisfaction of all the parties involved by the time it reaches the executive level, a vice president may have to intervene; but pity the poor vice president who can't handle the problem. The president's office is a bastion of corporate sanctuary. Woe to him who would invade it.

  When arranging sentences in order of climax, consider moving from the general to the specific or vice versa. Sometimes, moving from the familiar to the unfamiliar will soften the blow of dealing with a new idea.

  When we view each member of our office staff as an individual, we sometimes develop tunnel vision. We have to understand the larger picture in order to alleviate this problem. They are all a part of a much larger organism. Together they form departments. Departments form divisions. The larger company is composed of these divisions and the company is part of a much larger conglomerate. To take the analogy further, the conglomerate is only one of the hundreds of such groupings which help make our system of economics one of the most successful in the world.

Make logical transitions between sentences. Related ideas are given further unity by the use of logical transitions between sentences. A good transition usually refers to the sentences preceding it. Remember that a transitional word or phrase also has a meaning. Make sure the meaning adds to the understanding of the sentences or phrases preceding the transition.

> The floor plan was completely haphazard; furthermore, it appeared to crowd an already crowded office area. (*Furthermore* indicates an addition to the thought begun in the first clause.)
>
> Don Johnson was the first to try the new water fountain. On the other hand, he was the last to try the potato salad at the last company picnic. (The phrase indicates contrast.)
>
> Fourteen employees were found to be in violation of company policies forbidding alcohol on the premises. Consequently, inspection of employee lockers will probably become commonplace. (Indicates that the second sentence is a result of actions in the first.)
>
> The rate of consumption has tripled over the past 18 months. In short, we have a severe problem. (Indicates a summary or explanation.)
>
> Jeremy covered the news desk. Meanwhile, Judy was busy copying the report before Wally returned and discovered it was missing. (An indication of time placement.)

One of the major problems with the use of transitional words and phrases is the reliance on a very few common groupings. Many people tend to use words like *however* to bridge every transitional creek. After a while, its use becomes monotonous. The answer? Vary transitional phrases. There's always another word you can use. Think about it.

The same applies to transitions between paragraphs. Use words and meanings which tie the thoughts together and form a smooth bridge between subject changes. After all, even dissimilar ideas need to be linked. If they were so dissimilar that you couldn't link them logically, they wouldn't belong in the same document.

Paragraph Development

There are a number of ways to develop your paragraphs to show unity and coherence. Notice that all of the examples below supply relevant details in support of a main idea.

You will often find that **developing a definition** will add unity to a paragraph.

> There are a number of ways of viewing the office water cooler; however, to a social scientist, it is a communal gathering place at which ideas and information are freely disseminated. It is an informal location, usually outside the territorial boundaries of any one employee and therefore accessible to all on an equal footing. It is the traditional "oasis," shared by any who

> are in need of water and at which all are free to share. To imply that this communal ground is the "property" of any one individual or department is to negate its real value. At it, we not only quench our thirsts for liquid, but for information outside the formal boundaries of protocol.

Frequently, **classification** will serve to relate like ideas in a paragraph.

> There are three categories of clerical aid within the company. At the lowest rung of the pay scale is the clerk. A clerk's job includes light typing, no shorthand, much filing, and a tremendous amount of running around. Next up on the scale is the secretary. More typing is involved (at a much faster speed and with more accuracy), much filing, some shorthand, and a great deal of running around. At the top is the executive secretary. Typing is a must (at great speeds and accuracy), good shorthand, much filing, and more running around than the Stanford University track team.

The main idea can be made more coherent by **comparing or contrasting** it with a like idea.

> *Comparison:*
> A committee meeting is like a football game. The chair is the quarterback, and so is the directing force; however, the members are the players without whom no goal can be obtained. The key to the game plan, then, is to coordinate the players into a single unit with a single goal. The players must be made aware that a unified, or team, effort is integral to the accomplishment of that goal and that the quarterback is the director—not the coach. The director recommends; he does not command.
>
> *Contrast:*
> The typical office environment is orderly. Without order, little can be accomplished. Remember the recess periods of your school days? You were able to act freely, without consideration to the restrictive environment of the classroom. You were free to explore your voice, your agility, and your mastery of fast-paced games not suited to the indoors. Once inside, however, you were required to conform to the needs of the classroom—quiet and order. Within these confines, work can be accomplished with a minimum of disturbance; and the accomplishment of that work is as important in an office environment as in a classroom.

One of the best ways to develop a paragraph and its central idea is to show cause and effect. Most things in life are a result of something else. For most of us, though, it takes some thought to trace that development.

> The so-called "open office" environment popular in newer buildings today has its roots in several trends. Since the mid-1970s, energy conservation has been a major concern in the United States. The open office requires less heat in the winter and less cooling in the summer, due mainly to the lack of walls. In the place of these walls, we now have "dividers" which, although they serve to mask sound, allow for the free circulation of air throughout an entire floor. In addition to conservation, open offices serve to homogenize workers by removing the traditional boundaries of high walls and closed doors. Employees now have access to each other through a network of openings, yet maintain the margin of privacy needed for individual productivity.

Obviously, a paragraph need not be restricted to any single method of development but can benefit from a combination approach. The key, of course, is to be clear, and any method which promotes clarity is a good one.

Planning and Writing

A sentence usually contains a single idea. A paragraph contains a number of sentences related by a single theme. So too, a complete piece of writing, whether it's a press release, a backgrounder, or an article for the company newsletter, contains a series of paragraphs unified by a single theme and related by logical transitions.

For many of us, the writing is the easy part—planning is the snag. And the toughest part of planning is deciding exactly what to say and what to leave out. Most of us tend to overwrite. In the words of one observer: "Writing is like summer clothing—it should be long enough to cover the subject, but brief enough to be interesting."

The first task in writing, then, is to choose your subject and limit yourself to the information needed to cover it. There are several ways to accomplish this. One of the easiest ways is to work from a very general topic to a specific topic.

> banking > withdrawing and making deposits > avoiding waiting in lines > using automatic tellers > using automatic tellers in the lobby

This may seem simple, but it does help clear your thoughts and crystallize your ideas through the act of putting them on paper. Naturally, the theme of any piece is intimately tied to its purpose. If, for instance, your purpose is to encourage patrons to use the automatic tellers in the banking lobby, it may be necessary to come directly to the point in your pitch.

However, in doing so, you will probably use one of the traditional writing approaches.

Most of us remember our high school English classes in which we were taught to write various papers for different purposes. Among the most common approaches were:

Exposition—used to inform or explain
Argumentation—used to convince or persuade
Narration—used mostly for entertainment value
Description—used to explain through verbal "pictures"

In public relations writing, narration is the least frequently used except in feature-type stories. The other methods are often used and combined to present information to readers. A lot depends on whether you are trying to be persuasive, or are simply presenting information—the two most common goals of public relations writing.

The Central Idea

Once you have decided on the purpose of a particular piece, you should try to write down a central idea in a single sentence or *thesis statement*. Suppose, for instance, that your goal is to convince employees to come to work on time each day. This will be a persuasive piece. The method you have chosen to use might be exposition, which will inform your employees. What is your thesis statement? It might be something like this:

> Coming to work on time puts you in step with the other employees who work with you, gives you time to adjust to your daily environment, allows you thc leisure of some pre-work interaction with others, and impresses your employer.

So, in a single sentence, you have set down several controlling ideas which can now be elaborated upon. The next step is to develop a working plan or rough outline.

The Outline

Before you begin an outline, it helps to put down some ideas which are appropriate to the topic. These can be in the form of a simple list. For instance, to continue the previous example, perhaps you have decided to stress promptness by comparing the benefits of being on time with the disadvantages of coming in late.

Advantages of coming to work on time
—Allows time to adjust to daily routine

—Allows time for interaction with fellow workers
—Impresses employer
—Allows time to eat breakfast or have coffee
—Allows time to read through the paper

Disadvantages of coming in late

—You are rushed into daily routine without adjustment period
—You have no time to interact informally with fellow workers
—You do not impress employer
—You have no time for breakfast or coffee
—You have no time to read the paper

Now you have a starting point. It might be that you want to address the points one by one, covering the advantages first, then the disadvantages. Or perhaps you want to compare the advantages with the disadvantages one at a time.

Outline Organization

Outlines are extremely useful as a checklist of key points. You may use the outline simply to check your final written piece against to make sure you have covered all points (regardless of final order), or you may have each point represent a complete paragraph or section of your finished document in the order presented in the outline.

In either case, make sure that your ideas are related within each paragraph and that each paragraph follows logically from the previous one. The same methods you used to arrange your sentences within the paragraph can be used to arrange your paragraphs within a larger composition: time order, space order, or order of climax.

Unity and Logical Thinking

Clarity

We've already learned something of unity by studying the placement of ideas in a logical order within sentences, paragraphs and whole compositions. Now, let's turn to logic itself. In writing, we should try to present our ideas as logically as possible so that our message seems as coherent and reasonable as possible to enhance understanding.

A major problem hindering understanding is semantics. Semantics involves the meanings of words individually and as they appear in a context. We should be extremely careful to select words that hold the same meaning for the reader as for us. One way to do this is to define terms which are likely to be either misunderstood or not understood at all.

> The major cause of antenna malfunction is the lack of foundation stability. The antenna cannot be properly anchored due to permafrost, a permanently frozen layer of ice and soil some three feet below the surface.
>
> All copy to be printed by the in-house print facility should be camera ready (properly sized, clean, and pasted in place).

Often a word can be defined by inserting a synonym.

> The altercation, or fight, lasted only three minutes.
>
> Sled dogs are not only used to running over muskeg—boggy terrain—but often relish the softness of the ground.

Some words or concepts, however, require more careful treatment. Abstracts such as freedom, liberty, and democracy have meanings far beyond those found in the dictionary. We must be careful when we write to give some thought to a word's connotative meaning as well as its denotative, or dictionary, meaning.

> Productivity is the major responsibility of the individual employee. Although management is usually associated with and responsible for rises or drops in productivity, individual employees remain the sole determiners of these fluctuations. Do they arrive at work on time and refreshed, ready to work? Do they spend too much time on breaks or at lunch? Do they perform only the required duties, or do they work beyond those requirements? So, then, productivity is more than producing a greater number of "widgets." Productivity is a state of mind carried over into the workplace. Productivity means caring; and caring means taking responsibility.

The determining factor in deciding to go with a simple or expanded definition is knowledge of your target audience, and that is a concern of planning, not style.

Generalizations

A generalization is an assumption based on insufficient evidence. It is a belief that what is true of a few members of a group (regardless of how you categorize that group or what it composes) is true of the entire group.

> Women are lousy drivers.
>
> Orientals are inscrutable.
>
> Blacks are great dancers.
>
> Tall people are good basketball players.

Generalizations can be harmless or they can be dangerous. In writing, generalizations such as these should be avoided. If you do make a generalization, you must support it. This means that you must present adequate evidence that what you are saying is true for most of a particular group.

> The most striking figure given out at today's press conference indicates that four out of every five workers take some kind of drug on the job. A recent survey conducted by a Chicago-based firm within the various divisions of Associated Products Corporation shows that out of the 500 employees questioned, at least 400 indicated that they had taken drugs on the job. According to an Associated Products spokesman, the term *drugs* is defined to include prescription medicine, coffee, liquor, and the less traditional (and more notorious) illegal compounds.

In this paragraph, the writer has made a generalization, given supporting information, and defined terms. This would certainly be considered adequate support.

Cause and Effect Relationships

Logic is simply reason. What most people see as reasonable, they also assume is logical. It seems reasonable to assert that you *seldom* fall asleep before midnight, but any reasonable person would detect the unreasonableness in "I *never* fall asleep before midnight."

Illogical statements often result when the writer fails to set up adequately a *cause-and-effect* relationship. We can construct such a relationship based on either *inductive* or *deductive* reasoning. Inductive reasoning proceeds from the particular to the general. It implies a kind of generalization, in that generalizations are made based on specific evidence. That evidence is usually deemed sufficient to support a generalization. The results of scientific experimentation, for instance, are based on induction.

> A recent study by the Association for Scholastic Testing shows that school children between the ages of 7 and 14 learn quicker and absorb more knowledge when the lesson is interactive. Additional studies by National Employment Associates indicate that high-school students with computer skills attain higher-paying jobs upon graduation. It is clear that computer training is fast becoming a necessary component in the education process.

The deductive process involves working from the general to the specific. Specifics are usually determined from generalizations. If you know, for instance, that a high fever usually accompanies influenza—and you have a high fever during the flu season—then you might seek a doctor's care. You have deduced a specific need from a generalization. You may not, in fact, have influenza, but you have made a valid decision based on deduction. The basic assumption, however, must be sound for our deductions to be valid.

> It is clear that computer training is fast becoming a necessary component in the education process. Through this training, students will become better equipped to deal with a burgeoning technology. Teachers will be eased of the responsibility to be all things to all students, because of the interactive nature of computer learning. And students will ultimately benefit through higher-paying jobs.

As you can see, this deductive process was based on a previous inductive process. Most deductions are, in fact, based on previously collected information from which generalizations are made.

The inductive-deductive processes are prone to problems in construction. The following are the most common:

1. Because one item follows another chronologically, don't assume that the latter is a result of the former.

   > Helen came in late this morning, and everything has been going downhill since then.

   > Fred wouldn't be seeing Marge "on the side" if everything was all right at home.

2. Because one thing is true doesn't mean that you can infer another truth from it. This is commonly called a *non sequitur*.

   > The recent, sharp upturn in the economy will certainly result in lower unemployment.

   > Liz is something of an "air head." She'll never make it in the business world.

3. Don't beg the question. Sports interviewers frequently do this.

   > Champ? Was that the greatest match you ever fought or what? (Implies that the match *was* the greatest, thus biasing the response.)

   Begging the question assumes the truth of a statement you are trying to verify.

   > Janice snuck in at half past eight this morning. What do you suppose she's up to? (Maybe she slept late and isn't up to anything.)

4. Don't set up an either/or situation unless it really is one.

   Either you're going with me to the meeting or you're not. (Obviously a reasonable statement.)

   Either you're on my side or you're not. (Why can't I see the value in two different arguments without being on anyone's side?)

   This is often called the all-or-nothing fallacy because it sets up a false dilemma ignoring the fact that other variables or possibilities exist.

   Dedicated employees either come to work on time or they're simply not dedicated.

   School systems are either innovators, because they acquire and use computers, or they're traditionalists who choose to ignore the future.

Finally, never argue a point that you can't back up with facts simply because you *believe* it to be true. Although much of what we believe is based on personal predispositions formed throughout our lifetimes, it is never too late to learn something new or to add facts to our existing knowledge.

If you are to be a good, persuasive writer, you must learn to be objective. For most writers, subjectivity indicates that you have a stake in what is being argued or, at least, a personal opinion. Opinions are best left for newspaper columnists or editors who are paid to express their opinions. Objective writing is the hallmark of the logical (reasonable) writer. If you present the facts objectively, and they support your argument or point of view (whether that point of view is one which is personally held or not) your argument will be logically sound.

Correspondence

A discussion of style is an appropriate place to cover two of the writing forms not usually associated with public relations: the business letter and internal correspondence, or memoranda. Frequently, the public relations writer acts as a typical business correspondent, sending letters accompanying PSAs, writing letters of inquiry, or simply taking care of any of the myriad details that accompany everyday business and which require written correspondence.

Writing a business letter is much like any other type of writing. It requires conciseness and clarity. When reading the following information, remember everything that has preceded this section—it applies to correspondence too.

The Business Letter

A good business letter is clear and to the point. Most of us learned how to write business letters on the job. We learned from what we read and, unfortunately, much of what we read was clichéd and unnecessarily formal.

> As per your letter of March 21, I have enclosed the aforementioned donation to the United Way.
>
> With reference to your letter of April 1, I beg to inform you that a check in the amount requested is being forwarded to your office as of this morning. In light of this action, I request a meeting at your earliest possible convenience.

Can you spot the clichés in the above sentences? Do they add anything except a false, too-formal tone to the messages? If they don't, why use them at all? It is a mistake to think that if we don't write business letters this way, we won't be thought of as business-like. Business people don't have the time or the inclination to decipher such jargon. As with any type of writing, clarity and conciseness are valuable tools. Use them. Consider the following letter.

> Dear Mr. Alcroft:
>
> In compliance with your letter dated June 2, you will find the requested information enclosed.
>
> In addition to the information you have requested, you will also find a complete listing of all of the merchandise relating to the category in question listed alphabetically. It was deemed necessary to provide said information to prevent possible misquoting of prices.
>
> In accordance with our policy prohibiting the dissemination of pricing information to unauthorized personnel, we request that the aforementioned enclosure be limited to your perusal.
>
> Thank you in advance for your cooperation.
>
> Yours truly,

Even though Mr. Alcroft may understand the context of the letter, the message could certainly be communicated in simpler terms. This would clear up any possible misunderstanding and would definitely be easier on the reader, no matter what his or her familiarity with the subject of the letter. Now look at this revised version of the same letter.

> Dear Mr. Alcroft:
>
> I have enclosed the information you requested on the new product line along with a complete list of related items and their prices.
>
> Because our company has a strict policy against giving out prices to unauthorized personnel, please keep the list confidential.
>
> Let me know if I can be of further help.
>
> Sincerely,

Not only is the revised letter easier to understand, it is markedly shorter. One of the keys to successful business writing today is brevity. Using the active rather than the passive voice will also make your business letters more direct and personal. Moreover, phrases such as "you will find" or "as per your request" are superfluous as well as stilted, while including the pronouns *we* and *I* in the active voice indicate that you, the writer, have initiated the action. Remember, however, that *we* refers usually to the company. Don't use *we* if you mean *I*. In the above example, for instance, it might be inappropriate to say "We have enclosed the information" if you are the only person signing the letter. The use of what is known as the "editorial we" is intended as an indicator that the person speaking represents a group. It is certainly more personal to use *I* in most business correspondence.

The same preparation that goes into any type of writing should be used for letter writing. This means plan the letter in advance. Put down your central idea and supporting ideas in a brief outline form so that you will be able to cover the subject completely, yet concisely. And, above all, edit each letter for wordiness and proper style and grammar.

Letter Format

Formats for business letters vary from organization to organization. There is an accepted "military" style, for instance, that is common to all correspondence written in the military. Your company may have its own format as well. Learn that format and follow it. The following, then, is a generic format for business correspondence.

All business letters have certain elements in common. These are:

- Inside address (as it will appear on the envelope)
- Date (placement varies with format)
- Salutation

- Body
- Complimentary closing
- Signature
- Identification of signer.

The inside address

If your organization has a letterhead, use it. Type the address of the person to receive your letter four or five lines below the letterhead exactly as it will appear on the envelope flush with the left-hand margin.

The Date

The date the letter is prepared (or due to be sent if prepared in advance) usually goes next. The placement of the date will be discussed below in more detail.

The Salutation

The proper salutation deserves some detailed discussion here. It is usual to follow the salutation with a colon, but format varies (see below). Salutations can be problematic. How, for instance, do you begin a salutation for a person you don't know and whose sex is undeterminable from his or her signature? For instance, you have received a request from a "J. Harrington." You can't determine from this signature whether J. Harrington is a man or a woman. Make sure you don't create this problem for others—make your signer's identification clear.

> (Mr.) J. Harrington
> Office Coordinator
>
> (Ms.) J. Harrington
> Office Coordinator

Of course, you may use the tried and true:

> Dear Sir or Madam:

This smacks of too much formality for some tastes, especially if the sender knows that you know his or her name. Moreover, it may delay receipt of the lettero, or it may go to the wrong person. A better solution would be to drop the honorific from the salutation.

> Dear J. Harrington:

Informal salutations, such as *Dear John* or *Dear Judith*, are best left for personal letters or for business contacts with whom you have worked closely.

The body

Little can be said here about the body except that it should be to-the-point and as brief as circumstances allow. When you have covered the subject, you are finished. Don't embellish unnecessarily and don't be redundant.

The complimentary closing

Use the closing which suits your letter. Don't be too informal unless you are writing to a friend, and don't offend a friend or close business contact by being too formal. The most common closings are:

Sincerely,

Sincerely yours,

Yours truly,

Respectively yours,

Signature

If you have an extremely long name or if you write large, you might want to develop an abbreviated signature. Some people spend a great deal of time developing a distinctive signature. Distinctive, however, is often synonymous with illegible. Remember, clarity is the best policy. For those who do end with a flourish, the signer's identification will clear up any problems in translation.

Signer's identification

This is where you can be explicit concerning your preferred title or honorific. It is not usual to include college degrees as part of your title, but it is acceptable to use job titles or any other title which will aid your reader in judging your appropriateness as a correspondent. Normally, if you have a one-word title, it can be included on the same line as your name.

Martha Heyer, Treasurer

Paul Foyer, President

Titles of more than one word, however, should be placed on the line following the name. If they are extremely long, they should be broken appropriately.

Jamison Welty
President and Professional Advisor
Public Affairs Society of America

Typical Formats

There are a number of accepted formats for business letters. You should determine which one is standard for your organization and stick with it. If your company doesn't have a standard, it might be a good idea to develop one. The following formats are the most common.

Full-blocked

In the full-blocked style, all elements are flush left. Lines are single-spaced and paragraphs are double-spaced.

April 7, 19__

Geoffrey B. Alcroft
1459 Alder Place
Wilmington, Delaware 19808

Dear Mr. Alcroft:

I have enclosed the information you requested on the new product line along with a complete list of related items and their prices.

Because our company has a strict policy against giving out prices to unauthorized personnel, please keep the list confidential.

Let me know if I can be of further help.

Sincerely,

Susan Beach
Marketing Representative

Exhibit 14.1— Full-Blocked Letter Format

Blocked

In the blocked format, all elements are flush left except the date complimentary closing, signature, and signer's identification.

```
                                    April 7, 19__


Geoffrey B. Alcroft
1459 Alder Place
Wilmington, Delaware 19808


Dear Mr. Alcroft:

I have enclosed the information you requested on the new
product line along with a complete list of related items
and their prices.

Because our company has a strict policy against giving
out prices to unauthorized personnel, please keep the
list confidential.

Let me know if I can be of further help.


                                    Sincerely,



                                    Susan Beach
                                    Marketing Representative
```

Exhibit 14.2—Blocked Letter Format

Semi-blocked

Semi-blocked is the same as blocked except that the beginning of each paragraph is indented, usually five or six spaces. There are some variations in this style due to the paragraph indention. The original purpose of paragraph indention was to signify to the reader, visually, breaks in thoughts. The indentions represent new paragraphs. An alternate method, developed later, separated paragraphs by extra spaces (as in the full-blocked and blocked formats). Reason would tell us, then, that extra spacing between indented paragraphs is superfluous; however, some semi-blocked formats require indention *and* extra spacing.

April 7, 19__

Geoffrey B. Alcroft
1459 Alder Place
Wilmington, Delaware 19808

Dear Mr. Alcroft:

I have enclosed the information you requested on the new product line along with a complete list of related items and their prices.

Because our company has a strict policy against giving out prices to unauthorized personnel, please keep the list confidential.

Let me know if I can be of further help.

Sincerely,

Susan Beach
Marketing Representative

Exhibit 14.3—Semi-Blocked Letter Format

The Memorandum

Memoranda, or memos, are short messages exchanged within an organization, and, therefore, are less formal than other forms of correspondence. Naturally, the informality of a memo will be dictated by the working relationship of the parties using it. You wouldn't want to be too informal in a memo to the company president, but an informal note might be quite acceptable between you and someone else in your own department.

The beauty of a memo is its brevity and clarity. Unfortunately, too many memo writers think that the memorandum is a forum for obscurity and longwindedness. The very form of the memo lends itself to clarity. Where else will you find explicit directions as to who receives it, who is sending it, and what it is about before you even get to the body of the message? Like other forms of business correspondence, the memo follows some basic format guidelines. First, the word *memorandum* is usually typed or printed somewhere near the top of the form. This is followed by the information mentioned above.

MEMORANDUM

TO:

FROM:

DATE:

SUBJECT: (or sometimes, RE:)

Be sure to include all of the information necessary for the receiver to pinpoint exactly who sent the memo, including your name, department, and sometimes telephone number or extension.

Although we've all seen memos that were long enough to be small novels, the intent of a memo is to be brief. A memorandum is, in fact, a reminder, not a report. Come straight to the point in your opening sentence, which will serve as an introduction to the subject of the memo. Follow the "lead" with the body of the memo. This should include, in the most concise terms, the information necessary to get your point across. Most memos end with a brief conclusion, usually a "call for action" of some sort.

And, by the way, memos are not normally signed at the bottom. Instead, they are usually initialed after the sender's name at the beginning of the memo.

MEMORANDUM

TO: James Sutton

FROM: William J. Hoffman, Project Coordinator

DATE: April 10, 19__

SUBJECT: Upcoming marketing strategy meeting

I have some suggestions for the marketing strategy meeting scheduled for next Wednesday (April 17). I think these are worth talking over in advance.

1. We should seriously consider taking on a professional marketing firm to handle the logistics.

2. We should also consider hiring an outside ad agency to work with the marketing firm, through us.

3. In order to prevent "hurt feelings" among our own marketing people, we should remind them of the size of the project and the money involved. We may have to provide some visual info on this.

4. We should consider inviting Herb Simmons from the "Plaget" development project to the meeting. He worked out a similar plan for their big product push two years ago. He might be able to back us up.

Let me know if you want to get together on this before Wednesday. If you can't reach me on my line, give my secretary a ring.

Exhibit 14.4— Interoffice Memorandum

Some Final Thoughts on Writing

Now that you have come to the end of this book, you should have mastered the basics of writing and produced most of the documents common to public relations. This will not, however, make you a good writer—it will simply make you a good technician. Good writing takes skill and imagination. Skill can be gained by practice. Imagination can only be gained by your willingness to experiment. Don't settle for the dry phrase or the lackluster sentence—bring creativity to every aspect of your writing.

Naturally, not every piece of public relations writing lends itself to greatness; however, as writers, we should always strive to present our ideas in the best possible light. In this way, even the most mundane may shine. It is not an easy task. As Alexander Pope said, "True ease of writing comes from art, not chance." Never look at writing as simply a job—it is an art and should be practiced with the care of an artist.

And read. Collect the writing of other professionals whose styles strike you. Read everything that you can in your field. Understand what you are writing about and never be afraid to experiment with your style. Of course you will be edited, and sometimes by those with less skill than you. Don't give up. In the end, good writing pays off—not only monetarily, but in the knowledge that you have the tools to write anything with the clarity and style of a professional, and an artist.

All the rest is mere fine writing.

Paul Verlaine

Glossary

Accompanying script. The version of a television script sent with the taped spot to the stations who will run it. It is written on the assumption that the shooting script has been produced as it was originally described. The accompanying script is stripped of all but its most essential directions. It is intended to provide the reader a general idea of what the taped spot is about and is to be used only as a reference for broadcasters who accept the spot for use.

Actualities. Audio or video tapes that feature newspeople describing an event, interviews with those involved in the event, or ambience or background of the event itself for a voiceover.

Advertising. The controlled use of media ensuring that your message reaches your public in exactly the form you intended and at the time you want. Advertising can be print or broadcast.

Annual reports. One of the most-produced organizational publications. Annual reports not only provide information on the organization's financial situation, they also act as a vehicle for enhancing corporate image among its various internal publics.

Articles and editorials. Usually for newsletters, house publications, trade publications, or consumer publications. In the case of non-house publications, PR articles are submitted in the same way as any other journalistic material. Editorials can be either paid for, as are Mobil's editorials and *Fables*, or submitted uncontrolled and vie for placement with other comments from other parties.

As-recorded spot. A radio spot produced by the originating agency and ready to be played by the stations receiving it. They are usually sent in the format used by the particular stations or on reel-to-reel tape which will probably be transferred to the proper station format. As with television spots, an accompanying script is sent along with the standard cover letter and response card.

Audio. Refers to the sound portion of a TV commercial.

Backgrounders. Basic information pieces providing background as an aid to reporters, editors, executives, employees, and spokespersons. This is the information used by other writers and reporters to "flesh out" their stories.

Body copy. Text material set in blocks in relatively small type. Distinguished from display copy (headlines and subheadlines and other larger type).

Body type. Type set 12 points and smaller, used for body copy. Distinguished from display type, 14 points and larger.

Brochures. Technically called folders, brochures are usually formed of a single sheet of paper folded one or more times. The typical folded brochure may be stored conveniently in a pocket, making it literally pocket sized. Brochures may be either stand-alone information pieces or part of a larger package.

Captions, or cutlines. The informational blurbs that appear below or next to photographs or other illustrations.

Cliché. A word or phrase used too often to be effective in either headlines or copy.

Collateral publications. Such as brochures, pamphlets, flyers and other direct marketing pieces. These are usually autonomous publications which should be able to stand on their own merits but which can be used as supporting information for other components in a package. They might, for instance, be part of a press packet.

Color separation. Process of breaking down full-color art into its primary color components.

Commercial. An announcement or spot. A radio or television sales message.

Compatibility. The degree to which different types of either hardware or software interact successfully with each other.

Comprehensive (comp). A layout prepared to resemble the finished ad as closely as possible.

Consequence. One of the characteristics of newsworthiness of information. Relates to whether the information has any importance to the prospective reading, listening, or viewing public. Is it something that the audience would pay to know?

Controlled information. Information over which you have total control as to editorial content, style, placement and timing, is controlled. Examples of controlled information are institutional and advocacy advertising, house publications, brochures, and broadcast material (if it is paid placement). Public service announcements (PSAs) are controlled as far as message content is concerned, but uncontrolled as to placement and timing.

Corporate advertising. Advertising paid for by corporations, but not relating directly to products or services. Corporate or institutional advertising takes three basic forms depending on the purpose of the message.

- **Public interest** usually provides information in the public interest such as health care, safety, and environmental interests. In order to have these placed for free, they have to meet stringent guidelines.

- **Public image** tries to sell the organization as caring about its employees, the environment, the community and its customers. Unlike the public service ad, the public image ad will always focus on the company and how it relates to the subject.

- **Advocacy advertising** presents a definite point of view. This may range from political to social, and positions, by inference, the company as an involved citizen of the community or the nation.

Daisy wheel printer. A printer utilizing a circular type element that rotates into place as each letter is chosen by the computer program.

Dateline. A brief notation at the beginning of a press release used to indicate the point of origin.

Demographics. The statistical description of prospects in physical terms, such as age, sex, occupation, marital status, education, household income, etc. See Psychographics.

Desktop publishing. The creation of publications utilizing computer hardware and software.

Display type. Type larger than 12 point, used for headlines and other emphasized elements.

Dot-matrix printers. Printers utilizing a fast-moving head to strike an inked ribbon, compiling letters and forms from individual bits.

Downward communication. Communication within an organization that imparts management's message to employees. Ideally, even downward communication channels such as newsletters permit upward communication through letters to the editor, articles written by employees, surveys, and so forth. Newsletters can also provide horizontal communication, but this type of newsletter is rarely produced within an organization; rather it originates from outside.

Drop shadow. A shadow created, usually behind a box, in a page-layout program.

Dummy. A mockup of the finished product, showing where the elements will be placed.

Exclusive. A press release or other information intended for only one media outlet. The same information may not be released to other outlets in any form.

Extemporaneous delivery. One of the four basic modes of delivering a speech. In this type, a speaker studies notes carefully and is theoretically prepared to speak knowledgeably and fluently on the topic.

Face. The style or design of type.

Feature style. A less objective style of writing that provides less hard information than straight news style. Features generally take a point of view or discuss issues, people and places. The style is more relaxed, more descriptive and often more creative than straight news style.

Font. A complete set of type characters of a particular typeface and size.

Formatting. Setting up guidelines for the placement of text within word-processing or page-layout programs. Indents, line length, spacing, etc. are examples of formatting.

Four-color process. A printing process that reproduces a full range of colors using red, yellow, blue, and black. *Full color*.

Halftone. The traditional method of rendering a continuous tone photograph into a series of dots of varying sizes that can then be printed.

Hardware. The machinery of computing comprised of the computer itself and all physical peripherals attached to it.

Headline. Also *head*. Larger type lines used to get attention in an ad or other document. Usually at top of ad. See *subhead*.

Horizontal publications. Any publication distributed horizontally, across a narrowly defined group with a common interest (such as newsletters on management techniques within a certain industry, or technical publications within an industry).

House publication. Any publication produced within and directed toward an in-house audience—typically employee publications such as newsletters and corporate magazines.

Illustration. Usually a drawing or a painting.

Importing/exporting. Transferring data from one software program into another.

Impromptu delivery. One of the four basic modes of delivering a speech. In this type, a speaker is expected to speak knowledgeably and fluently on a topic proposed on the spot.

Interest. One of the characteristics of newsworthiness of information. Relates to whether the information unusual or entertaining. Does it have any human interest?

Laser printers. Printers utilizing a laser-read photo transfer method for reproducing text and graphics.

Lay out. To put the elements of an ad in a pleasing and readable arrangement in a given amount of space. *Layout* is the noun form, the resulting physical "blueprint."

Lead. The opening sentences of a straight news story or feature article. In a straight news story, the lead should include the who, what, when, where, why and how of the story. Feature leads generally begin by setting the scene of the story to follow.

Live copy. The copy read by an announcer, in contrast to taped commercials.

Live tag. A message added by the announcer to recorded commercial giving local address, local price, etc. Often used when a national manufacturer's radio commercials are aired by local stations.

Master pages. In *PageMaker*, the initial pages on which elements to be repeated from page to page are created, such as page numbers, headers, etc.

Medium. A means of communicating: newspapers, magazines, television, radio, direct mail, outdoor, etc. Plural: *media*.

Megabyte (MGB). 1,048,576 bytes, equal to 1,024 kilobytes.

Memorized delivery. One of the four basic modes of delivering a speech. The speech is delivered from memory, but with cards or script as a backup.

Newsletters. A brief (usually four pages) printed publication distributed either vertically or horizontally. A newsletter usually contains information of interest to a narrowly defined target audience. The various types of newsletters include the following.

- Association newsletters help a scattered membership with a common interest keep in touch. Profit and nonprofit associations and almost every trade association in the United States publish newsletters for their members, often at both national and regional levels.

- Community group newsletters are often used by civic organizations to keep in touch with members, announce meetings, and stimulate attendance at events. The local YWCA or Boys Club newsletter might announce its schedules, while a community church group newsletter distributed throughout surrounding neighborhoods might be a tool for increasing membership.

- Institutional newsletters, perhaps the most common type of newsletter, are usually distributed among employees. Used by both profit and non-profit organizations, they are designed to give employees a feeling of belonging. They frequently include a balanced mix of employee-related information and news about the company.

- Publicity newsletters often create their own readers. They can be developed for fan clubs, resorts (some resort hotels mail their own newsletters out to previous guests), and politicians. Congressional representatives often use newsletters to keep their constituencies up to date on their activities.
- Special interest newsletters developed by special-interest groups tend to grow with their following. *Common Cause*, for instance, began as a newsletter and has grown into a magazine representing the largest lobbying interest group in the United States.
- Self-interest or "digest" newsletters are designed to make a profit. The individuals or groups who develop them typically offer advice or present solutions to problems held in common by their target readers. These often come in the form of a sort of "digest" of topics of interest to a certain profession. In the public relations profession, for instance, you'll find PR Reporter, PR News, Communicate, O'Dwyer's Newsletter, Communication Briefings, and many more. If you have the money to produce it, and an audience willing to read it, you can probably sell it.

News releases. The most widely used of all public relations formats. News releases are used most often to disseminate information for publicity purposes and are sent to every possible medium, from newspapers to radio stations. News releases generally are of three types.

- **Publicity releases** cover any information occurring within an organization that might have some news value to local, regional or even national media.

- **Product releases** deal with specific products or product lines. These are usually targeted to trade publications within individual industries. They can deal with the product itself, consumer use of the product, or a particular business or marketing angle.

- **Financial releases** are used primarily in shareholder relations; however, they are also of interest to financial media and many local, regional, and national general media have financial highlights sections.

Objective setting. A primary step in the planning process spelling out the purpose of your message. Objectives should be realistic and measurable. For public relations writing, there are three types of objectives: informational, attitudinal and behavioral.

Offset lithography. The printing process based on the principle that oil and water don't mix. In offset lithography, the nonprinting area of the printing plate accepts water but not ink, while the image, or printing, area accepts ink but not water. During the printing process, both water and ink are applied to the plate as it revolves. It is named *offset* printing because the plate isn't a reverse image as in most printing processes. Instead, the plate transfers its positive image to an offset cylinder made of rubber (which reverses the image), and from there to the paper.

Output device. The device by which you print your document from a computer. It can be any type of printer (e.g., LaserWriter) or typesetter (e.g., Linotronic) or any number of graphic plotters or other such instruments.

Pasteup. A layout in which all types and illustrative material are combined for reproduction as a single unit.

PC (personal computer). A generic term for a single-user microcomputer, typically an IBM or IBM clone.

Perfect binding. A binding for publications that are expected to receive a great deal of use and/or be around for a while. The backs of the collated signatures are trimmed or ground off and dense adhesive is applied. While it's still sticky, a bonding/lining is placed atop the adhesive and the cover is glued on. The adhesive maintains its flexible bonding strength for a long time.

Pica. A unit of horizontal type measurement. Six picas equal one inch.

Placement agencies. Organizations that will take information, such as a press release, and send it out to media outlets using their regularly updated media lists and computerized mailing services.

PMT. Photo-mechanical transfer. A photostat produced without a negative (like a Polaroid process). Faster than *Velox*. Screened print.

Point. A unit of vertical measurement of type: 12 points to a pica; 72 point to an inch.

Positioning. A marketing strategy which takes into consideration how consumers perceive a product or idea relative to competitive offerings.

Press kit. One of the most common methods of distributing brochures and other collateral information pieces. Press kits are produced and used for a wide variety of public relations purposes, including product promotion presentations, press conferences, and as promotional packages by regional or local distributors or agencies

Process color or **four color**. Used for reproducing full-color artwork or photography. The illusion of full color is accomplished by optically mixing the three primary colors—yellow, red (actually **magenta**) and blue (called **cyan**)—along with black. Four color plates are shot through a screen to reduce solid areas to printable, graduated dot patterns. Because each color is shot through a slightly different angle screen, the screened halftone of each blends through the overlaid dot patterns.

Profile. A feature story written specifically about a person, a product or service, or an organization or some part of it. It literally profiles the subject, listing facts, highlighting points of interest, and tying them to the organization.

Prominence. One of the characteristics of newsworthiness of information. Relates to whether the information concerns or involves events and people of prominence.

Proximity. One of the characteristics of newsworthiness of information. Relates to whether the information is local.

Psychographics. Refers to describing prospects according to their personality and lifestyle traits. See *demographics*.

Public service announcement (PSA). A radio or television spot aimed at providing an important message to its target audience. The PSA is reserved strictly for non profit organizations—those that qualify as non profit under federal tax laws.

Pull quotes. A magazine or newsletter device of "pulling" out quotations from the text, enlarging the point size, and setting them off from the text as a device to draw a reader's attention to a point within an article.

Quick copy. A xerographic printing process. The larger model photocopiers used in this process can turn out multiple copies, collate, and often staple them.

Quick print. A printing process involving a small cylinder press using paper printing plates. The plates are creating using a photo-electrostatic process that results in a raised image created with toner (much like the toner used in photocopy machines). This raised image takes the ink and is imprinted directly onto the paper.

Rough. A preliminary sketch showing where type and art are to go.

Saddle stitching. A simple, inexpensive procedure for binding that nests the signatures atop one another and drives two to three staples through the spine and cover of the publication. Magazines and annual reports are most often bound this way.

Sans serif. In typography, a type that has no cross strokes or serifs at the tops and bottoms of characters.

Scaling. Enlarging or reducing an element in some increment of its original size.

Scene. In radio and television spots, a locale in which the spot takes place. A spot may be composed of several scenes.

Scripted delivery. One of the four basic modes of delivering a speech. The speech is delivered entirely from a script.

Serifs. The short cross strokes at top and bottom of characters in certain typefaces, especially those in Roman face.

Shooting script. A script constructed from a working script. A director will use it to produce a spot for television. It must include all of the proposed camera shots, transitions, narrative, audio of all types, and acting directions.

Shot. In radio and television spots, a camera or lens designation indicating location of action within a scene.

Signature. Groupings of pages printed on both sides, usually sixteen to a signature, but sometimes less, as long as they're in multiples of four (pages printed for binding are usually printed four to a two-sided sheet of paper).

Slice-of-life spot. A television spot that sets up a dramatic situation complete with a beginning, middle, and end. In the slice-of-life spot, the focus is on the story, not the characters. The message is imparted through an interesting sequence of events incorporating but not relying on interesting characters. Slice-of-life spots, usually use a wide variety of camera movements and post-production techniques, such as dissolves and special effects.

Slogan. Sometimes called a tagline. A cleverly written statement that communicates quickly everything a particular product represents.

Software. Computer programs.

Special. A press release or other information written in a certain style, intended for a specific publication, but being released elsewhere as well.

Speeches and presentations. The interpersonal method of imparting a position or an image. Good speeches can inform or persuade and good presentations can win support where other, written, methods may fail.

Spiral binding. A method of binding that allows the publication to open flat. Holes are drilled or punched through the gutter of the publication after the signatures have been collated and trimmed, and either wire or plastic is inserted or "spun" through the holes.

Spot color. The placement of a second color (black—or whatever the primary inking color—being the *first*) in a publication.

Spots. Broadcast messages, either paid-for advertising or PSAs.

Storyboard. An artist's rendition of a commercial, usually drawn on paper in separate frames.

Strategy. An approach to problem solving aimed at defining target audience, competition, product/service benefits, and message.

Subhead. May be (1) a display line enlarging on the main headline, usually in smaller size, or (2) a short heading inside the copy used to break up a long patches of gray.

Swipe file. A collection of publications and designs done by other people or companies. They help a great deal with design, layout ideas and writing style as well as with communicating ideas to typesetters and printers.

Talking heads spot. A television spot in which the primary image appearing on the television screen is the human head—talking. This style is often chosen for reasons of cost—talking heads spots are relatively cheap to produce—but it can be very effective.

Target audience. Those prospects to whom the product you are communicating is most relevant.

Thumbnail. A rough layout in miniature, at the doodling stage.

Timeliness. One of the characteristics of newsworthiness of information. Relates to whether the material is current. If it isn't, is it a whole new angle on on old story? Remember, the word *news* means "new."

Tint block. A shaded rectangle created in a page-layout program into which text is inserted.

Tone. An attitude or expression natural to a message.

Trade journals. Magazines produced for specific industries that provide news and stories dealing with the concerns and products of that industry. Trades typically accept product press releases and articles that deal with any aspect of the industry they represent.

Treatment. In television, a written narrative version of a television spot. A treatment is not written in a script format but may include ideas for shots and transitions.

Typography. The field involving designing, setting, and using type.

Uncontrolled information. Information which, once it leaves your hands, is at the mercy of the media, is uncontrolled. The outlet in which you want it placed has total editorial control over the content, style, placement, and timing. Such items as press releases are totally uncontrolled. Others, such as magazine articles, may receive limited editing but are still controlled as to placement and timing.

Upward communication. Communication within an organization that provides employees a means of communicating their opinions to management.

Vertical publications. Any publication distributed vertically—that is, intended to be read by everyone up and down the hierarchy (within a corporation, everyone from the mailroom clerk to the CEO).

Video news releases (VNRs). Originally, pre-packaged publicity features meant to be aired on local, regional, or national television, now VNRs are literally news releases designed as feature stories, usually for local television news programs.

Voice-over. The off-camera voice of an announcer who is heard but not seen.

White space. The space in an ad or publication page not taken with any other element, type, pictures, etc. An important design element in itself.

Word processing. Creating text with a computer. Word-processed documents may be used as is or imported into a page-layout program.

Working script. In television, the working script includes all of the information necessary for a complete understanding of an idea. A first draft in which camera shots, transitions, audio—including music and sound effects, and approximate times are fleshed out.

Glossary of Grammatical Terms

Adjective. Adjectives modify nouns or words acting as nouns. There are two basic types of adjectives: **descriptive** and **limiting**. **Descriptive adjectives** name some quality of an object.

> white house; small car; worn carpet

Limiting adjectives restrict the meaning of a noun to a particular object or indicate quantity. There are five kinds of limiting adjectives:

> **Possessive**: *my suit; their office*
> **Demonstrative**: *this suit; that office*
> **Interrogative**: *whose suit? which office?*
> **Articles**: *a suit; an office; the office*
> **Numerical**: *one suit; second office*

Adverb. Adverbs modify other adverbs, adjectives, verbs, and most other words. The most common way to recognize an adverb is by its -*ly* ending. Although not all adverbs end in *-ly*, most do.

Antecedent. An antecedent is a word or group of words referred to by a following pronoun.

Case. Case indicates the function of nouns and pronouns in a sentence. Personal pronouns (*I, you, he, she, it*) have different forms for the nominative, possessive, and objective cases. See **Chapter 13** for the proper uses of case, especially the troublesome use of *whom* versus *who*.

Clause. Clauses are complete thoughts which may or may not be complete sentences. The two type of clauses are **independent** and **subordinate**.

- **Independent clauses**, sometimes called **main clauses**, always have a subject and a verb and make a statement independent of the rest of the sentence. A sentence always has one main clause; however, sometimes it has more than one.

- **Subordinate clauses**, sometimes called **dependent clauses**, contain an idea less important than that of the independent clause. A subordinate clause relies on an independent clause for meaning, and is frequently introduced by a **subordinate conjunction**.

Complex sentence. A sentence that has a main clause and one or more subordinate clauses.

Compound sentence. A sentence that has two or more main clauses.

Compound-complex sentence. A sentence that contains two or more main clauses and one or more subordinate clauses.

Conjunction. A conjunction is used to join words, phrases, or clauses together. There are several frequently used conjunctions that serve to separate independent clauses. These are called **coordinating conjunctions**.

Subordinate conjunction. Subordinate conjunctions such as *because, if, since,* and *when* join dependent or subordinate clauses with main or independent clauses.

Conjunctive adverb. Conjunctive adverbs, like coordinating conjunctions, join complete clauses which are linked by a common idea.

Degree. Adjectives and adverbs show degrees or quantity by means of their **positive**, **comparative**, and **superlative** forms.

- The **positive** form expresses no comparison at all: *slow, quickly.*

- The **comparative** form permits a comparison between two (and only two) by adding *er* or the adverb *more* to the positive form of the word: *pretty, prettier; rapid, more rapid.*

- The **superlative** form which involves a comparison between three or more is achieved by adding *est* or the adverb *most* to the positive form: *pretty, prettiest; rapid, most rapid.*

Gerund. A gerund is the form of a verb which ends in *-ing*. The gerund is always used as a noun.

Indefinite prounoun. Indefinite pronouns act like nouns and therefore take no antecedent (*everybody, anybody, someone*).

Linking verb. Verbs that connect the subject of the sentence with the subject complement (the word that modifies the subject).

Noun. Nouns are words that usually name a person, place or thing. Subjects of sentences are usually nouns as are objects of verbs and prepositions. Although most nouns form the plural by simply adding *s*, some are irregular, such as *sheep*, and *woman*.

Parallel structure. Parallel structure involves putting similar ideas into the same kinds of grammatical constructions. Parallelism helps keep the meaning of sentences clear by organizing the elements into the same kind of construction. This applies to phrases, clauses, sentences, and longer constructions such as paragraphs. The problem may be as simple as making sure that you are using the right form of verbs within a sentence, or as complex as sticking to the same tense from paragraph to paragraph.

Prounoun. Pronouns substitute for nouns. Common pronouns are *he, she, you, they, it*, etc. Pronouns usually take an **antecedent**—a noun to usually preceding the pronoun and to which the pronoun refers.

Preposition. Prepositions are used to connect parts of the sentence. A preposition usually relates a noun, pronoun or phrase to some other part of the sentence.

Simple sentence. A sentence that has a single main clause.

Participle. A participle is the form of a verb which ends in *-ing* in the present form and in *-ed* or *-en* in the past form. A participle acts as an adjective.

Verb. Verbs are usually action words that make some sort of statement about the subject of the sentence.

Index

D

E–F

G

H–I

N

O

P

Q–R

S

T

U–V

W–Z

TITLES OF INTEREST IN PRINT AND BROADCAST MEDIA

ESSENTIALS OF MEDIA PLANNING, Second Edition, by Arnold M. Barban, Steven M. Cristol, and Frank J. Kopec

STRATEGIC MEDIA PLANNING, by Kent M. Lancaster and Helen E. Katz

MEDIA MATH, Second Edition, by Robert W. Hall

MEDIA PLANNING, by Jim Surmanek

ADVERTISING MEDIA PLANNING, Third Edition, by Jack Sissors and Lincoln Bumba

HOW TO PRODUCE EFFECTIVE TV COMMERCIALS, Second Edition, by Hooper White

HOW TO CREATE EFFECTIVE TV COMMERCIALS, Second Edition, by Huntley Baldwin

THE RADIO AND TELEVISION COMMERCIAL, Second Edition, by Albert C. Book, Norman D. Cary, and Stanley Tannenbaum

CHILDREN'S TELEVISION, by Cy Schneider

FUNDAMENTALS OF COPY & LAYOUT, Second Edition, by Albert C. Book and C. Dennis Schick

HOW TO CREATE AND DELIVER WINNING ADVERTISING PRESENTATIONS, by Sandra Moriarty and Tom Duncan

HOW TO WRITE A SUCCESFUL ADVERTISING PLAN, by James W. Taylor

ADVERTISING COPYWRITING, Sixth Edition, by Philip Ward Burton

THE ART OF WRITING ADVERTISING, by Denis Higgins

STRATEGIC ADVERTISING CAMPAIGNS, Third Edition, by Don E. Schultz

WRITING FOR THE MEDIA, by Sandra Pesmen

THE ADVERTISING PORTFOLIO, by Ann Marie Barry

PUBLIC RELATIONS IN THE MARKETING MIX, by Jordan Goldman

HANDBOOK FOR BUSINESS WRITING, by L. Sue Baugh, Maridell Fryar, and David A. Thomas

HANDBOOK FOR PUBLIC RELATIONS WRITING, Second Edition, by Thomas Bivins

HANDBOOK FOR MEMO WRITING, by L. Sue Baugh

HANDBOOK FOR PROOFREADING, by Laura Anderson

THE PUBLICITY HANDBOOK, by David R. Yale

NTC'S MASS MEDIA DICTIONARY, by R. Terry Ellmore

DICTIONARY OF BROADCAST COMMUNICATIONS, Third Edition, by Lincoln Diamant

PROFESSIONAL ADVERTISING PHOTOGRAPHY by Dave Saunders

ADVERTISING MEDIA SOURCEBOOK, Third Edition, by Arnold M. Barban, Donald W. Jugenheimer, and Peter B. Turk

HOW TO PRODUCE CREATIVE PUBLICATIONS by Thomas Bivins and William E. Ryan

For further information or a current catalog, write:
NTC Business Books
a division of *NTC Publishing Group*
4255 West Touhy Avenue
Lincolnwood, Illinois 60646-1975 U.S.A.
800-323-4900 (in Illinois, 708-679-5500)

Footstool in Heaven

Other novels by Brett Singer

THE PETTING ZOO

A Novel

Footstool in Heaven

Brett Singer

DONALD I. FINE, INC.
New York

Published in the United States of America by Donald I. Fine, Inc. and in Canada by General Publishing Company Limited.

Library of Congress Catalogue Card Number: 86-81478
ISBN: 0-917657-72-1
Manufactured in the United States of America
10 9 8 7 6 5 4 3 2 1

This book is printed on acid free paper. The paper in this book meets the guidelines for permanence and durability of the Committee on Production Guidelines for Book Longevity of the Council on Library Resources.

The author wishes to acknowledge the Vassar College Committee on Faculty Research for their support. And, profoundly, her husband—a gentleman and a maggid.

For my mother and father
That thy days may be long . . .

The highest thing a woman can hope for
is to be her husband's footstool in heaven.

(Yiddish folk saying)

1

Angel Dust

1

When Sophie was eleven and the world much older, her brother played a too-delicate Shark in his junior high school production of *West Side Story.* It was 1963 and children everywhere carried in their hearts the memory of a small boy saluting a man-sized grave.

In the auditorium, Miriam, her mother, sat on Sophie's right, her ears plugged with cotton. The noise of human voices filled her mother with terrible pain. And so it had been for the long and talented years of the children's adolescence: Sophie would sing and dance and play drums, her brother would act and do card tricks, speak French, and their mother would sit, hearing nothing at all but some voiceless interior music—the sound of oceans breaking? the punch line of some terrible joke? the noise of a language untranslatable into the words of men?

Years later, Brian, Sophie's brother, would sit in a darkened room in Berkeley, his shaved head catching what little light, and tell his sister over and over: "She never heard a word I said. She never heard one word."

Nineteen sixty-three and the mothers and fathers are clapping wildly around them. Sophie nudges her mother's hand whenever the music breaks. But this time, Sophie ignores her mother, who sits staring straight at the exit light. Brian wasn't in the number, leave Mother alone unless Brian is singing. Sophie doesn't care that the other parents must think her mother is weird.

Up on the stage, bathed in pink light, appears a girl who hangs out with the Jets. She isn't Maria. ("*Say it loud and there's music playing— Say it soft and it's almost like praying. . . .*") She isn't Maria or any of her friends. This girl wears basketball sneakers and jeans and her hair is styled like a guy's. Her name is Anybodys. She wears a duck's ass, just like the guys.

After the show, Brian finds them sitting on benches in the lobby. Most of the other families have left to order enormous ice cream concoctions at a restaurant on the highway. Kitchen Sinks, they call them: eight or ten flavors of bright ice cream, enough whipped cream to bring on angina, chocolate syrup and butterscotch sauce, hunks of cherry and crushed walnuts. . . .

"Where've you *been*, Bri?"

"Talking to the guys," Brian says.

"Talking to the *girls*, you mean," says Sophie. "And what's that on your face? Look!"

Penciled across Brian's right cheek is a sooty railroad track.

"That's my scar," Brian says.

"Well, why don't you wash it off?" Sophie says, but she's just being mean.

"Can't get it off," Brian whispers.

"I bet *I* could get it off," Sophie says, swiping at his cheek.

"Quit it," Brian says. "Just quit it."

"Use cold cream," Sophie says wisely.

"There's a *cast* party at Ronny DiPrima's. Mother, can I go to the cast party, please?"

"You were wonderful," their mother says. "You were wonderful. I was so proud."

"Can I please go to the cast party? Mom?"

"I thought we were gonna go to Maud's for Kitchen Sinks," says Sophie.

"That's where the fags are going," says Brian. "The *cast* is going to Ronny's."

"I want to eat a Kitchen Sink," Sophie says sadly. Marshmallow cream, pistachio nuts, gooey raspberry syrup . . .

Their mother rests a hand on each of her children's hands.

"So can I go?" Brian says.

"Take your sister with you."

"Will you drop us?" Brian asks. "Will you drop us?"

Their mother smiles and agrees.

"You'll be the youngest person there. Nobody'll even look at you," Brian warns his sister on the DiPrimas' brick stoop.

"I don't care," Sophie says as Mrs. DiPrima opens the door.

"It's Chino, isn't it?" Mrs. Di says. "And who are you, honey?"

"My sister Sophie," Brian says. "Sophie Spivack."

"I know Sophie . . . from Brownies. You were one of Rose Merman's girls."

"That's right," Sophie says. "I was a cookie princess. You were in charge of the cookies, weren't you? We came here to pick up our cookies."

"Cookie princess," Brian sneers. "Mother bought sixty boxes."

"I never forget a face," says Mrs. Di. "And no one forgets a cookie princess . . . ever."

Mrs. Di shows the children the stairs that lead down to the rec room. From below wafts the oil of potato chips, the high sound of girls acting bossy. Brian tugs at her sweater. "You wanna cut this princess shit? Hanging out with you is embarrassing. They'll nev—"

"Eh Chino," a boy says, slapping Brian's hand. He's gorgeous, Sophie thinks. He is a dream date for sure. "Who's the chick?"

"My sister. She ain't a chick," says Brian.

The boy takes a penknife out of his pocket and wipes it against his thigh. "Ever seen one of these?" he asks Sophie.

"Everybody's seen a penknife."

"Oh yeah?" the boy says. "Lots of people ain't never seen penknives. Savages in Africa haven't seen penknives. The wild men of Borneo haven't seen no penknives. And this ain't no pussy whittling knife anyway. This is a knife you could cut with."

Sophie looks into his swimming-pool eyes. He takes out a pack of Spring. "You smoke?" Sophie's heart fills with terror. This is a smoking party.

"I'm in sixth grade," Sophie says.

"Sixth grade? Sixth? Like one, two, three, four, five, *six*?"

"Yeah," Sophie says. "Sixth."

"Well, you're very *mature* for sixth grade," he says, looking right at her breasts. "You're very *developed*, aren't you?"

"Hell," Sophie says, "I don't know."

"Hell? You talk dirty, and everything. Are you allowed to swear?"

"I do whatever I want," Sophie says, meeting his eyes.

"Oh yeah? You wanna go sit in my car?"

"Your *car*? How old are you anyway?"

"Fifteen this July."

"You can't drive at fifteen."

"Uh-uh. You're wrong. If you live on a farm or your father is an invalid or—"

"*Is* your father an invalid?"

"My father's an alcoholic," he says, "but they don't even count that. The car's really my mother's. '56 Plymouth. You like Plymouths?"

"Um-hum." Sophie smiles brightly, flashing perfect teeth.

The boy whips his head to the side and a long sandy curl bounces across his eyes. Sophie longs to grab the curl, to pull it like a Slinky toy and watch it boing and boing. She has never touched a boy's hair except for Brian's. Brian used to let her play beauty parlor on him, even a year ago. Now he is thirteen and surly and sneaks her bras out of the hamper and reads dirty magazines, sniffing at her brassieres. She has never touched a boy's hair except for Brian's. Tonight she will touch a boy's hair and never quite recover.

"Lenn-n-n-y," a girl whines from across the basement. "Lenn-n-n-y, get over here."

To Sophie's surprise, Lenny, her Lenny, follows the thin whiny voice to the far corner of the rec room. "Lenny," the girl says, "sit on my lap." Lenny sits down on the girl's lap. And suddenly Sophie realizes it is no ordinary girl. It is Maria and Maria's lap. ("*Say it soft and it's almost like praying . . .*")

Maria is beautiful. She has hair as black as Veronica Lodge. Or National Velvet, or Connie Francis. Maria scratches her leg and creates a delicious noise: the sound of nails on nylon.

"You were great," Sophie says.

"Why thank you," says Lenny who is sitting in Maria's lap.

"Ow," Maria whines. "Get off!"

"I was talking to Maria. I meant you were great in the play."

"I have a voice coach," Maria says. "Get off, Lenny! Get off! He's in Manhattan. I *mean* it, Lenny. His name is Lorenzo. He worked with Kim Novak once."

"What's a voice coach?" Sophie asks.

"He's teaching me to sing. He's helping me with my range. He says I have an amazing range."

"How's your range, Sophie?" Lenny says, looking from her breasts to another boy. The two exchange wise looks. The other boy is small and blond. He is wearing make-up over his freckles. In the dim light, he looks a little like Gypsy's sister, Baby June.

Sophie doesn't answer. Instead she says, "I'm Brian's sister."

"Brian's a jerk," says Maria.

"Why? What's wrong with Brian?" Sophie says.

"He doesn't wear deodorant," one of the other girls says, squeezing her nostrils. "Tell Brian he stinks, would you mind?" Maria and her friend start laughing.

"Who are you?" Sophie asks.

"Whaddya mean, who *am* I?"

"Who were you in the play?"

"Anybodys," she says. "If you ask me, it was a dumb part. But they wouldn't let me be Maria because my hair is too blonde."

"That's not why," Lenny says. "They wouldn't let you be Maria because your tits are too small."

Everybody starts laughing, even Anybodys.

The girl, Anybodys, takes an ice cube out of the punch bowl and slips it down Lenny's shirt.

Maria and Anybodys tell Sophie to sit down and soon Sophie discovers that Maria is really Jane and Anybodys is Randi. Randi and Jane start whispering and all Sophie can hear are a few mysterious numbers: third, second, sixty-nine, fifty-seven or something.

"Do you know what sixty-nine is?" Randi asks.

"Sixty-nine what?" asks Sophie. She thinks of the corner of Sixty-ninth Street and Central Park West in New York. A day in the rain with her father. Italian ices and Macy's window. Her father's blond part in the rain.

"See," says Randi. "I told you," Randi says.

Across the basement, standing alone, examining a portrait of a cowboy, Brian looks lonely and sad. Sophie has an urge to hug him and smooth his scar.

"Sophie, you wanna see my car *now*?"

Sophie smiles at Lenny. Her legs feel light as matchsticks—they cannot hold her weight.

"Sure," Sophie says. "Let's go."

She follows the boy into the loamy night. The Plymouth is red and white, two-toned. Lenny opens the driver's side and ushers Sophie in. "Shove over, Sophie. *I* get the driver's side."

Sophie moves to the other side. She feels like she's never before seen a car. The dashboard is dazzling: Speedometer! Fuel gauge! The ashtray and lighter are lovely.

"I don't got the ignition key. I only got the door key," Lenny admits.

"*Could* you drive? If you had the keys?"

"This baby? Sure I could drive. But it's true, I *am* a great driver."

Sophie pulls open the ashtray. Inside the rusty drawer sits a clot of dark hair and a piece of bubble gum covered with ashes.

"Have a smoke," Lenny says, sticking two cigarettes in his mouth at once, lighting them both on the car lighter. Sophie takes one of the cigarettes and watches, mesmerized, as the luminous coils of the lighter fade: red-orange, pale orange, black. . . .

Outside the air is wet and the windows fog up from their breathing. Sophie inhales the cigarette—it tastes like burned popcorn. Lenny waits for her to cough, but the girl is a natural smoker. She inhales again like a goddamned pro. He watches her, fascinated. Her spiky eyelashes, her chubby nose, her eyes like grown-ups' eyes. Lenny's right hand reaches over, then walks like a delicate bird across Sophie's breast. Sophie pulls one of the curls at the base of Lenny's neck. The curl is as springy as a diving board. Sophie gasps for breath. "I love you, Lenny," she says moonily.

Lenny looks at her like he's dying. "Get out of my car, sixth grader."

2

Sophie wants to be a hippie, now that all the beatniks are dead. She works as a baby-sitter on weekends, a library aide after school, and she uses the money to buy Mexican blouses, cotton skirts, hoop earrings to stick through her ears. She reads in the *New York Times Magazine* about the trouble in Tompkins Square Park, the runaways and the dopers. Timothy Leary, Arlo Guthrie, Bobby Kennedy, Bobby Seale. It is 1967 and the Sexual Revolution has come to New Jersey—the Garden State, the Garden of Eden, the Mafia state, New York's whore.

Melanie Szasz and Sophie lie sprawled on Melanie's baby blue rug.

"What do you know," Melanie asks, "about lesbians?"

"Gertrude Stein was a lesbian."

"I know. I remember your book report. But what do you know about the sex?"

"You mean, what do they do to each other?"

Melanie nods.

"The same stuff as regular sex. Sex is sex," Sophie says.

"C'mon, Sophie. They can't *do* regular stuff. You need a penis for sex."

"There's other sex besides fucking."

"What do you mean?" Melanie asks. "Tell me everything."

"The French, they are a funny race. They kiss the cunt and fuck the face." Sophie read that in a book once, baby-sitting for intellectuals.

Melanie blushes. "I *thought* that's what you meant."

"You can have an orgasm from being kissed down *there*." Sophie points.

"I doubt it," Melanie says.

"I'm positive," Sophie says. "I read it."

"You can't," Melanie says. "There's no *sperm*, right? You need sperm for an orgasm."

"Uh-uh. You don't. You only need *sperm* for a baby. An orgasm is different."

"What's the difference?" Melanie asks.

"You're *kidding*, Melanie." Sophie is disgusted.

"I'm not. I'm not allowed to baby-sit. I never get my hands on anything. . . ."

"I'll bring you a book from the Freemans'. Or you can come over with me some time. They've got everything. *Lady Chatterly's Lover*, the Marquis de Sade. . . . They hide them in the linen closet along with their television."

Melanie goes to the vanity and sits down on the little stool. "I'm getting contacts," Melanie says.

"You're lucky," Sophie says. "You can get purple contacts. You can have violet eyes."

"Really?" Melanie asks.

"Really."

Sophie reads sex manuals. Her father's valuable Havelock Ellis. Kinsey. Masters and Johnson. She reads and rereads *The Interpretation of Dreams*, which is her favorite book. It is much more stimulating than *Facts of Life and Love for Teen-agers*, the only book she was given legally—a birthday present from her father's new wife.

Sophie wants to be a femme fatale. Cleopatra is her favorite. Sophie has less respect for courtesans than queens.

In the guidance assembly that afternoon, when they'd broken up into small groups, Sophie realized she couldn't *say* what her career objective was. Mrs. Le Fond, the youngest counselor and a sex bomb in her own right, had gathered the folders of the ninth graders, stacking them in the center of the cafeteria table.

"Spivack, Sophie," she'd called out. Mrs. Le Fond liked to sound official.

"That's I," said Sophie, causing the other ninth graders to titter.

"You have a very good record, Sophie. And your verbal scores are really very high. You show a real interest in helping others. And your grammar, of course, is very good. . . . Can anyone imagine what careers Sophie might consider?"

"An English teacher," said Kirby Spear, a small girl with haunted eyes.

"A good idea," said Mrs. Le Fond, her cleavage shifting as she raised an arm to scratch behind her neck. "Any other ideas?"

"A grammarian," said Larry Spofford, who everyone thought was a genius.

"A philologist," said Mrs. Le Fond. "Does anyone know what that means?"

"Sounds dirty," said Donnie Stanken, under his oily breath.

"What was that, Donnie?" Mrs. Le Fond crossed her leg, revealing pink pettipants.

"I said a go-go girl. I think Sophie would make a really bitchen topless dancer."

Melanie looked at Sophie, amazed.

"If you don't apologize right this second, I'll see that *you're* topless by this afternoon." Mrs. Le Fond was pissed.

"Sorry, Sophie," Donnie whispered. "I meant it like a compliment."

Sophie fixed Donnie with her most Monroevian moue. "I want to be a sex therapist," Sophie said suddenly. "It's a very important field and I can talk and help people. Many marriages break up because of sexual problems. Isn't that true, Mrs. Le Fond?"

"You want to be a counselor, like a marriage counselor—right? That's what you mean, isn't it?" Mrs. Le Fond looked at Sophie pleadingly.

"Yes, that's right," she'd said, but that wasn't at all what Sophie had had in mind.

Walking home from school with Melanie, Sophie discovered that Donnie Stanken was following them. "Melanie, it's Donnie Stanken. What'll I do? He's following us."

"Act like you forgot about the assembly completely. Ask him about the Mets' line-up."

"But I looked at him—like—you know . . ."

"Like you'd do stuff with him?"

"Yeah."

"Well, you looked cool anyway. Everyone thought it was really neat the way you handled Le Fond."

Donnie catches up with the girls.

"Hi," he says. He is much shorter out of school than in. He stares at his sneakers when he talks. "Like, there's this party this weekend. . . ."

Melanie walks to the corner and pretends to examine a pine cone. Her glasses are tucked inside the case and she can't see a thing.

"I've got to baby-sit," she hears Sophie say. "Maybe the next party."

"Can't you get out of it?" Donnie asks. "Like we have a whole bottle of Jack Daniel's and like a half a bottle of gin." Donnie looks desperate. Maybe he has blue balls this very instant. Sophie looks down at his leg where she expects to see something terrible, a blue halo encircling his crotch.

"I promised away all my Saturdays," Sophie says. "The Freemans—the people I baby-sit for—go to this marriage group every Saturday. If they don't go, they'll get a divorce. It'll be *my* fault."

"Well okay," Donnie says, still looking at his sneakers. "How about Friday? We could see *Georgy Girl*. I heard it's really neat."

"I already saw it," Sophie says. "Maybe next weekend."

"Well okay. I think you're a pretty nice person. I'd pay for you," he says. "In the movies."

"I always pay for myself," says Sophie, who's never gone out on a date with anyone. "It's part of my philosophy."

Donnie looks at her like she's the strangest girl alive. He turns around, then waves, then starts running east towards the less ritzy section of Hudson Heights.

Sophie's mother lies asleep on the living room floor. The phonograph is turned on, the needle scratching relentlessly in the same dead groove. Sophie's mother looks eerily pale, her aquiline nose tilted toward a dusty chandelier.

Upstairs in his bedroom, Brian's door is locked. Sophie rattles the lock.

"Bri?" she calls out. Silence.

Sophie goes into her own room and locks the door. She steps on a chair and pulls down from the top of the closet a stack of books. Pamphlets. *Lolita* and *Boys and Girls Together*. A life of Mata Hari slips out of her grasp. Inside this book are tucked away her own investigations and memoirs. The oldest entry describes her moments in the car with Lenny Schultz:

"*The car was beautiful. There was no radio, but the cigarette lighter worked. Usually they are always broken. Aunt Rose was visiting that day from Red Bank, but Lenny didn't seem to realize.*"

Sophie makes burgers for dinner. Brian comes out of his room, dressed, as always, completely in black.

"Whose funeral?" Sophie asks.

Brian doesn't answer. Sophie says, "Whose funeral?" every single day.

Their mother puts two of the patties on her plate and begins chewing. They look terrible, but taste good. Inside are bits of pepper, pieces of onion, rosemary and wine.

"Turds," Brian says.

Sophie glares at him.

"I want seconds," Brian says. "And then I want turds."

"So," Miriam says, "what's new in school?"

"I got asked on a date," Sophie says.

"How nice for you," says their mother.

"I'm not going."

"Why not?" their mother asks.

"I'm saving myself," giggles Sophie.

"How about you, Brian?"

"No one asked me on any dates."

"Well," says their mother. "Your father called. He wants you both to visit him."

"Fat chance," says Brian.

"His wife is in the hospital."

"Is she having her tits lifted?" Brian asks.

Miriam laughs. "She just had a miscarriage," Miriam says. "And your father seems very sad."

"I'll visit him on Saturday," Sophie says.

"I'll call him up," says Brian. "I know plenty of dead baby jokes."

Saturday, Sophie takes the bus to Manhattan to visit her sad father. Her father is a tall man with blue eyes and a head of blond hair. He looks like a college professor or a T.V. anchorman. He sits on a midnight blue pillow and holds a midnight blue cup.

"How pregnant was she?" Sophie asks.

"Four months. Skullcap," says her father, pointing to the cup. "Supposed to be good for depression."

"Don't be depressed, Sid. Dori's young. She'll have plenty of babies."

"I know," he says. "You're right, princess. How is your mama?"

"She's been talking more lately. It's Brian who's getting really strange."

"Brian hates me," her father says.

"Brian hates everybody. He sits in his room all day, listening to the Stones. And wears only black clothes."

"You're the only well-adjusted person in the family." Sid, her father, starts to cry. "When you were a baby, I was so happy. All of us were happy. We were a little family then. We went on picnics. The Botanical Gardens . . ."

"It's okay," Sophie says. "I don't even hate Dori. . . . But Dori really hates *me*."

"It's hard for her," says her father, warming his cheek on the cup, "to come into a family like ours. And now the baby . . ."

"Did she *see* the dead baby?"

"What a question, Soph."

"I'm curious," says Sophie. "Did she see it dead?"

"Yes," says her father. "It was a little boy. We were going to call him Forrest."

"I'm sorry." Sophie touches his cheek. Gray bristles pop from his face like tiny feelers. Underneath, Sid's skin is smooth and pale.

"When I was a boy, I remember sitting under my bed. We were on vacation in the Adirondacks. I remember sitting under my bed and dreaming of being an explorer. A fur-trapper or a pilot."

"And now?"

"Now I dream of going off to a tiny cabin in the middle of nowhere. Arizona or somewhere. And drinking myself to death."

"C'mon, Daddy. No you don't."

"You never call me Daddy."

"Daddy, daddy, daddy." Sophie sticks out her tongue.

"Let me look at your tongue," says her father.

Sophie starts to giggle.

"Really. It looks funny."

Sophie sticks out her tongue.

"What have you been eating?"

"Why?"

"Your tongue is all *coated*."

"Cigarettes," says Sophie.

"How many a day?"

"Four or five."

"You're too young to smoke."

"I've been smoking since I was eleven."

"Well, don't you think you'd better quit while you still can? A smart girl like you . . . Didn't you ever hear of the Surgeon General's Report? Hmnn? And don't start drinking or smoking—anything."

"Look who's talking." Sophie walks over to the coffee table, a slab of midnight blue marble, and removes a silver cigarette case. Inside are four thin joints.

"How'd you know?" asks her father.

"I've always known you were a doper. All dentists are dopers. They get hooked on nitrous and then they go on . . ."

"You talk like a grown-up," says Daddy.

"I am practically grown-up," says Sophie. "I am fourteen, you know."

Sophie lights the reefer and inhales professionally. A circle of smoke surrounds her dark head. Her father watches her, bemused. "You do everything," he says.

"Not *everything*," Sophie says, meaningfully.

"Give me some of that," Sid says, inhaling the smoke his daughter blows out.

"Wait your turn, Daddy-o," says Sophie.

Sid walks over to the stereo and puts on a Woody Guthrie record. He settles back into the love seat and starts to tap out a hokey rhythm on a delft fruit plate.

"Everything in this apartment is blue," Sophie says. "It's depressing."

"Dori believes in monochrome." Sid laughs gently. "She says it relaxes her."

"Even the flowers are blue. How depressing. I'm surprised you don't dye the food."

"Don't laugh. Dori *did* dye the fruit once. Some decorator was coming over to look at the apartment. Some photographer or something from some fancy magazine? You know? And Dori dyed these pears." Sid starts laughing. His laughter grows enormous and Sophie watches his tennis shirt bubbling up at his abdomen, the laughter making his shirt ripple over his soft belly. "And I *ate* one of the pears once. The room was dark. I couldn't sleep. I'd forgotten she'd dyed the fruit."

Woody Guthrie starts singing about the redwood forest and Sophie listens in amusement as her sad, handsome father begins to sing along in his manly Whiffenpoof tenor. Sophie knees her way across to where her father is sitting and lays her fuzzy head in his lap. She nestles against his warm calf where it crosses his knee, and both of them feel a lost sweetness in the place where curls meet calf. The telephone rings musically and, for a second, they have forgotten where they are.

Sid picks up on the third ring. "Of course," he says, winking at Sophie. "Of course I can. I'll be there in a little while. . . ."

"It's Dori," her father says. "She woke from the sedative hysterical. You want to come with me? I have to go over to Lenox Hill. . . ."

"I'll probably just make her feel worse."

"No, pumpkin, c'mon. First we can go for a nice long walk through the park. It's beautiful out. We can walk through the park and catch some air. . . ."

Outside, the May afternoon is overwhelmingly sunny. A perfect day for goody-goodies, Sophie thinks to herself. Her father puts his arm around her delicate shoulder blade and Sophie feels a charge of pride. This tall young-looking man could be anyone: a fiancé just returned from Da Nang with the Purple Heart in his pocket, the sexy-throated dee jay on WNEW, a professor of Zen Buddhism who wandered uptown from the New School to dip into Zabar's for goat cheese. . . .

"Sophie, look!" Her father points.

Up in the perfect afternoon sky a message is being inscribed in smoke: "Hey, hey, LBJ . . ."

"Anti-war slogan," her father says. "There's a big protest going on. Every weekend in the park naked kids are leafleting. Are you for or against, Sophie?"

"For or against what?"

"The war."

"I don't know, Sid."

"I don't know either, baby. But I'd like to think I'm *with* these kids. They remind me of something—ideals, full of opinions. . . . It was so different in my day. I wanted to rebel so much."

"*Did* you rebel?" Sophie squints against the sun. A Frisbee the color of limeade lands next to her foot and she tosses it back to a man wearing nothing but leather short shorts. His long blond hair moves romantically in ripples around his shoulders.

"Hippie boys are really sexy."

"Sexy?" her father asks. "Sexy?"

"Sexy," Sophie says meaningfully, "you know what sexy means." Overhead, the anti-war slogan disappears into a cloud.

At the reception desk, Sid picks up two green passes and hands one to his daughter. Sophie is too small to be mistaken for his lover, though her face is another matter. Her eyes are slanty Jewish eyes that summon up the desert: citrus flowers blowing apart in the dry khamsin, the imaginary smell of warfare.

"Four-fourteen," her father says to the elevator man.

"Maternity," the man winks, managing to make it sound dirty.

"Dori," Sophie's father whispers.

"What took you so long?"

"I've brought Sophie. We took a little walk."

"Honestly, Sid . . . Why'd you bring *her*?"

Dori's face looks swollen and dopey. Her nail polish is flaking off and her thumb looks like she dipped it in marinara sauce.

"What's this?"

"I pick my cuticles in my sleep. I take out my anger on my poor thumb."

"Poor thumby," Sid says, kissing it wetly. Sophie feels nauseated; she has seen this before in a movie.

"Dori," Sophie says, staring into the bathroom where a bumper seat of vinyl is attached to the porcelain. "Dori, I'm sorry about Forrest."

"How does *she* know my baby's name?"

"*She* is my daughter and *she* has a name. So, how are they treating you here? How's the food? I said you were kosher so they'd give you the best." Sophie's father smiles weakly.

"It's ridiculous," Dori says. "I've Episcopal down as my religion, and then I have kosher down as my diet. Last night I sucked fish sticks while everyone else was eating strip."

"It's not so bad here, baby, is it? You're just bummed out you missed the steak. I'll send you a steak in a cab later all by its little self."

Sophie is seeing if she can find all the letters of the alphabet in the sign explaining visiting policies. The husband and wife go on as if she doesn't really exist.

"What I *do* like, strangely enough, about this hospital, is the toilet. It's Royal Doulton," Dori whispers, "can you believe Royal Doulton?"

"Stick with me, kid, and you'll be farting through silk." Sid kisses his wife. Sophie thinks, yecch, and prays they don't start making out.

"I'm sorry she acted so bad," Sid says as they walk out of the hospital and into the sultry afternoon of East Seventy-seventh Street. "Walter Cronkite—over there, getting into a cab. History, Sophie! Look!"

"You're getting cornier and cornier. You're worrying about getting old—right?"

"Who are you?" her father asks. "You're turning into some little sphinx."

"I'm a grown-up woman. I'm fourteen. I'm growing up and I make you feel old. It bums Dori out that you have a teen-aged daughter, so she's bitchy to me. That dumbhead going on and on about shitting on Royal Doulton. Her head is up her ass," says Sophie, trying out something she's read. She looks at Sid appraisingly.

"Get in the cab," her father says, admiring his prize.

3

Brian is not going through a phase. Brian is just loony. His psychiatrist, whom he calls Bev, depresses him, she's so unhappy.

"Life *is* terrible," Bev says, trying to cheer Brian up. She lights two cigarettes, one for each of them, because she thinks giving him cigarettes demonstrates her trust. Brian is happy for the smoke, but Bev won't stop asking him questions about sex. He's sixteen years old. Does Bev want to ball him?

"So, do you ever think about pretty girls . . . and what you'd like to . . . do with them?"

"You mean do I wanna fuck 'em or do I wanna off 'em? Is that what you mean?" He points his finger like a gun.

Bev lights a third cigarette.

"Who's *that* one for? Elijah?"

Mrs. Spivack picks Brian up at Aquarian Associates in a rented car.

"Why'd you rent a car, Miriam? Busted yours up?"

"Oh, I was just in the mood to drive a red convertible. Can you believe it? Your old mother?"

"Let me drive," Brian says.

"No sweetie, doctor's orders."

"I'm driving, Mim. Pull over."

Miriam pulls over. She is terrified of her own son.

"Now I'm gonna show you bitches how to drive." At the first turn off the main road, he leaves a trace of rubber and a charnel burning smell. He changes a lane, changes back, guns down on the accelerator, flashing both turn signals. He screams out the window into the gathering air, "I'm crazy, Miriam! I'm crazy!"

Sophie calls her father.

"Dr. Spivack's service."

"Tell him to call Sophie."

"Call Sophie."

"Right."

Sophie sits down in a pile of pamphlets about venereal disease, a collection she scored earlier at the community health center. She had gone with Melanie that afternoon for her friend's first pregnancy test. And all because Laura Cabell, Melanie's cousin in nursing school, said there was a one-in-ten-thousand chance that a really sexy sperm could fight its way through a pair of Carter's.

The pamphlet on syphilis gives the etymology of the word 'syphilis': from the Greek, meaning pig-love. Sophie imagines a swineherd making love to a sow.

Sophie checks the time, 6:15, and realizes Melanie must know by now if Peter Rabbit is dead.

"Hello, Mrs. Szasz, it's Sophie."

"Can't you call back on Melanie's line? I'm too bushed to run up and down."

"I'm sorry," Sophie says, "I forgot." She dials Melanie's new number.

"I'm bleeding!" Melanie says.

"Then you're not pregnant." Sophie's a tiny bit disappointed.

"I went to call the lab, you know, and I *felt* the blood start dripping."

"You can *feel* it?" Sophie asks. "I never felt it." Sophie is envious.

"I always feel it," Melanie says. "Boy, am I lucky!"

"Melanie, now that it's over, I just want to tell you you can't get pregnant from dry-humping."

"Laura says—"

"—I don't care. But I think we should both go into the city and get diaphragms or the pill. I know where the Planned Parenthood is. I passed it with my father."

"Sophie, you've got to be sixteen."

"Not in New York, you don't. There's ten-year-old runaways who fuck every day. You think they don't give *them* diaphragms?"

"I don't *want* to get a diaphragm. If I have a diaphragm, I'll have no excuse. . . ."

"Don't tell Ricky."

"Won't he see it?"

"Not if you stick it in beforehand."

"Stick it in?"

"What do you think, Melanie? You eat it?"

"Is it shaped like a penis?" Melanie whispers.

"No. It's shaped like a little Frisbee."

"Does it feel, you know . . . sexy?"

"I don't know. I'll read some stuff and call you back. Anyway, congratulations."

"Yeah."

Melanie Szasz and Ricky Cooper have been seeing each other since October. Sophie counts on her fingers—over six months. Soon Melanie will have to give him a hand job, and soon after that she'll have to kiss it, and once you've kissed it, Sophie figures, you might as well stick it in.

Sophie's a little envious, though not of Ricky Cooper. Ricky is president of library council, very studious, with big ears. Ricky is someone to go out with maybe when you're older. There is no doubt that he'll get into Harvard, or at least Brown, and after that MCATs in the high 700s and Stanford or Hopkins. But now he's a skinny little nothing with depressing acne on his back. Sophie saw his back once when Melanie's parents weren't home and the three of them played strip poker down to their underwear.

Sophie is waiting for someone glamorous—a married man or at least someone older, someone with experience. A man who will sing opera to her in flawless Italian, like on her mother's records. A man who will buy her diamond earrings and take her to hear real music instead of dopey Janis Ian. . . . In bed he will read from the *Kama Sutra*, and wearing a velvet smoking jacket, he'll tell her about his love affairs—the pregnant geisha he left in Kyoto, the Russian spy in Brest-Litovsk. Still, Sophie thinks it's unfair that myopic Melanie has gotten so far, and all on Sophie's own steam.

Sophie is examining her breasts for lumps, lying on the fun-fur rug and consulting a hot pink pamphlet that lies open beside her: With the left hand, fingers flat, press gently in small circles— Sophie sits up, startled. Someone is watching her. She unbolts the lock and opens the door. By the time she gets to the top of the stairs, she sees a flash of black Levis disappearing into the attic.

By the time she knocks on Brian's door, he's already turned on the Rolling Stones; lying in his messy bed, he pretends he's absorbed in *The Dharma Bums* and listening to "Paint it Black."

"To what do I *owe* this visit?" Brian sounds like Ringo Starr, but is trying to sound like Oscar Wilde. He doesn't look up.

"Brian, quit *spying* on me. And leave my dirty underwear alone. In the hamper."

"You're beautiful," Brian says. She can't tell if he's kidding. "A beautiful woman with breasts that could break someone's heart." She is standing there with a ratty towel tucked around her chest.

"Thanks for the poetry. I'm really mad. Why don't you find someone to fool around with for real?"

"What about you, Sophie? Who's the lucky faggot? Still spreading your lips for Lenny Schultz? Or what do I hear about you and—"

"—Brian! Stop! You're perverted. I think you're crazy."

Sophie feels dizzy.

"You and everyone else. I *am* crazy, darling. Your dear crazy brother. Now they're trying to find out if brother Brian is a *faygeleh*."

"What's *faygeleh*?"

"A little bird."

"You mean a homo," Sophie says.

"Listen, Sophie, I'm not a faggot. I'm a very devout hetero who wants to suck his sister's breasts. C'mon, Sophie, let me."

He gives her an evil look.

She looks down at the pink towel. "I'm sorry. Give me a T shirt." Is her brother *really* crazy? Crazy like schizophrenic? Like Tony Perkins in *Psycho*? Or is he merely . . . peculiar? She looks down at his book. "What's Derma Bums?"

Brian starts laughing convulsively. She notices he is drooling. "Derma Bums . . . you're a scream. I don't believe it. Anyway, Sophie, no T shirt. You came up here to show me your titties and now you can't pretend you were kidding."

"What do you mean, Bri? You mean you think I came up here on purpose, to turn you on like?"

"Sophie, they say you're sophisticated. Dr. Bev thinks you're the new Jeanne Moreau. And I keep telling her you're just a little sex fiend is all. You and Melanie. I hear you two talking about whether a little spermie soaks up the menstrual flow. You are *fixated* on menstruation. It's practically all you talk about."

"You've been *listening* to all my phone calls." Sophie feels sick.

"You're right," Brian says. "You're stuck on bleeding, and I'm stuck on you."

"What do you mean, Brian?" She hopes he's kidding. She crosses her fingers under the towel.

"I want you, Sophie. I think you're hot. That night—remember?—with Lenny Schultz . . . I *saw* you, Sophie. I *saw* his grubby little fists. . . ."

"This is ridiculous," Sophie says. "I *know* you're kidding. I *know* you're just trying to freak me out."

Brian's voice breaks; he's dropped the English accent. He seems himself again: a tall peculiar teenager who wears no underwear, takes uppers and downers at the same time, has a reputation at school for being a nosepick-eater, a warlock, a creep. He wears peculiar buttons—FRODO LIVES and EAT YOUR HONEY, and black shirts and black pants. Brian's in training for an army of bad boys hungering for recognition: Montgomery Clift, John Garfield, Saint Jack Kerouac, Jimmy Dean. Motorcycles and magic mushrooms, Mick Jagger lookalikes all jerking off.

Suddenly, he turns pale.

"Brian, are you all right?"

He runs downstairs and Sophie runs after him. In the bathroom he vomits up angel dust, and Sophie stands there holding his head.

Sophie doesn't know what to do—whether to believe Brian or not. After all, he'd said he was high on angel dust and Jack Daniel's. He was probably hallucinating from all that shit at once. No one was *really* in love with his sister. But still, maybe she should tell her father or Brian's psychiatrist. She can't tell her mother—she knows that. Her mother's already afraid of him. Then she'd just start drinking more.

She remembers that party after the play when Lenny—she can't believe Brian even remembers that day—that Brian was watching them in the car—she remembers when Lenny told her his father was an alcoholic. She wonders if her mother is an alcoholic, too. Do alcoholics listen to opera? She's seen these booklets around the house . . . purple pamphlets from Alcoholics Anonymous. She's seen her mother reading these booklets, then hiding them away in a drawer when Sophie comes into the room. Once she'd caught her mother reading *Sex and the Alcoholic Marriage*. Maybe Sophie should tell her father. Sid was a dentist, after all. . . . Sid would know what to do.

"I'm getting to be sort of friends with my brother," Sophie tells Melanie, who is sitting in front of the mirror doing something disgusting to her pimples.

"The best thing is leave them alone," Sophie says, sitting down on the bed so she can't see Melanie's nails digging away at her chin.

"Got it!" Melanie sings, flicking the delicate blackhead into her pencil jar. "Anyway, Soph, tell me about Brian."

"What do you mean?"

"You know. Like you said you were getting to be pals."

"He takes angel dust and he drinks a lot. Daniel's. So does my mother," Sophie says wistfully. "They're terrible. Maybe they could drink together. That way it wouldn't be so bad."

"Tell me what he's really like," Melanie says. "Everyone in the high school thinks he's really perverted."

For the first time in three years, Sophie doesn't feel like telling Melanie everything. Brian's confession yesterday has to be her secret. And because she is sure there will be further secrets bubbling up between them, sister and brother, secrets as hot and sticky as lava, Sophie just smiles mysteriously. "Brian—perverted? Nah."

Sophie is sitting on her bed when the telephone rings.

"Daddy," she says.

"Pumpkin. I got a message."

"That was yesterday—today I'm feeling much better."

"What was going on yesterday?"

"Well Mom *did* rent a car—a red convertible, for no reason—"

"—What do you mean—no reason?"

"She said she wanted to go for a ride in a red convertible."

"That's a reason," Sid says, moved for the first time in years by Miriam. "Your mother's got to have *something*," Sid says.

"She drinks a lot. Chivas."

"She's entitled to Chivas."

"No, Daddy. You don't understand. . . . It's not the Chivas I mean. I mean . . . she drinks too much and Brian . . . Brian drinks a lot, too."

"Brian's how old—sixteen? I can't tell him what to do. Brian won't listen to *me*. . . ."

"What about Mom?" Sophie asks.

"Mom won't listen to me either. . . ."

When her father called her mother "Mom," it made her want to cry. She remembered the way it was before Dori, Dori the Bitch, had come into the picture. . . . Her mother used to drink then too. But at least her father had been around to wash the dishes when Mom passed out; to sign the various permission slips—Brownies and Burpee's, sick notes and class trips. . . . It was Sid who bought the cupcakes when it was her turn to bring the refreshments: hot dogs for cookouts, cupcakes for Halloween or Valentine's Day. . . . And now he lived in the Big Apple with the Big Cunt and was never home. . . .

"Well what *is* it, Sophie? Try to tell me what's wrong."

What was wrong with her father that she had to explain it to him?

"Well, how's Dori?" she asked. He couldn't tell that she was crying.

"Dori's back home now. She's busy doing something—slip covers for the lawn mower no doubt."

"When's the funeral?" Sophie asks. "For little Forrest, I mean." She imagined what she would wear to the funeral. She owned a black sweater, but not a skirt.

"Little miscarriage babies don't have funerals," Sid says.

"They ought to," Sophie says, teary, feeling sad for the dead baby. The books say they look like liver. Already she has looked it up. A bloody ball of calves' liver with tiny feet? Or is it just a river of blood?

She can't blame her father for not understanding. She can't bring herself to tell him what Brian really said. She'd better keep it to herself. She owes her brother *something*—he was high and only kidding. She owes her mother something, too. *They* didn't abandon her to go live in New York in a blue apartment. They were here . . . she was stuck with them . . . they were her family.

Sophie decides to work on her book report on Ernest Hemingway. She reads a bit of *The Sun Also Rises*, the part where Jake goes on the fishing trip with his friend. And reading the words she feels sleepy, falling into a deep dream that takes place in Mexico City.

In the dream Sophie wears a grass skirt and dances in front of a bonfire. Someone from the FBI, a man with a fat Havana cigar, tells her he is happy he's finally found her. He shows her a badge and Sophie gets into his car, a pale green LTD. She drives with him for a while through a deserted tropical landscape and when she looks into the rearview mirror, she realizes she is blindfolded. She begs the man to take off the blindfold, but he says it is impossible.

"Dinner," Brian calls from downstairs. "Dinner . . . Sophie, Mom!"

Brian is wearing a checked apron and matching chef's hat.

"Where'd you find *that*?" Mrs. Spivack asks. "Didn't that belong to your father?"

"I found it in the broom closet," Brian says. "I gave it to him for Father's Day. He never wore it."

"Maybe he'd wear it now," Sophie says. "He's gotten unbelievably corny. Did you know Dori dyes the fruit blue to match the wallpaper?"

Mrs. Spivack smiles.

Brian brings a heaping bowl of something to the table.

"What's that?" Sophie asks.

"It's little rat turds," Brian says. He winks at her lewdly. "Rat turds in tomato sauce."

"Bri-an," Sophie says, giggling, letting her kimono slip from her shoulder. "Brian, what *is* it?"

"One of Mom's favorite recipes. Didn't Grandma used to make this dish in Lithuania? Little Russian rat turds? The rats were tastier in the old country." Brian licks his lips.

"Mother, make him stop!" Sophie says.

"Nonsense," Mrs. Spivack says. "We're having a lovely casserole."

"Cocktails, anyone?" Brian asks, taking a long draft from a silver flask.

"I'd like a daiquiri," Sophie says.

"Fresh out of dykeries," Brian says. "How about a little sip of Daniel's?"

"Mother, may I?" Sophie asks. She has never tasted anything but Manischewitz Concord Grape.

"Why not," her mother says.

Brian gets a few mugs from the little wrought-iron mug tree and fills a cup for each of them.

Mrs. Spivack downs her cup, then starts to fan herself with her hand. "Pretty stiff cocktail," she whispers to Brian. "What *is* this?"

"Whiskey, Mim," Brian says. "Remember whiskey?"

"Campari for me," says their mother. "Could you fetch the bottle, Soph?"

For once, Sophie doesn't mind that her mother is drunk for dinner. Cocktails is such an elegant idea. From now on they'll drink together.

Sophie lifts the mug to her lips and tastes the Daniel's. Her brother watches her closely, waiting for her to gag. She drinks it down in one shot, then wails, "Brian, we forgot to toast!"

"To brotherly love," Brian says.

"*L'chayim*," Mrs. Spivack smiles, a tad crookedly.

"*Ciao*," says Sophie, giggling as the warm whiskey drizzles down to her bowels.

Three shots later, Sophie is telling her mother and brother about Gertrude Stein and Alice B. Toklas. "Was it a bell that rang?" Sophie asks. "You know, Brian. To show that Gertrude Stein was a genius?"

"Gertrude Stein," their mother says. "I remember a funny story about Gertrude Stein. Or was that Lytton Strachey and Vanessa Bell?"

"Mother's getting her literary history and her Hadassah all mixed up," Brian snickers.

"Brian, I was a smart girl," their mother says. "You may grant that I am an alcoholic, a manic-depressive, whatever you want. But when I was a girl I was smart as a whip, and don't you punks forget it."

"Oh, Mother," Sophie says. It's the first time Sophie remembers her mother sticking up for herself. "Oh, Mother, Brian and I both think you're wonderful."

"*I* don't think Mother is wonderful," Brian says. "Wonderful? No. I think Mother is quite inadequate as a mother. As a person. As a spiritual being. We might put up with her," Brian says. "We might decide not to blow her brains out, but we don't think she's wonderful, now do we really, Soph?"

Mrs. Spivack has gone to bed. Now she lies in her nun-sized cot, listening to *Lucia di Lammermoor* and sniffing the insides of tulips. Later she will fall asleep to dream of a piano recital she gave at seventeen, a tall dark-haired girl in Akron, Ohio, the only daughter of a Greek fisherman Jew and his wife.

In the dream she is naked at the piano. Everyone is clapping. A tall man in the audience stands up and gestures for her to follow. He crooks his finger, he is wearing gloves. She leaves the piano and follows him down a dense corridor that smells like the factory on West Waterloo. In America her father had been a foreman at the bread factory, Esposito's. Miriam discovers in the dream her father had been a holy man: a life of fishes and loaves.

Downstairs in the kitchen, Sophie is giggling huskily. *Tristan und Isolde* plays on the stereo from the living room. Her peach kimono is undone; her breasts are radiant, Biblical. Brian kneels on the kitchen floor and starts to caress her breasts. He looks into Sophie's eyes. Brian *thinks* she is conscious. Her breasts cradle Brian's face like halves of a perfect sourdough, yeasty from the oven.

Upstairs in the attic, he eats her. Opening, opening, opening her up, like a Chinese puzzle or a plump walnut, unfolding phenomenologically. In the center of the center is Sophie's heart, beating like a wing.

A pigeon in heat, her sweetness draining, her small song for the first time trills in the attic room. He swings above her like a crane. When he's come inside her, he kisses her. He kisses her like a signet sealing a letter in creamy wax.

Miriam awakens from the dream when she hears a tiny, painful cry. She recognizes the sound, but can't place it. Or is it the girl in the dream?

4

Sophie awakens with a hangover. The room reels and her eyes rest on *The Sun Also Rises*. She remembers the rat turd casserole and talking about Gertrude Stein, the three of them putting it away like the Kowalski family down in the kitchen. Then she remembers *Tristan and Isolde*. The rest of the evening she half-remembers only as a sickening smell lingering over her body. She feels an ache inside her, a shooting pain above her eyebrow. Her head feels like the inside of some forgotten Gouda cheese. Then she remembers.

She realizes Melanie must know a thing or two about hangovers. Melanie and Ricky's crowd come home from the "Y" dances and start in on the airplane bottles of Bacardi and Smirnoff that decorate the Szaszes' recreation room. Now that Melanie has a boyfriend, Melanie has a crowd.

She dials Melanie's number.

"Sophie, can't you *remember* to call Melanie's phone? I can't keep running up and down. My arches!" Gladys says.

"What time is it?" Sophie asks.

"Maybe 10:30."

"Well, Melanie must be at school."

"Don't bet on it," says Mrs. Szasz.

Sophie puts on a terry cloth robe and steps into the shower. Coming out of the stall, she slips on baby powder and bruises her thigh. She tries to get up, but feels dizzy. She reaches for the towel bar and begins to retch.

Downstairs, her mother calls. "Sophie, it's the school. You there?"

"Tell them I'm sick," she squeaks from the bathroom.

"*Are* you sick?" her mother asks, coming up the stairs.

"I'm dying."

Sophie's mother has hardly even had a hangover in her life. That's because she mixes the Chivas with Sealtest, she tells herself. She doesn't know what to give for a hangover. She decides to call up Sid. Maybe Sid knows. The bastard.

"Can I speak to him?" Miriam asks.

"Who's calling Doctor?"

"Mrs. Spivack, and he's a dentist, not a doctor."

"Mrs. Spivack! I was sorry to hear about little Forrest."

"What little forest? Could I please speak to my ex?"

"Symphony Sid," says Dr. Spivack, remembering a radio show he used to like in the fifties.

"Sid, it's the other Mrs. Spivack. The *real one*," Miriam says.

"I could tell it was you, Miriam. I caught the vibes. Well, what's up?" He sounds so jaunty, Miriam feels like saying, "your ass."

"Little Sophie has a hangover."

"What a family," Sid says.

"Well, I don't quite know what to *do* with her."

"You got a blender?"

"You *know* I have a blender." *Do I have a blender? What do you think*, you *leave and I throw away the blender*?

"Well, stick in some tomato juice and some Worcestershire and an egg or something. I don't know. What does she have? Diarrhea?"

"Just a second, I'll peek."

"Miriam, what's going on over there?"

"The kids have problems. They drink. They smoke pot. They screw. They're kids."

"Well, don't let them be drinking."

"I don't tell them what to do." Miriam feels bad. Just a moment ago she and Sid were kind of having fun, bantering. Now he sounds moralizing, superior, distant, and even his voice—Miriam is sure—sounds younger than hers.

"Well, be good, Miriam."

"Why don't you come over or something?" Miriam says. Her voice sounds small and pathetic, but she can't bring herself to stop. "Come over some night and I'll make you dinner. Chow mein out of a can. Dori makes snails and sticks real violets on the cakes, doesn't she? And she probably wears little boys' size-ten T shirts. Doesn't she?"

"Miriam, I have a kid in the chair waiting for me. Tommy Orlander. You know the Orlanders."

"I know the Orlanders," Miriam agrees, pouring herself a taste of Chivas and mixing in some milk. "They're perfectly nice people."

Sophie is sitting at the kitchen table drinking black coffee. "That was your father," Miriam says. "He says you should drink tomato juice and an egg in the blender."

"No thanks," Sophie says. "I feel a little better."

"Well, I know it's ridiculous. I know *I'm* ridiculous in you and your brother's eyes—so maybe you don't want to hear it from me. But Sophie, you mustn't start drinking. At my age, it's a different matter."

"Mother, you don't have to justify yourself."

"I hate words like *justify*."

"Sorry, Mom. Anyway, I know what you mean about drinking. I won't drink, I promise, and I haven't had a cigarette in a few weeks."

"And what about sex?"

"What about it?" Sophie asks.

"Don't tell me," her mother says. Sophie is so pretty, Miriam thinks.

"I never will. Don't worry."

"Never tell or never screw?"

"Never tell," Sophie says.

"But if you want to see a gynecologist, that's your business. Maybe you should. You can tell them to send the bill to your father. After all, what's a father for?"

"You're really a good mother," Sophie says. "I know Bri—Brian—didn't mean any of that stuff last night."

"Yes he did, Sophie. But I don't mind. I did what I could and it turned out to be not a whole lot." She watches her mother pour Scotch into a glass of milk. Wilma Flintstone and Betty Rubble pose on the glass with Stone-Age shopping carts.

"Mommy, please stop drinking."

"Soon," her mother says.

"You should go out on dates and stuff," Sophie says.

"Where would I go? To singles bars on the highway?"

"You're *still* pretty."

"The reason I was happy when your father left—I mean I wasn't *happy* —but the one consolation was I didn't have to walk through parking lots with a man who looked half my age anymore."

"Daddy doesn't look twenty," Sophie says.

"What about Dori? How old does she look?"

"Thirty, thirty-two," Sophie says.

"She's twenty-eight," her mother says. "How do you think that makes me feel?"

"Poor Mom," says Sophie.

"It makes me feel like old flesh."

Sophie watches television.

"All right, husbands," the announcer says. "What will your wife say her mother's surefire cure for constipation is?"

"How about a whole mess of prunes?" giggles Husband Number Two.

Sophie remembers the feeling of Brian inside her. Her brother's lips on her lips, his muscular thighs beating, his transfixed face staring endlessly into her vagina.

She has stumbled into a new country and she's really just a little kid dragging a Howdy Doody lunchbox. What if she's pregnant and gives birth to a Mongoloid? She'll be showing her very first day of tenth grade! The retarded baby will even *look* funny underneath her maternity blouse—the bump in her belly will appear abnormal, the head of the fetus hanging dully, the tiny fists pushed open, struggling against sanguine walls.

She will run away to the East Village, sign into the Chelsea Hotel, assume a new identity. She'll be Sally Jones from Shreveport. When people ask her questions, she'll chatter about Antoine's, the costumes at Mardi Gras. . . . The child will be a retarded boy and he'll look beautiful, but never talk. A little boy in a velvet suit, an angel with golden curls. Or maybe he'll look like a Mongoloid, but really he'll be a genius. A dwarf who becomes world-famous. . . . Oh God, Sophie thinks, if I make it this time—I promise, God, if I'm not pregnant, I'll become a *rebbitsin*.

5

Sophie is mortified. Only a total asshole would go to bed with her own brother. If it takes two to tango, it certainly takes two to bang. Even if Brian got her drunk on purpose—which she knows he did—she knows too she is partly to blame. She flirted with him at dinner. She flirted with her own brother. She wore her peach silk kimono and let it drift from her shoulders. . . . After the day he told her he loved her, then vomited angel dust, she should have done something to stop it. All she had done was fantasize about making love to her own brother. She was a pervert, too.

She had imagined his naked body. The naked body of her own brother was not that hard to conjure up, even if he looked nothing like her. Where she was round and soft and buoyant, Brian was angular and narrow. She'd imagined the two of them making love in the basement where her parents had made a pathetic attempt to create a rec room. Not a real rec room, of course, like Melanie had—with a real bar and bar stools covered in zebra fur. Bottles of Galliano as tall as the Eiffel Tower, clocks with the face of Mr. Boston smiling impishly down. Crystal decanters bright with claret, a motley collection of swizzle sticks from hotel bars all over the world: the Hotel David in Jerusalem, Harry's Bar, the Georges V. The Szaszes knew how to live.

Nothing in her life was *real* like Melanie's. As much as she hated Gladys and Brad, Melanie's torture-parents, at least Melanie's parents were *real*. Gladys sent away for things—cashmere throws for the living-room couch, porcelain place-card holders. She gave tons of dinner parties with hired slaves who wore white aprons. Gladys went shopping with other ladies, worried about her furs drying up, took to her bed with migraines, had her hair and her nails and her legs cared for, worked on, massaged.

All Miriam did was drink and listen to endless operas. Sophie hated opera —all those crazy fat people chasing each other around on a stage.

Melanie's father was a big shot in the liquor business. Sid thought Brad was connected to the New Jersey Mob. Sid thought *everyone* was connected to the Mafia—even their next-door neighbors, the perfectly normal Lazarowitzes. Brad seemed like a real father even if he *was* a Mafioso. He yelled at Melanie, he mowed the lawn on Saturdays, he'd even interrogated Ricky when he'd shown up for his first date with the Szaszes' only heir.

She bet Brad didn't sleaze around with people he met on airplanes. And if he did he'd pick someone more normal than Dori. Only her father was weird enough to fall in love with a bitch whose biggest thrill was checking out the brand name on a toilet.

She thought about her parents' fake rec room. Some dumb molded plastic chairs that made it look like a doctor's office for poor people. One dumb poster of W.C. Fields whom Sophie despised. A red light bulb stuck into one of the lamps. Even the ceiling depressed her—acoustic tiles with myriad holes, sagging and yellowing from the leaks Sid never bothered to fix. Brad was always fixing things in his woodworking shop.

Brian and Sophie had almost convinced Sid to buy them a record player so they could have real parties downstairs. A few days later he was gone, hiding out somewhere in Connecticut in a barn with Dori. The record player was forgotten and Brian and Sophie had given up trying to have a real rec room. No wonder they'd both turned out weird—they'd never had the right equipment for a normal childhood.

She was ten when Sid moved out and Brian a gawky twelve. She couldn't admit to anyone that her father had left them with the ceiling coming down. She thought it was her fault. For a long time she'd lied about it, pretended Sid was coming home, that he was on a business trip that lasted months, then years. He was off in Arabia making dentures for a black king; he was in Monte Carlo fitting gold braces on Princess Caroline.

Finally, in seventh grade, she had met Melanie Szasz in homeroom. Spivack and Szasz. Thank God for alphabetical order! Both of them were misfits. Melanie was heads taller than even the boys and wore glasses. Sophie was just—strange. She said the most unbelievable things out loud in English classes. Once when they were doing some dumb Emily Dickinson poem about death, Melanie remembered, Sophie had raised her hand and said that Emily Dickinson was sexually repressed. Another time Sophie was caught hiding *The Story of O* behind her copy of *The Old Man and the Sea*. Nobody understood why the book was such a shocker; no one else in seventh grade had ever heard of it. Melanie had thought at first it had to be a children's book: O is for ostrich and also for oats; O is for oceans chock full of big boats. Mrs. Le Vine had blushed as red as a jar of borscht.

And even if Sophie hadn't stood out as a weirdo on her own, there was her brother in ninth grade whose reputation for weirdness followed her like a family curse.

Sophie thanked God she finally had a friend. Brian didn't have one. She told Melanie the whole truth—how Sid had left her mother for Dori; how Miriam spiked her morning tea, then spent the rest of the day and night passed out on the living-room rug, listening to opera. She taught Melanie everything she knew about sex and the wide world and Melanie never told anyone—not even Brad and Glad—her secrets.

Now, almost three years later, Melanie had purple contacts and the figure everyone wanted—tall and thin like an English model—like Jean Shrimpton, like Twiggy. Melanie was learning how to be regular, how to fit in. She'd even joined a sorority now that she'd landed a boyfriend from the student council crowd. Sophie thought she was wasting herself on those whiny *yenta* girls who seemed like miniatures of their mothers: Jewish girls with slanty eyes and frizzy hair they ironed flat. In the corridors of junior high, their hair always smelled burned, like toast. They'd all grow up and marry doctors and spend their lives going to luncheons. Sophie wanted to barf. Melanie had more potential—Melanie deserved more than a Bloomingdale's credit card and a doctor husband. Though Sophie wasn't sure what it was. . . .

As for herself, she knew she was doomed. She couldn't explain it to anyone. She simply knew in her deepest self that her life would be a difficult one, that God had picked her out somehow—like in "The Lottery" by Shirley Jackson. No one in her English class had understood the story but her. She was not like other people—she was a bug, like Gregor Samsa. She'd asked her teacher if they could read something by Kafka in English that spring, that final spring of ninth grade. Outside their classroom, the delicate lilac and hydrangea hung in the chemical New Jersey air.

"Who?" the teacher had asked.

"Kafka, Franz Kafka," she'd said. Sophie had rolled her eyes.

The teacher had no idea whom she meant.

"You have no business teaching English if you don't even know who Kafka is! You should resign immediately! Resign!" Sophie called out.

Before the teacher could send her down to the assistant principal's office, Sophie had run out of the room, out of the school building itself, James Madison Junior High; and although there was no one chasing after her, she'd felt there was a posse of bloodhounds sniffing for her blood.

She'd run for a while, exhilarated, then collapsed in Diehl Park, where everyone went to cut school. In the bushes behind her she'd heard the wet sounds of a couple kissing, then committing fellatio; zippers scratching like insects' songs. The smell of semen mixed in the air with the other smells of first spring.

A few weeks later she lost her virginity to her brother.

She'd called up Brian's psychiatrist, Bev, who'd said, sure, she'd give her an hour.

On the walls of Bev's office hung enlargements of butterflies' wings, assassin bugs, ephemerids, dog-day cicadas.

"It's about Brian. . . ." Sophie said.

"Is he in danger of hurting himself . . . or hurting anyone else?"

"No. Not really."

"Then I'm afraid I can't discuss him with you. Confidentiality, you know." Bev's fingernails were a mess, all chewed-up, like Dori's. *I take out my anger on my poor thumb. Poor thumby*, Sid had said.

"Okay, forget it."

"I can refer you to someone else. . . ."

"No." She'd left the office then, feeling her doom like a stone inside her; a stone stuck inside her throat, a lump in her heart, a weight in her womb. She had done something terrible, something deranged, insane. As she walked over to Plaza Street and the safety of the bagel store, the head shop, the five-and-ten, she began to cry for her utter loss—the loss of a normal, a regular childhood. She wished she were a sorority girl with Bass Weejuns, a plaid skirt, a circle pin as round as Saturn. She wished she were going with Ricky Cooper, someone boring and safe—like a husband. She needed to find a husband.

She was like a heroine in a novel—a bad girl in Thomas Hardy who needed to be saved. Her sin she would wear like a badge, she decided. A red "I" for INCEST as big as her own body. She'd turn her shame into a cause, her tragedy would give her noblesse. She'd become a Puritan martyr like Hester Prynne. Or else a burlesque dancer, famous for her tits. She could play her cards either way.

Either she was already lost and her life was free—she could be a whore, a *bummekeh*, a woman with six abortions under her belt—or else she could become a nun, or, at least, a rabbi's wife. She'd visit the sick and elderly; she'd rub the calves, the varicose bulges, the chubby tumors of the dying. She'd learn calligraphy and make ornamental marriage contracts to support her husband's life of study. She'd singe the feathers off chickens and sell them in the marketplace—a stall of meager birds. . . . But where? The Bergen Mall?

Modern life provided no room for true repentance. This was the thought in Sophie's head as she entered Larry's Bong, the head shop on Plaza Street. Larry was examining a brand-new shipment of trip glasses—turquoise sunglasses with dodecahedral lenses. Around her were kaleidoscopes, rolling papers, strobe lights, candles smelling of coconut. Massage oils, emollients—everywhere the lubricious. A man grazed her in the aisle next to the books: *The Beginner's Garden of Grass, The Lovers' Massage Handbook*. Comic books featuring Mr. Natural and Harold the Head, lesbians with abundant biceps.

"Excuse me," the man said. He was really cute. Thirty-three with a hint of gray in his Jewfro.

He looked at her appraisingly.

She realized she was a virgin no longer. Now it was only a question of who.

6

Melanie and Sophie are lounging in the waiting room of the Women's Rites Clinic on St. Mark's Place.

"This is my third pregnancy test. I'm up," Melanie says. "My number is *up*."

Sophie is brushing kohl underneath the rims of her eyes. "It'll be legal any minute," Sophie says. "Don't worry."

"Well go call my congressman, okay, Sophie? I promise if I squeeze by one more time, I won't screw till it's legal. I'll sign my trust fund over to Gloria Steinem."

"Melanie, you were using a rubber, a diaphragm, and rhythm. Or was it foam and the pill?"

"Don't laugh, Sophie. Remember Anita." Anita, the president of Melanie's sorority, got pregnant using a diaphragm *and* an IUD.

"But her IUD *perforated*," Sophie says. "It perforated her uterus when it was inserted."

"What about her diaphragm?" Melanie says.

"Probably her diaphragm was sitting under her coleus. You know—catching the overflow."

"The overflow?"

"From the coleus."

"What's a coleus?" Melanie asks.

"Oh, you know—the rear entrance to the cervix." Sophie tries not to laugh. Melanie knows nothing.

"You're kidding! There's a *rear* entrance?"

"You've heard of Greek love," Sophie whispers.

"C'mon," Melanie says. "What about this coleus?"

"They're calling your number," Sophie says.

The receptionist, a messy redhead maybe six months along, calls hoarsely. "Number thirty-four, will you please come to the lab. With your pee."

"Don't worry," Sophie says, hooking her arm through Melanie's. "If you *are* pregnant, you can always get a job working here."

"They've got a lot of nerve," Melanie says. "Pregnant women leaking baby-juice into the airwaves . . ."

Outside, Melanie vomits on the corner of Second Avenue and St. Mark's Place.

"Soon you'll make us stop at a deli for pickles," Sophie says.

"I've *got* to call Ricky," Melanie says. "Ricky's gonna *kill* me."

"Let's hang out before you call Ricky. Get your head together. What do you want to do? You wanna go over to Fantasy and look at the earrings?"

"Uh-uh."

"We could go to the museum. There's always cool guys in the gift shop."

"With what money?" Melanie says. "That lab test cost fifteen dollars." They are leaning against a telephone pole. A tough-looking boy hangs his head out from a window across the street.

"Hey, baby, wanna come up here and share a can of beer?"

"Eat it," Melanie says.

"Let's go somewhere," Sophie says. "I know! We can go uptown—to Sid and Dori's."

"I thought you swore you'd never see her again," Melanie says.

"I haven't been up there since ninth grade," Sophie says. "I haven't laid eyes on the bitch since last year."

Melanie whips her head to the side.

"What *is* it?" Sophie asks.

The boy sticks his head out the window just as Melanie vomits again.

"Gross-out ladies," the boy yells. "You wanna see something grosser?" He sticks his butt out the window. It's white as notebook paper, fleshy as Chinese mushrooms.

"Get a cab," says Melanie.

"Right," says Sophie. "We'll take a cab to Sid's and ask for the money when we get there."

Sophie walks toward First Avenue, looking for a taxi. Melanie stands against the pole, listening as the boy's wild farts resonate in the afternoon.

Sophie leaves Melanie in the cab as collateral. Melanie has thrown up again, and the driver, a skinny Ukrainian, is listening to Miles, unperturbed.

Sophie comes down with a ten-dollar bill which she presses into his hand. "C'mon Melanie. I had to liberate the money from Dori's wallet. She was sleeping and I just saw it—"

"—I don't care," Melanie says. "I just have to lay down."

Melanie lies on the Persian carpet. The love seat is too short for her, though not for Sophie, who's four-eleven. The girls stare at the plaster ceiling; the haunted faces of gargoyles suggest to both of them the unborn.

Sophie remembers the silver case. Inside are two skinny joints rolled in blueberry paper. Sophie lights one and takes a deep hit.

"Give me some of that," Melanie says. "I've got to call Ricky. If I get stoned and call him, it won't be as bad."

"Don't tell Ricky right away."

"Why not?" Melanie says. "Who's gonna stake me for the big A?"

"You have money, Melanie."

"My money's so locked-up, I can't even visit it."

"You could sell your ring. You could hock it. There's a hock shop right next to the Woman's Rites. I saw a great fur coat in the window. Eighty dollars," Sophie sighs.

"Do I *have* to hock my ring? It belonged to my Nana Rachel. She's only been dead like two months. I'd feel so *ungrateful*. . . ."

"One thing I know about abortions is they cost, Melanie. They cost a lot. Where's Cooper gonna get hundreds of dollars together?"

"Shit, Sophie, you're scaring me. Tell me what to do. Can't I get something from a doctor? Like to have a miscarriage or something? How about if you push me down the stairs like Scarlett O'Hara—remember? Remember when Rhett pushed her down the stairs?"

"I'm not pushing you down any stairs. *Your* parents would definitely sue."

"I loved *Gone With The Wind*," Melanie says sadly. "Sophie, I'm scared. Please tell me what to do."

"Try to figure out how to get the money. Try to get the money. I'll try to figure out the rest."

Just as Sophie feels herself drifting off into a great daydream about the guy in the head shop, Melanie starts to cry.

Sophie sits down on the carpet next to Melanie's head. She takes her friend's horsy face into her hands and holds it. Melanie sits up and takes off her glasses. She has left the purple contacts home, safe on the vanity. Instinctively, she wipes her glasses on Sophie's Mexican blouse. Melanie snuggles into Sophie's bosom. "You have great boobies for snuggling. You'll be a wonderful mommy."

Dori walks into the living room naked.

"Girls! Sophie!" Dori says. Her body is perfect, Sophie thinks. No cellulite. No tits. "What are you doing here?"

"Melanie's sick," Sophie says. "So we came up here . . . to rest. I took ten dollars, I'm sorry. The cabbie was waiting. I can't pay you back. We had no other place to go."

"Just a minute," Dori says. She turns around and walks down the hall. Her ass has no dimples or creases.

"That's a groovy kimono," Sophie says when Dori returns to the living room.

"You *like* it?" Dori says enthusiastically.

"I love it," Sophie says. "I love kimonos." Then she remembers the peach kimono drifting away from her . . . and Brian.

"Then I'll give it to you," Dori says. She stands up from the corduroy love seat, unties the obi, and hands Sophie a raw silk kimono her father brought home from China in the twenties.

"You're kidding," Sophie says. She rubs the silk against her cheek.

"I want you to have it," Dori says. She sits with her legs spread wide apart. Sophie can't help staring, afraid she might fall in.

"Dori, Melanie's pregnant," Sophie says suddenly. Melanie looks shocked.

"Do you want to have it?" Dori asks.

"I'm not married or anything," Melanie says huskily. "I can't have a baby. My boyfriend would disown me."

"Well, do you want an abortion?"

Dori is pretty, Sophie thinks. She never saw it before: the uptilted, second-chance nose, the slanty gray eyes, the vaguely rodenty cheek bones. A sexy Episcopalian mouse.

"Sure I'd like to have an abortion," Melanie says. "But where?"

"How does Puerto Rico sound?" Dori asks. "The three of us could fly right down there. My sister-in-law had a perfectly safe abortion there just last fall. I do own a bit of real estate there. A little cottage—a guest house, really. We'll go down Friday, have it on Saturday, fly back Sunday! We'll say we went to check on the cottage. I'll call my sister-in-law, Porter, right now if you want. She'll talk to you."

"How much do I need? Money, I mean," Melanie says.

"I'll worry about that for now," Dori says. "Sid won't mind if I lend you the money. And we'll keep the whole thing a big secret. Don't worry, Melanie. . . ." Melanie looks at Sophie, bewildered.

Friday afternoon Melanie wears the maid's housecoat and a platinum wig. The bangs extend from an odd-shaped hat. "And I'm gonna wear baby blue glasses," Melanie says.

"You look like a nut. They'll arrest you at the airport."

"I'm incognito," Melanie says.

"Who's gonna *see* you?"

"Anybody could see me in Puerto Rico. Half my father's friends fly down there to gamble."

"Well, you look even more conspicuous dressed like a bag lady."

"I'm wearing what I'm wearing. I don't care how I look. But I think I'm *showing*," Melanie says. She lifts up her housecoat and flashes a stomach as flat as Kansas.

"C'mon, Melanie. We've gotta get to the city."

In Fort Lee, last stop till Manhattan, someone they know gets on the bus. It's Rita Passelini whom Sophie knows from Health. Last week in health class, Rita Passelini asked Mrs. Roman what an orgasm was. Everyone knows Rita's sister Janis had an abortion. Maybe Rita knows what it's like. Sophie thinks of the big claw inside those amusement park boxes. A big claw hangs from a crane and you work the crane with a red button, pushing for fifty cents. For fifty cents you won thirty seconds of control. The crane lifts up, then dead-ends into the side of the glass. The toy watch, the inflatable Pluto, the false money, the fright wig, do not get hooked by the claw.

Melanie has an old *Daily News* pushed against her face and Sophie says nothing to Rita until the three of them get off at the George Washington Bridge Terminal. This terminal is less frightening than the one at Port

Authority. No one stands up here recruiting New Jersey girls into a life of crime. But downtown, Sophie knows, the girls flock in from Amarillo and Hendersonville. They are looking for the hippie good life. They hang out at the bus station trying to figure out which way is Greenwich Village. They have a twenty-dollar bill or a piece of jewelry they hope to pawn. They carry a stepmother's flatware all the way from Decatur only to find out the stuff is stainless. They eat at Bickford's or Orange Julius. They see some guy with long greasy hair. Maybe he knows about one of those places the magazines call crash pads. They sit at the counter and practice what they are going to say. "Like, hi," they say to themselves, practicing. They see their faces reflected in the mirror above the counter. In the greenish cast of the fluorescent light, they see they are still pretty. And young. They remember that a pretty girl never has to worry. They touch their crucifixes for luck and check inside their billfolds to see if the twenty's still there. Tonight they will sit in the bus station, careful not to fall asleep. If they fall asleep, the cops will come and haul them off to the station. Where is Radio City? they wonder, drinking their third cup of coffee. Where is Washington Square Park? Where is the Empire State Building?

Melanie walks behind Rita and Sophie, pretending she doesn't know them. The long walk down the ramp to the token booth takes forever. The maids are returning to Manhattan, carrying discarded suit jackets and fur coats that have gone out of style. The executives return to New Jersey, carrying Cake Masters cheesecake and leftover veal Marsala from lunch. Melanie decides she will not have a maid no matter how rich she and Ricky are by the time he graduates med school. By the time Ricky graduates med school, their baby would be about seven.

"Rita," Sophie says, "I heard from one of my—you know, I heard that Janis had an abortion."

Rita turns red. She looks at Sophie meanly.

"You're in trouble, aren't you?" Rita says. "Don't ask me. Ask Maria Farducci. Ask Jill Grinspan. Ask your friend Anita the big shot. And don't go around saying stuff about my sister. My sister's a nicer person than a lot of people."

Rita's voice fades into nothing now that the A train is coming. She's hurt Rita's feelings, and Sophie feels bad. She sits down next to a fat man; the seat next to Rita is taken. Rita is sitting next to a nun. The nun is beautiful.

She looks like that lady in *Gigi*. Leslie Caron. No one has ever touched the nun's vagina. Not even the nun is allowed to touch it, not even in the bath. The nun's eyebrows are blondish, her eyes are gray or green. Probably she's blonde "everywhere," as the boys say. Sophie imagines the nun's vagina: a fragile blonde nest cradling delicate eggs.

Sophie once heard her mother talking on the telephone. "Get married again at *my* age? Have a baby at *my* age? My eggs are old," Miriam had said. My eggs are old. My eggs are old. Sophie imagines her mother's eggs—two thin-shelled Ping-Pong balls, one sitting in each ovary. Miriam's eggs are old, used-up, the shells grown thinner and thinner, translucent. The shells have grown black with age. Sophie remembers the burnt egg that sits on the *seder* plate at *Pesach*. Sophie remembers her mother readying the plate: her mother's slender hands tearing leaves from a celery stalk; her mother's delicate fingers striking a match, holding the flame up to an extra-large grade A.

The flame grows large and blue in the dusk. It is Passover and guests are expected! It is Sophie's job to take the guests' coats. Sophie will carry the coats into her parents' room. And there in her parents' messy bedroom she'll rummage through all the pockets. Lee Freund has the best stuff: pieces of tickets from Broadway plays, the lipsticky ends of cigarettes, purple swizzle sticks, paper parasols from drinks served in pineapple halves. . . .

Sophie looks into Rita's face. I'm sorry, Sophie thinks. And next to Rita sits the nun who looks like the girl in *Gigi*. What does it look like? A vagina that no one has touched?

On the AA train, Rita gone, the friends sit together. Melanie looks like a Martian. The bangs are now plastered against her forehead; she's wearing peculiar sunglasses. People must think she's crazy.

Melanie lays her head on Sophie's shoulder. Her pointy chin digs into Sophie's collar bone, and Sophie feels vulnerable. Inside Melanie's housedress, inside Melanie's panties, inside Melanie's vagina, a baby embryo yawns.

Delicate conduit, opulent port, messy catchall for jism and blood. Home for enthusiastic microbes, playground for sperm cells, oven for yeast. Vagina, container, receptacle, hopper. Cannikin, casserole, crucible, caddy. Mess kit for some, milk pail for others. Cream pitcher, cuspidor, loving cup, urn.

Sid is sitting on a cushion in the middle of the floor. He laughs, embarrassed. All the furniture has been removed and replaced by tapestry pillows.

"Sid, you weren't supposed to know. You were supposed to be working late," Sophie says.

"I won't tell. Hello, little Melanie. You poor delicate child. Your secrets are safe with Uncle Sid."

Melanie says, "You *recognized* me."

"Of course I recognized you, baby."

"She's supposed to be incognito," Sophie says slyly.

"Don't worry, Melanie. We have your cover all worked out. Dori has some real estate down there. Nothing fancy mind you."

"A small guest house," Sophie says. Sid and Dori are *so* bourgeois.

"Exactly," says Sid. "You have a perfect cover. You've gone down with Dori to help her open the cottage. Anyway, dear, no one will see you."

"Half my father's friends go down there to gamble," Melanie whines.

"What do they play?" Sid asks. "Low ball? Craps?"

"I don't know," Melanie says. "They have these junkets or something. Every liquor distributor in Jersey goes down on the weekend."

"Well, if you see any of those guys, I bet they'll be doing something worse than you. . . . Anyway, Dori's delighted to help."

"Dori's a trip," Sophie says. "Where is she? Are we still going?"

"Meditating," Sid says. "These days she spends half her time on her head."

"Where's all the furniture?" Sophie asks. Wait till she tells her mother the latest.

"Dori's facilitator told her it's bad to sit on couches. Something to do with vertical and horizontal energy or something. Don't ask me." Sid rubs his coccyx and smiles.

"Dori seems a lot different," Sophie says. "When we came up here last week, she acted like we were best friends."

"I know. She has changed a lot. But people change, Sophie. And she really wants to be close to you. And that's why she's helping you out. Poor Melanie," Sid says. Sid is really starting to age, Sophie thinks. His blond hair is going thin; the skin around his eyes is baggy, his eyes look sunken. Is Sid happy? Does it make a middle-aged man happy to have a twenty-nine-year-old wife? Or does he live in constant fear that she'll find someone more pliant? And what about penises? Does a penis collapse one day without any warning, like a worn-out chaise longue?

Dori is wearing a denim jumpsuit appliquéd with Mexican designs. Her hair is cut geometrically; her eyes are done up like Twiggy's.

"Well, girls, the limo is coming in thirteen minutes. You'd be surprised, Sid, you know? It's not much more than a cab with three."

"I've got to call Ricky," Melanie says. She fluffs her polyester bangs in a tin sunburst mirror.

"No dice," Sophie says. "You decided to call him afterwards. *Remember*, Melly?"

"All right," Melanie whines. "I look shitty as a blonde."

Melanie sits next to Sophie on the plane. Dori's by herself in No Smoking. They eat teeny club sandwiches—bacon and turkey and processed cheese.

"This beats baby-sitting and watching 'The Twilight Zone,' " Sophie says.

"You know, Sophie, I've been wanting to ask you. Don't get mad. Why you're always baby-sitting on weekends and all. You've got to start going out with guys and all. You're practically sixteen."

"I don't know anyone I want to screw. And at our age you've gotta screw. Or else you're a total fag, right? I mean, the guys I'd like to screw don't go to Hudson Heights High School and belong to the fucking glee club."

"That's really mean, Sophie."

"Mean? Whaddya mean? Why?"

"You're making fun of Ricky."

"I am not." Sophie runs her fingernail across the bottom of the peanuts container. She scrapes up a few grains of salt and licks them with her tongue. "I am not."

"You think Ricky's a fag."

"A fag-fag you mean? A homo?"

"No, I mean a douche—you think all my friends are douche-bags."

"Douche-bags! Melanie, you're so funny."

"Well do you?" Melanie asks. "Do you think Ricky's a douche?"

"No. I like Ricky. And he'd be really good-looking if he'd get rid of that student council pompadour and stop trying to talk like he's in graduate school."

"I know he's pretentious. But he'll outgrow it. He's eighteen, Sophie. No boys are cool at eighteen."

"Keats was cool at eighteen. Rimbaud—"

"—Is that who you're gonna screw? Rimbaud's great-great-grandson?"

"I have great dreams," Sophie says. "Dreams of incredible passion and wild beautiful boys." Sophie looks out the window. There is blackness and stillness and strange negativity. Seven miles down is Fairfax, Virginia.

"In the meantime," Melanie says, "how about Jay Kintsler?"

"To screw?" Sophie asks.

"To talk to. Go to a football game with. He's very intelligent. 74s on his pre-Sats, math *and* verbals."

"Oh . . . could I have a drink?" Sophie asks the stewardess as she passes.

"How old you supposed to be?" the stewardess asks.

"Nineteen," Sophie says. "Nineteen in July."

"Ask someone to order it for you. Okay, do you mind?"

Sophie walks down the aisle to where Dori is sitting in the No Smoking section. When Sophie approaches a small silver spoon enters Dori's nose, then emerges. She thinks of the salt dishes and little spoons her Grandma Spivack used to have.

"Ssh," Dori says. She puts her finger to her lips. "This is Barney. He's an importer-exporter in Puerto Rico. And this is my little stepdaughter Sophie."

"Sophie, what a funky name." Barney nods his head as he finishes each sentence. "Really."

"Dori, could you order me and Melanie some piña coladas?"

"They don't make piña coladas on airplanes," Barney says. "They don't like to mess around with small appliances in the air."

"Well, how about two Scotch and sodas?"

"Should Melanie be drinking? She'll vomit," Dori says. "That girl is a born vomiter. Nothing repressed about Melanie."

"Maybe you'd like a little toot?" Barney asks. "Take this into the bathroom." He hands her a glass vial and a small spoon.

Barney wrinkles up his nose and snorts to show Sophie how. "Just one spoon in each *loch*," Barney winks. "One shot each'll be plenty. Really."

In the claustrophobic bathroom, Sophie snorts cocaine. For a second she thinks she's going to pass out.

She returns the bottle to Barney, who is singing the title song from *Oklahoma*! Dori is snuggled against his Mexican wedding shirt, fooling around with his chest hairs.

By the time she returns to her aisle and her seat, Sophie feels happy. She feels a deep buzzing within her being. She longs to stroke the brown velour shirt of a bald-headed man three rows ahead.

The pilot is announcing the weather in Puerto Rico when Melanie awakens suddenly. "Oh, Sophie. I was dreaming about the baby. He was a Negro, can you believe it? And he had blue eyes. He was wearing the sweetest little suit—the darlingest little Negro baby."

* * *

The three of them sit in the Avis lounge waiting for the silver Cadillac Dori has insisted upon.

"It'll be another twenty minutes. We've got to clean out the inside. It looks like they had the Democratic Convention in there. Why don't you take the black Cadillac?" The Avis man is earnest.

"Black is depressing," Dori says.

"How about a little red Mustang?" the Avis man asks. "We've got a little red Mustang, brand new."

"I kind of wanted a silver Cadillac. Okay. I guess I'm just being silly."

The Mustang pulls up to a pink stucco house with an overwhelming garden. The air is charged with jasmine and bougainvillea; the atmosphere smells like the junior prom.

"What a wonderful little house," Sophie says. "A dollhouse," she says, "with palm trees."

"Are there coconuts?" Melanie asks. "I love fresh coconuts."

Inside there's a bedroom with a canopy bed, a small living room and a kitchen. "Melanie gets the bedroom," Dori says. "And you and I can camp out on the floor in here. I have a sleeping bag *somewhere*."

"Do you come down here a lot?" Melanie asks. "For vacations?"

"Sid and I had our honeymoon here," Dori says. She pats the bed. "First he had his divorce and then he married me the same day." Dori gasps. "I'm sorry, Sophie. I didn't realize what I was saying. I'm sorry. Sometimes I just run on."

"Can we go *out*?" Melanie asks. "I've never *been* to Puerto Rico."

"We *could* drive down to the casinos," Dori says. "But just for a little bit. Melanie can't eat or drink *anything* from midnight on. And we've all got to wake up very early. Eight o'clock's your appointment."

"Shit, I'd practically forgotten. I wish this was a vacation," Melanie says.

"It *will be*," Dory says. "Tomorrow as soon as you're rested up, we'll all have our hair done and go to the casinos. We can see a show or something. Barney—that nice importer-exporter from the plane—invited us over any time. He has a jacuzzi and everything."

"Maybe I'm making a big mistake," Melanie says in the back seat on the way to the Grand Casino.

"What do you mean? The abortion?" Sophie turns around.

"Yeah. I mean what if the baby turned out to be president—or a banker. A great man or something . . . I don't know."

"I lost a baby once," Dori says. "It was awful. I cried for six weeks straight.

And then when your dad, Sophie's dad, wanted to try to have another—I couldn't do it. I couldn't make love."

Sophie imagines her father trying to pry Dori's legs apart. She imagines her father's soft belly banging against Dori's flat chest.

"I really *love* Ricky," Melanie says. "He's a really good boyfriend. He buys me presents for half-birthdays and candy on Valentine's Day. He lets me pick most of the movies. He *baked* me a cake—from a mix, but still, when I didn't fail Algebra II. . . ."

"It sounds like you've got yourself a winner," Dori says. "Husband material. But listen, Melanie, there's an old saying—'Don't Advertise Your Man.' Get it?" Sophie's curls snap in the wind. Outside on the one-lane highway, tar bubbles pop beneath their wheels.

Inside the Grand Casino, Melanie plays blackjack. She stays good on a soft seventeen and the dealer busts with two aces, a queen, and then a jack.

"Lucky me!" says Melanie, who's up seven dollars. Seven silver coins sag heavily in her purse.

"I want a drink," Sophie says, mesmerized by the pair of bazooms on the six-foot waitress. "Get me a Cuba Libre," Sophie tells Melanie.

"Cuba Libre," Melanie tells the waitress.

Sophie looks at Melanie's hand. Melanie has blackjack.

After ten minutes, Melanie has twenty-four dollars. She has started to double-down on tens, and she's raised her bet to four dollars.

At the far end of the green felt room Dori has lost eighty dollars of Sid's money at craps and has, surprise! run into Barney, that nice man from the plane.

A bald man in dark glasses edges in toward their table and Sophie gives up her seat to him. He puts three C-notes down on the table and takes off his shades. "Melanie Szasz!" he says. "Are your charming parents here for the 'end?"

"Uncle Morty," Melanie says, then she vomits all over her hand.

"Well, you made twenty-eight dollars," Dori says. "You can buy yourself some perfume at the duty-free."

"I know Uncle Morty's gonna call Daddy," Melanie says. "He's not really my uncle. He's—"

"—I'll call up Sid and Sid'll work it out," Dori says. "Now get to sleep and rest up. Tomorrow'll be over as soon as a jiffy." Dori tucks the sheets in around Melanie's hips and kisses her on the forehead.

Melanie holds her ovaries, one hand on each of the places she imagines them to live, invisible beneath her pelvis. Inside her, Ricky Cooper's daughter lives and dies.

Dori has made piña coladas for herself and Sophie. Melanie is in a daze. "Can't I have just the pineapple juice or some coffee? Can't I have a Valium or *something*?" Melanie asks.

"No, baby, they'll give you a little pre-operative shot. Don't worry, you won't feel a thing. My sister-in-law said it was less traumatic than having her bikini line done. . . ."

On the way to the clinic, Melanie starts crying. "I never even had my tonsils out or anything. I never even had appendicitis," Melanie whines.

"They don't call it labor for nothing," Dori says. "Being a woman is a very demanding business. The species—the human species—keeps screwing up the feminine will to live an individual life. I took this course at the New School—a course in feminist consciousness. The professor was a close friend of Betty Friedan's. Shared a house with Betty over in Easthampton."

"Betty Friedan," Melanie says. "Does she live in Hudson Heights?"

"She's a feminist thinker," Sophie says. "Feminism is the new thing in politics."

"Now that civil rights isn't the big issue," Dori says, passing a Rolls doing twenty, "we're recognizing that the real oppressed class is women. All women, even wealthy women are oppressed." Dori smiles.

"Would you mind pulling over?" Melanie whispers.

"I couldn't hold it in," Melanie says. She is wearing a paper hospital gown and paper slippers. When the nurse asked her weight, Sophie heard her mumble 150, though Melanie weighs much less. "I thought I'd get a bigger shot," Melanie confides to Dori.

"Do you feel the Valium?" Dori asks. "Did they give you Nembutal?"

"I'm high as a kite," says Melanie. "I feel like I could fly."

In the corner of the room Sophie sees what looks like her mother's old Hoover.

"A vacuum cleaner," Sophie mouths to Dori. It looks just like the vacuum cleaners they sell from door to door.

"You girls will have to leave now," the dark-skinned doctor tells Sophie and Dori. "Don't worry about a thing." His accent is romantic.

"Ricky, Ricky, I love you," Melanie whispers, drugged.

* * *

Melanie is wearing the blue glasses and the yellow bangs and a new straw hat that has her name embroidered across it. *Melanie, Puerto Rico*. She is reeling a bit in the hot afternoon, yet Dori decides she can break doctor's orders and order a coconut drink.

"Coconut's so good for the complexion," Melanie says, slurping.

"So's semen," Sophie says. "It's also cheaper."

"You ought to know," Melanie says.

"You girls are crocked," laughs Dori.

"Maybe now's a good time to call Ricky up," says Melanie, "while I'm still high and all."

Sophie tries to talk her out of it, but Melanie is really high, high as John Glenn or Walter Schirra. It is ninety-six in Puerto Rico and Melanie is gone on Valium and rum.

"Richard," Melanie says.

"Where are you? Your parents said—first they thought you were in the city. Then your Uncle Morty said—are you in Puerto Rico? Why are you in Puerto Rico?"

"I'm with Sophie's father's wife. It's okay. She has this small— She . . . listen, Ricky, I had an abortion and I'm sorry. Don't be mad."

"An abortion? Were you pregnant?"

"I hope I was pregnant. Remember? I vomited twice on Thursday. Remember? Remember my breasts—"

"Oh, Melanie." Ricky thinks of her tiny breasts, little insect homes. "Melanie, is it over?"

"Yeah and I'm fine. So don't tell anybody. Not even your cousin in Flushing."

"Why didn't you t-t-tell *me*?" Melanie loves Ricky's stutter. He's so vulnerable when he stutters.

"I couldn't tell you, Richard."

"Why are you calling me Richard?"

" 'Cause I want to marry you," Melanie says. "I'll go to whatever college you go to. If I can't get into—if you get into Harvard, I'll go to a junior college. I'll—"

"Don't go to a junior college," Ricky says. "That's ridiculous. You never can be sure they'll transfer all your credits."

"Oh, Ricky," Melanie says. He's *such* a good boyfriend.

2

Divining Rod

1

"*Yo," Barney says*, opening the door. "Really."

"We're doing fine," Dori says, gesturing toward Melanie. She takes off her sundress and hands it to Barney. Sophie is relieved to see she has a bathing suit on underneath.

"Poor Melanie," Barney says. "Get right in that jacuzzi." Barney feels Melanie's shoulder. Like a Russian girl-gymnast's, he thinks.

Sophie and Melanie disappear into the bathroom. "I can't even use Tampax," Melanie says. "They gave me the biggest Kotex I've ever seen."

"Hospital Kotex," says Sophie. "Like they use when you have a baby."

"You *bleed* when you have a baby?" Melanie asks. "Oh God."

"You bleed when you have a baby. You bleed when you don't have a baby. Whatever happens, you bleed. Women bleed."

"I don't want to keep *bleeding* for the rest of my goddamned life." Melanie starts crying. "Ricky's goddamned penis. I wish I'd never seen it. Never laid eyes on it."

"Don't ask me," Sophie says. "I'm a virgin." She smiles.

"You're kidding. Sophie, I know you're kidding. I've never believed you. You knew about sex before anybody."

"I *know* about it, but I don't practice."

"Lots of boys like you. Ben Kalisher, Ricky said—"

"I don't care about the sex part. It's the kissing I dream about. I think about making out for hours in a field somewhere. . . ." She imagines the guy from the head shop throwing her down in the hot sun.

"I don't believe you, Sophie. I *know* you're not a virgin. Ever since last year . . . you started acting . . . mysterious. Tell me who it was."

"Don't be ridiculous, Melanie."

"Who was it, Sophie? They say—Ricky told me after a woman makes love, you can just tell she's different."

"Oh, yeah?" Sophie says. "Like boys say a girl *walks* different afterwards? You're so gullible, Melanie. You think a woman has sex once, then she walks funny with her legs spread apart for the rest of her life?"

"I don't believe you," Melanie says. She sticks out her fat tongue; her breath is coconuts and ether.

Sophie pulls up the acetate straps of her yellow bikini. Melanie flushes the toilet and poor little Ricky, Jr. is dead.

When Melanie and Sophie get out to the patio, they realize they're the only ones wearing bathing suits. Two men stand casually nude in the swimming pool. And Dori is making out with Barney in the jacuzzi.

Sophie feels sick. She spots a bottle of rum glinting in the sun. "Let's make *real* drinks," Sophie says, "in the blender." She goes into the kitchen where a woman is bent over butcher block, snorting cocaine. She offers a straw to Sophie, the smallest stub of a red-and-white-striped plastic straw. She chops away on a mirror with a shiny razor blade.

"Is Barney out back?"

"Uh-huh," Sophie says.

"I like your suit," the woman says. She cuts the cocaine over and over, chopping on a dime-store mirror. She lines it up, then cuts the line, then lines it up again. "Here."

Sophie sticks the straw in her nostril. She imagines she tastes the tiniest remnant of root beer syrup. And then the burn of cocaine as it shoots through her sinuses. In the mirror she makes out the interior life of her nostrils. The shy hairs. The little pink rooms.

"That line's yours," says the woman. She watches Sophie snort the second line. "I'm Lynn," she says.

"I'm Sophie. Thanks for turning me on." Sophie opens the freezer compartment as if she lived there. With Barney and Lynn and who-knows-else. The metal ice tray sticks cruelly to Sophie's fingers. She drops the tray; her fingers burn. Like napalm, Sophie thinks.

"This woman in the kitchen is chopping up cocaine," Sophie tells Melanie.

"You're kidding. Cocaine? The drug?"

"I snorted some. Through a root beer straw. You still could taste the root beer."

"I never even *heard of* anyone *having* cocaine. Except in film strips in Health. What does it look like?"

"Crushed-up aspirins. You cut it up with a razor blade. It feels great. Like sex. Tingles everywhere. I did it on the plane yesterday. This is my second time."

"You shot it? You took it?"

"I snorted it up my nose. Like remember when in seventh grade Barry Geffner was eating soup? And the chicken noodle came out of his nose?"

Melanie starts laughing, guffawing.

"Go do some, Mel. And go into the kitchen and get some tonic. I don't think he has a blender. Or maybe we should have juice with rum. Is rum and tonic a drink?"

"Take cocaine? Ricky would kill me."

"Do it, Melanie."

"I can't have an abortion and take cocaine in one day. What's gonna become of me?" Sophie watches fondly as Melanie parts the glass doors.

One of the men lumbers out of the pool and Sophie watches the golden sun glistening against his thighs. Puerto Rico, opulent port. His penis hangs like a piccolo—suspended to catch the note. It's Aaron's rod, a pogo stick, a pencil, a nightstick. A poker, a rapier, a dipstick, a crook. Cattle prod, tomahawk, totem pole, tower. Divining rod, pecker, Long Tom, shiv.

"Mind if I join you?" the man asks. He has slipped on a tiny bikini, red, and Sophie can see the bulk of his balls pushing against the synthetic.

"Rum and tonic," Sophie says. "Is that a real drink?"

"A drink's a drink," the man says. "You want me to get you something? Is rum and tonic your drink?"

"Not usually."

"What *is* your drink?" He squints and looks shady in the sun.

"My usual drink is a piña colada. What about you?"

"I don't drink. I used to drink. Now I toot."

Sophie watches Dori's nipples under the fingers of Barney's hands. What is she supposed to think? Does her father know she cheats? Is she supposed to tell him?

"Ernie Longanesi," the man in the red bathing suit says, extending a tan arm. She wonders if he is Connected. Her father would say, yes.

"Dori's my father's wife. I'm Sophie."

"But Dori's not your mother. Is—?"

"Second marriage," Sophie says.

"Second marriage," Ernie says languorously. And rolls his eyes.

"What do you mean?" Sophie asks.

"I had a second marriage," Ernie laughs. "I also had a third marriage. I'm through with marriage. How about you?"

"I'm fifteen," Sophie says.

Flowers are falling from the hibiscus. Hibiscus flowers fall into the pool. Dead mosquitoes float on the surface. A forgotten net hangs over the pool. The other man, who is standing still in the water, picks up a piece of hibiscus petal, inhales the fragrance slowly. Sophie prefers the man in the pool to this suspicious Mafioso.

Around the neck of the man in the pool there hangs a glinting golden chain. St. Christopher, the saint of travelers? A hammer and sickle? A *Mogen David*? Sophie studies the genitalia of the man in the swimming pool who is sniffing the insides of flowers. Purple-stained petals, pendant and white.

"You wanna snort?" Ernie asks. Ernie looks like a bit actor, somebody's stand-in, a supe. His face is a little mean. Pockmarks, three-o'clock shadow. His hair is Italian without the sheen. There is no halo in Ernie's hair, no blue luster, no Mediterranean oil.

"Sure," Sophie says. In the heat, she looks Levantine.

Ernie goes into the house, and the man in the pool waves to her. Sophie waves back. She wishes he would come out now and rescue her from Longanesi. She feels the sexual tension as doom. The hideous bleating of a cat in heat.

Ernie comes out of the house with an expensive tote bag. He takes out a piece of paper. The paper is folded like origami. As Ernie unfolds the colored paper, an advertisement for Virginia appears. Williamsburg. Colonial houses. Thomas Jefferson freeing the slaves.

"So where's your third wife?" Sophie asks. Lynn and Melanie part the glass doors. Lynn is naked; Melanie is wearing her bottoms. Sophie can make out the outlines of her sanitary belt: the blood of the child, his dark blood, spilled in the hospital's utility steel. Melanie's body looks fragile and strong. As

Melanie holds her long nose and dives into the pool, Sophie remembers the doctors have vacuumed her uterus.

Lynn sits on the edge of the pool. Sophie watches the crook of her spine as Lynn smokes Dunhills and flicks the ashes delicately into the chlorinated water. In the drain at the bottom cling myriad hairs—venereal, axillary, cilial, crine.

Dori ducks her head. Everyone can tell she is going down on Barney. Sophie's too high to be embarrassed.

"My third wife?" Ernie asks. He's scraping the powder from the paper onto a woman's compact. Flakes of powder cling to the compact, grains from another life. "Annie? Annie is living in Brooklyn. With this cowboy named *Robert*. Some phony. Some phony barbecue king out on parole."

"Which wife did you love?" Sophie asks. "Any of them?" Sophie is watching Barney. He is diving into the shipwreck of Dori's thighs. Do the thighs belong to her father? Or if not the thighs, the vulva? The clitoris? The glands of Bartholin? What?

Together they'd buried a baby. Together they'd picked out a tiny blond coffin without metal hinges. Together they'd worried about circumcision. Dori had laughed and told stories about the uncircumcised Greek student, Costos, she'd made love to in the *bagno pubblico*. His Attic penis. His foreskin as motile as a machine. In the *bagno pubblico* in Florence, they'd drunk espresso and played Flipper and paid extra lire for tiny vials of pink shampoo. And then they'd gone to a single stall and made love for minutes and minutes, the old water of Florence falling, falling, falling between them.

"Which wife did I love? I loved all of them," Ernie says. "What d'ya think? I'm an animal? Here, Sophie." He hands her a silver tube.

"That's good," Ernie says. "Now do the other line." Sophie notices the white powder dappling the inside of his nose.

Sophie watches Melanie and Lynn fighting over a Styrofoam kickboard. The hook of Melanie's sanitary belt shimmers evocatively in the heat. The tenterhooks of women. Lynn's breasts bobble as she leans off the deep end to grab the board.

Ernie is snorting his fourth line. Then he holds Sophie's hand. Her palm throbs under his fingers.

"I'm really high," Sophie laughs.

Ernie's hand lands like D-day on Sophie's shoulder.

"There's a cabaña behind the pool. There's a bedroom no one's using. There's my office downtown. . . ."

"What do you do for a living?" Sophie feels like an inflated toy. A funny balloon in Macy's Parade.

"A living? C'mon, I want to make love. Baby, I want to make love to you on brown sheets."

"Careful with the teeth," Ernie says.

He groans as Sophie's tongue fires against the ridge of his penis. It was here that the young Chinese intern, a sad-faced Ning-Gau Ho, had taken the brand-new scalpel to the infant Ernest Matthew in the Bronx in 1931.

Sophie looks in the mirror on the closet door. Her face is covered with semen. She looks in the closet. A pair of suede Keds with the price tag still on, the flash in the mirror of her hipbone circling madly in the mirror. It seems to be working without her.

Ernie falls asleep. Sophie puts on her bikini bottoms and goes out to the patio. Melanie and Lynn and the man from the pool are smoking a fat reefer rolled in newspaper. She watches as a bilingual Snoopy burns into nothingness.

"Give me a hit," Sophie says.

Melanie winks.

Sophie gives her a look. Melanie can't stop smiling.

"Lynn's an art history major at the university. And Kyle is Lynn's cousin," Melanie says.

"What were your SATs?" Sophie asks. Melanie glares at her.

"We used to live next door in Chicago," Kyle says. "Me and Lynn."

"And your sexy stepmother is beating my time," Lynn says gaily.

"Is Barney your boyfriend? How embarrassing." Sophie closes her eyes.

"Don't be embarrassed," Lynn says, relighting the doobie and inhaling. "It happens all the time." A seed catches fire and pops out, landing in Sophie's cleavage. She sticks her finger into a glass and rubs the remains of someone's Tom Collins onto her tender chest.

Dori and Barney finally emerge. Dori is pruny from the water. Sophie watches their behinds huddling off to the house. Barney's butt is a little too big. Golden and hairy, low-slung. Dori's is smaller—even though she's the woman. A small bum the color of a newborn gasping for air.

2

"*You wanna be an old maid*?" Melanie asks.

"Why not," Sophie says. "Old maids have more fun."

Melanie is tweezing Sophie's eyebrows.

"Ow." Sophie winces.

"You've got to suffer for beauty," Melanie says.

"My mother used to say that." Sophie remembers her mother combing the snarls out of her hair. Sophie remembers her mother's nails piercing through knots of gummy frizz. "You must suffer for beauty," Miriam had said, readying her daughter for the day the photographer came to school.

"Did your father find out about Dori and Barney?" The girls have been back from Puerto Rico for over a month.

"I don't think so. *I* never told him."

"I feel bad for your father."

"My father was horrible to my mother. Now it's his turn to get it."

"*Was* he horrible to your mother?"

"He must have been," Sophie says. "*Something* happened to my mother. She wasn't always an alcoholic. She used to sing opera. She used to be in some kind of chorus. She sang once in Town Hall."

"The concert is at *Carnegie* Hall. Saturday night. And you're *coming*."

"Melanie, I'm *not* going. I refuse. Get someone else. Get Anita."

"Bobby wouldn't *like* Anita. He's *smart*, Sophie. An intellectual. He's already heard from five schools: Chicago, Johns Hopkins, Harvey Mudd. . . . "

"Harvey *Mudd*?"

"It's a school for smart people. In California. He's supposed to be some kind of genius. I'm telling you, Sophie, he's a real person. A *mensh*," Melanie says.

"Then how come *you* have to get him laid?"

"He *has* girlfriends in Flushing, I'm sure. He wants to meet someone new. Ricky showed him a picture of you. At the beach in Puerto Rico. One of your famous tit shots."

"Don't mention Puerto Rico," Sophie says. "My cookie still hasn't recovered from Puerto Rico. That wop had the biggest dick. Like a thermos bottle."

"Really?" Melanie says. "Here." Melanie pushes her French take-home test over to Sophie. "Draw his penis."

"*You* draw Ricky's penis," Sophie laughs.

"I'd need a bigger piece of paper," Melanie says, giggling.

"I bet you could draw the whole thing on this matchbook."

"Sophie . . . "

"G'head."

Melanie draws the head of Ricky's penis. Her hand rests lightly on her French test. *Que signifie l'heroïsme dans* "Le Cid"?

"Mel, you're wearing too much lipstick again," Ricky says in the car driving across the George Washington Bridge. It is nearly summer and the Hudson shines with a poisonous gleam. Overhead an arc of gulls cuts across Jersey to the Apple.

Jonathan Schwartz is clearing his throat over the fragile airwaves, and Sophie's blind date is whistling the Donovan song, "There Is a Mountain." He's Bobby Buchman from Flushing, Queens—Ricky Cooper's whiz-kid cousin. Sophie catches him staring at her breasts.

"Is Flushing where the World's Fair was?" Sophie asks. She remembers the puppet of Abe Lincoln, the pickle-shaped pin from Heinz.

"That is correct," says Bobby. He talks like a fucking emcee, Sophie thinks. Who does he think he is—the fucking emcee on "College Bowl"?

"I hear your SATs were fantastic," Sophie says, teasing him, but really, ribbing Melanie.

"Rick? Ricky? What did you *say* about me? This girl already hates me."

"I didn't tell Sophie you were a Westinghouse," Ricky says.

"A Westinghouse?" Sophie asks. "Are you one of the T.V. Westinghouses? You must be loaded." Melanie glares at her in the mirror.

"Oh no. Ricky meant I won a national science search. It's no big deal. I found out something slightly interesting about DNA. That's all."

"DNA? Like genetics?" Sophie looks past his glasses into his watery blue eyes. Watery blue like a puddle in an impressionist earth.

"That's right, genetics. I hear you're interested in literature. Is that correct?"

"I have no interests," Sophie says. "This semester I'm taking Latin. And French. I used to think I wanted to be a therapist. They don't even have psychology until senior year. . . ."

"Yes they do," Melanie says. "They have Issues and Answers."

"That's really philosophy," Sophie says.

"Philosophy," Bobby says. "I'm very interested in epistemology."

"I thought epistemology was an operation," Ricky says. "Before a woman goes into . . ."

"Episiotomy," Sophie says.

"Episiotomy, that's right," Ricky says.

Carnegie Hall is wonderful for the fashions. It is 1968 and everyone is wearing purple. Every woman who walks down the aisle looks hipper and more beautiful than the woman before her. And the men! The men are dreamy. They are wearing caftans and flowers; they are carrying *Demian* and the *Realist*; they are high on opium and psilocybin; they live on Broome Street or Avenue B. A bearlike man sits down next to Sophie. She sits between Old College Bowl and the Incarnation of Eros.

"You go to high school around here?" the handsome man asks.

"I go to high school around New Jersey. You know, Hudson Heights."

Bobby reads the program. He is furious with Sophie. "The Proof of the Pudding," Bobby reads. "Let us seduce you for dinner. Sweet baby Ipswich clams nestled in a bed of chilled greens . . ."

"Hudson Heights. Where all those high-rises are?" He looks straight into her eyes.

"The bedroom community of the world," Sophie says, then blushes.

"Soph, let's find the bathroom." Melanie stretches her arm past Ricky and Bobby to pull Sophie's hair.

The friends push through a swelling crowd of stoned women and musky men. A barefoot toddler in a Carnaby Street dress steps on a smoldering cigarette and screams.

"Pick her up," says the mother. "Pick her up and suck her foot."

"Goddammit Sophie, you're flirting with some forty-year-old guy instead of talking to Bobby. Ricky's gonna kill me."

"I think Bobby's a bit of a retard. C'mon Melanie, you *know* he's a fag."

"He's handsome without his glasses," Melanie says.

The bathroom, when they find it, is overflowing with women. Everywhere glorious women in Indian saris, Arab wedding dresses, Moroccan djellabas. Everywhere women carrying purses from Guatemala, jangling earrings from the Ivory Coast. Everywhere silver and abalone. T shirts with the faces of Bob Dylan and Virginia Woolf; pierced ears, pierced noses, smooth shoulders unmarried by brassieres. No one is wearing a brassiere. It is 1968 and no one in Carnegie Hall will ever wear a brassiere again.

"Anyway, Sophie, if you saw him without his glasses . . . He looks a little like Dustin Hoffman without his glasses."

"Dustin Hoffman? Melanie, Dustin Hoffman is a *hunk*. That *older* guy is really sexy. Don't you think?" She wants to go back to her seat and flirt with the other guy. He has great sideburns, his jeans are thin as paper.

Sophie sits down dramatically. The sexy guy is reading something and misses her breasts as they fly for a moment, momentary sparrows.

Bobby hasn't missed a thing. "So tell me, Sophie, what you think of *Oedipus Rex*." He pronounces it funny: "Ead-a-puss."

"I think it's a swell play, Bobby."

Bobby laughs. She's impossible. "Swell? What do you mean?"

"I mean I liked it. I read it last year—in ninth grade—and thought it was good."

"What about hubris?" Bobby asks intelligently.

"Hubris, right. English teachers are very into hubris."

Bobby blushes. This girl is a tough guy. But if I don't make out with her, I'll kill myself, Bobby thinks. I'll kill Ricky first, though.

"Well don't you think that the hero is— Uh, don't you think that Oedipus's *pride* . . ."

"Do you want to make it with *your* mother?" Sophie asks.

"You're being a jerk," Bobby says. "Don't you give a shit *at all* about the gods?"

Phil Ochs is singing about the Flower Lady and Sophie feels high, stirred by the words of the songs, and by sex. Phil Ochs says something about Vietnam and the audience starts to holler and clap. Vietnam sits in the audience like a stain. A purple stain on Carnegie Hall.

It is 1968 and Phil Ochs cries imperceptibly on the stage.

Odetta starts to sing "He's Got The Whole World" and Sophie writes her phone number down on a slip of blue paper. A detention notice from last Thursday. She slips the paper to the man who is wearing the yellow T shirt and the dungarees so faded Sophie is moved by their longevity. The man looks at her and smiles. Bobby looks at her like she's an insect.

In the Automat, Bobby is acting really depressed.

"Tell me about your science project," Sophie says.

Bobby is eating apple pie with vanilla ice cream and drinking tea.

"Well . . . the fundamental idea of the project—conceptually speaking—was to isolate—"

"Of course," Sophie says. She stares languorously into his pale eyes. Dustin Hoffman? "Take your glasses off," Sophie says.

Bobby takes off his glasses. He *is* better-looking without them. And besides, he *listened* to me, Sophie thinks.

"You don't want me to talk about DNA? Or do you?" His voice has softened and Sophie feels interested. Something about him has caught her off-guard. He asked her in Carnegie Hall if she cared about the gods. Maybe a smart boy would understand her.

"Tell me about *your* genes," Sophie says. "Are the Buchmans a great dynasty in Flushing with geniuses in every room?"

Bobby laughs. Be nice to me, Sophie, he thinks. Mother me at your beautiful breast. Feed me and open your cunt to my lonely, intelligent cock.

"My father went to Harvard," Bobby says. "When he was forty he went back to college and became a Harvard man. Even though he already owned a carpet store and everything, he had this thing about Harvard. . . . He already had a degree, too. From Long Island University. But he wanted to go to Harvard."

"Why?" Sophie asks.

"He got an apartment in Cambridge. He probably would've lived in a *house* if they'd let him. He probably would have gone out for *crew* if they'd let him." Bobby laughs.

"How funny," Sophie says.

"Yeah. He got his own apartment. And we'd drive up, you know, me and my mom and my sister Muffin who's married."

"*Muffin*?" Sophie asks. "I thought you were Jewish."

"Her real name is Martha."

"Muffin Buchman?"

"Muffin Buchman-Mayerall. She married this guy Michael Mayerall. She's a corporate lawyer. *His* profession is rich person. . . ."

"So why'd they call her Muffin? Did she like English muffins? I hate English muffins," Sophie says.

"She just wanted a nickname. Like all her friends in her prep school had nicknames and she wanted one."

"What were the other girls' nicknames?"

"Bunny," Bobby says. "And there was one called Boo."

"Boo?" Sophie asks.

"Boo."

Ricky and Melanie want to go home, but Bobby and Sophie want to take a walk through Central Park.

"My parents won't be home till *three*. Or even *four*," Melanie pleads. "Four o'clock," Melanie repeats meaningfully. Melanie and Ricky are dying to make love. Melanie makes him wear two rubbers and Ricky doesn't feel a thing. Sophie can't believe she's back in the saddle so soon.

"The park isn't safe," Ricky says.

"Yes it is," says Sophie. "We want to buy some loose joints."

"Buy a joint in the park?" Ricky asks. He slaps his forehead.

"Melanie and I *always* buy joints in the park."

"Melanie, you do? How could you after all the times I've—" Melanie gives Sophie a filthy look. She shakes her head.

"*I* buy the joints," Sophie says. "Melanie waits in the lobby of the Plaza. Anyway, I want to get high." Sophie turns to Bobby. "Tell Ricky it's okay to buy loose joints in the park."

If Bobby has to risk getting jumped; if Bobby has to jeopardize his college career because he's doing time in the Tombs; if Bobby has to take a crap on a gonorrheal toilet in the middle of a cell peopled by ax murderers, he'll make sure Sophie gets high. A girl who's high is bound to be more willing. . . .

In the Automat, Ricky and Bobby confer in front of the jellos and puddings. Melanie whispers to Sophie, "You *do* like him, don't you? I *told* you he wasn't a douche-bag."

Melanie and Ricky make love on Gladys's side of the bed. Ricky puts on a Ramses and then he puts on a Trojan. Melanie puts on her glasses, examining him for holes.

In the living room, Sophie has turned on *Good Neighbor Sam*.

"I love *Good Neighbor Sam*," Bobby says wistfully.

"Me too," says Sophie.

Bobby smiles eagerly. *See*, he's saying, *see*? We *do* have things in common.

The mailman throws the mail down on Jack Lemmon's lawn.

Fifteen minutes later Melanie walks in, and, seeing them, giggles. "Sorry," she says, "wrong movie," and closes the door.

3

Sophie is sitting on the bathroom rug, shaving her legs. "Bobby Bookman is on the phone," Brian calls. He comes into the bathroom without knocking. "Bobby Bookman? What is he—a fucking encyclopedia salesman?" Brian follows Sophie into her bedroom.

My blind date, mouths Sophie. "Hi," Sophie says, "what's happening?"

"I think I fell in love with you," Bobby says. "You think it's scientifically possible?"

"Don't be silly," laughs Sophie, lighting up an L & M.

"When can I see you?"

"Let's just forget it," Sophie says. "It was only a fluke kind of thing." Like lightning striking twice, Sophie thinks—striking the same beech. "It was only a fluke thing that happened."

"I like you," Bobby says. "I know you think I'm a dork. Let's give it another chance."

"Melanie says you got into Stamford, Connecticut."

"Stanford. In California. I'll be going there," Bobby says. "In September."

"Well have a good time. In college," Sophie says. "Pick a good major."

"Wait a minute," Bobby says. "I want to see you. Be serious. I want to go to the movies with you and make out. So I won a stupid contest. So don't hold it against me."

Sophie motions to Brian to leave the room. Brian is sitting on her bed reading the *Daily News* and peeling his calluses. Brian stays put, picking his toes on the Indian spread.

"I don't hold it against you," Sophie says.

"Hold it against *me*," Brian whispers.

"People think I'm smart," Bobby says. "So, I'm not as smart as you. So, go out on a date with me. I think you're beautiful."

"Okay."

"I loved making love with you."

"Okay," Sophie says. "All *right*."

Bobby Buchman arrives in his mother's yellow Camaro. Sophie opens the door wearing a see-through Indian blouse. She realizes virgin-boys can be sexy. His eagerness is daunting.

Bobby takes one look at her and feels the energy drain from his groin; a delicious weakness loosens his thighs.

"Where are we going?" Sophie asks.

"I'll take you anywhere you say."

"Take me to the Plaza," Sophie says. She looks at his hooked nose, his watery eyes, his furrowed brow. They both have high brows, Sophie thinks. They are two smart Jewish kids. He's really into me, Sophie thinks. She leads Bobby into the living room. "This is my mother, Miriam Spivack."

Miriam takes off her headphones. "Are you Ricky Cooper's cousin? I know your Aunt Layeh. She is your aunt, isn't she? We used to work together, do the book club together at the JCC. Layeh's a very smart woman."

"She is?" Bobby asks. "That's news to me." Everyone laughs.

"Remember Layeh Cooper?" Miriam asks Sophie. "From the book club at the center?" Her mother is drinking a tall glass of amber milk on the rocks.

"I went to the book club with you when you talked that time."

"It was *Herzog*. I led the discussion."

"I read *Herzog*," Bobby says.

"I did a funny job, huh? I mixed up Herzog's first name. I think I called him Mitchell."

"No one noticed," Sophie says.

"Everyone noticed, are you kidding? Mitchell, I called him. You want me to make you something to eat? Some eggs or something? You like eggs, Bob?"

"Sure," Bobby says.

"We're going *out* to eat," says Sophie. "We're going to New York."

New York, Miriam thinks. Sid's office on York Avenue. The Feast of San' Gennaro when she was young and pretty and respected at The Lion's Head. Hudson Heights is five minutes away, and she hasn't been to New York in two years. What if she ran into Dori on the East Side? Dori would be buying miniature onions in Gristede's, little imported onions she'd cook with a *goyish* cream sauce and feed to Sid, spiked with sherry. Expensive sherry from somewhere in Portugal . . . "New York," says Miriam. "That sounds like fun."

"Well thanks for the eggs," Bobby says. "That is—"

"I could make you frozen pizza . . . with anchovies or sausage." He is the first boy Sophie has ever brought home. A little skinny, not too good-looking. His aunt is a smart woman, a bit of a gossip. She wears her Phi Beta Kappa key to book talks on her sweaters. A bit of a showoff, a very nice bust. Someone had told her Layeh's sister was a real bitch. She wouldn't mention it to Sophie. . . . What did it matter? She wasn't going to marry this boy.

A second time they cross the Hudson River. The sun is going down over New York Harbor and for some reason Sophie starts to cry. Bobby puts his arm around her shoulder; the coins jangle absurdly on her belly-dancer blouse.

"I'll be your friend," Bobby says. "I'll make you laugh. C'mon."

"Where are we going?" Sophie asks.

There is a magical feeling in the car, a warm feeling catching between them. They are two smart Jewish kids driving across a man-made bridge.

"We could go anywhere," Bobby says.

They see *Jules et Jim* at the Waverly and Sophie touches his hard-on during the lyrical parts.

"You're just like her," Bobby says after the movie. Sophie can't get served, so they sit in a coffee shop on Eleventh Street. "You're just like her," Bobby says, chewing Canadian bacon.

"Who?" Sophie asks. She spreads her arms sensuously across the length of the vinyl booth. Under her left armpit, one surviving curl glistens.

"Jeanne Moreau. The woman in the movie. I bet everybody is always falling in love with you." Bobby looks at her searchingly; she doesn't give anything away.

"I think I'll have another sandwich. Is that okay?"

They walk around in the April air. They pass a lot of couples, wandering around, lost like themselves. High school kids from Verona, New Jersey, whooping it up outside A Kettle of Fish. Sixteen-year-olds from Hewlett sneaking into the Café Wha, with IDs they bought in the cafeteria. They come to the edge of Washington Square Park. Music is being made on guitars, spoons, kazoos, Jew's harps, drums. Fingers snap; voices rise; lungs lift in harmony, lungs filled with the acrid smoke of Marlboros, Gitanes, Lucky Strikes.

"So tell me about your life," Sophie says.

In the soft heat, Bobby stammers. "You probably think I'm impulsive. On account of the other day and all . . . I'm no Don Juan," he says.

"Don Juan," Sophie repeats. No, she thinks, not a chance. She studies his angular face, his sad eyes, his sideburns. She notices the skin beneath his sideburns, the pale skin underneath. The skin of the Pale. She runs her fingers beneath his sideburn. He looks down at the pavement below him. He sees a silver nickel glowing in a pile of garbage: the wrapper from a Whammy Stick, the cellophane from a pack of Pall Mall. . . .

"A lucky nickel," Bobby says, giving it to Sophie.

Sophie puts the nickel away and doesn't spend it. Three years later, hung over and broke, she will find the nickel in a travel-clock box and spend it on espresso in Berkeley.

"Anyway, so I'm not exactly a Don Juan—you know, guy. You're really the first girl I ever had intercourse with. Of course you could tell, anyway, so I don't know why I'm making this a giant confession—"

"What makes you think I could tell?"

"Well, you've probably made love with a lot of people."

"Well *that's* pretty crass," Sophie says.

"Oh, I didn't mean it the—"

"Yes you did," Sophie says. "You're trying to get out of it, but you just called me a whore." Around them, full of drugs and wine, women call out plangently; teen-agers wrestle.

"A whore?" Bobby says. "C'mon. I meant something entirely different. I meant more like a femme fatale."

"You know what that means?" Sophie asks.

"Yeah. A heartbreaker, a goddess, Brigitte Bardot."

"Do you know what it means literally?"

"A fatal woman," Bobby says.

"Or a dead woman," says Sophie.

"Uh-uh. Dead would be *femme morte*."

Sophie thinks of Mata Hari, Cleopatra, Lady Brett, Marlene Dietrich in

The Blue Angel. The stiletto heel of the enchantress, the hollow laughter of the Sirens, the musky allure of Lorelei crouching on the Rhine.

Around them the night is dark and bright, the park is full of stars.

"Don't get technical," Sophie smiles.

4

All spring they make love. All summer they kiss in suburban back yards. Sophie's yellow bikini top glistens among the stars. Now her bikini is tied to the brace of a rusting chaise longue, and she and Bobby lie in the grass making love under Brian's window.

She realizes she loves Bobby. His head is full of a future for them—bookcases bursting with poetry, matching night stands, season tickets to the opera. He a local Albert Schweitzer giving his life away. He sees himself as the Great White Father and Sophie as his Great White Sidekick. Sidekick, mother, maidservant, wet nurse, *rebbitsin*, dancing girl, changeling wife. What happened to femme fatale? In exchange for season tickets, the enchantress gives up her magic.

The hibachi lies abandoned, next to Bobby's head. It is blackened with dirt and charcoal, the traces of dessicated grease. The ashy memory of pork chops from 1964. She moves his head away from the grill. They hadn't used the hibachi once since Sid had gone away. It lay there next to the broken hose, the soggy roll of fiberglass, the heavy blocks of concrete, cracked bricks, old tires.

There was a birdbath where Brian peed, late at night, coming in drunk. The face of a cherub carved in black marble puckered its lips to make a fountain. And every time Brian aimed to squirt it in the mouth. The only other love object in his life was his sister Sophie.

She hardly ever looked him in the eye. She never ate dinner with him anymore. All of them ate separately, if Miriam ate at all. Sometimes he would catch Sophie eating a thing of yogurt, sitting at the breakfast nook. She would read her magazines and not look up. He knows he's freaked her out. Bev told him she'd come to her office, a year or so ago, right after it had happened. . . .

He realizes Sophie had no one, that they were both orphans. So maybe it was good she had this skinny whiz kid from Queens banging her. He wondered if they fucked outside his window on purpose. To torture him. They always managed to end up coming right under his window.

Sometimes he'd be up in his room, listening to Miles or Bird, and he'd hear their voices—high and cheerful, lifting up from the grass. He wondered if he'd ever have a girlfriend. He'd only gone to bed with his sister. And almost with this prostitute once. She was off-duty, he'd met her downtown, on the street in Little Italy. She wasn't even bad-looking, young and a little dumb. Her complexion was terrible. He thought she was probably an addict. He couldn't get it up. The girl didn't seem to notice that much. They'd lain together on a sleeping bag and eaten English muffins with margarine. Actually, looking back now, it hadn't been a bad experience. The prostitute—her name was Sally—had had really nice blonde hair, silky between his fingers. It was the closest thing to a date Brian had ever had.

He heard Sophie's high laughter. She and Bobby were drinking champagne. The chump was going off to Stanford in a few days. Brian himself was heading west in another week. Though he'd never applied to college, Bev had talked to some guidance counselor who'd looked up his scores and his high IQ and made some telephone calls. He was offered admission to Reed College over the telephone. He was glad it was a hippie college with a lot of crazy girls. There had to be someone somewhere—like maybe in Portland, Oregon—who could love a guy like him.

Soon, summer is gone. Ricky goes off to Harvard and Melanie feels like a widow. Eleventh grade has to be the most useless year on earth. Sophie is sick of all the bullshit about Ricky at Harvard. Today Ricky bought a Harvard mug at the Harvard Co-op! Today Ricky went to his first Harvard home game! Melanie wakes her up on a Saturday morning at seven o'clock to read her an interview with freshmen in the Harvard newspaper. Richard B. Cooper, '72, from Hudson Heights, N.J., says he can't get used to the word "frappe" *at all*, and hates the greasy hot-dog rolls they used even for tuna fish.

Melanie is planning a trip to Cambridge for Rosh Hashanah. Sophie can't help but think of Brenda Patimkin. Melanie's supposed to stay with her cousin Laura whose husband works for Polaroid. Melanie thinks Laura might let her and Ricky sleep together in their guest room. What does Sophie think of her chances of flying out to Palo Alto?

"I'm sick of all this war-bride crap," Sophie says. "Can't we stop talking about those *boys*?"

They are cutting school at Melanie's house. They are lying, stoned, underneath the Szaszes' baby grand, eating peanut-butter cremes and drinking diet soda.

"I'm not married to Bobby, you know. I'm not planning to marry him either. Here you are in eleventh grade planning your dream kitchen."

"You used to *like* to play that game." Melanie pushes away the cookies.

"You know, I do sort of love Bobby," Sophie says. "It's just that . . . I can't explain. I just don't feel what you feel. I'm not ready to start planning my honeymoon with him. There are other guys out there—more interesting guys than Bobby."

"Like who?" Melanie asks.

"Like . . . different people," Sophie says. "Like remember that guy at Carnegie Hall?"

"What about him? That was so long ago."

"Don't you ever wonder?" Sophie asks.

5

Sophie sits in the back of the hall listening as Bobby's professor discusses de Sade and the modes of pleasure.

"Sartre, indeed, would have a *lot* to say about this falsification—" Bobby is writing in his notebook, partly to impress Sophie. Sophie seems more engaged in her cuticles than *Justine*.

"Pain," the professor is saying, "and the language of pain, serve as an evocation of the deepest *subjectivity* . . ."

Bobby looks at Sophie. Her shoulders are lovely. Soon he'll take her back to his room in Twain and ravish her. How lucky he is to have her for a whole five days. The teacher looks up at the class suddenly, as if he is startled to find them there—a roomful of rangy kids. "Well, I guess we're caught up for today. Go home and think about pain. And the midterm will be Wednesday as scheduled."

"So what did you think of the lecture? Professor Dobbins is really smart, don't you think, Sophie?"

Sophie still finds the campus amazing, even twenty-four hours after her arrival. Stanford looks like a retirement home for Republican Hollywood actors.

"Pain 101," Sophie says. "Is that what it's called?"

"Special Topics in Ethics," Bobby says. "Maybe I'll be a philosophy major. What do you think, Soph? What would you major in?"

Bobby and Sophie sit down at a table outside the Union. The president of some club or something is giving a speech with a megaphone in White Plaza. ". . . Only sane and responsible action . . ."

"Anti-draft rally this afternoon," Bobby says. "Last time the cops came and thirty-six people were busted."

"Were you busted?"

"Uh-uh, I'm a coward. I was studying differential equations. No way I'd pass calculus if I ended up in the clinker."

"You're a pragmatist, aren't you?" Sophie asks him, her eyes iridescent in the noonday sun.

"I'm a lover," says Bobby, touching her breast in front of everyone, touching her nipple in front of professors.

"Well, let's have some tuna melts," Sophie says suddenly.

"You're always hungry," Bobby says. "You're *al*ways hungry."

"I really should lose about twenty pounds. I don't know why I do it. Let myself get fat. Maybe I'm a masochist when it comes to—"

"A masochist," Bobby chuckles, poking Sophie in the ribs. "You're the biggest hedonist I know. If you *are* a masochist," Bobby says, "then let me take you to my room and tie you to the bed."

"You mean it, Bobby?" Sophie asks. Sophie's eyes widen and Bobby can't read them. Does she want him to say he was only kidding? Was he?

"You want me to tie you up and make love to you?" Bobby asks. She can't tell if he's bluffing.

"Okay," Sophie says, "let's go."

"What about those tuna melts?" Bobby asks cautiously. "Mmm . . . I can already taste all that American cheese."

On Bobby's roommate's side of the wall, Miss November 1968 looks exhausted. She is as creased as a racing sheet. Sophie goes up to the roommate's cot to examine the pinup's face. There is faint writing on one of her breasts, there are tiny pinholes across her butt.

"Did your roommate—what's his name—do *this*?"

"Well it certainly isn't mine."

"I bet you hang your math exams on your side of the room."

"I mail them to my mother."

"You're kidding," Sophie groans.

"I'm not. I mail my mother my math exams and she sends me care packages of cookies and stuff."

"Cookies and condoms?"

"Spice bars, spritz cookies, chocolate macaroons."

"I'd love a macaroon," Sophie says. What *was* it with him and his mother? "I thought you were gonna *Justine* me," Sophie says.

"Is that what you *want* me to do?" Bobby asks.

"It was *your* idea," Sophie says.

Sophie's left arm is tied to her right with the flannel tie-belt from Bobby's new robe. Her legs are tied to the frame of the bed with the rope Bobby's father had used to keep his trunk closed, going cross-country. It's hard reeling over the Rockies.

"Now blindfold me," Sophie says.

"I want to see your eyes," Bobby says. "And quit bossing me around. You're supposed to be my slave."

Bobby takes his clothes off. Sophie begins to giggle at the sight of Miss November, at the thought of them doing *this* at one o'clock in the afternoon in Palo Alto, Califo—

"Hey," the big blond boy says, Bobby's roommate. "Hey Buchman, what *is* this? Your birthday?"

"Stop crying," Sophie tells Bobby in the rare books room.

"I can't help it. I'm upset. I mean the fucking dork *promises* me he's playing football in Oregon. I mean, what am I supposed to do?"

"Relax, Bobby. Forget it. No one even knows me here. What do I care?"

"Will you make love with me again?" Bobby asks.

"Of course I will," Sophie says. "But stop being such a baby. Once a philosopher, twice a pervert." She sticks out her tongue.

"At least you enjoyed the lectures. At least you're enjoying that part, right? And tonight the law students are showing *Belle de Jour*. Want to go?"

At the airport a few days later, Bobby is weepy.

"Stop crying, Bobby. Shut off the waterworks," Sophie says.

"Stay here a few more days. Don't go back to New Jersey. I'll get rid of that dumb jock. I'll . . ."

"You're being silly."

"And I broke the sash on my brand new robe. Aunt Layeh bought me that robe. In Saks . . ."

"Big deal," Sophie says. "Saks."

"Whenever I put on that robe, and I don't have the sash, I know I'm gonna be bummed out. Like I feel like you don't *love* me anymore on account of my stupid room—"

"Did I ever say I *did* love you?"

"Actually you never did." He looks so sad she can't bear it. She can't believe how mean she is. "But I—you never did, that's right, but I kind of thought . . . Oh, Sophie, you're torturing me. Your plane is leaving in twenty minutes. The least you could do is not torture me."

"I'm sorry, Bobby. But you're really overreacting. Forget about your roommate. It *was* kind of funny. I'll never forget him asking if it was your birthday."

"Like someone bought me a hooker for my birthday, I guess. I guess that's what he meant—"

"Do I look like a whore?" Sophie asks. Another one of her trick questions. She was always imagining he thought of her as a whore. That was his one insight into Sophie's soul. How could he convince her she was not a bad girl?

The airport is eerily empty at 11:00 P.M. in November and Bobby can't stop feeling he's really blown it. When dumb Mike walked into that room and saw the two of them—Sophie tied up, his poor Sophie trussed like an oven roaster . . . Some light had gone out in Sophie's eyes, some green stars had gone out in the world. He'd made her think she *was* a bad girl after all. He never should have tied her up. It wasn't as funny as she thought. He'd never treat her that way again, even if she begged him to. He'd domesticate her, he'd clean out her belfry, he'd treat her only as a radiant wife. . . .

The plane to La Guardia is boarding and Bobby watches Sophie's legs ascending into the cabin.

"Au revoir, Justine," Bobby calls.

As Bobby pulls his R.A.'s car out of the parking lot, he is sure it is Sophie's plane he sees lifting into the air. As the green lights flicker in the atmosphere, flicker and die, Bobby sees thousands of green Sophie-eyes fading into extinction.

6

When Sophie gets home from school, her mother is sitting on the couch and the house is silent. What happened to lying on the floor and listening to opera?

"Rise Buchman called from Flushing. She wants you to call and tell her how Bobby is and everything."

"His mother?"

"Uh-huh. You never told me anything about your trip, Sophie. Your father was at Stanford once for some seminar. I visited him there. I remember all these red tiled roofs. And Hoover Tower," her mother says, "do they still have Hoover Tower?"

"That giant penis?" Sophie says.

"Penis?" Miriam asks.

"Yeah, everyone says it looks like a giant penis."

Penis, Miriam thinks. I think I remember penises. Kind of long and pink with a little cap on top? Or was it only Sid's that looked that way—so slender? Are other penises much thicker? Miriam hasn't seen a penis except for Brian's in five years. . . .

She tries to remember Brian—two months ago? Three months ago? Right before he'd left for college. She'd gone into his room to put all his black T shirts away, and there he'd been masturbating on her Aunt Stella's hand-hooked rug. She hoped Stella wasn't looking down on them from her footstool in heaven. She hoped Uncle Leo, smug in his Barcalounger, was looking the other way.

Miriam was relieved he hadn't climaxed with her standing there, holding his shirts against her chest. She'd left him lying there on the rug, brought his laundry back downstairs and fixed herself a tall one.

She was a ridiculous figure. She deserved her son's contempt, his cruelty. Forty years old, she looked older. Her blood vessels were bursting like the Fourth of July. She'd gone to A.A. twice last week in the Baptist Church where she thought she'd be anonymous. Two people she knew came up to her with coffee, cigarettes and pamphlets. This time she'd stay sober. Sophie had a boyfriend. Sophie deserved a chance.

"So, you in love with this Bobby?" Miriam asks. "Let's have a talk," Miriam says. "Come lie down next to me. I'm just used to the floor."

"What's the matter, Mommy?"

"I'm nervous," her mother says.

"About what?"

"Well, Brian, for one thing . . ."

"Did he ever call you?"

"No. But I called up Reed and supposedly he *is* registered."

"Don't worry, Ma. Did you talk to Dad while I was gone? Maybe you could talk to Dad about Brian."

"I don't know. I can't *go* there, can I? Up to York Avenue and sit on the blue sofa?"

"They don't have sofas anymore. They only have hammocks. I'm not kidding."

Miriam laughs.

"Two macramé hammocks from Dori's own sheep dog. She cards—"

"Stop," Miriam says, "stop. *Mein* bladder. If my bladder drops any lower, if I'd had the one more baby . . ."

"What baby?"

"Well . . ." Miriam says. "When I—when Sid left, when your father left, I was pregnant and I knew if I—"

"Why didn't you have it?" Sophie asks.

"I didn't want him not to leave me because of a little baby. I mean I thought—you see—I loved him. Did I ever tell you I *loved* your father? Anyway, I *begged* Dr. Louise to do something—give me something—"

"He's Catholic, isn't he?"

"Not strict. Anyway, he kept saying how he couldn't do anything, but the whole time—he kept me on the table for half an hour. . . . The whole time he was digging away. And then, about two days later, I was peeing and the baby . . ."

"It died."

"The baby was dead. A little girl."

"Did you see the baby dead?"

"I kind of remember a little foot. Maybe I imagined it. Your father was out. Banging little red sticks on a table, no doubt. At the Copacabana with Dori."

"Did Daddy ever know?"

"He came home at four o'clock smelling like Nina Ricci. But I'd never said anything before. I mean, he just thought I was fat."

"*You* fat?" Sophie laughs. Her mother had always been a wraith.

"I don't know what your father thought. He wasn't thinking about me. He was in love with this young girl. She was a Connecticut-Yankee type. The Madeira School and then the Sorbonne . . ."

"*You* went to Barnard," Sophie says, sticking up for her mother. She thinks of Melanie and Ricky devouring *Barron's Profiles of American Colleges*, naked in Melanie's rec room. Melanie holding his limp penis; Ricky comparing the SAT scores demanded by Bowdoin and Grinnell.

"Oh, Sophie. You're the only one who realizes I was a real person once."

"Oh, Mom." Sophie looks into her mother's yellow eyes.

"I decided to go on the wagaroon," her mother says, smiling. "This is my fourth day."

"That's great, Mom. Maybe you should go back to school. Or start playing the piano again. You could start singing again."

"*My* voice? My voice is gone. I can't get up there anymore. Not even in the shower."

On the coffee table lies a laminated card: *Let go and let God.*

"Why did Daddy marry Dori?"

"Young flesh," her mother says. "They met on an airplane. Sid was going to some convention for dentists in Las Vegas. Hah. I always hated those conventions. . . . And there she was. This young thing—"

"Were you and Daddy still—you know—were you happy together before he met Dori?"

"I don't know. Happy? He'd been having affairs for years. I kept him by never asking questions. He knew I knew and so forth. We never talked about it."

Sophie is surprised to hear that marriage can be like that. Never talking about it. Two people sleeping in one bed; two people shifting underneath sheets—sleeping together and not talking. Her father off in New York making love to debutantes. Her mother abandoned to bleed alone and drink alone, her father a mere stain in the bed.

She is starting to figure out that her father is a bastard. And then she remembers his blue eyes crinkling up with humor, his comforting dry hands. She remembers that Dori saved Melanie. She remembers Dori stepping out of the silk kimono, exposing herself to them—two fifteen-year-old girls—one pregnant, both their lives billowing before them.

"I think Dori's gotten nicer. She used to be a real bitch. Now she's pretty nice. She reads Herman Hesse and worries about her karma."

"Another Mother Teresa," Miriam says.

"Who's Mother Teresa?"

"She feeds all the lepers."

"Someone has to feed the lepers," Sophie says.

"You're right. Better she should get nauseous."

Sophie calls Bobby's mother. As the number rings in Flushing, Sophie imagines the Buchmans' kitchen. Wallpaper with repeating motifs of teapots and toasters. Bobby's exams stuck to the fridge with magnetic pears.

"Hello, Mrs. Buchman?"

"Speaking."

"This is Sophie Spivack. I just came back from Stanford."

"I do wish Bobby had introduced us during the summer. In any case, Layeh—Mrs. Cooper—tells me you're a very smart girl."

"Well not like Ricky. Or Bobby," she lies. She knows she is smarter than both of them. Put together.

"Well the boys in our family *are* superior. We make a rule of it." Rise laughs nervously; her voice is as strained as purée. "So dear, tell me, how's Bobby?"

"He's fine. He talked twice in his history seminar in one day."

"Does your mother know you went to visit a college man, unchaperoned? Or doesn't she care?"

"Yes, my mother knows." *A college man, my bunghole.*

"And who paid for your ticket? Bobby's been saving silver dollars from his Bar Mitzvah yet."

"None of your beeswax," Sophie says. If Rise were there in person she'd moon her. Bobby's thing with his mother was getting to be a bore.

7

Miriam goes into New York to meet Sid for lunch. They eat fettucine all' Alfredo at an Italian restaurant no one has heard of. He tells her the joke about the dentist who gets braces in his fifties. They laugh at the punch line. He pours her more Chianti, which she spills on her dress. An Anne Klein from the thrift store she's sure once belonged to Layeh Cooper. He pats up the wine with his handkerchief. Their hands meet in her lap. They go uptown to his office and lock one of the treatment rooms. They make love in the dental chair, her charm bracelet from the forties striking against the sink.

"Miriam, I still love you." The chair jerks back suddenly and Sid gives out a *geshrei*. "I threw out my neck."

Miriam buttons up her dress. Sid cries out again. "Shit. My neck is really fucked up. What should I do?"

"Why don't you sue me?" Miriam says.

"Oh, Mim. C'mon."

"Maybe we shouldn't have done this. You know I haven't had a drink in two months. Till today. I go to A.A. twice a week—"

"You're kidding. That's why you look so good. You really *do*, Mim. Your skin is really looking lovely. Very elastic."

"Elastic? Oh yeah? Well yours looks like brocade."

"Now I know where Sophie gets her sarcasm from. I'd forgotten how sarcastic you are."

"Is Dori sarcastic?" Miriam asks.

"Not really. She's Episcopalian, first of all. And anyway, let's not talk about her. It's not fair."

"I bet you two talk about *me*." Miriam pours some wine into a Dixie cup. Will she tell them at A.A. how she made sure to slip the bottle into her doggie bag, soaking the fettucine? Ruining her new wallet?

"Miriam, no more wine. You said you'd stopped."

"I'm bummed out," Miriam says. "I haven't made it with anyone since you left. It's only been five years. . . ."

"What about Morty Kates? He was always sniffing your skirts at parties."

"Morty Kates? He's awful. His wife is awful. You don't know my taste at all."

"Who?" Sid asks. "That guy in the Golden Griddle? That maître d' you always said was sexy?"

"They don't have maître d's in pancake houses. My, we're starting to sound like East Siders."

"Now, Miriam . . ."

"Who would have thought you'd end up an *Esquire* subscriber?"

"What's wrong with *Esquire*?"

"You know what I mean. . . . We used to make fun of those people. And now—you're one of them." Miriam sits on the revolving stool and starts to cry. It is early January and the sun is going down fast. Miriam is starting to get a headache. Sid can't move his neck. The sudden darkness in Sid's office pushes her over the edge into weltschmerz.

"Why don't you take a Valium and I'll get a cab. Sophie will be wondering where I am," Miriam says.

"How *is* Sophie? You *have* a Valium?"

"Beautiful. Healthy. Lousy grades except for French. She may have trouble getting into the best college."

"So she'll go to a second-rate college. She'll find a nice boy. Preferably a Jew—"

"Look who's talking," Miriam says.

"So she won't marry a Jewish boy. So she'll marry a Puerto Rican. What should I say, Miriam?"

"Say you'll take care of her."

"What do you mean?"

"I mean—don't abandon her. She's special."

"Of course she's special."

"You don't know her like I know her," Miriam says. "I just hope she's safe."

"What do you mean?"

"I don't know. It's 1969."

"The Year of the Tongue," says Sid.

"Something like that . . ."

"Well so long, Mim. Call me. We'll have lunch again."

"We will?"

"You want to?"

"I want to," Miriam says, unlocking the treatment room.

"I'll walk you to the elevator. No, I'll get the car out and drive you to Hudson Heights."

"No."

"No?" he asks, looking young, looking like 1949 when he sneaked into her dorm room during a tea dance. "No?"

Miriam mouths no, and closes the door behind her. By the time Sid cleans up the office, downs the rest of the Chianti, throws the bottle into the trash, retrieves it—a souvenir? For old times' sake? For what? Purple candles dripping into a Chianti bottle circa 1949? By the time Sid looks for her in the lobby downstairs, she has one foot on the cross-town bus and her head is full of a memory of the two of them riding the cross-town bus when Truman lived in the Blair House and only Lincoln, Garfield, and McKinley had been killed in office. . . .

8

Sophie sits in her brother's room, trying on shirts he's left behind and listening to Simon and Garfunkel. Brian is out in Portland—hitchhiking up and down the West Coast, developing sinusitis, having sex with weirdos, flunking out of his classes.

Sophie tries on a pink-and-white stripe Brian hasn't worn in years. She is doing the buttons when Melanie shows up at the door.

"Anita's pregnant," Melanie says. "She's afraid to have an abortion."

"Didn't she already have one?"

"Yeah, like two years ago. They botched it; she almost died. Anita had this cousin . . . Her cousin's roommate—who wasn't even pre-med . . ."

"*He* did the abortion?"

"He almost killed her. An American Culture major."

"What did he use? A coat hanger? A turkey baster? Did he make sure to sterilize it on his little Bunsen burner?

The cow swings from the rusty hook in the abattoir. The tampon strings swing in the breeze as women walk, moving their legs in black suede pumps on the way to the bank. They kill the castrated bulls for meat and save the she-cows for their milk. Do they also kill the slow-breasted cows? The poor capons, the poor eunuch steers. But their balls and their woes are second-most in Sophie's woeful imagination. First, she sees the she-seals barking, black and rubbery, feeding their whelps. Females huddling on a rock. First she sees chickens laying their elliptical eggs—the act so much an act at once of defecation and creation, the whole life of the universe singing in one ragged cloaca. Poor exhausted cloacas, poor weary cervixes, dilating and constricting, bleeding and not bleeding, moving in and out to make the dissonant sounds of creation. The cervix a flesh flute bleating through time.

"Who's the father?" Sophie asks.

"I promised," Melanie says, sitting down on Brian's bed. Picking up Brian's pillow and smelling it absent-mindedly.

"Melanie, who's the father?"

"Wayne Voekler." Melanie looks faint.

"She must have been hard up to screw Wayne Voekler." Sophie shakes her head.

"Screw him? I think she's gonna marry him. Her mother is making her. And then they're supposed to get a divorce the second the baby's born. And Wayne's parents signed this form saying they would let the baby be a hundred percent Jewish. And if it's a boy, they can circumcise."

"What? Already you're circumcising? The kid isn't even born and already you're cutting off his *shlang*."

Lee Freund and her brother stand next to the rabbi. For this I bought her playsuits in Bonwit Teller, Lee is thinking. "The brother's a lawyer in Washington," someone whispers across the pew. "Washington the state."

Anita is wearing a Mexican wedding dress even though it is February and cold. There are green parrots sewn to the bodice and purple grapes if you look close.

"What kind of dress is she wearing?" the secretary in Lee's office asks Wayne's grandmother. "It looks like a nightgown." The grandmother is crossing herself and muttering aloud. Sophie is sitting behind her with the girls from the sorority.

Wayne is wearing a rented suit. Shiny turquoise blue in the bright light of the ark.

The rabbi is speaking now about the responsibilities of marriage. There's an occasional lapse into Hebrew.

"They paid off the boy's family. To make it Jewish," someone whispers to Gladys Szasz. "They've already begun the paper work for the divorce."

Anita is crying audibly on the *bimah*. The rabbi gives her a dirty look and instructs Wayne it is time for the ring.

"At least they skipped the *chuppa*," Gladys Szasz says to her husband. "At least they didn't go totally crazy."

"It could have been us," warns Brad.

The cars follow each other as if it's a funeral procession. Lee's brother Maury almost forgets and turns on the lights. It *is* like a funeral. In the front seat sit the chauffeur and Lee and Maury. In the back seat the bride sits with her sisters, Roberta and Felice. Anita has refused to drive to the Sherbrooke in the same car as Wayne Voekler, or any of the Voeklers. Mrs. Voekler—Vi—is wearing air freshener behind her ears. Anita is positive.

"I fucked him twice," Anita tells Roberta for the hundredth time. "I fucked the creep twice. *Now* look at me."

Felice Freund starts to cry. She is thirteen years old and has never been so depressed.

"Felice, I'm gonna kill you," Lee says. "If you don't have a good time at this goddamned party, I'm gonna take you over my knee during the dancing."

"Dancing," Anita says. "Why'd you have to have dancing?"

"It's a wedding, Anita. We're gonna dance, eat chopped liver. The whole business. I know what I'm doing."

"I'm not dancing with Wayne," Anita says. "That creep has to wipe his hands every ten seconds."

"Maybe you should have thought of that—" Uncle Maury begins.

"*Shah*, Maury, it's too late. Now we're all going dancing."

There are no yellow matches with Wayne, Jr. and Anita Rain embossed upon them. No champagne squirting out of fountains, no alternative to the beef tips entrée.

"She had to act fast," Glad Szasz tells a woman from Lee's office. "With two weeks' notice, who could have done better?"

The Voeklers sit at their own table—Vi and Wayne, Sr., Wayne, Jr. and Wayne's sister Abbie, Granny Voekler and Abbie's little girl, Kimmie. Where is Abbie's husband? Lee Freund wonders. Is Kimmie another love child? Meanwhile Vi wants to know where Old Man Freund is. So far no one's explained that Tootie is dead, or otherwise suggested the unutterable—that perhaps Tootie is better off under the ground. Perhaps he was spared after all—to die at thirty-seven, giving blood at the bloodmobile on Willow

Lane—instead of having to witness this. Anita, five months pregnant, dancing the lindy with Wayne Voekler, Sr., a mortician of German descent.

No one jokes it would have been cheaper if Lee had just gone ahead and had the affair at Voekler Brothers. No one says anything bad about the herring appetizer; the chicken soup is a little fatty, but no one has the nerve to say. The forty or fifty adult guests fall upon their tips of beef with enormous hunger. They are eating in a hurry; they are hungry.

The teen-agers are eating nothing. The boys are drinking Seven and Sevens, the girls are drinking champagne cocktails. Gazelle Kupferberg has taken off her dyed-to-match peach pumps and Bobo Kleinbrenner pours matzo ball soup into her shoes. Arnie Comac takes a strip of onion from the herring and sticks it up his nostril.

Melanie begins to cry and then so does Lauren Small. Sophie doesn't cry along with the other girls. She is flirting with a bartender named Enrico and dabbling in apricot sours.

Felice Freund gets sick and Lee leaves to take her home. The photographer spills rye all over his negatives. Anita's grandma from St. Louis calls up the Sherbrooke person-to-person to Lee and the operator puts Grandma on hold. Lee is delayed in Hudson Heights tending to Felice. Felice started her first period the night before Anita's wedding and is now scared to death of bleeding, of pregnancy, of boys. Afraid in the dark of her own vagina.

Anita goes off on a honeymoon to her own recreation room where she and Wayne Voekler are given an hour together. They sit in the makeshift basement kitchen and Anita imagines this is her home with Wayne. A bridge table for a dining set, waxy paper cups full of Sprite.

Anita refuses to talk or make out with him. Wayne keeps drinking Seagram's and Fresca and the new Mrs. Voekler falls asleep. When Lee comes down to get her daughter, she sees the Voekler boy is drunk and talking to himself. His shoes are untied, his fly is unzipped, he seems to be losing an argument with his sock.

"Wayne," Mrs. Freund says, "you'll sleep down here. Here is your pillow. Here is your pillowcase. Here is the lever to make the bed come out. All right?"

Wayne keeps muttering, touching his ankle. "I bumped it," Wayne says. The ankle does look swollen. "My ankle hurts," Wayne says.

Lee puts some ice cubes in a bar towel and hands it to him. "Here." When

Wayne doesn't take hold of the ice, she crouches down in her miniskirt and holds the towel to his ankle. His skin revolts her. This drunken *goyisher* ankle, she thinks. This whitebread's semen has taken hold of my daughter's uterus, ruining all of our lives.

My own daughter, Lee thinks. Anita is asleep in the wicker rocker. Her face is red and blotchy, but she is still beautiful. So she'll have a little baby and she'll finish up her high school, and after that we'll see, Lee thinks. She isn't frightened. Anita will survive. Better she go away somewhere—the University of Miami. She, Lee, will raise the child, and when Anita finishes college and the baby is ready for school, Anita will take him. A little blondie with pale ankles. They'll teach him that mayonnaise only goes on salads and read him Bible stories about King Solomon. He could have his Bar Mitzvah right at the Wailing Wall! If Lee Freund can't make a Jew out of a pig's ear of a gravedigger's grandson— Well isn't she the one who sold the old Pinkus elephant on Grand Street for seventy-five Gs? She only hopes the girls in Anita's sorority don't make Anita step down as president.

9

On July 1, 1969, Anita gives birth to a five-pound, eight-ounce boy named Sasha Kripke Freund. Because his mother does not speak, the child is named by his grandma: 'S' for Seymour, Tootie's real name; Sasha because Lee thought Anita would like it. Anita was enrolled in Russian II at the high school when Wayne Voekler screwed her after the first pep rally of the year. Thinking Anita would want the name to be both groovy and romantic, and knowing Anita liked best of all her Russian class, Lee had settled on Sasha.

"It sounds like tushy," Felice had said irritably in the hospital cafeteria. "It's a good name for an asshole," Felice had said.

Lee had drunk still another cup of lukewarm coffee and thanked God that at least her middle daughter, Roberta, hadn't gone crazy or been afflicted with a menstruation complex.

It must be a terrible reflection on me, Lee had thought that humid day in New Jersey when she became a grandmother before her time. The sins of the children, she thought. They go around, these children, whose lives we elaborately save at any expense to ourselves. They go around sleepwalking from Bloomingdale's to Hong Fu's, hating us because they hate themselves. They go around whining and complaining and not knowing what it entails to wash a dish by hand until they grow up and have a little *goyisher* baby before they've learned how to use a sponge. And everywhere it's the parents. And how we should screw in front of them. Or not screw in front of them. Or bottle-feed them or definitely the breast. Or Montessori is no good and throw away that old-school Spock.

It is 1969 and Dr. Spock has sold out the parents. He is arrested for civil disobedience, but they don't lock him up. Maybe they ought to lock him up. Lee is angry. You betrayed us by telling us to let them do what they wanted, she thinks. Tootie, God rest his soul, used to let them draw cartoons on the dining-room walls. You told us to pamper them, Lee thinks sadly. It is 1969 and Dr. Spock is suddenly *vieux chapeau*.

Seven days later, Lee stages an old-fashioned *bris*. Dr. Dorkin sets up his surgical layout in the library. Everyone watches as the rabbi holds up the circumcision cup Gladys had sent from Tiffany's. (Was it gauche to have it engraved?)

Afterwards, the rabbi—enough is enough, forget the *mohel*—whatever you want, darling, Grandma Millie had said. Afterwards the rabbi had given a brief sermon about the special importance of men in Judaic law. The rabbi had held the wine to the baby's lips and Sasha, wearing a white stretchsuit and wrapped in Tootie's *tallis*, had sucked hungrily at the rabbi's finger. Poor little sucker, Lee had thought. But there was no way on God's earth that Anita was able to breast-feed. She hadn't spoken one word since the baby was born. Already the psychiatrists were talking psychotic episode. Anita was still in the hospital. They were thinking of having her moved to the psychiatric ward. Her absence at her son's *bris* hung over the gathering like an Old World curse.

Everyone toasted to Sasha's life as a Jew and a man. "May you live to introduce him to Torah, marriage, and good deeds." The rabbi's blessing to the (absent) parents made Melanie start to cry. Lauren Small began to join in and Glad pinched her daughter's shoulder. "Don't cry. It's bad luck. This is a joyous occasion." The birth of a boy, thought Sophie, who stood between Melanie and Lauren, watching them cry. Wimps. The cutting off of the foreskin of another boy's penis. Another *shmuck* hits the heap.

Ricky was there and Bobby Buchman, home from Stanford for the summer, smug and sophomoric. Sophie suspected he'd been screwing other girls.

He was avoiding her in a room with twenty other people. He stood there in a wine-colored *yarmulkah* reciting the words to the prayer. Probably the prayer thanking God he wasn't born a woman. Every man's favorite prayer, uttered with particular relish.

She'd wanted Bobby to be the strong one. He should have laughed when his roommate came in and she lay there, trussed, a make-believe chicken. He was a mama's boy. She was sixteen and ready for life. Something real. Powerful. Dramatic. Here was Anita—psychotic, a mother, married to a future mortician. Time was catching up with them all.

Bobby looked sexy. She longed to throw him down in a pile of sacred books and make love. Something about a man in a skullcap and *tallis* brought out the beast in her, the anti-Eve, the Lilith.

Here was Sasha, eight days old, bleeding into gauze. Let the men bleed for once.

Everyone was clapping hands, stomping their feet, drinking wine. When a girl was born, the most she could hope for was her grandpa gave the rabbi a ten-spot to have her named in *shul*. Nobody got dressed up and ate cocktail franks for a girl.

"Take that thing off!" Sophie knocks Bobby's skullcap to the floor of Glad's Mercedes.

Bobby picks up the *yarmulkah* and kisses it. Just like they taught him in Hebrew School, Sophie thinks. "Mama's boy," she whispers into his ear.

"Look Sophie, let's go to your house. I want to talk to you. Rick, drop us at Sophie's."

"What makes you think I want to talk to *you*?" Sophie asks.

Melanie, embarrassed, turns on the radio. The Beatles' song about the girl who runs away from home. Melanie turns it off. The anti-parents lyrics seem sad now, not romantic. After the *bris* and all, Melanie is feeling sad. And serious. Ricky will be going back to Harvard again in two measly months. She doesn't know if she can take another year like this—seeing Ricky, kissing Ricky, only on national holidays. . . .

In the back seat, Bobby is begging Sophie for a half-hour, no more—no touching, just talking. Melanie can't believe how mean Sophie is to Bobby. She can't even figure out why Sophie's so mad at him. Sophie just says the same thing over and over—mama's boy, weakling, yeshiva boy, *shlemiel*.

In the living room, Sophie and Bobby look at each other. Sophie sees him again. His vulnerable blue eyes. His Lithuanian nose, his high cheek bones, his skinny face. His stiff, tundrous hair.

Once, in his dorm room, before Mike had come in and shamed him and driven her off, ashamed of his shame; once, before his miniature Eve had run off and abandoned him to a cruel horniness—a wet winter, a dry spring in Palo Alto—the hills burned as brown as his roommate's dope—Sophie had told Bobby, the two of them snuggling in his cot, how nice she thought his ass was. And Bobby had replied, "We both have nice bottoms." Sophie had loved that line, had thrown her arms around him and kissed him, and now he loved that line, too.

"Sophie." He speaks first. "We both have nice bottoms." She kisses him, she holds him, she checks her mother's room to see if Miriam is asleep, then takes him into the living room and onto Miriam's floor.

10

Dori is planning to leave Sid and emigrate to Russia. This proves she's crazy, Miriam thinks. On the eve of their break-up, Sid brings Dori to Hudson Heights. The two Mrs. Spivacks finally check each other out. It is Sophie's graduation from high school dinner and even Brian is there with friends from college. The times are so strange that even Brian has friends. At least Miriam is being polite to Dori, Sophie thinks.

Brian's friend Dodie passes the turkey to Dori, then starts to laugh uproariously. "My God, this really *is* a bird," Dodie says. She is a hefty cattleman's bride of a girl with wide hips and a loping stride. While Brian screws her she calls out, "My well is deep! My well is deep!" She used to think she was a witch; now she thinks she's a Will to Power.

"Don't you kids ever eat?" asks Sid. He waves at Dodie. "Tune in, kids. This is Sid the Chopper-Copper."

Everyone starts to laugh.

"Get it?" Sophie nudges Brian. Brian looks really good. College and sex are good for his complexion. He's barely looked her in the eye since he arrived that morning. Maybe she can go out with them—Dodie and Murdoch, who doesn't talk at all, and Brian. Maybe she'll have a chance to talk to Brian later.

She'll be on the West Coast herself in a few months. Maybe once they're away from New Jersey, away from the ghosts of Miriam and Sid, away from the attic room, she and Brian can be friends, ordinary sister and brother.

She wonders if she chose Berkeley partly to be close to him. Now that her parents were getting back together, now that her mother was making a total ass of herself, she was glad she'd be far away.

And then there was Bobby. She knew he was becoming more and more religious. What had started out as bagel breakfasts at Hillel had blossomed into late nights studying Rashi's commentaries, watching the sun come up. Melanie had come over one day last month, and letting the screen door bang behind her, announced she had two things to tell her best friend: Sid had been seen, during Easter vacation, signing into a hotel in Miami with Lee Freund. The second piece of news was Bobby was becoming a religious fanatic.

Sophie wasn't surprised to hear about her father and Lee. Her father probably went to bed with everyone he met. He was a womanizer, a two-bit Casanova, a cheater. A suburban Lord Byron. The night of Miriam's miscarriage he was carrying on at the Copa. And still her mother was letting him move back in. Her father was about to become her mother's boyfriend.

She wasn't surprised about Bobby either. She knew he would end up a rabbi, no matter what. His philosophy major was a cover-up for secret fanatacism. At any moment this well-behaved philosophy student might turn into a raving Jew. At any moment, day or night, Bobby might grow earlocks, perform a sacrifice, rend his garments, start praying in caves. It was she, Sophie knew, who held him anchored to the world of flesh.

She hadn't seen him in ages. He was off in a few weeks to the same *kibbutz* he'd lived on the summer before. He'd left right after Sasha's *bris* and she'd seen him only briefly at the end of last summer. Melanie told her about girls who wrote to him—love poems from the orange groves, haikus from the sands of the Sinai. Ricky had told Melanie about Bobby's conquests in Israel, his sudden popularity. Israeli women were probably dying to come to America and collect their share of the Jewish princes. Sophie had heard how sexy these women could be: Tall beauties carrying rifles, tanned infantrywomen named Tzippi and Gila, with gold sandals and amazing fingernails. Sabras lounging in string bikinis on the Dead Sea.

She realized that Bobby was attractive to women. Good husband-material, as Dori used to say. She didn't know if she wanted a husband. Look at her parents. Look at Dori. Marriage was nothing more than black comedy. All Melanie thought about was honeymoons and linen closets, joint checking, embossed matches, engravement, imprimatur. Mr. and Mrs. Richard Cooper was all Ricky had to say to bring Melanie over the edge into orgasm.

Melanie had failed to get into Brown, Wellesley, Radcliffe, Smith, Tufts, and Mount Holyoke. Ricky had been really great about it. He told her she'd gotten in—indisputably—to the best liberal arts division of Boston University. He'd told her how glad he was they'd both be in Beantown, that that was the main thing—the two of them would be together. Melanie promptly immersed herself in equipping her dorm room: blender, popcorn maker, hotplate, waffle iron, bedspread, curtains. She went around singing that song about the man who disappeared on the M.T.A.

"Sophie!" Miriam calls. "Pass the gravy!"

"And what are you studying?" Sid asks Murdoch. Murdoch is tall and very skinny, one of those guys who always shows an inch of skin at the ankle.

"Murdoch's dropped out," Brian says. "The man without a major."

"So Murdoch," Sophie says. Murdoch appears neurasthenic. "Why'd you drop out?"

"Reed's polluted," he says.

"Problems with the ecology?" Dori asks knowledgeably.

"Problems with the cosmology," Dodie says.

Dodie spoons some gravy onto her plate. So far she's passed on the turkey, the crab-apple rings, the green beans, and the potatoes. Then she decides what the hell and takes a few ladles of gravy.

Sophie is gorging herself on the matzo-and-bacon stuffing which she doesn't pass around. She eats about a third of it straight from the serving bowl, until her mother signals her furiously to pass it.

Brian takes some stuffing, but doesn't eat it. He stares into the madder heart of the turkey which lies there, bleeding and shrinking, on his plate.

Sophie realizes they're all high on hallucinogens. No wonder they can't eat. Sophie has eaten the wings, her favorite part, and suddenly it makes her sad: Those awkward gawky turkey arms, those elbowy, graceless wings.

Brian and his friends take off in Miriam's car.

"Are you sure you can drive?" Sid walks up to the driver's side and looks at Brian. "Just tell me what drug you're on. *Please*."

"MDA," says Murdoch.

"The love drug," says Dodie. She bats her eyes.

"I see," says Sid, taking in Dodie's size, her enormous behind. What does Brian see in her?

"Don't crash, Brian," says Sid. "The insurance is—" He indicates "going-up" with his fingers. His skilled dentist's fingers take little steps in the air. "Brian, can *you* drive?"

"Sure, Pops," Brian says. "See you later, Pops."

Sophie can't believe how stupid her father is—letting Brian drive off, tripping, in Miriam's car. Still, she wishes she'd gone with them instead of staying at home—even if her mother had made the dinner for her. Even if they all ended up wrapped around a pole.

Melanie was off at the Steak Pit with Brad and Gladys, having a normal graduation dinner. She was stuck at home with Sid's jokes, her mother fawning all over her father, her spacy stepmother who was leaving her father to go to Russia. Nobody *went* to Russia.

Sophie was really surprised. Her mother had told her just last week that she and Sid were back together, that Sid was moving back in after all these years. She'd wanted to take her mother by the shoulders and shake her. And tell her what Melanie had heard about him and Lee Freund.

She was glad she was leaving for Berkeley. The whole situation depressed her. Now that she didn't need him, the big shot was moving back in. Soon his gray bristles would coat the sink in a grizzly foam. Back on top of her mother's dresser would sit his depressing calfskin caddy with all the little compartments: his loose change, his keys, his gold fingernail clippers.

She remembered playing with his caddy when she was a girl of five or six. The magic the leather had given off; the masculine smell of his driving gloves, his cashmere scarf, his Russian hat. One day he'd gone off and with him had gone his pennies, his roll of butter rum, his magnifying glass, his camera.

She used to look for things of his in the far corners of closets. When she was ten and he was first gone, she'd found a book with his name from college —a book of poems by Delmore Schwartz. Another time she'd found a photograph of Sid with his arm around a brunette she didn't know; her father wearing army clothes, the girl in a light two-piece suit. The photo had the crinkly edges of a coupon book.

She'd stored these souvenirs of her father in a shoebox which she pushed way back behind her diaries. After a while she stopped looking for his gloves, his fingerprints, his smell in the crannies of the house.

Sophie is glad she is going off to California. She hopes she can make it through the summer. She wishes Bobby were in Queens instead of the Promised Land.

"So, Dori, *why* are you going to Russia?"

"Dori's fallen in love with a Russian spy she met at the U.N. gift shop. She claims. She is leaving me for a Russki with bandy legs."

"Really?" Dori asks. "I thought you were leaving me. Not that I mind, Mim, but— Anyway, he's not a spy."

So now it's Mim, Miriam thinks. She steals my husband and gives him back seven years later and probably no wiser. With gray in his pubes. Probably dumber, Miriam thinks, looking at Sid who is drunk on vodka that Dori probably got for free from her Russian.

"And you two are really getting back together?" Sophie tries to act ho-hum. Miriam smiles. Sophie feels like slapping the grin right off her mother's face.

"We're gonna live together," Sid says. "At least at first." They are idiots, Sophie thinks.

"And I'm probably staying in Russia a while," Dori says. "If you know someone who wants to sublet the apartment . . ."

"What if there's a nuclear war?" Sid asks suddenly. "If Nixon's re-elected in '72—well look at his record on nuclear weapons."

"It's not all Pasternak and Tchaikovsky. I've read articles," Miriam says.

"The tundra," Dori says, "the cruel winters." She closes her eyes.

Sid laughs. "I can just see you in a sable coat, digging for roots and worrying about rust under the troika."

"I must make this trip," Dori says. "I had a dream," says Dori.

Later, Miriam and Sophie are washing dishes.

"I had a dream," Miriam says, and they both start laughing. "Who does she think she is—Martin Luther King?"

"But what did you think of her? After all these years?"

"It's funny. I wasn't jealous *at all. She's* not so pretty. You know who she looks like?" Miriam hands Sophie the turkey platter to dry. Sophie notices the monogram etched into the glass. She remembers the tray was a wedding present from her parent's hurry-up wedding in city hall. Her mother had put all the presents away when Sid had left seven years before. For seven years the dishes had lived in the attic, wrapped in newspaper. Unwelcome boarders dressed in old news.

Sophie almost drops the tray. Accidentally on purpose?

"Watch it," Miriam says. "That was a wedding present."

Sophie catches her mother's eye. Miriam looks embarrassed.

"You know who she looks like? She looks a little like Cousin Fred."

3

Bodies and Anti-Bodies

1

Sophie sits down in the coffee shop with Melanie's letter and a cup of coffee. There is a demonstration going on in the background, protesting American involvement in Cambodia. Sophie has gotten used to the protests, the cops on campus, the riot gear. The cops look like comic-book fascisti with strange goggles and walkie-talkies. Someone is calling out, "Every school is Kent State!" and beating a heavy drum. A chorus begins: "Kent State, too late! Kent State, too late!" It is just a few months since they were killed, shot down in the middle of the quad like Frisbees. A funeral in mid-spring. The chapel sticky with heat. The dead girl's hair moving eerily in the sudden breeze.

Dear Sophie,

Hi. How are you? I am really depressed. I couldn't get your phone number from student information. You're a fool not to have a phone in your room. Now that Mr. 3.9 (that's his GPA), Ricky, is a Harvard junior, he's too groovy to hang out with me and I think he's fucking this girl. I really think so. Or at least they are copping feels in their ethics course where she is a big genius with big tits. She looks a little like Jill Grinspan without the nose job, if I have the right one. I spy on him sometimes. I sneak into his dorm, into the dining room and the TV room. Once I looked through his keyhole. All I saw was his messy bed and the bedspread I bought him covered with *her* period stains. (Not really.)

So anyway, Ricky comes over to my dorm. He can't stand B.U. Either can I. Today I burned cigarette holes in the little B.U. terrier my dorky roommate Annette bought the first day. I think I'm losing my mind. So Ricky hates B.U. because it's not pure and full of geniuses like Harvard, and he even acts really condescending to my roommate. Like everyone at B.U. is a big home ec major compared to those Harvard crew majors. Everyone knows that Harvard has millions of dumb rich people with SATs in the 400s.

If I even look at that word SAT or MCAT or LSAT, I feel like killing myself. It is over between me and Ricky. It really is, Sophie. He has contempt for me because I go to a bad school and he is embarrassed in front of people and you'll never believe it, but suddenly everyone is calling him "Dick." Dick. Can you believe it? Why don't they just call him Dork? Because he is the biggest, smelliest dork that ever lived. I go swimming in the low-class B.U. pool and try to do the doggy paddle until I drown. I'm desperate, Sophie. Please call me as soon as you receive this and make arrangements for my funeral with Voekler Brothers. Speaking of which, Anita is talking again, but is crazier than ever. If anyone mentions her baby, she gets hives. Otherwise she acts kind of like a Martian. My mother saw her mother at a bazaar at B'nai Yeshurin. Speaking of which, Happy New Year. See you in a better world. Call me, collect. I'm dying.

Love,
Melanie

P.S. How are you? Do you like your roommate? Have you *seen* Bobby yet? Is he still in Israel? Is Brian coming to Berkeley? Have you gotten on the pill like you said? Fly out to Boston. I'll pay. I mean it. Call me. Glad has a TWA card & I know the number!

Just twenty feet from Sophie, a man gets hit with a billy club. An enormous thwack which must crack his skull. The man's high screams echo across the campus. Sophie grabs the letter and runs back to her dorm. As she runs through the crowd, she glimpses people she distantly knows from the dormitory or Art History. The crowd swings haphazardly from one side of the plaza to the other. A man has been wrestled to the ground. Sophie smells the scent of blood, the fumes of Mace, the scent of death, the imaginary smell of warfare. She runs and a shower of gravel rains down; pebbles bounce off her sneaker.

The phone rings in Melanie's room and Annette the roommate answers. "Melanie isn't here. She's in the infirmary. Who's this?"

"Sophie, her friend at Berkeley."

"Oh, yeah. I know about you. I saw a picture of you in a bathing suit in Puerto Rico. You had a nice tan," Annette says.

"What's wrong with Melanie?"

"She took about six Quaaludes and drank some beer. When she drank the beer she vomited, so she didn't die. God, I can't believe I finally get to college and they give me a psycho for a roommate. It's funny, her wardrobe seemed so normal."

"Is there a number for the infirmary?"

"I think her boyfriend isn't worth it, personally. Dick Cooper—what a jerk. I went out with a friend of his on this double date, this guy named *Lance* if you can believe it."

"Look, Annette, we'll rap about your date another time."

"Yeah. So anyway, Dick is really mean to her. When he broke up with Melanie, he brought his new girlfriend along. I mean, when you break up with somebody, the least you could do is take them to a really expensive restaurant."

Melanie can't stop crying long enough to talk. "If I'd had the ba-a-a—"

"C'mon, Melanie, you think if you'd had the baby, this wouldn't have happened? I'm telling you, it's not like that. Men are rotten. That's all there is to it. Men leave women with babies every day—"

"But at least then I'd have the ba-a-a—" She starts to cry again.

"Don't think about that. Melanie, do you have any friends? Doesn't Gazelle go to Northeastern? Can't you call up Gazelle and ask her to come over?"

"Gazelle? I can't face anybody. I feel so ashamed. He *abandoned* me. Sophie, if I pay for the ticket, will you come? You're the only person I know who even knows who I am. I mean I knew *you* before I knew—" And then Melanie's voice dies out in a series of coughs.

Sophie goes to her history of philosophy class. The teacher is a gorgeous blond graduate student; he looks like Robert Redford playing the Marlboro man. He is talking about flux; he is talking about the pre-Socratic philosopher, Heraclitus. He stops for a second in the middle of his lecture and strokes his yellow mustache. Sophie writes a poem in her notebook: There is something about a blond mustache/ Splashed with cunt water/ Next to white buttocks.

* * *

He is talking about Heraclitus when this short girl in the first row opens up her legs. She is wearing nothing, no underwear. He blushes and a rosy glow suffuses his handsome face. He looks Sophie in the eye. She holds his gaze.

After class, she walks out, neither hurrying nor loitering. She can hardly believe she showed her cookie to her philosophy teacher! A tall girl with flaming red hair—much prettier than I am, Sophie thinks—stays after class to ask Mr. Pfahl a question. Will there be true or false questions on the midterm? You want to have a cup of tea over at The Med? Chew the fat a little about the Eleatic Stranger? Sartre? The world experiencing the world as flesh?

2

Melanie starts to cry as soon as she steps off the plane in San Francisco. They head off, arms locked, to reclaim her baggage. She carries a Vuitton bag packed solid with memorabilia: Pictures of Ricky and Melanie at the College Fair, of Melanie's beautiful prom dress from Fred Leighton's. The butt of the first cigarette Ricky ever smoked—Silva-Thins. Ricky's sequence honors pin for getting all As—engaged to be engaged to be engaged, he'd said. A piece of chewed-up gum in a Baggie. She plans to show the loot to Sophie, then toss it into the ocean.

"Our first date," Melanie says while Sophie drives her roommate's car down Highway 101. "I was dumb enough, like a fool, to keep a piece of —remember?—Tiger-Striped Gum? A piece of Tiger-Striped Gum from 1967. Isn't that disgusting! I heard of a girl who saved her corsage from her sixteenth birthday. It had all these sugar cubes on it, you know? And the sugar cubes rotted and worms hatched. There were worms in her panty drawer."

"Give me that joint," Sophie says. Sophie inhales the Michoacan that Melanie brought from Boston. "Worms in her panty drawer," Sophie repeats. She sees the worms—brown and squiggly, their greedy bodies insinuating into the pink Sateen ribbon, the sugar cubes half-eaten away, the panties stained with shiny excreta. In all of our panty drawers, Sophie thinks. "We all have worms in our panty drawers," Sophie says.

"Four years of my life," says Melanie. "He brought this girl with him to break up with me. . . . She wasn't so much *pretty*, as—"

"It's a long time," Sophie says.

"Four years. I had his baby; I mean I could have had his baby. I should have," Melanie says. "Hey, California!" Melanie says. "Berkeley, I can't believe it. I'm really in Berkeley. Just like on TV."

"Wouldn't it be fun to have a date with someone else? With a college guy?" Sophie asks. "A graduate student, a pre-med?"

"You know pre-meds?" Melanie asks.

"Do *I* know pre-meds?" Sophie says. "Does Gazelle Kupferberg shave her armpits?"

Melanie's intimidated by Lonnie, Sophie's roommate. Lonnie is tall and blonde with even features. "She looks like she's never had a pimple in her life," says Melanie.

"She's from Pasadena," Sophie says. "That's just how everybody looks in Pasadena."

"Boy," Melanie says. "Like we're really in California. Palm trees and no pimples."

"No mosquitoes," Sophie says. "No underpants. I went to class today with no panties on and I showed my cookie to my philosophy teacher. On purpose. I flashed him. Actually, he's a graduate student. He's really gorgeous," Sophie says.

"Isn't that a bit radical?" Melanie asks.

"So maybe I *should* go to Palo Alto and talk to Bobby. I called his mother. He's back from Israel. Don't you even want to see him? Maybe Bobby will talk to Ricky, you know? See what's gotten into him. Can you believe they call him Dick? It's a nightmare," Melanie says.

"So, look. His class—that teacher I told you about—is in this building," Sophie says. "It's his other freshman class. It started ten minutes ago."

"Are you gonna just *wait* here till he comes? Don't you think you might be turning him off?"

"I know," Sophie says. "Let's just look through the keyhole right now. I know it works. I've looked through that keyhole already. Last week. I could see him, but not that good."

Melanie looks through the keyhole. She's an old hand at this. Tad Pfahl is sitting on top of the desk, swinging his legs. Melanie feels a charge of mistrust for the blond philosophy teacher swinging his muscular legs. "He looks like a hippie lifeguard," Melanie says. "Does he—is he the kind of guy who thinks he's really cool? He looks like the kind of guy who thinks he's really cool. Doesn't he?"

"I don't know," Sophie says.

"I'm really sick of teachers who are like thirty and they really try to act cool," says Melanie.

"I think Tad is like twenty-eight or so," says Sophie. "This is California. People aren't as uptight. The teachers act like regular people."

The girls are whispering in the hall outside Tad's classroom. He hears a rustling, then girlish laughter in the hallway. Probably another chick waiting for him to get out of class. The world is full of sexy bitches, Tad thinks. And for some reason they get turned on by philosophy. He realizes the students have stopped talking and that the classroom is strangely quiet. The giggling in the hallway begins again, and Tad can't remember how long it's been since the last kid stopped talking.

"How long has it been?" Tad asks.

"How long has what been?" A boy calls out from the back.

"Nothing," Tad says. "I'm talking to myself. Okay, people, I'll see you later." Tad dismisses the class after twenty minutes.

"Wasn't he kind of weird today?" A guy asks one of the women as they leave the classroom.

"I think he's wonderful," she says. "I worship his every bicep."

In the slant of open doorway, Tad sees Sophie Spivack, that weird freshman from his other section. Yesterday she'd opened her thighs and flashed her pussy from the first row. He remembered he was talking about Heraclitus, the principle of eternal flux. Was he imagining it or had he honestly seen her vulva—flickering—magenta, fuchsia, rose madder—beckoning to him?

3

"*Hellow Sophie*," her mother wrote from Antibes. "Your father and I are having our second honeymoon. Don't worry. We're not really married. If you ask me, it's more like the first honeymoon I never had. Your dad was in dental school cramming for exams. We were living with your Grandma Harriet and she was dying. I stayed in the apartment with her and read her *Uncle Tom's Cabin* while she died which she loved. Dori got Puerto Rico; I got death. Antibes is beautiful. Love, Mom and Dad."

Her father had drawn a dog's paw below which her mother had written "Dad." From the shape of the toeprints, she knew it was her father's drawing.

Sophie has a date with her philosophy teacher. He called her up and right away she knew it was Tad Pfahl. His voice as plaintive as a Western ballad; cognac with a hint of peach; the loamy smell of tobacco.

She is wearing tight jeans and a white silk scarf knotted into a kind of bra. Bobby had brought her back the scarf from Jerusalem. As Sophie strides down the street, she feels the knot loosening around her neck, giving way at her back. She remembers the lesson in the bowline at Camp Caledonia when she was nine and had a father. "See," the counselor, a perky girl named Cricket had said, "see how the little rabbit slips down the tree and into his home?"

Apron strings tied into a cuckold's neck; the fragile fringes of *tallises* tied into rolling hitches. A piece of string from a cake box—a piece of string with a chocolate stain from a Mocha Log Miriam served in 1963. (Imagine Sid walking across the George Washington Bridge with a white box.) Tie this string into thirteen knots, then tie it to the tail of a dog who pees real gold. And then Mrs. Gerry Pfahl, Tad's mother, a Fresno widow with rubbery arms, will appear in her housedress and say, "Marry my son, Sophie. Make me a grandson with pale ankles."

Sophie imagines Mrs. Pfahl sorting the clothes for the laundry. Her bloated fingers rubbing away at a chili stain on a nylon blouse. Her boxes of Cheer and Fluff-On, her tired legs aching in the cold launderette . . .

Tad is sitting outside at the Creamatorium. Heat wafts up from the electric floor. He smiles at her majestically—his blond mustache is wet with artificial creamer. There is something about a blond mustache . . .

"I'm glad you could come," Tad says.

"I'd like to get to know you," Sophie says lamely.

"Why do I feel like I already know *you*?" Tad smiles devilishly.

"I don't feel like I know *you* at all," Sophie says.

"Well, maybe after we have our coffee, then I can show you *my* cherry and we'll be even," Tad says.

Sophie blushes.

"You're an interesting girl. So have a cappuccino and then we'll go back to my place and have some Scotch."

"You ate already?" Sophie asks.

"I don't eat," Tad says. "I only drink." He laughs like Charles Bronson. Or Richard Boone. "But I'll make you a scrambled egg." When he smiles, the wrinkles around his eyes look sinister.

When the waitress comes, she is beautiful, and Sophie feels funny-looking, whory in her harem top. The waitress wears a man's jacket with no shirt and tailored pants. She looks classy. And Sophie looks like the runner-up for Miss Louisiana.

"Two cappuccini," Tad says. He winks at the waitress in the artificial light.

"So, where do you come from?" Sophie asks.

"I've been in Berkeley for ten years. I've been a graduate student since 1937."

Sophie laughs. "Were you *alive* in 1937?"

"Not more than an itch between my mama's legs," says Tad.

"Where were you from before Berkeley?"

"I went to high school in Fresno. I played football and I played a lot of chess." Tad laughs shyly.

"Are you good at chess?" This is the dumbest conversation she has ever had.

"Yeah, I was a real crack. I won a competition once. Took the bus to Sacramento to shake the governor's hand."

Sophie thinks he is exquisite. She'd rather go to bed with him than look at Bobby's photographs of the Wailing Wall.

"It was the first time I'd been out of Fresno. I remember eating fried chicken on the bus on the way up. . . . So what're we talking about *that* for? Fried chicken? So what about you, Sophie?"

"I come from New Jersey, Hudson Heights. A commuter town right on the Hudson. You know—the New York suburbs."

"And why'd you come out here, Jewess?"

"Berkeley just seemed kind of exciting on TV, I guess. I saw all the stuff going on here, on the news—you know?—and it seemed like maybe something was *happening* here. But then, when I saw that demonstration the other day, I just got scared and ran back to my room."

Tad looks bored. Probably he has his pick of all the women he wants. She saw him in the post office the week before with a beautiful foreigner. Maybe if she talked about philosophy . . .

"I guess I'm afraid of violence," Sophie says.

"Violence," Tad repeats, drumming thick golden fingers on the tabletop.

Tad's apartment reminds Sophie of some other time, some other place. The smell of eggs and old rooms; horses whinnying and dragging their feet in the dust. The smell of the curtains in the kitchen, their yellow peonies faded tan; the sniff of Scotch and the grease from the eggs; the imaginary smell of warfare.

"*The Devil's Dictionary*." Sophie picks up a library book from the kitchen table.

"Ambrose Bierce," Tad says. "One of the greatest neglected American visionaries."

"Yeah?" Sophie says, drinking the Scotch straight-up.

"So you wanna see the TV set in the bedroom?" Tad asks, unbuckling his belt. What did she think? They were going to discuss The Third Man Argument? He walks up behind Sophie and begins to massage her neck. He lets his dungarees drop to the floor. She thinks of Bobby in Palo Alto.

Probably he has a great tan. She and Mel will go down there and check out Bobby's tan tomorrow.

Sophie awakens at 6:00 A.M. to hear the birds of autumn squeaking outside Tad's window. Tad is sleeping soundly in the king-sized water bed. The only thing about him she doesn't like is his bed. When her head hits the pillow, she wants it to stay there. When she moves her pelvis, she wants to feel solid mattress underneath.

She puts on her clothes and slips away, Tad still dreaming the dreams of philosophers. Her head is fuzzy, her tongue is thick from all that Scotch. After the Scotch had run out, a half-gallon of Safeway brand, they'd started in on Barbera wine. She'd drunk so much she only dimly remembered the night. The wine—that's right—he'd poured the wine inside her and drank it from down there—or pretended to, scratching at her like a cat.

Sophie got into her jeans. Seeing the silk scarf from Israel, suddenly seeing it on the floor, used-looking and dirty, so tiny it hardly looked large enough to use as a handkerchief, Sophie realized she was a fool. She picked up Tad's T shirt from the foot of the bed and smelled it: whiskey and Bull Durham, horses beating their hooves in the dust; the chimerical smell of TNT. She pulled his T shirt over her curls. She wanted to live inside his smell, his smell was testosterone. Bottles of Guinness slapped down on a bar, the sound of cue sticks clicking at balls, the low sound of men acting ballsy. Eating a hundred hard-boiled eggs like Paul Newman in that movie. The silver glint of a switchblade glimmering in the darkness of Fresno or Carson City. Men wearing Stetson hats telling stories of runaway pussy; men roasting over a fire the young balls of castrati sheep. . . .

To live inside Tad's world, his smell, his yellow-at-the-armpits T shirt, was to live in a John Wayne western of wise words uttered at the point of death in a world where men loved horses. And Sophie didn't love horses *or* westerns. Sophie liked movies with Barbra Streisand acting funny and making her cry.

4

Sophie finds Lonnie Chapman snoring in her bed. She has fallen asleep with the light on and a piece of orange cheese on her pillow. There is no sign of Melanie. She must have slept over with her blind date. Before going off to the Creamatorium, she'd fixed Melanie up with some guy Lonnie kind of knew. Now she was worried.

Sophie imagines little scars on Melanie's uterine walls—marks from the abortion. On *my* uterine walls, Sophie thinks, there's probably graffiti: Yankee go home; Bigfoot was here; For a great BJ, call this number. . . .

She felt bad about setting Melanie up with that guy. Always she had believed only Ricky Cooper would pinch Melanie's big behind, coming up behind her while she washed the dishes. She'd always imagined that Ricky and Melanie would get hitched the minute Ricky finished Harvard. And probably Melanie would get knocked up right after the wedding. Melanie had never wanted anything but Ricky and Ricky's baby boys. And driving the kids to see the pumpkins at Tice's Farm. *That's* a kind of ambition, Sophie decides—spreading your legs to receive the seeds, becoming a flower box, a garden, a greenhouse for the husbands. All those special human lights beating down upon the fetus, illuminating the embryo in the darkness that surrounds. Feeding your blood and your vitamin B, your body and your antibodies, through the circuitous umbilical cord and into the heart of the blue-veined child. Being a woman was a service profession. Mothers and prostitutes serve the same need—bodies and anti-bodies.

Sophie gets into her bed and kicks off her dungarees. She smells Tad's T shirt. Already she misses his legs around her. He had the most remarkable thighs—as large and developed as a wrestler's, covered luxuriantly with blond Jungle Boy fur.

Sophie dreams about Brian. They are getting into a car and Brian is wearing a coffee can—Chockfull O' Nuts—over his head. She tries to pry the can off, but it doesn't work.

Melanie wakes Sophie up in the middle of her dream. "Sophie, wake up. I'm tripping. You've got to come with me. Drive me to Palo Alto. I realize I have to see Bobby, you know?"

"What, Melanie? You're tripping?"

"Yeah. That guy—what's his name—my date?"

"Larry, right?"

"Right. Larry. That guy gave me some LSD or something. I was in this big hippie house and people were dancing naked."

"Was it okay?"

"I started to get really depressed. All these fat people dancing naked with yucky bodies. I missed Ricky, you know? And then I got really high. Like I didn't even know where I was or anything. Like I even forgot at one point who I *was*. Like I knew I was Melanie Szasz, like that was my name, but I didn't know who I *was*. You know?"

"Of course I know what you mean."

"So, like this guy—"

"Melanie, let's go downstairs. We can have coffee. I don't want to wake her up."

"She doesn't look so perfect now," Melanie whispers. "With that cheese in her bed and those noises, she looks like a mouse or something. A rodent."

"So could you borrow Miss Pasadena's car or not?"

"I *like* Lonnie," Sophie says. "Try to get along with her. With three people in one room—"

"Okay, I'm sorry. But could you like borrow her car and drive me to Palo Alto? *Please* Sophie," Melanie says. "Please do it. I'm tripping. And you can see Bobby."

"I don't want to see Bobby."

"Why not? He's really nice. And—"

"And he goes to a great college, right?" Sophie looks at Melanie. As if to say, haven't you learned your lesson? About boys who go to good colleges? "Boys who go to the Ivy League will break your heart, but not your knees."

Melanie imagines Ricky attacking her knees with a doctor's mallet. "I'm still hallucinating," Melanie says.

"You are? How do I look—like a rodent, too? A rat?"

"No-o-o," Melanie says. "You look beautiful, like a madonna."

"One thing about LSD—people you love are supposed to look nice. Are you having a good trip, Melly?"

"Well, now I am. But before—see, I never told you, but I fucked that guy. What was his name again, my date?"

"Larry," Sophie says sadly. "Larry from Queens."

"Queens, New York?" Melanie asks.

"Uh-hum," Sophie says. "Another Jew-boy from Queens."

"I thought that guy was from Pasadena. No shit," Melanie says. "I only fucked him because I thought he was some major Wasp from Pasadena. Tell him I take it back."

"I'm not going back to B.U.," says Melanie. "No matter what. I've decided. Maybe I'll go to Berkeley. Or how about the University of San Francisco?"

"That's a Jesuit school. No husband material *there*. There's San Francisco State. The tuition is free or else low—"

"Well, I'm not going to B.U. I'm going to wash that boy out of my pubes completely."

"Then why are we going to see *Bobby* in Palo Alto? Not for my sake," Sophie says. "I don't want to go to bed with him," Sophie says. "I don't even want to *see* him."

"Well I *do*," Melanie says.

"Ricky? Or Bobby? You want to go to bed with Bobby?"

"Sure," Melanie says.

"Well don't you think you should slow down? I mean you just screwed some guy—Larry from Queens—last night."

Melanie is waving her hands wildly at passing cars and jumping around in the back seat of Lonnie Chapman's stepmother's Ford.

"Melanie, get down. There's a cop. Stop acting crazy."

The cop puts on his siren and the two girls are pulled over by the state police.

Sophie reaches for her lip gloss.

"Let's see your driver's license. New Jersey, eh?" He peers in at Melanie who looks pretty high; her pupils are as spacious as Versailles. "The armpit state," the cop says, looking at Melanie.

"Let's see the registration." When Sophie opens the glove compartment, the registration sits there, as legal as married sex in its U-Seal-It case. "Pasadena, eh?" says the cop. "Who's Ann Chapman?"

"My college roommate's mother," says Sophie. "I go to U.C. Berkeley.... My friend . . . "

"College girls, get out of the car."

Sophie feels like she's going to die. At least a quarter of a lid in her very own leather purse; Melanie acting weird and obviously up there with the angels.

He tells Sophie to dump the contents of her purse onto the hood. As Sophie upends the bag, several grams of tobacco mixed with marijuana pour out. Bits of gum wrappers, old Kleenex, myriad plastic tops of pens, empty packages of Marlboro, and one of Gitanes. And then a pair of sunglasses, broken, and then a Baggie of marijuana flops onto the hood.

He tells them they're under arrest.

In Redwood City (Deadwood City, Sophie remembers, walking through the parking lot with her arms cuffed), Sophie has her body searched by a young black woman. As Sophie separates her legs, spreading them to allow concealed weapons to fall out, she wonders if the matron can smell Tad's body upon her.

Lucky Melanie is eighteen. She is booked and put in a holding cell. Sophie is put in a room to wait for her parents to do something. She prays they aren't still in Antibes.

They won't let Sophie talk to Melanie, who is probably too high to make a phone call. If you give a tripping hippie one dime for the telephone, she is likely to call Dial-A-Horoscope from the cell. She crosses her fingers that Melanie will call Bobby Buchman. But how will she get his number? What if Bobby's not in his room? What if he's playing Ping-Pong or screwing one of his Jewesses? That's what Tad had called her—Jewess. She decided that was a second thing she didn't like about him. Besides his water bed. Even if she wasn't ready to marry Bobby and keep kosher, to shave her head and wear a *shaytl*—neither was she ready to join the anti-Semites.

She remembered a post card Bobby had sent her from Israel in August. Something he'd read in one of his courses. Something like this: *The sufferings of the Jews could not be recorded, even if all the seas were full of ink, and all the reeds were pens, and all the men were set to work, writing the story . . .*

Naturally, it was the *men*.

Just then the matron called her. They had her father on the line. Sid was sending a fancy lawyer, the brother of his college roommate who lived in Los Altos Hills.

Sid and Miriam had flown in from France the evening before. Maybe there *was* a God. But even if there was, Sophie was convinced He never would have chosen *her*.

5

"*You poor girls*," Bobby says. He has borrowed a car from one of the guys in his dorm.

"I wish Sophie could've come with us. They're calling her parents or something. Because she's seventeen," says Melanie.

"You think her parents are gonna be really mad?" Bobby asks. "You *know* she hasn't visited me. She's been at Berkeley a month and she hasn't even called me."

"Why don't you call *her*?"

"She doesn't love me," Bobby says. "I write her these twenty-page letters pouring out my heart and then she sends me some really cryptic post card. . . . Did Ricky tell you that—"

"Ricky doesn't tell me anything. Ricky broke up with me," Melanie says.

"You're not serious."

"Ricky—you'll never believe it. I'll tell you, Bobby, Ricky's going around like he's Lévi-Strauss, Jr."

"How do *you* know Lévi-Strauss?"

"I go to college," Melanie says. "I've taken classes," Melanie says. "Everyone thinks I'm a retard. Even you think I'm a mo-mo."

"No I don't Melly," Bobby says. "It's just you never *studied* in high school."

"And now I'm gonna have to pay for it my whole life. My whole life is in the garbage because I didn't do the homework in tenth grade. I was too busy reading *Glamour* so Ricky would like my outfits. You can't win,"

Melanie says. "Sophie tried to tell me that a long time ago. All men are rotters one way or the other. Why didn't I listen to Sophie?"

"You think Sophie knows so much? About love? About men? What does Sophie know? She's very mixed up about men. Because of her father and everything . . . There's a guy here from your high school—Larry Spofford? He graduated with you."

"I remember Larry. How is he? Does he like Stanford?"

"He said that Sophie went to bed with everybody in Hudson Heights. He said she was a famous whore. Black guys. White guys. What did she care? *I* have to fall in love with a whore."

"Larry Spofford called Sophie a whore? That pimple-faced virgin. He *wishes* Sophie was a whore so he could screw her. He sat across from her in homeroom. He only asked her out about eighty times in one semester. He used to stare at her tits in homeroom. I *saw* him," Melanie says.

"Well is she a whore or not?" Bobby says.

"Ask me again and I'll flatten you."

"I have to know. I *love* her. I haven't seen her since that *bris*. . . . I think about her all the time . . . but if she doesn't want me, *is nisht*. Right?"

"Well Sophie never screwed one person in our high school. Except I'm not so sure about her brother. . . . Well, I know she didn't go to bed with anyone else. . . . "

"Are you *serious* about her brother? She's even crazier than I realized. I can't deal with her—"

Bobby looks sad. Melanie is afraid he'll cry. She looks into his blue eyes, eyes the color of flowers. Forget-me-nots. He begins to hiccup. Melanie puts her arm around Bobby; she snuggles her head against his chest. Bobby is thinking of Sophie's breasts. That first time in Melanie's den. That first time they'd flown out. Their springy flight from her black brassiere. Like birds they'd flown into his face, like momentary sparrows.

In his dorm room, Bobby makes camomile tea. "And then he must have met that girl. A philosophy major or something. He brought her over to break up. Her name is Catalina Crawford. Could you *plotz*? He calls her Cat. I wish someone would call *me* Cat."

"*I'll* call you Cat," Bobby says, rising from the desk chair and sitting down on the bed. "Cat," Bobby says. "Meow," Bobby whispers.

"Don't," Melanie says suddenly. "Don't meow anymore."

"I'm sorry," Bobby says. He takes off his glasses and puts them down on the pillow. "I'm going to kiss you," Bobby says.

Melanie awakens stiffly. "What time is it? Bobby, wake up! We've got to call the prison. Bobby!"

"Hmmm." She looks at him. He is opening his suburban blue eyes.

"Sophie. What about Sophie?"

"Screw Sophie," Bobby says.

"We've got to call Redwood City. See if her parents are coming . . . "

Bobby starts kissing Melanie's ear. Boy, Bobby thinks, girls really *feel* different than each other. Sophie's legs were so different than Melanie's. Sophie's round knees. Her soft calves. She used to go wild when he kissed her calves. But here was Melanie—all angles—her shiny hair sliding between his loose fingers. Melanie had long skinny hands. She wore an enormous pear-cut emerald. Sophie's hands were tiny, her thumbs like dolphin's thumbs. He'd always thought that Sophie had to be part dolphin.

Her blood was Jewish-dolphin blood. An elegant dolphin from Odessa—dark and sleek as the Baltic, a manhandler of herrings, a swigger of vodka, a swaggerer—had raped the wild-eyed daughter of some learned Cracower rabbi. A Pisco-Judean coupling with blood spilled on the Russian rocks. Gelatinous algae, pieces of shell, the secret purple heart of the conch. And dolphin semen splashed everywhere, thicker and whiter than any man's. The lost tribe of Israel was really these secret dolphin Jews.

"What are you thinking about?" Melanie is lying on Bobby's cot, smoking a Kool. Her legs are brazenly spread apart. She's athletic and easy in her nakedness. He could count the beauty marks on her neck and run out of fingers.

"I was thinking about—Poland."

"Why Poland?" Melanie asks.

Sophie had always acted so shy after sex. After her first brazenness, Sophie closed up like a flower.

"I don't know. Poland. Where are *your* grandparents from?"

"My Nana Rachel—who died a couple of years ago . . . See, this is her ring. Look, it has an inscription."

Bobby puts on his glasses. Suddenly he's seized with a mad desire to look inside Melanie as far as Poland, and beyond. Sophie had seen her own cervix once. She'd told him how a midwife had asked, "Do you want to see your cervix?" during an internal exam, and how Sophie had been afraid to say no.

Bobby gets down between Melanie's legs. Her hair is soft and unusually straight. Has Melanie had her pubic hair straightened? He'd read *Vogue* and *Cosmopolitan*. He had an older sister. He knew there were places they tortured women to make them beautiful.

"What are you doing?" Melanie laughs. "I wanted to show you the inscription."

"I can read it from here," Bobby says.

"What does it say?" Melanie pants. He is holding apart her labia and looking for Cracow, for Warsaw, for Mars.

"It says *Ingresso libero*."

Melanie laughs. Bobby isn't sure if she understands his joke or not. That's right, Bobby thinks, that's what Sophie had said. The cervix looks like the moon, Sophie had told him once, making love in a hammock in her back yard. The cervix looks like the moon.

6

Sophie fails out of college right before Christmas. She and Melanie buy Cold Duck at the grocery store and start celebrating at eleven in the morning. Lonnie has been living with her boyfriend off-campus, so Melanie and Sophie share the same room and the same man. Once a week Melanie goes down to Palo Alto to see Bobby. And once a month—if he's lucky—Sophie lets Bobby come up to Berkeley. If Sophie were paying attention, which she isn't, she would notice easily that Melanie and Bobby are making it. Melanie is always leaving hints as broad as noodles.

"You never ask me what I *do* in Palo Alto," Melanie says, slurping Cold Duck.

"You want me to ask you?" Sophie says. "I figure you do the same thing you do here. Nothing." She looks at Melanie. "You want me to ask you?"

You never pay attention to me, Melanie thinks. "Yeah, ask me." Melanie is dying to own up and make up. She can't stand it anymore. *No* sneaking around. *No* disguised phone messages. Sophie doesn't notice anything. She walks around in a stupor. That goddamned Nazi boyfriend of hers, Melanie decides. He's a little *too* cool, Melanie thinks.

"Okay. So, like, what do you *do* in Palo Alto? Buy earrings? Go to department stores?"

"You won't act so superior and déclassé when I tell you I've been humping your boyfriend."

"Tad? You and Tad?" For a moment Sophie feels a fierce pinch in her heart. "Tad?"

"No, stupid. Bobby."

"Bobby!" Sophie looks genuinely surprised. "Melanie, you double-crossed *me*? *Me*? Your little friend from New Jersey?"

"But Sophie, you acted like you didn't care. I figured you knew—"

Sophie starts to cry. Is she drunk? Where is the old Sophie who never cried at weddings or *brises* or even at funerals? Where *is* my little friend from New Jersey?

"I can't *explain* it, Melanie. It's like Bobby *belonged* to me. Do you know what I mean?"

"Are you trying to make me feel bad?" Melanie asks.

"No. I'm really trying to tell you what it was like. I mean I don't know *why* I feel he belongs to me. Any more than . . . I don't know. I remember going over the George Washington Bridge with him. How old was I? Like fifteen? I remember how he acted so nervous. It turned me on. Isn't that funny? *He'd* blush and I'd get turned on. What a role reversal."

"This is turning into a major guilt trip," Melanie says. "How could I know you love him? You spend all your time with that Nazi boyfriend of yours. I thought you loved the Nazi."

"I do love the Nazi," Sophie says. "And I love Bobby, too. In a different way. And look, Melly, I never said you had to stop *seeing* Bobby, did I?"

Melanie is incredulous. "Keep screwing him? Right in front of you? Even though you love him? Just keep doing it?"

"Maybe we both need him," Sophie says. She takes another swig of Cold Duck and smiles. "Bobby's gonna flip out when he finds out both his women are college flunk-outs. He was supposed to be here by now. I wonder if they notify the parents?" Sophie asks.

"Huh?"

"You know. The parents. Remember them?"

"I was still thinking about what you said—*both his women*. I mean, Sophie, this is just getting too fucked up."

"It's okay, Melanie," Sophie says. "We're just not good girls. So we might as well have what bad girls have. Fun."

Bobby walks in. Except he's not walking—he's swaggering, Sophie realizes. That tricky bastard.

"You bastard," Sophie says, "you've been plugging Melanie this whole time." Sophie throws the bottle of Cold Duck against the door. Some drops stick to the ceiling. The bottle spins crazily, doesn't break. For the next fifteen years, Berkeley freshmen will see, late at night, the traces of fake champagne flickering down from the ceiling.

The only problem was Bobby loved them. He loved them *both*. Of course Sophie was his true love, the woman he wanted to marry, impregnate with his Chosen seed, the woman he'd cherish till death did them part. . . . Of course, the only wholesome thing was to declare his love right now. The only wholesome thing. He'd have to break it off gently with Melanie. She needed him and Sophie didn't. But, maybe, Sophie needed him more. She was the lost soul. Melanie wasn't lost, she was only confused. But no one was as confused as he.

7

The administration gives Sophie a last warning to vacate her dorm room. Her grade point average for the fall semester is a 1.2. Three Ds and a C. The C is her Christmas present from Tad along with a pair of crotchless panties. So much for the consolations of philosophy.

She sits in his lousy apartment, drinking eggnog from the 7-11 mixed with Meyer's rum. He is snorting Locker Room, amyl nitrate, he buys in a gay bookstore.

"Tell me a Christmas story. Then let me spank you. Nothing heavy," Tad says.

"What do you mean, nothing heavy?"

"What do you mean what do I mean nothing heavy?"

"I don't feel like it," Sophie says. "I want to watch the Charlie Brown Special."

She turns on the television and there is Charlie Brown dreaming of the little red-haired girl. That's what he wants for Christmas. The heart of the little red-haired girl. Sophie understands Charlie Brown. He's perverse like me, Sophie thinks.

Lucy tricks him over and over, but still he hangs out with her all the time. Every time she lines up the football, every time she lines up the pigskin and Charlie puts out his fat little leg, ready to kick it over the goal, Lucy takes it away. Every time she promises she isn't going to take it away and every time Charlie Brown believes her. Or does Charlie *know* she'll take it away, and is *that* what he really wants for Christmas?

* * *

Tad is snorting Locker Room and reading *Beyond Good and Evil.* And playing with his pud. She realizes she hates him. Charlie Brown is walking over to the red-haired girl's house to deliver his Christmas present—a picture of himself wrapped with a big red bow. On television Charlie Brown's head shines like a halo, an aureole, a fleshy crystal ball.

The little red-haired girl takes the package and begins to untie the bow. Poor Charlie Brown. Is it hubris? This gift of his very own face?

"I'm leaving," Sophie says, getting up from the sofa. "I'm leaving and I'm not coming back to this stinking apartment. You disgust me," Sophie says. She puts on her rabbit coat. A beautiful white rabbit coat her father had sent her from Bloomie's. I hate him too, Sophie thinks, buttoning the buttons, feeling the little rabbits' kisses on her soft neck.

"You'll be back," Tad says. "And you want to know why?"

"No, I don't want to know why."

"Because you *love* it," Tad says. "You need it. You worship it."

Sophie picks up a plant and throws it against the TV where Charlie Brown is explaining how giving is better than receiving. The clay pot hits the stand and the TV merely blinks. On the carpet lies the dead plant—a wandering Jew Tad hadn't watered in two years. She puts on her white fur earmuffs. They press down her curls so comically, her hair sticks out from around the fur like the hair of one of the girls on TV. She looks just like one of the girls who is singing the carols with Charlie Brown. Their little cartoon mouths make a series of tender Os.

Tad is shaking his head back and forth as if to say what an ass she is, as if to say he knows her better than she knows herself. Her last glimpse of his apartment is neither his smug expression nor the comic strip kids on the TV. Her last glimpse takes in the dead plant lying on the carpet. Brittle brown leaves which once shone purple, which once shone purple and lustrous and green. A wandering Jew like me, Sophie thinks. Throw another Jew on the fire. A dead Jew like me.

8

Melanie's Louis Vuitton tote bag sits packed in the corridor. The bag is filled with everything Melanie could get her hands on. Filthy washcloths with green checks, her special set of Revlon eye shadows—every color in the cosmos from Scared Yellow to The Gang's All Here Green.

Sophie leaves behind her books, her notes from classes, most of her wardrobe. She even leaves behind her sheets, contour sheets with lovely flowers! Even her high school yearbook, *The River*. On page sixty-two of the yearbook, next to Sophie's name it says: MOST LIKELY TO SINK A SHIP. In the square where the photo was supposed to go, the photo Sophie never got in, the editor had drawn her face, delicately and well. Among all the glossy photos of identical Jewish girls with matching slanty eyes and Dr. Diamond schnozzolas—carefully carved into mere schnozes—among the future wives of men named Mark and Alan and Jeffrey, among the wives of these Jewish princes—and that's what this yearbook surely was—a book of wives like the mail-order catalogues of long ago—a book of wives, and from among them, Sophie's face—round and delicate, Semitic as old gaberdine—from among them, Sophie—penciled-in, created alive through the skill of a high school boy's hand—Sophie shone like a ghost girl, a ghost girl among the wives.

And there on page sixty-three was Melanie—her long nose, her unsinkable smile, her Kovno dimples. And in her myopic blue eyes there were Ricky-vibes, for surely she thought only of Ricky in those old high school days before she'd gone off to Comm Ave. and the wrong side of the Charles. In her eyes there were years of sex, devotional blow jobs, hum jobs whose melodies could move the spheres. Years of washing his Jockey shorts, spraying on every new enzyme the moment it first came out. And then the years of no enzymes and worrying about the effects of diethexelyde on your husband's soft balls. All those years were in her eyes—twentieth anniversaries at corny French dives in the suburbs; golden rings on Mother's Day—old Art Nouveau rings wrapped by the children—the *kinder*!—in Snoopy wrapping paper; Thanksgiving cards shaped like pneumatic turkeys; the ear infections, the bumped heads, the waiting on lines for movies starring Volkswagens as the heroes. All of these years floated from Melanie like a consummation. If Sophie was the girl in pencil—half-whispered, half-there, half-washed-away—then Melanie was Queen of the Jewesses, wife-wizardess among the wives.

9

Sophie and Melanie find an apartment in a borderline neighborhood in Berkeley. Brian comes down from Portland to visit, and soon he is sleeping with Melanie. He's become a real carpenter with a union card in his wallet. His running shorts and jock strap hang brazenly from Melanie's door.

Soon he realizes he is supporting both of them. Melanie has been cut off completely from her trust fund. Sophie picks up whatever money is the closest.

They've been doing a lot of crystal and Melanie gets crazy on speed. These days it's Sophie who's got to watch out for the two of them. Brian's been working construction. He supported them willingly for a month. But the other day he came home exhausted—he'd been hit on the head with a beam at work—and told them the least they could do was pay for their magazines. Everywhere *Glamour* and *Vogue, Mademoiselle* and *Cosmopolitan*. The *National Enquirer* and wrappers from Chunkies. And boxes of Rit. All the girls did, it seemed to Brian, was smoke reefer and snort crystal. And then maybe they'd sleaze on down to the Laundromat in the afternoon and dye everything in the house Electric Blue or Orchid or once, even, Tan. Finally he told them to go to work.

Work. Yikes! The word flipped them out. Maynard G. Krebs playing the bongos and wearing a beard through their black-and-white girlhood of 1959.

And so they stood at three o'clock in the darkened bar of Harry's, talking to the manager. He asked the girls to change into something.

"Like what?" Sophie asked.

"You ever do this before?" the man asked. He looked like a shoe salesman, a conventioneer in the cocktail lounge of the Holiday Inn. A guy with a Shriner's fez. "Can you dance?"

The jukebox was playing "The Letter" and Sophie's dance was more funny than sexy. She bumped her ass and stuck out her breasts; she arched her back. She remembered the strippers in *Gypsy*. She *wished* she had a trumpet. She made faces at Melanie and couldn't stop laughing. At one point she became hysterical, laughing and crying on the splintery stage.

Melanie did a real dance from Modern Jazz. Brush-brush stamp. Brush-brush kick.

"I'm glad Gladys bought you those lessons," Sophie said later, as they sat laughing, remembering each other's dances. "Now that we're going into show business."

They were both hired on a probationary basis. They started that very weekend. They had to show their breasts to the boys, but not their cookies. He was starting them at $150 for four nights a week. It wasn't a whole lot of money for showing your tits to the tourists.

When they told Brian, he laughed, and Melanie was a little pissed he didn't even mind. Suddenly, Melanie missed Bobby. Bobby at least would have minded.

10

That summer Ricky Cooper comes out to visit Bobby in Palo Alto. Rick was looking great, Bobby told him, really hunky.

"What do you mean *hunky*?"

"That's what the girls say," Bobby says.

"Oh, so now you know what the girls say, eh?"

Bobby laughed shyly. "I meant *the girls—our girls*."

"Our girls? Oh, Sophie. She still breaking your balls, Bob?"

"I see her, you know, once in a while. We're not lovers anymore. But I *love* her," Bobby says.

"Then why *don't* you screw her? Christ, screwing is amazing, isn't it? I mean—they never *told me*. I mean—with Melanie—hell, she was fourteen years old. Can you believe we were ever so young? Christ, when I think how long I stayed with Melanie, I can't believe it. And she really had me *sold*, you know? I thought I wanted to *marry* her. Marry *her*. Could you *plotz*?"

"Would that be so bad? Marrying Melanie?" Bobby feels bad. Melanie is such a nice girl. Great wife-material. If only he didn't love Sophie so much his heart beat like Big Ben if he even saw her bra strap. Otherwise he'd claim Melanie for himself. Her blow jobs more joyous than Handel . . .

"Marry Melanie? Christ." The cousins are sitting in the coffeehouse at Stanford. "Marrying Melanie would be like, like subscribing to The Book-of-the-Month Club and maybe *The Harvard Classics* . . . and no other books in the house, you know?"

What a jerk you are, Bobby thinks. "Melanie isn't stupid."

"She failed out of B.U. Only a really dumb chick fails out of B.U."

"You're an asshole," Bobby says. "She wasn't exactly working for the dean's list. She was in school maybe five weeks. . . . She's here 'cause you dumped her. *You* fucked her over, *Dick*."

On the stage a comedian tells a joke about Vietnam, about eating Vietcong ears and thinking they're dried apricots.

"Christ, Bob. Who are you? The defender of all the chicks? St. Pussy?"

"I'm glad I didn't go to Harvard," Bobby says. "I'm glad I haven't turned into a complete asshole."

"You didn't get *into* Harvard," Ricky says. "Remember?"

"Who cares?"

"You do. You're really jealous. The class of woman who sucks my cock—well you wouldn't believe these girls. And it doesn't make them frigid, you know? Their high IQs . . . They've studied it over at Radcliffe—I think—sexual response in—"

"You're disgusting. Talking about women that way. It disgusts me, Ricky."

"It disgusts me, Ricky," Ricky says mincingly, implying Bobby sounds like a fag.

"Well, I'm not going to try to elevate your thinking," says Bobby. "But I want you to know it's bad for your head. Women are special. Making love to a woman is—"

"I gotta laugh, Bob. I'm sorry, but I just gotta laugh. I remember when you were threatening to kill yourself—I think it was Rosh Hashanah. . . . Anyway, Grandma was there. We had brisket. Anyway, I remember, we were hanging out in your room and you were moaning away how you were gonna cut if off. Slice off your own prick. Do mankind a favor. Remember? Because you couldn't get *near* a pussy. Remember?"

"It seems a long time ago," Bobby says. I used to like you so much, Bobby thinks. You used to be like me, Bobby thinks. Or maybe, I used to be like you. If nothing else, I've learned a lot from Sophie and Melanie, Bobby thinks. And now he has neither one of them. Melanie started sleeping with Sophie's weird brother, and Sophie said it was bad for their relationship to have sex. She said if she slept with him, she couldn't love him. Why wasn't she so virginal in the old days when he was stuck in Palo Alto and she was off in New Jersey selling blow jobs on the boardwalk. . . .

He imagines Sophie in a faded dress, wearing a *shaytl* and a bright babushka the color of desert fruit. She's selling the world's most blissful blow jobs on the boardwalk in Belmar, New Jersey. Even the sea gulls slow down to watch as she sells love songs by the seashore. Sophie sells *shlang*-songs by the sea. . . .

"It seems a long time ago," Bobby says.

11

Driving from Palo Alto up to the city, Bobby tells Ricky he'd slept with Melanie for months and months.

"You're kidding." Ricky turns down the tapedeck. It's Miles doing "Nefertiti." "Christ. Melanie? My old Melanie?"

"You're not going with her anymore. And now neither am I."

"Melanie? You and *Melanie*? What did you do with her? Did she ever blow you?"

"I'm not gonna discuss that stuff. Sorry, Ricky, I'm a gentleman." Bobby looks out the window. There is a big drop and below them the beach. The smell of wet Keds and riptide; the violent shrill of the gulls.

"Well, the problem with Melanie—like, you see, Bobby, this woman—she really *is* a woman. She's twenty-*eight*, Bobby—"

"Who?"

"This woman I'm seeing. It's a whole different ball game with a married chick. These older girls know how to come. Man, these older girls are *something*."

"I'm surprised you care if they come," Bobby says.

"Aw, c'mon, Bob. Who do you think I am? Hitler? And besides, you know, the greatest lovers *always* cared if the woman came. Byron, Don Juan . . . "

Don Juan, Bobby thinks. He remembers the heat coming up from the asphalt in the spring of '68. The year he went off to the West. And Sophie wearing a gypsy blouse covered with mirrors. She'd eaten ten dollars' worth of sandwiches in the coffee shop. She'd touched his hard-on in The Waverly

Theatre. He'd confided miserably, trusting her, "I'm no Don Juan. . . . "

"Don Juan was a homo anyway. And so was Byron. And a lot of these big lovers really *hate* women if you must know. I think you're getting turned around in a really lousy way," Bobby says. "Hey, Ricky, look at that sculpture. That's Junipero Serra. . . . "

"I was telling you about Solange."

"What's that—a cold cut?"

"Solange is my woman in Cambridge. She's married, you know? Her husband owns half of Gulf Oil."

"Does that make her good in bed?"

"Bob, I'm telling you. With Melanie it was not *like* this. I mean, Solange's *hands* have Ph.D.s. You know, once these girls hit twenty-five, they start to *like* fucking. Especially if they're dying to get knocked up. Solange is dying to get knocked up, you know?"

"You better be careful," Bobby says. "You're fertile Fred."

"Huh?"

"Melanie's abortion?"

"Yeah. That's probably what made me stay with her for all that time, you know? I felt really guilty about knocking her up. Christ, and I *did* think about the kid. The kid would be about two or three. It blows me away just to think about it. Shit all over the house . . . "

"It's not like a dog, you know. It's not like babies go around leaving turds in the closet," says Bobby.

"Anyway, I recommend you find yourself a married girl—late twenties, you know? You don't have to always be spending money either. They make you dinner all the time. Veal chops. Last week Solange made me veal chops."

Bobby looks at Ricky. He's really a little nuts.

"Veal chops," Ricky says. "Eh man, that's my favorite."

At City Lights, Ricky stations himself in the Women's Books section. He picks up a copy of *Sisterhood is Powerful*, starts reading a piece about high school girls and sexism. He has an amazing hard-on. The woman standing next to him is really nice-looking. Could use some attention in the armpits. Middle-aged hippie chick, maybe thirty-two.

He saw her giving him the eye—really subtle the way she did it, sizing him up. He was sure she was staring at his feet—trying to figure out how big his willy was. He wagged his toes in his Cons, even tried flexing his foot to make it look bigger. Though 11½ wasn't too bad.

"Eh, like," Ricky says, giving the woman a nudge in the ribs. He glances over to see what she's reading and this babe is actually studying a diagram of a twat. A twat. Ricky can't believe his luck. He winks conspiratorially and narrows his sexy Bar-Mitzvah-boy eyes. He points to the book. "Any good?"

Later the cousins walk up Broadway. Down the street on Grand, Wavy Gravy is performing at the Coffee Gallery. They are pulled over by hawker after hawker outside the topless bars. The hawker over at Big Al's has Ricky in a half nelson.

"Free look," Ricky says, shrugging his shoulders, "come on."

"You can't get the clap from looking," the hawker tells Bobby.

"No thanks," Bobby says. He is more interested in the sign over the ice-cream shop. Piña cola ice cream. He thinks of Sophie—her piña coladas, how they revealed her true nature. Sophie was about as sophisticated as a musical comedy put on by the Teaneck, New Jersey JCC.

"C'mon," Ricky says with irritation.

"Uh-uh," Bobby says as Ricky goes in for his free look.

"Please, let's go in," Ricky says. He looks so crazed and desperate, Bobby looks down at Ricky's crotch to see if he's making a spectacle. What a goon, Bobby thinks. How my mother could possibly be his mother's sister . . . But then again my mother is an amazing bitch, Bobby thinks.

"No," Bobby says. "It's not sexy, it's disgusting."

"Well sex *is* disgusting if you think about it," Ricky says. "I mean—like, what's a cunt? It isn't a flower, let's face it." Ricky smiles.

"Let's get a drink," Bobby says, "in a regular place. And don't show your ID." It seems funny to Bobby all of a sudden that he can feel so ancient and still be considered too young to drink a beer. He was sure it was true—the only pleasure of growing old was tormenting the young.

The cousins sit listening to a girl singer with bad skin. She sings Joni Mitchell songs in a beatific voice.

"I can't believe this," Ricky says. "I really feel like getting down, and I've never been in Frisco before, and instead of staring up pussy . . . You should have *seen* the girl in there. She was jerking off," Ricky says, "with a bottle of root beer."

"C'mon, Ricky, I'm *tired*."

"If you go into one of those places, I'll do whatever you want. Anything."

"Will you call up Melanie and explain why you broke up with her? Why you're such a shit . . . "

"*That's* what you want to trade?"

"Okay, I'll do it. But you have to do two things. You have to pay for me. I bet we get soaked in there. You've got to pay for me, and you've got to call up Melanie and explain this macho-pig shit—"

"All right, Bob. Let's go back to Big Al's."

"How about this place?" Bobby points to Harry's across the street.

"No, the guy didn't proof me at the other place. Let's go back there."

"Okay," Bobby says. He is thinking about what the hawker said: "You can't get the clap from just looking. . . . " But you could, Bobby knew, you just could. . . . *What is the sound of one spirochete clapping*?

The girl on the stage is wearing a red-and-white checked apron and a French baker's hat. She holds the wooden end of a spatula between her labia. She removes the spatula and tells the audience how she's going to cook the egg. First she passes the raw egg to a shy guy in the front row. He is eager and young—a bridegroom out for his stag party? He checks the egg to make sure it's raw. He passes it back to the naked woman who pushes the egg into her womb.

She times two minutes with a kitchen timer. And then she removes the egg, cracks it open, and shows the men the egg is hard-boiled. The center is dark yellow with a faint tracing of green.

She slices the egg into two halves and puts it on a paper plate. She asks the bridegroom-to-be to stand and she takes a handkerchief, red-and-white checked, and tucks it into his shirt. She gives him a plastic fork and knife; she hands him exaggerated cellars of pepper and salt.

"I feel like killing myself," Bobby says.

"This is fascinating," says Ricky.

A bottle of cheap champagne and two acts later, Ricky is eager to move on.

"The second act was good," Ricky says. "I really liked that Asian girl's ass."

"I feel like puking," Bobby says. "Let's get some air," says Bobby.

"One more club, all right?" Ricky asks. He is wobbly from champagne.

Exhausted, Bobby agrees. He vomits mournfully in an alley. As he throws up his Chinese dinner—delicate steamed pancakes!—he thinks of the irony of the egg passing out of her vagina. Creation working backwards. What is the sound of one spirochete clapping?

12

Ricky doesn't seem to notice anything familiar about the girl dancing on the stage. She is wearing a red G string. She's tall and thin with wide hips, a horsey mien. Bobby doesn't know what to say. Should he tell Ricky? Is Ricky liable to make a scene? Probably he won't care. Sophie's idea, natch. And then he realizes Sophie will be out next doing something worse.

"Dynamite," Ricky says.

"You like this one in the red thing?"

"Like her? I worship her."

"I'm pretty sure I could get you a date with her. In fact, I'm positive," Bobby says.

Ricky slaps Bobby on the back and orders another bottle of pissy champagne.

Two other dancers come on and neither one is Sophie. Bobby looks them over to make sure they aren't Sophie wearing a wig. One girl is over six feet; the other girl is black.

He says he's going to the head. He tells the bouncer he's got to see one of the dancers. Right away. It's his wife and the baby's sick.

The bouncer looks at him. "Sure."

"Hey, it's my woman. I'm not starting anything. Just tell Melanie Bobby is here. You better tell her Bobby Buchman."

"How long you two been married?"

"The baby is sick. My child has cholera and you won't let me talk to my wife?"

The bouncer looks at Bobby. He looks about nineteen. If he calls the cops, they'll proof the kid, and he'll get into trouble too.

"Our girls don't talk to customers. Forget it, college boy. Now go sit down or I'll call the cops."

Bobby looks around, then goes back to his seat. Melanie is back for an encore wearing some kind of tiger G string and now she's down on all fours, her butt pointing into the air. Her claws scuttle across the stage.

"This is it," Bobby says.

Ricky is practically passed out.

"Ricky, I can't believe you can't tell, but that's *Melanie* on the stage."

"Melanie?" Ricky says.

"I'm going to get them," Bobby says. "I'm going backstage and dragging those asshole girls out by their hair."

"You're kidnaping the strippers?" Ricky starts laughing moronically.

"Look, I know Sophie's back there, too. Melanie could never think this one up by herself. You coming with me or what?"

Bobby can't tell if Ricky's laughing or crying. Ricky picks up a cigarette butt from the ashtray and goes to light it.

"Why you smoking for?" Bobby asks. "I'll buy you a pack of cigarettes. Don't you know any better? Germs?"

There's no possibility of taking Ricky with him. He was gone. They'd arrest him or kill him. Who knew what kind of creeps hung around backstage here. Bobby feels like going back to the table and crying, too. Ricky's turned into a creep. Sophie's probably sucked off half the guys in the Bay Area. Bobby knew she was going out with borderline guys who Melanie thought were beating her up. Something about a nerve going dead in Sophie's hand last winter . . . Melanie had told Bobby something very dangerous had been going on with Sophie and Tad. I'll have to kill him too, Bobby thinks. If he so much as hurt one hair, even if Sophie let him.

He remembered the way she used to look up at him when they were making love. Such knowledge had seemed to shine from her eyes. He remembered when they were high school kids and he was still a virgin. If I can save her, Bobby thinks, I won't make love with anyone else until Sophie gets better. And he'd make it up to Melanie, too, though he wasn't at all sure how he could.

Melanie shakes her ass in a last obscene finale. And Bobby remembers a line from a Wallace Stevens poem. "*Let be be finale of seem*." He'd never understood the poem he realizes as he runs toward the dressing room door. Or what he thinks is the dressing room door. He ends up in a closet full of a terrible chemical smell and hits his head on a pipe. His head is killing him, but he thinks he sees the curtain that leads backstage. His head pounding, he slinks through a couple of cheesy curtains and ends up in a dark hall. There are little rooms along the hall and lights shine out from some of the doorways. He hears the sound of a man coming for the first time since the Korean War.

As he stands in the hall listening, he hears a faint giggle. The giggle is unmistakably hers. He'd know her giggle in a laugh riot. What is going on? She's fucking guys in these little rooms. She's taking their money and sucking their cocks. His woman was in one of these rooms sucking some farty old guy's dick. He crashes through the plywood door as easily as in a dream. And then the girl starts screaming. A girl he'd never seen before in his entire life. And this guy was sitting there, calm as hell, wearing a three-piece suit and holding his pud in his hand. And before he knew it the bouncer had knocked him out and the cops got there just in time to see him coming out of it. The stars were blinking in his face as the cops gently scooped him up and took him off. The last thing he remembered before he came to in the parking lot of the station was understanding those lines from the Wallace Stevens poem.

13

"*I understand how you feel, Bob,*" his lawyer says. "I had a daughter who went bad. Ran away to Greenwich Village. She was a speed addict when we found her. Toothless and practically bald. She didn't recognize her mother." The lawyer shakes his head gravely. "All this freedom's no good for the girls. You should call up their families. Get the fathers out here with shotguns."

"Yeah," Bobby says, imagining Sid whom he'd never met. He'd sooner come out here with a fur coat, if I know my Jewish fathers. And the thing is, Bobby realizes, I don't even know my *own* Jewish father. Comes home from the carpet store and reads back issues of the Harvard alumni magazine. His father was a bit loony. A harmless, barrel-chested man who looked like Zero Mostel, but was hung up on the Ivy League and the Yale-Harvard game. His father's secret dream was to move to Compton, Rhode Island and open a souvenir shop. Conch shells made into lamps. A *goy* locked in a Jew's body. The heart and soul of Ashley Wilkes locked in the body of a counterman on the Lower East Side . . .

The lawyer gives him a ride to downtown Berkeley, and he walks the three blocks to the girls' apartment feeling unbearably sad. What is he supposed to tell them? Did they even know their place had been busted up last night? That *he* had busted it up?

He buys a pretzel from a vendor, eschews the bright mustard. The pretzel is doughy, and he throws it into the street. An enormous gull swoops down and carries the pretzel off whole. As the gull flies off in an arc, glides off like a long chain of handkerchiefs bound luminously together, he thinks of her. Sophie as miraculous and white as this bird. In the distance, as the gull flies off, Bobby sees the glints of silver—the flecks of salt grown holy.

And now he's in their living room. Melanie lies asleep on a mattress on the floor and the door to the hallway is wide open. He hopes Brian isn't there. Brian is a little scary. What kind of brother would allow this to go on?

"Sophie!" he calls like a father, "Sophie!"

She's wearing an outrageously short purple skirt and what looks like a child's T shirt: I LEFT MY HEART IN SAN FRANCISCO. The blue heart is plastered against one nipple.

"Oh yeah?" Bobby says. "Well, don't look now, but I think you left something else there, too."

"Huh?" Sophie asks. She leans coquettishly on one hip.

"I feel like spitting right on the floor," Bobby says. "Well, wake her up. The other *bummekeh*. I want to talk to both of you. . . ."

"Cool out, Bobby. What's the big deal?"

"I was busted last night," Bobby says.

"For what? Impersonating a douche-bag?" Sophie stands there with her hand on her hip. She looks great, Bobby thinks—it must be all that jism she swallows. She's semen-crazy, Bobby thinks. Maybe she has some biochemical problem. Get her to take protein tablets and yeast, Bobby thinks.

"Look, you stupid bitch, I was busted last night at Harry's. I was busted for breaking down a door 'cause I was positive I heard *you* cackling away in there. Like a whore. But there's no more *like* is there, Sophie?" He takes her chin roughly in his hand. "You are a whore," he says, "aren't you?"

"Yes," she says.

He slaps her across the face so hard he can see his hand on her cheek.

You belong to *me*, Bobby thinks. I can see my hand on your cheek.

They sit down on the edge of the mattress where Melanie is still asleep. Sophie pushes Melanie's leg away with her elbow.

"I was at Harry's last night," Bobby whispers.

"You can talk regular. She won't wake up. She took three Seconals. She'd been speeding for a week."

"Look, there's a reason you're telling me this. You wanted me to find out. About *everything*. Sophie, how could you?" He lays his head down on her breast. He'll kill the next guy who comes near her. Hell, he'll kill the next thirty-five guys who come near her. "Look," Bobby says.

Sophie sticks her tongue in his mouth, between his lips. Sophie's mouth tastes no longer like the insides of peaches.

"You kiss those guys?" Bobby asks. "Just answer me. Do you kiss them?"

"No," Sophie says.

"How can I believe you?" Bobby asks. He knows he can never kiss her again.

"You can't believe me," Sophie says. "When are you going to accept it? I'm just a bad girl." Her look is beautiful and defiant.

"I'll never accept it," Bobby says. "And I'll never believe it. And you're *not* a bad girl, either, you know. You know that as well as I do. You're a good girl, Sophie. But you are really crazy. And all your craziness has to do with sex."

Sophie snorts. "You're telling *me* about sex?"

"You didn't invent sex," Bobby says.

"No, maybe not. But I invented *you*," Sophie says.

"You're probably right," Bobby says. "But didn't I invent you, too? A little?" Bobby asks.

"I never thought about it," Sophie says.

"Never?" asks Bobby. "I thought you said you loved me. Didn't you say you loved me?"

"Yes, I love you," Sophie says. "But I just can't *do* anything about it."

"Why?" Bobby asks.

"I don't know. You think I'm seriously crazy?" Sophie asks. "I mean—nuts?"

"Yeah, as a matter of fact I do," Bobby says. "Any girl who has sex with men for money—"

"I don't actually have sex-sex with them," Sophie says.

"You *admitted* you were a whore," Bobby says. "I won't believe you if you take it back now."

"I'm a hand-jobber," Sophie says. "I only do hand jobs. And I take off my clothes. Yeah. I do that. And I talk dirty to them."

He feels like slapping her again. She looks so miserable and lost. Her eyes are dull as textbooks.

"Well maybe if we cut off your hands," Bobby says, using his hand as a knife. "Like the Venus De Milo." And then he looks at her. "What about venereal disease?"

"I told you I don't *do* anything except jerk them off. That's it."

"Well, I hope you wash off their cocks," Bobby says. And then he gets mad again. "I can't believe I'm sitting here discussing this with you. Like whether or not you washed their penises before you touched them. It's disgusting." He looks at her and she laughs. "*You're* disgusting."

Melanie turns over and opens one eye. "Bobby," she says, "was that Ricky last night? At the club? Was I tripping or what?" Melanie looks terrible. Her eyes are bloodshot and puffy and ringed like Dracula's.

"You look terrible," Bobby says. He gets up and starts pacing. He slaps his hand against his forehead. "*Oy gevalt*!" he says, slapping. "Now listen to me, Miss Handjob, and you, too, the other bum. If you ever go near one of those joints again, either of you, if you ever so much as go *near* one of those places . . . Either of you. I'm calling your fathers. I'm calling your Aunt Tillie. Do you hear me? Both of you? I was *busted* last night for breaking down one of those hand-job rooms. I broke down the door because I thought I heard Miss Spiritual Tramp of 194—"

"J.D. Salinger," Sophie says. " 'A Perfect Day for Bananafish,' " Sophie says brightly.

"A perfect day for a murder, you mean. I'll kill you first. Both of you. I'll kill you before I'll stand by and watch you become *sewers*."

Bobby feels proud of himself. They sit down at the butcher-block table in the dinette—the dinette! These girls are loaded. He'd seen the Farberware coffeepot in the kitchen. Farberware! They were living out some suburban drama—some made-for-television movie. Two nice girls from New Jersey—well, one not-quite-so-nice girl and one really nice one . . .

"How much are you girls making?" Bobby asks. He loads up a pita with Melanie's homemade hummus. Not bad, Bobby thinks.

"One-fifty," Melanie says. "And Sophie's making over three hundred. But I don't want to do handjobs." Melanie giggles.

"Three hundred dollars a week?" Bobby asks. He's stunned. "My old man is thrilled to see three hundred a week."

"My father says the carpet business is doing terrible," Melanie says.

"And what do you do with the money?" Bobby asks.

"We *live* on it," Sophie says.

"We *live* on it," Bobby says, imitating Sophie.

"I *loathe* being imitated," Sophie says.

"Who cares what you loathe?" Bobby asks. "So what are you going to do?" Bobby asks.

"About *what*?" Sophie says.

"You quitting that place or what?"

The girls remain quiet.

"Well?" Bobby grabs the neck of Sophie's T shirt. "Well?" Bobby asks.

Melanie is really impressed. She's practically falling in love with him. Who would ever have thought Bobby Buchman was such a *mensh*?

Sophie laughs. "No, Bobby, I'm not quitting."

"Why not?" Bobby asks. He looks at her incredulously—the face that launched a thousand tips.

"The money's too good," Sophie says.

"You know that's not it. I'm willing to believe that with Melanie. Or Melanie's doing it because you *told* her to. Because she *believes* you and *trusts* you."

"Hey!" Melanie says. "Don't I get any credit? I really resent the way you act like everything I *do* is 'cause somebody else *made* me, you know? I mean, if I want to dance with feathers coming out of my ass—"

"You do that already," Bobby says.

"Well, it ain't nobody's business if I do," says Melanie.

"You stupid neurotic girls."

"Don't give us that macho condescension rap," says Melanie.

"I'll condescend you ass, Szasz. I've had it, do you understand? I can't stand either of your spoiled little faces another second. That's all you are. Two crummy little JAP girls from New Jersey."

"I don't believe *Flushing* is dumping on Hudson Heights," Sophie says.

"Spivack, I loved you," Bobby says.

Melanie looks up, more interested than Sophie.

"I loved you, Sophie— At least as much as anybody *could love* somebody like you. I used to read this poem—from the Bible. 'And who can find a woman of valor? For her price doth far exceedeth rubies.' I used to read *that*, and think of *you*. The *Bible*, Sophie. That's the way I thought of you. And now if I didn't feel so *sorry* for you . . ."

"There were whores in the Bible," Sophie says.

"Sophie, you're so awful. Bobby is trying to *tell* you something. Maybe I should go out. Anybody want some coffee from the 7-11?"

"I want you to hear this too, Melanie. I love both of you very much. In different ways," Bobby says.

"And I'm the side dish," Melanie says. "Put a paper bag over my head and fuck—"

"Fuck, fuck, fuck. I'm sick of the way you talk."

Sophie opens her mouth to say something, stifles it.

"What? What were you going to say?" Bobby looks up at her. She gets up from the table and puts her arms around his neck. She hangs from his neck, she lets herself go loose.

"All right, Buchman. I love you. You're irresistible," Sophie says. It's only then that she notices the tiny suede *yarmulkah* bobby-pinned to the back of his head. He *is* a religious fanatic.

"You gonna quit your job, Sophie?"

"No," Sophie says.

"Why not?"

"The money. I told you. I like the money."

"What do you plan to *do* with the money?" Bobby asks.

"I'm gonna buy myself a bike and ride with the Angels," Sophie says.

14

"*Hello*," *he'd said*, "this is Bob Buchman."

"Bookman? You selling encyclopedias?"

"No, I'm a good friend of your daughter's."

"Oh, my God. Mim, it's happened. Tell me. Is she alive? Arrested? Was she arrested again?" There's a touch of annoyance in Sid's voice.

"Look I'm a very *good* friend of your daughter's."

"What are you getting at, son? I have high blood pressure. Could you maybe speed this up?"

"This isn't so easy. Your daughter—"

"A fire," Sid says. "Was there a fire? Car accident?"

"Your daughter's a prostitute, sir."

"What? You call me up long distance to insult me?" Sid says.

"I'm not insulting you, sir. Maybe I could talk to Mrs. Spivack. She met me a few times. She offered to make me eggs—"

Bobby hears Sid talking to Miriam. And then he hears the click of Miriam getting on the line.

"Remember me? Layeh Cooper's nephew," Bobby says.

"Of course I remember you, Bobby."

"Well, I hate to have to tell you this, but Sophie works as a prostitute. . . ."

"Is this some kind of practical joke? Because if you're pulling my leg, young man—"

"I mean it, Mrs. Spivack, Dr. Spivack. I'm sorry. Sophie and Melanie both. Melanie claims she's only a dancer. . . ."

They said they'd call him back in the morning. The father had taken it much harder. Bobby wasn't even sure Dr. Spivack believed him. He'd expected them to fly out right that second. Drag her back by the hair.

Sophie is waiting for Brian to come home from work. He's fixing up a Victorian house over in Oakland. And making really good money. They haven't seen a lot of each other. With her working nights and Brian working days . . .

When Brian walks in, his head is shaved. Sophie starts to laugh. "Who scalped you?" Sophie asks.

"I don't know," Brian says. "I just got sick of all that hair. It's hot, you know?" Brian says, peeling off his sweaty T shirt.

"I've got bad news," Sophie says.

"So what else?" says Brian. The sun is going down around them. The sun is sinking into the water. Only 8:15 and it's practically dark. Sophie feels sad for the loss of summer. For the loss of all those green-hearted days.

Brian puts on a record, a sweet and sentimental song—Crosby, Stills and Nash. Not his usual.

"Well, what's the bad news?" Brian asks, settling down on the mattress next to Sophie. He is eating cottage cheese with chives out of the container.

"Well, Miriam and Sid are coming out."

"That *is* bad news," Brian says. "I thought it was something minor. Like you found out you had cancer. I'm really not in the mood for them. When are they coming? Bummer."

"Tomorrow. I think."

"What the hell for?"

"Well, Bobby called them, you know? Bobby *told them* about me."

"What about you?" Brian asks.

"You know. That I work at Harry's . . . He told them I was a prostitute—"

Brian starts to laugh.

"You think it's funny? I'm terrified. What do you think they'll do?"

"I don't know. If you ask me, they're both full of shit. Especially her."

"I thought Daddy was the one you hated."

"Well I'm not crazy about him either. But Miriam's a class-A cunt."

"Why?" Sophie asks. "I always thought it was Sid you were mad at. For leaving us, you know?"

"Yeah. How old was I when Sid left?"

"I don't know. Twelve? I was ten. Yeah, I was ten." Sophie remembers her tenth birthday. The Barbie Dream House her father had bought her. The birthday party where everyone wore clown hats except for her. She had worn a tiara.

"Yeah, I remember. I remember him coming up to my room. Sitting on my bed, you know? Fluffing my hair and all that crap. Well, son, and all that crap. And he told me how much he loved Dori. How beautiful and pure she was. *Pure*, could you barf? Pure as my bunghole."

"That *is* pretty sickening," Sophie says. "And remember that first time we met her? How Mom got us new outfits and sent us up to his office? I remember we took a taxi. A taxi all the way from New Jersey. It seemed so glamorous," Sophie says. "Going over the bridge in a taxi."

"George is washing the bridge . . ." Brian sings her a song from their childhood. Their long-ago and faraway childhood. Never had it seemed so far.

The sun goes out suddenly. Suddenly all the sunlight has vanished and there they sit in a darkened room. Brian's head is so closely shaven, the light catches strangely on his skull.

"But why do you hate Miriam so much? I can understand about Sid. But why her? Because she drank so much? I guess she was drunk most of the time."

"I'll tell you why I hate her," Brian says. "She never heard a word I said. She never heard one word."

Sophie puts her arms around Brian and holds her brother close. Suddenly there sneaks up the memory of Brian inside her. She feels herself stiffen, and senses Brian knows why.

"I'm sorry, Sophie," he says in a reedy voice.

She doesn't ask him what he means. She knows he knows she knows what he means.

"It's okay, Bri."

"It's not okay," Brian says. "It'll never be okay. It's probably all my fault."

"What's all your fault?"

"Your life. Your life's a mess," Brian says. "I guess I fucked you up. About men. And sex. God, it's not like I knew what I was doing. . . . I *was* in love with you," Brian says. "As weird as that sounds, it's true."

"So you think my life's a mess, eh?"

"Well what do you think, Sophie? You think you're doing great?"

"Well not *great*," Sophie says. "But not terrible . . ."

"You're a whore, Sophie. Eighteen years old and you suck dick for a living."

"I do not," Sophie says. "I told you I was a hand-jobber."

"You pull them. You suck them. What's the difference?" Brian asks.

"I don't know," Sophie says. "Maybe there is no difference."

"They say prostitutes hate men. Do you?" Brian asks.

"I don't know. I guess I must," Sophie says. "But then again, what's to like?"

"What about old Bobby? You like him, don't you?"

"I like Bobby. He's crazy about me. He worships me. He'd probably do anything for me."

"Even try to rescue you." Brian laughs. "The way he busted down that room, 'cause he thought you were in there. It kinda made me like him. I was never crazy about him, you know that. But that was great—you know? It reminded me of Dustin Hoffman in "The Graduate," you know? The way he barreled in there . . . Remember when Dustin Hoffman broke into that church? . . . It reminded me of that. . . ."

"I love Bobby," Sophie says. "I never thought I'd love anybody. But I think I really do love him."

"Then do the right thing," Brian says. "Be his lady," says Brian.

15

The Spivacks and the Szaszes rent an Oldsmobile at the airport. They call up the kids for directions, and, naturally, no one is home. Brad says they should go to the bar in the airport and keep trying; Gladys insists they head for Berkeley right away.

"We can go to the school and look for them. Sproul Plaza," Glad says. "That's where all the bums hang out. Or we can go to Haight-Ashbury and look for them there," Gladys says. "Haight-Ashbury. That's the hangout."

"No, no," says Miriam. "Haight-Ashbury's old hat. No one hangs out there anymore."

"Look," Glad says, "I know what I'm talking about. I asked that psychiatrist. I called the same guy Lee Freund used with Anita. Dr. Popkin—or Pipkin? Which is it, Brad? Pipkin? Popkin?"

At the mention of Lee's name, Sid blushes deeply. He remembers Lee's heavy breasts, her downy thighs, her tight tummy. And everywhere he'd looked—gold leaf. The headboard. The night stand. Everywhere gold as thin as paper. Miriam looks at him and knows what he's thinking.

"Why? You think that Pipkin did such a great job? Sophie told me all he did was imitate Anita. She drooled, so he drooled. You need a doctor to drool? You think Lee Freund knows what she's doing?" Miriam waves her hand. And looks at Sid.

"Well Pipkin says the thing to do—" Gladys begins.

"Fuck Pipkin," Miriam says. "Anita's been in Passaic Pines two years now. You want Melanie in Passaic Pines two years talking baby talk?"

"It's terrible," Sid says. "It's a *shandeh* what's happening to these kids. I still can't believe it," Sid says. "Little Sophie a prostitute . . ."

"Little Sophie was always a bum," Gladys says. "I used to listen to them talking. Twelve years old, they were talking already blow jobs and who knows what. Jobs you never heard of . . . And Sophie was always the ringleader. Melanie was like a little girl. I'm sorry," Glad says, "but I blame Sophie. I'm sorry, but she was always no good."

Miriam looks at Sid. Sid starts to say something, but Miriam looks at him—let it go. The last thing they needed now was to start fighting with the Szaszes.

Sophie and Melanie are sitting in the Creamatorium. Melanie looks at the waitress's watch. "It's 12:40," Melanie says. "Their plane's landed. We can't just leave them at the airport."

"Why not?" Sophie says. She orders another piña colada. "Have another drink, Melly. You're gonna need this one," she says.

Around three the girls head back to their apartment. By now the parents are driving down Telegraph Avenue, looking for them on the street. "Look," Gladys says, squinting. Two young girls walk down the avenue. One is small and curly-headed. The other is tall and gawky. Brad, who is driving, slows down.

"That's not Sophie," Sid says.

When they pull up to the curb, they see these girls are much younger. They could have been Sophie and Melanie four or five years ago. They are wearing too much makeup. Their eyes are lost in a smut of grease and kohl. Their eyes are full of mania. They would do anything, these girls. Pay to have swastikas tattooed on their behinds, have sex with perverts, shoot drugs into their eyes. And everywhere you looked you saw them: Giggling on Ritalin in the Port Authority; strung out, in plastic chairs; investing quarters in TVs. "I Love Lucy."

"I failed her," Miriam says.

"You did what you could," Gladys says.

In the back seat Sid takes her hand, the elegant fingers of his wife, and holds them tight. He strokes Miriam's knuckles. "I failed *you*," says Sid.

"For once you're right, Sid. I'm not sure *you* did everything *you* could," Gladys says.

"Gladys!" Brad says.

"Gladys, Shmadus, it's time we spoke our minds. Look where it's gotten us, all our politeness. You had no right going on and on with that Eve Giletti, Sid. The Boy Scout Dinner, in front of everyone. The Blue and Gold Dinner, and Eve was the chairman. . . ."

"What were *you* doing at the Boy Scout dinner?" Brad asks. "You got a son, I haven't met him?" He winks at Miriam through the rearview mirror. For a moment their eyes catch and Miriam knows Brad wants her.

"Gladys, you're a *yachna*," says Sid.

The mothers and daughters are sitting in the dinette. The fathers have left them alone. The fathers are eating egg foo yung and talking about *their* salad days—the worst things *they'd* ever done. Compared with their daughters, they were wimps. Gladys, like Bobby Buchman, notices the Farberware, the Marimekko tea towels. At least they have some nice things, Gladys thinks.

"So, like I just *danced*," Melanie says.

"*Der gantze tuches ist geveyn nokkit*," Gladys says to Miriam, raising one penciled eyebrow. Melanie had always been fascinated by her mother's complete baldness in the eyebrow department.

"One and a half bathrooms," Gladys says, glancing meaningfully at Miriam: Maybe these girls don't have it so bad.

"Two sinks to clean," says Miriam. "Two Johnny-mops."

"Melanie, are you pregnant?" Gladys asks.

"No, Ma," Melanie says for the third time.

"Are *you* pregnant?" Gladys asks Sophie. Miriam can't help but laugh. This Szasz woman is pure theater. Miriam feels closer to Melanie and Sophie than she does to Gladys. Perhaps Miriam is just another *bummekeh* at heart.

Mothers and daughters—the cruelest subject? Gladys Szasz at fourteen skipping to dancing school? Melanie thinks of her mother's hands, their innocence at fourteen. Now they are covered with brown spots, with dilated capillaries; the cuticles yellow as wax beans. It wasn't always this way. Girls grow into mothers; yet sometime between your mother's head emerging from your grandmother's body and the trick of menopause, your own mother falls in love.

Melanie's mother sits in civics class, thinking about Mortimer Wilder—his legs, his loins. . . . Her own mother thinking about boys' penises, as she, Melanie, sat and thought, squirming through World Literature, wiggling through Earth Science. Her own mother, Gladys, wearing white pedal-pushers and a pink cashmere cardigan, swinging her calves from a hammock in 1944. Next door, in another cabin, Mortimer Wilder is practicing how to put on a condom and her mother's best friend, Rhoda Lemmel, goes all the way *by accident* with her mother's boyfriend.

"Could you explain again how it was an accident?" Gladys asks Rhoda.

"Well, I just didn't realize. All I knew was if you didn't take off your panties, the fella couldn't get in. And all of a sudden, I'm still wearing my bloomers and all, but I've got this big thing inside me."

"Anyway, Ma, I *said* I'd go to a psychiatrist," Melanie says. "In the Bay Area . . ."

"You're coming back to Hudson Heights," Gladys says. "Your father and I have decided. I'm not going to be a weakling," Gladys says.

"And you're coming home, too," Miriam says. "Aren't you?"

"I don't know," Sophie says.

"You're going to be a prostitute as your career? That's intelligence, Sophie?" Gladys looks at her. "That's Honors History, Sophie, and the prize you won for writing those haikus? What are you doing to your parents?" Gladys remembers Sophie's honors better than her own mother. Did Miriam know about the haikus she'd won the prize for in ninth grade? Gladys seemed to remember everything Sophie had ever done.

"You never liked me," Sophie says. "You didn't want me to be Melanie's friend."

"That's true, Sophie. You always were a *bummekeh*, I'm afraid. But we always knew how smart you were. Even as a little girl, you always knew everything. And my Melanie—" Gladys pinches Melanie's cheek, and chuckles. "My Melanie was always a simple type."

"A simple type? Ma! Doesn't anybody care what they say about me? Everyone thinks Sophie is the interesting bad one and I'm just the copycat moron. I'm *sick* of it. And I'm sick of *you*." Melanie walks over to Sophie and pulls a hunk of Sophie's curls.

"Ow. Quit it, Melanie. What's the matter with you? You on the rag or something?" Sophie claps her hand over her mouth and looks at Glad.

"Incorrigible," Gladys says.

Brian stays in Oakland the two days his parents are there and never sees them. On the plane back to New York, Sophie remembers Brian talking as the sun went down—explaining why he hated Miriam. How she'd never listened to him, how she'd never heard one word Brian ever said. She feels sad about Brian. She wonders how long they'll make her stay in New Jersey. She wonders when she'll see her brother again. And Bobby. The stewardess hands her a diet soda in a plastic tumbler. The soda splashes into her lap. She remembers the name of a movie she saw every day for a week on "Million Dollar Movie" when she was sick with the measles: *Nobody Waved Goodbye*.

16

Melanie and Sophie see their psychiatrists, then get permission to visit Anita in the locked ward. Anita is getting married tomorrow for the second time. Sasha has just turned two. He has a full head of blond hair and goes around saying to everyone, " 'Bye Doo-doo. 'Bye Doo."

Sasha calls Lee "Mama," which makes Lee nervous, but what can she do? The doctors keep saying soon, soon, when she asks about Sasha visiting Anita. Soon, soon, she's making progress. What kind of progress is this? A second doomed marriage and she is barely nineteen. Lee is sitting in front of her vanity removing part of her eyebrows. She's thinking about Sid Spivack. If she invites them to the wedding, she will get to see Sid. She remembers the line of golden hair leading down from his navel. His treasure trail, he'd called it. Men.

Lee is not paying attention and has tweezed away too much. If I keep this up, I'll end up looking like Glad Szasz. She'd always wondered about Gladys's eyebrows. Had they just fallen out? Probably from aggravation. How ironic and terrible that Melanie and that funny Sophie should both end up as out-patients in Passaic Pines. . . . The way the class of 1970 was headed, they'd be having their five-year reunion in the hospital cafeteria.

She supposed she ought to invite the Szaszes *and* the Spivacks to the wedding. It wasn't going to be much of an affair, though her mother had insisted on flying up from St. Louis. "Don't worry," Millie had said, "so Anita will be like Liz Taylor. She'll have five husbands. So?" Five husbands wasn't the point. . . . Even Wayne Voekler, that pale gravedigger, was better than this Snowboy or Snowbunny. Whoever he was, his prognosis was worse than Anita's. Too much LSD or something, Dr. Pipkin had said. Snowboy was twenty-three and he acted about eight. He carried around a stuffed Humpty Dumpty that sang a little tune. Pipkin, to Lee's annoyance, had encouraged the romance. Anita was *talking* to this Snowboy. And that was the main thing. She talked only to him, or through him. It was the only progress Anita had made in two years. Who could imagine what they talked *about*? And yet they talked for hours. She'd seen them whispering herself through one of those special mirrors, had heard her daughter's gravelly voice under the snow of static.

The phone rings and it's the caterer. "Smoked mackerel?" Lee considers. "How much a pound?" Lee asks.

"You did a nice job," Gladys says, patting Lee on the shoulder. "As usual."

"Did you try the mackerel?" Millie asks Sid. "It's mackerel," she says, pointing. Hadn't she seen this guy somewhere? In Florida during *Pesach*? A year or so ago?

"Which is the mackerel?" Sid asks Miriam. Miriam knows Sid is uptight around Lee Freund. Gladys volunteered last night, over the telephone, that Sid had slept not only with Lee, but also with Lee's sister, Betty Ann.

Sid looks good, Lee thinks. She pops into her large mouth what the caterer calls a coronet—little horns of mortadella stuffed with cream cheese and pimento, stuffed with cornichons and crème fraîche.

"So how's old Betty Ann?" Miriam asks Lee's mother.

Millie opens up her bag, inside is a half-pint of vodka. "Vodka?" she asks.

"I have," Miriam says. She is drinking ginger ale.

"It's the only drink you'll get around here," Millie says. She makes the child's sign for crazy: She points to her head and twirls her finger: I curl my hair and I brush my teeth . . .

"And Betty Ann?" Miriam asks.

"I didn't know you knew Betty Ann, you girls up here. . . ."

"My husband knew her in Miami. . . . I've never met her," Miriam says.

"Well, you're lucky," says Millie.

"Lucky?"

"She's a real bore, my younger daughter. Stu-*pid*," Millie says. "Not at all like Lee, you know. You never know with children, do you?"

"You sure don't," Miriam says, drinking off the ginger ale from the paper cup. On the cup are wedding bells with perky little faces. The bigger bell, the groom bell, conjures Akim Tamiroff.

"Ssh," Millie says, "there's the kids." Roberta and Felice walk into the dayroom holding baskets of daisies and mums. Roberta looks down at her feet; her eyes are ringed in black. Felice's stockings bag in folds around her soft ankles and knees. They are wearing identical white shifts with big collars and middy ties. The nautical look, their mother had said. When in doubt, the nautical look will always pull you through any ambiguous occasion. And what could be more ambiguous than a wedding in a mental ward performed by the hospital chaplain? And the groom's head is riddled with holes. And the bride's heart is missing in places. And the bride's son is home with the maid playing with sturdy Swedish toys. " 'Bye Doo-doo."

Dr. Pipkin—call me Elliott—is coming down the improvised aisle with Anita on one arm, Snowboy on the other. Anita turned down the nautical dress her mother had chosen for her. She is wearing what looks like a nursing gown, blue terry, tied under the bosom. Her long hair is up in a knot and she's wearing little paper flowers around the bun. Her gaze is otherworldly. Lee looks at her and starts to cry. Millie digs her nails into her daughter's wrist. Lee smiles exaggeratedly through a mantilla of tears.

She sees Anita as a baby, fat and red and crusty—a victim of hives and rashes. Allergic to cow's milk and orange juice, skittish at egg yolks and cat hair and wool. She remembers Anita on Tootie's knee, scratching her eczema, rubbing her hives. And Tootie trying to calm her, playing the harmonica. She smiles at Anita then, and waves. Tootie putting his big lips up to the harmonica and blowing out "Ain't She Sweet." And Anita crying harder.

Snowboy looks awfully proud of himself. He is waving enthusiastically though he has no people here. When Lee called up the boy's folks—a number in Moonachie, New Jersey—just to see what was what in case this lasted beyond the ward—whoever had answered had said something about Christ-killers and hung up. And so here they were again, the enemies of Jesus, eating smoked fish and chattering, and if only Millie had a bigger bottle in her bag. . . .

The chaplain is a girl minister named Reverend Butterfass. She looks about twenty. The most Protestant face Lee has ever seen—lips as thin as carpaccio: "Dearly Beloved, we are gathered together . . ."

Lee remembers Anita at three in the back yard on Glenham Court. Blonde and pudgy and laughing. Tootie comes out in a madras shirt with his Leica around his neck. It is 1955 and the air is buzzy with flies. Roberta is taking her first steps and Lee is nine months pregnant, trying to figure out the name if it's another girl. "What about Freida, if it's a girl? What about Florence? Like the city?" Tootie sticks out his tongue.

Later that day they go next door and there in the middle of the Wassermans' pool, her water breaks. Chickie Wasserman is swimming around when suddenly she's positive someone has peed. Lee Freund, a grown woman, peeing in her pool? And just when Maury had finally finished fussing with the pH.

"My water broke," Lee says.

"Oh my God, the baby! Hurry, Maury, hurry!"

"Another baby?" Anita asked. "We already got Bertie, Mom. I don't *want* another sister."

"Why not?" Lee asked, letting Maury Wasserman hoist her out of the pool.

"You can't play beauty parlor with *babies*. They don't have hair," Anita says.

Why had it seemed, when she came home from the hospital a week later, Anita's toddler days were over? That suddenly, in seven days, she'd become a real little girl?

17

Sophie sits in her parents' living room. Miriam is making buckwheat blini in the kitchen. Sid is sitting on the couch, reading "The Girls in Their Summer Dresses."

"Daddy, where is Dori now?"

Sid puts his finger to his lips. Sssh. Mom-my, he mouths.

"It doesn't matter," Sophie says. "Mommy doesn't care."

"How do *you* know?" Sid says.

"Mom!" Sophie shouts.

"Butter," Miriam says.

"Mom, do you care if Sid and I talk 'bout Dori?"

"What?" She comes into the living room wearing jeans with flour dust all over the knees.

"Do you—"

"Sophie!" Sid shakes his head.

"What's the matter?" Miriam asks. "Sophie, remember the blini we had at the Russian Tea Room?"

"The Russian Tea Room?" Sid makes a face. "Who took you to the Russian Tea Room?"

"Just a friend," Miriam says. "Anyway, remember those blini? Well, come taste mine and see if you think it tastes right."

"I was asking Daddy about Dori. He thought you would mind."

"Why should I mind?" Miriam asks.

"See," says Sophie.

Sid shakes his head, dismayed.

He turns to his book. The Girls in Their Summer Dresses. "Women," he says.

"Well, tell me what happened to her," Sophie says.

"Dori, you mean?" Her mother dips a piece of blini in a container of sour cream. "Mmm," she says. "Yummy."

"Yeah, Dori. Where *is* she? Still in the loony bin?"

"She's very depressed," Miriam says. "Sid went to see her just before you came home. She's taking a lot of strong drugs and you'll never believe how fat she got."

"She's fat?" Sophie laughs. "You're kidding. Wait till I tell Melanie. . . ."

"Never gloat over another woman's weight," says Miriam. "Any one of us could become fat at any minute."

"Not you," Sophie says.

Miriam pats her thigh. "I'm spreading. . . ."

"Does Daddy give her money?"

"I don't think so," Miriam says, "I honestly don't know. Ask him. Maybe he pays her insurance. They're still married," Miriam says.

"Well, isn't he going to get a divorce like a normal person?"

"You know, I don't care. I'm never gonna marry him again, I've decided. Only a total nut marries the same guy twice, don't you think? Me marry a dentist? Twice?"

"Do you . . . trust him?" Sophie asks.

"Not to two-time me you mean? I don't know . . . I know all about Lee Freund and Betty Ann, her sister. If that's what you're getting at. . . . Your father's almost fifty. His bladder's a little weak. He's tired. You know what I mean? That girl—Dori—broke his balls. The whole time they were married, she drove him crazy. She still drives him crazy. And you know what? I'm glad. I actually love it when she calls and breaks his chops. Let him suffer a little."

She's glad her mother isn't the sucker in all of this. She'd been really teed off when her parents had started getting back together, acting all lovey-dovey the second she graduated from high school. Where was Sid the Kid in the old days when she was upstairs having sex with her own brother? Where was Sid with his Mexican serape and his stupid puns when Brian was tripping his brains out on LSD cut with strychnine? Where was Sid when she came home from seventh grade and her only mother was passed out on the living room floor at 3:35?

She goes into the living room and sees, or thinks she sees, the outline on the rug of her mother's sleeping body. There is a stain or a faint aura around the place where Miriam had lain, listening to *Salomé*, weeping through *La Bohème*.

She knocks the paperback out of her father's hands.

"What?" Sid looks up. He's wearing his glasses; he looks old. His eyes are pale and baggy. He looks no more like an anchorman. He looks just like some guy, some husband, some middle-aged Jew.

"Talk to me," Sophie says. "About why you left. Why you abandoned Mom . . . and us."

Her father looks so vulnerable in his faggy mohair sweater, Sophie is sorry she's started up.

"I was young and stupid," Sid says. *Just like you are now.*

"That's not good enough," Sophie says.

"I'm still your father," Sid says. He looks at her, his *kurveh*, his whore. "Aren't I?" he asks.

4

Diaspora

IN PUERTO RICO

for M.S.

In Puerto Rico the jasmine drips
From the trees and the bougainvillea bleeds.
They open you up like a bald turkey,
A smoked duckling,
A fragrant goose.
I hear the Electrolux humming
As the brown doctor empties your insides,
Gravy of skin and dust and blood.
Later, we dog-paddle in Barney's pool
And your sanitary belt
Glints in the sun like a proposition.
We snort cocaine in the kitchen, giggling.
We think we've got it all:
Nice titties, good-looking boyfriends—
The future's as rosy as blood.

Sophie Spivack
San Francisco
1972

1

Bobby graduates from Stanford in the spring of '72. His senior essay is entitled, "Versions of the Good: The Old-Testament Notion of *Hokmah* vs. The Platonic Ideal."

He wins the Dinkler Prize for the best senior essay, the Elizabeth Bonner Elicott Prize for the highest grade point average, and a cash award from the Women's Club of Flushing, N.Y., which pays for summer study in Europe.

"So I *told* your aunt Layeh we'd only be in Frisco a day or two— Are you listening, Bobby?" He looks up, surprised, to see his own mother sitting across the table. Her lips are oily with pork fat; flecks of seaweed are trapped in her teeth.

"What'd you say, Mom?"

"Didn't you hear a word I was saying? Honestly, Bobby. You're such a *luftmensh*. Isn't he? Ben? A *luftmensh*?"

Ricky is staring down a magnificent pair of knockers. Nipples the size of hundred-lira pieces struggle against red net. He is drinking Campari on the waitress's recommendation. It tastes like dirty bubble bath. He has been in Florence for two days and still hasn't managed to get laid. Italy. Hah. Across the piazza he recognizes what have to be American girls. You can tell the American girls by their contraptions—ridiculous luggage carts with wheels they drag across cobblestone.

If necessary, he'll have to settle for an American girl. And better one of these pampered types with frosted hair and a luggage cart than one of those other American types—the dirty hippies in flannel shirts who've been wearing the same waist-high panties since check-in at Icelandic. You could catch a disease from one of those girls.

He's seen them on the trains. They wash out their one pair of Levis in those disgusting bathrooms—no wonder they call them water *closets*—and then they hole up in the bathroom for the rest of the trip, waiting for their jeans to dry. You know how long it takes for a pair of jeans to dry? The bathroom is off-limits all the way across the Alps and enormous Italian women with weak bladders bang on the door for the rest of the night. And no one gets any sleep.

What's wrong with these girls? Didn't anyone tell them about Yankee ingenuity? And what's wrong with their sinuses that they can spend hours in there reading Agatha Christie?

He'd rather *shtup* one of the princesses—spring for a thirty-dollar hotel room, and maybe even a second hotel room for her ugly friend—than dip his dork into a hippie spittoon.

Remarkably, he's won the showdown with the pair of tits. For suddenly their mistress is standing lasciviously beside him. He doesn't take out his traveler's phrase book. He simply narrows his eyes and beckons her to have a seat. "Twenty thousand," the girl says.

Melanie is living in a women's cooperative house in Cambridge. She spends her summer training to be a midwife's assistant and working on a women's newspaper called *Xantipi*. Most of the women in the house are lesbians, or at least bisexuals. In any case, none of the women bring men into the house. Melanie feels like a bit of a sneak running upstairs from her typewriter and locking herself in the bathroom. There she takes from its hiding place, behind the toilet-bowl cleaners, behind the derelict douche-bags, the sponges gone fuzzy and fetid and foul, a Louis Vuitton tote bag brimming with the weapons of old: Love's Lemon-Scented Body Splash, Andrea eye make-up pads, Nudit hair-remover, cotton balls and Co-et pads; lip shine, lip gloss, lipstick, balm. There's even a tube of Cupid's Quiver which wraps the vagina cunningly in four feminine flavors: Strawberry, Peaches 'n' Cream, Brandy Alexander, Banana Split.

Melanie spits languidly into a cake of eye liner and tests the brushstroke on her wrist. She runs her hand against her leg to see if the stubble's coming in. She's thinking about the piece she's writing for her column, "Pudenda and Addenda." It's a miscellany of things—a random collection of news items, excerpts from other papers, detailing the oppression of women. Scented douche was *exactly* the kind of thing she'd run down in her column. And here she was *shtupping* it up her very own pudendum. Brandy Alexander indeed! She knew she was a hypocrite, but she'd rather be anything than a fool. She'd never be a fool again.

"Mel, what's going *on* in there? I've got a bladder infection."

It was Moonchild banging on the door. She couldn't come out with one eye done and a douche syringe stuck halfway up. Moon would surely notice.

"Sorry, Moon, I'm bleeding to death. I'll come out in a second. Promise."

The cabbie drives them around the Cascine. They pass a pair of Italian girls with lustrous hair holding hands. The Italian women grow enormous, with arms like Rocky Marciano, asses like the Apennines, but the young ones are svelte as sylphs. And they are all virgins. A country full of virgins and whores. He wonders if he's paying too much—twenty thousand lire must be about twenty-five dollars. In Boston you could buy a blow job for fifteen dollars, or even less.

For graduation they'd had a party and he'd been in charge of the entertainment. They'd hired these two strippers—sisters—Annemarie and he forgot the other one's name. The girls were pretty doggy, though their bodies weren't too bad. For fifty dollars apiece the girls had eaten each other as the climax of the show. And sisters, yet; the girls had been sisters. Ricky doesn't know if it's funny or sad. Probably they just made it up as a gimmick.

Yup, it had been one hell of a party. Who knew when all of them would get a chance to party again? He felt like his crowd at Harvard had served somewhere like Korea together. Making it through Harvard *was* kinda like surviving a war. And now old Sokol was going off to Berkeley for law, and Sigalow was off to the London School of Economics. Only he and Kralich would be living in Cambridge next year. He had no idea how he'd finessed his own admission to Harvard for med school. There must have been a mistake somewhere. Sure he had a 3.8, but lots of guys had 3.8s. A 3.8 at Harvard meant *bubkes*.

Yup, it had been one hell of a party. He remembers going down that silky night in May to the Combat Zone to audition the entertainment. He remembers going into a club, The Velvet Glove, and waiting for a stripper to come up to their table. He and Sigalow were doing coke; he remembers how mellow they were. Coke, then champagne, then more coke. He remembers this one girl on the stage, dressed in a fireman's hat. And then he remembers

Melanie dressed like a tiger—her butt stuck into the air—Melanie scuttling her tiger claws across the splintery stage. He remembers that Melanie once was his. He imagines the two of them naked in the Szaszes' rec room, the *Barron's Profiles of American Colleges* spread-eagled before them. Melanie's devotional lips wrapped around his penis . . . And then the girl in the fishnet T shirt gives a tricky lurch of her head and Ricky is lost to bliss.

2

Bobby is lost in a dream of halvah. He wakes up with the taste of sesame gluing his lips together. In his dream he was walking through caves of halvah—marble, chocolate, vanilla, honey, pistachio, walnut, coffee, cream. There had been nothing but walls of halvah, a grotto of sweetness and sticky delight. He'd go into the Armenian Quarter first thing after breakfast and buy enormous hunks of halvah. And then he'd sit in a café and write in his journal exactly what he was feeling in this land of bulrushes and milk, this country of bone and sand and law.

The one thing that became very clear as he walked the melancholy streets of Jerusalem was that he had already made his choice. He had spent the last years of his college career pulled like taffy, like Turkish delight, between the hands of Faith and Reason, Aristotle and Maimonides, Philosophy and God. Philosophy was easier. Ethics was easier than Law. He had wanted philosophy to win. He had rooted for her with his high IQ, with his SAT scores and his 3.9 cume. He could see himself more easily as a philosopher than a rabbi.

A graduate student in philosophy, reading St. Augustine into the night, cooking hamburger Stroganoff on a hotplate in an attic room. Staying up all night long, learning Greek and Arabic. Living the life he was meant to live—rational, empirical, scholarly, sane. He had come to Israel to figure it out; now he realized he had already made up his mind. Coming to Jerusalem to choose between faith and reason was like going to Sodom to choose between lechery and restraint.

He lifted himself out of his cot and looked at the map someone had tacked to the wall of the hostel. Sodom was not too far away, just a bit south of the Dead Sea. The thought of Sodom made him think of Sophie. A philosopher could marry anyone—even a fornicatrix like Sophie. But shouldn't a rabbi marry only a woman noble like Sarah, faithful like Ruth, courageous like Deborah? If he chose Jerusalem over America, was he also choosing to abandon Sophie? Or was she anchored in his heart until the end of days?

She'd come back to California after six months with Miriam and Sid. At first he'd seen a lot of her. Then she had grown, more and more, incommunicative and mute. She'd spent her days selling rainbows in a head shop on Embarcadero, and when he saw her, nights, she was listless and pale. He'd tried to talk to her, but she wouldn't. He'd tried to get her to come with him to *Havdalah* services, bagel brunches at Hillel. She'd only look at him and her eyes would tell him she thought he was nuts. He'd felt unbearably optimistic when she'd first come back and found an apartment in Menlo Park, just minutes away from the Stanford campus. Within a few months she left the Peninsula and headed back to San Francisco—the city of sin and sailors and sex.

Bobby imagined the little chair where Sophie sat while she did her work. A wrought-iron chair with curlicues, like the chairs in soda fountains. Bobby imagined his Queen of the Sabbath wearing a pair of leather hot pants; the cheesy look of the curtain behind which she plied her trade. Bobby imagined Sophie's hands—tiny, underdeveloped hands, the secret hands of secret dolphins—Sophie extending her pliant hands to milk the penis of a stranger.

Again she was lost to him.

Melanie and Danny De Vries—that cute guy from Sociology—have each taken a Quaalude. They loll on Danny's mattress in an attic apartment in Brookline. Across the bed a game of Monopoly lies in messy progress. It is Melanie's turn to go, but they can't find the dice. Danny lifts up one of the pillows. Underneath is a plastic bag of sinsemilla and a pair of women's panties.

"Those aren't *mine*," says Melanie.

Danny can't help but start laughing.

"What're you laughing at, like a moron? Whose panties are they?"

"I don't know exactly," Danny says, laughing harder.

"Well, this is typical," Melanie says. The panties look like real Puccis, though Melanie's too high to be sure. She wants to check the label, but doesn't particularly want to touch them.

"C'mon, Melanie. Don't bum out. So who cares whose panties they are?"

"I care," Melanie says. "How did they get here?"

"They walked here," Danny says. He takes Melanie into his arms and kisses her. "They took the A train," Danny says.

"This is typical," Melanie says. "Roll me a reefer, Danny. I didn't know you had pot."

"I always keep it under my pillow. Otherwise my roommates steal it. That's why I keep my panties there, too."

"What do you mean, Danny?"

"God, Melanie, I can't fool around with you anymore. Here," he says, handing her a long skinny joint.

"I hate skinny joints," Melanie says. "In California, at least people knew how to roll a doobie."

Danny undoes his pants. His penis rolls out like a practical joke. "Oh Ricky!" Melanie says. She clasps her hand to her mouth.

"Ricky?" Danny says. "Bummer." He takes a swig from a can of soda. The soda's been sitting on the radiator since early April and now it's June. The sickly green of the can shimmers in the wet heat.

"Now we're even," Melanie says.

"Even?"

"For the panties."

"Let's forget everyone else."

"I'm thinking of giving up men."

"That's silly. Because of a pair of panties?"

"I'm a columnist on a *serious* feminist paper. I'm supposed to be serious," Melanie says. "I'm the press."

Danny kisses her; inhales the citrusy smell of her arms as she inhales the reefer.

Ricky is lonely in Paris. He goes to Pigalle and looks for whores. He can hardly tell the prostitutes from the regular girls. He is afraid of catching some exotic strain of syphilis. He is afraid of paying too many francs for a blow job *français*. He sits in an L-shaped café and points to the baguettes smeared with *rillettes* the woman beside him is eating. The waiter makes a joke in French and doesn't serve him. He can't understand a word, but Ricky knows the joke is on him. The woman sitting next to him laughs. He takes out his copy of the *International Herald Tribune* and reads the headline out loud: "NIXON LEAD STRONG IN POLLS."

He turns to the crossword puzzle and takes one of the croissants from the basket. He stuffs it into his mouth and chews defiantly, his mouth open. He looks up at the snotty bar-man with a mouth full of croissant; the bar-man puffs languidly on his cigarette. The woman moves down to another stool. He notices her long nose, her full lips, her Gallic sneer. He curses her beneath his breath. He grabs another croissant; gobbles it, then another. He decides, what the hell, he'll go down to the Louvre and take a gander at the Mona Lisa. He'd seen her once before. In sixth grade.

They'd all had buddies on the way to the museum. He remembers the buddy system with warm nostalgia. A yellow school bus full of children driving over the George Washington Bridge. He remembers the dull gleam of the Hudson; the civilized smell of carbon dioxide; the scratchy feel of his woolen pants—charcoal gray, his mother had called them—rubbing against his legs.

His buddy had been Aviva Cohan, a red-haired girl whose father was Reverend Cohan, the cantor at the Jewish Community Center of Hudson Heights. He wondered where Aviva was now that he needed her. A buddy. A tiny girl with tiny hands. A voice as squeaky as Alvin the Chipmunk's. He thought of Alvin and the Chipmunks singing Christmas carols over the New York airwaves. He began to choke on his fifth croissant. Maybe when he got back to Hudson Heights, he'd call her up, what the hell, just for the fun of it. Eh, Aviva, what's happenin'?

The bartender pushes his bill across the counter. Twenty-four francs. Twenty-four francs for a cup of coffee? And then he realizes, the croissants weren't free. They just put them there so you'll smell them and absent-mindedly eat them. Another ploy to fix Whitey, get the American greenback. He wasn't a bit surprised. He decided to walk to the Louvre. He could use the exercise and he wasn't exactly flush. When he got there, he would head straight for the post-card rack and mail out a dozen. Maybe he'd find something sexy to send to Sigalow and Kralich. He'd even send one to Bob the Boob who was off in Israel on a fellowship from the Women's Club of Flushing. What a dork, Ricky thinks. Trust old Bob to land a fellowship from a *women's* club. They probably raised the money having little bake sales and giving a prize for the best *hamantashen*. And now the *putz* was going to Israel to become a goddamned *rabbi*.

Probably he figured he couldn't get laid anyway, so he might as well get paid for being celibate. And then he could marry some Jewish girl with a wig on her head and a mustache. All those religious girls had mustaches. He'd read somewhere that religious girls had to shave off their pubic hair and wear pussy-wigs called merkins. He began to laugh, to guffaw, in the streets of Paris. He saw a really beautiful woman in a leather jumpsuit getting out of a cab. She must have been six-feet tall. He gave her a nasty American look, the look of the ugly American. He flexed his feet and began to run. He knew what he'd write on all those postcards. Dear ______, Paris is a rip-off.

3

Bobby is in the Hadassah Hospital looking at the Chagall windows. He is standing in front of the window of the tribe of Zebulun. He reads from the little tourist pamphlet describing each of the windows: "And Moses proclaimed that Zebulun would 'suck of the abundance of the seas.' " He looks at the window: Two fish rubbing noses, two fish grazing gills, a marriage of water and salt and blood. The woman next to him blows her nose loudly. He looks at her. She is very pretty, though not in the American way. Not pretty like Lori—the girl from Atlanta he'd taken out—who looked like she served drinks for Braniff. Not pretty like Sophie, but closer to Sophie's look.

The woman was stuck there with no Kleenex. Bobby took out the linen handkerchief that had seen him through many a woman's crisis. The same *shmatte* handkerchief Sophie had soaked with the salt of her tears; the same rag Melanie had used to wipe his seed from her belly; the same innocent square Lori had used to blot her lipstick—Love That Damson. Bobby loved lipstick. It was just his luck to have reached puberty during the era of no lipstick . . . the bleached-out, lipless look of the sixties. . . . The girl with no Kleenex was walking away. "No!" he exclaimed.

"What?" She was no-nonsense. Her eyebrows were absurdly bushy. Bobby was charmed. This pretty girl had a Yiddish accent.

"You want to have some Nescafé?"

"I never touch coffee."

"You want to have some lemonade?" He gestured toward the door of the chapel.

"One lemonade can't hurt." He took her arm. She smelled like Europe. No American girl smelled this way. He thought of his mother's mother,

Runia. The silk kerchiefs she wrapped around her blue-veined throat; her Persian lamb coat, the loose powder spraying her dresser. The dainty doilies that covered the arms of her dignified *Europaïsche* armchairs.

"Ach, there's a line," the girl sighed as they entered the cafeteria.

"Don't worry," Bobby said. "I'll wait in line. You sit and rest." There was something ageless about this girl. Probably in real life she was only twenty-five, and yet she inspired in Bobby an appreciation he preserved for older women. One lemonade can't hurt. Waiting with the tourists and the occasional native Israeli, these words made Bobby smile. One lemonade can't hurt. How many lemonades *did* it take to hurt a sturdy girl like this? A girl with the faint whiff of Europe: Bucharest, Budapest, Buchenwald, Berlin. . . . A girl born forcibly wise, her flesh burnished by history; a girl who didn't smile much, who blew her nose shamelessly, proudly—as if it were the *shofar*.

Melanie can't believe it, but Danny has said he loves her. No one had said he loved her since Ricky except for Bobby. And what good had it done her to be Bobby's side dish? A small fluted paper cup filled with macaroni salad. A side dish of spaghetti while everyone else is devouring prime rib.

For the first time she felt really angry at Bobby. That crypto-misogynist, that crypto-pseudo-philosophy major. She'd only given him about ten thousand blow jobs in a row, when all he'd been thinking about was Sophie the entire time. Well she was sick of them both. Bobby was off in Israel becoming a rabbi—what else? And Sophie was living in San Francisco with an unlisted phone. She'd written to Sophie three or four times, sent her copies of the newspaper, *Xantipi*. Sophie never wrote back. She sent only a Polaroid of herself in sunglasses in front of an apartment-house pool. Probably, Sophie thought women's liberation was lame. Well, what wasn't lame? Sophie's nihilism was beginning to seem rather childish. It was 1972 and Melanie was twenty years old. She'd already had an abortion, worked as a stripper, lost the only boyfriend she would ever love. She'd even had an affair with her best friend's boyfriend. Wasn't it time to believe in something?

She was glad she was in Boston, a columnist on a feminist paper. Just this morning she'd written a truly far-out article on fertile and infertile mucus. She'd discovered a pamphlet at the Health Food Co-op on Boylston, a slim green volume that would revolutionize birth control forever. Even blind women could use the mucus method. Her piece would be only the third article on the subject to appear ever in the feminist press.

She was glad she was here in Boston, carrying on the serious work that needed to be done. She was tired of being a laggard, a *bummekeh*, a wastrel. Let Sophie spend her life kissing penises and petting balls and trying to exploit men, so men couldn't exploit her first. Wasn't that what it was about—giving men hand jobs for a living, pulling their puds for nickels and dimes? Sophie had always acted like the joke was on the men, but wasn't the joke really on her? Didn't the men just pull up their zippers and sashay off into the night? Wasn't Sophie the one, after all, left holding the bag?

The men returned to wives with big hips and generous overbites. In the middle of the night, with the glow of the street lights balancing on the snow, these Curtises and Bos lie awake and remember Sophie's hands. In the bed, next to them, their wives give off the musk of sleep; powder blue contour sheets strain from the corners of the mattress. Underneath their bodies, mattress-protectors from Sears shine in their dull opacity. And underneath the mattress covers, the ticking is as regular as the heartbeats of their wives.

In the middle of the night they remember Sophie—her sad eyes, her nasal accent, the alarming dexterity of her hands.

Melanie hears someone at her door. It's Moonchild practicing mandolin in the drafty hallway.

"It bothers me that we can't reach her. *I'll* pay for a telephone if she can't afford one." Sid is rinsing the breakfast plates—French toast and rib-eye steak. A river of maple syrup and blood swirls into the sink.

"She *has* a phone. It's unlisted. No one has her number. Not even Melanie. What do you make of the picture?" Miriam examines a Polaroid Sophie sent by way of reply to their two-page letter. It had been hard to fill two pages—*two* yellow legal pages—with chatty words and no advice. What could she tell her daughter at this point? She was sure psychiatry had done Sophie no good. Miriam knew they had screwed her up—both of them, she and Sid.

She didn't blame Sid exclusively, though how many years had he been gone before he'd really left? The night of her miscarriage he'd been off at the Copa, pounding the table with little drumsticks they gave out for free. And there had been others before Dori. That crazy Anita's mother, Lee. And Gladys had said something in Berkeley about someone named Eve Giletti. Miriam remembered a baby-sitter they'd had in 1961. A tall redhead with bad teeth named Marci, or was it Darci? Sid was supposed to be showing her around the house—emergency phone numbers, extra bottles of soda. Miriam had come downstairs wearing a leopard-print jumper she'd bought that day in Orbach's. She'd taken time with her hair. She was only thirty-two, but she'd felt matronly next to these coltish baby-sitters of seventeen and less. Did they even have hair under their arms? (Yes, yes, Sid would have said. Orange fluff. Like cotton candy.) She'd come downstairs in ballet slippers and there on the stairs to their own rec room—their wreak room—Sid and Darci were kissing. Miriam had slammed the door, whacking the baby-sitter's ear.

Miriam couldn't believe what a nerd, what a clod, she had been in those days. She'd fetched an ice bag for the girl—they still had that same *farshtinkener* ice bag rotting upstairs in a bathroom drawer. And then she'd gone off with her cheater husband to a dinner dance at the JVFW, the Jewish Veterans of Foreign Wars. What could she have been thinking? Slurping down barley soup? Spooning up baby peas? It wasn't that she'd been smiling bravely, putting up some kind of front, patching her marriage for the public. She had merely pretended the kiss had never happened. As if she'd gone down to the basement landing, and seen, instead of her husband kissing the baby sitter, an apparition, hallucination, the visitation of a ghost.

She remembered the stacks of canned goods lining the way to the basement, food stockpiled to keep them eating during the Cuban Missile Crisis. She remembers how happy those stacks had made her, how secure their amount had made her feel. It would take thirty years to eat up all those canned carrots, those jarred beets, those tinned hams. Why, she could make a hundred baked zitis out of all those cans of sauce—Aunt Millie's from the sixties.

In reality the cans had dwindled remarkably after Sid left. Miriam remembers sending the kids over the bridge to visit their father and his new wife. Her skinny obedient children. Sophie wearing patent shoes, Brian's tender cowlick. They had survived the Missile Crisis only for Sid to abandon them for some skinny bluestocking of twenty-four. She'd seen those girls at Barnard in the forties. They'd wear the same cashmere sweater two weeks in a row, while insecure Jewish girls like herself changed their outfits every ten minutes. She remembers the trunk from her college days. She remembers her father's foreigner's lettering on the genuine leather ID tag he'd bought for her going away. Her Greek fisherman father, dead at forty-six—her sophomore year. Her mother dead two years later in a movie-house fire. Watching *One Way Street* with James Mason, Marta Toren, and Dan Duryea.

By the time she'd sung at Town Hall with an all-girls' choir, by the time she was graduated from Barnard Phi Beta Kappa, by the time she'd landed a husband—a dentist!—a blond Jew, Yale '50!—Old Eli!—she'd buried both her parents in a small cemetery run by the Sephardim of Northern Ohio.

She'd met Sid in the Catskills at a convention of college choral groups. It was spring of 1947, the air was sweet with apple blossoms, and still with the victory of the Allies. Their hotel was very modest compared to the splendor of Grossinger's down the road. Sid and his roommate, Jody Fox, another Jewish Yalie, had been at the center of everything. Jody was the handsome dark one, and Sid was the gorgeous blond one, and all the women at the convention were determined to have one of them.

They'd all gone over to Grossinger's for the entertainment. Warming up for the comic was a magician named Nick Romancer. Somehow, a tipsy Miriam had ended up the stooge in a trick. He'd pulled a brassiere out of her blouse, a black brassiere with transparent cups. No one had seen such a daring brassiere in 1947. How innocent she had been. How susceptible to Sid. One of the girls who went to Vassar had told her Sid was a famous Lothario, a smooth-talking seducer who'd made every Jewish girl in the class of '49. Big deal, she wasn't impressed by this Sidney Spivack. God, they even called him Sid the Kid.

She thought his hair was too long, she thought his gut was a little soft. She though his tenor was only this side of so-so. When he came to her room in the Gold Mountain at three in the morning, she was fully dressed and reading—of all things—Bertrand Russell's *Marriage and Morals*. She'd come to the door remarkably groomed and perky for 3:00 A.M. She'd been lost in Lord Russell, oblivious to the romantic tendencies of their setting. The apple blossoms in the wind, unchaperoned youth after the war, a supernumerary black brassiere pulled out of her sweater by a swarthy magician named Nick Romancer.

"Can I help you?" she'd whispered. In the next bed Lily Shnee was smiling smugly in her sleep.

Sid had laughed drunkenly and shrugged his arms. "The apple blossoms are falling," he'd said.

"And what do you propose I do? Make applesauce?" Miriam had said.

He'd laughed and kissed her lightly then, lightly on the shoulder. No one had ever kissed her on the shoulder before. The convention was ending the next day and Sid was determined to have her by check-out nine hours later. This smart dignified brunette girl reading Bertrand Russell.

"You're very funny," Sid had said.

"Maybe Lily could make room for you in *her* schedule," Miriam had said. She gestured to her sleeping roommate. She realized she was milking it. He shook his head. This girl was tough.

"Do you want to have breakfast?" Sid had asked.

"By the time I finish this chapter and do my exercises and go to sleep and have a dream and wake up and take a shower . . ."

"I meant right now," he said thickly.

"You seem to have had enough breakfast for one night," she'd said, smiling. She knew she was losing ground. If she didn't close the door right now . . .

"There's a coffee shop open across the road."

How much harm could be done at a coffee shop at 3:00 A.M.? No one she knew had lost her virginity in a coffee shop. She'd put aside her Bertrand Russell and gathered up Lily's shawl. She let the big shot take her arm and together they'd walked across the road. In the distance she thought she heard the sounds of Tommy Dorsey or Harry James—the rich people laughing and clicking ice. He'd been right about one thing—the apple blossoms were surely falling. The breezes were wild with delicate petals. McIntosh. Wealthy. Delicious. Winesap. Rome Beauty. Grimes Golden. Northern Spy.

"She looks okay," Sid says, picking up the snapshot of Sophie.

"Who?" asks Miriam.

"Your *daughter*," Sid says, his fleshy arm rummaging in the fruit bowl. "What were you thinking, Mim?" Sid bites into an apple. "These apples are old." He makes a face.

"Older than you know."

4

Bobby receives a letter from Sophie at American Express in Jerusalem. He savors the unopened envelope. Inside is an instant photograph, with not so much as her name, or "love." He goes to the Biblical Zoo, the envelope shifting in his pocket. He hadn't heard from her since Christmas. She'd quit her job at the head shop, then moved to San Francisco and an unlisted phone. Probably she was back with her Nazi boyfriend. He'd suspected she'd been having an affair even before that. Maybe with Luc, Bobby's French roommate. Maybe with a customer who'd wandered into the head shop to buy a carton of Sex Trip—this special sex cream he'd once found, snooping around in her knapsack.

He'd come home one day from Saturday morning services when she was staying with him. He'd planned to take her to the beach at San Gregorio and have a talk. He'd planned to make the kind of sandwiches they used to make as their special treat: avocado, smoked turkey, lettuce, tomatoes, good bacon.

Sophie had gotten really pissed off when he'd decided to become kosher—the bacon had been his concession. To show he was still reasonable, to show he was willing to give up even his principles for her. He'd found a note instead saying she had to break off with him for good. There had been no explanation. One day she evaporated.

A few days later he'd called her apartment in Menlo Park and the telephone was disconnected. He'd driven over, and by the time he arrived, a whole family was living in the two-room apartment that had belonged to Sophie only days before. The new family spoke no English except for a little boy, maybe three years old. "Sophie Spivack. So-fee," he'd said to the little boy. The boy had giggled as if the whole thing were a joke.

He bought a lemonade from the concession and some crackers to feed the goats. Even these goats are Jewish, he thought, smiling at them. *Landsleit*. And then he felt the pleasure of tears. He took out the linen handkerchief he'd given to that Yiddish girl in the Hadassah Hospital. Her name was Sheva Grunig. He'd written her phone number on his wrist, an affectation he'd picked up in high school. It used to drive his mother crazy. She'd leave his room muttering about his death by ink poisoning. He remembered the look on Sheva's face when he wrote her number on his wrist. . . .

They'd sat in the cafeteria, drinking lemonade, and Sheva had asked him to bring her back a little sandwich, nothing special. Nothing shy about Sheva. He'd gotten back on the line and picked her out a sandwich filled with *baba ghanouj*. She'd examined the bread carefully; she'd sniffed the eggplant suspiciously. What could be more kosher than the Hadassah Hospital cafeteria? Her peasant directness attracted and put Bobby off, at once. He'd never seen a woman so young exhibit so much caution and brashness. The way she'd blown her nose, as if she were making an announcement. The way she'd taken off her shoes in the cafeteria. No American girl would have taken off her shoes and rubbed her feet in public—groaning. In a cafeteria, mind you, groaning with mixed discomfort and pleasure. He supposed it was her fierceness, her inelegance, that turned him on. Her sturdy, solid, peasant ways.

Bobby looks up and sees a camel nursing its baby. He looks at his wrist, her number's still there. (02) 222537. He holds a telephone token in his fist. He's tired, he wants to go home. For now home's a shared room in the Beit Atid Hostel with three guys he doesn't know. You're not even allowed in your room till the hostel reopens at 5:00. He can't decide whether to call Sheva and invite her to dinner. Why does he feel so much would depend upon one dinner? She's probably twenty-five or so, she's probably looking for a husband. She probably doesn't have one casual bone in her body. If he showed up at her door, a rabbi would probably answer his knock and he'd spend the rest of their first date answering the rabbi's questions: Was he acquainted with the laws governing ritual purity? What does the following mean in the *Baba Mezi'a*: "Thy wife is short, so bend down and consult her"? Why did Spinoza receive the sentence of *herem*?

After the rabbi was through with him, they'd give him a meal of soup and bread, or maybe pottage—whatever that was. He'd eat his supper with her great-uncles, smelly old men in ancient clothes. The women would serve them, then eat alone— cackling together in the kitchen. The funny thing was he liked this fantasy date he'd imagined. The evening would end with slivovitz and maybe, a short impassioned *kazatska*.

5

Dori has been released from Payne Whitney and lives downtown on Thirteenth Street. She's still married to Sid legally. From time to time he visited her in the hospital. She hadn't minded his visits. He'd sat there in his tight jeans and faded Mexican wedding shirt, staring at her, or staring past her. If she'd had the strength, or the wit, to ask him what he was thinking about, and he had told her the truth, she would have realized he thought about tax shelters; a jazz combo he hoped to start with other dentists; even Miriam, his real wife, whom he had never understood.

It wasn't that he felt nothing for Dori. He felt guilty for one thing. When he'd met her, her whole life had stretched dazzlingly before her. She was twenty-four and beautiful. Beautiful? Not exactly. But classy and elegant. Her butt was small and hard as a rock. Her butt was the hardest live thing he had ever felt. She was the only Episcopalian girl in the world to have a nose job. Was that why he'd fallen for her? He'd seen a photograph of her before the nose job and she'd looked exactly, but completely, the same. In the photograph she was riding a horse the color of fresh rust. Even during his days at Yale, he'd never fantasized that such a girl could be his. Thighs that smelled of saddles and horses. A girl who could have modeled Patagonia walking shorts for L.L. Bean. What could he offer such a girl? A forty-year-old dentist who made an okay, but not great, living? And what could money mean to her who was related to robber barons?

In the beginning he'd been afraid of her—afraid of her genealogy, her worldliness, her sweaters. When they were first married, he used to go through her drawers and feel her sweaters. He'd never felt anything as soft as her sweaters, as hard as her smooth Yankee butt.

The worst thing he'd ever done was not to abandon his children and wife, but to do so so heartlessly. He remembered the night he'd come home from the Copa and Miriam was bleeding all over the breakfast nook, a bottle of Chivas empty beside her. She had waited for him, bleeding alone. She hadn't even called the doctor. Boy, had he been pissed! She didn't do it to make him feel guilty. She'd been too drunk to dial the doctor's number, too drunk to deal with this fresh death slipping down her legs.

Sid hadn't known it was a baby until he heard that word—*miscarriage*. As euphemisms go, it wasn't too bad, he thought. He pictured a baby carriage, the old-fashioned sort with a hood, gray-blue. He imagined the layers of netting and lace, layers of ribbon and eyelet and silk. In the depths of the carriage, a baby goo-ed and gaa-ed. Next to this carriage there stood another, a doppelgänger carriage, rusted and broken-down. Instead of lace, there were spider webs; instead of flannels, mold and moss. The carriage was filled to the top with blood.

Sid shakes his head like a dog. He is staring into the face of Dori—his second, his legal wife. Two miscarriages his seed had spawned; two misfirings his gun had fired. He blames himself—a failure of manliness. If he hadn't been such a middle-aged fool, he wouldn't have left his elegant wife for a simple girl. And he was sure the psychiatrists blamed him for what had become of his children. Brian was uncommunicative, sullen, an utter loner; Sophie had said he never went out with girls or had any fun. When Brian wasn't working, he sat and stared out the window. The only person he'd ever liked was Sophie. And Sophie—what could he say? If he thought about her he got sick. He felt as though the lid of a can, the corrugated lid of a can, were buried within his heart. He bled slowly and painfully; the jagged metal festering in his heart.

His own daughter. He remembered the pale ballet shoes hanging over her canopy bed. At least he'd given her canopies and ballet lessons before he'd abandoned her. He remembered how much she'd adored him. How she'd loved to come to his office and sit in the magical dentist's chair. She'd played spaceship in his office. Alan Shepard and John Glenn. She'd loved even the special sinks shooting water in helical jets. . . .

His daughter was lost to him. He knew that Bob Buchman was right. "Your daughter's a prostitute, sir." He'd never forget those words. At least the boy seemed to love her. At least the boy had been polite. "Your daughter's a prostitute, *sir*."

Miriam had met him years ago when he and Sophie had gone off to the Big Apple on their first date. Miriam had offered to make the boy eggs. Sid had never met him.

He stares at Dori, his legal wife, and she stares back at him. He hasn't said anything in half an hour. How could he ever explain to her that it wasn't her fault? That he's the *shmuck*, not her. "Dori . . . ," he says, "it's not your fault. You're only thirty-three. Big deal. I'll be fifty soon. Fifty. The big five-O. Don't you understand that . . . I don't know how to say it, honey. But life's a trick. Get it? Life's a joke, get it?" Sid the Kid starts to cry. "I guess nobody gets it. Life's a joke that no one gets. A shaggy-dog joke." He takes her raw-knuckled hand into his own paw. He kisses the place where their knuckles meet. "Here's the church and here's the steeple . . . Open it up and here's the people. . . ."

Now she was out of Payne Whitney. And bound to find someone else. Someone more worthy . . . anyone was worthier than he.

6

Brian receives a letter from Sophie. It's been a long time since he's heard from her. He doesn't open the letter, but saves it for his lunch break. He puts it in his metal lunchbox and clips the buckles closed. He wonders if his thermos will spill and soak the letter with iced tea. He made iced tea out of sticks and stems of leftover marijuana. It doesn't actually get you high, but it's better than nothing. And besides, he was worrying about getting high and ending up in the hospital minus his dingus. Last week on this same job, some joker named Tip had brought a thermos of grape juice spiked with LSD. The guy had ended up tearing his leg pretty seriously, and Brian was pissed that he'd endangered all of their lives.

For all of his nihilism, Brian was a great believer in fairness, in team spirit, honor among thieves. He'd refused to chip in for the lame present the rest of the guys had bought Tip. A hookah shaped like a giant twat. Brian was a puritan underneath it all, which was why his sister really got to him. She'd done it all, or so he thought—he hoped she hadn't really—but she'd understood nothing. If you descend into the gutter, wasn't it supposed to *mean* something? Weren't you supposed to see the shit transformed into flowers? Wasn't *that* the genius of the poets of the sewers? Baudelaire? Genet? The transformation of the sewer into a garden of pale fluorescence?

He is riding down the Peninsula in a pick-up truck. The other carpenters are smoking a number. To his right is the Pacific, the ocean of lunacy and peace. He hopes the thermos will not tilt and soak his letter from his sister. He remembers the soaked sandwiches of old; he remembers his sodden mother. He could never figure it out. The other kids at day camp, at school, always had model sandwiches. Tuna-fish sandwiches that never gushed, normal white bread from the bakery. Some of the mothers trimmed the crusts; some of the mothers cut the bread with cookie cutters into shapes. Heart-shaped sandwiches on Valentine's Day, log-cabin sandwiches on Lincoln's Birthday. A little bunch of chocolate chip cookies, cookies wrapped like exquisite sachets.

You don't even want to know what the Spivack kids brought for lunch. First of all, the bread was weird. Sometimes the halves didn't match. A piece of week-old raisin bread paired up with a heel of sour rye. Instead of tuna fish, weird mixtures—pieces of hot dog cut up and a smattering of ketchup. Peanut butter and cream cheese on a hoagie roll. If there was anything on the side, you can be sure it wasn't Oreos or even potato sticks. On a good day, a rotten peach; on a bad day, a jelly doughnut from the half-price bin. And everything soaked with juice. Brian expected fumes to escape when he unlatched his lunchbox at day camp. He'd lock himself in the latrine and open the box with no one looking. Sometimes he took a bite before he tossed it down the latrine. Often he would go hungry until Canteen opened at three. And then he would console himself, blowing his nickel on peanut logs, on Likamaid, on candy buttons.

How could his mother have expected him to grow up normal, a regular guy? He'd told Bev, his psychiatrist, about the lunches his mother had made, but she had thought he was only kidding. How could they've expected him to turn into a regular kid? While the other guys were trading halves of their identical lunches, he was locked in the latrine mailing his sandwich to the void. Creeps are made, not born. His parents had made him into a reject, a kootie kid, a pathetinoid. It wasn't his fault. He was doomed.

"I don't get it," one of the carpenters says.

"The guy was just circumcised. I told you, he'd just been circed. He wasn't allowed to get a hard-on. So the bitch nurse, naturally—"

Brian looks out the window. He sees a girl with long hair dancing alone on the beach. Brian feels sure she'd waved to him before running into the ocean. He tapped his lunchbox and heard its echo over the roaring of the sea. Inside was a message from his sister. For now that would have to be enough.

"Dick Cooper passed out," one of the first-year medical students giggles to another woman.

"It's always the macho creeps who pass out."

Ricky comes to in the nurses' lounge. Around him several women are laughing. And then it begins to come back to him. The young girl on the table. The shot of novocaine in her vagina. The resident selecting a dilator, then the twitch of certain pain, the sick look on the girl's face. . . . He thought of Melanie at fifteen, cruciform in Puerto Rico. Melanie offering up her insides to the dark-skinned doctor. He thought of his baby, his own child, diminished to nothing, a clot of dark blood.

He left the lounge where the nurses sat, smoking Benson & Hedges menthol; gossiping; *menstruating* for all he knew. Women. More and more, he was beginning to see that women were complicated, a species apart. He realized he would never understand them.

He tried to go about his business, attending anatomy classes, reading medical journals. *Obstetrics Today, Gynecological Newsletter*. He called up Kralich who was working at Back Bay Savings. Kralich suggested they go down to the Combat Zone. How about Pandora's Box where the drinks were cheap and the strippers were fat? For the first time in years, the idea of naked women exhausted Ricky. If anything, he wished to be spared another view of a woman's insides. Didn't they call them private parts for a reason?

One night Brian and this drummer he knows smoke heroin. A third guy drives them around in his '60 Valiant. Brian looks out the window. In the Mission in San Francisco, he sees a young whore who looks like Sophie. "Pull over," he tells the guy driving them around. By the time Brian convinces him to pull over, the whore is gone. They stop and have a drink in this bar. Other whores come in, but not Brian's sister. Later he wonders if the whole thing had been a mirage—or if he'd really seen her—laughing, beckoning to him.

7

Bobby and Sheva spend every evening together. She lives with a cousin a few years older than she. Her cousin is a nursery school teacher and Sheva works as a proofreader for the *Jerusalem Post.* Bobby is learning modern Hebrew in a class for foreigners and studying the Talmud at night. At ten o'clock, when the class is over, he goes to see Sheva and her cousin. They drink tea and discuss the politics of their adoptive country. Only the cousin, Orit, was born here.

Sheva's father, a Sabra, went to Germany to attend University. He survived Nordhausen to die in the DP camp where Sheva was born. Her mother went to Brooklyn where Sheva was brought up lower-middle-class in a mixed ethnic neighborhood. She attended a yeshiva for girls, although her mother was not religious. By the time she was sixteen she couldn't stand Brooklyn another minute. She had come to America at six, but she never felt it was her country. For one thing she hated American Jews. The girls talked about nonsense. Boys. Sex. Hairdos. Sweaters.

She preferred the girls of her own neighborhood—the Italian girls who quit school and worked as beauticians, the girls who came home from work and started cooking for their families. The Polish girls who handed over their pay checks to their mothers. They seemed closer to real life. They talked about real things. Relatives who were back in Poland watching Poland disappear. Relatives who lost everything to the Communist regime. Relatives forced to kneel in pigshit and declare their loyalty to the Communist Party. These were the lives, the stories, that Sheva understood. While the girls she knew wrote fan letters to TV stars and sent away to Modess for booklets explaining the facts of life, these girls sent money to distant cousins starving in the Ukraine.

Sheva listened, but never told her own story, her own history. The father who impregnated her mother, then died before she was born. The grandmother dead on the train to Treblinka. The young uncle—the beautiful boy named Asher, the family's bright hope—who'd died in the final days of the Warsaw Ghetto Uprising. A comrade of Asher had written to Sheva's mother. Asher had died a hero's death, perishing of dysentery in the sewers under the ghetto. The Nazis had burned out the ghetto building by building. The survivors had entered the sewers, swimming through excrement to the Aryan side. Uncle Asher had died en route.

As a child Sheva had built a whole mythology about Asher. Where the other girls in the Chaim Weizmann Day School fantasized about Ricky Nelson, Edd Byrnes, and Tony Dow, Sheva made up romances about Asher. Even if he'd lived to carry her off to the Promised Land, he would have been too old. By the time she turned fifteen, he would have been close to forty. And besides he was her *uncle*. . . . And yet she grew up dreaming of him. Dead, he never grew older. He would always be twenty years old—muscular, virile, moral and brave.

Once when she was ten years old, her mother's friend Vivi had asked her if she was going to marry Vivi's fat son Arthur when they both grew up. Very seriously, Sheva told Vivi what she had known since she'd first heard her uncle's name. "I'm going to marry Uncle Asher."

"You can't marry your own uncle," Vivi had said in Yiddish, laughing. "*Deine fetter*!"

"Uncle Asher is dead," said her mother. She remembered the look on her mother's face. Her mother looked really angry.

"He's not *really* dead," Sheva whispered. "The Nazis—" Her mother had slapped her face.

"Come, come," Vivi said. "It's your turn," Vivi had said. The two women were playing hearts. "*Luz das kind zein. Du sheest die levuneh*?"

Sheva ran off to the bedroom she and her mother shared. She lay down on the lumpy bed and looked out the window. Even though it was dead winter—February and raw—a cardinal appeared on the sill, a bird as red as the real ruby earrings Vivi always wore. Sheva knew the bird was a messenger from Uncle Asher, alive in Warsaw. The Nazis had him locked up in a prison cell. Even though he'd been in prison thirteen years, he looked pretty good.

Sheva had him dressed in a maroon smoking jacket and white slacks. He looked like Clark Gable. He smoked cigarettes and played the accordion and talked to the birds outside his window. The Birdman of Auschwitz. He wrote books that were smuggled out into the free world. He wrote of valiant Jewish soldiers who fought off the Nazis with magic swords. He wrote of Israel, the Promised Land; but his Israel had no deserts, no irrigation systems, no hospitals, no Arabs. His Israel looked like Knott's Berry Farm.

Later that night, her mother came in, holding a photograph of her father. She'd seen the photograph before. Her father squinting into the Teutonic sun. The picture had been taken in Germany a few months before the war. He'd mailed it to his mother in Palestine and Orit's mother had kept it safe during the war.

He was a student of German literature at the University of Freiburg and everyone thought he would be a poet. Sheva's mother had copies of one or two of his poems—poems he'd memorized, then written down in the DP camp in the months before his death. He'd tried at first to keep all his poems alive in memory. After a short while in the concentration camp, he could remember nothing. Even the names of his fellow inmates he could not etch in his brain. Later his brain would grow sharp again as the years of incarceration stretched on; but in the beginning he remembered nothing. The loss of the poems of a Jewish schoolboy struck him later as silly. He had lost nothing. He remembered a pile of photographs, a pile of photographs of their children the inmates were forced to surrender. A pile of photographs of pale children stirring in the breeze of the camp. He was lucky to have lost his words; speechlessness had become a blessing.

"Your father is dead," her mother says.

"I *know* he's dead," Sheva says.

"He's not hiding out somewhere in a barn or something. He's dead. His body is buried in Israel. Someday, when you're older, perhaps you can see the grave." Her mother's accent annoyed her. The way she rolled her Rs drove Sheva out of her mind. "Your father's brother Asher died of dysentery."

"He was a hero," Sheva said meekly. Would her mother slap her again?

"Yes. They were all heroes. Your father was a hero, too."

"But Uncle Asher *fought* in the Resistance. They told us all about it in school. The Warsaw Ghetto Uprising. All they had were a few homemade guns. The Nazis had cannons—and bombs."

"Your uncle died of dysentery. You know what dysentery is? Dysentery is diarrhea."

"Uncle Asher did *not* die of diarrhea," Sheva says. "Why, that's ridiculous," Sheva says.

"I'm afraid so. What did you think?"

"He was a hero," Sheva says. Her mother is the cruelest person she has ever met. She will leave her in Brooklyn. She will run away to Israel. Uncle Asher dead of diarrhea? Impossible. A stupid joke.

"They were all heroes. What do you think a hero *is*? What do you think happened in those camps? They wore costumes like Errol Flynn? They wore eye patches? What do you think? Don't they teach you *anything* in that yeshiva of yours?"

The girl lay crying in the bed. "I'm sorry, Sheva. I can't let you have these ideas. Not after everything that's happened to us. I can't let you believe it was like a fairy tale. Someday I'll give you books, your father's diary."

Sheva stops crying. "My father had a diary?" The idea seems crazy, absurd. Sheva imagines a little pink book, pink leatherette with a gold latch and key. *Dear Diary: Today I went ice-skating. That cute girl who sits next to me . . .* "My father had a diary?"

"After the war. After the camp. He was trying to write it all down. He wanted to write it down for *you*."

Her mother who never cries starts crying. "He very much wanted a little girl. Just like you," her mother says. "Your father would have been very proud."

"Mama, did Papa die of diarrhea, too?"

"No, no. Your father died of pneumonia. It's kind of like a bad cold."

Uncle Asher dies of diarrhea. Her father dies of a cold. Honestly, didn't anyone in her family know how to die a proper death? She was disgusted with all of them. But mostly with her mother.

8

Brian starts hanging out in the Mission nights. He's looking for his sister. He sits in the Cock's Tail drinking his fifth or sixth Dos Equis. A whore comes in and sits down beside him. He buys her a drink and asks her name. They leave the bar together. Brian hasn't made love to a woman in over a year. The whore's name is Dolly. She takes him to a flophouse. She wears a T shirt that says: *I like to boogie*. She smells a little pissy. She falls asleep while Brian is taking off his clothes. On the mirror a message is written in the dust: *Meado de la araña*. He leaves a twenty on the dresser and hitchhikes home across the Bay.

Melanie is busy with the feminist archives the women are organizing over in Allston. Tonight there's a slide show on battered women in the basement of a Methodist church. This weekend their whole collective was going over to Simmons for their Women's Weekend. There was going to be a panel on women's motorcycle gangs and Melanie thought she could get a column out of it. And yet the idea of meeting those women secretly terrifies her. Once she had gone with Moonchild and Moon's ex-lover, Christeen, to an all-women's bar on Mass. Ave. A lot of the women looked regular, but a few of them were really scary. One was wearing all leather and must have weighed three hundred pounds. Around her neck hung a bicycle chain; her lover was connected to her arm at the waist.

Melanie wished her friend Joanne Micheldorf wasn't off in Italy for Junior Year Abroad. She realized she didn't know any regular girls. How could she talk to Moonchild about her problems with Danny? Moonchild was convinced that men were psychically inferior. She wasn't a political lesbian; for Moon it was spiritual. She spent her time in her room, drinking weird herb teas—mixtures she would blend to gain heightened states of awareness. All her clothes were sensuous costumes: satin cloaks, velvet robes, abalone jewelry, kimonos made of raw silk.

She made her rent money reading the tarot on the Commons, casting the I Ching in Harvard Yard. In her room she practiced shiatsu, learned the fundaments of reflexology, practiced the recorder and the mandolin. She had the oddest record collection of anyone Melanie knew: Medieval Sephardic chants, Hungarian operas, the Everly Brothers, Nina Simone. Usually she listened to recordings of natural sounds: the oceans breaking, birds chirping; she even had a record of silence.

Everyone in the collective admired Moonchild, wanted Moonchild for her special friend. The other women argued brashly—politics, the effects of pornography, whether or not to vote at all in the upcoming election. ("Look at it this way," Nini had said over breakfast—chili-and-cream-cheese omelettes—"who would you rather have blowing the president? Eleanor McGovern or Pat Nixon?") Moonchild would be doing her Kegels and working on inner peace.

Melanie thought it was strange that of all the women around, Moonchild had picked Christeen. Christeen was as ordinary as mashed potatoes. A friendly backslapper of a girl, she was a hail-gal-well-met, a healthy freckle-face from Nebraska. She was also a little dull. The other women made fun of her, made her the target of cruel jokes. They couldn't stand the idea that Moonchild—their exotic, graceful gazelle—had chosen such a workhorse, a mule. When Christeen and Moonchild broke up, news traveled fast on the lesbian switchboard. Deliveries of flowers came to their tumble-down house so often in those first weeks of Moon's independence, they learned to recognize the delivery boy's knock. Moonchild remained independent. She had been "very close" to Christeen and claimed she simply wasn't ready to open up to other souls.

Melanie was glad her next-door neighbor had so much free time. They'd spend hours in Moon's room, listening to Gregorian chants, drinking bright-colored teas, painting their toenails with rainbows. Even though she felt reluctant to bring up Danny with Moon, her neighbor's company was refreshing. The other women in the house were noisy and combative. Visiting with Moonchild was like a month in the country.

9

Bobby and Sheva go to see Dirty Harry. To show their enthusiasm, the audience throws soda bottles at the screen. "I don't understand you Americans," she says, then goes outside to wait in the lobby.

Bobby watches a few more minutes, then comes looking for her. "You're an American too," he says.

"Naturalized," she says. "And I'm going to keep dual citizenship. After what my parents went through, I can't imagine giving up American papers. Can you?"

American papers. She sounds like someone out of a movie from the 1940s. Ingrid Bergman or Lauren Bacall. "Did you ever see *Casablanca*?" he asks.

"Sure, sure," Sheva says. "Who didn't?"

"You remind me of her. Ingrid Bergman."

"Why? Because she has an accent? Because you think of me as exotic?"

"It's a compliment, you know." He leads her into a café. She orders *mitz*—grapefruit juice; he orders rosé from the Carmel Valley.

"You Americans and your violence." He smiles at her. He does not love her. He admires her courage, her forthrightness, but he doesn't love her. Why is it he can't turn affection and respect into love? Is it that she's too serious? He thought *he* was serious until he met her. She put serious on the map. She takes a bag of pumpkin seeds out of her embroidered bag and begins to split them with her teeth. She spits the seeds out the side of her mouth like a gangster's moll. "Explain to me," she says, "about Americans and violence. Explain to me about cowboys."

"Cowboys, hmm . . . I'm not sure I understand cowboys. *Goyisheh kop* . . . Lyndon Johnson is a cowboy."

"I mean real cowboys . . . like the Marlboro man."

"That's funny. That you think the Marlboro man is more real than a president." The waiter comes to take their order. They'd eaten dinner two hours before—Orit had made turkey cutlets. Bobby orders some pickled herring. Sheva orders a whole chicken in the pot with dumplings.

Two Israeli soldiers walk in. He's been in Israel a few months; he ought to be used to soldiers and guns. Yet Bobby looks up, freshly surprised. The soldiers are younger than he is—healthy teenagers wearing khakis and *yarmulkahs*. "You talk about Americans and violence . . . what about the Israelis?"

She shakes her head sadly, that superior sadness of the Israeli in the face of American naïveté. "These guns are a symbol *against* violence. Jewish guns," she says. "This is no country for American liberals. . . ."

"Jewish guns are *not* innocent. They fire bullets, don't they? They make holes, don't they?" Bobby slams down his fist. The sprightly rosé from the Carmel Valley spills all over the table. Sheva takes out her handkerchief, a pink bandana, and begins to wipe up the wine. That's what he likes about her, about her Israeli soul. The way she uses her own bandana to wipe up a public spill.

He remembers going to the *Mogen David* when he cut his hand in the middle of the night, wrapping a package. He remembers that everything was public. The patients had their own cubicles; they even had curtains; yet no one bothered to draw them. Everything was immediate: Old men holding their *kishkas* and moaning, babies wailing with high fevers, a teen-aged girl with a broken leg. Pain and the language of pain were a public concern in this country. This country built upon wailing and keening, this country built upon howling and prayer.

The waiter brings Sheva's soup, a serving big enough for a family of four. She lifts her spoon and digs in, not waiting for the broth to cool. An American would have blown on the spoon. This *proves* she is not American. There are vapors as dense as chimney smoke issuing forth from Sheva's bowl. The furnaces of Majdanek.

"Save me a *knaydl*," Bobby says. All of his women were good eaters.

It worries Miriam that Sophie only sends photographs. She'd been in California two months. She called Brian on the phone; Brian only had photographs, too. She would not answer anyone's letters.

She sent a telegram to Sophie's return address: URGENT. CALL YOUR MOTHER. And only a Polaroid had come back, Sophie smiling lyrically in front of a green dumpster. Miriam felt like one of those people in an ad in the *Village Voice*: DEBBIE MC INTOSH: CALL YOUR MOTHER. ALL IS FORGIVEN. YOUR OLD ROOM IS WAITING. WE LOVE YOU, MOM. She remembers the articles in the sixties: the runaways and the dopers, the trouble in Tompkins Square Park. The storefronts littered with Xeroxed photos of runaway girls. It was heartbreaking to pass those windows. You knew that half of the kids were dead. LAURIE BENSON. 13. Blue eyes. Light brown hair. 4′10″. Freckles. No distinguishing marks.

Ricky is still upset about the abortion. He keeps dreaming about death. Graveyards full of fetus bones, utility pails splashed with blood. It's Christmas Eve in Boston. He's invited to a tree-trimming party at one of the nurse's apartments. He imagines the scene so completely he feels he doesn't have to go. Cubes of Swiss cheese stuck with toothpicks. Four-dollar pink champagne. Holly Bicall, the hostess, will sidle up against him. He'll put his hand on her big ass. They'll start to make out in the kitchen. She'll start to huff and puff like a car. (He's never heard a woman warm up as automotively as Holly.) Then, when they're both turned on, she'll pull away from him and laugh. It's happened three times before. He doesn't understand why. In the last few months he's stopped trying to figure women out completely. The closer you get, the more mysterious they become.

A man is simple. All his mystery resides in his dork. He gets excited, his dork gets big. He gets bummed out, his dork gets small. That's all there is to it. Women are secretive and se*cre*tive. You never know what's going on inside their circuitous, farfetched bodies. Their concentricity was daunting. You couldn't see what they were feeling. You'd think they were feeling one thing; but always they were feeling something else.

Like take this woman Solange he used to screw a while back. Married chick. Her husband practically *owned* a refinery. While he was nailing her, this girl used to cry. At first he thought he was hurting her. He'd shrivel up and ask her what was wrong, should he fetch the Vaseline? He'd seen a tub of it big as the moon on her night table. Then the chick would be mad at him, mad at *him*—could you *plotz*?—because she was just about to come, to come like she'd never come before in her entire life—a double vaginal-clitoral orgasm with multiple after-rushes, and he'd pulled out at the wrong moment to talk about Vaseline.

How come she only threatened to have these extravaganza orgasms when he pulled out or lost his erection? How come she never had them all those times he kept it up for three hours at a clip? Once her husband had flown to Brazil on a business trip and they'd stayed in bed for two days. He must have made her seven times a day for two days. The girl had so many orgasms, Walt Disney had wanted to lease her as a ride.

It didn't pay to be generous, Ricky decided. After Solange, he'd decided no more Mr. Nice Guy. He was probably too *nice* to women, he should probably restrain himself.

He'd started screwing prostitutes. He hadn't intended it as a *policy* change or anything. He and Kralich had just fallen into it during their senior year. At first he'd thought they were just lazy. Kralich was a real slob. Going to a prostitute meant you could just be yourself, you didn't have to powder your balls. Just like that joke about masturbation—you didn't have to dress up.

They'd go down to the Combat Zone. Their favorite club was the Velvet Glove where the girls were fairly regular—cheap-looking, but normal. Waitressy kinds of normal girls. Fifteen dollars for a blow job, even less for a lay. You paid your money, you had your come. You didn't have to worry about your technique. The girls could be a little sardonic, but compared to regular girls, not bad. They'd look at you contemptuously—trust a girl to turn it around—they're the whore, but you're the sleaze. But compared to the wisecracking girls he knew, and he knew the real ball-crackers, the champs—the prostitutes were all right.

What had happened to innocence? Where were the sweet farmers' daughters he'd read about all his life? The girls who starred in dirty jokes, the virgin-girls who posed for *Playboy*? Where did you go to meet these girls? Platte River? Abilene? Suddenly all the girls in the world were cynical, psychologically damaged, bitter, pissed off. Was it Women's Lib that had done it? He remembered Lauren Small from Melanie's sorority. Women's Lib had done a real number on her. She used to spend her Saturdays gluing stickers to advertisements on the New York subways: A woman in a bathing suit, smoking a goddamned cigarette. *This ad insults women*. He wasn't a bit surprised. *Everything* insulted women.

Lauren had been a perfectly regular Jewish girl. She and Allen Goldwasser had had a perfectly normal relationship. He'd paid for *plenty* of her egg rolls, Ricky remembers, before she became a women's libber and went to consciousness-raising sessions where she complained about Allen's *shlang*. Well Lauren, you think you're so smart? Allen Goldwasser is making $700 a week as a stockbroker in Fort Lee, and you're probably selling macramé belts in Big Sur. Or maybe you've graduated to full-fledged dykedom by now, you twat. Congratulations, Lauren. Melanie always thought you had a certain lesbianic vibe. *Melanie*. He thought of Melanie. He remembered Melanie's satisfied face between his avid thighs; he remembered Melanie's long fingers. He used to tell her her hands were made especially to hold his prick. That used to drive her wild.

Melanie had been a very sexy girl. Why hadn't he realized it then? He'd gotten to Harvard, and suddenly he was surrounded by Protestant girls in camel's hair coats. Their coolness had turned him on, their aloofness. Melanie was always right there, waiting for him. She'd screw him on the dime. All he had to do was give her a minute's, a second's, notice. Melanie, take off your panties, I'll be there in four minutes. Melanie, spread your legs, I'll be there in four hours.

It had come like a revelation to him. The world was full of Protestant girls with nonchalant beavers. A Jewish girl you could make come by looking at her fiercely enough. Hadn't Henry Miller warned them of Jewish orgasms that lasted twelve hours?

When he'd first broken up with Melanie, he'd discovered Cat Crawford. Even her name gave him *frissons*. He remembers the look of her profile the time he'd first spotted her, leaning against a brick wall—cashmere, camel's hair, Oxford cloth, duck.

She came from San Marino, California. Her people—not her family—her *people*—had settled Catalina Island, and so they had called her Cat. He remembered trying to make her laugh on their first date. He realized these Wasp girls didn't understand his jokes. After five or six of his funniest lines, Cat would break down and crack a rusty smile. If he tickled her for an hour with an ostrich feather, he'd be lucky to get a tee-hee. That's rich, Dick, Cat would say. Dick. No more Ricky. Ricky was suburban, Jewish; Ricky was bourgeois. From now on it was Dick. "Hi there, Dick. How're the mater and pater faring? Good morning, Dick, old boy, how's your vicuña lining?"

After three dinners at Ferdinand's and the Iruna, he'd spent his whole book allowance for the second semester, and all he'd managed was casually to flick her left nipple. They'd have to sail to Portofino for the weekend before she would let him near her pussy. Cat's pussy. Meow. It drove him crazy. Then one afternoon he was sitting in Dunster, watching "Hollywood Squares" when suddenly she was naked beside him, grabbing for his *shvantz*.

When he broke up with Melanie he'd brought Cat with him. Otherwise, he was afraid, he wouldn't be able to do it. If Melanie saw him with Cat, she'd know it was really over. Now he regretted it. He remembered Cat in her Burberrys raincoat, her slouchy Bogart hat, her suede jeans from Florence. And Melanie in some hippie dress she'd shoplifted in the East Village—some *shmatte* Indian bedspread made into a dress.

He remembered the look of Melanie's dorm room. Her dorky roommate's side of the room all done up in Design Research. The funny thing was she'd decorated only her half of the room. Ricky remembered she'd hung one curtain on her side of the window.

Cat had slouched against the roommate's bulletin board. Tall girls never sat down, they preferred to slouch against walls. Ricky remembered the notices for registration, tours of the library, meetings of La Tavola Italiana. . . . Thinking back, he wanted to cry. How could he have come to despise her—his Melanie, his girlfriend, his babe?

The year was 1966. Sonny and Cher were singing "I Got You, Babe" over the airwaves. Cousin Brucie. Melanie's first pair of bell-bottoms from Gimbel's in the Garden State Plaza. At Hong Fu's in those long-gone days, you could buy a bowl of wonton soup, a side order of steamed rice and an egg roll for $1.10. Melly and he would go down there after school. They'd slurp their soup, holding hands; they'd kiss with wontons in their mouths. They'd trade wontons from tongue to tongue, the dough unwrapping soulfully between their lips. . . .

When he saw her in Palo Alto, at Bobby's insistence, the summer after they broke up, she looked really bad. In the space of seven months, Melanie had gone to hell. It was funny now that he thought of it; it was funny he was so hung up on strippers. And his own high school girlfriend, his own bourgeois Melly had turned into just that. He'd seen her about a year ago. She and another girl in Brigham's eating ice cream sundaes and laughing. They looked like they were having fun. He was walking by with some girl —maybe Solange—he couldn't remember. At the time he'd been growing a beard and Melanie hadn't recognized him at first. And then the laughter had left her face and an expression of shock had taken over. He remembered the O her mouth had made, the terrible vacant O of her mouth.

He called Information. There was no listing for Szasz, Melanie or Szasz, M. Girls were always doing that. Using their first initial. Didn't they realize any rapist using the telephone directory had already psyched them out? He called Student Information at B.U. It wasn't so hard—was it?—despite what everyone said, to recapture the past?

10

It's like a nightmare. One minute he's sitting in Lod Airport, innocently drinking *mitz*; the next minute he's kissing the greasy lips of his mother. She is talking about the food on the plane. "Kosher, Posher. It doesn't mean they have to feed you the garbage, does it?" Next to his own mother, Aunt Layeh is a sight for sore eyes. The sisters are wearing matching outfits—turquoise knit suits with white shells underneath. His mother is wearing a giant *chai* around her neck. Just in case anyone has doubts about her religious preference. Aunt Layeh is wearing her Phi Beta Kappa key. He looks down at his mother's sandals; her engorged toes depress Bobby.

"So how's my genius?" Rise asks, grabbing a hunk of Bobby's cheek. "How's my little yeshiva *bucher*?"

Aunt Layeh kisses him modestly on the forehead.

"Matching outfits?" Bobby asks, waiting for the taxi driver to give him a hand with the luggage.

"The colors of the Israeli flag. We wanted to give you a little thrill. You know, Bobby, you could still get your rabbinical degree, whatever it's called, and still go to law school. Not every rabbi needs his own congregation. Where is it written? Am I right?" She turns to the cabbie for confirmation, a beefy man in his forties.

Bobby laughs to himself. The driver is clearly an Arab.

"I bet lots of young men, like my son here, come to your beautiful country and study your Torah. It doesn't mean that every one of them has to become a rabbi. Am I right?" Rise nudges the cabdriver's arm. He smiles at her indulgently.

"You speak Yiddish?" Rise laughs. She is having a good time already. A country where everyone speaks Yiddish! All she needs is a deck of cards. " *Du redst Yiddish*?"

"Lady, I am a Moslem," the driver says.

"An Arab?" Bobby's mother says. "You're pulling my leg. An Arab?" She mouths the word for Layeh, beside her. She grabs Bobby's arm. *Yiddish* she spoke to an Arab. If she doesn't watch her step, she'll be tried as the next Ethel Rosenberg.

When they arrive at their hotel, Rise is still recovering. "The food on El Al is fit for pigs," she tells the woman beside her on line. "*Chozzerai* like I've never tasted. So where you from? I'm from Flushing. So, would you believe it, I'm still suffering from an indigestion, when my son over here, the rabbinical student—the genius—he gets me an Arab cabdriver. . . . An *emeser* Arab."

Brian leaves Tony's Bar and Grill. Tonight he's had too much to drink. Six bourbon and sodas. Rotgut bourbon. He wishes he knew a regular girl, a girl he could just call up and say, Can I come over? Do you need anything from the 7-11? Cat food? Cremora? A box of Kotex? He could just go over there and they'd watch Johnny Carson or reruns of "Dragnet." He'd bring a few reefers. Maybe they wouldn't make love. It didn't matter. He wanted to see a girl in her bathrobe. He wanted to run his hand across the top of her dresser. Little baskets of potpourri, antique antimacassars, different colors of make-up. He wanted to sit with her in the morning and listen to the weather report on the radio: It's forty-two degrees at Oakland Airport; the barometer is falling. . . .

Brian finds his yellow Fiat parked on Dolores Street. He turns the key in the ignition; he accelerates swiftly into the night. On the tapedeck is *Die Fledermaus*.

Sophie goes into Tony's Bar and Grill. Tad Pfahl sits down beside her. He orders a shot of Jack Daniel's. "Jack," he tells the bartender. He downs the whiskey in one gulp. "I'd better go," he says.

"Stay," says Sophie.

"If I stay, there's no point." He looks around to see who's there.

"Stay," Sophie says. She is sitting on the same stool Brian sat on ten minutes earlier. She doesn't notice the stool is warm, tingling with his aura. She's been snorting a mixture of coke and heroin the pusher calls Boy and Girl.

Tad gives her a pat on the shoulder. It is one o'clock in the morning and the bar will be open a while. She doesn't feel like working. She's high and not in the mood to be alone.

Tad is gone a few minutes when a guy comes up to her and asks her what she wants to drink. Is she supposed to know this guy or what? She can't remember if she'd dated him before.

"I said, do you want something to drink?"

She notices his front teeth are gold. She's pretty sure she's not supposed to know his name.

"Hmm?"

"A drink?"

"No," she says. She shakes her head. She smiles sweetly. Is she supposed to know him?

"Ginger ale?" he asks her. "How about a Shirley Temple?" He grazes his knuckles against her cheek.

"Shirley Temple?" She starts to laugh. She *knows* who Shirley Temple is. The Little Princess. Little Miss Marker. Where's Tad? Is she supposed to laugh? "Shirley Temple."

The trick orders a Shirley Temple. The bartender gives him a dirty look. What is this? A big joke? He pours grenadine into ginger ale and Sophie gasps as the soda turns pink. For a second she'd thought it was blood.

Melanie sees the message that Ricky Cooper called. She's sure it's a practical joke, but who would even know Ricky's name? The only person who could have done it was Sophie. She hadn't heard from Sophie in months. Once in a while a Polaroid picture would come in the mail. These weird pictures—they were spooky. There was something staged about them. As if Sophie had been abducted and her kidnappers had posed her at gun point, smiling against a picket fence.

"Ricky Cooper" had left no message. She knew the real Ricky was in med school just a few blocks away. Bobby had told her. She was surprised he'd gotten in. Compared to the other guys she knew who'd gone to Harvard, Ricky really wasn't too bright. She wondered why Harvard kept taking him while she would be stuck forever at Boston University with the rest of the middle class. If Long Island and New Jersey seceded from the Union, B.U. would have to close its doors in three days.

But who cared if Ricky went to a male-chauvinist racist sexist imperialist university and became an overpaid, overweight quack? Why should *her* consciousness be polluted with his karma? Moonchild would tell her to transcend her envy and her rage. Who was he to call her up out of nowhere and mess up her head with memories? Hadn't she forsaken his memory when she'd moved into a feminist collective? Wasn't each word she wrote another stake buried in his misogynist's black heart?

Against her will, against her judgment, she remembered anyway the night of Ricky's junior prom. The Mexican dress from Fred Leighton's. Dinner at The Old Salt. The orchid corsage she'd meant to preserve in her mother's freezer. The orchid was crushed when Ricky straddled her in the back seat of his parents' Chevy. Ricky had parked the car on a side street around the corner from Melanie's house. Sophie's coaching had promised more. Sophie had read her descriptions of sex that had prepared Melanie for Valentino, for Jim Morrison, for Aly Khan. Instead there was a spot of blood on her Mexican wedding dress, her left leg had fallen asleep, and Ricky was staring down at her, his eyes glazed, winking like a big shot.

She started to cry in his arms and he soothed her by singing "I Got You, Babe." And then he'd listened patiently, cheerfully even, as she'd described their wedding: The color scheme of off-white and peach, the appetizer of rumaki, the little papier-mâché couple waltzing across the marzipan ice.

By the time they made love a second time and planned their engagement party and the *bris* of their first-born son, it was three o'clock in the morning in June and the streets of Hudson Heights were as quiet as the grave. When she'd gone to retrieve her orchid, it sat no longer on the rear hump where she'd placed it for safekeeping. She found a confetti of orchid sprinkled across the back seat, sifting into the carpet. Twice in one night she had been deflowered.

Ricky promised her other orchids, other proms, other nights like this night —fourteen and madly in love. She'd taken a fistful of petals and tossed them out the window and into the night. She'd felt like Zelda Fitzgerald or Isadora Duncan, a woman of large gestures. She'd put her key into the lock of her parents' sturdy front door and blown her boyfriend, her *lover*, a kiss. Ricky watched her enter the house. Yahoo, he said. He'd finally gotten inside her. Before he backed out of the driveway, he picked up a piece of the orchid she'd overlooked and stuck it in the ashtray.

New Year's Eve, 1972. Auld Lang Syne. Should old acquaintance be forgot . . . Tad Pfahl has arranged a gig for Sophie in Marin County. Tad is at the party with a beautiful physics professor. The other guests are tax consultants, marijuana farmers, professors, drug lawyers, salesmen of saunas and jacuzzis. There's a Bang & Olufsen stereo playing bootleg Rolling Stones, pâté with real truffles, a Revere sugar bowl filled with cocaine. There's live entertainment—a short girl with curly hair and a tattoo on her thigh. She looks a little out of it and she's not a very good dancer, but Tad says she'll do whatever you want.

Ricky gets Melanie on the phone. She hangs up on him twice. He's at a really depressing party. He wants to see her. How come she's home alone on New Year's Eve? Couldn't she get a date? He wants to talk to her. Just talk. He tries to tell her over the phone about that girl's abortion, how he fainted, how he finally understands what she's been through. How bad he feels about everything—the abortion, bringing Cat to her dorm room. He tells her how he saw her, just a year or so ago, eating a sundae in Harvard Square. Butterscotch syrup on her chin. He tells her he's going through changes. That women didn't like him. That she was really the only girl he'd ever known who'd *liked* him. He knew he had sex appeal, but none of them ever *liked* him. Why did she think girls didn't like him?

"I can't handle this," Melanie said.

He began to sing to her. "I Got You, Babe." Then the Turtles—"Happy Together." All she could do was hang up, then leave the phone off the hook. She *had* been invited to a party. Danny had asked her to a party and so had all the women. She wasn't in the mood for a party. She'd planned to watch a Jimmy Stewart movie on television and make herself rumaki. She'd just changed into her robe and started to fry up some bacon when Ricky Cooper—Ricky Cooper!—had called her up and blown her mind.

No one would understand. Except for Sophie. She couldn't tell the women in the house; not even Moonchild would understand the longing she sometimes felt for Ricky's arms, his sideburns, his big hands. Ricky was a bastard, the worst sort of macho pig. He'd humiliated her, he'd pissed on her heart, he was going to be a pig doctor with a Harvard diploma on his wall. Harvard Medical School. Pen and ink drawings of Widener Library hanging in the waiting room. The waiting room. The words made her tremble. The words had not lost their magic, despite her political transformation. Despite her column in the feminist press, despite her reading of Simone de Beauvoir, of Shulamith Firestone, of Robin Morgan; despite the words of Sojourner Truth—Ain't I a woman?—and Ti-Grace Atkinson, she could not overcome her pleasure in that mantra: Waiting room.

He had once been hers, this doctor-to-be, this Jewish prince with an attitude. She had been his lady-in-waiting, wife-in-waiting, mother-in-waiting to his waiting heirs. But what was it finally she had been waiting for? Moonchild would tell her it was maya, the veil of illusion. She wanted a Jewish doctor-husband because she thought he would heal her. It was only a metaphor, Moonchild would say, for Melanie's hunger to be healed. The waiting room was an emblem for Lourdes, it was the Jewish Lourdes.

She hated herself. It was one thing to sneak eye liner, to shave her legs on the sly and pretend she wasn't hairy. It was quite another to remain in love with an enemy of the people, to long secretly for marriage and the bourgeois thump of the mail on the stoop: the fall catalogues from Bendel's and Saks, the P.T.A. newsletter, the *Harvard Magazine*, the *New Yorker* and *Parents*. She realized she was politically hopeless, her whole feminist commitment a pathetic charade. She was about as deep as the toilet bowl, she decided, and just as serious.

She wished she had gone to a party. Danny's party would have been more fun than the all-women's party. These events always depressed her. Women sitting around with their blouses unbuttoned. Women kissing and dry-humping, rolling around on the floor. Women cultivating mustaches—and even beards. Women doing "rituals" with feathers and drums and silk scarves and listening to Laura Nyro. She felt trapped in both worlds. She feared she wasn't really a feminist; she'd promised herself she'd never be tricked by heterosexual love again. Danny was gentle and soft . . . she knew she could never fall in love with him. In the meantime he offered her friendship, marijuana, a couple of laughs. She'd never fall in love with him or understand his soul.

The other women respected her because she had been a stripper—that was the funny part. The political types admired anyone who was black or poor, anyone who had been in jail or a mental hospital, anyone who had been a criminal, a prostitute, a bum. They saw the whore as revolutionary, which Melanie thought was silly—bourgeois romantics glorifying the debased. What did she know that they didn't, except that they were all wrong?

She'd shaken her nipples for strangers; she'd dressed up in weird costumes; she'd let smelly old men stick five-dollar bills down her crotch. What was the lesson in it? That degradation was a state of mind? That even a pampered New Jersey girl with a trust fund could grow up to be a whore? And what had she learned from her shrink in Passaic Pines, except how to get the drugs she wanted? Valium, Demerol, Dalmane, Meprobamate. And waiting for an appointment in the clinic, she'd learned the names of all the characters on "All My Children."

Moonchild came in on tiptoes wearing a silver kimono, glitter in her hair. On her arm was a black woman who must have weighed in at two hundred. Her head was completely shaved.

"This is Pammy," Moonchild said. "You're not eating nitrates *again*? This is Melanie, one of my housemates."

"Happy New Year," Pammy said.

"Happy New Year," said Melanie.

11

Sid knew they were going to play Switch at the New Year's Eve Party, and as he dressed he took extra care. Powdering his genitals with Miriam's French powder, putting on turquoise bikini underwear. When he saw the state of Miriam's underclothes, he wanted to tell her to wear something nicer. He'd bought her a luscious red camisole for the previous Valentine's Day. How could he get her to put it on without letting his secret slip? If he told her he knew what Morty and Diana were planning, there was a chance she'd want to stay home, and he couldn't risk it.

So he said nothing about the dingy waist-high panties she'd bought in the Food Fair for eighty-nine cents, nothing about the gray brassiere that had taken one tour too many through their ancient washer. He watched her slip a white jersey dress over her lithe body. Her figure was still terrific. In the forties she'd been too thin, too small-breasted. For the seventies, she was perfect.

"Not bad for forty-four," Sid wolf-whistles. He rubs her butt with the palm of his hand. He remembers Dori's hard ass. Was Miriam's any flabbier? Was the ass always leaner on the other side? He wishes he could tell her his pun.

Brian doesn't leave his apartment. He stays home and watches television. On PBS is *Die Fledermaus*, performed by the Metropolitan Opera. He turns up the sound to full volume. He wishes he had a color TV. He wishes he had a girlfriend.

He remembers his mother, Miriam, lying on the soiled carpet, her ears plugged with headphones, a Flintstones giveaway glass of Chivas by her side. He'd wanted to listen with her. He'd developed a taste for opera in spite of himself. Probably because his mother had played opera all through her pregnancy. *Their* pregnancy. His and hers. It was probably all they had ever shared, that watery friendship in the womb. Later she had played opera for him in his nursery. His father had wanted to play show tunes, "South Pacific," and "Let 'Em Eat Cake," but his mother wouldn't allow it.

And then, and then, what? What had happened? When had she stopped playing opera for him? When had she simply plugged in her headphones, abandoning him to the culture, to Lawrence Welk and Elvis, to Frank Sinatra and Patti Page? He hoped his mother was home tonight watching the same broadcast, listening as Eisenstein fell in love with his own wife. Just as Sid, his dumb father, had fallen back in love with her. What did his parents know about love? Whatever else you could say about them, the Spivacks were lousy at love.

Sid looks up into the Kates' mirrored ceiling. His erection points oddly to the side. Somewhere he'd read about the decline of the angle of erection. *Cosmopolitan*? In a few years he'd be lucky if his penis could manage twenty degrees.

Diana Kates is in the powder room whistling "The Long and Winding Road." She's been in there twenty minutes. Already, two other couples have knocked on the bedroom door. When she comes out, he is holding his penis foolishly in his left hand and watching television. A broadcast of *Die Fledermaus* straight from the Met. He wonders if Miriam knows it's on. He wonders who she's with right now. What does Macy's do the day after the Parade? Die Fledermaus.

Diana is wearing a cranberry-colored nightgown. Her blonde hair is piled professionally on top of her head; her eyelids are shadowed with silver. He kisses her swany neck. He runs the tip of his finger down the length of her bumpy nose. He feels a sudden rush in his bladder. The major transformation he's discovered in approaching fifty is the greater urgency of Nature's call. He pulls himself up from the bed and goes into the bathroom. He watches the urine leave his body, the extravagance of his water. From the next room come the gay notes of "Trink Champagne." Rarely has he felt so mortal. 1972. He remembers his father who used to announce every New Year's Eve: "1933—I'm glad it's over with already. 1933—worst year of my life. 1934—gone. I'm glad it's over. Worst year of my life."

He looks into the medicine chest. Glycerine suppositories. Neomycin. A bottle of Liquid Chin Strap. From the next room, the twins' bedroom, he hears Lee Freund giggling at one of Herbie Brockelman's jokes. *I* tell much better jokes, Sid thinks. Brockelman's strictly an amateur. He wonders if he'll get to see Lee without her clothes. Tonight.

Bobby holds Sheva in his arms. "Your mother is a bitch," she says. "I thought *my* mother was a bitch; but compared to Rise, my mother's a saint. A *tzaddik*," Sheva says.

"I think she was trying to help you," Bobby lies. "She probably went into fifteen drugstores before she found it. It doesn't strike me as a very Israeli product somehow."

"Why do you say that?" Sheva runs her finger along her mustache. It doesn't *feel* like a big deal. She'd never even *thought* of removing it.

"I don't know," Bobby says. "I guess I meant that Israeli women don't strike me as particularly vain."

"A lot of Israeli women are beautiful stunning girls," Sheva says. "As pretty as your American girls with their nail polish and their *halter tops*. Did you ever see those girls working in the fields at the *kibbutzim*? Wearing bikini bathing suits and straw hats from Bloomingdale's? Well, it's enough to make you sick," Sheva says. She starts to cry again. She throws the depilatory out the window onto Rehov Mekor Haim. "Tell me the truth," Sheva says. "Do you think I'm . . . too hairy?"

She *is* pretty hairy, Bobby thinks, though he's never really considered it. Her arms are as hairy as a boy's, and except for through the veil of stockings, he has never seen her legs. "I think you're beautiful," Bobby says. And in her own way, Bobby thinks, she is.

"In America it's New Year's Eve," Bobby says, holding her tight. "You want to go to a café and have a glass of champagne?"

"It's 5733," Sheva says. "And don't forget it, American boy." She strokes his hair maternally. She looks searchingly into his eyes. He's not a bad soul, her Bobby. "1973." She makes a face. *Puch*. 1973 is nothing.

"You want to have a glass of wine? We could go to Habourekis. You like that place, don't you?"

"I guess one glass of wine couldn't hurt."

Melanie is eating a bowl of Swiss muësli with honey and milk and sliced bananas.

"What's this?" Moonchild asks, sniffing at the frying pan.

"I think Lorraine made it. It's Hopping John or something. Hopping Jack? I think it has ham in it."

"You know, I saw Danny last night. Your friend Danny. At the New Year's Eve party."

"Oh yeah? I thought it was all women."

"Uh-uh," Moonchild says. "Though most of the men there *were* queens. And Danny, I thought I should tell you, Melly . . ."

"Tell me what?" Melanie says. She is reading an issue of *Parade*. An article about Pat Nixon. Her old-time family recipe for creamed corn.

"He was in drag," Moonchild says.

"So, it's New Year's Eve. Weren't other people—wearing costumes?"

"I don't think it was a costume. He had on a garter belt—and a bra. He was wearing false eyelashes. His legs were shaved. He had his hair—"

"What are you trying to *say*, Moon?"

"I saw him making out with a guy. Really making out," Moonchild says. "The other guy's hand—"

Melanie pushes away her bowl. The cereal topples over, soaking Pat Nixon and her daughters. Melanie runs upstairs.

"Don't get mad at *me*," Moon calls up the stairs. "I was trying to *help* you," Moon says. Idly, she dips her finger into the pan of Hopping John and tastes it. *Yuck. Pork.* Moonchild gags.

Sid and Miriam make love. Then they make love again. "I can taste Morty Kates' paws all over your body," Sid whispers, licking his wife's neck.

"Does that turn you on?"

"Yes," says Sid. "Everyone wants you. Because you're a beautiful lady."

The phone rings next to their bed. Miriam starts to pick it up. "Let it ring," Sid says. "It's probably just Morty Kates. He can't get enough of you. They probably want us to come right over and give it another round."

They are sitting outside in a café on Noe. It's a warm day for January in San Francisco. A young girl, maybe sixteen, is wearing only a cub-scout hat and regulation shorts. Her tiny breasts are bared to the sun. She is wearing red sunglasses and going around from table to table. Now she sits on the lap of a bearded man with a bald head. The man ignores the girl and keeps talking to his friend. She slides a bit from his lap as he gesticulates, talking to his companion.

"Her breasts are perfect," Tad says. He elbows Sophie, who is drinking Emperor's Choice and nodding out.

"Hmm?" she asks, looking at Tad.

"Look at that girl. Her tits are amazing."

Sophie smiles indulgently. She hasn't heard a word. She rubs Tad's elbow fondly.

When the girl gets up from the bald man's lap a few minutes later, Tad follows her inside the café. "Hey," he says, following her.

Sophie nods out in the sun. She doesn't notice Tad is gone. Café business is slow today; the sun is making everyone mellow. The waiter serves her more hot water and does not rouse her. Brian is leaving the café, full of jalapeños and eggs, when he sees her sleeping in the sun.

Melanie won't come out of her room. She won't take calls from Ricky Cooper or from Danny De Vries. Her column will be omitted from this month's special issue on vaginal infections if she doesn't get out of bed and write something right away. Moonchild is the only person Melanie agrees to see. Moonchild massages Melanie's feet. She rubs herbal compresses on Melanie's forehead. She reads her astrological explanations for her psychic decline. She paints a mural of nymphs and unicorns across the facing wall. Nymphs and unicorns making love, a sinuous chain of girls and horns.

"You've got to eat *something*," Moonchild says. "How about a milk shake? How about some onion soup? I'll even get you a bacon burger. You want a bacon burger? Nice and greasy with onion rings and extra BHT?"

Melanie smiles at Moonchild. She reaches out and touches her hair. Moon's crown of mythic curls. Melanie looks into Moonchild's eyes. Eyes the color of cucumber skin, the color of succulent. Moonchild rests her hands over Melanie's ears. They stare at each other a full moment. Tears come to Melanie's eyes. Moonchild wipes the tears away with a scarf of violet silk.

"It's not complicated at all," Sheva tells Bobby. "Either you love me or you don't."

"Of course I love you," Bobby says. "Haven't I told you I love you?"

"Only when I ask you directly," Sheva says.

"Well stop asking," Bobby says. Sheva gives him a fierce look. Now he's done it. In a second or two she'll slap him. "C'mon, Shevy," he says, pressing his lips against her face.

"Is it because I don't sleep with you?"

"Is *what* because you don't sleep with me?"

"That you don't love me," Sheva says.

"I love you," Bobby says. "I love you."

"Does it bother you that we don't make love?" Her face is wildly beautiful in this moment. Her eyes are wide and smoky, her hair is black and wild; he longs to connect her beauty marks, a lover's game of dot-to-dot. And yet, he doesn't want to make love to her. Even when they are kissing, he feels no passion. He wonders if it's all the studying he's been doing; he wonders if he is coming to observe—involuntarily—the rabbinic prohibition against pre-marital sex. But that isn't it. When he sees women on the street, he desires them, he undresses them, he even makes love to them in his head. With Sheva he feels something else, something less murky than desire. There is no mystery to her flesh. Her hardy legs, her sturdy arms, her hale and hearty body. He doesn't wish to see her revealed. He does not wish to enter inside her. Inside her is a memorial, the eternal flame of remembrance, inside her are the ashes of the crematoria.

"We'll make love when we're married," Bobby says.

"Are you proposing?" Sheva asks. Her voice catches. She squeaks, "Is this a marriage proposal or what? Are you joshing me, Bobby?"

He looks into her smoky eyes. The smoke of the factories at Auschwitz, the burning furnace of Chelmno. He thinks for a second of Sophie. Of losing himself in Sophie's body. Inside her is forgetfulness, the damp river of Lethe. "Yes," Bobby says. He kisses her on a beauty mark. Bingo. "That's right. I'm asking if you'll marry me."

"What about the children?" Sheva says. "Is it all right if we give them a religious upbringing? Can we name the first boy after my father?"

Bobby starts to laugh. He pulls her hair. "You forget I'm going to be a rabbi."

"An American rabbi," Sheva says. "What does an American rabbi know?"

"He knows his fate when he bumps into it. He knows his destiny," Bobby says.

Sheva starts to cry.

"You are my *zivug*," Bobby says. "My intended wife."

5

Paper Birds

1

Brian brings her back to Oakland. He puts her in his bedroom. By the end of the first afternoon she is straight and demanding heroin. She claws at his face like an incubus, a *dybbuk* from the other side. He brings her to a clinic he's passed in the neighborhood. The doctor gives her methadone and tells Brian, "You can't decide for someone else they're giving it up."

"I know all that," Brian says. "I know. But she's my sister."

The doctor is a tired blonde of thirty-five or so. Underneath her left eye is a prominent scar. "Sister, wife, my uncle Louie," the doctor says. "If she's not ready to kick, she won't. Most of the clients go home and shoot up an hour later. The methadone is a little extra—an extra kick. If I were you, I wouldn't let her even *look at* the other clients." The doctor gestures across the room where Sophie is whispering with some guy in a black beret.

Brian shakes the doctor's hand. "What did you say your name was?"

"I didn't say," she says.

Melanie and Moonchild spend the next two days in Moonchild's bed. Melanie feels like she's living underwater. Underneath the water she discovers a white-boned mermaid with pieces of shell stuck in her hair.

"What's your real name?" Melanie asks. It surprises Melanie how comfortable she feels, lying naked with Moon in the bed, tangled together—mythic, nymphic, naiadic, yin. They were mermaids, mergirls, sea-maidens with silver tails, undines diving into each other's bodies.

* * *

Brian plays her *Die Fledermaus* on his crummy portable player. He brushes out Sophie's curls. He mixes her milk shakes: Pistachio. Honey vanilla. Heavenly hash. He reads to her in theatrical French Baudelaire's *Les Femmes Damnées*.

Melanie is in love with Moonchild. Moonchild loves Melanie, but still sees Pammy—the black woman she met at the party on New Year's Eve. Melanie rouses herself from bed and goes back to her classes; back to the prenatal clinic where she assists the midwives—speculum, diaphragm, Dalkon Shield. Back to her typewriter where she churns out a breakthrough article on lesbian jealousy. She writes intimately of her feelings towards Pammy, the Other Woman. Pammy making love to Moonchild. Moonchild making love to Melanie. She writes about the great chain of female interconnectedness. She describes the mural Moon had painted on her bedroom wall. Virgins making love to unicorns, an endless chain of girls and beasts, an endless chain of girls and girls.

For her article she wins a prize, The Golden Tampon Award, for the best personal essay published in the feminist press.

One day in early March she makes love with Moonchild and Pammy at once. Her own words gain flesh. She feels connected to Pammy, and through Pammy to Pammy's mother, Pammy's daughter, and so forth, backwards and forwards at once in time. Afterwards the women eat a feast in Moonchild's bed: oysters and clams and yeasty bread, a bottle of fruity Beaujolais. They drive out to Revere Beach. Melanie jettisons to the water her secret tote bag of make-up. She casts unto the waters her guilty arsenal. Into the Atlantic Ocean, the ocean of *mythos* and loss. First they dump the bag on the sand and gather up handfuls of make-up: little jars of eye cream, miniature palettes of shadow, the Cupid's Quiver scented douche. Strawberry. Banana Split. Peaches 'n' Creme.

Gladys Szasz is in bed with a migraine when the maid brings her the mail. Bills from Bergdorf's and Bonwit's, another tuition bill from B.U., a birthday card for Brad from his sister Alene. There is also a letter with no return address, postmarked Worcester, Massachusetts. On the envelope, Gladys notices, their name is grossly misspelled: Mr. and Mrs. Barford Zasz. Inside is a newsletter printed on cheap paper; the ink comes off on Gladys's hands before she begins to read:

Only once before in my life had I tasted another woman's nectar. I spread the damp dark hair gently with my lips and tongue. I sent my tongue as a messenger, an ambassador to this unfamiliar cuntry. . . .

Gladys clutches her heart. She calls to the maid for Valium. She glances down, full of dread, to the bottom of the page: *Melanie Szasz, who regularly writes the* Pudenda and Addenda *column, is a sophomore at Boston University and a member of the Sappho's Cave Collective.*

By the time Lindy returns with the Valium and a glass of water, Gladys is out cold.

Brian won't leave her alone for even ten minutes. He makes her go with him to the 7-11 for cigarettes or a six-pack of Beck's. He hasn't worked in weeks, but still has a few thousand marinating in the bank. She hasn't had any junk at all as far as he can tell. Once he caught her smoking a reefer with the landlord's twelve-year-old son.

Her methadone has been cut down to the minimum. Dr. Rogers says the next step is up to Sophie. There is nothing else Brian can do. He has her eating and exercising, she's taking stress vitamins and drinking gallons of goldenseal. How long, the doctor asks him, does he think he can go on, baby-sitting her day and night? As long as he has to, he tells her. As long as she needs him, he says.

Gladys and Brad fly to Boston. They take a taxi to Melanie's address. When they arrive at the front door of the Sappho's Cave Collective, Pammy answers the door. She is wearing a pair of overalls covered with buttons: SISTERHOOD FEELS GOOD. BE HEALTHY—EAT YOUR HONEY.

During the Yom Kippur War, Bobby falls in love with Sheva. The two of them work side by side at the Hadassah Hospital. The bodies are flown in and Sheva and Bobby ID them. Sheva does not cry. She is tough like Golda Meir.

In the evenings they sit in the student bars and watch the news on television. They hold hands and drink wine in the livid light. For the first time in the sixteen months he has lived in Israel, Bobby feels he is one of them. A Jew among Jews. Sheva has stopped calling him American Rabbi. When college boys start flying in to fight the war, winging in from the Five Towns, from Cleveland Heights and Beverly Hills, Sheva doesn't make fun of them. Her bitter tongue grows sweet with the luxury of Bobby's love. In the middle of the war they go back to Bobby's apartment and make love for the first time. She wonders if she is too hairy. He wonders if he will ever be worthy of her virtuous arms. Outside the apartment it is eerily quiet on Rehov Tchernichovsky. It's okay, he tells himself. She's tough. Like Golda Meir.

2

Sophie kisses Brian good-bye at the Oakland Airport. She holds a ticket to Tel Aviv and $2000 of Brian's money.

"You got your ticket?" Brian asks. They cry openly in the gift shop. She loads up on chewing gum, on Chapstick, on magazines. Dramamine, cough drops, the *International Herald Tribune*.

He watches as she passes through Security. Her dark curls bounce as she maneuvers her duffel bag onto the belt. She turns around and waves to him. He waves back awkwardly. He's not sure, but he thinks he sees her blowing kisses into the air.

He goes to the telephone booths and calls up Miriam and Sid. "She's leaving now," he tells their mother, "in a few minutes she'll be in the air."

"I wish she could have stopped in New York on the way," says Miriam. "You really think the political climate is—"

"She's fine, Mom," Brian says. *Remember, Mom. It's hard to be a Jew.* Miriam passes the phone to Sid. He called me Mom, Miriam thinks, as Sid picks up the phone.

It's chilly in Jerusalem. It's been raining for ten days straight. The weather is Biblical. Sophie is in the Hadassah Hospital looking at the Chagall windows. She stands in front of a scarlet window. The tribe of Zebulun. She reads from the little tourist pamphlet describing each of the windows. "And Moses proclaimed that Zebulun would 'suck of the abundance of the seas.' "

Later she goes to the cafeteria. She eats a plate of vegetables with sour cream, and drinks coffee. The Israelis use three times too much instant coffee per cup. She reads the *Jerusalem Post* and feels lonely. She's been in Israel for a week. She is working up her courage to call Bobby. Next week she'll be twenty-one. She hopes that she and Bobby will celebrate her birthday together. She doesn't know if she'll be able to find him. The last letter she has from him was postmarked December '72. Now it was nearly a year later.

She'd called Melanie at her commune before she left for Israel. Melanie had acted distant—not exactly cold, but removed, and didn't have an address for Bobby. What did she expect, Brian said. Sophie had to understand Melanie had gone through changes; Sophie had turned everyone off. She'd hurt people; she couldn't expect everyone to shine her back on immediately.

"I know," Sophie had said. "But don't you realize, doesn't she realize, I've been through changes, too?"

"You were always the tough one," Brian said. "Melanie worshiped you. Whatever you did, she did. She wanted to be just like you."

"How could anyone think *I* was tough? How could anyone want to be like *me*?"

"Like the sabra fruit," Brian said. "Tough and prickly on the outside. Tender and sweet inside."

Sitting in the cafeteria, she realized she hadn't tasted a sabra fruit. That was something she'd have to try. Maybe it would help her know who it was she was supposed to be.

"I want you to quit calling me," Melanie tells Ricky. The creep won't leave her alone. Like every other month or so, he calls her up and complains to her. How lonely he is. How miserable. How tired he is. His schedule.

You want to be a pig doctor looking up women's cunts? Then you gotta pay the price, Dick. "Don't bother me with your problems. I don't even *believe* in male obstetricians. I'm a dyke," she says. "Why don't you leave me alone?"

It turns Ricky on that Melanie's a lesbian. He fantasizes about kissing her and she has the taste of other women lingering on her tongue. He fantasizes Cat Crawford spread-eagled on his bed and Melanie devouring her twat.

"I delivered a *baby*," Ricky says. "My first baby," says Ricky.

"That poor baby," Melanie says, hanging up the phone.

Miriam and Morty Kates are celebrating their anniversary in a motel on Route 4. They've been screwing each other every Thursday for the last ten months. It is four o'clock in the afternoon and Morty has an appointment with a jobber at four-thirty.

"I can't go on this way," Morty says. A stringy piece of hair dangles in front of his face. He tries to compensate for his baldness by parting his hair in left field, then combing the hair laterally over his bald spot. His vulnerability doesn't bring out Miriam's maternal nature. His bald spot makes her laugh. In fact, while they are making it, she thinks up jokes about it. Hairless old coot. Billiard-ball head. Let me look into your head a sec, Mort. I have to redo my lipstick. In her monologues with herself she refers to him as Mr. Baldini. Sid has all his hair.

"I can't go on this way," he says. He is sitting on the side of the bed, his red-knit Jockey shorts pulled down to his knees.

"Sure you can," Miriam says, grabbing the waistband of his shorts and giving it a nice zing.

"I love you, Mim," Morty says. The nickname annoys Miriam. Only Sid calls her Mim.

"C'mon, Morty."

"I love you. I worship you. Don't you believe me?" He takes off his aviator glasses and rubs his eyes.

"C'mon, Morty. Why can't we just screw like normal people?" Miriam asks.

"I don't *feel* normal," he says. "I feel like a kid."

"How old *are* you?"

"Forty-eight," Morty says. "I've been selling men's sportswear since I was twenty-four," Morty says. "I do all right. Nothing great. In a good year, I make thirty thousand."

"I just asked you how old you are. I didn't ask for your autobiography. Can't we just screw?" Miriam asks.

"But what does it mean?" Morty asks. "I mean, tell me, Miriam. You're smart. You went to Smith or somewhere, didn't you? Tell me what it all means. Now take Diana," Morty says.

"Not Diana," Miriam says. "You promised me you wouldn't complain about Diana."

"So, who's complaining?" Morty says. "Now take Diana," Morty says. "She's pretty smart. Maybe you don't think so. She has *nothing*. I gave her nothing. She can't even go *shopping*—I mean *really* shopping, like other women. I never made enough money for that kind of shopping," Morty says. "How much does Sid make? A dentist does pretty good, huh?"

"I refuse to answer," Miriam says. "I thought we weren't going to—"

"So don't tell me. It's all right. So, Diana, anyway, she takes up sculpture. I bought her a piece of marble as big as the Taj Mahal. So she starts *hokking* away at this piece of marble, in the garage. I made her a little studio. Nothing fancy, mind you. But I set her up in the garage. . . ."

"Get to the point," Miriam says.

"I'm trying to tell you a story."

Miriam takes out a tweezer and starts plucking her eyebrows in the streaky motel mirror. She can't stand listening to this. Morty is making her really nervous.

"Okay? Can I go on? Leave your eyebrows alone, Miriam. Your eyebrows are fine," Morty says.

"Anyway . . ."

"Anyway, so I set up this little studio for her. It's really nice. You should come over and see it. On a Saturday sometime, you and Sid should come over. I *like* Sid," Morty says.

Melanie and Moonchild have a giant fight. Moonchild has Melanie pinned. Melanie tries to remember her moves from self-defense class, but Moonchild has her pinned to the Tibetan prayer rug and it's all Melanie can do to breathe.

"Say uncle," Moonchild says. "Say aunt," Moonchild laughs. She is sitting naked on top of Melanie. Her breasts sway lyrically over Melanie's face. Melanie feels a quick desire to suck her nipples until the colostrum comes, flooding her face with moony milk. Did she ever feel so passionate with Ricky, she wonders. With Brian Spivack? With Danny De Vries?

Finally, Moonchild lets her up.

"I'm sorry I called you a stinking twat," Melanie says. "I love you. I just can't stand it that you're such a whore."

Moonchild pins her in four seconds.

Ricky goes down to the Velvet Glove. Kralich is really stewed. A Portuguese girl with glossy hair nestles in Kralich's lap. On stage, a girl in a red G string teases herself on a bare mattress. Ricky looks at the G string and thinks *babies* come from that hole. Babies slick and sticky with blood, babies with arms and legs and toes. Babies who swim through the uterus, somersaulting through evolution, dog-paddling through history. Ontogeny recapitulates phylogeny; each baby the first baby reenacting the journey through time.

He slaps a ten-spot on the table and mumbles something in Kralich's ear. Outside it is bitterly cold and the wind blows garbage into his eyes.

Yesterday was her twenty-first birthday. She called the information office at Hebrew University; she called all the youth hostels and youth hotels she could find in the book. She thought of calling Rise Buchman in Flushing, but lost her nerve at the last minute, waiting at the post office.

She can't remember why she came to Israel. She feels like shooting up, she feels like getting high on pot. She's sure she could find some great hashish with hardly any trouble. All she'd have to do, she was sure, was ask the night clerk at her hotel, a Palestinian kid about sixteen. She thinks of Brian, her only brother. She thinks of the days he sat beside her, rubbing her shoulders, patting her hair, playing her the operas their mother used to listen to in the chiaroscuro fifties. Their mother lying alone on the floor, her ears plugged with arias, her ears full of romance, her head full of Chivas and memories of their handsome father in the days just after the war.

Except now her mother and father were living together again. Now Dori was out of Payne Whitney and rich as fettucine. An ancient aunt had died, leaving Dori all her money. No longer did Miriam lie alone dreaming the days of her girlhood. Now she had a husband again. A blond husband to mow the lawn, to wait on line at the bakery, four poppy-seed and six garlic. And give me a nice fresh piece of that *pletzl*. A husband to check the fuses, to turn the heat down at ten o'clock, to make witty comments together during the Barbara Walters special. A husband to wake up in the middle of the night when the refrigerator noises, the settling sounds of the house, and the strain of insomnia conspired into a waking nightmare. A husband who smelled of the dentist's office and Niagara Spray Starch; a husband who made terrible puns and ogled every waitress in every New Jersey diner. A husband to worry with over the children, lying in bed, eating peanuts. Sid wearing his reading glasses and looking like a professor. Did anyone have worse children, crazier children than Brian and Sophie? Why didn't they have normal children like everyone else—lawyers and doctors?

Sophie goes back to her hotel room and reads Hart Crane until dawn. Tomorrow she'll go to Yad Vashem, the memorial to the Holocaust. Tomorrow she'll write a poem sitting in a café. It has been a long time since she's written a poem. She will write of Israel: the bony air, the citrus blossoms blowing apart in the dry khamsin.

"Godammit, Ruth!" Ruth is Dr. Rogers of the methadone clinic. She and Brian are watching TV. Brian has plugged in the space-heater and made a bowl of popcorn. The jar said it was gourmet popcorn. Why not, Brian had said, whistling in the kitchen. Why the hell not, indeed?

Ruth was complaining that she and Brian were seeing too much of each other. She didn't want to get serious. She didn't want him to think she was going to fall in love with him. She didn't know any other guys; the only men she ever met were junkies and cops. But if she met someone she liked, she would go out with him in a second. "In a *second*," she said, "do you hear me?"

"Godammit Ruth," Brian said. "Let's just watch TV and then I'll take you home. Okay?"

"You're twenty-three years old. What do you know anyway? When I was your age, I was already supporting two people."

"I'll take you home right now." Brian goes to the closet and takes out his down jacket. He zips up the jacket an inch or two. A solitary goose feather sneaks out from a torn seam. He places the feather on his finger tip, then brings it over to Ruth. "Here."

She smiles at him. She is not from the smilers. There is something different about this boy. Maybe he *is* too young for her, but still there's something about him. And besides, he's a wonderful lover.

December 22, 1973

Dear Mother and Dad:

I am sorry about the big fight we had last month when you came up here to Cambridge to see me. You could have at least called me first to tell me you were coming. I think it's unfair for parents to show up without any warning. I am a real person and you've simply got to face the fact that I am grown-up now, even if it makes you feel really old. I am twenty-one years old and that's that.

Whomever sent you that clipping of my column from *Xantipi* was trying to do a number on all three of us and I can't figure out who it could have been since the only enemies I have are political and don't know you. Maybe it was Ricky Cooper who calls me up all the time after everything that happened, and I simply refuse to sympathize with his existential problems as a second-year medical student at the biggest and most misogynistic university in the world.

Now for the hard part: I know it hurts you that I am a lesbian. It is not something I chose, but something that chose me. The Zeitgeist of the times requires me, perhaps, to be a lover of women. I know this is not what you had hoped for when you brought me up in Hudson Heights and made all the sacrifices to send me to dancing school, etc.

I know it hurts you that I am in love with a beautiful woman. Moonchild is the gentlest, most poetic, most serious person I have ever known. Sexual relations with Moonchild are a natural, organic expression of our enormous and precious love for each other. You wanted to know what we *do* to each other and you, Mother, made some rather crude remarks about dildos and stuff which really was a big downer. What we *do* is love each other and love each other's beautiful, womanly, procreative bodies. As far as Pammy is concerned, Pam and I have been *lovers*, but we are not in love. Also, Moonchild's real name is Marilyn Dellabough, since it seemed such a big deal to you that she had a strange name. Lots of people change their names. What about all the people who change their names because they don't want people to know they're Jewish, like half of your friends including the Grahams?

I am happy with Moonchild. I don't want to know particularly the details of your sex life, and neither do I expect that you want to know the details of my sex life. If it upsets you that I am happy, I am very sorry. I am sorry about the mean things I said, but you hurt me, Mother, when you said those mean things to me about vaginas. If you don't want to pay my tuition bills anymore or my rent, I really *do understand.* I don't want you to be hypocrites and so I don't want you to feel like ones.

Maybe some day you can accept the beauty and happiness of my new life. I have never been happier.

With Daughter-love and respect,
Melanie Jane

3

Sophie was not prepared for the power of Yad Vashem. The Memorial to the Name of God. The plaques with the names of the camps. The eternal flame. The hush of immortality. The photographs of little girls tiptoeing balletically into the fire.

She pauses to read from the list of writers whose books were burned by the Nazis: Spinoza, Einstein, Heine, Zweig, Maimonides, Rosenzweig, Buber. Halevi, Rashi, Philo the Jew, Leone Ebreo, Freud, Herzl. Marx, Proust, Disraeli, Peretz. Agnon, Cohen, Sholem Alecheim. . . .

On the wall above her is an excerpt from the diary of one of the commandants. He describes the dignity of an old woman who holds her grandchild in her arms, whistling and cooing, reassuring the child. Behind the *bubbe* and baby stand the infant's parents. The mother who wears a printed handkerchief. She stares sharply past the tourists into the jaws of history. The father who holds the mother gently around the waist. His arms are an apron of devotion. "The children's goldfish died today and we were all very sad . . . ," the Nazi's diary goes on.

Sophie is sitting on a bench outside the women's bathroom. Her heart is full of death and fire, the butcher-cauldron of Europe. The Jews a death-stain on the map, a yellow-green stain on the globe. Ashes and a confetti of bones. A heap of golden watches, a mess of golden teeth. Smoke, blood, Zyklon-B, statuary of excrement, bas-relief of bones. A pile of broken eyeglasses, Nazis whistling in the bath, Jewbabies without eyes rolling down a hillside. Post cards from Buchenwald, from Belzec, from Chelmno. Mint tea. Soapsuds. Black kettles of roiling fat. Inmates dancing in the dark. Corpses cooking *kolishkes*, dead men praying, half-men dreaming, banquets of blutwurst, *Trockenbeerenauslese* splashing in a wineskin.

Bobby is walking Sheva to the women's bathroom. He sees Sophie before she sees him. His mouth makes a terrible O.

"You don't understand," Bobby says.

"*You* don't understand," says Sophie.

"What don't I understand?" They are eating raspberry soup in a small vegetarian restaurant just outside the Old City.

"I love you," Sophie says. "I've always loved you. And don't act like you didn't know. Like this is some kind of giant surprise."

"I'm getting married to Sheva. I've asked her to marry me. I . . . love her." She hears the quiver in his voice, the moment's hesitation. She knows he doesn't really love Sheva, that sturdy girl with the mustache. He couldn't. She knows he could only love her.

"Give me a chance," Sophie says. "We'll go out . . . on dates. To the movies. We'll get to know each other again. I'll go to the Hebrew University. I want to study something—Jewish. I'm not the same person, Bobby. I've actually been reading Jewish philosophy. Halevi. Saadya Gaon. I'll marry you whenever you want. Please, Bobby. Can't we start over?"

She looks at him through a veil of tears.

"I don't know, Sophie. You *can't* start over. We have a whole history together. I'll never stop loving your memory. You were fifteen. It's such a long time ago," Bobby says. He remembers driving with her across the George Washington Bridge. The oily sheen of the Hudson below. "The Hudson River is smelly and rank; *shvartzes* and knishes on the other bank." He remembers this song from the Maccabee Day Camp. The Musicale of 1959. He touches her hand and feels a thrill.

"Bobby, I didn't *mean* to hurt you." He won't be able to stand it if she cries. "I only meant to hurt myself. I never meant to hurt *you*."

"I believe you, Sophie. Now don't ask me to hurt Sheva. Hasn't everyone been hurt enough?"

"But what if I can't live without you? What if I can't find the strength to go on without you?"

"You're very strong, Sophie. You're tough as nails," Bobby says.

"Not really," Sophie says. "That's what everybody thinks. But not really. Really. I'm not."

In a few minutes he'll pay their check, he'll lead Sophie by the arm into the Old City. They will walk through the ancient streets and come to the Wailing Wall. From their separate sides, men and women, they will write messages to the same God. Meager slips of pale paper they will tuck into the Wall. Their prayers will flutter like paper angels, like paper birds in the paper air.

"He *won't* leave you," Orit tells Sheva. Sheva has taken to her bed, a convertible couch in the living room. Around her are boxes of chocolate cherries, balled-up tissues, fashion magazines from the States and France.

"He's seeing her again tonight. She was a prostitute in San Francisco. A prostitute," Sheva says. "A Jewish prostitute, can you imagine?"

Bobby is sitting in a café reading *Ha'aretz* and drinking a bottle of Coca-Cola as dusty as a museum. He is struggling through an article about plumbing complexities in the Old City. He is thinking about Sheva and Sophie. Pictures of Sheva and pictures of Sophie. Sheva wiping up wine stains with her pink bandana, Sheva taking off her shoes and rubbing her feet in the cafeteria. Sheva's eyes like black raisins, her heart as pure as a blessing. He loved her now. He really did. Her strong capable hands. Hands you could believe in. Hands that could plant an orange grove; hands that could hide a baby boy in a basket of rushes. He believed in Sheva the way he believed in *Eretz Israel*. The future shone in her dark eyes like a benediction.

He could marry Sheva and teach school. Rabbis were a shekel a dozen in Israel. He'd still need to find a job, even after he'd received his ordination. It was almost impossible for a foreigner to become a professor—especially in philosophy or Judaic studies. Coming to Israel to teach philosophy was like bringing owls to Minerva, carting coal to Newcastle, importing sin to San Francisco. . . .

If he married Sheva they would have four children, four Jewish babies with black hair and flashing eyes. Jacob. Rebekkah. Joshua. Ruth. Sheva would be a social worker, helping immigrant families to find jobs, apartments, food. Sheva would make extra loaves of *challa*, extra pots of fatty soup, and leave them on the doorsteps of families whose fathers and sons were dead in the wars. Sheva would work with the *Mogen David*, collecting money for ambulances, oxygen tanks, mosquito nets, blood. They would send their sons to *cheder*. They would *kvell* together into the night, both of them wearing clean pajamas, listening as their faithful children repeated the words of the evening prayers. Their sons' bodies *shukling* and *davening* through time.

If he married Sophie, they would make love in the snow on the top of Mt. Hebron. . . . No, he wouldn't marry Sophie. It was impossible. Yet . . .

He would marry Sheva. She would wear a simple white dress and carry an armful of desert flowers. He would wear a white *kittel*. They would have an Orthodox ceremony. Women dancing with women. They would invite the whole community. *Le tout* Jerusalem would dance at their wedding. They would receive practical gifts, presents out of Sholem Alecheim: Fat geese, eiderdown quilts, pairs of fatted calves. Children would laugh and women would cry. He would meet Sheva's mother. *Mazel tov* on your head, on your head, on your head . . . To see your daughter wed, daughter wed, daughter wed. . . .

What does the Talmud say about a man who takes two wives? Bobby does the only thing a man in his position can do. He goes to the bank and withdraws the last of his Women's Club money. He stops at a travel agency on Rehov Abraham Lincoln and buys a boat ticket to Piraeus. He checks the bus schedule from Jerusalem to Haifa. His boat would leave from Haifa the next morning at 7:30. He stops in a grocery and buys blood oranges, bread, cheese, olives, yogurt, sardines. He has always wanted to see Athens, to walk around in the Agora where Socrates walked, instructing his students, adumbrating the Good.

Sophie goes to see Sheva at home. She has managed to wrangle her address from the *Jerusalem Post* offices. When she opens the door, Orit realizes right away who it is. That prostitute ex-girlfriend of Bobby's. She goes up to her bedroom where Sheva is darning panty hose.

"It's that girl," Orit says. "The prostitute. Do you want me to tell her to go away?" Orit knows instinctively that Sheva should change her clothes. She is wearing a housedress that once belonged to Orit's mother, a housedress as old as Israel's independence. She knows that Sheva should look her best. She ought to put on lipstick and rouge; she ought to run a comb through her curls and change into something American. A tight pair of dungarees. A T shirt with a message. Something: The Pepsi Generation.

Sheva goes downstairs. Sophie is sitting on the couch looking at *Elle*. She gets up to shake Sheva's hand. Sheva wonders where Sophie's hand has been last. Sheva is wearing a circus-striped duster, her curls are wild and glistening with sweat. She is wearing a pair of men's cheap socks. They pool thinly around her ankles.

"I'm Sophie Spivack. I saw you at the museum."

"Yad Vashem. The Remembrance Authority."

"I thought the museum was . . . amazing. . . . I'm very interested in the concentration camps. I've been reading Nelly Sachs. *O the Chimneys* . . . Do you—"

"I'll bring you some Nescafé," says Sheva. She leaves the room to compose herself. She puts the water on to boil. She looks into the courtyard where a small boy with curly *payess* rides a tricycle. He bangs, on purpose, into a garbage can. Sheva listens for the clang.

When she comes back into the room, carrying a small copper tray, Sophie is caught cleaning her ear with a wooden matchstick.

"So, you've heard from Bobby?" asks Sheva. Sophie notices she has an accent. So you've heard from "*Bubby*?"

"Yes. And you?"

"He called me. Long distance," Sheva says. "You know he's in Athens?"

"Yes."

"Rather cowardly, don't you think?"

"Um, I guess," Sophie says.

"We are going to marry," Sheva says. "You know that, don't you?"

"Bobby told me."

"Well." She sits down in a wooden chair. She looks like a beautiful deranged housewife. She could be thirty or older. "Well. You came to tell me something?"

"I . . . I'm sorry," Sophie says.

"Sorry?"

"For disrupting your life," Sophie says.

"Disrupting *my* life? How?"

"I . . . this is really hard for me," Sophie says.

She's very pretty, Sheva thinks. Sheva looks at her smooth legs. Pretty, but tiny, Sheva thinks. *Too* tiny. I could kill her with my bare hands. She looks like she weighs forty-five kilos. I could sit on her and take her neck right between my hands. No one would ever know. Orit would help her hide the body. *I'm really interested in the concentration camps.*

"Maybe I'd better go," Sophie says.

"You didn't touch your Nescafé. Do you want a piece of honey cake? I made it yesterday," Sheva says. Honey cake, Sheva thinks. Am I going insane? She goes into the kitchen. The tricycle lies abandoned in the small yard. She notices the rusty wheels, the little bell.

"I love Bobby," Sophie says from the living room. Sheva cuts her an extra-large slab of honey cake, then licks the knife. She goes into the living room, wielding the knife and the honey cake.

"I love him or I wouldn't be here."

"Love," Sheva says, shaking her head. Love, shmove, Sheva thinks. American love, big deal.

"And I know you must love him, too. And he told me how much he loves *you*. He really loves you," Sophie says.

"Of course he loves me," Sheva says. She lifts her arm and Sophie notices the heavy sweat stains, the lusty axillary hair. "Why shouldn't he love me?"

"Yes," Sophie says. "Of course. I'm sorry, I just don't know what to say. How to apologize. The last thing Bobby wants is for you to be hurt."

"I should be hurt?" Sheva asks. She points to her own chest. She forgets she is holding the knife. The cake knife grazes her chest. "Why should *I* be hurt?"

Sophie is exasperated. She can't talk to this girl. She's bitter and ironic like all the Israelis. Like Israel itself. She stuffs the honey cake into her mouth. One slice must weigh a pound.

Sheva smiles at her bitterly. Sophie sees the strain in her neck, the tendons tightening there. Sophie gets up and takes her hand. "Thanks for the cake," Sophie says. She buttons up her raincoat. Outside a gentle snow falls over the city. In a few days it will be Chanukah, the Festival of Lights. She wishes she had a friend.

After they'd gone to the Wailing Wall she and Bobby had made love. He had initiated it, not her. A farewell gift? An apology? The simple act of his desire? He'd seen the tattoo on her thigh. A swastika inscribed in red and black. She remembered the look on Bobby's face when he'd seen the tattoo. She'd never bothered to explain that she didn't remember having the tattoo made. That she'd awakened one morning and there it was. That Tad had probably done it to her as the ultimate punishment when she was too high to know or care. Probably he and his friends—rich psychiatrists from Marin County—had gotten a big kick out of it. Dragging the Jewess to a tenth-rate tattoo artist while she was nodded out. And branding her.

She was glad Bobby hadn't seen it until after they'd made love. Certainly, once he saw it, everything became clear. She hadn't intended it to work out this way. Now she realizes he would never understand if she explained herself for the rest of her life.

He'd looked at her—stunned, sick, paralyzed, speechless. He'd looked long into her eyes. The next morning he was gone.

Why hadn't she had it removed in Oakland? It would have been simple enough, she was sure. Lots of people got tattooed when they were young —anchors on their arms, hula dancers on their chests—then changed their minds.

Why was this so different?

Sophie was never sure if it had happened that way. Tad dragging her down there as a joke. Maybe she had sleepwalked to the tattoo parlor all by herself. Maybe the mark had appeared on its own—as innocently, as magically, as piously as the stigmata on the palms of virgins.

4

Ricky shows up at Melanie's collective. Lorraine answers the door. She is not used to seeing men at their threshold. Ricky senses she is frightened. He brushes the snow off his shoulders. His hair is very long and his beard covers most of his face. He hasn't looked in a mirror in ages. Ever since he stopped shaving. Maybe he looked weird.

"I'm looking for Melanie Szasz. She lives here, doesn't she?"

"Yes. Um-hum. She lives here. But usually we don't allow men in the house. Wait here, I'll see if she's home."

Ricky stands on the stoop. There's a cracked urn filled with black stones. Flat stones from a Zen river. In the corner of the porch is a rotting pumpkin, orange and pulpy, spilling its seed. He is kicking a fragment of concrete against one of the rotting posts on the front porch. He looks up and sees her. She is tall and skinny and older somehow. She stands behind the storm door wearing a thin peasant blouse. She's delicate and ironic. The wind whistles in the cold air.

"Well, if it isn't Dick Cooper." She nods her head appraisingly. He is sure she can see straight through to his soul.

"Hi, Melanie," he says meekly.

She laughs and opens the storm door. She stands next to him on the stoop. He watches as her thin arms fill up with goose bumps. He takes off his parka. It's neon orange and very dirty. He hands it to her and she takes it. She refuses to put her arms in his armholes, but she lets the jacket drape lightly across her shoulders. Her hair blows in the wind. Her eyes hold a faraway look.

"I'm sorry, Melanie," he says.

It takes her a few seconds to hear him. "Huh?"

"I said I'm sorry."

"For what?"

"Well. For coming here. For bothering you. For calling you on the phone. For bringing that girl to your dorm room when we broke up."

She laughs. "That was so long ago," Melanie says.

"The last time I saw you you were sitting in Brigham's eating a sundae. You looked like you were having fun."

"And you were starting to grow a beard. I remember noticing that your beard was red, like . . . "

He blushes. "I wasn't sure you saw me."

"I saw you," Melanie says. "You were with some very tall girl. Anyway," Melanie says, "like I said, that was ages ago."

"Not so long ago," Ricky says. He runs his big foot against one of the steps. He is wearing his Cons. Melanie looks down and sees the insignia—Chuck Taylor it says on his heel. In spite of herself she is flooded with memory. His foot is so unabashedly masculine. She thinks of Moonchild's narrow feet. Her calisthenic arches. She catches a whiff of Ricky's BO. She remembers she is wearing his jacket. Both of them watch as a pregnant woman wheels a stroller down the street.

He looks at her. Babies. The nurses laughing when he fainted.

She looks at him. His big feet. His flannel shirts. Chuck Taylor.

The macho pig has tears in his eyes.

"What do you *want*, Ricky?"

"Just to talk," Ricky says.

"All right," says Melanie. She goes back into the house and comes out wearing a red velvet cape, Moonchild's cape she wears as a totem. It is early Saturday morning. She leads the way to Central Square and a coffee shop out of Edward Hopper. The menu says "Good Morning!" The talking menu. The vinyl booths. The graveolent coffee. The whiskery men in thin jackets. The Christmas decorations hanging between the stanchions. Evergreen. Ketchup. Thin napkins. Garbage spilling from green bags. Scruffy children with chocolate spittle leaning into the wind.

Ruth has moved in with Brian. They do fine as long as they don't talk about the future. Sometimes Brian comes into the bedroom and looks at their setup from the doorway. On Ruth's night table lie *Women and Madness*, the

Chocolate Lovers' Newsletter, an old prescription pad, pearls. Do they *look* happy? Brian asks himself. Are these the props of a happy couple? Will Ruth forget she's ten years older? Will she marry him anyway? Will she have his baby?

He is happy driving home to her from the Peninsula. He whistles in the supermarket, buying her panty hose and Woolite. He is happy watching her disappear behind the aqua shower curtain, happy watching her reappear from the other side. Each time she reappears he allows himself to be surprised. A miracle. He fears he will lose her.

He makes dinner for her. Cuts up chicken livers, sautés them in leftover wine, offers them on a bed of Minute Rice. He's happy when she calls him from work on the weekends. Just to say hello because the junkies are unruly today and the bureaucrats are getting her down. He is happy when she gets in the bed and snuggles her body against him. He wants to make her pregnant.

Sid meets Morty on Saturday morning in Nussbaum's Hardware. Morty is buying screws. Sid is buying a shaver head. They meet in the check-out line. Morty is very friendly. Sid hasn't seen him in almost a year. Not since that funky New Year's Eve when Morty had turned over his bed to Sid and his own wife.

In the parking lot the snow is dirty, black with the mortal exhaust of cars. "So," Sid says, tapping Morty conspiratorially on the arm. "What you got on for New Year's Eve?"

Morty blanches. "Look, Sid. Can I talk to you?"

"Sure." Sid is sure Morty's gonna hit him up for a loan. Miriam had once intimated the Kateses had problems with money. Fifty bucks?

"Man to man," Morty says.

A hundred bucks, Sid thinks.

"Miriam and I—"

Sid starts to laugh. "You're banging Miriam. I don't believe it." He studies Morty's plaid hat, the green pinfeather at the brim.

"You think it's *funny*?" Morty is nervous. He didn't expect Sid to laugh. "Why are you laughing?"

"What do you want me to do? Cry?" Sid imagines Morty and Miriam. Miriam kissing Morty's thing. He starts laughing. It *is* funny. Morty in bed eating Entenmann's while Miriam massages his dong.

"I think I'm in love with her," Morty says.

"Now *that's* not funny."

Morty looks at his own feet. He's wearing pointy black boots that went out of style a decade before, Beatle boots from the sixties. "I'm serious."

"What about Diana?"

"I love her too."

"Don't be so serious, Morty. Life is too short."

"Is Miriam married to you?"

"No, I'm still married to my second wife. Dori."

"Does that mean Miriam's free?"

"You want my permission or my blessing?" Sid remembers Tevye, his nubile daughters.

"I mean . . . would you let her marry me? If I divorced Diana?"

"Morty, are you nuts?"

Sid looks over at Morty's car. A '72 Cutlass. Yellow. Leatherette interior. A little cardboard pine tree dangles from the rearview mirror. On the shelf above the back seat, he sees a calculus textbook, an AAA travel guide, a straw hat with a pink chiffon scarf tied around the brim. He thinks of Diana in pink chiffon—her pointy erotic profile, the erotic surprise of dark roots under her yellow hair. He thinks of the elegance of her neck, the smoothness of her legs.

"I want more poetry in my life," Morty says.

Bobby cables her from Athens. When she passes the desk of her hotel, the Palestinian teenager stuffs the telegram into her hand: THE MORE FLESH, THE MORE WORMS. THE MORE WIVES, THE MORE WITCHCRAFT. GO BACK TO N.J. I MUST CHOOSE SHEVA.

Morty and Sid get bombed in the basement of the VFW. The Veterans of Foreign Wars. *Goyim* everywhere, working men with purple noses. Juice glasses full of beer. Calendar girls from the fifties nestling above the urinal. Georgia Tech vs. Louisiana State. Howard Cosell is showing his age.

" 'There was an old hermit named Dave . . . who lived all alone in a cave . . .' You want more poetry in your life? I'll give you poetry." Sid is ordering boilermakers. "Did you know I used to sing with the Yale Glee Club?" Sid asks. "Do you know I never *wanted* to be a dentist? Do you know what it's like to spend your life digging around in the decaying trap of some *alter kocker*?"

"A dentist makes a good living, Sid. A dentist always makes out. Even in the depression . . . Am I wrong? Two thousand dollars for braces? Both the twins I had to buy braces. Three hundred dollars for Diana's cap on the side."

Sid downs another shot.

"How much for a root canal? How much for cutting the gums? I heard that that's *really* painful. I bet it costs a mint. Am I right?"

Sophie flies to Boston on El Al. The man sitting next to her is a Jesus freak. He'd come to Israel, to settle, with fifteen dollars in his pocket. He'd gotten into a fight with Immigration at the airport and ended up, his first night in the Promised Land, in a detention center. He makes cracks against the Jews all the way to Logan Airport. "So tell me, young Jewish lady, is it true what they say about matzo?" He lowers his voice. "Do they really put blood in it?"

She calls Melanie from the airport, but Melanie isn't home. This person named *Moonchild* assures her that Melanie would be *delighted* if she came and stayed with them. She doesn't figure it out right away, that Melanie has become a dyke. If she'd known, she wouldn't have come to Boston. A whole house full of dykes. It's more than she can deal with. But what else can she do? She doesn't know anyone in New York. She's afraid if she went to New York, she'd end up downtown, getting high or going to bed with some weirdo. She couldn't go back to New Jersey and see her parents. Her mother was an ass for taking Sid back. Sid was a terminal dork. He'd call her Pumpkin or Princess. "What's wrong, Princess?" he'd say. Well maybe one of these days, she'd tell him. "You're a dork, Dad."

She didn't want to admit to her mother she'd gone all the way to Jerusalem in pursuit of Bobby, and he'd turned her down for a girl with a mustache. She was too ashamed. The more flesh, the more worms. The more wives, the more witchcraft. His telegram annoyed her. He was using Jewish mysticism as a way of avoiding her. Go back to N.J. I must choose Sheva. Go back to the Garden State. Go back to the Garden. What made him think there *was* a way back? The only way back was through his arms. Now that she knew she really loved him, she knew she'd never stop.

She knew he'd never tell Sheva that they'd made love in the Arab hotel while the streets of Jerusalem filled with rain. She wondered which Sheva would think was worse—their making love or patronizing an Arab hotel.

Maybe he wouldn't marry her. Maybe no one would ever marry her. But of one thing she was sure—she could always get Bobby Buchman into her bed.

They hadn't made love for years. For a long time there had been no years, no months, no days, no afternoons. Heroin killed time. She had worked mostly at night. The darkness around her hadn't existed. The street lamps had not shone. The moon had gone away.

She couldn't expect Bobby to understand what her life had been like or why she had chosen it. The world was full of two kinds of people—reets and semi-reets. Fools and bigger fools. Everyone kidding himself. Everyone dying. She thought of her father whoring around with the mothers of all her friends. She thought of Anita's mother, Lee Freund, imagined Lee beneath her father. She thought of Anita wasting away in Passaic Pines. All because she and Wayne Voekler had flung care to the wind, their damp bodies pressed together behind the football field. She saw Anita and Wayne kissing, imagined Anita's golden hair stuck to his face with kisses. She saw Wayne's football number—62—his damp jersey balled up under Anita's head.

Where was Wayne Voekler now? Tender divorcé of twenty-one; football hero, retired; father to a damp-haired boy he would never hold in his arms. She thought of Sasha, Anita's son. Sasha was over four years old—ready for kindergarten: the candy fragrance of Play-Doh, necklaces wrought from macaroni, the transfiguration of paper plates into talismans. . . .

Bobby shouldn't marry Sheva. Bobby should marry her. Rise Buchman in a splashy print dress, Bobby's father wiping his eyes with a Harvard hankie; both fathers misty-eyed in the fluorescent light. As she sat in the molded chair, hungry and homesick in Logan Airport, nostalgic for the New Jersey air, the oily gleam of the Hudson, she let herself grieve for all she'd lost. She remembered the demonstration against the invasion of Cambodia, the smell of tear gas in the air, the smell of souvlaki and body heat, patchouli oil and marijuana. She remembered getting dressed for her first date with Tad, how she'd creamed and oiled and perfumed herself into a sacred offering. . . .

Not even then had he been romantic. She'd invented all the romance herself. She'd made Tad into a cowboy, a he-man, the Marlboro man made flesh. She'd invented for him a sexy past involving courage and booze and honor. She'd loved his blond hair as thick as ropes, his eyes as green as counterfeit money. Later his eyes looked hazel to her, and still later, she was sure they were brown. His hair, which once had shone from his head as yellow as crayons, turned dirty blond, and later, light brown. Where once he'd been muscular and tight—the skin of his belly resilient as Spandex—she discovered in time a premature softness, a fleshiness that repelled her.

How had she found him, her Mussolini, her personal führer, her private de Sade? Had she caught the cruelty in his wink, the viciousness in his voice? She remembered the first time he'd had the idea to tie her hands to the wicker bedstead. She remembered the strange look in his eyes as he'd taken the rope from the night table drawer. He'd opened the drawer and she'd seen a cruel flash of metal and leather and rubber and rope. Once he'd gotten her high on junk, then clipped a clothespin onto her nipple. Blood had spurted from a duct—fantastically, as in a myth.

She remembered the spare room in his apartment, the extra room he hid from view. This room would come to her in her dreams—the spare room, the extra room, a supernumerary chamber stuffed with the death-sick detritus of dreams. She remembered the piles of *Hustlers* tied together with frayed twine. She thought she'd glimpsed a giant doll made of thin flesh-colored plastic. When she'd asked Tad about the doll—she knew such creatures existed—he'd acted as though she'd lost her mind. She thought she'd seen a trapeze in there; she thought she'd seen a bale of rope; she thought she'd seen a cage of reptiles, a vat of blood, a dead woman, a penis lying in a box. He'd laughed at her, he'd told her she was seeing things. It's just the spare room, he'd said. You've taken too many reds. Don't be insane, he'd say. It's just the extra room.

5

Melanie sits beside her in the back seat of an old Chrysler. Around Melanie's slender neck there swings an ankh on a golden chain. Sophie doesn't notice that Moonchild and Melanie and the husky black girl are wearing matching lavender T shirts.

"I think you should know," the black girl says, "that politically we—the collective— don't support the racist Zionist state of Israel . . . and for another thing—"

"C'mon Pammy," Melanie says, giving Sophie a big squeeze. "Give Sophie a break."

Moonchild turns around from the front and pats Sophie herself. "Pammy's a PLO groupie," Moonchild says in her annoying spiritual voice.

Sophie wishes she'd gone to New Jersey. Even Miriam and Sid would be better than this. Even Sid in his chef's apron with the sayings on the front —FOR THIS I WENT TO COLLEGE—would be better than this. She looks at Melanie and tries to figure out what the years have done with her friend. Melanie looks prettier. Her pale eyes shine with confidence, with self-possession. Gone is that gawky *who-me*? look, gone is her boy-crazy, husband-mad fervor. Pussy must agree with her, Sophie tells herself later that night.

"Sophie, don't laugh, okay? Sophie don't laugh, but I'm a dyke."

No kidding, Melanie, Sophie wanted to say.

It is New Year's Eve 1973. Pammy is dressed in a giant diaper. Her breasts hang like two loaves of yeasty pumpernickel. Sophie sits on the edge of a couch reading back issues of feminist rags: *Big Mama Newsletter, Bitch, Rat, Kali*, the *Anti-Eve(ning) News*. Next to her on the couch two of the women are having a fight. "C'mon, Les. Leslie, c'mon. I just don't want you to go in there. Remember what happened the last time?"

Next door, in one of the bedrooms, some kind of orgy is going on. Melanie had disappeared into the room and come out a half-hour later, giggling and naked. Then she'd gone back in, carrying a stainless-steel punch bowl filled with popcorn. Sophie thinks it's pretty weird that Melanie brings her to a dyke convention their first weekend together in almost two years. Maybe Melanie was trying to convert her. It was pretty funny, all things considered, that Sophie should end up the one obsessing about a boy, complaining that Bobby had tricked her.

She'd been sitting on the bed last night, in Moonchild's sensuous bedroom. Melanie and Moon had been wearing identical flannel nightgowns and all three of them were smoking grass. Sophie told them about Tad, about doing heroin for the first time. Sophie told them how Brian seduced her when she was fourteen. Sophie told them how much she loved Bobby. Melanie had never known that Sophie was so vulnerable, so dreamy, so romantic. The idea of Sophie and Bobby together seemed off to her now. Bobby was too bourgeois, as well as a Zionist, and a rabbi. Sophie should forget him. Jewish men prayed every day: *Blessed are you, Lord our God, Ruler of the universe, who has not made me like a woman.*

"I just can't imagine Bobby Buchman—the rabbi—with a prostitute," Melanie says.

"Are there any *real* cigarettes in this house?" Sophie asks. "I think I better lay off the pot. It makes me feel too self-pitying." Sophie imagines Bobby and Sheva at the Wailing Wall. She imagines Sheva in a white *shaytl*, Sheva's hands kneading the dough for Bobby's sacramental *challa*.

"You really love him," Melanie says. "I guess I never knew that. Remember when he tried to save us? Remember when he knocked down the wall at Harry's?"

"I remember everything. Going over the bridge. I'd do anything to be back there in Ricky's car, listening to the radio."

Sophie imagines walking over the bridge. She imagines the spray-painted initials of surly boys she'll never know. She imagines the feel of the steel ropes, their shifting shadows over the Hudson.

"Ricky Cooper came by about a month ago. I know you won't believe this, but he wanted to start *seeing* me again. He wanted us to go out on dates and screw." Melanie starts laughing. She runs a hand across Moonchild's back. Her back is white and creamy with brown moles like chips of carob.

"I'll go out with him," Sophie says.

Melanie starts to laugh. "I only hope you're kidding," Melanie says.

6

Moonchild goes to Chicago for the weekend, and while she's gone Sophie and Melanie go with Ricky to a movie. Just for old times' sake. They sit in the Brattle Street Cinema in 1974 with Ricky Cooper between them. They eat popcorn with fake butter. On the screen before them Faye Dunaway looks sultry and desperate in white silk. Later, they go back to Cambridge. All of the women are gone. The three of them sit on Moonchild's bed and talk about old times. Anita Freund was sent home on her first weekend pass. . . . Jill Grinspan is married and living as a Hare Krishna. . . . Above the bed hangs a fisherman's net—pale as the insides of shells. Stuck in the net are bits of flowers, fragments of jewelry, smidgens of lace.

From time to time Sophie catches Ricky staring at Melanie. Melanie throws her head back in laughter. Sophie can't get over it, the transformation of Melanie. Melanie makes love with Moonchild, but she and Moon are still friends. They giggle together like best friends under the pink canopy; they giggle amid bits of lace, the pale viscera of flowers. They share camisoles and money, they share their twenties in Cambridge. A midwife's assistant, Melanie takes the Red Line Saturdays to a clinic where she looks inside the bodies of women. Pregnant housewives, teenagers, women afraid of cancer, of candidiasis, of babies. She feels sometimes like a stargazer, an astronomer gazing through a telescope into the Milky beyond.

Sometimes she finds herself attracted to men. Sometimes she notices a man is flirting with her—taking in her long legs, appraising her behind. She thinks of a Russian waiter in a restaurant in Somerville. His sibilant consonants, the curly hair at the base of his neck. She can recreate the thrill she felt when his leg rubbed accidentally against her thigh. Sometimes she daydreams about his long arms—extended to her, bearing blini.

And even stranger is the desire she feels for Ricky Cooper. Threatening was the desire he aroused in her that day on the stoop in late November. The pumpkins rotting, the gray sky, the emanations of body heat wafting up from his jacket, his odor. In the theater she'd felt his thigh stirring beneath the popcorn.

Lately she'd started thinking—why *not* make love with him? Moonchild would never object; Moon believed in changing partners. There was no more danger. She did not love him. This time she would do it for pleasure. In her early days she'd done it for love—a pliant girlfriend's obedient gift. Later she'd done it to keep him, to keep the boy with the high SATs interested in little her. She'd had no special gift for sex. What it took, it seemed, was mostly endurance and patience, a willingness to withstand whatever—the car-door handle poking into her ribs, the eternity it took for Ricky to release himself into her mouth.

With the customers in Harry's she'd learned to provoke the men. None of them could touch her. She'd come to them on the dim-lit stage, dressed as a tiger, a whore, Lolita; served as a fireman, a gypsy; served to them as their very own daughter. And none of the men could touch her.

With Moonchild, Melanie had healed herself; their bond was much stronger than sex. With Moonchild she'd grown whole and wholesome. It was funny how her parents considered her a pervert with Moon. Her parents had it all wrong. Moonchild loved her. She'd been a pervert with Ricky.

And yet, she liked the new Ricky Cooper. He'd given up the prep school bullshit. He looked like a dirty leftist now with his wild hair and his red beard. She liked it that he'd lost his nerve; now he was afraid of her, afraid of women and their bodies. She wanted to show him, to express her power, to wrench her private pleasure from his solid man's flesh. She longed to feel his rough hair, his sinewy skin, his hard calves. She'd siphon the last shred of arrogance from his masculine body. She'd go to bed with him and then she'd write about it! An exposé in the feminist press! She was good at writing about sex. Hadn't she won that Golden Tampon Award for her article about sex with Moon? That piece had been a serious turning point. She'd freed herself through language of her fears and her shame. The whole world had come to know that she was an eater of women, a lavender cannibal, a cunt-happy muff-diver, a proud lady of Lesbos. And now she'd do the same thing for heterosexual sex. She'd go to bed with Ricky and tell. Boy, would she tell.

"Look-it," Ricky says. "I guess I had it coming to me . . . but this does come . . . Well, look. Read it."

Bobby Buchman and Ricky Cooper sit in a coffee shop on Madison Avenue. Bobby has just had his interview with the Jewish Theological Seminary. If things work out all right, he and Sheva will move to New York in September. She'll live in Brooklyn with her mother, he'll live in the JTS dorms; and sometime in the next year or so they will get married. His mother will want the affair to be an extravaganza—the Ten Commandments carved in ice, flaming shrimp kebabs, trained lovebirds flying above the canopy. She saw it on Merv—the birds. Bobby knows enough to make sure that Sheva has it her way. Sheva's mother will make the party. Egg salad instead of shrimp; the neighborhood Hasids instead of birds.

Bobby starts to read the article Ricky pushes across the table.

> "My old boyfriend had dumped me a few years earlier for a tall Protestant girl whose name was Cat. The significance of her name is certainly noteworthy seeing as how we are all trained—women—in this culture, to see each other as the enemy, complete with claws. Somehow my old boyfriend had started to desire me again, despite the fact that I had come out as a dyke. The world—as certainly we in the feminist avant-garde well know—has changed revolutionarily in the past three years. My old boyfriend had spent these years doing, ironically, the same thing as I—looking inside the bodies of women. He was, ironically, considering the fact that he was a fascist pig at best, who, by his own admission, had spent the best part of his undergraduate days at Harvard going to girlie shows . . ."

"Melanie's not much of a writer." Bobby takes off his glasses. Ricky notices he looks older, better-looking, more relaxed.

"That's not the point," Ricky says. "This beginning part isn't too bad. Read the middle section. She describes"—here he lowers his voice—"she describes our *lovemaking*—if you can call it that. Well, read it, Bob. I'm not kidding."

"His penis was as limp as an old brassiere. I began to talk to him about making love with my woman, Moon, since I knew it would be a real turn-on for him. I described in passionate detail what it was like to make Moon come."

"I don't know," Bobby says, pushing the newspaper away.

"She used my real name," Ricky says. "Now the whole world can find out I was impotent with a dyke."

"She shouldn't have used your real name. I suppose if you really wanted to, you could sue her and the newspaper both."

"The Jewish Final Solution. Suing. I don't want to *sue* her; I want to *see* her," Ricky says. "I know she's a dyke and all that. I know she hates me and everything. I don't even care. I don't blame her either. I was pretty rotten to her. I brought Cat along when I broke up with her. I even cheated on her in high school when she was off in Puerto Rico flushing our kid down some Puerto Rican toilet. Really, Bob . . . I never told anyone this. But I went to a motel with Connie Fass while Melanie was in Puerto Rico."

"It doesn't matter anymore," Bobby says. Ricky's tears embarrass him. He's no good as father-confessor. It's a good thing rabbis are not confessors. "It doesn't matter anymore who you went to bed with. We all do things we wish we hadn't." He pats Ricky on the shoulder. "It's okay, Rick, let it go. Try to let it go."

"I can't let it go, Bob. You don't understand. I'm in love with Melanie and I . . ."

"Eat your muffin," Bobby says. He picks up the serrated knife and smears it with butter. "Here. *Ess*."

"Tell me how to get her back," Ricky says, pleading.

7

Sophie lives all alone in Cambridgeport. She'd stayed with Melanie in the collective longer than she'd intended. After a while she felt too strange living among the lesbians, going to women's parties, women's movies, women's bookstores, women's openings. She found a job in a Laundromat right in her neighborhood. All she had to do was be there, a witness to the ablutions of the neighborhood. Occasionally, she'd sweep the floor, empty the lint traps in the dryers, post an Out-of-Order sign on one Speed Queen or another. She'd organized a Lost & Found: the hand-me-downs of other lives. Weltschmerz everywhere: one thin rayon sock, one milk-stained turquoise stretchsuit with Baby All-Stars on the chest, one orange oven mitt covered with hex signs. A royal blue gymsuit with the owner's name embroidered expertly across the back: ANN FLEMING. One pair of maternity jeans with a yellow daisy on the rear pocket.

Sophie liked her job. From eight to six she sat in the Laundromat, watching the women come and go. Their pillowcases were not glamorous. They carried the stains of their lives in their arms: gooey blots of fried egg, small islands of store-brand oil, blood, tuna fish, turpentine, semen—they carried their overflow in their arms.

A skinny redheaded woman comes in wearing a plastic rain hat. "Wet enough for you?" she asks. A young couple comes in, carrying nothing. The boy goes into the bathroom and hands his clothes out to the girl: a stiff pair of dungarees, a Jefferson Airplane T shirt. The girl puts his laundry in. Her hair is long and silky, she looks Portuguese. She hands Sophie two quarters and three shiny dimes. She enters the room where her boyfriend is waiting. She undoes the elastic from his ponytail. She hands her clothes out to Sophie who drops them into the machine: a faded blue knit top with dingy ruffles around the armholes, a homemade denim skirt. Sophie adds some Joy liquid abandoned to the Lost & Found. She watches the clothes as they spin together; from the bathroom come the teenagers' cries.

8

Sophie and Melanie are both wearing nylon stockings and real shoes. They are wearing tacky thrift-store dresses they bunch up with plastic belts. It's Easter Sunday among the Jews. Balmy April in the back yard of Miriam and Sid. It is Sid's fifty-second birthday and everyone has brought a dish. Diana Kates is there with her famous miniature knishes; Dori is there with some take-out ambrosia and her latest beau, an actor. Lee Freund has a man on her freckled arm, and surprise! he's richer than she is.

Gladys and Brad walk into the yard. Gladys is pretty happy today—Melanie is wearing a dress. Even if it's some old *shmatte* that belonged to a corpse. Melanie had told her that morning that Miriam had invited Bobby and Ricky, a sort of surprise for her and Sophie. The girls had driven to Pennsylvania earlier that morning to attend a "Happening." They'd driven all the way to Bucks County only to stare at a hole in the ground two art students had dug themselves as their senior project. One of Melanie's dykes had called her from New York to invite her. These dykes were everywhere, Glad thought. There were probably dykes at this very party! Why wouldn't there be? Everyone at this party had done *something* ridiculous, anti-social, dirty, in the last few years. Take that Dori over there. She'd done some time in a loony bin before her aunt died and she became a millionaire. Now she buys herself men. This new one looked about thirteen. And Miriam who walks around as if it's all a dream. Nothing seems to get to her. When Sophie came home last Christmas with an earring through her nose, Miriam laughed.

Morty Kates flirts gingerly with Miriam who is wearing shorts, barefoot in April. Miriam laughs at his opening line. "So how's the most sensual lady in New Jersey today?" Morty lowers his voice. "Can we talk?" He points in the direction of his car. She follows him out to the car and they spend most of the party there—talking, parked, across the street.

Ricky and Bobby show up with a twenty-dollar platter of cookies from the Butterflake in Teaneck. Their Sunday morning on the bakery line has suburbanized their stance. They don't look like little kids, standing there at the garden table, pouring slivovitz. They look like young men, like husbands.

Sophie feels a little sick when she sees it's Bobby with the thick Jewfro and starched Mexican shirt. She'd been eyeing him from the back for the last few minutes, thinking he was Dori's boyfriend, some other woman's younger man. She has the urge to run upstairs and bolt herself in her old bedroom. Now it's Sid's music room. Posters of Bessie Smith. A set of drums. A fancy stereo. Sophie goes up to him and takes his wrist in her hand. He is wearing a Timex watch with a hand-tooled leather band.

"What's this?" Sophie says, flicking his Mexican shirt. "Gidget goes Nogales?"

Bobby smiles. He kisses her cheek. "You look beautiful," he says.

"Can I interest you in a bicentennial blow job?" Sophie asks.

He blushes. "I see nothing's changed."

"Nothing," she says in a sexy voice. Bobby blushes deeply down to the V of his Mexican shirt.

"How about if we go for a walk?" He looks into her green eyes; as always he sees in her eyes a challenge. She was the most pugnacious girl he'd ever met.

They walk out to the street where Miriam and Morty are having their talk in Morty's car. Bobby waves to Miriam; Miriam waves back. Mother and daughter pass a look full of love and confusion and loss.

Melanie avoids Ricky. She wonders if he is still mad about her article in *Xantipi*. Where was his sense of humor, she thinks. That's the trouble with these men, she thinks delightedly to herself, they just don't have a sense of humor.

Bobby and Sophie take a walk through the neighborhood. On an impulse they try the back door of the Szaszes' house. All the Szaszes are at the party. When they find the back door closed, Bobby starts to pry open a window. The housekeeper presses a button and five minutes later, half the Hudson Heights police are buzzing around with red lights.

* * *

Ricky and Melanie, Bobby and Sophie, are down in the Szaszes' rec room. They are drinking daiquiris and listening to Harry Belafonte. They sit at the Szaszes' African bar. Carved heads, bright masks, rhinoceros and zebra skins covering the stools. There's a giant bottle of Galliano and lewd signs printed to look like Hebrew: Please piss in the bowl.

Bobby is describing a party at the seminary where a girl jumped out of a giant *hamentash*. Melanie is laughing at the face Sophie made at Bobby while his back was turned. The paneled walls, the stainless-steel sink, the oversized brandy snifter filled to the top with restaurant matches, the humming of the refrigerator at the other end of the room—all conspire with the sexy sound of Calypso. Ricky's arm slides tentatively around Melanie's back. She doesn't push him away. Bobby is the drunkest of all. His drawstring pants droop at the heinie. Sophie knows he will sleep with her. Didn't they break into Melanie's house in order to do just that?

Wasn't it clear this afternoon that he still loved her? *Did* he love her? She didn't know. She wanted to ask him if he and Sheva were still getting married. She wanted to ask him if he could wait a little while longer. She felt she was almost ready to marry him, to be a rabbi's wife for real. She'd even gone to the *mikva*—the ritual bath—to cleanse herself of her old life. She couldn't ask him. He was drunk and he wouldn't want to discuss it. That was how it had seemed earlier that afternoon when they'd walked around her old neighborhood. "So how's Sheva?" she had asked, trying to sound casual, ho-humsville. "Is she doing all right?" She hadn't seen Bobby in over a year. He still hadn't married Sheva.

"Sheva's fine," Bobby had said. That's all he'd said, but she could tell they were still together. She felt a weight just then on her elbow. He had passed out on top of her arm.

9

Moonchild has fallen in love with a man—a guru named Norman. He lives in a house in Jamaica Plain with all his followers. Moon met him and his disciples at a health food fair on the Boston Commons. One day she was Moonchild, Spacewoman of Bilitis; the next day she was sleeping with a male guru from Cleveland Heights. Lorraine and Pammy try to deprogram her, with memories, with politics, with sex. One June morning she leaves while the other women are sleeping, tangled together in feminine arms.

When Moonchild changes her name back to Marilyn, Melanie realizes Moon is lost. Marilyn becomes one of Norman's thirteen wives. Within a few months she graduates to number-two wife. When Melanie comes to visit her, Marilyn is a stranger. Along with her name and Melanie, she has given up her jewels and her satins, her kimonos and feather boas. Today she is wearing a powder blue shirtwaist with somebody else's monogram and a matching plastic belt. Her cloud of hair is plaited into two long braids held with rubber bands. Melanie is surprised most of all by the rubber bands—everyone knows they break your hair.

Melanie tries to talk to her, to get Moonchild to laugh. It is hopeless. The whole time Melanie's talking, Moonchild's slender fingers move back and forth on a rusty washboard. She is washing Norman's socks in a cracked enamel basin. Melanie tells her the collective seems to be breaking up. Lorraine, Nini, and Pammy have all joined another, more radical, group in Boston—a group whose members plan to start their own society on an island. They call themselves New Lesbos. They are busy learning the practical trades: plumbing, bricklaying, auto mechanics, against the day when they will live on their separate island, totally independent of men. Melanie jokes how they'll buy back Manhattan for twenty-four dollars' worth of macramé.

Moonchild smiles serenely. She lifts one rosy hand from the water and pats Melanie's hand. Melanie lifts her hand in pain. It is then that Melanie realizes the extent of Moonchild's conversion. The sock water had to be near boiling. She leaves Moon to the twelve other wives, to Norman and his soft-boiled socks. She walks aimlessly around the block, returns to the front stoop of the house. She longs to spirit Moon away—back to the collective, to a feminist psychiatrist, even to her parents in Chicago. On the porch of the sagging house, two of the wives sit in thin dresses, braiding midsummer flowers into their hair. As she leaves the house and Moon, this time for good, she tastes in her throat her unspent tears, her memories and regrets. She waves to the wives, but they do not see her. They are lost in their work, they are weaving wreaths.

A few days later, Melanie shows up at Sophie's door on Putnam Avenue with a U-Haul. Of all her matching Vuitton bags—once they numbered six—only one tote remains. When her mother and father come for her in their '75 Mercedes several months later, Melanie about to move to a Long Island town, Gladys will ask her about the rest of the luggage. Melanie will laugh and recall the day she dumped her make-up into the Atlantic; the day she threw Ricky's petrified gum, his ancient cigarette butt, even his sequence honors pin—fourteen-karat gold—into a green dumpster.

Melanie and Sophie are roommates once more, best friends one more time. Sophie takes courses in Jewish Studies at B.U. and works in the Laundromat nights. Melanie works full-time at the Free Women's Health Clinic. She's planning to go back to school and get her master's in public health. They seem these days like regular girls, like anybody's suburban daughters. Dr. Ricky Cooper calls to tell her he can't stop thinking about her. None of the women he meets mean anything to him. He tells her he can't help it, despite the article in *Xantipi*, he wants to see her again, he loves her. Melanie says—yes. Yes.

This time she makes love with him and means it. She kisses his belly, his face, his legs. Walking across the B.U. Bridge, she knows she belongs to him, that she is his intended one, that fate has led them to this moment: the leaves falling from the trees and she falling into his arms. There will be a waiting room after all. And she will be a doctor's wife. The hand-me-down copies of magazines—the back issues of *Parents* and *Time*—will have *her* name on the mailing label. She'll convince Ricky to subscribe to *Ms.*, to warm up the speculum, to tack interesting pictures onto the ceilings of the exam rooms, to support midwifery. She *will be* Mrs. Ricky Cooper even if she hyphenates: Melanie Szasz-Cooper. This time she won't let her sawbones slip away.

Ricky bends to pick a flower—the last wildflower of the season—from a crack in the sidewalk. "Dream-weed," Ricky says.

"I've got it," says Melanie. "After you finish your residency . . ."

"Why do I get the feeling you're about to get down on your knees?"

She waves her hand at him. "After you finish your residency, we'll start a clinic. I'll be licensed by then . . . OB-Gyn. Someplace groovy. Like Oregon. Or the South of France."

"The South of France? Are you crazy?"

"Why not? A free clinic."

"For all the poor women on the Côte D'Azur?" Ricky laughs. His Jewish princess. *Plus ça change, plus la même chose.* . . .

They embrace in the stillness.

"I mean it," Melanie says.

10

Bobby and Sheva are watching TV in Sheva's mother's house in Brooklyn. David Susskind and three hermaphrodites. Why doesn't he ever have normal people on his show? Sheva thinks. Even this depresses her.

"Sweet child," says Sheva's mother coming into the parlor with a plate of babka.

"Huh?" Bobby asks.

"Susskind in Yiddish," Sheva says. "Sweet child."

"So, another month, and you'll be a rabbi," Mrs. Grunig says. She puts her hand on Bobby's hand and smiles, revealing gold teeth. Every time Bobby sees her teeth, he thinks of the concentration camps. She cuts Bobby a piece of babka and pours him a cup of Turkish coffee.

"Now *that one* has a nice bustline," Mrs. Grunig says, laughing. "That one has a better figure than me. So, Bobby," she says. Bobby knows what's coming next. "So, Bobby, what are your plans . . . after the ordination?"

"I don't know whether to look for a pulpit right away," Bobby says, "or go back to Israel."

"I say let's go back."

Bobby looks at Sheva. She's waiting for him to make a move and who can blame her? He's been stalling for years. She knows he's seen that Sophie again. She can sense it in his moods. She thought if she were patient with him, didn't push him, didn't *hok*, didn't *hok* him to China, as Bobby would say, she thought that finally he would be hers—lock, stock, and *tuches*. Now she had trouble believing they'd ever be married.

* * *

She's been working at the *Forvertz*, copyediting Yiddish, the only person under seventy in an office of dying men. Copyediting the Yiddish news. So . . . what could be new? And living with her mother. Evenings she spends cooking dishes she or her mother heats up for the next day's meal. *Cholent* and stuffed peppers, sweet and sour salmon, *gedempte fleysh*. Her curly hair stuck to her forehead with sweat, the vinyl tablecloth, the cracked photographs of relatives long dead, the smell of the D train in the distance . . .

She is thirty years old and she looks it. A Brooklyn housewife with red hands. Already she is making do and she isn't even married. Wednesdays Bobby brings his laundry down from the dorm and they make love. Her mother and Vivi Shapiro, her friend from the Holocaust, go to the opera on Wednesday nights. Afterwards they go to Sammy's or one of the other refugee haunts. They meet other survivors and over *kugel*, they reminisce: the look of Krochmalna Street at dusk, the *Bund* picnics before the war, the Iron Gate on Leszno Street, the *arbes* in paper cones they sold in the Krasinski Gardens. . . .

She should have married Vivi's son Arthur. Now he's a foot doctor in the Five Towns. Who did she think she was? Too good for Arthur Shapiro, an expert on hammer-toes? What was *she* an expert on? On spinsterhood? On the serial comma? On Yiddish? A dead language they called it. Her blood was musty from all the death, her heart carried a bad smell. Uncle Asher dead in the sewers. Her father dead of pneumonia in the DP Camp. Her mother and Vivi on Christie Street, chuckling over the jokes of ghosts.

In Israel the Jews were alive. In Israel they said the *Kaddish* and kept walking into the wind.

Bobby had made her feel alive. For the first time in her life, with Bobby, she had felt young. With Bobby she had understood life the way other people lived it. She should have demanded he marry her the day after they made love. She should have hung up their conjugal sheets in the yard for the neighbors to see. "And if a man entice a virgin that is not betrothed and lie with her, he shall surely pay a dowry for her to be his wife."

"Well, tell us," David Susskind says, "What does it *feel like* to be a . . . *mish-mosh*? Neither a man nor a woman? Don't you feel kind of peculiar walking down the street? . . . I mean, where do you fit in? I mean, aren't you a misfit?"

11

Sophie can hear Melanie giggling like a hyena. Ricky and Melanie are listening to The Blues Project and making love. All they do is make love. Even if she's gone all day—at the library and classes all morning, at the Laundromat all night—the minute she walks into the house, Melanie starts giggling. What's so funny, Sophie wants to ask them. All of a sudden sex is funny. I never found sex especially funny, Sophie thinks.

After Bobby's ordination they go out for lunch to a place on Long Island. They eat clam cocktails with little forks. Sheva had never *seen* a clam. It is the strangest, slipperiest, most disgusting thing she's ever seen. Didn't they use the expression, "happy as a clam?" What's so happy? She'd expected a smiling face—like those yellow smile-faces that showed up everywhere these days. America. *Goyisheh kop*. Even her mother was pushing clams onto her fork and smiling like a *goyeh*. And flirting with Bobby's father. And Bobby's sister Muffin was pregnant. She'd felt a moment of jealousy when she'd first heard Muffin was expecting. Would *she* ever have a baby, Bobby's baby?

Muffin was a hotshot lawyer who planned to turn the baby over to some governess or someone the second it popped out. Typical American career bullshit, Sheva thinks. She seems so complacent, this Muffin. Her skin is perfectly, evenly tanned, even though it is only May. She probably has her legs waxed, her eyebrows waxed, her "bikini line." Sheva runs her finger across her upper lip. Perhaps she should stop making fun, the pot calling the kettle, and find out the name of Muffin's salon. . . .

* * *

"With Mayerall you need something kicky . . . and personally I don't care for the alliterative approach."

"And, of course, Muff will return to work the next week . . . junior partner . . ."

". . . not enough pulpits in Israel . . ."

"Haifa had the best food. . . ."

". . . her father died *after* the War . . . I heard dysentery. . . ."

". . . not enough pulpits in Israel . . ."

"That was Caesarea . . ."

". . . too much *baba ghanouj* . . ."

". . . 100 percent inflation . . ."

". . . the *Sephardim* are taking over . . ."

". . . Harvard . . ."

". . . Stanford . . ."

"What about Gabrielle for a girl? . . ."

". . . too much *baba ghanouj* . . ."

Mr. and Mrs. Bradford Szasz

request the honour of your presence

at the marriage of their daughter

Melanie Jane

to

Dr. Richard Bernard Cooper

on the nineteenth of December

nineteen hundred and seventy-six

Temple Emanuel

Reception to follow at the Sherry-Netherland Hotel

They sit on the Promenade in Brooklyn Heights for what seems like hours.

"Yes or no," Sheva says.

"Don't pressure me," says Bobby.

"If you don't marry me in six months, forget it," Sheva says, crying. "Just forget it."

Bobby takes Sheva home. She sleeps all the way to Avenue P. The weight of her curly head in his lap is more than he can bear. He's ruined her life, Bobby thinks. He just can't make himself agree on a date. Melanie and Rick's invitation had come just that day in the mail. He'd taken it out of his pocket and shown it to her over dinner. Brisket and potato *latkes* at the Madison Deli. She'd ripped the invitation out of his hand and crumpled it up. He'd laughed, he didn't understand why she was suddenly mad.

"Everyone is getting married. Everyone is having babies. And I'm working with old men and living with my mother." When she wouldn't eat her dinner—she'd ordered the stuffed cabbage—he'd realized something was really wrong. He'd never known her not to eat.

She'd ripped the invitation up and thrown the pieces into his plate. When he'd pushed the paper aside and kept eating, sopping his gravy, then she'd really let him have it. In the middle of the deli, she'd started to scream at the top of her lungs. "Betrayer, deceiver, whore-monger! Perverted American rabbi!" Beige-haired ladies in Persian lamb had turned to stare at him. They'd had to leave before he was finished. He'd taken her hand and they'd walked and walked all the way to Fourteenth Street. A bitter wind had tossed them about in the dying November light. "When?" she had said. "When? If not now, then when?" Who did she think she was, Bobby thought—Rabbi Hillel?

When would he make her his *rebbitsin*? When would he leave his bourgeois job teaching in a rich man's yeshiva and take her to the promised place, the land of covenant and light? He couldn't answer, he didn't know. He *wanted* to be a noble man—a wise man like Saul or Moses, a kingly man like Samuel or David. He wanted to make his Bathsheba happy: a mother of sons, a queen of the Sabbath, a radiant footstool in heaven. And yet his dreams were full of her whom he could never forsake. Sophie's body came to him in his dreams every night. It had been many months since he'd seen her, all tarted up, at her father's birthday party. Inexplicably, she'd cleaned up her act. Now she was studying Jewish philosophy.

Melanie had called him up the night she and Ricky had become engaged. "Where's Sophie?" he'd asked casually, knowing she and Melanie were living together, expecting Melanie to say she was off working the bar around the corner. Expecting Melanie to say she was out with some middle-aged Shriner in town just for the night. . . .

"She's studying," Melanie had said. "She's reading Maimonides." Melanie laughed. "You want me to put her on?"

"Maimonides?" Bobby had said. The Rambam himself. Hadn't he been reading Maimonides just fifteen minutes earlier? He thought he could hear, over the wires, the ancient sound of Sophie's fingers turning sacred pages. Sophie's lips wrapping themselves around the syllables.

"You want me to put her on? I didn't realize Maimonides was such a turn-on," Melanie had laughed.

"No, no," Bobby had said. "Just tell her I miss her," Bobby had said. "Just tell her I said hello."

Hello.

Six months, Sheva had said. Either he married her by May, or else forget it, Sheva had said. And now her large curly head was bouncing in his bony lap. He saw her violet-veined lids; her yellow-green skin—the stain of the Jews, a yellow-green stain on the map. The right thing was to marry her. Why was the right thing so clear and also so difficult? If he'd meant to choose Sophie, after all, he should have done so years ago when she had flown across the seas, when fate had brought her to Yad Vashem on the day he and Sheva had gone there.

Then, he'd been angry with her. He'd thought her coming to Israel had been a shallow manipulation. Who was she to decide suddenly she was ready to be his wife? After the torture she'd put him through, after the years of silence and loss? After he'd rescued her from Harry's only for her to laugh in his face?

He'd fled to Athens like a coward. He'd slept in the open on the third-class deck. He'd heard the sounds of the sailors singing; he'd seen the distant earth of Rhodes; he'd wrapped himself in the *Jerusalem Post*, warming himself against the chill. He'd covered himself with *Ha'aretz*, the sacred letters lending sanctuary against the wind and air. He'd eaten blood oranges and sardines and listened to the phlegmatic music of ancient Greek men singing their sleep.

By the time the boat was moored in Piraeus, he knew he had made up his mind. He'd chosen Jerusalem over Athens, he'd chosen the promise of the World to Come. And Sheva would be his wife.

No matter that Sophie burned in his loins, no matter that sometimes, just once in a while, her face, her arms, her breasts, her hips, would come to him in a heady swoon while he was making love to Sheva. Sheva would give him sturdy sons; Sheva would keep the sacred Sabbath; Sheva would keep a solid roof over his *luftmensh* head. Hadn't he learned through philosophy that eros was the enemy of law? Didn't he know there could be no Israel without her stony laws? Didn't Jewish ethics demand that he marry a wholesome woman, a woman whose heart and body were pure?

The Christians had Mary Magdalene. Repentantly, she'd washed Christ's feet, drying his soles in her hair. Let he who is without sin cast the first stone. No Jewish girl he knew would wash anybody's feet. Wash your own feet; what are you, nuts?

Let he who is without sin . . . The Jews were simply not big on forgiveness. Where Mary Magdalene was spared and redeemed, Jezebel was stoned to death, the polished stones of Jerusalem striking her pale brow. . . .

Sheva Grunig would be his wife. He'd cabled Sophie as much from Athens: GO BACK TO N.J. I MUST CHOOSE SHEVA.

And yet he'd taken her to the Arab hotel just hours before he'd left for Greece. Making love to his Jezebel while the streets of Jerusalem filled with rain . . . No wonder she hadn't believed him then, never believed a word he said. Always he had given in.

He hadn't seen her in over a year when he'd shown up at her parents' door for Sid's birthday party. He and Rick had both thought it strange that Miriam had invited them. Rick hadn't seen Melanie since the exposé she'd published in that lesbian rag. He was still mad at Sophie—for being a junkie, a whore, a bum, for coming to Israel and screwing things up with Sheva. And he had been really furious that she'd gone to Sheva's apartment. God knows what she'd said. Where did she get the chutzpah? Had she told Sheva they'd made love just hours, just minutes, before his departure?

Who said the Jews were not big on forgiveness? Hadn't Sheva forgiven him that? Hadn't Sheva forgiven him a thousand times before and after? It wasn't her fault he was a fool. Nothing was Sheva's fault. For years he had led her on. Hadn't he asked her to marry him even before they'd ever made love? "And if a man entice a virgin that is not betrothed and lie with her, he shall surely pay a dowry for her to be his wife."

He looked down into his lap—his skinny, thankless lap. Hadn't his years at the seminary taught him anything at all? Survey of Practical *Halakhah*; Tragedy, Death and the Rabbi? Either he was a man or he wasn't; either he was a Jew or nothing. What did it mean to be a rabbi? Didn't rabbi mean *my teacher*? What did it mean to be a teacher if one could not teach oneself? How could he be sitting here, a presumptively pious man, riding the subway through Brooklyn, plotting a way to break his promise?

He leaned down and kissed her lips. Sheva had pretty lips. So what if they were cracked and raw? That was his fault. He'd made her cry. They'd set the wedding date in the morning. He'd make sure she took care of herself. He'd buy her cosmetics. Chapstick. Eye shadow. Nail polish. Powder. He'd send her to a beauty parlor. Every Friday afternoon like his mother and her friends. He'd make her into a Jewish Princess. Maybe he'd buy her a fur cape. White bunny fur. He'd take care of her. He had a little money now. The yeshiva paid him almost $150 a week. He'd buy her a bracelet or something, silver with little red stones. She'd had her engagement ring for years. Surely the ring had worn off by now. It was time for a booster, a second installment, the renewal of his promise. . . .

12

Sophie is the maid of honor. She is wearing the most magnificent dress Dori has ever seen. A delicate gray the color of oysters, the color of smoke, of evanescence, the very tincture of flight. And Bobby is the best man, mischievous in a gray tux. Dori is sure they planned their outfits; a match as perfect as this one could only have been planned. A match as perfect as these two could only have begun in heaven.

Dori watches as Bobby leads Sophie to the *chuppa*. From behind her comes an audible gasp. Dori turns and sees a young woman, a pale young woman with dark hair, who looks like she's going to faint. And then a very pregnant person she's sure she's never seen before leads the fainting one down the aisle. A procession in reverse. The interruption has screwed up the band. The *klezmer* group sighs and begins again. Layeh and Shelly Cooper are leading their Ricky down the aisle and all the mothers are weeping.

Morty Kates winks at Miriam across the sea of sniffling moms. A dry-eyed Miriam smiles inscrutably. She pats her ex-husband's hand. She's always loved his clean hands, the slenderness of his fingers, the perfect moons of his manicured nails. Why is Morty winking at her? She's always found winking especially vulgar. They hadn't been lovers for years. Why couldn't he just forget it? Take their affair for what it had been, a light-hearted romp in middle age? He thought he'd fallen in love with her. He'd told Sid he wanted more poetry in his life. *Poetry*. Then he and Sid got sloshed in the VFW bar.

Later that evening she and Sid had laughed their heads off. Lying in bed, the two of them drinking diet soda, he'd made love to her over and over. How's this for poetry, he'd said, entering her body. How's this little sonnet grab you? He'd tickled her ear with the sounds of his love. And now Sid wanted to marry her and she didn't know what to do.

They'd been living together ever since he'd split with Dori. Wasn't he due for the seven-year itch? As soon as she married him, she was sure, he'd find someone new to screw. He'd want somebody on the side. The only woman he hadn't made they both knew was Gladys Szasz. She tried to imagine Gladys and Sid, but it was impossible. Why does Gladys close her eyes when she and Brad have sex? It was one of Sid's favorite jokes. She doesn't want to see Brad enjoying himself.

And speaking of Gladys, there she was, she and Brad leading Melanie down the aisle. Brad looked great, he'd shaved his mustache. Gladys had been begging him to shave it off for twenty years, ever since the girls were small. He did look younger, Miriam thought. Funny how the men hit fifty looking terrific, Miriam thought, while the best the women could hope for was well-preserved.

She'd always hated that expression. It made her think of mausoleums. Mausoleums and museums. Maple leaves pressed into albums, old photographs, daguerreotypes, flowers covered with shellac. The golden color of shellac the same gold as autumn leaves. Autumn leaves and golden apples, the golden apples of the sun.

She found herself holding back tears. Around her everyone was weeping. Even Sid, Sid the Kid, had turned on the waterworks. Melanie stood next to Ricky under the velvet of the *chuppa*. Gladys and Brad stood on one side and next to them was little Sophie, resplendent in a lovely dress. She could no longer hold back the tears. She couldn't remember how long it had been since she'd had a real cry. She wasn't crying for Melanie and Ricky, their whole lives shining before them; she wasn't even crying for Sophie—the daughter she'd lost through sloth and neglect, the daughter she had lost to time.

She cried for herself, not even for Sid, she cried for her own lost girlhood. She remembered her own hurry-up wedding, the pale gardenia pinned to her suit, the apartment she and Sid had rented on Seventy-first street near Columbus. She remembered a wrought-iron free-style vase she and Sid had bought in the Village when she was twenty-two and an orphan; her father dead of a heart attack, her mother burned up in the Rivoli Theatre, sighing over James Mason.

She'd filled the vase with glossy eggplants and a trio of bright lemons. Sid had been impressed by her flair. He'd said she should be in a magazine:

Newlywed decorates first apartment on a shoestring budget. Even "budget" was old-fashioned now. Budget had gone the way of full-length slips, Aunt Millie's Sauce, and Contact paper on the bridge table.

In the beginning Sid had admired her. He was a mama's boy; his family had always had money. While she had sent herself through college, giving piano lessons to the children of her professors and sorting dirty clothes in a laundry, he'd been sent ten dollars a week just to take girls out on dates. Ten dollars a week in the forties! And he was a grown-up man by then, a veteran on the GI Bill.

She remembered the first time she'd seen him that night in the Catskills. She'd known right away he was out of her league. And besides, he wasn't even her type. She'd liked the scholarly boys with glasses who read Marx and Freud. Sid, to this day, thought Marcuse was a band leader—Herbie Marcuse and his existentialists. And yet, when he picked her out, singled her out from among the beauties, the buxom blondes with fur-trimmed sweaters, she'd given in, she'd thought, why not? He made her laugh. That was it. The scholarly boys didn't make her laugh. He still makes me laugh, she thinks, looking over at Sid who's crying.

The rabbi extends a silver cup, first to Ricky and then to Melanie. Miriam tries to catch Sophie's eye as the newlyweds are pronounced man and wife. Sophie is looking across the canopy at the eyes of the best man. Miriam is pretty sure Sophie is still in love with Bobby. If only she had loved him back when he had been in love with her. She remembered the time Bobby had called, waking them in the night: "Your daughter's a prostitute, sir."

She remembers she hadn't been surprised. Somehow she'd expected as much—or even worse—from Sophie. Always there had been something strange about her only daughter, some indefinable peculiarity. . . . She hadn't pressed her for details. She guessed she hadn't wanted to know exactly what it was she'd done at the topless bar. Melanie had insisted she was only a dancer. Sophie had said nothing; she figured Sophie must have done worse. Her whole generation was cursed . . . The sins of the parents were only the beginning.

She had to remember to tell Sophie the latest news about Anita. Some young doctor, a specialist, had come to Passaic Pines where Anita had been a patient for many years. A hopeless case. And somehow, he'd cured her. She wasn't sure about the details, exactly what happened after what, but basically he had cured her with love. He'd cured her with an engagement ring, a diamond as big as the King David. The doctor had fallen in love with her and through his love she had been restored. Miriam had run into Lee in Riverside Square. Lee was trying on cruise wear, checking her bum in the three-way mirror, when Miriam recognized her. Lee was trying a gilt sarong which draped craftily below her abdomen. Her belly looked appetizing at fifty. Playfully, Miriam had put her finger in the cleft of Lee's navel. "You need a diamond right *here*."

"Speaking of diamonds," Lee had said. Miriam surveyed Lee's face for wrinkles, for brown spots, for falling objects. "Can you believe that Anita's engaged—again?" She'd laughed.

"You look happy," Miriam said.

Lee was wearing a silk T shirt. "What do you wear on top with this thing? I *am* happy," Lee said. "The third time around . . . well . . . This time Anita is being released for good. And listen to this—marrying her psychiatrist."

"A doctor," Miriam said. "*Mazel tov*."

"Of course it won't be easy for her. I've decided she has to take full charge of Sasha herself now. I mean, I'll give her a few months. . . . He knows that Neeter is his mother. He's seven years old," Lee said. "Already he's in second grade."

"*Tempus fugit*," said Miriam.

"Time flies," said Lee, remembering her Latin. "It sure does. Now tell me, Miriam, what do you wear on top with a crazy skirt like this?"

"Bare bosoms," said Miriam, smiling.

Lee laughed her throaty laugh. "I wish I had the tits for *that*. Now *you're* nice and flat," Lee said. "You could get away with it."

"I can't get away with anything," Miriam said. She looked Lee right in the eye. One of Lee's lashes was coming loose. She was a funny girl, this Lee. A kind of minor-league Liz Taylor. Everyone knew her current boyfriend was filthy rich, a real estate developer. "Where are you going?" asked Miriam.

"A little cruise," Lee said. "To the Dutch Antilles. We're leaving the day after Melanie's wedding. Neeter is getting married in April. Now she and Eric are off visiting his family in San Francisco. It's too bad she has to miss Melanie's wedding. But Eric wanted her to meet the *mechutanim* right away . . . get over her nervousness. You'll come to Neeter's wedding, won't you? You've been to *all* her weddings."

"I'm a veteran," Miriam said.

"I hear Sophie's the maid of honor. When will we get to dance at *her* wedding?"

"We'll just have to wait and see," said Miriam. "I'm not sure she's the wedding type."

"She was always different," Lee said. "Your Sophie was always a little different than the other girls. I remember how she always refused to join the sorority." Lee remembered the tragic look in Sophie's eyes, what a sad little girl Sophie had always been. "Well I hope she's doing all right. Gladys tells me she's back in school. Studying Jewish something . . ."

"Jewish philosophy," Miriam said.

"Not the most practical thing . . ."

"You'd be surprised," Miriam said, patting Lee on her tanned belly. "You'd be surprised," Miriam said, inscrutable as ever.

In the garage of the hotel, Sheva vomits. Bobby's sister Muffin wipes her brow with a lace hankie.

"It seems to me *you* should be vomiting," Bobby says to his sister.

"I never vomited once," says Muffin. "I never had morning sickness once. I've had the most perfect pregnancy." Muffin smiles in the winter sun. She takes off her fur jacket and wraps it around Sheva's shoulders.

"Aren't you cold?" Sheva asks.

"My furnace is on overdrive. I'm burning up," Muffin says. "Go ahead in, Bobby. Sheva and I will sit in the car."

Muffin opens the door to her parents' Fleetwood and ushers Sheva inside.

"I *can't* get sick in here," Sheva says. "Can't we sit in *your* car?"

"Our car is teeny," Muffin says. She points to the red MG parked alongside the Caddy. "If I don't deliver pretty soon, we'll have to rent a car or something. A station wagon or something. I can barely fit in there. And besides, I'd rather you barfed in here."

"Your mother already hates me," Sheva says.

"My mother hates everybody. She's not crazy about me either. Or Michael, my husband, for that matter. She doesn't like my father either. The only person she respects—or likes—is Bobby. Although she's disappointed, I guess, that he only became a rabbi. No offense," Muffin says.

"When I first met her—in Israel—she gave me some cream for facial hair . . . to take off my mustache," Sheva says.

Muffin starts laughing. "How awful," Bobby's sister says. "Bobby never told me *that*."

"*Well*? Wouldn't you feel terrible?"

"It *is* pretty amazing," Muffin says. She takes out her compact. When she opens it, a little light comes on. Like magic, Sheva thinks. How perfect. How perfectly feminine. Why didn't she have anything like that? A compact with a little light? Femininity, she decided, was a matter of the right equipment. She'd never have the right props.

"Where do you get . . . something like that?" Sheva asks Muffin.

"A compact?"

"With a little light?"

"Any drugstore," Muffin says. "They have them everywhere," she says.

But Sheva knew it wasn't true. It simply wasn't as easy as that.

"Where's Sheva?" Sophie asks.

"She's in the car. With my sister. She isn't feeling well," Bobby says.

"She shouldn't leave you alone like this. If I were Sheva, I wouldn't let you out of my sight."

He couldn't tell if Sophie meant it or if she was goofing on him. The longer he knew her, the less he knew her. He never could tell when she was kidding. . . .

"So when's the wedding?" Sophie asks. "This has to be the longest engagement on record."

"Not so long."

"It seems like a thousand years," she says. She takes his hands into her own. "Dance with me, Bobby," Sophie says.

Holding her close to his rented tux, he feels the heat of her body against him. She is the most alive person he's ever met. The most passionate woman in the world, he thinks, pressing her close to his pulsing heart. Sophie sings along with the band, a hokey song from *The Fantasticks*.

"Pretty corny," Bobby says.

Her eyes closed tight against his tux, she sniffles into his rented jacket. She smells the scent of mothballs, of time, of time elapsed and time preserved; she smells his smell beneath the jacket. And like the jacket, he is on loan, he doesn't really belong to her. He belongs to her only for this dance, this finitude of sappy music, this sappy finitude of time. She knows that he loves her as she loves him. She knows that he wants her. And yet he is promised to another and she knows that he has to, will do, the right thing. The right thing is to break her heart. Just as she broke his heart a thousand times when she was young; young and foolish, or young and sick, it no longer mattered.

What mattered now was only this dance, this time, this moment which stretched between them—a moment whose limits were made in time. His arms encircled her moving body. A circle made of arms and arms. The rest of her life she would live in this moment. The rest of her life she would long for this circle, this circle of flesh, this circle of light. . . .

She notices a spotlight is shining on them. She sees that all the guests have formed a circle around her and Bobby. "The best man, Rabbi Robert Buchman, and the maid of honor, Miss Sophie Spivack . . ." The emcee was wearing a turquoise jacket with shiny lapels and a sequined skullcap. "Rabbi, would you mind starting us . . . and you, too, young lady. Isn't she beautiful, ladies and gentlemen? Okay Rabbi, Sophie, let's go. You put your left foot in, you put your left foot out. . . ."

13

Nineteen seventy-seven is the year for weddings. In January Miriam and Sid are married in the living room of their own house. Sophie flies down from Boston to be her parents' witness. The other witness is Glad Szasz. Miriam had called her up, simply asked her to pop over for a cup of coffee. She was the only woman they knew who'd never gone to bed with Sid. As far as Miriam knew.

And it's the mayor of Hudson Heights who answers Gladys's brisk knock. A young guy, maybe thirty-five, wearing clunky jewelry; his shirt unbuttoned to his waist, a gold *chai* as big as the Ritz dangling in his chest hair. The ceremony is short and legal. They haven't written their own vows. Not like Melanie and Ricky. Sophie remembers Melanie standing in her Bendel's gown, reading from Sojourner Truth. "And ain't I a woman? . . ."

Sophie had had to bite her lip to keep from laughing during the service. She'd been afraid to catch Bobby's eye, though Bobby wasn't the best partner for a laughing fit. And yesterday Mel had called from her honeymoon in Paris to tell Sophie they'd just heard Bobby and Sheva had set a date. Bobby and Sheva planned to get married in April on the anniversary of the Warsaw Ghetto Uprising. Melanie hadn't laughed. She didn't know whether or not Sophie would find this detail amusing. Sophie did, but she saved her laughter. She knew she was going to need it.

And now she stood next to her father. He looked no more like an anchorman; he looked no more like a New School professor stopping in Zabar's for a pound of chèvre. His blond hair had turned yellow-gray, his full head of hair looked almost indecent. He looked like the aging emcee in a bankrupt Catskills resort; he looked like a drama coach whose students had all OD'd. She looked at her father in the cruel light of the living room. He looked like a sex offender.

On his way out the door, the mayor of Hudson Heights asks Sophie what she's doing later. His name is Jedd Fink. After five minutes he'll take out a Cuban cigar and jump on top of her. He probably has French ticklers in the glove compartment.

"Not tonight," Sophie says. "We're celebrating . . . you know. . . ." Instead of champagne, there was bubbling cider from the health food store. Miriam had stayed on the wagon eight years. She closes the door on the mayor. In the bright foyer the *chai* on his chest catches the light, glinting good luck.

In February Sophie receives a telegram from her brother. Brian and Ruth were married just weeks after her parents' wedding. It strikes her as funny suddenly. Not only Melanie and Anita, but even Brian has landed a doctor! He and Ruth would be in Boston at the end of the week to attend some medical conference. Would Sophie have dinner with them?

It is more than a little weird to be eating sushi with the doctor who'd supervised her de-tox, and yet she likes Ruth Rogers. Their good news is Ruth is pregnant. Sophie looks into Ruth's face. "I'm thirty-seven," Ruth says. "I'm lucky there's any action down there."

"Plenty of action where that came from," Brian says, patting her belly. It's clear to Sophie in that moment that Brian really loves Ruth. She realizes she's never seen her brother happy before.

When Ruth goes to the bathroom, Brian takes his sister's hand. "There's something I have to say to you . . . now that everything is working out. I'm starting my own company. Fixing up Victorian houses. Anyway, so Ruth will feel free to stay at home . . . you know . . ."

"What's the matter?" Sophie asks. "You want me to pay you back? I have *some* money saved . . . not the whole $2000—" Why does she think she knows what's coming?

"No, no. Of course not. We have plenty of money. . . ."

"A *doktor*," Sophie says, putting on a Yiddish accent.

"I want to say this before Ruth . . . Sophie, you *have to* forgive me . . ."

"I know what you're going to say. Don't say it." She sticks her finger into her dish, swirling up the rest of her green tea ice cream. "It's okay, Brian."

"It's not okay," Brian says. And then he starts crying. She hates it when men cry. Bobby used to drive her nuts. Even her father had started crying ever since his male menopause. What was happening to the men? The men were turning to jelly.

"Please don't cry," she says. She blamed feminism for this. All the men were turning to mush.

"I was really crazy," he says. "I don't know how I could have done it . . . you were fourteen or something. I was a virgin too," Brian says, "as if that makes any difference."

Sophie laughs. How could it matter that her brother was a virgin?

"I raped you," Brian laughs. He's losing it, Sophie thinks. He rakes his nails into the tablecloth. She hopes he'll pull it together before Ruth comes back. She wishes Ruth would hurry.

"Now *stop* it. You didn't rape me. It was mutual," Sophie says. "Kind of, anyway . . ."

"You were drunk. You didn't . . . You were fourteen years old," Brian says. "I can't believe I did that to you. I went to see a psychiatrist. Not Bev. Recently. I told him the whole thing. How I was in love with you. It took me about six months to tell him—I raped you."

"I never thought of it as rape. I always thought it was mutual. Weird, but somehow mutual . . ."

"The time I finally spit it out . . . I was talking to him about something else . . . about Miriam, I think. And all of a sudden I spit it out. . . ."

Sophie sees Ruth ambling back to the table. She carries Sophie's niece. "*Tell me a joke, Aunt Sophie. Tell me about you and Daddy when you were kids.*" "*We'll talk about it another time. . . .*" She watches Brian's face light up as Ruth sits down beside him. It strikes her as a miracle that Brian's baby is swimming around inside this sober woman's womb. Maybe the next generation would have an easier time. She was glad new babies were coming into the world. Bobby had become an uncle in December. "You're lucky to have him," Sophie says, putting her hand on Ruth's hand. "You're lucky to have my brother."

Sophie decides not to fly to New Jersey for Anita's wedding. "I've already been to enough weddings," she tells her mother on the phone. "I think I've been to enough weddings to last me," Sophie says.

"I was invited to Bobby's wedding. Did I tell you that? I'm surprised they wanted me. I don't even *know* Bobby's parents. I only know Layeh slightly. Gladys really wants us to come."

"Probably because she's so happy Bobby is marrying someone else."

"I won't go if you don't want me to. I already bought them a wedding present. *The Treasury of Jewish Humor*."

"They're gonna need it," Sophie says.

"You love him, don't you?" Miriam says. "You still love him after all this time."

"Almost ten years," Sophie says.

"Well *do* you love him?" Miriam asks. "It made me so sad at Melanie's wedding . . . to see you two dancing."

"Of course I still love him," Sophie says. "But there's nothing I can do. What can I do?" Sophie asks.

"Nothing," Miriam says. "You want me not to go to the wedding?"

"It doesn't matter," Sophie says. "Do whatever you want," says Sophie.

Melanie calls up Sophie two days before Bobby's wedding. She's making tabbouleh for some Jewish event in Woodmere and wants Sophie's recipe.

"Are you in the Sisterhood or what? I can't believe it," Sophie says.

"It's good for business. I meet all the women, and then they'll go to Ricky for their tubal ligations—if they like *me*. I'm doing it for both of us," Melanie says. "It's going to be my clinic too. I made him put my name on the stationery."

"So how are the lovebirds?" Sophie asks.

"Ricky saw Bobby last night. And Ricky's making a stag party here tomorrow night. You aren't mad, are you? What could I do?" Melanie asks.

"What do I care," Sophie says. "Is Ricky having a stripper? Maybe I could be the stripper."

"You *are* mad, aren't you? What could I do? Forbid him to have it?"

"I'm serious, Melanie. I want to jump out of the cake."

"I'm not *letting* them have a stripper. I may have sold out my politics, but not *that bad*," Melanie says.

"Well give the old groom a kiss for me," Sophie says. "On the tush."

"You sound bummed out," Melanie says. "I probably shouldn't have brought it up."

"It doesn't matter," Sophie says.

"Of course it matters. I wish I could be with you that day. I *have* to go to the wedding, don't I? He *is* Ricky's first cousin and best friend, right?"

"I'm not arguing," Sophie says.

"If you think it's unethical," Melanie says.

"My *mother's* going," Sophie says. "And she doesn't even *know* them. *You* have to go," Sophie says. "Later you can tell me the details. I've accepted it," Sophie says. "I accepted it a long time ago." She only wished that were true.

"You'll find someone else. Someone better. Somebody really handsome and rich . . ." Melanie stifles her tears.

"Right, who graduated from a great college. So anyway, Melanie, I have to get off and write this paper. I'm writing a paper on Saadya Gaon. Tell Bobby the night before his stag party, I was writing a paper on Saadya Gaon and the foundations of the Commandments. He's the only person in the world who could appreciate the ironies."

"It's funny, isn't it?" Melanie says. "Both of you studying Jewish philosophy . . ."

"Not as funny as you think. I've come to believe in fate," Sophie says. "*Godal* in Hebrew. It's not as funny as you think."

14

The night of Bobby's stag party, Sophie goes to a bar in Cambridge and picks up a blond guy with muscles named Stan. So much for the Ten Commandments. She goes with him to his apartment in Brookline. He offers her a Heineken and turns on the radio. He moves closer to her on the couch. From upstairs they overhear a domestic argument. "Fascist!" the woman screams. "Wife-beater!" the woman cries. A child starts crying then. A dog starts to bark. She hears a lamp or something knocked over, the child crying, "Mommy, don't!" Stan turns to kiss her. His eyes are bloodshot, he smells of beer. She moves away from him. "Mommy, don't! Make her stop! Daddy, please, make her stop!"

"You want me to put on a record? Paul McCartney? Rolling Stones?"

"No," Sophie says. She looks around the room. A lobster trap made into a table. A back issue of *TV Guide*. A plastic lamp like they sell in the supermarket. "No."

"You want something to eat? I have some kind of dip or something my sister made last week. Cheese dip or something . . ."

"Okay." She watches his pants ride down his hips. She thinks of Bobby's bachelor party. She wonders if Melanie is staying upstairs pretending to read a book. *How To Do Your Own Hysterectomy*. She sees a trail of dark blond hair leading down the base of his spine. She sees his name on the subscription label of the *TV Guide*: Stanley Smith in computer letters. On top of the television, she sees a child's mitten. Emerald green with a white thumb. She wonders if Stan is a father. Whose mitten is it? A little girl with a jelly-stained face? A little boy with scabby knees? He comes back into the room.

The dip is in a cottage cheese container. He carries a couple of Heinekens, and a miniature bag of chips. "I only eat Lays," she remembers. A dirty joke from her childhood. On the window an azalea blooms in a plastic pot.

"Kiss me," Stan says.

Upstairs there is only silence. She wonders if the child has gone back to sleep. She wonders if the couple upstairs have made up; if right this minute, above their heads, the man and woman are making love.

Melanie wakes her up at ten in the morning. She is hung over on beer and relieved to be in her own bed. "I'll call you back," Sophie says.

"No," Melanie says. "You'll never believe what happened."

"What? I have to call you back. I have to go to the bathroom."

"I'll wait," Melanie says.

Sophie feels horrible. She hadn't been drunk in months, in years. She remembers Stan's bedroom—the dirty corduroy comforter, the bottles of beer under the bed, the scar as circuitous as Lombard Street running across his belly. She splashes water on her face and goes back to the phone.

"Sophie? You took forever. Bobby has disappeared."

"What do you mean?" Sophie asks.

"Ricky went over to the Buchmans' an hour ago. Bobby slept at his parents' last night, but he's not there. Bobby's father heard him come in. The wedding is at twelve o'clock."

"He'll show up," Sophie says. "He's not the type to disappear."

"I have this feeling, Sophie, he's gonna show up at your place."

"That's ridiculous," Sophie says. "I haven't seen him since your wedding."

"A week ago he asked me for your address. He said he wanted to write you a letter."

"I never got it," Sophie says. "He probably went for a walk or something. The bachelor takes his last walk . . . you know what I mean."

"I have a funny feeling," Melanie says. "I just have this feeling he's not gonna marry her. I think I always kind of knew he'd never go through with it."

"Well, leave me out of it," Sophie says. "I don't care *what* he does."

"Don't kid yourself," says Melanie. "You know you're still in love with him. Admit it, Sophie. Admit you love him."

"Forget it, Melanie. I don't care where Bobby is. Let him marry that hairy bitch. You think I care? I don't."

"I didn't know you were gonna get so freaked out. I'm sorry, I thought you'd want to know."

"I don't," Sophie says. "I don't want to talk about him."

"Will you call me if he shows up?"

"I told you, Melanie, forget it."

"Think of Sheva," Melanie says.

Think of Sheva? Sophie hangs up the phone. Why should she think of Sheva? She remembers that day in Sheva's apartment in Jerusalem. The honey cake that tasted like sand, the sweaty curls of underarm hair, the thin black rayon socks Sheva let pool around her ankles. She thought of Sheva in a white dress, waiting in the rabbi's study. A white dress as plain as virtue, a bouquet of violets, her mother's string of genuine pearls. She thought of a table prepared by the Sisterhood: Outsized bowls of egg salad, tuna fish, macaroni.

She slipped into a pair of jeans. Unconsciously she put on a T shirt that once belonged to Bobby. She took a walk through the neighborhood. The streets of Cambridge were shiny with rain. The parked cars, the bright litter, the teen-aged girls in lavendar parkas—the whole world filled her with a sense of wonder and pain. The anniversary of the Warsaw Ghetto Uprising! What a corny day for a wedding. She knew that Bobby would show up and marry Sheva after all. Perhaps he needed the false drama of making Sheva wait. He'd show up at the last minute, a little bit ruffled, in his tux. He'd say "I do," in a clear voice. He'd kiss her firmly on the lips when the rabbi said, "You may now kiss the bride." The rabbi had never said it at all at Melanie's wedding. Always that had been the high point of the wedding games of her girlhood. "You may now kiss the bride." It turned out they never said it. The kissing was beside the point.

She remembered playing Barbie's wedding with Melanie and Anita. The climax had always been squashing Ken into Barbie's hard face. And then the two of them would leave in a shoe-box limousine. Thom McAn 8½ AAA 9406.

The honeymoon would take place underneath Melanie's bed. They'd strip Barbie of her wedding dress, her little shoes, her paper bouquet. "My darling Barbie," Ken would say, naked as God had made him. "My darling Barbie, I've waited for you my whole life and now you're mine. Your rooted hair, your movable arms, and all your accessories."

Bobby Buchman sits at the bar at La Guardia, drunk as a peasant. He is carrying Maimonides' *The Guide of the Perplexed*. He is drinking whiskey sours—a woman's drink—what else? He doesn't like the taste of booze—another of his many insufficiencies as a man. He orders a Jack Daniel's and hopes the bartender can't tell he's crying. He looks at the watch of the man sitting next to him. 10:55. It's not too late to do the right thing. He could make it in plenty of time. Ricky was supposed to pick him up in Flushing at 9:30. He could call Ricky right now. Ricky would come in his new Volvo, a wedding present from Melanie's parents. They'd pick up his tux and rush to Brooklyn, listening to 1010 WINS the whole way. They could be at Sheva's door in less than an hour. Easy. He thinks of Sheva, her white face, her white hands, her white dress. She'd wanted to wear a regular dress. She'd bought a terrible street-length dress in Klein's for nineteen dollars, a cheap synthetic she'd modeled for him on one of their Wednesday nights in March. Didn't she know it was bad luck to let the groom see the dress before the ceremony?

He'd asked Melanie to take her shopping. Melanie hadn't wanted to do it. She'd thought it was disloyal to Sophie. She hadn't said so, but Bobby had known. Why else would Melanie Szasz refuse a shopping trip? Perhaps that was why he'd never believed Melanie could be a diehard feminist. He simply couldn't imagine her giving up on fashion. She'd even written an essay once: "Why I Can't Give Up Bloomingdale's." Of all her columns, that was the one Bobby believed.

He'd given Melanie $200 and begged her to take Sheva shopping. He knew $200 wasn't enough, but that was all the money he had. Melanie had agreed to do it if Bobby promised he'd never tell Sophie. And so he had promised. He remembered the day the girls had come home, carrying shopping bags. There was a dress, a veil, a garter, underwear, a negligee. He knew that Melanie wouldn't let him down.

Later he'd taken Melanie aside and asked her how she'd done it on $200. He remembered that his sister's dress had cost over $800. Melanie smiled mysteriously. "Think of it as our wedding gift," Melanie had said. "We found this place in *Modern Bride*. An outlet you wouldn't believe. Discounts you shouldn't know from. . . ."

His heart was full of love for Melanie. She was the best of all of them. He remembered making love with her while Sophie sat in Redwood City, waiting for her parents' lawyer.

He turned to the lines from Proverbs he'd read that morning in Maimonides' *Mishneh Torah*. He'd copied them down on an index card which he held now on the bar: "Nor should a man live without a wife, since married estate is conducive to great purity. But above all this, as the sages have declared, a man should direct his mind and thoughts to the words of Torah and enlarge his understanding with wisdom, for unchaste thoughts prevail only in the heart devoid of wisdom, and of wisdom it is said, 'a hind of love and a doe of grace, let her breasts satisfy you at all times, with her love be you ravished always.' "

Sophie returned to her apartment at twenty minutes after twelve. She knew that Bobby was safely married to Sheva by now. But just in case he was still missing, she took her phone off the hook. She didn't want Melanie calling her and filling her in on the latest installment.

Sheva has taken off the dress—the $600 dress Melanie found for $295. Her mother wrapped it in plastic and hung it in the "guest" closet. The closet that held her husband's suit from 1939. Always she'd planned to give it away. Whenever there was a rummage sale; whenever the Salvation Army called to say they'd be in the neighborhood—did she have any old clothes, any furniture she didn't need? She wasn't a sentimental type, Dina Grunig. Not like her friend Vivi Shapiro who cried at Doris Day movies. But how else could she explain the black gaberdine suit that hung in her guest closet?

Guest closet. It made her laugh. Ghost closet was more like it. And now her daughter's wedding dress hung next to her dead husband's suit. It was a suit from another age; now the Jews were somewhere else. In Hollywood taking drugs. In fancy diners ordering clams. Even the rabbis were nothings. Bobby Buchman she'd never forgive, no matter what happened next. Maybe the boy was having a breakdown. Her high-strung daughter lay on her bed on her wedding day. She wouldn't eat. She lay there dazed, her black eyes staring up at the ceiling. She didn't know what to do. She hung the dress in the closet next to Shmerl's suit. She called Vivi who came over wearing the hot pink flowered dress she'd put on for the wedding. In the refrigerator at the *shul*, the egg salad was getting mushy. She told herself not to worry; the egg salad would do fine, forget the food, the egg salad would outlast all of them.

15

Bobby goes to the telephone and calls Sophie's number. Busy. The noise drove him crazy. Who was she talking to? At a time like this? He called his sister Muffin. No answer. Everyone was at his parents', pacing the room, cursing him, yelling about what the wedding would cost them.

Three hours later he is riding the air to Boston. He expected her to show up at the airport, looking terrific, even though there was no reason for her to know he was there—the wedding called off, he unable to live without her. She was his *zivug*, his other self; she was his wife, his fate, his life. He couldn't cut out his own heart, then heal the hearts of others. He wasn't a rabbi, he knew that now. He wasn't even a teacher. In the yeshiva, the boys were Jewish only in their looks. Whom did he think he was kidding? God? Himself? His parents? Sheva? Sheva was the only one who knew he was really a fake. She was the only real Jew he knew. His only link to the other side—mournful men with hooded eyes *davening* in the dark.

Sheva lies there for a day and a night. Then she rises and calls Bobby's father. He promises to come over at seven o'clock that evening. He promises to close early. Buchman's Magic Carpets. Now she'd never see the inside of the carpet store.

Bobby always promised her he would take her there. She'd imagined the floor room many times—the bolts of rugs in every color. Shiny pseudo-Orientals. Sturdy dhurries. Hot pink shags. She told her mother to make something special, Bobby's parents were coming over. Maybe he'd never planned to marry her. Probably Sophie had been to the carpet store a million times. Probably they had walked around, having sex on every rug. She knew that was where he was, making love with Sophie. If she'd had any brains, she would have known a long time ago it would end like this: Sophie and Bobby married and living in a bourgeois town. Bobby would become something else. Rabbis did everything these days. They were thieves and pornographers, movie producers and lawyers. In America, Sheva knew, anything was possible. "God is dead," Nietzsche had said. "Everything is permitted." Rabbi Bob's Magic Carpets. Anything, Sheva thought.

Finally they are together. Bobby and Sophie. Bookman and whore. Rabbi and rabbi's wife. *Shlemiel* and *shlimazl*. Everywhere the *shlemiel* goes, he spills coffee on the rug. The *shlimazl* is the person who invites him back every week.

They lie in bed for two days. They eat soup out of cans. The next day, Bobby calls Sheva. He's surprised when she comes to the phone. She acts cool and distant, a little bit ironic. He tells her where he is. She doesn't seem surprised. She tells him, take care of himself, she's going to Israel in two days. "Where can I write to you?" Bobby asks. She has the sense to hang up the phone.

Bobby and Sophie are married in Boston City Hall. He knows the marriage is not binding according to Jewish law. He can't have a religious wedding. Forsaking Sheva, he knows, he's also forsaken Jewish law. He knows he has forsaken God. All he has left is *her*.

They stand, like *goyim*, in City Hall. Sophie is wearing a black suit that once belonged to her mother. She wears a gardenia from the florist. She thinks of her parents in 1950, also married in City Hall. She wishes her daughter something else—a lovely *chuppa* with latticework, a beautiful dress of ancient lace, pale attendants in pink organza, a wise rabbi, the crunch of glass under her husband's lucky heel.

Their honeymoon is daily life. They go to the Laundromat. They hold hands while their underpants roll around, having all the fun. They don't know what to do with themselves. Bobby knows he can't be a rabbi. Nor can he live in Israel as he had planned. He can't follow Sheva there—risk running into her at the university, on the beach, on line at the bank. Jerusalem was not big enough for the two of them. Sheva's heartbreak is bigger than Israel.

Life was smaller suddenly. He was married to Sophie, but he didn't know her. He didn't even know if he liked her. Fate had come to him finally, and he held out his arms to receive her. He remembered meeting a philosopher from the Hebrew University, an attractive Israeli man who studied Maimonides. It was the week after the Yom Kippur War and the taste of death hung thickly in the air. Bobby had spoken, or tried to speak, about the dead he and Sheva had seen, working in the basement of Hadassah Hospital. Their job had been to keep track of the records—searching out dental X-rays—the banal bureaucracy of death. Occasionally, by accident, they would see the faces of the dead. Bobby had tried to tell the philosopher how this had made him feel. The Israelis had been impatient with him, another eager American Jew-boy—they were professionals in death.

The city smelled of ashes and wax; the city smelled of remembrance and *Yortzeit*. The Israeli philosopher had been kind, his brown eyes had shone with compassion. "I understand," he had said in English. It was a week after the Yom Kippur War. Orit was celebrating her twenty-eighth birthday.

"I understand," the man had said. Later that night when the party was over Bobby had said good night to the man at the door. A cool rain was glistening on the windowpanes. The philosopher had stood at the door wearing a slightly absurd hat—a plaid hat with a little feather, the kind his own father wore. A suburban hat that looked out of place on his noble Israeli head. The smell of rain wafted up from the pavement outside. The smell of death was lifting from the streets of the city. "Good night Zevi," Bobby had said, and the man had looked at him, then at Sheva. "Life is not a joke," he had said.

He looked over at Sophie who was staring into the dryer. Her brassiere was stuck onto the glass. He looked at their clothes and he looked at her. He reached over and hugged her. "Life is not a joke."